The Aberconwy Register
and
Aberconwy Abbey

Castle Studies Research & Publishing

2018

First Published 2018 ISBN 1-899376–94-
9781899376940
by SCS Publishing

Produced and published by Castle Studies Research & Publishing,
Internet website: www.castles99.ukprint.com
e-mail: castles99uk@yahoo.co.uk

Cover Photograph, St Mary's church, Conway

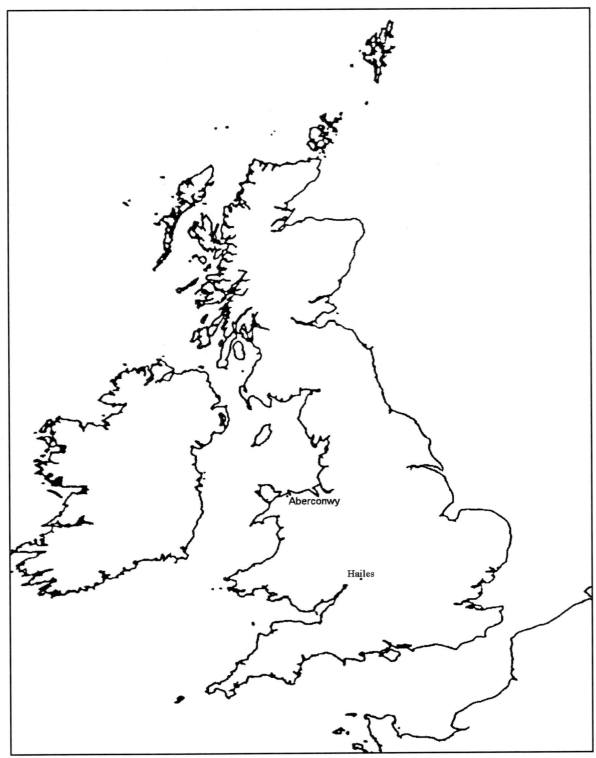

Figure 1, Aberconwy and Hailes Abbey in relation to Great Britain.

Conversion Factors

The conventions used throughout these books are feet and inches as I believe these to be of greater value in defining castle features. For conversion to the metric scale the following formula should be used. Divide the imperial figure by 3.05, ie. 1 foot is .305 of a metre. Dates in brackets referring to a person usually refer to the period when they held office or were of age and rarely to their date of birth.

Contents

Appendices

Abbreviations
Acts   *The Acts of the Welsh Rulers, 1120-1283*, ed. Pryce, H. [Cardiff, 2005]
ByS   *Brenhinedd y Saeson or The Kings of the Saxons*, ed. and trans. T.
            Jones [Cardiff, 1971]
CACW   *Calendar of Ancient Correspondence Concerning Wales*, ed. J.G.
            Edwards [Cardiff, 1940]
CAPW   *Calendar of Petitions relating to Wales*, ed. W. Rees [Cardiff, 1975]
CCR   *Calendar of the Close Rolls 1272-1500* [46 vols., 1892-1955]
CPR   *Calendar of Patent Rolls, 1232-1509* [1906-15]
Pen   *Brut y Tywysogyon or The Chronicle of the Princes. Peniarth Ms. 20
            version*, ed. and trans. T. Jones [Cardiff, 1952]
RBH   *Brut y Tywysogyon or The Chronicle of the Princes. Red Book of
            Hergest version*, ed. and trans. T. Jones [Cardiff, 1955]
Statuta   Canivez, J., *Statuta Capitulorum Ordinis Cisterciensis*
            [8 vols, Louvain, 1933-41]
TNA   The National Archives

Glossary

Aisle	A part of a church divided laterally from the nave, transept, or choir by a row of columns
Arcade	A series of arches making a pierced wall
Ashlar	A squared building stone cut to fit closely to similar stones, permitting minimal thin mortar joints
Bailiff	An officer who manages an estate for another
Blodwyte	A fine for shedding blood
Bovate	An eighth of a carucate
Buttress	Masonry built against a wall to give it extra strength
Cantref	Welsh administrative land unit, commonly of 3 or 4 commotes
Capital	The stone making the head of a pillar
Carucate	A ploughland, stated in the reign of Richard I to be either 60 or 100 acres depending on the quality of the land
Chancel	The eastern part of a church where the altar stands
Clerestory	An upper storey, usually of the nave, set above the aisle roof
Commote	Welsh administrative land unit, commonly equated to a Hundred
Corbel	A block of stone used to support a projection
Corbel Table	A series of corbels, usually used to support a roof or floor
Course	A continual layer of stones making up a layer in a wall
Cusp	The projecting point of intersection of two ornamental arcs
Danegeld	A land tax originally raised to fight the Danes
Demesne	Land held by a lord in his own hand
Dower	Land or goods given by a husband to a wife so that she had means of support should he predecease her
Escheat	Land that reverts to its previous holder
Flemefrith	The right to punish those who receive felons
Flemeneswite	A fine for the wrongful hanging of a thief
Flithwyte	A fine for harbouring fugitives
Forsteal	Violent affray in the streets
Frank Almoin	Tenure of holding land 'forever in pure and perpetual alms'
Gaywite	A fine for neglecting to keep watch and ward
Hamsoken	Offence of assaulting a man in his own home or the fine for such
Headstop	A carving at the end of an arch label
Hengwite	A fine for hanging a thief without due process
Hide	120 acres of agricultural land
Hue and Cry	The legal obligation to pursue a felon with loud outcry
Indult	A special, often temporary, dispensation
Infangenethef	The right to try and sentence a thief caught in the act within the district
Hundred	English administrative land unit subject to royal justice
Knight's Fee	Land held by service of providing a knight in time of war
Label	Projecting stonework above an arch or lintel - often called a hood mould
Lastage	A payment made by the holder of a fair or market allowing goods to be carried freely
League	Distance of usually three, but occasionally one mile

Marcher Lordship	Land held in chief of the king, but separate of royal justice
Mullion	The upright in a window dividing it into lights
Murage	A tax for building or repairing town walls
Nave	The main body of a church
Paage or Pedage	Protection money paid to travel a road
Panage	The right to let pigs roam in the forest
Passage	Toll to use a right of way
Perfeddwlad	The later name for the four cantrefs of Rhos, Rhufoniog, Tegeingl and Dyffryn Clwyd
Pilaster	A shallow buttress with no structural strength
Pipe Roll	Exchequer account of the Shires
Piscina	Recess in the wall for ritual washing
Plinth	A solid base on which to stand a wall or feature
Pontage	Toll paid for construction or maintenance of a bridge
Pura Walia	Pure Wales, or Wales under Welsh Law
Puture	The right to take food from tenants
Quatrefoil	A four lobed shape
Quoins	Large stones forming an external angle of a wall
Reredos	A decorative screen to obscure the altar from the nave
Respond	A half-pier or half-pillar which is bonded into a wall and designed to carry the springer at one end of an arch.
Rubblework	Rubble masonry consisting of undressed, rough stone in a mortar matrix
Scarp	Steeply sloping ground like the face of a ditch
Sok and sak	The right of holding of a court and cognizance of pleas as well as receiving fines made or imposed
Spandrel	The space between two arches
Springer	The lowest portion of an arch, usually where it starts at a pier
Stallage	The fee paid for having a stall at a fair or market
Stiff leaf	A stylized three-lobed carved foliage thought to be 12th or 13th century
String Course	A projecting course of masonry, usually in a horizontal line.
Suit	Attendance due at a court house of the lord
Tallage	A compulsory land tax
Tollage	Taxes paid to a town or market
Theam	The right to tax villeins and their progeny
Tol	The right to take toll on things bought and sold
Tourn	The circuit made by the sheriff to the hundreds/commotes of his shire
Transept	Part of a church built at right angles to the main structure to give it a cruciform shape
Trefoil	A three lobed shape
Uchelwyr	Leading Welshmen
Utfangenethef	The right to execute a thief on the local gallows despite them being sentenced outside the jurisdiction of the court
Vaccary	A place where cows or cattle are kept, later a dairy farm
Vill	Norman Hamlet originally equivalent to a manor or later parish
Virgate	A quarter of a hide or 30 acres

Introduction

There is only one copy of the 'Register of Aberconwy' and this appears in a fifteenth century manuscript that originated at Hailes abbey in Gloucestershire (Fig.1). The purpose of this book is to examine this manuscript and the 'chronicle' it contains and decide what historical value this has in relation to the abbey founded at Aberconwy in 1186 and the history of England and Wales in general. To achieve this aim the history and buildings of the abbey will be examined and the register and chronicle dissected for their factual value. This is especially worthwhile as much historical use has been made of the evidence recorded in the manuscript, unfortunately without understanding the nature or age of the source. Indeed, to understand the abbey itself it is also necessary to examine the history of Gwynedd between 1170 and 1246, as much of this period is woefully misunderstood. Hence the long historical chapters that intend to right the many misconceptions about Prince Llywelyn ab Iorwerth and his relatives.

If the contents of the register and chronicle were originally written at Aberconwy, which would seem likely considering its name, they would have been created in the scriptorium of that monastic house, along with many other works in Latin. Many such chronicles were created in the twelfth and thirteenth centuries, while registers tend to come later[*1]. In this Aberconwy would not have been alone and so it is probably best to begin this research with a look at the monastic tradition in which the register and chronicle began.

One of the most interesting things about the Cistercian houses of Wales, and the rest of Europe, is their unique building styles and histories. This in itself appears perverse, as the Cistercian houses were formed under strict rules of obedience passed down from above to achieve a uniformity of life. It is therefore somewhat surprising that all of their churches tend to differ so greatly in style and form, with no two such structures in Britain appearing similar in style of conception or decoration. In short, despite St Bernard's urging of 1125, it appears that all the Cistercian churches bathe in a sculptural paradise of magnificent masonry and often exalt in beauty and decoration.

> ...I say naught of the vast height of your churches, their immoderate length, their superfluous breadth, the costly polishings, the curious carvings and paintings which attract the worshipper's gaze and hinder his attention.... But in the cloister, under the eyes of the Brethren who read there, what profit is there in those ridiculous monsters, in the marvellous and deformed comeliness, that comely deformity? To what purpose are those unclean apes, those fierce lions, those monstrous centaurs, those half-men, those striped tigers, those fighting knights, those hunters blowing their horns? Many bodies are there seen under one head, or again, many heads to a single body. Here is a four-footed beast with a serpent's tail; there, a fish with a beast's head. Here again the forepart of a horse trails half a goat behind it, or a horned beast bears the hinder quarters of a horse. In short, so many and so marvellous are the varieties of diverse shapes on every hand, that we are more tempted to read in the marble than in our books, and to spend the whole day in wondering at these things rather than in

---

[*1] It has been stated that Strata Florida had its own register before 1248, Williams, D.H., *The Welsh Cistercians* [Bodmin, 2001], 220. However, what existed in 1248 is clearly a set of annals and not a register, Pen, 108, 206. Registers of this abbey and Neath certainly existed in the sixteenth century. There is also a lease book containing leases of lands by Abbey Cwmhir between 1492 and 1577, TNA, LR.2/76. Further there are copies of two books of Abbey Dore leases in Cantref Selyf, TNA.E.303/5, ff.88-130 & E.315/238, ff.58-97d. Other than these the Aberconwy Register appears a unique survival.

1

meditating the law of God. For God's sake, if men are not ashamed of these follies, why at least do they not shrink from the expense?[*2]

Bernard's preachings had obviously failed to grab the minds of the Cistercian founders by the time Aberconwy was constructed in 1186. At Abbey Cwmhir, only seventy miles away, it would appear that the monks allowed the head of its founder to be carved amongst the capitals soon after 1176 (Fig.2)[*3]. Despite Bernard's warning and the 'ridiculous' adornments of the abbeys, it is interesting to note that even before 1124 the English monk, William Malmesbury (d.1143), thought that the Cistercians were the most holy order in England and that their austerity in both their lifestyles and their churches, 'is now both believed and asserted to be the surest road to heaven'[*4]. Judging from the architecture of their buildings from the foundation of the order in 1098, their austerity dipped as the century progressed. Alternatively William had never left his cloister to see the reality of their buildings.

When Aberconwy was envisioned in the mid 1180s the Cistercians were attempting to reinvigorate the austere rule of St Benedict. This consisted of performing the liturgy, reading and manual labour. For the Cistercians this meant the return to hard physical work. This was made possible by cutting down on the daily routine of the liturgy which had been vastly expanded over the years and had compressed the time available for manual labour in other orders. The Cistercians were therefore not supposed to be initiators, but re-creators of the old purity of the founding fathers. From the time of Abbot Stephen Harding of Clairvaux (1109-34), the Cistercians were renowned for their simplicity and austerity as well as their desire for poverty - a desire that was certainly becoming outdated by the time of the writings of Giraldus Cambrensis (1146-1223) at the turn of the thirteenth century. Initially at least the Cistercians strove to be 'desert monks' like their Egyptian forbears. In the early twelfth century they sought their

Figure 2, The head of a young prince from Abbey Cwmhir. As the man is clean shaven, apart from a moustache, this seems likely to have been a Welshman. As he was wearing a crown it seems possible that this might represent Prince Cadwallon ap Madog (d.1179), the founder of the abbey. No English king is known to have sported a moustache.

[*2] Translation by Paul Halsall of Bernard's original letter of 1125 attacking the Cluniacs, www.fordham.edu/halsall/source/bernard1.asp

[*3] Ralegh Radford, L.C.A., 'The Cistercian Abbey of Cwmhir, Radnorshire', *Archaeologia Cambrensis* CXXXI [1982], 58-70. It should be noted here that the sculpture is dated in the article to 1250-1300 on the most flimsy of grounds. The subject is examined in some detail in Remfry, P.M., *Abbey Cwmhir* [forthcoming].

[*4] Willelmi Malmesbiriensis Monachi, *De Gestis Regum Anglorum. Historiae Novellae*, ed. Stubbs, W., [2 vols, 1887-89] II, 380-85.

habitations 'far from the dwellings of men' as their regulations stated or 'in lonely wooded places' as was thought by Orderic Vitalis. The Cistercians therefore rejected modern man's lifestyle and with them the manors, churches and tithes which formed the economic framework of medieval life. Instead they commenced with concentrating on the direct exploitation of their lands and the shunning of their fellow agricultural man. Regardless of this, the prohibition of tithes seems to have been soon discarded, possibly due to the incorporation of the order of Savigny within the ranks in 1147. The Savigniac houses had accepted tithes since their inception. Certainly Aberconwy abbey had tithes and appropriated parishes within its bounds by 1253.

The basis of the Cistercian order was its constitution or Charter of Charity/Love (*carta caritatis*). This was referred to in order to sort out any problems that might arise in the various houses which it had not been possible to solve without external intervention. Aberconwy was founded in 1186 as a colony or daughter house of Strata Florida in Ceredigion, a region of Deheubarth, itself founded in 1164 and apparently refounded by Prince Rhys ap Gruffydd (d.1197) on a new site completed only in 1201[*5]. Aberconwy abbey was therefore theoretically under the guidance and occasional supervision of Strata Florida from 1186 onwards.

The new house was supposed to follow the statutes of the Cistercian order, which allowed each house their own independent life and left the monks free to elect their own abbot and officials without any undue external pressure from either the secular or ecclesiastical powers. In this manner the community would organise itself and not be subject to outside interference in the running of its properties or in the use of its finances. However, this did not mean that the abbeys were totally autonomous, for every year in September the abbots of all the houses were required to make the journey to Citeaux for a general chapter meeting. Here the abbot of Citeaux would preside over the meeting and discuss the approved form of customs and obedience throughout the order. The purpose was that each house should base themselves upon the manner in which Citeaux operated.

The monks of new Cistercian houses in obedience to their orders sought out undeveloped lands and shunned the urban houses of the Benedictines. Consequently they resided in the wilder places in Wales, although Aberconwy was one of the least wild places they occupied, it being near a major river crossing and in time what must have become a major settlement with its own castle and princely connections (See p.167ff for the Welsh princely llys at Aberconwy).

The initial numbers of monks working an abbey could be large, while thirteen was the minimum number. Whitland was founded for 100 monks in either 1140 or 1153[*6], while

---

[*5] The idea that Strata Florida relocated in 1184 appears in Robinson, DM., *The Cistercians in Wales: Architecture and Archaeology 1130-1540*, Society of Antiquaries of London, Research Committee Report [London, 2006], 268. However, the early evidence for the site move seems fairly conclusive for the abbey's completion in 1201, Pen, 182-3. On the eve of Whit Sunday the community of Strata Florida went to the new church that had been built with fine workmanship (*nos Wyl y Sulgwyn, yd aeth cofent Ystrat Flur y'r eglwys newyd a adeilyssit o advwynweith*). The idea that the site move occurred in 1184 seems based on Rhys' charter of that year which notes that he had begun to build a monastery called *Stratflur* and that he both loved and cherished it, Acts, 171-5. Such could apply to either the early site of 1164 or the later one of 1201 which was 1½ miles from the Afon Flur which gave the abbey its name.
[*6] 'at the foundation it was so richly endowed that 100 monks and more used to reside in it', *CPR 1436-41*, 380.

Strata Marcella in 1170/72[*7], Cwmhir in 1176[*8] and Llantarnam in 1180[*9], were founded for 60 brethren. At an early date the Cistercian rules stated that an abbey was not to found a daughter house unless they themselves had at least 60 monks[*10].

There is no information for how many monks were intended for Aberconwy, but, from the above figures, sixty seems a reasonable assumption in 1186. Even if Aberconwy could have had that many monks at its foundation these men would obviously have proved insufficient to work the massive estates that they had acquired by the end of the twelfth century. Therefore, the Cistercian order allowed for the taking on of *conversi* on the abbey granges. These were illiterate peasant lay brothers who were under vows of chastity and obedience, but were otherwise free to follow their own lives and were not as bound religiously as their monkish counterparts. In this manner the monks of Aberconwy would have slowly brought their massive estates under pastoral and agricultural cultivation, if they had not been so utilised before. This was done by making the lands granted to them into granges administered from a usually central location. Often this would be the site of the grange barn, known in Welsh as ysgubor - a placename often found centrally in Cistercian granges. By definition a monastic grange was an estate or farm run for the production of agriculture. Some could be subdivided like the Aberconwy grange of Nanwynian into smaller estates or dairy farms known in Wales as hafod. By the time of Llywelyn ab Iorwerth (d.1240) Aberconwy would seem to have had some fifteen granges (Fig.3). These will be examined in detail later when it will be seen that already by the end of the twelfth century the monks were slipping away from their high ideals. By 1388 the number of monks living in abbey precincts within Wales had dwindled considerably from their initial foundation. Aberconwy was down to just six, while Cwmhir had eight, Cymer five and even Whitland was reduced to only seven from its initial one hundred[*11].

After examining the religious impulse for the founding of Aberconwy it is next necessary to see how the secular power brought this foundation about. Yet, before this is done, it is needful to comment on the spelling of the name of the abbey. In its earliest years the abbey seems to have been named as *Aberconewey* or variants. Therefore, throughout this book, the word Aberconwy has been used as the 'correct' modern spelling. Despite this, it is obvious that the name *Conwey*, or variants, was also used from an early era to name the district, town, castles and abbey that lay on the river of the same name. When dealing with the Welsh usage of the site and river the modern Welsh spelling of Conwy has been used. When dealing with the English conquest and the founding of the new town the English word Conway has been used to help differentiate between the two. Although this method is somewhat confusing, it seems the best way to bring forward the differences in spelling and the different languages that once fought for control of this area of the British Isles. Similarly,

---

[*7] The foundation date of 1170 for Strata Marcella rests on questionable grounds, despite modern assertions, while the earliest list clearly favours 1172. The probable date seems to be before 25 March 1171. In 1328/33 John Charlton, the lord of Powys and patron of the abbey, stated that it had recently held 60 monks, but there were now only eight as the abbey had been 'destroyed and almost annihilated', CAPW, 489-90.

[*8] 'The first foundation was made by Cadwallon ap Madog for sixty monks', *Joannis Lelandi Antiquarii de Rebus Britannicis Collectanea*, Hearne, T., [London, 1770, 6 vols], III, 52.

[*9] The foundation of Llantarnam is usually given as 1179 following the fourteenth century Bruts, Pen, 72. However, the Cistercian lists, though much confused, quite clearly give 22 July 1180. As a fourteenth century source the list date should be preferred, especially as the event is recorded in the Bruts after the 22 September 1179 death of Prince Cadwallon and before the comments of the virtually blank year of 1180. In 1317 the abbot of Llantarnam wrote to the king explaining that 'only 20 monks can be maintained there with difficulty... where there were formerly wont to be 60 monks and ... more serving god', CAPW, 286.

[*10] *Nullus de abbatibus nostris locum ad abbatiam faciendam accipiat, nisi prius sexaginta habeat monachos professos, et hoc licentia generalis capituli, Analecta Sacri Ordinis Cisterciensis* VI [1950], 29.

[*11] The bulk of the information within this paragraph is taken from Williams, D.H., *The Welsh Cistercians* [Norwich, 1983, 2 vols] I, 147-9.

although the name Aberconwy continued to be used concerning the abbey after 1283, in this work the new abbey will be referred to as Maenan, its final site.

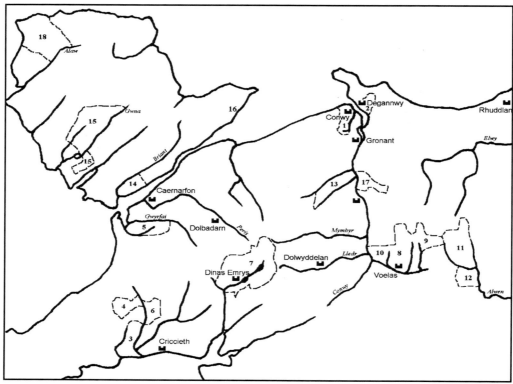

Figure 3, The estates of Aberconwy Abbey and the main Welsh rivers and castles.

Land	Acquired by	Land	Acquired by
1, Conwy Gyffin	1188	2, Creuddyn	1263
3, Ffriwlwyd	1282	4, Cwm	1282
5, Rhedynog Felen	1186	6, Nant Call	1282
7, Nanhwynain	1281	8, Pentrefoelas	1273
9, Ceirniog	1282	10, Llanfair Rhyd Castell	1273
11, Llyn Cymmer	1282	12, Lechwedd Cryn Llwyn	1282
13, Arddau	1278	14, Gelliniog	1199
15, Bodgedwydd	1282	16, Llanfaes	1485
17, Maenan	1283	18, Ghornwy	1283

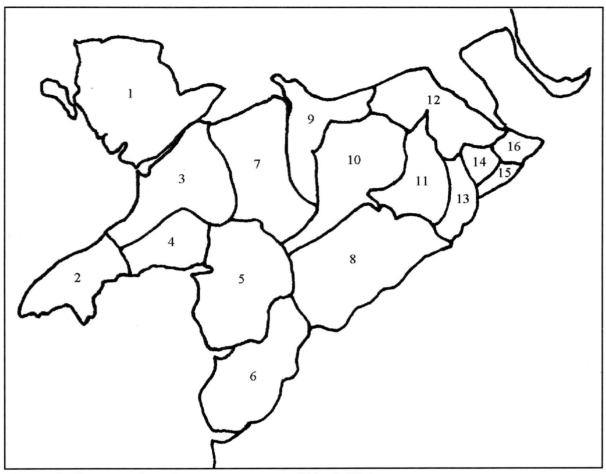

Figure 4, The cantrefs and some commotes of North Wales.

1, Mon/Anglesey	2, Llyn	3, Arfon	4, Eifionydd
5, Ardudwy	6, Meirionydd	7, Arllechwedd	8, Penllyn
9, Rhos	10, Rhufoniog	11, Dyffryn Clwyd	12, Tegeingl
13, Ial	14, Mold	15, Hope	16, Hawarden

The Foundation of Aberconwy Abbey, 1186

The early history of Aberconwy abbey has been shrouded in obscurity and confusion, but, as ever, going back to the original documentation soon removes the obscurity and clears the scene of unnecessary controversy. It is the purpose of this book to look at and translate in full the Aberconwy Register and explore further the routes open to us in understanding this short, yet complex document[*12]. To do this it is also necessary to explore the history and development of the abbey, as understanding the one assists in understanding the other. A glance at figure 4 also helps in explaining the layout of the political divisions in North Wales.

All history involves continuing research and examining new evidence, or rather rediscovered old evidence. This can often upset long held and venerable interpretations. The main starting point for all research before the examination of the usually voluminous and often obscure original data are 'modern' compilations of what is known of the site. Aberconwy has been lucky in being the subject of much research over the past few centuries. Unusually it is generally accepted that the abbey was founded in 1186, but not on which day. Usually given is either the second ides of June (12 June) or the ninth calends of August 1186 (24 July 1186). Despite this, later sources also suggest a foundation date in 1185 or even 1184[*13]. It is further suggested by modern historians that there was an unrecorded site move from Rhedynog Felen near to Caernarfon, to the Afon Conwy location in the 1190s, before yet another firmly recorded move was made in 1283/4 when the abbey was translated to Maenan[*14]. The late thirteenth century Maenan site was then operational until 1537 when the monastery was dissolved at the order of King Henry VIII (1509-47). In between these dates many things have been claimed for Aberconwy abbey and many more things were in fact done there. It is the purpose of this book to examine the original documents and from these untangle the truth, or get as near to it as possible until further evidence is found.

The first task is to untangle the true foundation date of the abbey. Two anonymous lists of Cistercian abbey foundations were probably made around the first half of the thirteenth century and both mention the foundation of Aberconwy abbey[*15]. The first list runs chronologically up to 1190 and is preserved in B.L. MS Cotton Faustina B VII, fo.36. This Latin text probably predates 1234 and its early portion may be as early as 1190 as the style of the document changes dramatically at that point. As such it is nearly contemporary and gives the foundation date for *Abbatia de Aberconuy* as *2 idus Junii mclxxxvi*, or 12 June 1186 as it would be termed today. Incidently, this day would have been a Thursday. A second text is found at B.L. MS Cotton Vespasian A VI, fo.54b, and probably dates to 1247 or soon after. This again places the foundation of *Aberconoeu* (*in Cambria* added in a later hand) in the year 1186 - a year which would appear to be correct - unfortunately no day is given. Further, from a seventeenth century document preserved in Cottonian MS Titus CX, ff 43-46, comes the statement that *Abercun* was the daughter house of Strata Florida. This statement is corroborated by the three fourteenth century copies of the Brut y Tywysogyon.

[*12] The manuscript has been printed twice in modern times, *Register and Chronicle of Aberconway from the Harleian MS. 3725*, ed Ellis, H., *Camden Miscellany* [1847] and Rees, T.M., *Mynachdai Cymru* [Newport, 1910], 38-61. A translation has also appeared in Lowe, W.B, *Heart of Northern Wales* [1912] I, 448-58.

[*13] *Originum Cisterciensium*, ed. L. Janauschek [Vienna, 1877] I, 186, lists the 'sources' for these. Most appear to be later attempts at forming a chronology of the foundation dates of Cistercian monasteries and their accuracy does not inspire confidence.

[*14] Allegedly Maenan's original name was Aberllechog, Hays, RW, *The History of the Abbey of Aberconway, 1186-1537* [UWP, 1963], 78, quoting *Gwaith Tudur Aled*, ed. Jones, TG [Cardiff, 1926] II, 390 and *History of the Diocese of St Asaph*, Thomas, DR. [1874] II, 308.

[*15] Birch, W. de. G., 'The Date of Foundation Ascribed to the Cistercian Abbeys of Great Britain', *Journal of the British Archaeological Association* XXVI, 281-299, 352-369. Aberconwy appears on pages 290 and 363.

1186 A community went from Strata Florida to Rhedynog Felen in Gwynedd.[*16]

1186 In that year, about the month of July, the community of Strata Florida went to Rhedynog Felen in Gwynedd (*Redynawc Velen yGwyned*).[*17]

1186 And the community (*covent*) of Strata Florida went to Rhedynog Felen in Gwynedd/Arfon (*Redynawc Velen yn Gwyned/Arvon*).[*18]

There is much argument about when the original Bruts were written, but it seems relatively certain that the original Latin text, from which all three above versions derive, was written at Strata Florida before the end of the thirteenth century. Interestingly, the older Annales Cambriae in their current forms carry, no mention of the foundation of Aberconwy[*19]. Indeed, in a particularly dearth time for the twelfth century annals, the year 1186 has been left totally blank, although it is possible to speculate that an original Aberconwy Brut account mentioned the foundation of the abbey[*20].

From the evidence accrued above there seems little doubt that Aberconwy abbey was initially founded on 12 June 1186. Yet this does not answer the question as to who founded the abbey and where and why this date is different from the 24 July 1186 date found in the Register. In modern times a story has grown up that the abbey was founded at Rhedynog Felen outside Caernarfon and then migrated to Aberconwy before 1199 due to the hostile environment of the first foundation. This erroneous assertion appears prominently in on-line versions of the abbey's story and can be summed up by the Wikipedia statement:

> A Cistercian house was founded at Rhedynog Felen near Caernarfon in 1186 by a group of monks from Strata Florida Abbey. About four or five years later they moved to Conwy, and in 1199 were given large grants of land by Llywelyn the Great who had recently become ruler of Gwynedd.[*21]

This assertion of an abortive foundation is unlikely as it is in no means substantiated by any surviving evidence. It should be noted that the fourteenth century Bruts name Rhedynog Felen as the place to which the monks of Strata Florida set out in 1186. Quite possibly to found an abbey here may have been their original intention as recorded for 12 June 1186, but before Easter 1188 the monks would appear to have been dwelling in an abbey at Aberconwy as Giraldus Cambrensis tells us when he passed by in early April.

> *Transnavigato deinde Cunewe fluvio, vel potius maris brachio sub Dugannu, monasterio Cisterciensis ordinis super Conewe ab occidua fluvii parte a dextra relicto, usque Ruthelan... pervenimus.*
> From there we crossed over the River Conwy, or rather a branch of the sea under Degannwy, by the monastery of the Cistercian order above the Conwy by the western

[*16] Pen, 73.
[*17] RBH, 169.
[*18] ByS, 186-8.
[*19] *Annales Cambriae. A Translation of Harleian 3859; PRO E.164/1; Cottonian Domitian, A 1; Exeter Cathedral Library MS. 3514 and MS Exchequer DB Neath, PRO E.164/1*, ed. Remfry, P.M., [Malvern, 2007], 96.
[*20] See p.51ff on the Aberconwy Brut.
[*21] https://en.wikipedia.org/wiki/Aberconwy_Abbey. Accessed 10 August 2017.

side of the river [which] we left behind on our right, [as] we reached up towards Rhuddlan....[22]

This tells us clearly that the archbishop's party crossed the river where it was narrowest, opposite Degannwy castle to the north of Aberconwy abbey, or the abbey above the Conwy as Giraldus correctly calls it. Further, when Giraldus actually visits the abbey over Christmas 1201, he makes no mention that it is not the same abbey that he saw in 1188[23]. This again strengthens the impression that Aberconwy abbey stood in its position by the Conwy within eighteen months of its alleged foundation at Rhedynog Felen[24]. As Giraldus makes no mention of building work or temporary structures, it can be presumed that the abbey was already functional. Further, Giraldus' route as described by him takes him along the Menai right past the site of Rhedynog Felen of which no mention at all is made. The implication from this, and the names used in the earliest foundation lists of the Cistercians, would seem to be that the abbey was always intended to stand at Aberconwy and that if the first monks from Strata Florida were of the intention of founding a monastery at Rhedynog Felen they were within weeks if not days, disillusioned of their purpose. Quite possibly the monks arrived at Rhedynog Felen on 12 June 1186, but then moved on to the Aberconwy site and actually founded the abbey there on Friday, 24 July 1186 and this was remembered as the foundation day when the Register was drawn up some 300 years later. It is interesting that a sister house of Strata Florida, Abbey Cwmhir, was also reported in modern times to have had multiple site changes and repeated foundations, although later research has found these to be totally foundationless as well as illogical[25]. Irrespective of this it is claimed that some third of Cistercian houses had early site changes[26]. Aberconwy and Cwmhir are, judging by the original evidence, wrongly included amongst those figures.

It is worthwhile stressing here that the foundation of Aberconwy abbey had nothing at all to do with Llywelyn ab Iorwerth (1172-1240), despite many modern claims to the contrary. This prince had no power in North Wales in 1186, being at that time a youth of some fourteen years. Giraldus himself mentions that Llywelyn was only 'now' beginning to demand his inheritance in the period 1188-91, although Llywelyn's bard stated that he was making a nuisance of himself to his uncles when he was aged ten, ie. in 1182. It is therefore ludicrous to suggest that the widespread grants to the abbey were the gifts made by 'Prince Llywelyn of the whole of North Wales' - see map Fig.3. Simply compare this with the lands known to be held by Llywelyn's uncles and cousins, the real founders of the abbey - Figs.8&9.

---

[22] Giraldus Cambrensis, *Opera*, eds. J.S. Brewer, J.F. Dimock and G.F. Warner [8 vols., 1861-91] VI, 136-7.

[23] Giraldus Cambrensis, *Opera*, eds. J.S. Brewer, J.F. Dimock and G.F. Warner [8 vols., 1861-91] III, 227

[24] It has been argued that Giraldus did not write up the second more detailed version of his trip until 1197 and therefore the abbey may not have been moved until then, Hays, RW, *The History of the Abbey of Aberconway, 1186-1537* [UWP, 1963], 5, quoting Lloyd, J.E., *History of Wales* [2 vols., 1911] II, 601. However, the argument that Gerald's 'memory may have failed him' is an old one that has little validity. The idea that Giraldus decided in 1197 that he had noticed an abbey besides the Conwy that wasn't even there in the Spring of 1188, especially as there is no evidence that he visited Gwynedd between 1188 and 1200, makes the claim he made up seeing the abbey unbelievable. The subject of Giraldus' geographical reliability is examined in Remfry, P.M., *Harlech Castle and its True origins* [Ceidio, 2013], 12-18.

[25] Remfry, P.M., *Abbey Cwmhir* [forthcoming].

[26] Williams, D.H., *The Welsh Cistercians* [Bodmin, 2001], 13.

The Confirmation Charter of King Henry II, 1186 to 1189

When the abbey was founded in the summer of 1186 it is likely that this was done with solemn undertakings which were supported by written charters listing the lands newly granted by lay donors to the monastery. Unfortunately these have not survived. The earliest known charter for the abbey comes from the king's chancery and was made within three years of Aberconwy's founding, but sadly this has not survived either. Sometime in the last three years of his reign King Henry II (1154-89) made a confirmation of the rights of Aberconwy abbey, a copy of which remains in the Register. This charter was apparently still extant when the Register was made and carried a date of 1 April 1202 (*primo die Aprilis Anno regni nostri tercii*). This was when the document was drawn up for King John after he had seen a copy and confirmed his father's act of granting protection to Aberconwy abbey. King John is solidly attested in Normandy at this time and was staying at Montfort sur Risle where he issued another document that survived on his patent roll on that very day[27]. The next entry is an undated one to the men of Eu and this is followed by the king's confirmation of the 11 July 1201 Shrewsbury peace treaty with Llywelyn ab Iorwerth. There then follows a letter of simple protection to Guy de la Vale and then a letter sent from Rouen to Geoffrey Fitz Peter on 8 April 1202. This tends to suggest that a delegation went from Aberconwy abbey specifically to see the king and at around the same time the king finally accepted the terms that his men had agreed with Llywelyn the previous July. Again it would seem logical that the party from Aberconwy returned to Wales with both their confirmation of their privileges and the confirmation of the July 1201 treaty to take to Prince Llywelyn. More will be said of this later while examining the rise of Llywelyn ab Iorwerth in Wales. John's grant to the abbey simply states at the end of his charter of protection that the provisions he granted were 'just as the charter of my father King Henry reasonably testifies'[28]. It is unfortunate that nothing further is known of Henry's original grant of protection, although it is possible to surmise some further details of this document, especially when considering the nature of John's grant.

It is interesting that neither this confirmation of 1202, nor Henry's original grant of protection, should have survived. This is even more curious as John's exchequer rolls of this period have survived, but no mention of Aberconwy occurs there at this date. This is no surprise and it should be taken as further proof, if any is still needed, that the exchequer rolls of John are not a complete record of his chancery. That John's confirmation was copied into the abbey register at a later date would suggest that at least this charter survived the abbey's many misfortunes during the thirteenth century - assuming of course that the charter copied into the register was an original and not a copy or even itself a forgery; for it is surprising that the confirmation of the peace treaty with Llywelyn was recorded in the rolls, but not the confirmation to Aberconwy.

A question also remains as to why King Henry II should have confirmed the foundation of a Cistercian house in the westernmost extremes of his Welsh lands in the period 1186 to 1189 - a time in which Henry was engaged in a desperate struggle with the king of France and his own son and during a time in which he never came to England, let alone Wales. The answer may lie in the course of this war. In the early stages of the dispute Henry sent a high-powered negotiating team to Wales to make sure that his Welsh rear was

---

[27] *Rotuli Litterarum Patentium in Turri Londinensi asservati [1201-16]* ed. T.D. Hardy [1835], 8b.

[28] *Register and Chronicle of Aberconway from the Harleian MS. 3725*, ed Ellis, H., *Camden Miscellany* [1847], 10.

secure while he fought on the continent. According to a contemporary chronicler King Henry:

> sent Ranulf Glanville, his justiciar, to Rhys ap Gruffydd and to other Welsh princes, to make peace between them and the men of Herefordshire and Cheshire, who a little while before had killed many Welshmen in some conflict, and to obtain serjeants to cross the sea with the king into Normandy.[*29]

Giraldus mentioned one such meeting taking place at Hereford between the king's representatives and Rhys where the newly installed Bishop William Vere of Hereford was present in the county town itself[*30]. As William was only elected on 25 May 1186 and consecrated on 10 August, it is to be presumed that the meeting took place in the later half of the year and that as a result of what was probably later negotiations between the justiciar's party and the men of Cheshire and 'certain Welsh princes' it was agreed that the king would confirm the newly founded institution of Aberconwy. Such a scenario would explain why Henry did not appear to make confirmations to most of the Cistercian abbeys in his Welsh domains. The extant abbeys found in Wales during his reign (1154-89) and those of his two predecessors (Henry I, 1100-35 and Stephen, 1135-54) in chronological order of their founding were Neath 1130, Tintern 1131, Basingwerk 1133/57, Whitland 1140/53, Margam 1147, Dore 1147, Strata Florida 1164, Strata Marcella 1170/72, Trawscoed 1170/73 (suppressed before 1214), Cwmhir 1176, Llantarnam 1180 and finally Aberconwy in 1186. Of these twelve abbeys only two others have royal confirmations of their lands by Henry II, these being Basingwerk and Strata Florida. Trawscoed, founded by Walter Clifford (d.1190) the father of Henry II's mistress, Fair Rosamund, did not get a charter which delineated its lands, merely the statement that they were to have the land of William Foria in Cantref Selyf. Presumably the land was so well known as not to need delineating and so it is possible that the extent of early Cistercian lands were not mentioned in detail in early charters. This is somewhat surprising when it is considered that kings normally took an interest in religious houses within the closely knit community that would have been their own intimate household. The two early recorded royal charters to Welsh Cistercian houses are undated, but, due to the witness lists and the foundation dates of the abbeys, are relatively easy to date.

The royal confirmation to Basingwerk almost certainly dates to the late summer of 1157 when the king was campaigning into north-east Wales from Cheshire against Owain Gwynedd (d.1170). The charter was dated at Chester, a place the king did not visit very often[*31]. The campaign of that year passed over much of the abbey's vast estates and supplies a credible reason for the charter's creation. Strata Florida received the second Henrician confirmation to a Welsh abbey in December 1181 when the king was working with Rhys ap Gruffydd (d.1197) to keep Wales peaceable[*32]. As such, the creation of this charter comes as

---

[*29] *Gesta Regis Henrici Secundi Benedicti Abbatis* ed. Stubbs, W. [2 vols, 1867] I, 355-6.

[*30] Giraldus Cambrensis, *Opera*, eds. J.S. Brewer, J.F. Dimock and G.F. Warner [8 vols., 1861-91] I, 57-60.

[*31] *Monasticon Anglicanum*, ed. W. Dugdale, Revised edition by J. Caley, H. Ellis, and B. Bandinel [6 vols., 1817-30] V, 262-3; Itinerary of Henry II, 29.

[*32] *Monasticon Anglicanum*, ed. W. Dugdale, Revised edition by J. Caley, H. Ellis, and B. Bandinel [6 vols., 1817-30] V, 633; Itinerary of Henry II, 246.

little surprise, especially when it has been suggested that the Lord Rhys was apparently making great new grants to the abbey around this time[*33].

As there is no accurate copy of the contents of Henry's charter to Aberconwy it is worthwhile taking a closer look at the two surviving confirmation charters to its fellow houses. The probably August 1157 charter to Basingwerk begins in common form and then lists the lands granted and confirmed by the king.

> King Henry of England and duke of Normandy and Aquitaine as well as count of Anjou greets his archbishops, bishops etc. Know that I have given and conceded and confirmed by this present charter to God and to St Mary and the monks of Basingwerk in free and perpetual alms the money tithe of lands in Longedendale, that is Glossop with the church which is there, with all lands and things and their appurtenances just as William Peverel (bef.1089-54) fully had them in the time of King Henry my grandfather (1100-35). And besides I concede to the same and confirm all their tenements which Earl Ranulf of Chester (bef.1100-53) and other barons of his gave and confirm with their charters, that is Holywell and Fulbrook/Greenfield (*Fulinbroch*, SO.194776) and the chapel of Basingwerk in which they first abode, with the mills and all their appurtenances. Also *Kethlenedei* the gift of Robert Banaster. Also Holway (*Holes*, SO.176766) and half Lloc (*Lecche*, SO.142768) and 100 shillings rendered by Chester which Earl Ranulf gave them. And *Calders* with the men and things and lands and all their appurtenances and anything which was reasonably given to them. Whereby I wish etc.... Witnessed by Chancellor Thomas (Jan 1155-23 May 1162), Constable Richard Hommet (bef.1130-81), Reginald Dunstanville (earl of Cornwall, bef.1115-Dec 1175), Joceline Balliol (bef.1115-70+) and William Fitz Hamon at Chester.

Similarly the December 1181 confirmation to Strata Florida follows a common form, but note at the end how the king has changed from the old standard 'I wish' to the new royal 'we wish'. This was following standard papal practice and shows how royal charters were evolving during the reign of Henry II.

> Henry by the grace of God king of England, duke of Normandy and Aquitaine etc. Know that it is conceded by me etc to the abbey of Strata Florida and the monks there serving God, the reasonable gift which Rhys ap Gruffydd has made to them of the lands written below; namely of the field which is between *Hendreskynavandu* and the torrent of *Buarchegre*, and thence up to the Teifi and *Hirgarth* up to the Flur and up to the Teifi. And of *Langhereth* up to *Hedegeu* with its bounds, and from the river which is called *Pastruth Akelly* it drives up to the Teifi and *Lispennard* and to Strata Florida with its bounds and to *Castell Keven* with its bounds. And to Pennal up to *Dyrondu* and up to *Camdimor* and to *Kevenpuet* with its bounds. And to *Kellyeu Urmdevoy* and to *Maysbre* with its bounds. And to *Fennan Noyr* by *Ritheuelyu* on high up to *Mayesbre*. And from *Drepoyth Riwardh* to the sea. Whereby we wish etc. Witnesses bishops Richard of Winchester (1173-22 Dec 1188), Geoffrey of Ely (1173-bef.1189), Seffrid of Chichester (1181-1204) and Peter Leia of St David's (7

[*33] *Charter Rolls, 1327-1341*, 382-386. A site move from the Afon Flur to the Afon Teifi appears most likely to be associated with this 'refoundation', but the new church does not appear operational until the eve of Whit Sunday 1201, Pen, 183.

Nov 1176-16 Jul 1198), Geoffrey my son the chancellor (1181/2-1189), at Winchester.

These two charters give a good idea of what the late 1186 charter to Aberconwy may have looked like if it were this complex and mentioned any lands[*34]. As it was of a late date, probably late 1186, it would in all likelihood have been more akin to the Strata Florida confirmation in form, but would appear to have been the most general of confirmations as several other charters of Henry were, as discussed below. It is unlikely that the charter stated which Welsh prince had granted which lands to the abbey. This is suggested as neither King John nor his successors ever thought to copy King Henry's charter into their records verbatim as they did with so many other documents. In any case it is possible that the original was destroyed with the abbey muniments in its 1245 sacking. Therefore, all that can be certainly said is that Henry's charter granted the monks protection for themselves and their possessions, which were to be treated as if they belonged to the king himself. If they were the same as those granted by King John, as he claimed, the monks were further quit from all toll, passage and pontage and from all customs pertaining to the king throughout his lands as well, as having quittance of all things that they or their servants could prove to be their own. This was a similar general confirmation of privileges that all Cistercian monasteries seem to have held. It is therefore possible that Henry just issued this general charter and did not mention any lands at all. Certainly no succeeding king thought it necessary to confirm any named lands before 1283/84 when King Edward I transferred the abbey to Maenan. It is therefore eminently possible that no lands at all were mentioned in the charter of Henry II. This was the case in most early royal confirmations to the Cistercian abbeys when these charters seem to have allowed for quittance of toll, passage and pontage through all the king's lands. These were granted by Henry II to Aberconwy (1186?), Margam (2 charters, the first almost certainly 1155 and contemporary and similar to the one to Tintern), Neath (lost but mentioned in King John's 1208 charter) and Tintern (1155). Further, similar quittances were granted by King John to Strata Florida (1200), Strata Marcella (1200), Aberconwy (1202), Margam (1205), Neath (1208) and Whitland (1214). Slightly differently, the grant to Strata Marcella on 11 April 1200, stated that the quittance of tolls excepted London and was only for the monks' own needs[*35].

The circa late 1186 charter of the king to Aberconwy opens up a long discussion that will continue throughout this book. For now it is sufficient to ask in what form were the original early foundation charter or charters to Aberconwy and indeed who made them? It has generally been assumed, without any reliable original evidence, but with the connivance of the fourteenth century monks of Aberconwy, that the main land grants to the abbey were made by Llywelyn ab Iorwerth (d.1240).

A Cistercian house was founded at Rhedynog Felen near Caernarfon in 1186 by a group of monks from Strata Florida Abbey. About four or five years later they moved to Conwy, and in 1199 were given large grants of land by Llywelyn the Great who had recently become ruler of Gwynedd. Llywelyn was regarded as the founder of the

---

[*34] Margam abbey was also taken under the protection of Henry II at least twice during his reign, but the documents that have survived were not confirmations of the abbey's rights, *Cartae et alia munimenta quae ad dominium de Glamorgan pertinent*, ed G.T. Clark [6 vols., Cardiff, 1910] VI, 2270-1.
[*35] *The Charters of the Abbey of Ystrad Marchell*, ed. Thomas, G.C.G. [Aberystwyth, 1997], No.24.

house, and thanks to his support it came to hold more land than any other Welsh abbey, over 40,000 acres (160 km²).[*36]

This ill-conceived statement, as has been seen, contradicts the original documentary evidence for the abbey on several levels. We are therefore left with the task of unravelling who granted what to the abbey and when, as well as what became of these original charters if they ever existed. It is a well known fact that Cistercian abbeys were careful with their documents as these were the proofs of the lands which they held and the key to their prosperity. It should come as little surprise to find that the earliest surviving grant to Aberconwy was not made by Llywelyn ab Iorwerth, but by a predecessor, Prince Gruffydd ap Cynan of North Wales (bef.1155-1200), the older cousin of Llywelyn. Unfortunately this grant has not survived but a copy remains within the Aberconwy Register (See below p. 251, 272).

This copy has every appearance of being a transcript of an original and as this grant was later claimed to have been made by Llywelyn ab Iorwerth in the spurious 'great charter of 1199' it can be seen how the later fabricated charter has swallowed up the gifts of at least one and probably all the original donors. A similar occurrence happened with Abbey Cwmhir, although King John's charter to that institution was not fabricated. Here the gifts of the original princes were consumed into the gifts of later princes when the Cwmhir lands were confirmed in 1215, some forty years after the original gifts were made[*37]. It can therefore be seen that there is absolutely no reason to accept any of the original grants to Aberconwy as having been made by Llywelyn ab Iorwerth, although it is possible, if not likely, that some of these were. To discover who is most likely to have made any such grants to the abbey it is necessary to delve deeply into the politics of Gwynedd between the death of King Owain Gwynedd in 1170 and the overthrow of his heirs and successors by Prince Llywelyn ab Iorwerth at the turn of the thirteenth century. Before that is done it is worthwhile examining the form of Aberconwy abbey and exploring how this church compared to others built in Wales around this time.

[*36] https://en.wikipedia.org/wiki/Aberconwy_Abbey retrieved 6 June 2017.
[*37] These events are examined in Remfry, P.M., *Abbey Cwmhir* [forthcoming].

The First Abbey Church at Aberconwy

According to Giraldus Cambrensis a monastery was standing on the present site of St Mary's church at Aberconwy in April 1188. Quite clearly the outline of the current parish church overlies that of the twelfth century abbey church (Fig.5). The structure has been much analysed and the general consensus is that the east and west ends of the church are the original twelfth century masonry structure, while the nave and aisles in between have been rebuilt between 1245 and 1300[*38]. This dating given for the remains is largely based upon guesswork and is used to fit in with the then suggested historical activities at the abbey. It is undoubtedly too simplistic, although it has been useful groundwork, as hopefully this will be for others to build upon.

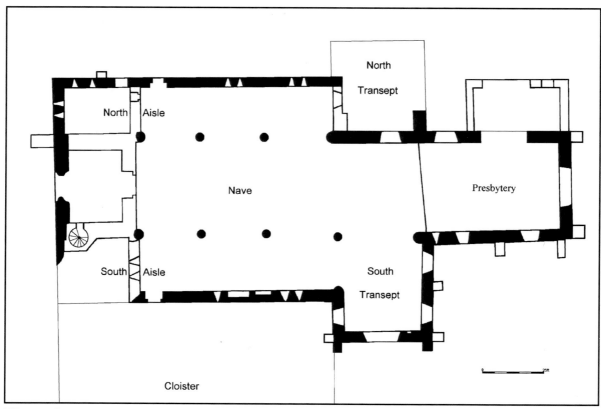

Figure 5, A reconstruction of Aberconwy abbey with the current surviving walls which may stand on original foundations in black.

Unfortunately the remains of the abbey church tell us little of the condition of Gwynedd at the time of the foundation, other than the church was rather small compared to other Cistercian houses in *Pura Walia*; this is shown in the table below - assuming of course that the suggested reconstructions for all these places are correct.

[*38] *Royal Commission on Ancient Monuments in England and Wales, for Caernarvonshire* [3 vols, 1960] I, 39-43, which on the whole merely reworks the conclusions and insights of Hughes, H., 'The architectural history of St Mary's Church, Conway', *Archaeologia Cambrensis*, [1895], 161-179.

Abbeys	Date	Church length	Nave width[39]	Transepts width
Cymer	1199	110'	60'	none
Llantarnam	1180	110'[40]	66'	125'
Strata Florida I	1164[41]	126'	42'	?
Aberconwy	1186?	140'	60'	80'?
Basingwerk	1132/57	150'	60'	90'
Margam	1147	160'	66'	105'
Valle Crucis	1201	170'	78'	115'
Strata Florida II	1184/1201	220'	70'	145'
Whitland	1140/53?	225'	58'	95'
Strata Marcella	1170/72	280'	72'	c.100'
Abbey Cwmhir	1179	300+'	63'	154'

As it seems likely from studies of the fabric that Aberconwy parish church does incorporate parts of the old abbey church, it would appear that this was nearest in congregation size to the first Strata Florida abbey and Whitland. Whitland abbey was founded in 1140, or more likely in 1153, for 100 monks, while Strata Marcella (1170/72), Cwmhir (1176) and Llantarnam (1180) were all founded in the same decade for apparently sixty monks[42].

At Aberconwy the two surviving 'twelfth century' church walls to east and west suggest that the abbey church was a modest 140 feet long. In style it seems most likely that Aberconwy resembled Whitland (1140/53), Strata Marcella (1170/72, Fig.6) and Strata Florida I (1164) in being a cruciform shape with a presbytery the same width as the nave without the aisles and transepts projecting beyond the widths of the aisles. This style was continued at Valle Crucis (1201)[43]. The earlier Savigniac house of Basingwerk (1133/57) follows a similar cruciform plan to that suggested at Aberconwy, but its sister house of Neath (rebuilt 1280?) does not. Instead it has ambulatories the same widths as the aisles surrounding the presbytery and making the east end the same width as the west end. This style apparently first appears in Wales at Margam (1147). Maenan (1284) also follows this plan and it is to be presumed that in this case it is possible that this represents an expansion of the original design of Aberconwy. Despite the similarities of all these Cistercian houses' layouts in Wales, Cymer abbey (1199) is totally dissimilar. This takes on a rectangular form, with the presbytery and choir flanked by the aisles. Further, it totally lacks transepts. The

---

[39] Including aisles if present.

[40] The plan of the church produced by A.G. Mein puts the nave at 200' long, 80' wide with aisles and 150' wide transepts, Williams, D.H., *The Welsh Cistercians* [Bodmin, 2001], 288.

[41] Williams, S.W., *The Cistercian abbey of Strata Florida* [1889], 19-21.

[42] Williams, D.H., *The Welsh Cistercians* [Norwich, 1983, 2 vols] II, 147-8. It has recently been suggested, that Cwmhir was built in two distinct phases, Ralegh-Radford, C.A., 'The Cistercian Abbey of Cwmhir, Radnorshire', *Archaeologia Cambrensis* [1982], 58-76, but this is unproven by excavation and appears an impossible scenario considering the history and documentary evidence for the site, Remfry, P.M., *Abbey Cwmhir* [forthcoming].

[43] For bibliographies of all these sites turn to the Monastic Wales website, www.monasticwales.org

transepts in the surviving abbeys also have subtle differences in size and style. Those at Basingwerk (4), Maenan (6), Neath (4), Strata Florida (6), Valle Crucis (4) and Whitland (4) have small internal chapels on the eastern sides. As the nearest houses in filial links to Aberconwy - namely Whitland, Strata Florida II (Fig.7), Valle Crucis and Maenan - all have these transept chapels, it is quite likely that Aberconwy once had them too, although no trace of them has survived the alterations to the site. The east end of Cwmhir abbey has yet to be excavated and it is impossible from the site to guess what form this took.

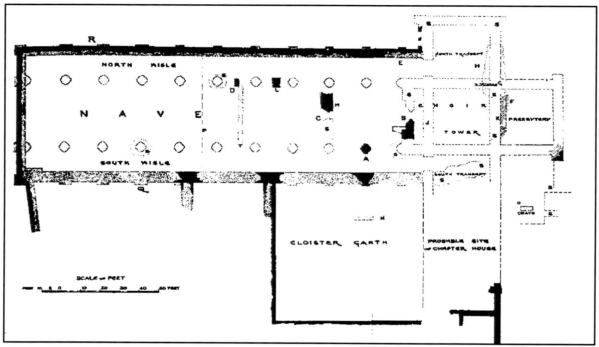

Figure 6, Strata Marcella from the excavation plan in Montgomeryshire Collections XXV [1891].

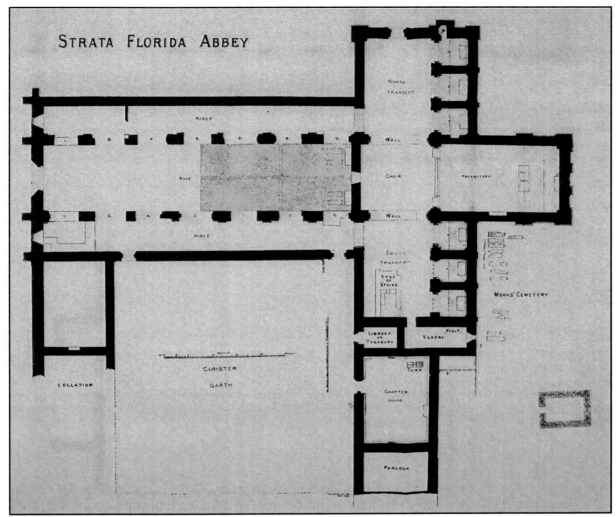

Figure 7, Strata Florida II abbey after excavation in 1889, showing a relatively standard layout of a contemporary Cistercian monastery to Aberconwy.

The Fall and Rise of Gwynedd, 1170 to 1188

To be able to make a reasonable speculation as to who invited the Cistercians into Gwynedd it is first necessary to look closely at political affairs in North Wales at the time of Aberconwy's foundation. Only when the lands held by various princes and when they were granted to the abbey are examined, does it become clear who is likely to have been responsible for the early development of the monastery.

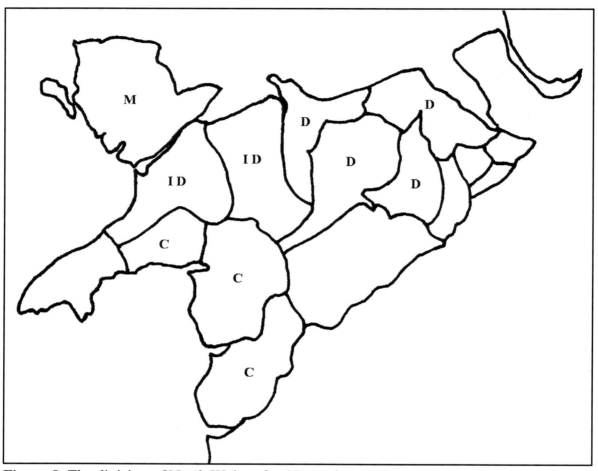

Figure 8, The division of North Wales after November 1170 as suggested by contemporary records.

C = Cynan ab Owain	D = Dafydd ab Owain
ID = Iorwerth Drwyndwn	M = Maelgwn ab Owain

After the death of Owain Gwynedd in November 1170 it has in modern times been claimed that his principality was to pass to his eldest son, the allegedly illegitimate Hywel ab Owain. In the event this did not come to pass and Hywel was assassinated in Mon (Anglesey) by his half brothers, Dafydd and Rhodri ab Owain[*44]. As a result of this, Gwynedd was split amongst several of Owain's surviving sons. Iorwerth Drwyndwn, the future father of

---

[*44] See Remfry, PM, *Medieval Battles: Wales, 1055 to 1216: Volume 2, part 1*, 182, for the killing of Hywel.

Llywelyn ab Iorwerth, received Arfon and Arllechwedd[*45], Cynan ab Owain received Ardudwy, Eifionydd and Meirionydd, Maelgwn ab Owain received Mon and Dafydd ab Owain the border country of Clwyd which later came to be known as the Perfeddwlad, the bowel or gut country which has lately been taken to mean the middle country[*46]. Rhodri seems to have gained nothing for his treachery, although he may have been granted Llyn as he was holding this later and its control at this time is otherwise unknown (Fig.8). Alternatively this cantref and Penllyn may have been held by Cadwaladr ap Gruffydd (d.1172), the younger brother of Owain Gwynedd. With this division civil war seems to have been averted, perhaps with the brothers accepting the tutelage of the much older Cadwaladr who was also known to have used the title 'king'[*47].

Unfortunately the historiography of much of what is thought to have occurred in Gwynedd during this period is coloured by the spite of Giraldus Cambrensis as well as later misunderstandings. When Giraldus came to write up his journey through Wales which had taken place in the spring of 1188, he was not feeling generous to either Rhodri or Dafydd and this can be seen in his text where he makes disingenuous play on their alleged illegitimacy. Despite this, he said nothing about the legitimacy of the sons of Cynan, who were probably the senior surviving descendants of Owain Gwynedd if primogeniture was at play in Gwynedd at this time. The reason for this confusion was simply because Giraldus was having a gibe at people who had not helped him, contrasting them to his 'friend', Llywelyn ab Iorwerth. The meaning of Giraldus' text has also been somewhat skewed in the most available translations. A copy of one is reproduced here as an example.

> I shall pass over in silence what was done by the sons of Owain in our days, after his death, or while he was dying, who, from the wicked desire of reigning, totally disregarded the ties of fraternity; but I shall not omit mentioning another event which occurred likewise in our days.
>
> Owain, son of Gruffydd, prince of North Wales, had many sons, but only one legitimate, namely, Iorwerth Drwyndwn, which in Welsh means flat-nosed, who had a son named Llywelyn. This young man, being only twelve years of age, began, during the period of our journey, to molest his uncles David and Rhodri, the sons of Owain by Christina, his cousin-german; and although they had divided amongst themselves all North Wales, except the land of Cynan, and although David, having married the sister of King Henry II., by whom he had one son, was powerfully supported by the English, yet within a few years the legitimate son, destitute of lands or money (by the aid of divine vengeance), bravely expelled from North Wales those who were born in public incest, though supported by their own wealth and by that of others, leaving them nothing but what the liberality of his own mind and the counsel of good men from pity suggested: a proof that adulterous and incestuous persons are displeasing to God.[*48]

The text of Giraldus is not straight forward and actually originally seems to have run:

[*45] This seems to be the best interpretation of Giraldus Cambrensis, *Opera*, eds. J.S. Brewer, J.F. Dimock and G.F. Warner [8 vols., 1861-91] VI, 134, and *The Myvyrian Archaiology of Wales*, eds. O. Jones, E. Williams & W. Owen [2nd edn., Denbigh, 1870] I, 338 (235-6).
[*46] The term seems first to have been used for the year 1211 in, Pen, 85. The term Perfeddwlad was apparently unknown to Giraldus.
[*47] *Cartulary of Shrewsbury Abbey*, ed. Una Rees [2 vols., Aberystwyth, 1985], No.313.
[*48] Giraldus de Barri, *The Itinerary of Archbishop Baldwin through Wales*, trans. Colt Hoare, R., [2 vols., 1806] II, 124-5.

Quid autem, mortuo Oeneo, vel etiam in extremis agente, filii ejusdem, pravo dominandi ambitu, fraterna non respicientes foedera, diebus nostris inter se gesserint, hic praetereo.

Illud autem, quod nostris hic diebus notabile censi praetereundum non putavi. Oeneus filius Griphini, princeps Norwalliae, inter multos quos genuit filios tantum unum legitimum suscepit, scilicet Ierverdum Troyndun, quod Kambrice simus sonat, agnominatum: qui et filium similiter legitimum suscepit Luelinum. Hic in transitu nostro patruis suis David et Rotherico, quos de consobrina sua cui nomen Christiana Oeneus susceperat, quanquam puer tunc quasi duodennis, infestare coepit. Et licet totam Venedotiam, praeter terram Canani, inter se pro herili portione divisissent; licet etiam propter hoc David Anglicano fulciretur auxilio, puta qui sororem regis Henrici secundi sibi matrimonio copulaverat, ex qua et filium quoque susceperat; tamen intra paucos postmodum annos, de publico incestu natos, divitiis pariter et divitum auxilio fultos, legitimus iste, terris omnino carens et thesauris, a Venedotia fere tota, divina opitulante vindicta, viriliter ejecit: nihil eisdem nisi ultroneo motu, bonorumque virorum consilio, misericorditer et ex pietate relinquens.

Argumentum adulterinos et incestuosos domino displicere.[49]

A more literal translation of this would therefore be:

Which however as Owain died, or even was driven to the point of death, the sons of the same, being corruptly ambitious to rule and not respecting fraternal agreements, in our days [what] they carried on amongst themselves, I will here pass over[50].

But however, I have not thought to neglect any other thing judged notable here in our days. Prince Owain ap Gruffydd of North Wales begot many sons among whom only one was accepted to be legitimate, that was Iorwerth *Troyndun*, whom the Welsh spoke of as snub nosed, [and] honoured; by which means also the son, Llywelyn, was similarly legitimate and supported. In this place we are passing, his paternal uncles, Dafydd and Rhodri, who from his first cousin, who was named Christina, Owain had received [Dafydd and Rhodri], [Llywelyn] although a boy then about twelve, had begun to harass. And although all Gwynedd, except for the land of Cynan, they had divided the superior portion between one another; further that Dafydd might be supported on account of this by the help of the English, thought that he would unite to himself in marriage to the sister of King Henry II, and from whom also he likewise received a son; yet presently within a few years, those [two] born from public incest, propped up equally through the aid of wealth and fertile land, that lawful [son, Llywelyn], altogether without lands and monies, [kept] from Gwynedd almost totally, by the aid of divine vengeance, he manfully drove [them, Rhodri and Dafydd] out; bequeathing nothing to the same unless voluntarily affected, or by the advice of good men, from either compassion or a sense of duty.

[This being] proof that adultery and incest is displeasing to the Lord.

In short, Giraldus does not say that Llywelyn conquered all of North Wales during the 1190s. Obviously writing after 1194 he states that Llywelyn drove out his half-uncles Dafydd and

---

[49] Giraldus Cambrensis, *Opera*, eds. J.S. Brewer, J.F. Dimock and G.F. Warner [8 vols., 1861-91] VI, 134.
[50] This would appear to be an allusion to the murder of Hywel ab Owain and possibly other crimes.

Rhodri, the products of what he alleged was a canonically unlawful marriage, from their domains in the superior or upper part of Gwynedd. Perhaps by this Giraldus was thinking of Llyn, Mon, Arfon, Arllechwedd and just possibly the Perfeddwlad. What he does not mention is any war waged by Llywelyn against the sons of Cynan who are specifically left out from Giraldus' recounting of the tale. It is also obvious that Giraldus does not consider the sons of Cynan to have been illegitimate, even though he claims that only Iorwerth was born legitimately. It would have been odd if he had, as both Cynan and Iorwerth would appear to have been the sons of Gwladys ferch Llywarch of Arwystli. Unfortunately this statement of Giraldus has been totally misunderstood in modern times as can be seen from the Wikipedia summing up of the affair:

> Giraldus Cambrensis refers to Iorwerth Drwyndwn as the only legitimate son of Owain Gwynedd. Following Iorwerth's death, Llywelyn was, at least in the eyes of the church, the legitimate claimant to the throne of Gwynedd.[51]

As Iorwerth, Cynan and probably Rhun (d.1146), were children of the same mother, the ridiculousness of this interpretation of Giraldus' statement that only Iorwerth was legitimate is made clear. The even more ridiculous implication that Giraldus Cambrensis was the eyes of the Roman Church needs no further comment. Checking what is known of their paternity, Owain Gwynedd and Gwladys were in fact half third cousins which placed them in the eighth degree of consanguinity. Before 1215 marriage in or below the seventh degree of consanguinity was considered improper, so by church standards they were properly married, if only by one degree. After 1215 the level was dropped to the fourth degree of consanguinity. By either this or the earlier form, Owain's second marriage to Christina ferch Goronwy before 1150 was then considered unlawful as they were first cousins. Yet there is no evidence that Owain was in any way related to his first 'wife' Pyfog, nor is there any evidence that they were not properly married, though whether by Irish, Welsh or English 'Catholic' rites is unknown. Pyfog would also appear to have borne Owain two further sons, other than Hywel (d.1170), in the form of Cadwallon and Cynwrig. These were both blinded some time after 1165. Therefore, all three of Owain's children by Pyfog had been removed from the succession equation before Giraldus made his statement as to their legitimacy. Similarly, Christina, as Owain's third wife and first cousin, was a suitable bride if the proper papal dispensation had been applied for. Apparently it had not been if Giraldus' word is to be taken for it - and yet can Giraldus' word be trusted? This is especially worrying as he was quite capable of presenting 'the truth' in any manner he chose. Further, he makes no mention of papal dispensation being sought or not. With the confusion of the legitimacy of Owain's children examined and the errors of Giraldus and later writers exposed and hopefully corrected, time must be taken to examine what else Giraldus has to say of affairs in Gwynedd and especially the doings of the sons of Cynan. Once more it is unfortunate that what he wrote has undoubtedly been misconstrued by later writers to further distort the evidence for the foundation of Aberconwy abbey.

In 1172 Cadwaladr ap Gruffydd died, but it is uncertain whether another bout of internecine warfare broke out now or later. Certainly there was fighting in North Wales when civil war raged in England from May 1173 until August 1174. Meanwhile, during 1173 in Wales, according to the later Bruts, Dafydd attacked his half brother Maelgwn and drove him

---

[51] Wikipedia, 'Llywelyn the Great', accessed 8 Nov 2015.

from Mon. This would appear to have been done to aid King Henry II against his enemies. At the time it was recorded that Dafydd and Owain were the only kings to remain true to their king in Wales[52]. The *Evayn* of the text probably stands for Owain Cyfeiliog, who was loyal to Henry in 1177 and often used royal forces to protect his lands[53]. Despite that, this statement is definitely in error for Rhys ap Gruffydd also remained loyal to Henry and even marched a Welsh army from Deheubarth to Tutbury to besiege the rebel earl of Derby[54]. Once more it can be seen that the Bruts were at best economical with the truth and at worst deliberately misleading.

It was probably as a result of Dafydd's services in 1173 that the king, before Michaelmas 1174, rather reluctantly allowed his half-sister, Emma Plantagenet, to marry the Welshman. Dafydd's intention was said to have been to instill fear in his Welsh enemies at the power of his new relationship and the pride he would feel in having sons from royal stock[55]. The sheriffs of London provided £28 17s for her wedding outfit, but there is no record of any dower[56]. Therefore Dafydd's purpose seems to have been correctly divined by the chroniclers as the wish for royal children and to overawe his enemies by the implied strength of his new in-laws. Certainly the Norman king did aid his new brother-in-law by sending the Welsh Marcher Lord Roger Powys of Whittington to aid Dafydd. Roger consequently marched a royal army at least as far as Degannwy (*Daggenot*) and possibly all the way to Mon, which was merely on the other side of the Menai straits from there[57]. It is interesting to note that before Michaelmas 1174 Simon the monk, the nuncio of Dafydd ab Owain, was given a gift of 20 shillings by the king apparently in London[58]. As the king was probably only in London from 14 to 17 July 1174[59] it seems likely that the messenger reached him then. Similarly, Simon the monk, nuncio of Dafydd ab Owain, received 13s 4d by the writ of Richard Lucy in Hampshire[60]. The king's gift to the monk would suggest that he had received good news - possibly that Dafydd had conquered Mon, or even the rest of Gwynedd. Certainly the sum given strongly suggests that the news was good and that it was more than merely the fact that Dafydd had successfully married Emma.

At this time civil war was disturbing all King Henry's domains, so it is to be presumed that Dafydd favoured his king, while Maelgwn and possibly other sons of Owain Gwynedd attempted to re-establish some measure of independence. In this they were obviously unsuccessful and Dafydd extended his influence throughout North Wales. It is also possible that Iorwerth Drwyndwn, the father of Llywelyn (1172-1240), died this year, perhaps

---

[52] *Gesta Regis Henrici Secundi Benedicti Abbatis* ed. Stubbs, W. [2 vols, 1867] I, 51.

[53] Giraldus Cambrensis, *Opera*, eds. J.S. Brewer, J.F. Dimock and G.F. Warner [8 vols., 1861-91] VI, 144-5.

[54] Ralph de Diceto, *Opera Historica*, ed. W. Stubbs [2 vols., 1876] I, 384; Roger of Wendover, Flowers of History [Llanerch], II, 30; *PR 20 Henry II*, 121. For the supply of Rhys' royalist soldiers see *PR 20 Henry II*, 21.

[55] Ralph de Diceto, *Opera Historica*, ed. W. Stubbs [2 vols., 1876] I, 397-8.

[56] *PR 20 Henry II*, 9, 16, 94. *PR 22 Henry II*, 57, describes her as the sister of King Henry.

[57] Suppe, F., 'Roger of Powis, Henry II's Anglo-Welsh Middleman and his Lineage', 15, suggests that this was Haughley in Sussex, which was then called '*Haganet*'. In 1173 Haughley was besieged and captured by the king's enemies, but there is no other evidence of a relief operation being launched from Whittington, nearly 200 miles away. It would have taken foot serjeants a minimum of ten days to march there. In any case any relief operation would surely have been undertaken from the royalist army at Leicester which went on to defeat the rebels at the battle of Fornham on 22 September immediately after the fall of Haughley, or *castello de Hageneth* as it was called in *The Historical Works of Gervase of Canterbury*, ed. W. Stubbs [2 vols, 1878-80] I, 246. In contrast Degannwy is only 54 miles from Whittington via Denbigh.

[58] *PR 20 Henry II*, 7.

[59] Eyton, R.W., *Court, Household and Itinerary of Henry II* [1878], 181.

[60] *PR 20 Henry II*, 133. As King Henry landed at Southampton on 8 July and set off for London the next day, Eyton, R.W., *Court, Household and Itinerary of Henry II* [1878], 180, it seems likely that Simon failed to find the king there and Richard Lucy gave him some way money and sent him on his way so that he finally caught up with the king at Winchester later in July. Alternatively, Simon came with a message for the king a second time and reached Hampshire after Henry returned to the continent via Southampton at the end of July 1174, *Idem*, 183-4. From there Lucy gave him his way passage either to cross the Channel to the king or to return home.

from a wound sustained in battle, though whether he was fighting for or against King Henry is another matter. The elegy to Iorwerth composed by Seisyll Bryffwrch styled him prince of Arfon and placed his burial at *Llandudclud*, now known as Penmachno in Arllwechwed[61].

Whatever else happened in Wales, the year 1174 saw not only the royal marriage of Dafydd, but also his successful occupation of all Gwynedd. Thus it was recorded in the Bruts that Dafydd:

> gained possession of all Gwynedd, after expelling all his brothers and [nephews]... Maelgwn was seized by Dafydd, his brother, and imprisoned. In that year Prince Cynan ab Owain of Gwynedd died.[62]

It was probably around this time that Gwilym Rhyfel, his court poet, described Dafydd as king of Cemaes (*Vreyenhin Kemeis*) and blessed with the strength of Hercules, the wisdom of Solomon and comeliness of Adam[63].

During the period 1173 to 1174 the fighting throughout North Wales may have been strenuous although unfortunately next to nothing of it has been preserved to posterity. All that is known is that the ultra-royalist Dafydd kept King Henry informed of what was happening and that after his victory he may have encouraged the clergy of St Asaph to regularise their bishopric. Thus it was that on 18 May 1175 the clergy of his diocese petitioned the archbishop of Canterbury that Bishop Godfrey of St Asaph (1160-75) should be forced back to his flock from Abingdon, where he was administering the abbey for Henry II, or else resign his place to another. Bishop Godfrey seems to have begun his exile in either 1164 or 1165 due to the revolt of Owain Gwynedd and his campaigns in the Perfeddwlad[64]. When pushed the bishop preferred resignation and Adam, a Welshman as well as a canon of Paris, was consecrated in his place[65]. It would seem likely that Godfrey did not like the warlike nature of his flock. Yet he benefited little from his resignation for on 11 July he was dispossessed of Abingdon abbey, of which he had hoped to have been made abbot[66].

Some time, probably early in 1175, Dafydd seized his uterine younger brother Rhodri and imprisoned him as the young man had dared to ask for his share of the princely patrimony. According to the Bruts, it was only now that Dafydd married the king's sister, though this actually occurred two years previously, so it is possible that Rhodri had initially fought with Dafydd and then claimed some form of territorial reward in the peace that followed. During this period of his supremacy Dafydd issued at least two charters in Llyn where he claimed to be King of North Wales[67]. In one of these he styled himself *David Rex Norwallie* and in the other *David Rex filius Owini*. The latter charter was witnessed by Roger Powys of Whittington, the man who had aided him in his march to Degannwy in 1173. The earlier charter was witnessed by Bishop Gwion of Bangor. As Bishop Gwion was only

---

[61] *The Myvyrian Archaiology of Wales*, eds. O. Jones, E. Williams & W. Owen [2nd edn., Denbigh, 1870] I, 338. One of the gravestones at Penmachno is associated with Iorwerth.
[62] Pen, 70.
[63] *The Myvyrian Archaiology of Wales*, eds. O. Jones, E. Williams & W. Owen [2nd edn., Denbigh, 1870] I, 274 and partial translation in Lloyd, J.E., *History of Wales* [2 vols., 1911] II, 551.
[64] See *Councils and Ecclesiastical Documents relating to GB and Ireland*, ed. A.W. Haddan and W. Stubbs [2 vols., Oxford, 1869-78] I, 362-3.
[65] *Gesta Regis Henrici Secundi Benedicti Abbatis* ed. Stubbs, W. [2 vols, 1867] I, 90-1; *Chronica Magistri Rogeri de Hovedene*, ed. W. Stubbs [4 vols., 1868-71] II, 78. Ralph de Diceto, *Opera Historica*, ed. W. Stubbs [2 vols., 1876] I, 587, states that he was consecrated at Westminster on 13 October 1175.
[66] *Chronicon Monasterii de Abingdon* [2 vols, 1858] II, 234, 293.
[67] *Cartulary of Haughmond Abbey*, ed. Una Rees [Aberystwyth, 1983], Nos. &785&786.

formally consecrated by the archbishop of Canterbury in May 1177 it has universally been asserted that Dafydd still retained power in Llyn at some point after this date[68]. Yet as Gwion's predecessor, Bishop Meurig, had died as long ago as 1162 it is far more likely that Gwion was acting as bishop of Bangor from way before the date he was officially consecrated on 15 May 1177 at Amesbury[69]. Certainly he is described as the bishop elect of Bangor before his consecration and even simply as bishop of Bangor at the 13 March 1177 council of Westminster[70]. It therefore seems almost certain that this is what he was when he witnessed Dafydd's charter almost certainly made during the tumultuous years of 1174 to 1175.

Towards the end of 1175 a revolution occurred in Dafydd's new kingdom. Rhodri escaped and drove his brother out of Mon and across the River Conwy[71]. The implication of this is that Rhodri held Gwynedd and Mon from the end of 1175 onwards, but this is uncertain, for quite obviously the sons of Cynan ap Gruffydd (d.1174) also obtained lands in southern Gwynedd at least, if they had ever been dispossessed. This can be confirmed from the Brut entry for 1178 when 'the sons of Cynan waged war against Rhys ap Gruffydd'[72]. The obvious implication of this is that they were holding Meirionydd and possibly more of North Wales at this time. During this period there were three sons of Cynan, Gruffydd (d.1200), Einion (d.1185) and Maredudd (d.1212). After 1178 the Bruts are again silent over the affairs of North Wales, but it may be significant that one of the sons of Cynan, Einion ap Cynan, died in 1185 at Strata Florida abbey, for it was the next year, 1186, that a community left that abbey to found Aberconwy. It is also apparent that Gruffydd ap Cynan and possibly his brother, Maredudd, were major donors to the new abbey. Quite possibly Aberconwy was founded in memory of the recent loss of their brother, but this is jumping ahead of the chronology.

In late 1175 Dafydd, after his expulsion from Gwynedd and Mon by Rhodri, was left as 'king' of the Perfeddwlad. He ruled this from his major castles of Rhuddlan, Denbigh and Ellesmere, the latter of which he held by the grant of King Henry II. This remained his powerbase for the next twenty years, although there is some evidence that he constructed or garrisoned other castles further west, viz. Pentrefoelas, Gronant and Degannwy. To the west Rhodri held Mon for certain, while his influence was felt strongly on the other side of the Menai west of the Conwy. The possession of Degannwy castle at this time is problematic and Giraldus tells us nothing other than he passed underneath its walls when passing to Rhuddlan. It was quite possibly held by Rhodri at this time, although without firm evidence Dafydd cannot be ruled out as being its lord during this period. The fortress would appear to have fallen to Gruffydd ap Cynan in 1194 and then to Llywelyn ab Iorwerth as is suggested in Llywarth ap Llywelyn's poem to the prince of circa 1204. This subject is examined in a later chapter. However, a poem of Prydydd y Moch states that Gruffydd ap Cynan (d.1200) held Degannwy at the time of his death. As such it would simply have been acquired by Llywelyn when he took over the bulk of North Wales in 1200.

Two bardic poems survive of this era of strife, one of which must date to 1175. In this Gwalchmai bewails the setback suffered by his patron Dafydd.

---

[68] As followed in Acts, 332-3, *Cartulary of Haughmond Abbey*, ed. Una Rees [Aberystwyth, 1983] etc.

[69] *Gesta Regis Henrici Secundi Benedicti Abbatis* ed. Stubbs, W. [2 vols, 1867] I, 165-6; *Canterbury Professions*, ed. Richter, M. [Torquay, 1973], No.113. Ralph de Diceto, *Opera Historica*, ed. W. Stubbs [2 vols., 1876] I, 420, says that Gwion was the best of those elected (*electus antisties*).

[70] *Gesta Regis Henrici Secundi Benedicti Abbatis* ed. Stubbs, W. [2 vols, 1867] I, 144, 154.

[71] Pen, 70.

[72] Pen, 72.

I shall be poorly bested without it,
The friendship of my renowned Dafydd
Rhodri will not keep me; he needs me not
He sets no price upon me.[*73]

Fortunately for the poet he misjudged Rhodri; within the next few years he went on to praise the prince as 'the great rampart of his people'[*74].

Why King Henry did not aid his brother-in-law in his time of danger is unknown and is in stark contrast to Dafydd's conduct in supporting Henry in 1173-74. The period of civil war in England had effectively ended by early August 1174, but King Henry still had to deal with continental enemies and consequently crossed to Barfleur on 8 August. The next year, 1175, was spent by the king in trying to repair some of the damage done during the fighting. In this King Henry was far from vindictive. One contemporary even felt it necessary to defend Henry's lenient policy towards his traitors. Diceto thought that Henry acted for the best of his sons and his country as he believed it was his duty as king to preserve his people from the horrors of war which included bloodshed and oppressions as well as the loss of law and order[*75]. This is a fitting testament to Henry II, a king who, according to Giraldus, 'dreaded the doubtful arbitration of war... and grieved more than any prince for those lost in battle...'[*76]. During 1175 and 1176 King Henry toured his English realm and demolished any castle that had been held against him as he saw fit[*77].

Despite his heavy schedule King Henry visited many places within his kingdom and came to Shrewsbury in mid January 1176 where he met with Bishop Adam of St Asaph[*78]. It is possible that Prince Dafydd sent the bishop of his lands to see his king. Certainly king and prince were acting in harmony concerning Hamner church in Mealor Saesneg at this time when they appear to have sent a joint petition to Bishop Richard of Coventry, *ad peticionem Domini Henrici Regis et David principis*[*79].

Thus it was only in May 1177 that Henry turned his attention to what had occurred in Wales and yet again he sought to mildly punish his traitors and reward his friends. By this time Dafydd had lost control of all North Wales west of the Conwy. Initially some unnamed Welshmen met King Henry at Geddington, probably on 2 May 1177, and there paid him homage[*80]. However, the main Welsh discussions obviously did not start for a further week, even though the baronage and ecclesiastics of the realm had come to Henry by 2 May at his command.

After 8 May and before 22 May 1177, many Welsh rulers met the king at Oxford just after Henry had returned the estates and castles of Earl Hugh of Chester to him. Earl Hugh was the hereditary enemy of the princes of Gwynedd and his armies often campaigned in the Perfeddwlad which was now held by Dafydd. Those who came to Oxford were King Rhys ap Gruffydd of South Wales, King Dafydd ab Owain of North Wales, King Cadwallon of Elfael as well as Owain Cyfeiliog, Gruffydd of Bromfield, Madog ab Iorwerth Goch and many other

---

[*73] *The Myvyrian Archaiology of Wales*, eds. O. Jones, E. Williams & W. Owen [2nd edn., Denbigh, 1870] I, 198-9, translated in Lloyd, J.E., *History of Wales* [2 vols., 1911] II, 552.
[*74] *The Myvyrian Archaiology of Wales*, eds. O. Jones, E. Williams & W. Owen [2nd edn., Denbigh, 1870] I, 199-200.
[*75] Ralph de Diceto, *Opera Historica*, ed. W. Stubbs [2 vols., 1876] I, 393-4.
[*76] Giraldus Cambrensis, *Opera*, eds. J.S. Brewer, J.F. Dimock and G.F. Warner [8 vols., 1861-91] V, 303.
[*77] Ralph de Diceto, *Opera Historica*, ed. W. Stubbs [2 vols., 1876] I, 398, 404: *Gesta Regis Henrici Secundi Benedicti Abbatis* ed. Stubbs, W. [2 vols, 1867] I, 126-7.
[*78] Eyton, R.W., *Court, Household and Itinerary of Henry II* [1878], 198.
[*79] *Cartulary of Haughmond Abbey*, ed. Una Rees [Aberystwyth, 1983], No's. 492, 494.
[*80] *Gesta Regis Henrici Secundi Benedicti Abbatis* ed. Stubbs, W. [2 vols, 1867] I, 159.

nobles of Wales[81]. These 'other nobles of Wales' would appear to be the followers of the above named kings and princes. Those who can immediately be seen to be missing from the meeting are Rhodri ab Owain as well as the three sons of Cynan ab Owain - Gruffydd, Einion and Maredudd. The reason for this soon becomes clear, they had and were continuing to oppose King Henry II. The chronicler goes on to state that at the conference, assembly or parliament (*colloquium*[82]), the king granted Dafydd the land of Ellesmere as he had already married the king's sister (whose name was left a blank in the manuscript) and for this Dafydd:

> swore there in that very place in person to his lord the king of England to be faithful from that time onwards as his liege; and he swore that he would keep the peace with the kingdom of England.

Similarly King Henry granted the land of Meirionydd to King Rhys of South Wales on the condition that:

> he himself swore faith and liege and to observe the peace.

These terms are themselves interesting. Both Dafydd and Rhys were given lands, but their terms appear different. Dafydd received lands that had previously belonged to the princes of Powys while Rhys was granted a territory that had intermittently belonged to the kings of Gwynedd since time immemorial. Further, Dafydd was allocated no lands in Gwynedd by King Henry, but was recognised as king of North Wales, which implied that all Mon and Gwynedd belonged to him. Perhaps this is why King Henry publically gave Rhys Meirionydd and this was to be Rhys' payment for aiding Dafydd in conquering the rest of his realm, which he had lost in 1175. It also appears that Dafydd entered into a more defined peace with King Henry in 1177, of a type that Rhys had submitted to as long ago as 1171 - hence the different wordings of their oaths. Unfortunately it is not possible to read too much into these statements. Certainly another contemporary chronicler saw matters somewhat differently. He stated:

> And in the same council there came to the king, Prince Rhys ap Gruffydd of South Wales and Prince Dafydd ab Owain of North Wales, who had married a sister of the same king of England, and Prince Cadwallon of Elfael and Owain Cyfeiliog and Gruffydd of Bromfield and Madog ab Iorwerth Goch and many other nobles of Wales and all became men of the elder king of England, and swore faithfulness to him against all men and to keep the peace with him and his kingdom. While in the same council the lord king of England gave to the aforesaid Rhys ap Gruffydd the land of Meirionydd and to David ab Owain the land of Ellesmere.[83]

The subtle difference of who swore what in this account is omitted, but the idea that Rhys and Dafydd were to launch a joint invasion of Gwynedd remains.

That such a war took place seems obvious from the scant mentions in the Brut, though it is to be regretted that more was not recorded.

---

[81] *Gesta Regis Henrici Secundi Benedicti Abbatis* ed. Stubbs, W. [2 vols, 1867] I, 162. The thirteenth century Walter of Coventry, *Historical Collections*, ed. W. Stubbs [2 vols., 1872-3] I, 289, copies Benedict virtually verbatim.
[82] Scottish parliaments were called colloquiums from 1235 and it therefore seems likely that this was an early English parliament.
[83] *Chronica Magistri Rogeri de Hovedene*, ed. W. Stubbs [4 vols., 1868-71] II, 134-5.

The sons of Cynan waged war against Rhys ap Gruffydd.[*84]

It is also interesting that Dafydd ab Owain was not mentioned in this brief entry. It is to be presumed that he waged war along the Conwy while the three sons of Cynan - Einion, Gruffydd and Maredudd - held their own in the west. The outcome of the war was obviously that Rhys was defeated, for when the political landscape is next seen clearly, Meirionydd still belonged to the sons of Cynan and Dafydd had failed to cross the Conwy. It is unknown on which side Rhodri ab Owain fought, but it is to be presumed that he allied with the sons of Cynan as he does not appear to have gone to Oxford, unless of course he was considered an underling of Dafydd and consequently not worth recording. This latter explanation seems unlikely.

Meanwhile some of the doings of Dafydd ab Owain came to the fore. While returning from Oxford Dafydd joined forces with one erstwhile enemy so it was recorded that:

> Earl Hugh of Chester took all Bromfield on 13 June, the second holiday on the day after Pentecost, while he was supported by Dafydd ab Owain and a small band of soldiers.[*85]

It is unfortunate that nothing further is known about this affair. Gruffydd Maelor of Bromfield (1147-91) was married to Angharad, the sister of Cynan and Iorwerth and therefore all were the children of Owain Gwynedd (d.1170). Gruffydd had been present at Oxford. It therefore seems somewhat unlikely that he was the target of this act of aggression, especially by a loyalist joined with a former rebel against Henry II. Perhaps then Bromfield at this time had fallen to Owain Fychan ap Madog, the probably elder brother of Gruffydd Maelor. Certainly he was said to be lord of this district in 1175, but at his death in 1191 he was recorded as prince of Maelor, Ial, Nanheudwy, Cynllaith and Mochnant Is Rhaeadr. As such this could have been an action by royalists against an outlaw of King Henry's peace.

Despite his defeat in North Wales, mainly at the hands of his brother, Rhodri, King Dafydd did not consider his eclipse terminal. Indeed, English chroniclers still regarded him as king or prince of North Wales, and this was a title that Dafydd himself apparently never ceased to use despite the disappointments that he met with. In the period between 10 August 1186 and April 1194, Dafydd described himself in his charter as *David filius Owini Princeps Norwallie*, when he made a grant within Ellesmere lordship with the consent of his wife Emma as well as his heir, Owain. This he notified to all his faithful men both French and English, but rather surprisingly not Welsh. The grant was witnessed by Bishop Reiner of St Asaph, Cynwrig ap Cadwgan who was Dafydd's chaplain, Ralph Lega and William Culemere. This grant was also confirmed by Dafydd's wife who described herself as the Lady Emma, the sister of King Henry and wife of Prince Dafydd ab Owain of North Wales (*Domina Emma soror Henrici regis uxor David filii Owini principis Norwallie*). The witnesses were more inclusive than those few of Dafydd and included Cadwgan ap Peiler', Cynwrig ap Cadwgan (without his designation as Dafydd's chaplain), Chaplain Arthur (who was presumably chaplain to Emma), Alan the seneschal of the Lord Dafydd, William Hortuna, Einion ap Cadwgan, Ivone Aelega, Chaplain Guy and William Colemere (again). Interestingly this grant was further confirmed by their son, Owain ap Dafydd, but his

---

[*84] Pen, 72.
[*85] *Annales Cestrienses, a chronicle of the abbey of St. Werburgh, Chester*, ed. and trans. Christie, R.C., Record Society for Lancashire and Cheshire XIV [1887], 25.

witnesses were far more powerful in English circles, being, William Fitz Alan (1154-1210), John Lestrange (bef.1159-1234), Hugh Pantulf (bef.1150-1224), Hamo Lestrange (bef.1161-1221), Vivian Rossel (bef.1185-1235), Stephen Stanton (bef.1175-1215+), Odo Hodnet (bef.1165-1201), Reiner and Ralph the clerks, Chaplain Martin of Ellesmere, Chaplain Robert, Einion Seis and Dwywg (*dooc*) the servants of Dafydd my father[*86]. As Odo Hodnet had died before 1 October 1201[*87] this charter was made while Dafydd was said to be still alive. However, it is possible that Dafydd was killed in 1200 so this charter may have been made either in 1197-98 while Prince Dafydd was in the custody of Llywelyn ab Iorwerth or immediately after his possible death on 1 January 1200[*88]. There is yet another charter to Haughmond that is made by Emma the spouse of Dafydd ab Owain (*Emma sponsa David filii Owini*) that probably again dates to the time after his release in February 1198, but before his death[*89].

When 'Prince Llywelyn of North Wales' took over Ellesmere in March 1205 as his marriage portion from King John[*90], he seems to have immediately confirmed this charter of 'his uncle, Dafydd ab Owain' as was witnessed by Bishop Reiner of St Asaph (1186-1224), Archdeacon Elise of St Asaph, Owain ab Ednowain (Gwyn ab Ednywain, d.1215), Gwion ap Jonas (the step father of Prince Llywelyn, bef.1171 - July 1210[*91]), Cleric Reiner of Ellesmere, Richard and Hugh his sons, William Horhtun and Ralph Lega[*92]. Many of these witnesses are similar to those who served Dafydd. Despite his claims to lordship in these charters, in another act to Haughmond abbey, Dafydd merely makes the grant as *David filius Owini et Emma uxor mea* and confirms that this was done with the consent of his son and heir, Owain, who later confirmed the deed[*93]. It has been argued quite cogently that this deed dates to after February 1198 when Dafydd was released by Llywelyn ab Iorwerth into the hands of the archbishop of Canterbury. It is possibly at this time that Llywelyn took over Dafydd's title as *princeps Norwallie*, that Dafydd seems to have previously used from the 1180s onwards. This might explain Dafydd not being given a title in this deed which certainly dates to after 25 April 1194, when King Richard I issued a confirmation to Haughmond abbey which does not contain this grant[*94].

It was probably also soon after March 1205 when Llywelyn described himself as *Lewelinus Princeps Norwallie* when he confirmed the grant of 'our uncle, Dafydd ab Owain' of the land of Kenwick in Ellesmere[*95]. Yet when these lands were confirmed on 4 June 1344 they consisted of gifts from Llywelyn formerly prince of North Wales (*Lewelyn nadgairs prince de Northgales*) as well as by Prince Dafydd ab Owain of North Wales (*David fitz Oweyn prince de Northgales*)[*96]. Presumably the formerly in the case of Llywelyn was due to the quashing of Llywelyn ap Gruffydd's title in 1282 or the terminology used by the Exchequer during the principality of Dafydd ap Llywelyn (d.1246). It is noteworthy that when Llywelyn confirmed gifts made in Nefyn in Llyn by King Dafydd ab Owain of North

[*86] *Cartulary of Haughmond Abbey*, ed. Una Rees [Aberystwyth, 1983], No's.1169, 1170, 1171.
[*87] *Pleas before the King or his Justices, 1198-1212*, ed. Stenton, D.M. [London, 1967] III, 65.
[*88] See chapter on Owain ap Dafydd, p.101.
[*89] *Cartulary of Haughmond Abbey*, ed. Una Rees [Aberystwyth, 1983], No.1173.
[*90] *Rotuli Litterarum Patentium in Turri Londinensi asservati [1201-16]* ed. T.D. Hardy [1835] I, 51b.
[*91] Jonas' career and marriage is examined in Remfry, P.M., *Whittington Castle and the Families of....* [2007], 49ff.
[*92] *Cartulary of Haughmond Abbey*, ed. Una Rees [Aberystwyth, 1983], No.1172. Owain ab Ednowain was Prince Llywelyn's seneschal and will be mentioned later.
[*93] *Cartulary of Haughmond Abbey*, ed. Una Rees [Aberystwyth, 1983], No's. 268, 269.
[*94] *Cartulary of Haughmond Abbey*, ed. Una Rees [Aberystwyth, 1983], No.200.
[*95] *Cartulary of Haughmond Abbey*, ed. Una Rees [Aberystwyth, 1983], No.657.
[*96] *Cartulary of Haughmond Abbey*, ed. Una Rees [Aberystwyth, 1983], No.658.

Wales, as well as by the untitled Maredudd ap Cynan and Gruffydd ap Cynan, Llywelyn did not use any title for his predecessors, although he did call Cadwaladr the brother of the Great or Senior Owain (*Owini Magni*)[*97]. This suggests that Llywelyn did not recognise the title of his uncles and cousins to rule North Wales and ignored that title when he confirmed their documents.

With the defeat of Rhys ap Gruffydd in Meirionydd some form of peace seems to have returned to North Wales and silence resumes in the records. It was during this time of relative peace, of which the Bruts are singularly uninformative, that Aberconwy abbey was founded. By 1187 at the latest, Rhodri ab Owain had penetrated as far south as Garn Fadryn in Llyn which had been newly fortified by the spring of 1188. Despite this evidence it is difficult to understand where his power extended to between Llyn and the lands of Dafydd. Between the two brothers lay the major power block in the hands of the sons of Cynan ab Owain (d.1174) and to better understand this complex geopolitical position it is necessary to take a closer look at the itinerary of Giraldus Cambrensis through Wales and what this actually tells of conditions in the North, rather than relying on the conclusions which have often been erroneously drawn from this tainted source.

Giraldus Cambrensis and the trip through North Wales in 1188

Giraldus Cambrensis made a trip around Wales in the spring of 1188 accompanying the archbishop of Canterbury and his party in raising troops for the forthcoming crusade. This religious expedition has been much discussed in historical terms, but few have delved deeply into the politics of North Wales and Powys[*98]. This was hardly surprising as both principalities were undergoing a time of turmoil which had ensued after the death of their respective kings, Owain Gwynedd in 1170 and Madog ap Maredudd in 1160. In the south things were somewhat more harmonious under the auspices of Rhys ap Gruffydd (d.1197), but by no means stable. This partially explains Giraldus' quick trip around Gwynedd, but leisurely progress through the more settled Deheubarth and its Marches.

The part of Giraldus' trip that throws some light on the political conditions in Gwynedd around the time of the foundation of Aberconwy abbey, is the section of his advance through Meirionydd and Llyn to Nefyn and from Nefyn via Caernarfon, Bangor and Mon to Rhuddlan. It is therefore worth examining what he first says about the district in general as well as copying in full and then translating the original text of the particulars relevant to Aberconwy and comparing them to how this evidence has been expounded in the past. This is necessary to see what he actually said, rather than what subsequent historians and archaeologists have thought that he said. Book II of his itinerary, Chapter 5, deals with the archdeacon's trip through Meirionydd[*99].

[*97] *Cartulary of Haughmond Abbey*, ed. Una Rees [Aberystwyth, 1983], No.789.
[*98] Giraldus Cambrensis, *Opera*, eds. J.S. Brewer, J.F. Dimock and G.F. Warner [8 vols., 1861-91]; Giraldus de Barri, *The Itinerary of Archbishop Baldwin through Wales*, trans. Colt Hoare, R., [1808]; *The Itinerary through Wales*, [Dent, J.M., London, 1908]; Butler, HE. & Williams, CH., *The Autobiography of Giraldus Cambrensis*, [1937]; Owen, H., *Gerald the Welshman* [1889]; Jones, T., *Gerald the Welshman* [1947]; *Gerald of Wales. The Journey through Wales / The Description of Wales* Trans. Thorpe, L. [1978]; Morris, R., *Gerald of Wales* [1987]; *A Mirror of Medieval Wales, Gerald of Wales and his Journey of 1188*, Kightly, C.,[Cadw: 1988]; Remfry, P.M., *Harlech Castle and its True Origins* [2013], 12-21.
[*99] The original Latin is transcribed in Giraldus Cambrensis, *Opera*, eds. J.S. Brewer, J.F. Dimock and G.F. Warner [8 vols., 1861-91] VI, 122-3. This translation is based upon Dent's 1908 version, Dent, *The Itinerary through Wales: Description of Wales by Giraldus Cambrensis* [London, 1935], 113-4, which in turn is based upon Giraldus de Barri, *The Itinerary of Archbishop Baldwin through Wales*, trans. Colt Hoare, R., [2 vols., 1806], II, 77-8. Roger Pearse's Quick Latin programme has been used to begin the translations throughout this book. This uses Whitaker's Words 1.97 dictionary and is an excellent tool for initial readings before using Latham, R.E., *Revised Medieval Latin Word-list* [Oxford, 1983]. Quick Latin can be found at http://www.quicklatin.com

Of the river Devi, and the land of the sons of Cynan

Approaching to the River Dovey, which divides North and South Wales, the bishop of St. David's, and Rhys ap Gruffydd, who with a liberality peculiarly praiseworthy in so illustrious a prince, had accompanied us from the castle of Aberteivi, throughout all Ceredigion, to this place, returned home. Having crossed the river in a boat, and quitted the diocese of St. David's, we entered the land of the sons of Cynan, or Meirionydd, the first province of Venedotia on that side of the country, and belonging to the bishopric of Bangor. We slept that night at Towyn. Early next morning, Gruffydd ap Cynan came to meet us, humbly and devoutly asking pardon for having so long delayed his attention to the archbishop. On the same day, we ferried over the divided river Maw, where Maelgwn ap Rhys, who had attached himself to the archbishop, as a companion to the king's court, discovered a ford near the sea. That night we lay at Llanfair, that is the church of St. Mary, in the province of Ardudwy. This territory of Cynan, and particularly Meirionydd, is the rudest and roughest district of all Wales; the ridges of its mountains are very high and narrow, terminating in sharp peaks, and so irregularly jumbled together, that if the shepherds conversing or disputing with each other from their summits, should agree to meet, they could scarcely effect their purpose in the course of the whole day. The lances of this country are very long; for as South Wales excels in the use of the bow, so North Wales is distinguished for its skill in the lance; insomuch that an iron coat of mail will not resist the force of a lance thrown at a small distance. The next morning, the youngest son of Cynan, named Maredudd, met us at the passage of a bridge, attended by his people, where many persons were signed with the cross; amongst whom was a fine young man of his suite, and one of his intimate friends; and Maredudd, observing that the cloak, on which the cross was to be sewed, appeared of too thin and of too common a texture, with a flood of tears, threw him down his own.

It should be remembered reading this, that translation is quite a personal enterprise and rarely will two people translate Latin the same way. There is always a different point of emphasis and multiple ways to reconstruct a sentence[*100]. Despite this, the text makes it clear that after having crossed the Dovey, probably from Borth to Aberdyfi, the party was within Gwynedd and in the cantref of Meirionydd, which was ruled by Gruffydd ap Cynan. This agrees with the Bruts describing the war between the sons of Cynan and Rhys ap Gruffydd of Deheubarth in 1178.

The next chapter of Giraldus is of greater relevance, for it describes the area where the lands of the sons of Owain (Dafydd and Rhodri were the only known surviving sons of Owain Gwynedd at this time) and the sons of Cynan (Gruffydd and Maredudd) met.

De Traitmaur et Traitbochan t[ra]nscursis de Nevin q[uo]q[ue] et Kairarvon et Bangor cu[m] not[abilibus] suis.

Transivim[us] inde Traitmaur et Traitbochan i[d est] t[ra]ctum maris majore[m] et t[ra]ctum minore[m] ubi duo castra lapidea de nova sita fueru[n]t unu[m] i[n] Evionyth v[er]sus montana borealia q[uo]d erat filior[um] Chanani cui nom[en] Deutrait alt[er]um v[er]o ex alia fluvij p[ar]te v[er]sus mare i[n] capite Lhein

[*100] Comments on Giraldus' trip through the southern lands of the sons of Cynan are examined in Remfry, PM., *Harlech Castle and its True Origins* [Ceidio, 2013], 12-21.

q[uo]d erat filior[um] Oenei cui nom[en] Karnmadrun D[ici]t[ur] a[utem] Trait ling[ua] Britannica sabulu[m] mari influente longi[us] et se ret[ra]hente nudatu[m] Transieram[us] tam[en] aq[ua]s antea n[on] ignobiles Dyssennyth int[er] Maviam et T[ra]itmaur Arthro int[er] T[ra]itmaur et T[ra]itbochan. Ea nocte jacuim[us] ap[u]d Newein vigilia videl[icet] Pasche floridi...[101]

Of the crossing of Traitmaur and Traitbochan also of Nefyn and Caernarfon and Bangor with their notable characteristics.

From that place we crossed over Traeth Mawr and Traeth Bychan that is the greater and the lesser drawing of the sea where two castles of stone had been newly sited one in Eifionydd towards the mountainous north, which belonged to the sons of Cynan, which was named Deudraeth; the second truly on the other side of the river towards the sea in the headland of Llyn, which belonged to the sons of Owain, which was named Garn Fadryn. It is said that Traeth in the Brythonic language signifies a sand flowed over by the sea a long way and left bare when it ebbs. Notwithstanding we had previously crossed over the not ignoble waters, the Ysgethin (*Dissenith*) between the Maw and Traeth Mawr, the Arthro between Traeth Mawr and Traeth Bachan. We slept that night at Nefyn, on the eve of Palm Sunday...

It is unfortunate, but true of many medieval texts, that Giraldus' words are ambiguous as to their true meaning. Regardless of this, what is clear is that Rhodri and apparently Dafydd (as overlord?) appear to have been holding Llyn and its castle of Garn Fadryn if *filior* is correctly expanded to *filiorum*. As the sons of Cynan are treated the same way this seems likely. Yet this cannot be taken as proof that Dafydd and Rhodri were acting in unison. All it means is that this is how Giraldus chose to describe the land of Llyn and that he groups the sons of Owain as inimical to the sons of Cynan. Giraldus was reporting something that everybody of influence at the time was expected to have known and therefore he was not listing the boundaries between the warring participants, merely stating the broad overview.

Continuing with the itinerary, the next day the party departed from Llanfair in Ardudwy and reached Nefyn on the north coast of the Llyn, with Giraldus saying little more than this of the journey. As there was no Porthmadog cob at this time, the party would have needed to go via Maentwrog to avoid the tidal Glaslyn and Dwyryd estuaries. Alternately, if they had taken ship at Llanfair, they could have sailed straight across the mouth of the estuary to Criccieth or Pwllheli, from where they would only have had a trip of either thirteen or six miles to Nefyn. Unfortunately no mention of a boat trip is made in these short passages. Conversely it seems unlikely that the party took the long land route as Giraldus does not mention any crossing of the Dwyryd or the Glaslyn. The land route would have made this a journey covering some 36 miles, the longest day trip of any made in Wales and one that was thought to take about a day from Harlech to Tremadog in the eighteenth century. Before the Porthmadog cob was built the usual way to cross the traeth was by boat from Tygwyn (SH.602349), which is now a station near Talsarnau, to Penamser (SH.553395), a mile west

---

[101] British Library, Cotton MS Domitian A 1, f.101. This, and many of the other original documents quoted were kindly transcribed by Simon Neal. This manuscript, between folios 56 and 111, contains the *Itinerarium Kambriae* as well as other works of Giraldus. These treatises are all on vellum in single columns of 29 lines per page which were all written by the same hand, probably in the first half of the thirteenth century. The MS begins with an earlier treatise by various writers on Isodore dating to between 1213 and 1220, but this would appear to have originally been a separate manuscript. After the Giraldus section comes the St David's copy of the *Annales Cambriae* which is in a different hand altogether and could not have been written before 1289. It therefore seems likely that these three works were compiled into one book sometime after that date. The text of the Itinerary transcribed here was possibly written within Giraldus' lifetime.

of Porthmadog*102. That said it is obvious that Giraldus did not mention every stop the party made or how long they remained at some places*103. Giraldus makes no further mention of land ownership, but as Nefyn was in Llyn and he continued on his way past Caernarfon to Bangor and then to Mon where he met Rhodri, it is to be presumed that all this land lay under Rhodri's control. It is worth printing Giraldus' meeting with Rhodri in full.

> From hence we crossed into the island of Mon over a small arm of the sea about two miles distant [from Bangor]. There Rhodri, the younger son of Owain, with nearly all the inhabitants of the island, and many others from the adjacent lands, came in a devout manner to meet us. Confession having been made in a place near the shore, where the surrounding rocks seemed to form a natural theatre, many persons were induced to take the cross, by the persuasive discourses of the archbishop, and Alexander, our interpreter, archdeacon of that place, and by Abbot Seisyll of Strata Florida. However, sitting on the opposite rock were the chosen juveniles of the household of Rhodri, of whom none could be prevailed upon, although the archbishop and others most earnestly exhorted them, but in vain, by an address particularly directed to them.
>
> However, within three days, as if by divine vengeance, that these juveniles, with many others, pursued some robbers of that land, who immediately were discomfited and put to flight, some were slain and others mortally wounded, and the survivors voluntarily assumed that cross which they had before despised.
>
> Rhodri, also, who a short time before had incestuously married the daughter of Rhys, related to him by blood in the third degree*104, in order, by the assistance of that prince, to be better able to defend himself against the sons of his brothers, whom he had disinherited, not paying attention to the wholesome admonitions of the archbishop on this subject, was a little while afterwards dispossessed of all his lands by their means; thus deservedly meeting with disappointment from the very source from which he expected support.*105

This text shows us clearly that Rhodri was in possession of Mon in 1188 and for a while afterwards. The defeat of Rhodri's household or teulu three days after Giraldus' visit could have been occasioned by Llywelyn ab Iorwerth who was sixteen at this time. It is also interesting to see Rhodri and Rhys ap Gruffydd allied against the sons of Cynan who were therefore caught with enemies to all three landward sides of their domains. To the north lay Rhodri, to the east Dafydd and to the south Rhys ap Gruffydd. To the south-east their lands would also have bordered with Owain Cyfeiliog who may have been more favourable to their cause.

From Mon the party passed back to Bangor and on along the coast to Aberconwy, where they crossed the river just north of Aberconwy abbey. At this point Giraldus commented on the river Conwy running up into the hills of Snowdonia and to the fortress of Dinas Emrys - which of course it doesn't, the Conwy swinging much further south than Dinas

---

*102 Ashton, W., *The Evolution of a Coastline* [London, 1920], 241-2.

*103 The time actually spent on the perambulation and the time allotted to stays have been examined elsewhere, Remfry, PM., *Harlech Castle and its True Origins* [Ceidio, 2013], 18.

*104 Agnes was actually first cousin once removed to Rhodri, so was related to him in the fifth degree and not the third degree as Giraldus wrongly asserted.

*105 Giraldus Cambrensis, *Opera*, eds. J.S. Brewer, J.F. Dimock and G.F. Warner [8 vols., 1861-91] VI, 126-7.

Emrys, although both the Mynbyr and the Lledr do rise nearer to the castle (Fig.3). Dinas Emrys quite possibly lay on the borders of the lands of Rhodri ab Owain and the sons of Cynan, ie the border between Ardudwy, Arfon and Arllechwedd (Figs.4&9). This view is confirmed by Giraldus' description of Snowdonia.

> Truly the mountains which are called by the Welsh Eyri and truly by the English Snowdon, that is the mountains of snow, which from the land of the sons of Cynan gradually rises up, and near Degannwy stretches itself out to the north, truly facing Mon the highest citadels towering immoderately growing up towards the clouds, are not to be passed over in silence. Accordingly so great and so immense in magnitude they are presented, that an ancient proverb is customarily said of it; just as the island of Mon the year's produce is for men, so Eyri in pasture, with all the herds collected into one, [this] can be sufficient for all Wales.[106]

Quite clearly in 1188 Snowdonia was held by the sons of Owain and the lesser mountains of Meirionydd by the two surviving sons of Cynan. This is important to the study of Aberconwy abbey, for the granges it later held spread across the rough borders of Eifionydd, Ardudwy, Arfon and Nantconwy. In short, the lands which the granges of Aberconwy occupied were held by mutually hostile princes in 1186. It therefore seems unlikely that Aberconwy held all these granges - Ffriwlwyd, Nant Call, Cwm, Nanhwynain - from the first.

From the River Conwy Giraldus passed into the lands of Dafydd ab Owain and proceeded to what appears to have been his royal caput at Rhuddlan. The party then continued on through St Asaph and over Coleshill by Basingwerk abbey to Chester, near which he left the lands of Dafydd without comment. It can therefore be seen that although Giraldus was not much interested in the politics of North Wales, it is possible to work out much of the political layout of Gwynedd and from this get a clear idea of who held which lands when Aberconwy abbey was set up in the last years of the 1180s. The suggestion from this is that the initial granges of the abbey in 1186 consisted of Rhedynog Felen, Conwy Gyffin and possibly Creuddyn and Arddau. There is no evidence that the abbey held lands in Mon until the coming of Gruffydd ap Cynan some time probably in the winter of 1190-91, although it is possible that Rhodri may have granted them lands at Bodgedwydd[107]. As has been noted above, it is unknown who was holding Degannwy castle in 1186. The grange of Creuddyn which lay south and east of the castle could well have been granted to the monks at the foundation, as the nearness of Aberconwy to Degannwy suggests. Unfortunately it is uncertain whether Rhodri, who would therefore have held both sides of the Conwy at this point, or Dafydd ab Owain, who appears to have held Gronant castle on the west side of the Conwy in 1194, were lords of this commote at the time. A study of the history of Gwynedd during the reign of Richard I (1189-99), unfortunately throws no further light on this question.

---

[106] Giraldus Cambrensis, *Opera*, eds. J.S. Brewer, J.F. Dimock and G.F. Warner [8 vols., 1861-91] VI, 135.
[107] All that can certainly be said about this grange is that it belonged to the abbey by 1282.

Aberconwy During the Reign of King Richard, 1189 to 1199

When King Richard came to the throne the political situation in Gwynedd was stable. Dafydd held the Perfeddwlad, but appeared to have no power west of the Conwy other than his uncertain relations with his brother, Rhodri. In his border domains Dafydd was one of the princes pointed out by Giraldus who was well-known for trying to keep the peace between the English and the Welsh and arbitrating between them entirely fairly[108]. To the west Rhodri held Mon and Llyn as well as the bulk of Arfon and Arllechwedd. To what extent he held these lands in association with Dafydd is unknown. Maredudd ap Cynan held Eifionydd and his elder brother, Gruffydd, held Meirionydd and Ardudwy, although their power possibly penetrated some distance into Arfon and Arllechwedd, though this cannot be certain.

On the death of King Henry II, it was Rhys ap Gruffydd of Deheubarth who rebelled against the new rule of King Richard I and attacked the Norman held lands in the south. This is best shown, not only by the Brut accounts, but also by the fact that the bishops of St David's, Bangor and St Asaph attended the king's coronation on 3 September 1189[109]. However, the bishop of Llandaff appears not to have attended and this was the diocese where Rhys was most active against the peace. The implication of this is that Rhodri and Dafydd maintained their peaceful status, while Pembrokeshire was as yet beyond the range of Rhys' attacks. More importantly, Rhys' uprising meant that Rhodri was now stripped of any aid his father-in-law may have been able to send him as first war and then civil war continued in Deheubarth until both their deaths brought their careers to an end in 1194 and 1197 respectively.

Soon after 17 September 1189, King Richard dispatched his brother Count John of Mortain, later King John (d.1216), to Wales with a great army to deal with the revolt of King Rhys of South Wales. John proceeded to Worcester where he met with 'all the rest of the Welsh kings' who 'immediately made peace with him'[110]. This peace would appear to have been recorded solely in the writings of Richard of Devizes who stated:

> The king received security from the tributary kings of the Welsh and the Scots that they would not pass their borders to the annoyance of England during his absence [on Crusade].[111]

Rhys too made a 'private' or 'personal' peace with John who induced him to go to Oxford to meet the king in October. Richard however, did not come to Oxford to take Rhys' homage and Rhys in a fit of pique returned to Wales and continued his war[112]. Thus the king left England with the country pacified except for Deheubarth and with agreements in place with all the tributary princes except for Rhys ap Gruffydd.

While Gwynedd was apparently at peace during 1190 (Fig.9), Bishop Gwion of Bangor died and Subprior Roland (*Rotoland*) of Aberconwy was elected, but not consecrated

---

[108] Giraldus Cambrensis, *Opera*, eds. J.S. Brewer, J.F. Dimock and G.F. Warner [8 vols., 1861-91] VI, 145.

[109] *The Historical Works of Gervase of Canterbury*, ed. W. Stubbs [2 vols., 1878-80] I, 457; II, 86, for Rhys' attack and *Gesta Regis Henrici Secundi Benedicti Abbatis* ed. Stubbs, W. [2 vols, 1867] II, 79, for the bishops present at the coronation.

[110] *Gesta Regis Henrici Secundi Benedicti Abbatis* ed. Stubbs, W. [2 vols, 1867] II, 87-8.

[111] Richard of Devizes, 'De rebus gestis Ricardi Primi', *Chronicles of the Reigns of Stephen, Henry II and Richard I*, ed. Howlett, R. [1886] III, 8.

[112] *Gesta Regis Henrici Secundi Benedicti Abbatis* ed. Stubbs, W. [2 vols, 1867] II, 97; *Annales Cambriae. A Translation of Harleian 3859; PRO E.164/1; Cottonian Domitian, A 1; Exeter Cathedral Library MS. 3514 and MS Exchequer DB Neath, PRO E.164/1*, ed. Remfry, P.M., [Malvern, 2007], 97; *Chronica Magistri Rogeri de Hovedene*, ed. W. Stubbs [4 vols., 1868-71] III, 23.

in his place[*113]. This was due to the fact that Archbishop Baldwin of Canterbury had died on 19 November 1190. As it turned out, Roland would have to wait until a new archbishop was enthroned and this occurred only on 7 November 1193, when Hubert Walter was made archbishop. By this time the political situation had changed drastically in North Wales. Rhodri had been overthrown and chased out of Gwynedd, though in this year he had returned with Manx aid and had a second time been evicted from Mon. This left the sons of Cynan supreme in the north-west. As papal correspondence shows that Rhodri married the daughter of King Reginald of Man on 15 June 1192 and that Rhodri had been on the Isle of Man since at least early May it can be seen that Rhodri lost control of Gwynedd before April 1192[*114]. This instability in Gwynedd may have been the deciding factor that made Archbishop Hubert refuse to accept Roland as bishop. Instead Bangor remained officially vacant, though it is almost certain that Roland remained bishop elect. Quite possibly he was involved with detailed discussions with the archbishop at this time.

Aberconwy abbey also briefly appears in the written record this year. At the September 1192 convocation of the Cistercians at Clairvaux, the king of the Danes and the Norwegians had his appeal against Aberconwy abbey referred from the general chapter of the Cistercians to the abbots of Whitland and Strata Florida (Tractus)[*115]. It is not too difficult to work out who the king of the Danes and Norwegians might have been, despite there being at the time no such person by modern parlance - the Danes and Norwegians being separate kingships. So more likely this was a claimant to the title and as such could well have been the king of Man. Indeed King Reginald is recorded on one occasion in a non contemporary source as Ragnall son of Gofraidh, king of the Fionngall (Norwegians)[*116]. If the man mentioned in 1192 was King Reginald of Man (bef.1165-1229), it is likely that this dispute was linked to the war waged between Rhodri ab Owain and the sons of Cynan over the control of Mon[*117]. This might also have been a factor in the Manxmen backing Rhodri in his attempt to regain his lands in 1193. If this was the case, then the lands in question were probably in Mon and would suggest that the gift of Gruffydd ap Cynan to Aberconwy abbey at Gelliniog, or even Bodgedwydd, included some lands claimed by Reginald and possibly Rhodri. This would suggest that the granting of these lands in Mon occurred soon after Gruffydd seized them from Rhodri. Gelliniog is attested in the Aberconwy Register as a gift of Gruffydd ap Cynan in the month of June sometime in the 1190s. Therefore it seems reasonable to assume that at least Gelliniog and possibly Bodgedwydd were granted by Gruffydd on his victory over Rhodri, probably in 1190/91, although whether his grants were new or merely confirming what had been granted by Rhodri is another matter for which there is no evidence. This would mean that Gruffydd's surviving grant, as copied in the Register, was probably made in June 1192. That this led to a dispute with King Reginald of Man

---

[*113] The use of Rotoland to mean Roland is examined on page 76.

[*114] These events are examined in the chapter, Llywelyn's Marriage and Aberconwy, 1195 to 1203.

[*115] Querela quam proposuit dominus rex Daniae et Norvegiae contra abbatiam de Alberconeu, abbatibus de Blancha Landa et de Tractus committitur, compositione vel iudicio terminanda. Statuta I, 152/34. Tractus was thought to have been Albus Tractus in comitatu et dioec Corcagiensi in Hibernia, but as this was only founded in 1225 it seems more likely that this was a garbled form of the Strata of Strata Florida.

[*116] The quote comes from a translation of part of the book of Clanranald, Skene, WF., Celtic Scotland: A History of Ancient Alban [3 vols, 1886-90] III, 400. There is also an uninformative panegyric to Reginald, Idem, 411-27.

[*117] It is possible that Rhodri was already allied with King Reginald as early as 1188, for in that year the newly crowned Reginald made a charter to Furness abbey confirming the grants of his grandfather, King Olaf (d.1153). The first lay witness of this was Rotherico, fratre meo, as appears in Monumenta de Insula Manniae or a Collection of National Documents Relating to the Isle of Man, Oliver, JR., ed & trans, [2 vols, Douglas, Isle of Man, 1861] II, 17-8. Reginald had no known brother Rhodri and considering their later alliances it is possible that this is Rhodri ab Owain and that the two already regarded each other as close associates.

would indicate that the land had not belonged to Aberconwy before this date and was purely a gift of Gruffydd ap Cynan and not of Rhodri at the foundation of the abbey.

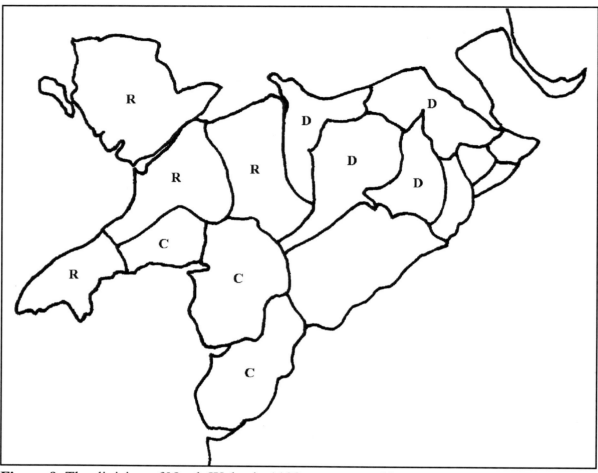

Figure 9, The division of North Wales in 1189 as suggested by contemporary records. Rhodri's lands were captured by the sons of Cynan by 1191.

C = The sons of Cynan ab Owain	D = Dafydd ab Owain
R = Rhodri ab Owain	

With the capture of King Richard on his return from Crusade in late 1192, the rebel barons under Count John moved against royal supporters and war began once more in Gwynedd. One of King Richard's supporters in Wales was most certainly his uncle, Dafydd ab Owain. Initially the fighting occurred further west when Dafydd's brother, Rhodri ab Owain, overran Mon in 1193 with the aid of the son or sons of Godred of Man[118]. The lost Aberconwy chronicle would appear to have detailed these events, but unfortunately nothing

---

[118] Pen, 74. Reginald IV (bef.1165-1229) was the son of King Godred III of Man who had died on 10 November 1187 and is probably the man mentioned in the Brut. Several versions of Peniarth have sons rather than son of Godred. This may mean that Reginald's half brother Olaf (1173-1237) may have been involved too. ByS, 189, also has sons, but RBH, 173, has son.

of these matters has been preserved other than the laconic statement in the 'chronicle' known as *O Oes Gwrtheyrn*:

> The summer of the Irish (*haf y gwydyl*)[*119].

This appears to mark the brief occupation of the island by Rhodri and his Manx in-laws. It seems that in this Rhodri took Mon from the two remaining sons of Cynan rather than his brother Dafydd. This view is reinforced when the statement in the Brut is looked at in full:

> Rhodri ab Owain subdued all the island of Anglesey through the help of the son of Godred and before the end of the year after that he was expelled by the sons of Cynan ab Owain.[*120]

It was long ago suggested that Rhodri was expelled from Mon between 1188, when Giraldus met him there and 1191, when Cambrensis published his first edition of his itinerary through Wales. In this he describes Rhodri as expelled from his lands 'a little while' after 1188[*121]. Giraldus also tells us that it was the sons of his brother who expelled Rhodri from all his lands and that he received no help from his father-in-law. Therefore this leaves us in little doubt that Gruffydd and Maredudd ap Cynan attacked Rhodri some time between late 1189 and early 1191 and drove him from his lands in Gwynedd. As Rhodri returned with an army of Manxmen to capture Mon it is to be presumed that he fled overseas rather than to the aid of his brother Dafydd. These political affairs are also linked with Rhodri's marriage in 1192 to a daughter of King Reginald and his recorded stay in the Isle of Man from April to at least 15 June 1192[*122].

Although there is no evidence either way as to whether the sons of Cynan swore not to invade England at Worcester in 1189, they would not appear to have sworn not to attack their Welsh neighbours. As the sons of Cynan had a grudge to bear against Rhys ap Gruffydd, who had attacked them after 1177 with the king's permission, it is possible that Gruffydd and Maredudd moved against Rhodri to break the pact between him and Rhys ap Gruffydd. As such, the move may have been looked on favourably by the English government and Dafydd ab Owain. There is no surviving evidence that Rhodri and Dafydd ever acted together in unison and certainly the only time they are known to have met in 1175, things obviously did not work out favourably for Rhodri. Once again, it is necessary to rely on Giraldus' vague statements for what was occurring in Gwynedd. He states that by 1191 Gruffydd ap Cynan had made himself supreme in Gwynedd and had overrun Rhodri's territories of Llyn, Arfon, Arllechwedd and Mon. This left the sons of Cynan with a border with Dafydd ab Owain running along the Conwy. It also meant that the castle of Garn Fadryn, only founded immediately before 1188, was rendered pretty much obsolescent by the sons of Cynan's victory by the Spring of 1191. Gruffydd ap Cynan was therefore prince of all North Wales west of the Conwy and north of the Dovey from around the Spring of 1191 until his death in the Spring of 1200. Therefore, although Rhodri was apparently in control of Arfon and Arllechwedd in 1188, this does not mean for certain he was prince there in 1186 when Aberconwy abbey was founded, although this is the most likely reading of the situation.

[*119] The chronicle is translated in Appendix 3, p.290

[*120] Pen, 74.

[*121] Lloyd, J.E., *History of Wales* [2 vols., 1911] II, 588, rehearses the argument.

[*122] See the chapter on Llywelyn's first marriage where the pope examines Rhodri's marital conduct from 1191 to 1194, p.79ff.

Again, these changes of control fit in nicely with the dispute between the king of the Isles and Aberconwy in 1192 when Rhodri was attempting with the aid of his new father-in-law, Reginald, to regain Mon. As such the political history appears to show that Rhodri ab Owain (d.1194) was the founder of Aberconwy abbey in 1186 as he appears to have held both Rhedynog Felen and Aberconwy at that date. Perhaps his lack of remembrance at the abbey was due to his overthrow in Gwynedd by 1192 and his fate by 1194. As ever, realpolitik trumped history. It is also possible that Rhodri was aided in his religious endeavour of foundation by his nephews of Meirionydd as they had recently lost a brother, Einion ap Cynan in 1185 and they also held lands which were later held by Aberconwy abbey - viz certainly Ffriwlwyd and possibly Nanhwynain. That said, the core original lands granted to Aberconwy were in Arfon and possibly Mon and these places can be shown to have been held by Rhodri around this time (Figs.3&9).

Regardless of the fate of his younger brother, Rhodri, the collapse of Dafydd's position in the Perfeddwlad clearly began with the revolt of Count John of Mortain and therefore came after his younger brother Rhodri's overthrow by the sons of Cynan. In this war King Dafydd and the Powys cousins in the Marcher lordships of northern Shropshire, clearly placed themselves on the side of royal authority and fought against Count John and his allies. Unfortunately for them, by 1194, King Richard's attentions were not fixed on Wales, but on France. As a consequence troops were pulled away from the royalists in Wales and sent to the Continent. To this end, troops were not sent westwards to aid Dafydd as they had been in 1173. Instead, initially twenty horse serjeants with two horses each from the Northern Marches, were paid for forty days to transfer themselves over to the king in Normandy[123]. At the same time Meurig ap Roger Powys of Whittington was given £5 7s for eight days marching to the coast with six mounted serjeants with two horses each and sixty foot serjeants, to sail overseas and join the king in Normandy. Further, rather than there being six serjeants drawing 6d per day, if Meurig counted himself as a sergeant, we get a sum of 42 pennies per day[124]. Such a force would have been the direct descendent of the small army which Roger Powys had led to Degannwy in 1173. This time the troops were going abroad to deal with a greater foe and King Dafydd was left to his own devices and no doubt a hope that royal troops would again flood west to his aid after the French had been defeated.

The campaign in France is not really relevant to the history of Aberconwy, but the loss of royal support rapidly undermined Dafydd's position in north-east Wales. To summerize, King Richard boarded ship from England for Normandy on 12 May 1194[125]. His Anglo-Welsh army landed at Barfleur on 12 May and the king marched directly against King Philip of France who was routed at Freteval on 4 July. From Freteval the king and his composite army swept south, until on 23 July a truce was arranged bringing the war to an end for the rest of the year. In total, the war in France had lasted 73 days from the king's leaving England[126]. At the same time as the bulk of the Anglo-Welsh forces were engaged in France, the king's uncle, Dafydd ab Owain, was decisively defeated by a combination of Welsh princes.

---

[123] *PR 6 Richard I*, 141.
[124] That Meurig was not a knight at this stage is seen when he acquired the accoutrements of knighthood early in the reign of King John.
[125] Roger of Wendover's, *Flowers of History* [Llanerch, 1994] II, 135.
[126] The campaign and the Welsh troops used in this war are examined in Remfry, P.M., *Whittington Castle and the Families of....* [2007], 62-4.

Llywelyn ab Iorwerth and the two sons of Cynan ab Owain [Gruffydd and Maredudd] and Rhodri ab Owain united together against Dafydd ab Owain and they drove him to flight and took from him all his territory except for three castles.[*127]

And then Llywelyn ab Iorwerth and Rhodri ab Owain and the two sons of Cynan ab Owain united against Dafydd ab Owain and they expelled him from all his territory except for three castles.[*128]

Llywelyn ab Iorwerth and the two sons of Cynan, Rhodri and Owain, took Dafydd ab Owain's territory from him except for three castles and they drove him to flight.[*129]

Even more bluntly the Annales have:

Dafydd ab Owain was expelled from his land by Llywelyn ab Iorwerth.[*130]

Obviously, there is a bigger story to be told here than the few lines recorded by the scanty Welsh chronicles of the time. It is also clear that the international picture was responsible for the fall of Dafydd ab Owain rather than merely internal Welsh politics as is usually stated in modern histories following readily in the insular view of the Welsh chronicles. It should also be noted that Llywelyn was undoubtedly the junior partner of the coalition. Quite obviously the later chronicles have anachronistically increased his importance and placed him first amongst the allies, when in reality at the time he would have been the least important of the four.

Figure 10, Gronant motte from the west. The ditch and slight rampart is visible to the left. The north side of the motte (not visible) has been heavily damaged/quarried.

There seems little doubt that Rhodri had initially turned against his brother and that the three united armies of the sons of Cynan, Rhodri and Llywelyn ab Iorwerth had crushed Dafydd's forces. Thankfully, due to the survival of poems in praise of Llywelyn, the course of this campaign can be better traced. The battle at Aberconwy, according to the poets, was hotly contested, while the name itself would suggest that it was actually fought near the

---

[*127] Pen, 75.
[*128] RBH, 175.
[*129] ByS, 191. The compiler of Brenhinedd has badly mangled this sentence.
[*130] *Annales Cambriae. A Translation of Harleian 3859; PRO E.164/1; Cottonian Domitian, A 1; Exeter Cathedral Library MS. 3514 and MS Exchequer DB Neath, PRO E.164/1,* ed. Remfry, P.M., [Malvern, 2007] (B Strata Florida), 99.

abbey[*131]. This certainly bore the name of Aberconwy by 1192 at the very latest, while the abbey appears to have been founded under this name as early as June or July 1186. However, it is possible that the actual fighting took place further south around Gronant (Fig.10), the castle at the natural crossing place of the river and five miles south of the ferry to Degannwy.

In 1188 Giraldus had used the Degannwy ferry north of the abbey to cross the river, but this would surely have been a poor place from which to launch an attack into the Perfeddwlad, necessitating as it would a battle being fought across a river where it would have probably been too deep to wade[*132]. Unless hopelessly outnumbered, it is to be expected that Dafydd would have crushed his enemies while they attempted the crossing. This is where the elegies to Llywelyn come into their own. Cynddelw, who probably wrote near to the time of the battle as he doesn't seem to have lived long into the thirteenth century, said:

> We and he were carried to battle at the fall of Aberconwy
> Porthathwy denominating a visit to Mon
> In Mon the head dragon, the peak of dragons - Prydain
> .....
> Battle was hard in the Aneu wood...[*133]

This suggests that Llywelyn fought first at Aberconwy and then at Porthathwy as he crossed over into Mon. Once on the island he won another 'great battle' at Coedana. The trouble is, how much faith can you place on a poet who also writes of the same action:

> Many were the foes of my lord, but there fell of them in the fight seven times the number of the stars.[*134]

Obviously some leeway has to be allowed for poetic licence, but there seems no reason to deny the series of events as portrayed by the poet. Though again it should be noted that Cynddelw was obviously writing in hindsight and that the sons of Cynan, the senior partners in the campaign, are totally and no doubt politically ignored.

A most prolific poet of this era was Llywarch ap Llywelyn, otherwise known as Prydydd y Moch[*135]. He appears to have been court poet to most of the princes of Gwynedd judging by the number of poems he wrote to them - three to Dafydd ab Owain, four to Rhodri, three to Gruffydd ap Cynan, one to Maredudd ap Cynan and nine to Llywelyn ab Iorwerth. In one panegyric to Rhodri ab Owain he talks of him being among the victorious dragons at Aberconwy.

[*131] The battles in the campaign of 1194 are examined in, Remfry, PM, *Medieval Battles: Wales, 1055 to 1216: Volume 2, part 1* [2017], 212-26.

[*132] In the eighteenth century the ferry crossing was some 150 feet at low tide with the water being a mere eight feet deep, but at high tide this could rise another twelve feet, Pennant, T., *Tours in Wales* [3 vols, London, 1810] III, 120.

[*133] *Ni bu ledrad cad cadr Aber conwy, Porth athwy myrdd ofwy mon, Ym Mon bendragon ban dreigiau - Prydain, Wyt prydfawr ith arfau, Cefeist a donaist yn dau, Cad anhawdd y coed aneu...* The *Myvyrian Archaiology of Wales*, eds. O. Jones, E. Williams & W. Owen [2nd edn., Denbigh, 1870] I, 262-3.

[*134] Lloyd, J.E., *History of Wales* [2 vols., 1911] II, 589.

[*135] Llywarch ap Llywelyn seems to have flourished between about 1170 and 1220 and may have held lands and a mill in Rhos at Dulas. In one of his poems he hints that his forebears were not poets. He was supposedly called Prydydd y Moch from a daring reference to casting pearls before swine in a poem rebuking Gruffydd ap Cynan; however, doubt has been cast on this identification. Thirty of Llywarch's works survive, totalling some 1780 lines. His first extant poems were addressed to Dafydd (d.1200/3) and Rhodri ab Owain (d.1194), but most of his output, totalling nine extant poems, were to Llywelyn ab Iorwerth (d.1240). That he mentions Dafydd as lord of Aberffraw would suggest he began writing before Dafydd's expulsion from this district in 1175.

At Aberconwy I existed amongst two dragons in glory.[*136]

From this it can be deduced that there was a general alliance of the surviving royalty of Gwynedd against Dafydd ab Owain, the man who claimed and had been king of North Wales. Llywarch also wrote poems to the otherwise unknown children of Hywel ab Owain (d.1170) as well as to the son of Gruffydd ap Cynan. After about 1200, when Llywelyn became prince of North Wales, Llywarch seems to have been solely his poet and sang his praises extravagantly. It is therefore thanks to him that much more can be said about the 1194 campaign that smashed the power of the two remaining sons of Owain Gwynedd, Rhodri and Dafydd. Despite this, it should be remembered that Llywarch was a poet first and last and never was what would now be thought of as an historian. Even so, it should also be remembered that modern historians as much as medieval bards are prone to error. For instance, the statement attributed to Llywarch that during the war of 1194 Llywelyn was ten is clearly false. Viz:

at ten, he was the bold darling of fortune, the terrible Llywelyn.[*137]

When the entire poem is looked at - it is translated below - it can be seen that this is not what Lywarch said. What is actually put forward is that Llywelyn began to make a nuisance of himself to his uncles when he was aged ten. Llywarch in a subsequent sentence goes on to describe the events of 1194 which it can be shown happened twelve years after Llywelyn was ten. In any case, as Llywelyn was actually 22 in 1194, surely no one living before about 1204, when Llywarch appears to have finished composing this poem, would have believed such an outlandish falsehood. Indeed, such a claim in even a panegyric would have made Llywelyn look foolish to contemporaries who would have known of his rough age during the battles of 1194. Once more a mistranslation has got the better of history.

The salient parts of Llywarch's poem about Llywelyn's career up to 1204 are translated below. The bulk of this deals with the capture of the Perfeddwlad which mainly occurred in 1194 and 1197. Some dates have been added in square brackets to help make historical use of the poem. Some of the placenames have also been tentatively identified.

Llywelyn is the ruler of Britain and her armour.
He is a lion-like brave prince
unmoved in action
The son of Iorwerth
our strength and true friend
a descendant of Owain the destroyer
whose abilities appeared in his youth.
He came to be a leader of forces, dressed in blue,
neat and handsome.
In the conflicts of battle, in the clang of arms,
he was an heroic youth.
When ten years old he successfully attacked his kinsman [1182].

[*136] *Ker aber congwy kynnognes dwy dreic Deu dragon yn ygres*, *The Myvyrian Archaiology of Wales*, eds. O. Jones, E. Williams & W. Owen [2nd edn., Denbigh, 1870] I, 284.
[*137] Lloyd, J.E., *History of Wales* [2 vols., 1911] II, 589. The poem appears in *The Myvyrian Archaiology of Wales*, eds. O. Jones, E. Williams & W. Owen [2nd edn., Denbigh, 1870] I, 297-300. Portions of it are translated below.

In Aberconwy (*aber conwy*) [1194], ere my prince, the brave Llywelyn, got his right [1197?]

he contested with Dafydd, who was a bloody chief,

like Julius Ceasar[*138].

A chief without blemish, not insulting his foes in distress,

but in war impetuous and fierce,

like the points of flaming fire burning in their rage.

It is a general loss to the Bards,

that he [Dafydd] is covered with earth.

We grieve for him.[*139]

Llywelyn was our prince before the furious contest happened [pre.1194?],

and the spoils were amassed with eagerness.

The purple gore ran over the snow-white breasts of warriors,

and there was an universal havoc and carnage after the shout.

The parti-coloured waves flowed over the broken spear

and the warriors were silent.

The briny wave came with force

and another met it mixed with blood

when we went to Porthaethwy (*Porth athwy*)

over the sounding surge we rode our steeds as they swam [1194].

The spear raged with relentless fury

and the tide of blood rushed with force.

Our attack was sudden and fierce.

Death displayed itself in all its horrors;

so that it was a doubt whether any of us should die of old age.

Noble troops in the fatal hour

trampled on the dead like prancing steeds.

Before Rhodri [ab Owain d.1194] was brought to submission [1194],

the churchyards were like fallow grounds[*140].

When Llywelyn the successful prince overcame near the Alun

with his warriors of the bright arms

ten thousand were killed

and the crows made a noise

and a thousand were taken prisoner [1199?].

Llywelyn though in battle he killed with fury

though he burned like outrageous fire

yet he was a mild prince when the mead horns were distributed.....

He gave generously under his waving banners to his numerous bards gold and silver,

which he regards not, and Gascony prancing steeds,

with rich trappings

and great scarlet cloaks,

shining like ruddy flame:

[*138] Julius Caesar was renowned for killing his high-ranking captives. Is this an allusion to what happened to Dafydd's half brothers, Maelgwn and Iorwerth Drwyndwn? Certainly Hywel ab Owain had perished at Dafydd's instigation in 1170.

[*139] This is obviously Dafydd who is dead and not Llywelyn, as his greater triumphs are listed in the poem. It therefore seems that the piece was composed between the death of Dafydd and April 1205 when Llywelyn married Joan Plantagenet, for surely the marriage would have been mentioned as Prince Llywelyn put such store by it.

[*140] The suggestion here is that there had not been a great deal of killing in the years immediately prior to the onslaught of Llywelyn and his allies in 1194.

warlike, strong, well-made destroying steeds,
with streams of foam issuing out of their mouths.
He generously bestows, like brave Arthur,
snow-white steeds by hundreds,
whose speed is fleeter than birds.

You that feeds the fowls of the air like Caeawg the hero
the valiant ruler of all Britain
the numerous forces of England tumble and wallow in the field before you.
He bravely achieved above ?Criccieth[*141] (*deu draeth dryuan*) the feats of the renowned Ogrfan.
Men fall silently in the field
and are deprived of the rites of sepulture.
You have defeated two numerous armies, one on the banks of the Alun of the rich soil
where the Normans were destroyed [1199]
as the adversaries of Arthur in the battle of Camlan [alleged 515].
The second in Arfon (*aruon*), near the sea shore........
And two ruling chiefs[*142], flushed with success, encouraged us like lions,
and one superior to them both, a stern hero,
the ravager of battles, like a man that conquers in all places
Llywelyn with the broken blade of the gilt sword
the waster of Lloegr, a wolf covered with red
with his warriors about Rhuddlan (*rutglann*) [1197?].
His forces carry the standard before him waving in the air.
You are possessed of the valour of Cadwallon ap Cadfan [d.634].
He is for recovering the government of all Britain.
He kindly stretched his hand to us,
while his enemies fled to the sea shore
to embark to avoid the imminent destruction,
with despair in their looks
and no place of refuge remained
and the crimson lance whizzed dreadfully over their brows.
We the bards of Britain
whom our prince entertains on the first of January
shall every one of us
in our rank and station
enjoy mirth and jollity
and receive gold and silver for our reward.....

... Chester (*Caer lleon*), the chief of Mon, he has brought you to a low condition
Llywelyn has wasted your land
your men are killed by the sea...............
He has entirely subdued Mold (*wytgrug*)

[*141] It seems likely that the real castle of Deudraeth was at Criccieth and not Portmeirion, Remfry, PM., *Harlech Castle and its True Origins* [Ceidio, 2013], 19-20. This reference to its apparent capture appears to add further evidence towards this identification.
[*142] These would appear to have been Gruffydd ap Cynan and his brother Maredudd ap Cynan. By 1205 Gruffydd was safely dead and Maredudd disgraced and dispossessed of his lands.

where the English ran away
with a precipitate flight
full of horror and consternation [1199].
Your fields are miserably wasted,
your cloister and your neat houses are ashes.
The llys of Ellesmere (*elysmer*) was with rage and fury burnt by fire[*143].
You all now enjoy peace by submitting to our prince,
for wherever he goes with his forces
whether it be hill or dale
it is the possession of one sole proprietor.
Our lion has brought to Welshpool (*trallwng*) three armies that will never turn their backs,
the residence of our enemies ever to be abhorred [1202?].
The numerous bards receive diverse favours from him.
He took Mold (*wytgrug*) [1199].
See you who succeeds in Mochnant (*uochnant*) when he victoriously marches through your country.
On its borders the enemy was routed,
and the Powysians (*argoedwys*) were furiously attacked
and covered with blood.
Let Powys see who is the valiant king of her people,
whether it argues prudence to act treacherously.
Whether a French chief is preferable to a conquering Welshman (*gymro*)?
We have a prince, consider it,
who, though silent doubt his own merit,
puts England (*loegr*) to flight
and is fully bent to conquer the land that was formerly in the possession of Cadwallon
the son of Cadfan the son of Iago [d.bef.632] ....
A noble lion, the governor of Britain, and her defence,
Llywelyn, numerous are your battles,
you brave prince of the mighty
that puts the enemy to flight.
May you my friend and benefactor
overcome in every hardship.
He is a prince with terrible looks
who will conquer in foreign countries
as well as in Mon the mother of all Wales.
His army has made its way broad through the ocean,
and filled the hills, promontories and dales.
The blood flowed about their feet when the maimed warriors fought.
In the battle of Coedana (*coed aneu*)
you supporter of bards,
you did overthrow your enemies [1194].

[*143] Ellesmere was a possession of Dafydd ab Owain. There is no other mention of its destruction during the wars before or after it was granted to Llywelyn in April 1205.

The other hard battle was fought at *dygen dyfnant*[*144]
where thousands behaved themselves with manly valour.
The next contest, where noble feats were achieved
was on the hill of Bryn yr Erw (*Bronn yr erw*[*145])
where they saw you like a lion foremost in piercing your enemies
like a strong eagle,
a safeguard to your people.
Upon this account they will no longer dispute with you.
They vanish before you like the ghosts of Celyddon.
You have taken Mold (*wytgrug*) and Degannwy (*Dygant*) by force
And Rhuddlan (*rutglann*) with its red borders
and thousands of your men overthrew
Denbigh (*dinbych*), Pentrefoelas (*voelas*) and Gronant
and the men of Caernarfon (*chaer vn aruon*), your friends, were busy in action
and Dinas Emrys (*Dinas Emreis*) strove bravely in your cause
and they vanquished with the renowned Morgant at their head
all that stood before them.
Your pledges know not where to turn their faces,
they cannot enjoy mirth or rest.
You were honourably covered with blood,
and your wound is a glory to you.
When you did resist manfully the attack of the enemy,
you we honoured by your sword,
with your buckler on your shoulders.
You did bravely lead your forces,
to the astonishment of England (*Lloegr*),
to the borders of Mechain (*mechein*) and Mochnant...[*146]

This long poem is primarily interested in singing Llywelyn's praises and therefore concentrates on battles in North Wales. Further, it is clearly written before Llywelyn made the momentous decision to imitate his Uncle Dafydd and marry into the Plantagenet royal family. The remorse shown at the death of Dafydd is interesting considering that Dafydd had been the main enemy of Llywelyn from his youth and the Register states boldly that Llywelyn killed him, probably in 1200. Obviously, the poem suggests that Llywelyn was happy to wear his uncle's mantle as the leader of Wales and this no doubt accounts for the change of heart in Llywelyn's apparent feelings for his uncle.

Of the fighting itself in 1194 Llywarch tells little, although he does give an idea of Llywelyn's progress to the south and east as his power spread at the turn of the thirteenth century when he lists the fortresses that fell under Llywelyn's power. It is instructive to see

---

[*144] This would appear to be in north-eastern Wales. Possibly this place is now 'Degannwy' Deunant (S.820738) just outside Llansanffraid Glan Conwy, in which case this could be another name for the battle of Aberconwy, which therefore took place east of the Conwy. It should be noted that the battle of Mold is repeatedly mentioned in the poem, and therefore a repeat of the battle of Aberconwy under a different name is not impossible.

[*145] This was the site of a battle in 1075, See Remfry, PM, *Medieval Battles: Wales, 1055 to 1216: Volume 2, part 1* [2017], 43. This is probably the battle mentioned above as being fought in Arfon. Presumably Maredudd ap Cynan was the enemy on this occasion between 1200 and 1202.

[*146] A translation of Llynwarch Brydydd y Moch, in Evans, E., *Some Specimens of the Poetry of the Ancient Welsh Bards* [Llanidloes, 1764], 30-35.

Dafydd's major fortress of Denbigh mentioned together with Pentrefoelas and Gronant, all three of which are alluded to as possessions of that prince. These were followed by the mention of Dinas Emrys, which lies actually within a grange of Aberconwy abbey, as does Pentrefoelas. Considering these details it is possible that the battle of Aberconwy began on the west bank of the Conwy with an assault on the motte castle at Gronant (Fig.10)[*147]. The river was then forded and the Perfeddwlad invaded with Pentrefoelas castle falling next, before Llywelyn swept through the rest of the cantrefs taking the allegiance of the people, but not of Dafydd's household who managed to hold out in the remaining 'three castles' of, probably Rhuddlan, Denbigh and Basingwerk/Colleshill. Dafydd would obviously also have retained Ellesmere. Possibly this place was the final 'palace' destroyed in the poem, although Dafydd's widow, Emma Plantagenet, and their son, Owain ap Dafydd, continued to live there until they exchanged the land and castle at the request of King John in May 1203[*148]. This was obviously after Dafydd's death. Certainly the evidence from the poem nowhere contradicts the surviving evidence concerning the careers of Llywelyn and his allies and enemies. Llywarch also gives us greater detail of the castles stormed by Llywelyn and provides the answer to the fate of Degannwy castle (*Dygant*). Note how contemporary writings have it as *Dugannu* and *Daggenot* as well as possibly *Dygen* in the same poem.

Figure 11, The possible circular tower base just north of Gronant motte on the line of the probable bailey.

To summarise, the victory 'of Llywelyn' was not as decisive as it might have been in 1194. Regardless of this, it would appear that the assault knocked Dafydd out of the war and, with his field army destroyed or in France, he played no further part in the subsequent battles fought for the control of Gwynedd. Instead, he appears to have sat impotently within his fortress defences. There is no solid evidence for Dafydd's age at this time, but, judging by their careers, he and Rhodri were probably in their mid forties around 1194. It should also be noted that the land of Pentrefoelas was later granted to Aberconwy. As the poetry evidence shows almost certainly that there was a fortress here in 1194, when it was probably destroyed, this is firm evidence that this grange was unlikely to have been granted to the abbey before this date and therefore

---

[*147] The motte stands on the west bank of the Conwy about forty feet above the current Tal y Cafn bridge. The oval mound is about 340 feet in basal circumference and fifteen feet high. The summit measures some fifty feet by 35, *Royal Commission on Ancient Monuments in England and Wales, for Caernarvonshire* [3 vols, 1960], 27, No.114. Some loose rubble can be seen around the summit of the mound. More has been made into a bank above the scarp down to the bridge. Possibly this suggests some element of stone defence on the motte. The entire structure has been damaged, either by a motte slighting or via the quarrying of the mound. A bailey appears to have lain on the north side where there are the possible foundations of a round tower (Fig.11).

[*148] *Rotuli de Liberate ac de Misis et Praestitis regnante Johanne*, ed. T.D. Hardy [1844], 36, 56; *Rotuli Litterarum Clausarum in Turri Londinensi asservati [1204-27]*, ed, T.D. Hardy [2 vols., 1833-44] I, 12a.

that this grange, and its two neighbours of Llanfair Rhyd Castell and Ceirniog were probably not within an original foundation grant of 1186. It therefore appears most likely that theses granges, later known as Hiraethog, were the grant of Llywelyn sometime between 1194 and 1240[*149]. Certainly Pentrefoelas and Llanfair Rhyd Castell were definitely held by the abbey by 1273, while Ceirniog was held by them before 1282. As they appear as separate granges they were presumably granted at different times, although it seems likely that it was Llywelyn who granted all three to the abbey. However, it is equally possible that Dafydd granted the two outer granges (Llanfair Rhyd Castell and Ceriniog) to Aberconwy and Llywelyn added Pentrefoelas after the castle's destruction in 1194 and his assuming full control of the region on his capture of Dafydd in 1197.

With Dafydd's defeat in 1194 the alliance against him fell apart. Whether Rhodri reneged on his agreement or whether the sons of Cynan decided to expel him from all his lands, if he still held any at this time, is unknown. The poetry quoted above may suggest that Castell Dinas Emrys was stormed around this time, but who was defending it against whom is unknown, although possibly it was defended by troops loyal to Rhodri for Llywelyn is later credited with the deed by the poets. That said, it is obvious that at this time Llywelyn remained in alliance with his more powerful cousins, the sons of Cynan. Whatever the reasons, and whatever lands he was still holding, the sons of Cynan with Llywelyn then turned against 'the Dragon of Mon', Rhodri ab Owain. It would seem unlikely that Dafydd's troops would have been holding a castle as far west as Eyri in 1194, so it seems likely that Rhodri was attempting to re-establish himself in Arfon and this may have been what united the sons of Cynan with Llywelyn, who claimed to be heir to his father in this district. The consequence was an important battle of which little but the name is now known. Most of the evidence for it comes from the *O Oes Gwrtheyrn* which was probably written at Aberconwy abbey (Appendix 3), the poem of Cynddelw quoted above and the few lines about Llywelyn's early battles by Llywarch.

The suggestion from the poems is that the remaining allies crossed the Menai Strait at low tide and forced their steeds to swim the water. This must have been a dangerous undertaking and it suggests that the attack was made purely as a cavalry action, unless of course the poor infantry following behind by whatever means they might were simply not thought worthy of mention. Presumably the defenders on the other side were mainly infantry. It is likely that the unnamed enemy at this battle was under the command of Rhodri, unless there had been an uprising in favour of Dafydd, who may still have had a naval base at Rhuddlan, the castle of which he continued to hold. Again, it is not possible to state with certainty what had happened here. Most likely the defender was Rhodri, who was attempting again to hold the northern portion of Gwynedd against Gruffydd ap Cynan and his relatives. Quite possibly there was no battle here, just a heart stopping cavalry charge made across the waters. What certainly happened next was a battle in the heart of Mon at *Coedaneu*, a placename that still exists as Plas Coedana (SH.421825). Here again 'the allies' won a decisive victory, and again the enemy is likely to have been Rhodri ab Owain, though again the defeated's identity is not mentioned by the poets. After all they were writing poetry at a time when everyone would have known who was defeated in Mon. The poets would not have needed to spell it out to their audience. The supposition that Rhodri was defeated in these

---

[*149] The idea that the Levelinus stone was raised near Pentrefoelas to commemorate the monk's love for Llywelyn ab Iorwerth for granting them this grange seems far fetched and can be fairly confidently dismissed. The story appears in Hays, RW, *The History of the Abbey of Aberconway, 1186-1537* [UWP, 1963], 15 and is commented on in Appendix 10, p.346.

battles is strengthened somewhat by the fact that he died in 1194, apparently in Caer Gybi on Holyhead[*150].

There is also the fact that this action against Rhodri could have been motivated by hurt pride. The pope himself informs us that in or a little before 1192 it had been mooted that the twenty year old Llywelyn should marry the eight year old daughter of King Reginald of Man. However, Llywelyn then went on to become engaged to a sister of Earl Ranulf Blunderville of Chester (1170-1232, Fig.12) and the Manx alliance was dropped[*151]. Yet this same year, Rhodri instead took up the marriage offer 'without the consent' of Llywelyn and acquired both the girl and the alliance with King Reginald. Subsequently, after Rhodri's death in 1194, Llywelyn proceeded to marry his widowed eleven year old aunt, while stating to the pope that the marriage between her and Rhodri had not been consummated - a statement he renounced in 1203 to assuage his conscience in asking for an annulment to the marriage. Once more these long overlooked details tell us how much the political actions of this era are hidden to us and how complex the changing maelstrom of alliances actually were.

Figure 12, The seal of Earl Ranulf of Chester and Lincoln reproduced from Ormerod, G., *The History of Cheshire* [3 vols, 1819] I, 41.

As the Annales Cambriae state that Llywelyn ab Iorwerth alone dispossessed Dafydd ab Owain in 1194, it is possible that the anachronistic compiler of this source was interested in the rise of Llywelyn and not the careers of his relatives. Consequently, he ignored the actions of the sons of Cynan when he came to compile what is now the final version of the Annales, compiled some time in the late thirteenth century. As a consequence, the question is left as to whether there was a copy of the Welsh Annales that was compiled at Aberconwy and contained details of affairs in North Wales that were ignored in the southern redactions of the Bruts which survive as the Red Book of Hergest and Peniarth Ms.20. Undoubtedly any

---

[*150] *Annales Cambriae. A Translation of Harleian 3859; PRO E.164/1; Cottonian Domitian, A 1; Exeter Cathedral Library MS. 3514 and MS Exchequer DB Neath, PRO E.164/1*, ed. Remfry, P.M., [Malvern, 2007], 99. John Gwydir stated that a Welsh chronicle copied by Sir Thomas Williams of Trefriw stated that Rhodri lay in the college of *Kerkyby*, Wynne, J., *History of the Gwydir Family* [Ruthin, 1827], 25.
[*151] See the Chapter, Llywelyn's Marriage and Aberconwy, 1195 to 1203, for the evidence about this.

Aberconwy chronicle or Brut would likely have carried much information concerning the wars that occurred in Gwynedd when the abbey was founded. Evidence shows that at least one such Welsh Brut made at Aberconwy did exist and survived down into the seventeenth century. This 'Welsh Chronicle' was in the hands of 'Sir' Thomas Williams of Trefriw (1545/6-1622), a noted collector of Welsh manuscripts. It was apparently later used by Dr Powell in his history[152]. A further link to this Welsh manuscript is the comment by John Wynne that:

> In a fragment of a Welsh chronicle, copied by Sir Thomas Williams, I find, that in the end Llywelyn killed his Uncle Dafydd and all his posterity at Conwy.

This is fascinating as this is the only piece of evidence to link a Welsh chronicle with the extracts printed in the Aberconwy manuscript which could be translated thus:

> In the year of our lord 1190, when Richard called the heart of a lion was reigning in England, on 1 January, which is the day of the Circumcision of the lord, Llywelyn ab Iorwerth Drwyndwn strangled and killed his prince, Dafydd ab Owain, at Aber, and thus he raised himself over the principality of all North Wales, also he brought together and subscribed the diverse possessions of the abbey with its liberties.

The year 1190 is an obvious nonsense which will be further commented upon later, but the fact that Dafydd was claimed to have been killed by Llywelyn is only found in these two North Welsh sources, one copied from an unknown Brut at the end of the sixteenth century and one from the fifteenth century Aberconwy Register. They would appear to be different versions of the same tradition, as one assigns the scene of the killing to Aber, the other to Conwy. It should also be noted that this version of the Register cannot date to before 1315, the earliest possible date on which Llywelyn's charters of 1199, noted in the extract above, were forged. This would again suggest that the Register chronicle is following an earlier exemplar.

The generally accepted version of events as relayed by the Bruts is that Dafydd was expelled to England in 1198 and that he later died there in 1203:

> In that year Llywelyn ab Iorwerth expelled Dafydd ab Owain from Gwynedd; and he died in England.[153]

> And then Dafydd ab Owain died in England, after being banished from Wales by Llywelyn ab Iorwerth.
> *Ac yna y bu varw Dauid ap Ywein yn Lloeger, wedy y dehol o Lywelyn ap Jorwerth o Gymry.*[154]

> In that year Llywelyn ab Iorwerth drove Dafydd ab Owain Gwynedd from Wales and he died in England.

---

[152] *Cambro-Briton, The*, [3 vols, London, 1819-22] I, 219.
[153] Pen, 82.
[154] RBH, 185-7.

Yn y vlwyddyn honno y gyrrodd Llywelyn ab Jerwerth Ddavydd ap Owain Gwynedd o Gymry; ac yn lloegr i bu varw.[155]

It is therefore quite clear that all our currently accepted knowledge of the death of Dafydd comes from the fourteenth century redactions of the Bruts and that no knowledge of it has been recorded from the various Latin Annales Cambriae. It therefore seems possible that a lost Welsh chronicle from Aberconwy placed Dafydd's death not in England, where he had allegedly been expelled to in 1198, but in North Wales, at Aber (or Conwy in which case the Register's Aber might just be an abbreviation of Aberconwy), the llys of the princes[156]. It should further be noted that Ellesmere llys remained in the hands of Dafydd or at least his family until May 1203. At that date Ellesmere was in Maelor in Wales and not in Shropshire. In fact this part of Wales did not become a part of England until the time of Henry VIII (d.1547). It is therefore eminently likely that Dafydd did die 'in Wales' and not in England as the fourteenth century Bruts have it. It is far more likely that any such record of his death would have survived in North rather than South Wales. In the fourteenth century the compilers of the Welsh Bruts were not much interested in the affairs of Gwynedd when they were related to non-direct ancestors of the Llywelyns. It is also apparent that in the poem to Llywelyn he is credited with burning down Ellesmere. These two events, the burning of Ellesmere llys and the death of Dafydd, could possibly be linked. Certainly in *O Oes Gwrtheyrn* (Appendix 3) all that is said of Dafydd's death is:

> the year after the death of Gruffydd [ap Cynan], Dafydd ab Owain died.

No place for Dafydd's death is mentioned here, although later, King John is stated to have come with an army to Aber in 1211. As Gruffydd ap Cynan died in the Spring of 1200 this would indicate that the author - who appears to be a contemporary at this time - thought Dafydd's death occurred before the Spring of 1201. From this it is possible to deduce that the place of Dafydd's death may have been recorded as Aber in the lost Aberconwy chronicle. Certainly, no other known source mentions the place of John's encampment in 1211 and so possibly the Aberconwy Register recorded a fact about Dafydd's death as recorded in the lost Aberconwy Brut. Alternatively, the fifteenth century compiler may have simply believed this to have been the fate of Dafydd, without any contemporary evidence whatsoever. It should also be noted that Llywelyn would have had no right to be resident at Aber in January 1200 as that llys then belonged to Gruffydd ap Cynan. However, he would have been in possession in January 1201 if the dating in *O Oes Gwrtheyrn* is correct. The origins of this chronicle is discussed in Appendix 3, but in the sixteenth century it was thought that the Bruts:

> Of the which collections there were several copies afterwards kept in either of the abbeys of Conwy or Strata Florida, which were yearly augmented as things fell out, and conferred together ordinarily every third year, when the Beirdh which did belong to those two abbeys went from the one to the other in the time of their Clera, wherein were contained besides, such notable occurrence happening within this isle of Britain, as they then thought worthy of writing...[157]

---

[155] ByS, 198-9.
[156] For the llys at Aber, otherwise Aber Garth Celyn see Remfry, PM., *A Brief Report on Pen y Bryn and Aber, Gwynedd* [2012].
[157] *David Powel's Historie of Cambria, now called Wales* [1584, London, 1811], ix.

Such evidence must be regarded with caution and it must be remembered that the Bruts are not contemporary sources, but are a compilation redacted in the fourteenth century.

Other evidence as to the existence and value of the lost Aberconwy chronicle comes from the fact that:

> In a fragment of a Welsh chronicle copied by my kinsman Sir Thomas Williams, I find that in the end Llewelin killed his uncle David, and all his posterity, at Conway. Soe that I think there is none descended from the said David and the Lady Emma his wife either male or female.[*158]

This would appear to be different from the information recorded in the Register, viz:

> In the year of our lord one thousand one hundred 90, Richard called the heart of a lion was king reigning over England, on 1 January, which is the day of the Circumcision of the lord, Llywelyn ab Iorwerth Drwyndwn strangled and killed his prince, Dafydd ab Owain, at Aber, and thus he raised himself over the principality of all North Wales...

This would therefore suggest that these two works have a different provenance, unless the compiler of one blundered with the placename. A little later Sir John Wynne stated:

> I find in a fragment of a Welsh chronicle, copied by my kinsman Sir Thomas Williams, that Rhodri ab Owain had another son called Einion (as is afore specified) by the daughter of the Lord Rhys, Prince of South Wales, beside Gruffydd before mentioned and Thomas.[*159]

Again, this is exactly the sort of thing that might be expected in a Venedotian version of a Welsh Brut. Certainly this does not appear in the Aberconwy Register or any other surviving Welsh chronicle. Finally, from the same lost Aberconwy chronicle Sir John notes:

> Rhodri lyeth buried in the colledge of Caergybi (*Kerkyby*). This I had out of the Welsh chronicle, copied by Sir Thomas Will of Trefriew.[*160]

This information points quite clearly to an Aberconwy chronicle or Brut surviving into the seventeenth century. The work of John Wynne (d.1627) is rightly regarded with much trepidation for some of his highly dubious guesses, but within his guesswork he certainly used original material. The pleasure of history is, as ever, sorting the wheat from the chaff.

Concerning the death of Dafydd there is also a record at the Citeaux Chapter General that a 'king of Wales' requested permission to found a Cistercian monastery[*161]. In response to this in September 1203 the general chapter of the Cistercians appointed the abbots of Margam and Buildwas to examine if the king had sufficient resources to follow through his plan and report back to the chapter, presumably for the next general meeting in September 1204. No report was apparently submitted the next September and nothing further is heard of

---

[*158] Wynne, J., 'History of the Gwedir Family', *Miscellanies*, ed. Barrington, D., [London, 1781], 362.
[*159] Wynne, J., 'History of the Gwedir Family', *Miscellanies*, ed. Barrington, D., [London, 1781], 362.
[*160] Wynne, J., 'History of the Gwedir Family', *Miscellanies*, ed. Barrington, D., [London, 1781], 363.
[*161] Statuta I, 294 (1203/48). This appears quite different to Gruffydd ap Cynan's request to build an abbey which is discussed in the next chapter.

the request. At this time the main contenders for those who may have still been calling themselves kings of Wales could have been, in no particular order, Hywel ab Iorwerth of Caerleon (d.1211), Llywelyn ab Iorwerth (d.1240), Rhys Ieunanc (d.1222), Rhys Gryg (d.1234), Hywel Saes ap Rhys (d.1204), Maelgwn ap Rhys (d.1230), Maredudd ap Cynan (d.1212), Gwenwynwyn (d.1216) and Madog ap Gruffydd (d.1236). Of these the princes of Deheubarth can probably be ruled out as being too insignificant after the death of Gruffydd ap Rhys in 1201 to be considered as kings. Maredudd ap Rhobert of Cedewain, although he founded a Cistercian nunnery at Llanllugan, was hardly in a position to claim to be a king of Wales in 1203 and was apparently landless until after 1210[*162], so he too must be ruled out. This really leaves Llywelyn ab Iorwerth, who was described in 1223 as king of the Welsh in a chronicle possibly composed during his lifetime[*163], but who in 1203 was really disputing that position with Gwenwynwyn of Powys who thought that this mantle naturally fell on him. Maredudd ap Cynan is another possibility if he was attempting to step into his brother Cynan's shoes, but really the only logical choice for any man claiming to be King of North Wales at this time was Dafydd ab Owain - or his son Owain ap Dafydd. Yet Dafydd's alleged death in May 1203, if not as early as January 1200, would surely have been reported to the general chapter by at least the abbots of Margam and Buildwas who should have been at the meeting in September 1203, as too should all of the other Cistercian abbots from Britain. Surely they too would have known that Dafydd was dead in 1203 for at least six months and probably several years. Whatever the case, nothing further was heard of the request. Yet Dafydd's son Owain did in fact have a monastery founded, possibly for him and certainly named partially after him, immediately after his death in 1212 by his cousin King John of England. This was founded in the manor of Hales in Staffordshire and was immediately known as Halesowen[*164]. Perhaps this is the abbey that Dafydd, or, if he was dead as the evidence seems to suggest, his son Owain notified his intention to found between the General Chapters of September 1202 and September 1203, assuming of course that he was the man claiming to be 'king of Wales'. If it was Dafydd making the request, then his death before May 1203 obviously ended any chance of the immediate fulfilling of his intention. It would also be a valid reason for the two abbots neither performing the task enjoined upon them or anything further about the new abbey being recorded at Citeaux. However, it seems impossible that any such commission would have been given in September 1203, a minimum of four months after Dafydd's death, for surely such an event would have been known to the Cistercian order. Consequently, the only sensible option seems to be that it was Dafydd's son Owain who was trying to step into his father's shoes and that obviously he did not have the resources to undertake such a foundation and indeed never did. In fact it was left to his cousin, King John, to found Halesowen abbey after Owain's death.

Although it has often been stated that the brothers Dafydd and Rhodri were usually in alliance on the strength of a 'throw away' comment by Giraldus[*165], the text itself can in no way support such a premise:

> his paternal uncles, Dafydd and Rhodri... although they had divided the superior portion of all Gwynedd between one another, except for the land of Cynan... yet

---

[*162] Remfry, P.M., *Native Welsh Dynasties of Rhwng Gwy A Hafren, 1066 to 1282* [2010], 96.
[*163] *Matthaei Parisiensis, monachi Sancti Albani, Chronica Majora*, ed. H.R. Luard [7 vols., 1872-83] III, 76.
[*164] The foundation of Halesowen is looked at later in this book.
[*165] Lloyd, J.E., *History of Wales* [2 vols., 1911] II, 588-9; Pen, 190, note 75, 26-8, and of course don't forget to visit the Wikipedia pages for a fantasy trip through the Gwynedd royal family!

presently within a few years, those [two] born from public incest, propped up equally through the aid of wealth and fertile land, that lawful [Llywelyn ab Iorwerth], altogether without lands and monies, by the aid of divine vengeance, he manfully almost totally drove [them] out from Gwynedd...

The linking together of the two brothers here hardly constitutes an alliance or any comment upon how they fought in 1194. The surviving historical evidence shows that Dafydd alone was the enemy of a united front of the sons of Cynan, Rhodri and Llywelyn in 1194. The possibility remains that Dafydd advanced over the Conwy this year and fortified Dinas Emrys while simultaneously sweeping across the small arm of the sea from Degannwy castle (if he still held it or had recently seized it) to take Mon. As a result the allies counterattacked at Aberconwy and then swept northwards to evict Dafydd's forces from Mon. Quite simply, without further evidence it cannot be certain and any claims should not be stronger than the fact that Rhodri fought against Dafydd at Aberconwy and that he may still have been the enemy of his brother at Porthaethwy and Coedana, although the poetry seems quite clear that the enemy of Llywelyn in Mon during 1194 was Rhodri and that Dafydd was not even mentioned in respect to this part of the campaign.

It should also be noted that although Llywelyn ab Iorwerth is regarded as the hero of the hour in the three battles by later poets, it is noticeable that he profited little from the affair. This strongly suggests that his part in the campaign has been anachronistically overstated. After the fighting was finished Gruffydd ap Cynan appears to have ruled in Mon, Arfon, Arllechwedd and Llyn. Further Prydydd y Moch implies his control over Degannwy (*dygannwy*)[*166] which suggests that this fortress too fell in 1194 and that Gruffydd also held Creuddyn from this date. Meanwhile, his younger brother, Maredudd ap Cynan, held Ardudwy, Eifionydd and Meirionydd as his portion. Llywelyn, despite the poets' praise, withdrew to the Perfeddwlad east of the Conwy where he also had to contend with his uncle, Dafydd, who still retained 'his three castles' probably Rhuddlan, Denbigh and Basingwerk/Coleshill. It is indeed possible that Llywelyn held little real power until he captured his uncle in 1197. Again, the details of this are sadly lacking, but English royal records do register some clear facts which will be examined after the next chapter.

[*166] *The Myvyrian Archaiology of Wales*, eds. O. Jones, E. Williams & W. Owen [2nd edn., Denbigh, 1870] I, 288-9.

Aberconwy and the Foundation of Cymer Abbey

Aberconwy does not seem to have played any part in the founding of Cymer abbey, but the new abbey's placing in Gwynedd did have an effect on the older monastery. If the chronology in the Bruts is correct, then between the capture of Gruffydd ap Rhys in the early part of the year and the battle of Painscastle on 13 August 1198:

> A community of Cwmhir went to reside at Cymer in Nannau in Meirionydd.[*167]

This is an interesting occurrence as it shows something of how an abbey was actually founded. If the Bruts are correct the community left Abbey Cwmhir before 13 August, but it was only that September that the petition to found a new abbey was received at the yearly Cistercian general chapter in France.

> Petition of Gruffydd to construct an abbey entrusted to the abbot of Clairvaux. Returned to our following chapter.[*168]

It is unfortunate that Gruffydd ap Cynan's original petition did not survive, but the request was taken up at the subsequent chapter in September 1199.

> Petition of Prince Gruffydd of North Wales wishing to build an abbey. The abbot of Margam is to join with the abbots of Buildwas and Whitland, who he will take with him to the place of foundation, that they may agree the place with him, and carefully examine that forwarded and subsequently report back to the chapter.[*169]

It is quite clear from this that Cymer abbey had been founded and maybe partially built by September 1199. That Cymer was a functional abbey within the year is confirmed from the next entry in the manuscript where it was shown that Cymer had already got itself into a land dispute with its neighbouring abbey of Aberconwy.

> The complaint which is pending between the abbey of Cymer and Aberconwy is entrusted to the abbots of Buildwas, Dore and Croxden, to be concluded by agreement or trial. The abbot of Combermere is to deliver this summons to the others.[*170]

The matter was apparently settled between the two abbeys without the interference of the abbot of Croxden who was put on bread and water for three days for his failure to do as ordered[*171]. Leastways, that is the last heard of the matter. It may well be that Prince Llywelyn ab Iorwerth settled the dispute after the death of Prince Gruffydd ap Cynan in March 1200. It is unfortunate that there is no information on why the abbot of Croxden failed to perform the arbitration. However, as Cymer was a foundation of Gruffydd and this led to tensions with Aberconwy abbey, it might suggest that Gruffydd was not overly fond of the

---

[*167] *RBH*, 181; *Pen*, 79.

[*168] *Petitio Gifini de construenda abbatia committitur abbati Clarae vallis (reversuri sequenti nostro Capitulo)*, Statuta I, 230/41.

[*169] *Petitio Gifini/Grifini, principis Norwaliae de abbatia aedificanda, committitur abbati de Margan, qui assumptis secum abbatibus de Bidoars et de Blanchalanda cum fundatore loci, ad ipsum locum accedant, et diligenter inquirant de praemissis et ad sequens Capitulum renuntient.* Statuta I, 236/21.

[*170] *Quaerela quae vertitur inter abbatiam de Quemier/Kemeria/Chemerium/Kemmer) et Arbercornii, committitur abbatibus de Bidoars, de Dora et de Crosquedane, compositione vel iudicio terminanda. Abbas de Crosquedane hoc aliis denuntiet.* Statuta I, 237/22.

[*171] Statuta I, 257/44.

house that was to bury him. Perhaps the solving of the dispute and Gruffydd being buried at Aberconwy marked his reconciliation with a house probably founded by his enemy, Rhodri ab Owain (d.1194).

The foundation of Cymer abbey shows how quickly things might progress with the establishing of an abbey. It therefore adds strength to Giraldus' implication that Aberconwy abbey was standing and viable in 1188, two years after its foundation, when he travelled past. In the sixteen years that the abbey had been in existence a lot had gone on there, from the troubled politics of the collapse of the hegemony of the sons and grandsons of Owain Gwynedd, to a subprior of Aberconwy being twice raised to the rank of bishop elect of Bangor. However, the strangest case during this period must have been the promotion of a mere monk of Aberconwy to a bishopric. It is sad that the only evidence there is of this comes from a meagre notice in the Cistercian records from September 1200.

> Philip, a monk of Aberconwy, who by his own authority appointed himself forward into a bishop, has up until Easter to appear at Clairvaux and there stand at the order of the abbot of Clairvaux. Otherwise he may be held as a fugitive. The abbot of Margam is to deliver summons of this to him.[*172]

Over the years Aberconwy abbey seems to have had more than its fair share of renegade monks.

The Rise of Llywelyn ab Iorwerth:
From Rebel Prince to Vassal of King John, 1195 to 1199

The war of 1194 must have severely disrupted life at Aberconwy abbey, just as the war of 1245 would do. To what extent this affected monastic life and the abbey granges - some of which were on Mon certainly before 1199 and probably as early as 1192 and others were right along the lines of the political frontiers along the Conwy (Hiraethog and Arddau) - is unknown, but life was quite likely problematical for the eight year old abbey. That said, there is no evidence that the granges that became Hiraethog yet belonged to Aberconwy and certainly the central one of Pentrefoelas did not, housing as it did the royal castle of King Dafydd ab Owain.

After the discomfiture of the royalist Dafydd in 1194, the government of King Richard paid more attention to Wales, but their first objective was Deheubarth, rather than Gwynedd. Thus during 1195, royally sponsored armies penetrated South Wales and the Middle Marches. In Shropshire the Lestranges refortified Carreghofa castle, only just clear of the north Shropshire plain. Action was also taken beyond the Perfeddwlad. Alan St Cross was made bishop of Bangor in place of the elected Roland, the subprior of Aberconwy, on 16 April 1195[*173]. This occurred a fortnight before Archbishop Hubert was made legate of England, Wales and Scotland on 30 April[*174].

[*172] *Philippus monachus de Albocornu qui sua auctoritate se dicit promotum in pontificem usque ad Pascha, Claraevali se praesentet, et ibi stet ad mandatum abbatis Claraevallis. Alioquin pro fugitivo habeatur. Abbas de Margan hoc ei denuntiet.* Statuta I, 262-3/70.
[*173] *Flores Historiarum*, ed. H. R. Luard (3 vols, 1890) II 113. Alan's profession to Canterbury was made the same day, *Canterbury Professions*, ed. Richter, M., [Canterbury and York Society, 1973] LXVII, No.134; Alan's seal is still extant, Williams, D. H., 'Catalogue of Welsh ecclesiastical seals as known down to 1600. Part I: Episcopal seals', *Archaeologia Cambrensis* [1984], 110. See also Hays, R.W., 'Rotoland, subprior of Aberconway, and the controversy over the see of Bangor, 1199-1204', *Journal of Hist. Soc. of Church in Wales* XVIII [1963], 9-19. Alan's elevation and death are also noticed in 'Annales de Theokesberia', *Annales Monastici*, ed. H.R. Luard [5 vols., 1864-9] I, 55.
[*174] *Flores Historiarum*, ed. H. R. Luard (3 vols, 1890) II 113.

Alan was no ordinary bishop, for before his appointment he had been the prior of the hospital of St John of Jerusalem in England, and was therefore likely to have been a man accustomed to warfare. He was certainly of age before 1181 and so would have probably been a vigorous youngish man in 1195[175]. It seems quite obvious that Alan could in no way make himself bishop of Bangor in the face of the hostility of Prince Gruffydd ap Cynan and his ally, Llywelyn ab Iorwerth. After his appointment Alan busied himself with supporting Dafydd ab Owain and his increasingly fragile grasp on what remained to him of the Perfeddwlad. Beyond his apparent three castles of Denbigh, Rhuddlan and Basingwerk, or Colleshill castle as it was otherwise known, Owain also held Ellesmere castle, which was described as a llys (palace or royal court) in the poem by Prydydd y Moch. Alan's appointment may have led Llywelyn ab Iorwerth, his new lands sandwiched between Dafydd ab Owain and Gruffydd ap Cynan, to try to negotiate with the English government, for in the Michaelmas 1195 pipe roll for London and Middlesex, one Vincent, the nuncio of Llywelyn (Lefwin), was allowed two marks (£1 6s 8d) for a robe at the instance of the archbishop of Canterbury[176]. If this was Prince Llywelyn's man, it is certain that any such negotiations proved abortive. As a consequence, the archbishop sent a force of a dozen mounted serjeants under the new bishop of Bangor to help maintain the situation in North Wales. The serjeants were paid 6d per day and cost £12 by Michaelmas 1195. Twelve pounds was 2,880 pennies. So if this figure is divided first by twelve for the number of serjeants and then by the 6d wage, we get the amount of days the serjeants were in action - in this case forty days. As the bishop was also allowed £5 to garrison Denbigh castle it is to be presumed that this was his base of operation[177]. Twelve serjeants were obviously insufficient to stop the ravages of Llywelyn ab Iorwerth or expel Gruffydd ap Cynan from Gwynedd, so Alan's job was obviously just to maintain the status quo while the main royalist Welsh forces, thousands strong, fought for King Richard in France[178]. Regardless of these actions, it is possible that some form of truce was arranged at this time. During his sojourn in Wales, Bishop Alan confirmed the charters of his predecessors, Meurig and Gwion, concerning Haughmond abbey: viz the gift of King Hywel of Arwystli of Trefeglwys church, from Cadwaladr and his sons Maredudd, Einion and Cadwallon, the church of Nefyn with appurtenances between the two rivers and the land of Cremioch, from King Dafydd of North Wales; the land Troitbremeth held in Boduan in Nefyn, from Bishop Gwion the tithes of Edern and a third of the tithes of the lordship of Nefyn and the church of Nefyn itself. This long document of confirmation was witnessed by Archdeacon Abraham ap Gruffydd, Archdeacon Gervase of Bangor, Archdeacon Philip the son of the bishop and Archdeacon Cynddelw (Candelauo) of Llyn[179]. It is of course possible that these archdeacons came to Bishop Alan at Denbigh to make this charter, but it is likewise possible that Alan himself went to Bangor, or even further into the Llyn. It is also possible that the Abraham ap Gruffydd might have been a later abbot of Aberconwy who died in 1233. In this case the abbey may have had two abbots before this date.

If the year of 1195 did end with peace in Gwynedd, it did not last. In April 1196 2,100 foot and horse were transferred from Wales under William Braose (bef.1170-1210) to

[175] He witnesses a charter as Brother Alan between 1178 and 1181, *Cartulary of the Knights of St John of Jerusalem in England, Secunda Camera, Essex*, ed. Gervers, M., [1982], 137, No.219. This was obviously before he became prior after the death of Ralph Dover (*Dyva*) on 13 May 1190, *Idem*, 242, No.423; 570, No.961.
[176] *PR 7 Richard I*, 113.
[177] *PR 7 Rich I*, 244.
[178] See Remfry, P.M., *Whittington Castle and the Families of...* [2007], 62-66, for the Welsh part in the French war.
[179] *Cartulary of Haughmond Abbey*, ed. Una Rees [Aberystwyth, 1983], No.794.

Brittany[*180]. Even more troops were sent from the southern Marches, although the archbishop did not skimp on supplying soldiers to keep the peace. In the London account of the Michaelmas pipe roll, £260 12s 3d had been spent on Wales and the Marches for knights and serjeants retained there on the king's business. Many further Welshmen were also paid wages in transferring themselves overseas while the archbishop of Canterbury himself accounted for a further £237 18s 3d spent in strengthening Welsh castles and on the king's business[*181]. In the northern marches of Gwynedd full scale war was obviously occurring. Over 250 Welsh foot and some cavalry marched to Normandy in the service of the king, while behind them the Welsh lords of Whittington and Overton castles strengthened the defence of the remaining lands of Dafydd ab Owain[*182]. Bishop Alan of Bangor was given ten marks (£6 13s 4d) to maintain himself in the custody of Denbigh castle, while Meurig Powis of Whittington and Gwion ap Jonas of Overton were granted twenty shillings each for clothing as well as the custody of Denbigh castle. They were further given two marks (£1 6s 8d) for their sustenance within the castle garrison and Meurig was given an extra £2 of the king's gift in payment for horses that were lost in defence of the castle and to discharge his debt. The mention of the three constables of Denbigh castle was undoubtedly due to the death of Bishop Alan of Bangor, which occurred on 16 May 1196[*183].

While Denbigh was obviously under attack the archbishop himself moved against another rebel, Gwenwynwyn of Powys, and besieged his castle at Welshpool. The Bruts are not much interested in this war, being much more occupied in the affairs of Deheubarth. That said, they do state:

> Archbishop Hubert of Canterbury, justice of all England and of all the kingdom, having gathered innumerable princes and earls and barons and knights and the princes of Gwynedd along with him, went against the castle of Gwenwynwyn at Welshpool. And after labouriously laying siege to it with various kinds of catapults and slings, at last, when through a marvellous device sappers had been sent into the earth and had tunnelled under the castle, they forced the garrison to surrender the castle; and all the garrison escaped with their arms free and in peace, except for one who was slain. And thereupon, about the end of the year, Gwenwynwyn gathered his men, and he manfully laid siege to that castle and forced it to surrender to him, upon his pledging the garrison their lives and freedom to depart with their arms.[*184]

The slightly later version of the Brut has 'all the princes of Gwynedd' while another version has 'the princes of Wales' as too does the Deheubarth version of the Annales Cambriae[*185]. That any prince of Deheubarth joined in with an attack on Powys while they were both at war with the English government and engaged in hostilities against them in Elfael is highly unlikely. This leaves the question as to whether Dafydd had buried the hatchet with Gruffydd ap Cynan and Llywelyn ab Iorwerth and that all three had marched together against

---

[*180] *PR 7 Richard I*, 205; *Chancellor's Roll 8 Richard I*, 60, 88.

[*181] *PR 8 Richard I*, 17-19.

[*182] *PR 8 Rich I (Chancellor's Roll)*, 41-2.

[*183] The day only is given at the end of Ms. Nero E VI. This dates to the years 1442 to 1447 and is printed in *Cartulary of the Knights of St John of Jerusalem in England, Secunda Camera, Essex*, ed. Gervers, M., [1982], 570. It would seem likely that his obiit is correctly remembered. The year comes from Pen, 75 and 'Annales de Theokesberia', *Annales Monastici*, ed. H.R. Luard [5 vols., 1864-9] I, 55, which both merely state that he died in 1196.

[*184] Pen, 76.

[*185] RBH, 177; ByS, 193; *Annales Cambriae. A Translation of Harleian 3859; PRO E.164/1; Cottonian Domitian, A 1; Exeter Cathedral Library MS. 3514 and MS Exchequer DB Neath, PRO E.164/1*, ed. Remfry, P.M., [Malvern, 2007], 100-1.

Welshpool. This seems a highly unlikely proposition, especially when considering what happened in 1198 at the battle of Painscastle. More likely only one prince appeared at Powis castle, Dafydd ab Owain, the increasingly isolated king of North Wales. However, the possibility that Llywelyn's envoy had been to London the previous year might suggest that a truce was in operation between Llywelyn and Dafydd and that Llywelyn did indeed march south with his uncle.

The English chronicles unfortunately add little to the story, not being much interested with the internal politics of Wales.

> Meanwhile the Welsh burst forth and concentrated in streams against the borders of England making pillagings and burnings. When he heard this the venerable Archbishop Hubert of Canterbury, as he was therefore the highest leader at that time in England, quickly assembling the army, hurried to Powis castle which he besieged and captured, and he put to flight the enemies and strongly reestablished the peace.[*186]

The Chester annals add a little to the story telling us that Powis castle fell to the archbishop on 14 September and that it was retaken before the year was out[*187]. Royal records add little more other than that the attacking force included 48 miners, eleven carpenters and crossbowmen as well as a stone throwing mangonel[*188]. There is no information of the new custodian's name after the castle fell, but William Bibbe and William Wainepain had thirty shillings accounted to them for two different suits of chain mail as was supplied by the sheriff of Shropshire for 'the garrison of Pole castle'. A further sum of £12 5s 9d was spent on the garrison and another £2 4s 7d on ropes, hooks, picks and brattishing, the transport (*passandum*) of the army and in payment of the carpenters as well as for the carriage of their materials[*189]. The garrison commander of Powis castle was probably John Lestrange, for, between Michaelmas 1197 and Michaelmas 1198, it was recorded that he had received ten marks (£6 13s 4d) for his custody of the fortress[*190].

In the same year as this siege of Powis castle was occurring, Denbigh castle disappears from the records. The fact that it is not heard of again for many years strongly suggests that the stronghold fell to Llywelyn ab Iorwerth before Michaelmas 1196. It is also notable that although Meurig of Whittington was seen to have lost his horses, probably when the castle fell, he escaped with his life. His cousin Gwion might not have been so lucky for the next year, 1197, he only received £5 5s for three quarters of a year rent he was owed by the Crown, the other £1 15s going to Geoffrey Fitz Peter. Judging from this Gwion was captured by Llywelyn. This can be ascertained from the reference to him redeeming himself in the pipe roll and the fact that he next appears as the father-in-law of Llywelyn ab Iorwerth - Gwion having married Margery ferch Madog ap Maredudd of Powys[*191]. From this it appears that Llywelyn had captured Gwion and the most likely time for this to have happened was at the fall of Denbigh castle - of which Gwion had been partially entrusted. While these actions

---

[*186] *The Historical Works of Gervase of Canterbury*, ed. W. Stubbs [2 vols., 1878-80] I, 543.
[*187] *Annales Cestrienses, a chronicle of the abbey of St. Werburgh, Chester*, ed. and trans. Christie, R.C., Record Society for Lancashire and Cheshire XIV [1887], 45.
[*188] *PR 8 Richard I (Chancellor's Roll)*, 42.
[*189] *PR 8 Richard I (Chancellor's Roll)*, 42.
[*190] *PR 9 Richard I*, 156.
[*191] Remfry, P.M., *Whittington Castle and the Families of....* [2007], 65-67.

were being played out in Gwynedd, Giraldus Cambrensis was paid £7 12s 1d for his unsuccessful attempts to bring hostilities with Rhys ap Gruffydd in the South to an end[192].

The war with Llywelyn obviously continued into 1197, while Roland, who had again been elected to the see of Bangor, was again rejected by Archbishop Hubert who in his place installed Robert Shrewsbury on 16 March 1197[193]. A month later, on 28 April 1197, King Rhys ap Gruffydd of Deheubarth died. This did not end the war in South Wales, but it did create a civil war within the ongoing war. This was fought out between Rhys' sons. The internal feud was only resolved by the intervention of Archbishop Hubert who went to the Marches and made peace between the waring factions[194]. Dafydd can have had little help from his neighbour, Earl Ranulf of Chester, for this year he is found in the retinue of King Richard fighting in France[195]. The year could not have been very favourable for warfare as plague was also sweeping through the land and 'an untold number of people and a multitude of gentlefolk and many princes' were carried off by it[196]. The Bruts suggest that it was after the capture of Gruffydd ap Rhys and the fall of Ceredigion and Arwystli to Gwenwynwyn that Dafydd ab Owain was finally overthrown when he was captured by Llywelyn, possibly late in the year[197].

The archbishop of Canterbury came to Hereford in Wales to celebrate Christmas 1197 and to militarily reorganise the Herefordshire and Shropshire marches. He then proceeded to Coventry in January 1198[198]. In early February he moved from Shrewsbury, where he had been hearing court cases from at least 14 January 1198, to Knockin in Shropshire with his fellow regents, Earl Roger Bigot, Geoffrey Fitz Peter and Geoffrey Bocland, as well as other faithful lords of the king[199]. There they decided the fate of the little Knockin lordship which they adjudged to John Lestrange rather than Gruffydd ab Iorwerth Goch of Powys (bef.1171-1221) and his wife, Matilda Lestrange (bef.1179-1242). It is interesting that an elegy to Prince Llywelyn ab Iorwerth by Dafydd Benfras states that at some time in his career he made English blood flow in the ditch of Knockin:

Oedd braw saw saeson clawdd y Cnwckin.[200]

An old translation of this part of the poem reads:

When he strove for superiority with Loegria's king
when he was wasting the country of Erbistock (*Erbin*)
his troops were valiant and numerous.
Great was the confusion when the shout was given
his sword was bathed in blood
proud were his nobles to see his army

---

[192] *PR 8 Richard I (Chancellor's Roll)*, 88.
[193] Giraldus Cambrensis, *Opera*, eds. J.S. Brewer, J.F. Dimock and G.F. Warner [8 vols., 1861-91], I, 114; III, 193; *Canterbury Professions*, ed. Richter, M., [Canterbury and York Society, 1973] LXVII, No. 136; Annales of Merton, Cambridge Corpus Christi College, MS 59 fo. 168rb.
[194] *Chronica Magistri Rogeri de Hovedene*, ed. W. Stubbs [4 vols., 1868-71] IV, 21.
[195] *Foedera, Conventiones, Litterae etc*, ed. T. Rymer and R. Sanderson, 4th edn, by A. Clarke, F. Holbrooke, and J. Caley [4 vols. in 7 parts, 1816-69] I, 30.
[196] Pen, 76.
[197] Pen, 79.
[198] *Chronica Magistri Rogeri de Hovedene*, ed. W. Stubbs [4 vols., 1868-71] IV, 35.
[199] *Feet of Fines, 9 Richard I* [Pipe Roll Society, vol 23], 78-80.
[200] *The Myvyrian Archaiology of Wales*, eds. O. Jones, E. Williams & W. Owen [2nd edn., Denbigh, 1870] I, 308

when they heard the clashing of swords
then was felt the agony of wounds...
[some lines missing]
Many were the gashes in the conflict of war.
Great was the confusion of the Saxons about the ditch of Knockin.
The sword was broken in the hand of the warrior.
Heads were covered in wounds
and the flood of human gore gushed in streams down the knees.[*201]

Immediately after the Knockin court case, during the week after 2 February 1198, the archbishop alone proceeded 'into Wales for the liberation of King Dafydd of Wales'[*202]. The implication of this is that Dafydd had only recently been captured, though in what manner is not even hinted at. However, the capture of Dafydd did not mean that the fight was over in the Perfeddwlad, as his son, Owain ap Dafydd, obviously continued the war, receiving twenty marks (£13 6s 8d) to sustain himself in king's service on the Shropshire account of that year[*203].

It would seem likely that with Dafydd's release from the custody of Llywelyn his claim to all the Perfeddwlad was extinguished. It is also possible that all his castles apart from Ellesmere had fallen to Llywelyn or were surrendered to him as a part of the peace treaty between the two. Concerning what appeared to be this conflict the poet Einion ap Gwgan sang:

In Rhuddlan he was like the ruddy fire flaming with destructive light.
There have I seen Llywelyn the brave gaining immortal glory.
I have seen him gallantly ploughing the waves of Deva,
when the tide was at its height.
I have seen him furious in the conflict of Chester,
where he doubly repaid his enemies the injuries he suffered from them...

When you invaded your enemies,
where Owain your predecessor invaded in former times;
full proud was your heart in dividing the spoils,
it happened as in the battles of Kulwydd and Llwyveion[*204].
Your beautiful steeds were fatigued with the labour of the day
where the troops wallowed in gore
and were thrown into confusion.
The bow was full bent before the mangled corpse
the spear aimed at the breast in the country of Eurgain[*205].
The army at Offa's Dyke panted for glory
the troops of Venedotia and the men of London
were as the alternate motion of the waves on the shore,
where the sea-mew screams

[*201] Evans, E., *Some Specimens of the Poetry of the Ancient Welsh Bards*, [1764], 18-9.
[*202] *Feet of Fines, 9 Richard I* [Pipe Roll Society, vol 23], 79.
[*203] *PR 9 Richard*, 156 - *Dauid Reg' Wall'*.
[*204] Battles fought between Urien Reged and his son Owain, against King Ida of the Northumbrians.
[*205] Llaneurgain is now Northop in Flintshire, so called from Eurgain, the daughter of Maelgwn Gwynedd.

great was our happiness to put the Normans to fear and consternation
Llywelyn the terrible with his brave warriors effected it;
the prince of glorious and happy Mon.
He is its ornament and distinguished chief.[*206]

The year 1198 proved decisive in the direction that Llywelyn ab Iorwerth was to take in his relationship with the Crown. Initially he seems to have made common cause with Gwenwynwyn as both would seem from the events of 1196 to have been enemies of Dafydd ab Owain. Probably in the aftermath of his release from the prison of Llywelyn, Dafydd came to London and while delaying there was granted just two marks (£1 6s 8d) towards his ransom by the Crown[*207]. This is to be compared with the 100 marks (£66 13s 4d) that the archbishop of Canterbury was granted to carry out the king's business in Wales and the Marches. Similarly in London, Bishop Reiner of St Asaph and Hamo Lestrange were given a further 100 marks (£66 13s 4d) to deliver to John Lestrange towards the garrisoning and custody of the king's castle of Pole and to drive back the siege of the Welsh from the castle[*208]. The Bruts had previously indicated that Powis castle had fallen back to Gwenwynwyn in 1196, which in this case they probably meant before the old year end on 25 March 1197. In any case there is no other evidence that Powis castle survived in Lestrange hands into 1198, so this entry probably dates to the previous financial year and just had not yet been entered.

In the meantime, with Dafydd ab Owain out of the way, Gwenwynwyn proceeded to counterattack in the Marches after securing his own castle of Pole. The story is best taken up by the Brut, followed by the Chester chronicle, which notes a detail more relevant to Aberconwy and the lands that surrounded it.

> In that year Gwenwynwyn gathered a mighty host to seek to win for the Welsh their original rights and to restore their bounds to their rightful owners, which they had lost through the multitude of their sins, and that about 22 July [feast of Mary Magdalene], with the help and support of all the princes of Wales. And after they had assembled together, they laid siege to Painscastle in Elfael; and for three weeks they were laying siege to it without any recourse to catapults or slings. And when the Saxons learned that, they were amazed; but nevertheless they then set free Gruffydd ap Rhys, the man who was in their prison. And they gathered all the might of England, and they sent to seek to make peace with the Welsh. And the Welsh said that they would burn their cities for the Saxons once they had taken the castle, and that they would carry off their spoils and destroy them too. And the Saxons, being unable to suffer that, as God showed thereafter, fell upon the Welsh and immediately drove them to flight and slew untold numbers of them like sheep. And in that wretched slaughter Anarawd ab Einion and Owain ap Cadwallon and Rhiryd ap Iestyn and Robert ap Hywel were slain; and Maredudd ap Cynan was captured and imprisoned. And so the Saxons returned joyfully to their land, enriched with the spoils of the Welsh.[*209]

> An infinite number of Welshmen, it is said up to four thousand, were slain by the French at Painscastle on 13 August [1198]. Many of the nobles of all of North Wales

---

[*206] Evans, E., *Some Specimens of the Poetry of the Ancient Welsh Bards*, [1764], 20-1.
[*207] *PR 10 Richard I*, 167.
[*208] *PR 10 Richard I*, 172.
[*209] Pen, 79-80.

and especially the men of Llywelyn were slain and dispersed, and the castle of Mold was captured by Llywelyn on 6 January 1199.[*210]

The texts are therefore clear that Gwenwynwyn united to himself not only the forces of those princes remaining in the Middle Marches, but also those of the new princes of Gwynedd. Hence the appearance of both Maredudd ab Cynan and the troops of Llywelyn ab Iorwerth at the battle. Further, the statement in the Chester chronicle that many of the nobles of Gwynedd were slain there suggests strongly that Gruffydd ap Cynan also supported the enterprise. It is not clear from the Chester text whether Llywelyn accompanied his men of Gwynedd to the battle or not. Whatever the case, after the slaughter and dispersal of his forces he was still strong enough to take Mold castle six months later. What is also clear is that the alliance between the two sons of Cynan and Llywelyn survived the overthrow of Dafydd ab Owain and continued apace until death ended it.

What has previously been missed about this reasonably well known event is that on 7 January 1199, the day after Mold castle fell, Llywelyn was supposed to be at Aberconwy making his great charters to the abbey 'in the tenth year of my principality' (Appendix 2). Obviously the dating clause of this charter is false. A close examination of the text also shows that the rest of the charter is also a forgery, riddled as it is with contradictions[*211]. Consequently, not only Llywelyn's known actions, but also the contents of the charter show it to be spurious. One of the most remarkable features of this forgery is that the monks, who undoubtedly fabricated this charter, probably early in the reign of Edward III (1327-77), did not know that Llywelyn in his true charters never made his grants for the health of his successors' souls. Possibly this was due to Llywelyn's own matrimonial problems and the disputes he later had with his sons. Then, there is the problem of the lands themselves. Even if it is accepted that Llywelyn somehow got himself to Aberconwy in one day after the fall of Mold and made a grant virtually refounding the abbey with Prince Gruffydd ap Cynan's lands without even asking his permission, it is impossible to believe that he also granted Ffriwlwyd in Eifionydd, which until 1201 was undoubtedly in the hands of Llywelyn's rival, Maredudd ap Cynan. At this time Maredudd was held in an English prison and Llywelyn could have had no rights to his Eifionydd lands, which must have fallen briefly into the hands of his elder brother, Gruffydd ap Cynan. Further, although it is possible that Llywelyn was holding Creddyn at this time, it being east of the Conwy, it is again impossible that he was holding the lands of Gruffydd ap Cynan, viz. Aberconwy itself, Cwm, Rhedynog Felen, Nant Call, Gelliniog (which in any case has an extant charter of Gruffydd granting it to the monks), Bodgedwydd, Llanfaes, Nanhwynain, Arddau and Darlas. That said, Llywelyn was probably holding the Perfeddwlad which would have given him control of Pentrefoelas, Ceirniog, Llanfair Rhyd Gastell, Llyn Cymer and Llechwedd Cryn Llwyn. Despite this, the statement that in the tenth year of Llywelyn's rule he granted the monks free passage over the Dovey and Abermaw is simply ludicrous. Llywelyn in 1199 had no rights over these rivers whatsoever, both lands being under the jurisdiction of Gruffydd ap Cynan. There is no way that Llywelyn had any form of principality in 1189 as has been seen, and indeed he could have had no rights over these two rivers until 1202 at the very earliest. In short, there is nothing in the charter which argues for a twelfth century date, neither in its style nor in its content and the argument that it must contain some core of originality bears no merit. Consequently, the

---

[*210] *Annales Cestrienses, a chronicle of the abbey of St. Werburgh, Chester*, ed. and trans. Christie, R.C., Record Society for Lancashire and Cheshire XIV [1887], 44.
[*211] See pages 67, 74, 183-4, 193-5.

information contained in the forged charters of Llywelyn must be discounted from any discussion of the history of the abbey before 1315 at the very earliest. This of course bears much on the story of Aberconwy abbey.

Some months after Llywelyn's non-foundation charter was alleged to have been drawn up, on 6 April 1199, King Richard died and was succeeded by this only surviving brother, Count John of Mortain, who became King John (1199-1216). Notwithstanding that Wales was still in a state of turmoil and civil war, Llywelyn ab Iorwerth, the new prince of the Perfeddwlad, was the first of the Welsh princes to break ranks and come to terms with the new government of King John.

> King John to all his men etc... Let it be known we have accepted into our hands the custody and protection of our beloved and faithful Llywelyn ab Iorwerth, with his lands, men and all his properties; and you are ordered to accept this and strengthen, maintain and defend this in all things, nor inflict or allow to be inflicted injuries or molestation. We concede and confirm to the same all his rights and all his lands which he holds by his right. Witnessed Bishop R of St Andrews, Earl William Longspey of Salisbury, Earl William of Arundel. Dated at Le Mans, 28 September 1199.[*212]

This is very interesting as Llywelyn was the first major Welsh prince to make his peace with King John after the chaos of Richard's reign. Llywelyn's actions may well have made the other princes of Wales think of their positions and they rapidly set out to also obtain the new king's goodwill. Otherwise it is possible that Llywelyn ran quickly to John as he faced considerable opposition in his own lands. Certainly the agreement with Llywelyn shows that John did not regard him favourably, for although he was pardoned his previous sins against the Crown, the king only confirmed him in the lands which he held 'by right' and obviously this left a lot of room for lands to be removed from him if it could be shown that he had seized them by force majeure.

It was not until the beginning of December 1199 that John made peace with the other princes of Wales under the title 'The Charter of a Welshman' (*carta Wallensium*). In total there are four instruments, of which the probably most important is printed first, but is dated as the last on 4 December 1199. The other three following documents are dated 3 December. It is therefore possible that the first document was misdated, or considered the most important and placed first in this copy on the roll. The first charter was to Gwenwynwyn and, as it is dated the next day, will be considered last. Therefore the first charter chronologically was that to Gruffydd ap Cynan which was titled, *carta eo'd'* which should be expanded to *carta eosdem* or 'The Charter of the Same'. Obviously Gruffydd ap Cynan was not the same Welshman as Gwenwynwyn and so this should be taken as meaning the charter of another Welshman. This charter is quite different from the one given earlier to Llywelyn.

> Know that we concede and by this present charter confirm to our beloved and faithful Gruffydd ap Cynan, for his faithful homage and service, all his lands and castles and tenements in North Wales, so that his acquired rights, and any others that might be acquired from our enemies, wholly and fully, may be held from us and our heirs by you and your heirs, so that the same Gruffydd may serve us faithfully and be faithful

---

[*212] *Rotuli Chartarum in Turri Londonensi asservati [1204-22]*, ed. T.D. Hardy [1837], 23.

to us against all men. Witnessed Earl William Marshall of Pembroke, Count Ralph of Eu, Ralph then constable of Chester. Dated by the hand of Archdeacon S of Wells and John Gray at Poitou, 3 December first year of our reign.[213]

This charter clearly shows that John thought Gruffydd the most powerful magnate in North Wales and that the sons of Dafydd, Rhodri and Cadwaladr were not even considered as powerful enough to warrant an agreement. Llywelyn ab Iorwerth himself had of course already made his peace with the Crown and was presumably still holding to this, unless it is assumed that the clause mentioning the rights that might be taken from royal enemies, issued to all three of these princes, was aimed at Prince Llywelyn. From this it appears that John thought that Gruffydd was the major or possibly even the sole power in North Wales to be dealt with. The phrase 'all his lands and castles' should be taken into consideration when that glib platitude that all the native Welsh castles of North Wales owe their genius to Llywelyn ab Iorwerth is regularly put forward as it is these days[214].

The next two similar charters concerned Maelgwn ap Rhys (bef.1169-1230) and the burgesses of Cardigan whom Maelgwn handed over to the king. No charter was made with Maelgwn's brother, Gruffydd ap Rhys (bef.1165-1201), as he was already within the king's peace. The final charter, dated 4 December 1199, but placed first amongst the charters recorded, was that to Gwenwynwyn of Cyfeiliog. This was in the same form as those charters issued to Gruffydd and Maelgwn, but included the statement that Gwenwynwyn's lands were 'as much in North Wales as in South Wales and Powys'. This clearly indicates that John thought Gwenwynwyn the greatest of the four princes he had dealt with and that his power stretched throughout Wales. Despite this, it is noticeable that only Maelgwn and Gwenwynwyn sent hostages to John for their good behaviour[215]. There is no record of Gruffydd ever doing likewise.

It is interesting that one prince that King John did not give a charter to was Maredudd ap Cynan. He had languished in a London jail since the battle of Painscastle, but this year was transferred from London to Bridgnorth and probably freedom[216]. Perhaps this was a consequence of Gruffydd's agreement with John, or was a goodwill gesture from the king to the man he hoped would become the king's new prince of North Wales. Whatever John's intentions for Gruffydd, he did not bask in the king's goodwill for long as his life was nearing its end.

During this year Prince Llywelyn had also been having problems. In January 1199 he had taken Mold, possibly after fighting the battle recorded there by his poets. He had then either been politically attacked for his uncanonical marriage or had thought it worthwhile to ask the pope for a confirmation of his marital actions, as he now had at least one son and maybe even two, who could potentially succeed him - Gruffydd ap Llywelyn was born before 1200 and there is a slim possibility that another son, Tegwared, was born before 1204[217]. As a consequence, Llywelyn wrote to the pope outlining his version of events leading to his espousal of his aunt by marriage. Unfortunately this letter has not apparently survived, but the pope's reply of 24 November has. In this he states that he is satisfied that Llywelyn's

---

[213] *Rotuli Chartarum in Turri Londonensi asservati [1204-22]*, ed. T.D. Hardy [1837], 63.
[214] See Remfry, PM., *Harlech Castle and its True Origins* [Ceidio, 2013], 22-3, for the demolition of the idea that Llywelyn ab Iorwerth was a great castle builder.
[215] *PR 2 John*, 1199-Mich 1200, 119.
[216] *PR 1 John*, 1198-Mich 1199, 80, 214.
[217] Tegwared's lack of mention in the treaty of 1211 all but proves his non-existence, below pp. 86, 109-10.

marriage is valid due to Llywelyn's statements, but that he was setting up an ecclesiastical court to confirm this. This would suggest that Llywelyn had written to the pope during the summer and certainly no earlier than mid October 1199. The tone of this reply would strongly suggest that Llywelyn was seeking to legitimise his marriage to the daughter of King Reginald of Man and not to revoke it or see if it would be legal to marry her as has been otherwise suggested. As such it would indicate that political pressure was being brought on him by ecclesiastical sanction, or that he had a bad conscience about his actions some four years earlier. It should also be remembered that in the middle ages it was not uncommon to marry your deceased opponent's wife, cf. Earl Harold and the widow of Gruffydd ap Llywelyn in 1064. However, this marriage would in the end prove the ruin of Gwynedd and all Llywelyn's hopes for a dynasty. This affair will be dealt with in full in a subsequent chapter after examining the politics of the next few years.

Prince Llywelyn ab Iorwerth from 1199 to 1202

It is uncertain when Llywelyn began using the title prince of North Wales, especially if Giraldus' use of this title was forged just like Llywelyn's two spurious charters of 1199. Nevertheless, there are undated charters to Basingwerk abbey which could date from the time of the battles of 1194 onwards, by which time Llywelyn's power could have reached various lands of Basingwerk. These charters were certainly made before October 1202[*218]. One of these charters (No.216) was by *princeps Norwall* and was witnessed by the bishop elect, Roland of Bangor, Abbot Abraham of Aberconwy, Gwyn ab *Ednywain*[*219] and Richard ap Cadwaladr (bef.1172-1230+). As both Aberconwy and Bangor lay in the lands of Gruffydd ap Cynan this would at least suggest that this charter dated to the time after Gruffydd had died in the Spring of 1200. The other charter (No.213) was by *Lewelinus princeps Northwall* and was witnessed by Richard ap Cadwaladr as the first witness and six other men, two of whom, Horin Fitz Ulf and Hitel Fitz Kenred, could possibly have been English. As such it is probably the earlier of the two and marked Llywelyn's earliest days in control of the Perfeddwlad. Quite obviously there is no evidence, other than the suspect writings of Giraldus, that Llywelyn used either title before 1200, although this is not impossible. Certainly the letter from the pope to Llywelyn of 24 November 1199 suggests that he used the title before this time in private correspondence.

Early in 1200 King John visited his English kingdom and on 11 April granted Prince Gwenwynwyn two charters. In the first he gave him the Derbyshire manor of Ashford and in the second the right to hunt in the king's forests with four greyhounds and a bow when he travelled to and from the royal court[*220]. The same day John again confirmed Maelgwn ap Rhys in Ceredigion and then confirmed the lands of the abbey of Strata Marcella (*Stratmarthell*) which had been given by Owain Cyfeiliog and Gwenwynwyn his son. The king also made a confirmation in favour of Strata Florida (*Stratfulr*)[*221]. A further charter on 11 April 1200 confirmed Meurig Powis in Whittington, while the day before the king took the lands of his Aunt Emma Plantagenet, the wife of Dafydd ab Owain, into his own hands for their protection from molestation by anyone, particularly the manors of Ellesmere and

---

[*218] Acts, 344-46, Nos. 213, 216.
[*219] This man is probably synonymous with Owain ab Ednowain, the first known seneschal of Prince Llywelyn.
[*220] *Rotuli Chartarum in Turri Londonensi asservati [1204-22]*, ed. T.D. Hardy [1837], 44.
[*221] *Rotuli Chartarum in Turri Londonensi asservati [1204-22]*, ed. T.D. Hardy [1837], 44b.

Halesowen granted to her by King Henry II[*222]. Such an event strongly implies that Dafydd ab Owain was now thought to be dead, as he was most likely only just over fifty years of age the implication of foul play, as alleged in the Register, remains.

All this was occurring at exactly the time a revolution took place in North Wales. Around the end of March 1200, Gruffydd ap Cynan took himself to Aberconwy abbey, had himself made a monk and died there soon after.

> Gruffydd ap Cynan ab Owain died, making a good end, after assuming the habit of the Order at Aberconwy, the man who was known by all in the island of Britain because of the abundance of his gifts and his gentleness and his goodness. Nor is it strange, for so long as the men that now are shall live, they will remember his fame and his praise and his deeds.[*223]

At this point his principality should have devolved upon his son Hywel ap Gruffydd, or even may have been claimed by his other relatives, Maredudd ap Cynan and Owain ap Dafydd, or even the sons of Rhodri ab Owain - Thomas, Einion and Gruffydd. No claim was apparently put forward and it is quite possible that all these claimants, apart from Maredudd ab Cynan who was at least 35 years old, were at this time too young to claim the principality. It was therefore Llywelyn ab Iorwerth who seized control of North Wales without the sanction of his king or Prince Gwenwynwyn. It is also possible that Gruffydd relinquished his principality to his nephew, but if so the Bruts are surprisingly quiet about this. Unfortunately, the royal records remain silent over North Wales during this period, although on 22 October 1200, King John issued a safe conduct for Gruffydd ap Rhys [Deheubarth] to come to the king for discussions[*224].

To keep this narrative on track it is necessary to diverge here into modern debate to dismiss a faulty reading of the original sources. In recent years a proposition has been advanced that Gruffydd ap Cynan had been defeated in battle in early 1199, forced as a monk into Aberconwy abbey and replaced by Llywelyn ab Iorwerth. To achieve this all the poetry and chronicle evidence listed above has to be dismissed as 'shaky foundations' for Gruffydd's continued rule of Gwynedd until his death in 1200[*225]. The proof of this pudding is stated to be the two 7 January 1199 charters of Llywelyn to Aberconwy. To accept this argument it is first necessary to disregard all the contemporary evidence and then selectively read the poetry. Consequently this theory has been succinctly quashed[*226]. And this is without going into the fact that the two Llywelyn charters are undoubtedly forgeries. Once again, it can be seen how a deliberate fabrication of the past for financial gain in the 1330s has led to the distortion of history and the confounding of historians. That said, it is a happy historian who can say that they have never got it wrong.

In 1201 Prince Llywelyn moved to safeguard his position by turning on the only near relative with sufficient stature to oppose him, his first cousin, Maredudd ap Cynan.

[*222] *Rotuli Chartarum in Turri Londonensi asservati [1204-22]*, ed. T.D. Hardy [1837], 43b, 44.

[*223] Pen, 80. Whoever wrote this epitaph, and it only appears in this version of the Brut, was obviously working with great foresight, for as soon as Gruffydd's contemporaries had died, his name certainly faded from public remembrance. That Gruffydd was dead by mid April is strongly suggested as King John busied himself about the affairs of Wales at this time and no mention is made of Gruffydd. Similarly Llywelyn appears to come to the fore after this time.

[*224] *Rotuli Chartarum in Turri Londonensi asservati [1204-22]*, ed. T.D. Hardy [1837], 98.

[*225] Carr, AD, 'Prydydd y Moch: ymateb hanesydd', *Trans. of the Honourable Society of Cymmrodorion* [1989] 162-3; Stephenson, D., *The Governance of Gwynedd* [Cardiff, 1984], 199-200.

[*226] Insley, C., 'The Wilderness Years of Llywelyn the Great', *Thirteenth Century England IX: Proceedings of the Durham Conference* [2001], 167ff.

Maredudd was also from the elder branch of the descendants of Owain Gwynedd and therefore according to primogeniture - something that had not taken root in Wales yet - could be thought by later opinion to have a greater right to rule in North Wales. Consequently, during the year:

> Llywelyn ab Iorwerth, being a young man graced with generosity and worthiness, gained possession of the cantref of Llyn and Eifionydd, after driving out Maredudd ap Cynan because of his treachery.[*227]

The Deheubarth version of the Annales Cambriae adds little to the Bruts, but does place the action in the first half of the year.

> This year Llywelyn ab Iorwerth, still a juvenile[*228], but well equipped with the gift of probity and largess, manfully won through his merit the cantrefs called Llyn and Eifionydd expelling Maredudd ap Cynan. A little after, around 24 June...[*229]

This bald outline can be somewhat expanded from what survives of the royal correspondence of this year. On 13 January 1201, the king wrote to Gwenwynwyn informing him that he was sending Hugh Bardolf from the household of the archbishop of Canterbury to Powys concerning the truce proposed between the Crown and Llywelyn[*230]. This is fascinating information, because the last thing heard of Llywelyn was his agreement with King John in September 1199. It can therefore be seen that Llywelyn's seizure of Gruffydd's lands had been done against the peace and that not only the king, but also Gwenwynwyn was worried at his actions. Hugh Bardolf was apparently successful in his mission, for on 3 April 1201, the king wrote that he had granted a safe conduct for Llywelyn and his men in coming to see the king at Westminster during a period of some forty days until 7 May 1201[*231]. As John had been in England from October 1200 until about 14 May 1201 it is possible, but unlikely, that this meeting actually took place. Indeed, all the evidence points to John staying on the South Coast during this time and not visiting Westminster. It would therefore seem likely that Llywelyn wrote refusing this safe conduct and that as a consequence, before the time ran out, the king, a little before 2 May, sent his council to Shrewsbury instead. Presumably by this time Maredudd ap Cynan had been forced out of Llyn and Eifionydd, if this had not happened as early as January and resulted in the king's letter to Gwenwynwyn in reply to an apparently lost letter. The upshot was that Archbishop Hubert of Canterbury, Earl Geoffrey Fitz Peter of Essex and other faithful men met at Shrewsbury concerning the business (*negocia*) with Llywelyn ab Iorwerth[*232]. The result was a very interesting peace agreement that is worth quoting in full.

[*227] Pen, 81.

[*228] This statement is apparently a deliberate falsehood, for contemporaries must have known that Llywelyn was married to his Manx wife. Therefore, the comment has likely been added after 1205 when Llywelyn married a second time, his first wife by then being conveniently repudiated. A juvenile was the medieval word for a bachelor and had nothing to do with age. The great Earl William Marshall of Pembroke remained a juvenile until his 42nd year when he married Isabella Clare in 1189. This version of the Annales was put together possibly for use in the Hopton Commission in Deheubarth in the late 1270s.

[*229] *Annales Cambriae. A Translation of Harleian 3859; PRO E.164/1; Cottonian Domitian, A 1; Exeter Cathedral Library MS. 3514 and MS Exchequer DB Neath, PRO E.164/1*, ed. Remfry, P.M., [Malvern, 2007], [D, Deheubarth], 106.

[*230] *Rotuli Chartarum in Turri Londonensi asservati [1204-22]*, ed. T.D. Hardy [1837], 100.

[*231] *Rotuli Chartarum in Turri Londonensi asservati [1204-22]*, ed. T.D. Hardy [1837], 103b-4. Easter was on 25 March 1201, so the Tuesday after the close of Easter was probably the 28th, while the Sunday after Ascension was 7 May 1201.

[*232] *Rotuli Chartarum in Turri Londonensi asservati [1204-22]*, ed. T.D. Hardy [1837], 103b-4.

In the first court of bishops Robert of Bangor, Reiner of St Asaph and Earl Geoffrey Fitz Peter, justiciar, and many barons and others, Llywelyn has sworn, and the great men of his lands after him, to observe fealty to King John forever in respect of his life, members and all his earthly honour. And Llywelyn received from the hands of the lord justiciar seisin of all the tenements which he then possessed, to hold them in peace until the king came to England. And when the king should come to England the same Llywelyn at his mandate will come to him and pay homage to him as his liege lord for the aforesaid tenements. And having given homage in peace he will return to his own land and not be impleaded by anyone until he has received relevant summons and the king will forgive all the former forfeits made before the day of peace, if there were any. If afterwards anyone should move a cause over any of these tenements, he [Llywelyn] will have the choice of it, whether that cause will be dealt with following the law of England or following the law of Wales, and he will not respond to anyone unless concerning the ownership of the land, excluding entirely the question of possession. And if he elects to follow the law of England, the king will convene his court in a suitable place in England and justice shall be judged there following that law. If however he elects Welsh law, he may handle it at any time before the same in the cause, it will first be seen whether Llywelyn himself may have his own court or not; if he is to have it, that cause will be handled in his court. If he is not able to have his court; the king shall send distinguished men to the land of Llywelyn which was in dispute and in whose presence by Welshmen chosen to this and not suspected by the parties, that justice may be done and firmly observed by the parties. The same shall be done for all other pleas brought to the king or his justiciar concerning Llywelyn himself. Further, if the said Llywelyn or his men do injury to the king or his men after the aforesaid peace, the king will receive amends by the faithful counsel of the archbishop of Canterbury and Justiciar Geoffrey Fitz Peter, or one of them if both are not able to be present, and of other faithful men, regardless the aforesaid peace [will be] observed. Furthermore the archbishop, Geoffrey and the bishops, earls and barons concerned with the composing of this peace to the honour of God and the lord king, will cherish the cause of Llywelyn after [that of] justice. In addition, if any who cause damages in the king's land and come into Llywelyn's land and sufferers of the injuries or others with cries and horns up to Llywelyn's land may come after them, the same Llywelyn should make good the damages and do justice to the wrongdoers. If wrongdoers truly from the king's land may pass furtively through Llywelyn's land or hide themselves there, he has promised on his oath that he will use all diligence to this as it requires to be corrected, just as he might if those damages had been done to himself or his land. This peace was made on 11 July 1201 [*iii anno regni Reg Joh'is v idus Julii*]. And to securely complete this thing the lord of Canterbury and Geoffrey Fitz Peter have put their seals to this script and they have stipulated that the king will confirm this peace with his seal.[*233]

This in itself is an interesting treaty and, as it turned out, boded ill for the rest of the thirteenth century in the carrying out of either English or Welsh justice. Eighty years later the inability of king and prince to agree whether English, Welsh or Marcher law was best for Wales led to the war of 1282-3 and the destruction of the principality of Wales. It should also be noted

---

[*233] *Rotuli Litterarum Patentium in Turri Londinensi asservati [1201-16]* ed. T.D. Hardy [1835], 8-9.

that the terms of the agreement suggest that Llywelyn had been illegally acquiring lands and that his gains would stand until the treaty was ratified by the king, after which justice would be done by Welsh or English law if anyone should claim land from Llywelyn. It would be most interesting to know what earlier agreements between Welsh rulers and English kings looked like, but unfortunately, although many existed during the twelfth century, none have survived.

It is instructive to see how hollow the peace seems to have proved. At some time, probably in the Spring of 1202, Llywelyn continued his action against his elder cousin and neighbour.

> Maredudd ap Cynan was expelled from Meirionydd, because of his treachery, by Hywel ap Gruffydd his nephew, his brother's son, and he was despoiled of all his possessions except his horse.... Llywelyn ab Iorwerth moved a mighty host to Powys[234] to subdue Gwenwynwyn and to gain possession of his territory: for though he was a kinsman to him by blood and a near relation, yet he was a man most hostile to him in deeds...[235]

The Deheubarth version of the Annales also appear to have disliked Maredudd, somewhat similarly stating:

> As his just deserts Maredudd ap Cynan was expelled from Meirionydd (*Meironyd*) by his cousin Hywel ap Gruffydd, and, as was seen, he was plundered of all his goods except for his own horse.[236]

It is possible that this war had begun by 16 March 1202, when Geoffrey Fitz Peter at Worcester wrote to Prince Llywelyn of North Wales that he had been granted safe conduct with the bishops of Bangor and St Asaph, William Fitz Alan, John Lestrange, Hugh Pantulf and the sheriff of Salop and Stafford, in coming to and returning from the king before 7 April[237]. During this time King John was highly distracted with Continental problems. April 1202 found him besieging Montfort sur Risle castle in Normandy rather than meeting Welsh princes. Even so, in the Aberconwy Register, he was said to have granted protection to the abbey from his siege camp on 1 April[238]. The deed appears to be genuine, but has not been preserved amongst the royal rolls (see above p.10). This again shows how careful it is necessary to be about the completeness of these documentary lists. Again there is no evidence that Llywelyn or any other Welsh prince made any effort to meet John and instead Llywelyn would appear to have gone to war with Maredudd ap Cynan against his recently made agreement with King John about settling matters via English or Welsh law. This makes it even more peculiar that John seems to have confirmed this treaty only on 1 April 1202, some nine months after it was made, when he made his confirmation to Aberconwy. Presumably he had yet to hear of Llywelyn's treason in attacking Maredudd ap Cynan against the peace he had made in July 1201. Alternatively, Llywelyn may have thought that as John had not

---

[234] About the first feast of Mary in the Autumn, which was 15 August 1202, RBH, 185.
[235] Pen, 81.
[236] *Annales Cambriae. A Translation of Harleian 3859; PRO E.164/1; Cottonian Domitian, A 1; Exeter Cathedral Library MS. 3514 and MS Exchequer DB Neath, PRO E.164/1*, ed. Remfry, P.M., [Malvern, 2007], 106.
[237] *Rotuli Litterarum Patentium in Turri Londinensi asservati [1201-16]* ed. T.D. Hardy [1835] I, 39.
[238] *Register and Chronicle of Aberconway from the Harleian MS. 3725*, ed Ellis, H., *Camden Miscellany* [1847], 10.

confirmed the Shrewsbury treaty then he was free to act as he wished. Llywelyn's embassy had arrived at the justiciar's court on 2 February 1202 and had there informed the justiciar, Geoffrey Fitz Peter, of what Giraldus had been doing in Wales and that it was in no way against the peace and that the archdeacon had not gone to North Wales to persuade Llywelyn to ally with the princes of Powys and South Wales and to raise the whole of Wales against the king in revolt[*239]. Again, as this was only recorded in Giraldus' own work, whether such an event actually happened is open to question. Once more the current lack of evidence makes any certainty in the matter impossible to obtain.

It has always been taken for granted on the word of the Bruts that Maredudd was guilty of treason against Llywelyn, but was he? Was he actually remaining solid in his fidelity to King John and this was seen by the young Llywelyn as provocative? The attack on Meirionydd, followed by an advance through Bala and the taking of its castle on the way to an attack on Gwenwynwyn, looks very much like a well-thought out plan to bring about Llywelyn's dominance in central Wales[*240]. Although it is not stated, it seems likely that the attack on Maredudd was masterminded by Llywelyn as Hywel ap Gruffydd ap Cynan is always seen as under Llywelyn's tutelage and working in tandem with him. It is also noticeable that after Hywel's death in 1216, Meirionydd was treated as Llywelyn's personal domain. Nonetheless, delving into Llywelyn's later career is not the point of this chapter. Instead it has been necessary to examine Llywelyn's early actions so that it can be better judged if he was capable of making the well-known charters to Aberconwy in 1199 in the terms which have been attributed to him and is widely accepted as genuine by modern historians. Quite obviously the answer to this is no. Llywelyn ab Iorwerth could not have made the two charters recorded by Dugdale from the royal confirmations of 1332. Not only is it most unlikely that he was at Aberconwy abbey, rather than waging war on the confines of Chester itself, the terms and extent of the charter are simply not those to be found in twelfth or early thirteenth century charters. As these were the charters presented to chancery in 1332, and not in the 133 years before that date, they quite obviously had been forged during that time. Therefore, the only question remaining to be answered, is when they were forged and why? Both questions can be satisfactorily answered when the chronology of the abbey and its charters are examined.

[*239] Butler, HE. & Williams, CH., *The Autobiography of Giraldus Cambrensis*, [1937], 225, 231.
[*240] Pen, 81; Giraldus Cambrensis, *Opera*, eds. J.S. Brewer, J.F. Dimock and G.F. Warner [8 vols., 1861-91] III, 221-6

Giraldus Cambrensis, *Rotoland* and Llywelyn ab Iorwerth in 1202

As has been noticed, Giraldus was a firm 'historical' friend to Llywelyn ab Iorwerth, to the point where he poured calumnies on the heads of the prince's enemies and ignored Llywelyn's superiors or cast them as enemies of the 1188 Crusading mission around Wales, viz. Dafydd, Rhodri and the brothers Gruffydd and Maredudd ap Cynan. The reason for this would seem to be twofold. Firstly, Llywelyn was not powerful enough to play any part in opposing the Crusade supported by Giraldus in 1188, while the princes of Gwynedd and Powys who were, were not helpful. It is possible that Giraldus met Llywelyn then, when the fledgling prince was sixteen, and the two decided they had something in common. Certainly, it is clear that Llywelyn solidly supported Giraldus' claims to be bishop and hopefully then archbishop of St David's. Giraldus famously stated that Llywelyn claimed that the cleric's fight for an archbishopric of St David's would be remembered 'as long as Wales stands' and Giraldus thought this speech so important he recorded it twice in his works[241]. With Giraldus' distortions of the truth, it is to be wondered if such words were ever uttered[242]. Regardless, this apparent attitude most likely explains Giraldus' exceptionally kindly treatment of Llywelyn and his demonising or ignoring of the other princes of Gwynedd and Powys, though he did castigate his enemy Bishop Cadwgan of Bangor of having achieved election to that office through the influence of Prince Llywelyn in 1215. Indeed, most of the surviving comments on Giraldus' enemies seem favourable, unless recorded by Giraldus[243]. It is therefore worth looking at what actually happened between the prince and the bishop-elect in 1202 and how this involved Aberconwy.

The year 1202 proved crucial for Giraldus in his relationship with Prince Llywelyn. After appearing in Rome during his dispute over his election to St David's, Giraldus returned to Wales and reached his episcopal seat on 20 December 1201[244]. He then immediately set out for Gwynedd, arriving there before Christmas. On route he set about reconciling prince Llywelyn with Subprior Roland of Aberconwy and ensuring that he received back the custody of the see of Bangor of which Llywelyn had stripped from him and returned it to Bishop Robert Shrewsbury. At this point, Bishop Robert was apparently in England in exile from his see. Giraldus then spent Christmas 1201 at Aberconwy abbey where he gave a sermon which he thought was well worth preserving. Unfortunately this sermon and those made at Bangor, Strata Marcella and Valle Crucis on this expedition have since been lost. Consequently, it is unknown what Giraldus preached to the monks and probably Roland and Llywelyn that winter. Neither has the chapter on how Giraldus was treated with honour in Gwynedd survived[245]. Presumably Giraldus did not remain long at Aberconwy, before moving on to the south and east of Wales via the Cistercian abbeys of Strata Marcella and Valle Crucis. By 2 February 1202 he was with the archbishop of Canterbury and the justiciar when an envoy of Prince Llywelyn appeared at court[246].

---

[241] Giraldus Cambrensis, *Opera*, eds. J.S. Brewer, J.F. Dimock and G.F. Warner [8 vols., 1861-91] I, 128; III, 209.

[242] Giraldus in his works repeatedly claims that the outlook of the canons and clerks at St David's was purely Welsh, bar for two Englishmen, yet the tone of the St David's chronicle during this period is solidly English, *Annales Cambriae. A Translation of Harleian 3859; PRO E.164/1; Cottonian Domitian, A 1; Exeter Cathedral Library MS. 3514 and MS Exchequer DB Neath, PRO E.164/1*, ed. Remfry, P.M., [Malvern, 2007]. Also Giraldus accused Abbot Peter of Whitland of betraying him as a former member of his own household, claiming that the members of the chapter of St David's supporting Peter were of his kith and kin, Butler, HE. & Williams, CH., *The Autobiography of Giraldus Cambrensis*, [1937], 197, 223. As such it is surprising that the chapter (according to Giraldus) voted unanimously for Giraldus in 1198.

[243] Viz, Williams, D.H., *The Welsh Cistercians* [Bodmin, 2001], 20.

[244] Giraldus Cambrensis, *Opera*, eds. J.S. Brewer, J.F. Dimock and G.F. Warner [8 vols., 1861-91] III, 193-4.

[245] Giraldus Cambrensis, *Opera*, eds. J.S. Brewer, J.F. Dimock and G.F. Warner [8 vols., 1861-91] I, 10.

[246] Butler, HE. & Williams, CH., *The Autobiography of Giraldus Cambrensis*, [1937], 231.

Sometime between 29 July and late August 1202, the bishop-elect attended meetings at Bedford and then St Albans, before he travelled on to North Wales after holding his own chapter at Brecon[247]. It was probably in late August that Giraldus found himself unable to get the money that had been promised him from North Wales[248] and Powys even though he often sent messengers there. Giraldus concluded that:

> the archbishop infected even those parts and dissuaded them from fulfilling their promises by means of the abbot of Whitland and other corrupt seducers.

Consequently, the bishop-elect decided to travel through Elfael, Maelienydd, Ceri and Cedewain and then on to Gwynedd. Penetrating the thick forests of Powys he found Gwenwynwyn on an expedition against Llywelyn with whom he had previously been dwelling in peace. The prince received Giraldus with honour, but of all the princes of Wales Gwenwynwyn alone refused to give an aid to St David's in his own land. According to Giraldus this was because Llywelyn had been the first to promise aid in Giraldus' quest. Obviously Gwenwynwyn, as a vassal of King John, would not abide this slight to his king's wishes, though of course the bishop elect did not record this. Giraldus also blamed the prince of Powys' actions upon avarice as well as thinking that by doing this Gwenwynwyn would appease the archbishop of Canterbury as well as the English whom the prince had joined against Llywelyn. Quite obviously Giraldus thought that Gwenwynwyn had decided that he was better off opposing Giraldus' claim and having royal backing in his dispute with Llywelyn. Giraldus immediately and joyfully explained to his readers that soon after this meeting Gwenwynwyn was the victim of divine retribution for opposing the instrument of God - Giraldus himself - for the prince's horse subsequently trampled Gwenwynwyn and badly injured his foot. Yet in contradiction of himself Giraldus elsewhere records at this time that Gwenwynwyn was full of praise for the archdeacon's actions in fighting for an archbishopric of Wales[249]. Obviously his contradictory views suggest that Giraldus played fast and loose with recording 'history'.

After the bishop-elect left the prince of Powys he entered Gwynedd on his way to Llywelyn and met with Roland of Bangor, who was again trying to gain that see[250]. The two bishop-elects subsequently encountered the prince and conversed with him at Aberconwy concerning the money which had been collected for Giraldus' cause and deposited with Roland at Aberconwy. Llywelyn is said to have welcomed Giraldus with joy and cheerfulness. Giraldus put this down to Llywelyn being a generous and kindly man. He further suggested that if the prince had contracted any taint from the contagion of his neighbours, as soon as he saw the face of his friend, Giraldus, he cast all traces of enmity aside and ordered the money to be paid him, amounting over and above that which he had from Powys, the sum of £20. With this done Giraldus took his leave of Wales via

---

[247] The bulk of this story is taken from Butler, H.E. & Williams, C.H., *The Autobiography of Giraldus Cambrensis*, [1937], 247-53, and is based upon Giraldus Cambrensis, *Opera*, eds. J.S. Brewer, J.F. Dimock and G.F. Warner [8 vols., 1861-91] III, 221-7.

[248] Giraldus describes Gwynedd as North Wales. No doubt this is because Llywelyn was yet to become all powerful in the district and was still facing opposition from Maredudd ap Cynan in Meirionydd and possibly elsewhere.

[249] Butler, H.E. & Williams, C.H., *The Autobiography of Giraldus Cambrensis*, [1937], 234-5.

[250] Roland had recently been excommunicated by the Cistercians at the bidding of the archbishop of Canterbury, although the sentence may not have been acted upon until the general chapter of the order met that September. Statuta I, 281/34. His full story, as far as it is known, is given in Hays, R.W., 'Rotoland, subprior of Aberconway, and the controversy over the see of Bangor, 1199-1204', *Journal of Hist. Soc. of Church in Wales* XVIII [1963], 9-19.

'Whitchurch', the medieval name for Oswestry and passed via Shrewsbury to Haughmond abbey, which he reached on the fourth day after leaving Llywelyn.

Here there is an obvious problem in his narrative, for Giraldus claimed that he left Powys empty handed in August 1202. Yet, when in December he set off for Rome, he claimed to have had with him letters with seals attached from the princes of Wales, namely Prince Llywelyn ab Iorwerth of North Wales, Gwenwynwyn (d.1216) and Madog (d.1236), princes of Powys, Gruffydd (d.25 July 1201) and Maelgwn ap Rhys (d.1230), as well as Rhys (d.1234) and Maredudd ap Rhys (d.2 July 1201), princes of South Wales[251]. Quite noticeably Maredudd ap Cynan (d.1212) is not included amongst these princes. Was this because Maredudd had been overthrown by Llywelyn that Spring, or because he, together with Gwenwynwyn, had stood on his royal fidelity to King John? In the latter case, it is strange that Gwenwynwyn sent a letter, unless it was written before his meeting recorded above with Giraldus that Autumn. Quite obviously Giraldus' narrative fails here. This problem has been competently examined before, so it is not necessary to go into great detail about it here[252]. What can be said with certainty is that the joint letter as copied by Giraldus was his own composition and whether such an original document or documents, sealed by all the above princes, ever existed is open to grave suspicion. Certainly Maredudd ap Rhys (d.2 July 1201) and Gruffydd ap Rhys (d.25 July 1201) were dead well before Giraldus alleges the letter was written and signed. If the letter was genuine it would have been composed at some point prior to his setting off for Rome in December 1202 - yet he appears to claim he had no such letter in August 1202. Obviously with two of the princes dead they would have had trouble legally sealing such a document between August and December 1202. The letter was alleged by Giraldus to have been presented to the pope on 6 January 1203. It is also notable that by this date all the princes other than possibly Llywelyn were now hostile to him and his cause. Further damning the letter's authenticity is the opening structure, for it puts the princes of Wales in a power order that only Llywelyn himself would have accepted. Gwenwynwyn - as noted in King John's charters to the princes of Wales in 1200, to which Llywelyn was not even a party - would have deemed himself superior to Llywelyn and any such letter would surely have come from him. Further, any other prince at this time would have seen themselves as superior to Llywelyn in lineage, seniority and prestige. Therefore they would not have accepted Llywelyn as their leader at this time.

Previously Giraldus claimed to have presented another letter to the pope from the princes of Wales in early 1200, for he himself recorded the pope's alleged reply of 5 May 1200 to 'our beloved and noble men, Llywelyn and the other princes of Wales'[253]. Once again the same complaint of precedence can be raised against this letter, as why would the other princes of Wales write to the pope under Llywelyn's implied supremacy before the death of Gruffydd ap Cynan in March 1200? It is beyond belief that Llywelyn had the authority at this point to obtain the agreement of his fellow and established rulers in Wales to write to the pope on their behalf. If the 'other princes' were Llywelyn's magnates, then surely they would have been recorded as nobles rather than princes. The similarities between this letter and the Aberconwy forgeries as well as that of Cymer with its *conprincipes* must surely urge towards extreme caution in regarding any such letter as authentic.

---

[251] Giraldus Cambrensis, *Opera*, eds. J.S. Brewer, J.F. Dimock and G.F. Warner [8 vols., 1861-91] III, 244.
[252] Acts, 368-70, No.220.
[253] The pope's alleged reply is printed in Davies, WS., 'The Book of Invectives of Giraldus Cambrensis', *Y Cymmrodorion* XXX [1920], 149 (III.4). It does not appear in the papal registers, but this does not prove that it may not once have existed. Unfortunately this document in reply to the alleged letter of Llywelyn does not appear in Acts of the Princes.

Finally, it must be noted that the pope's reply recorded on 5 May 1200 in *De Invectionibus* is unlikely to be any misplaced reply to the princes' letter Giraldus alleges was delivered on 6 January 1203, as it seems couched in terms not related to any extant letter. It is just possible that Giraldus presented the same letter twice to the pope as it would seem most unlikely that Maredudd and Gruffydd, being dead, and Gwenwynwyn, being hostile, would have sanctioned any such letter in or after 1202, although they could well have done so in 1200. If this were the case then Giraldus altered the pope's reply when he wrote up his notes to make the reply to Llywelyn alone and his princes - an idea impossible in May 1200 but feasible after 1212. It is also apparent that there is no corresponding entry in the pope's register to any letter, which may suggest that the whole affair is the product of Giraldus' febrile imagination. Indeed, if such a letter of the Welsh princes was ever written, it may best be placed with Giraldus' second visit to Rome between 4 March and November 1201. Therefore, if there was an earlier letter (whether simply imagined by Giraldus or not) from Llywelyn and the princes of Wales to which the pope replied on 5 May 1200, there is no trace of it other than in Giraldus' own works. As the evidence stands it suggests that this letter is likely a forgery by Giraldus; otherwise the reader would have to accept that Prince Llywelyn was paramount throughout Wales and recognised by such by all the Welsh princes before April 1200 at the very latest and that the other princes had authorised him to deal with the pope for them. Alternatively, Llywelyn may have just been 'trying it on', in which case Giraldus must have known that the letters he took to Rome were worthless and would crumble at the first light shone upon them by the archbishop of Canterbury's proctors. This can be stated, for if any letter had been sent to the pope by the princes of Wales before April 1200 then it would have been by Gruffydd ap Cynan, Gwenwynwyn or another senior prince of Wales and he would have addressed the letter and not a much less significant prince of the Perfeddwlad. In short, both this letter of 1202 and its alleged predecessor of 1200 would appear to have been forgeries of Giraldus' creation, as too was apparently the pope's reply. This, of course, is exactly what Archbishop Hubert Walter of Canterbury accused Giraldus of doing to bolster his position in his campaign to have himself made archbishop of St David's[254].

> Thus it came about that at that time my name was ever on their lips as that of a traitor, a Welshman, useless and unfaithful to the king and his realm, an expert in forgery, a skilful fabricator of false seals.[255]

It should further be noted that Llywelyn would also at the time of the alleged second letter appear to have been on reasonable terms with King John, for in the pipe roll of Michaelmas 1202 he, as Llywelyn the Welshman, was recording as paying fines for lands he had acquired via escheats under Shropshire. He paid a £2 10s 6d fine for an unnamed escheat as well as £2 10s for six months for the farm of *Lega* (possibly Lea near Ellesmere) and a single shilling for the farm of Kingsland[256]. If the fine of £2 10s 6d was for the lands of Gruffydd ap Cynan in Gwynedd the prince had gained a great victory as well as a bargain. As such it seems unlikely that he and Gwenwynwyn would have risked annoying their king by trying to set up St

[254] Davies, WS., 'The Book of Invectives of Giraldus Cambrensis', *Y Cymmrodorion* XXX [1920], 85-7.
[255] Butler, HE. & Williams, CH., *The Autobiography of Giraldus Cambrensis*, [1937], 144. Giraldus was also a man who thought nothing of breaking the seal and reading a stolen letter, *Idem*, 165.
[256] *PR 4 John*, 1201- Mich 1202, 42.

David's as an archbishopric against the king's specific instructions and when his ministers were persecuting Giraldus.

The only other letter from the princes of Wales that Giraldus is recorded as having around the summer of 1202 is that from the queen of North Wales[257]. At such a time the only person likely to be using such a title was Emma Plantagenet, the wife of the ex king of North Wales, Dafydd ab Owain. Unfortunately the letter itself is in the lost part of Giraldus' *De rebus a se gestis* and only exists as a chapter heading, *Literae reginae Norwalliae Giraldo directae* - The letters the queen of North Wales send to Giraldo[258]. What the last Plantagenet queen of Wales told a man who was intimately bound up with her enemy, Llywelyn ab Iorwerth, can only be guessed at.

Finally, a last point should be raised about Subprior Roland of Aberconwy abbey and that is his name. At some point between 1187 and probably 1226, King Reginald of Man had the story of Charlemagne and Roland translated into Latin. This, some hundred years later, was translated into Welsh. According to copies of what may be the original colophon this original Latin work was simply undertaken by a scholar known to King Reginald.

> Thus far is related the history which King Reinallt of the Isles caused a good master/teacher to translate from the Acts of Charles from Romance into Latin, namely his quarrel with the queen as related above throughout, which Turpin did not bother to relate...[259]

The work is now conveniently known as *Can Rolant* and included a translation of the *Chanson de Roland*. There were also Welsh versions of the *Historia Karoli Magni et Rotholandi*[260]. From this it becomes obvious that our Subprior *Rotoland* was actually called Roland. Roland may have been an unusual name in 1190s Wales, but obviously it was well-known at this time. The prince of Galloway, the son of Uchtred Galloway (d.1174), was called or took the name Roland. He died on 19 December 1200 and was buried at St Andrew's priory, Northampton, while on a visit to pay homage to King John[261]. This Roland was first cousin once removed to King Reginald of Man. Whether Subprior Roland had anything to do with the Can Rolant is open to speculation, yet the work being done for King Reginald does impact on the story of Aberconwy abbey.

A later colophon than King Reginald's survives in the Peniarth 5 and Peniarth 9 manuscripts. These state:

> And Madog ap Selyf translated this book from Latin into Welsh at the wish and desire of Gruffydd ap Maredudd ab Owain ap Gruffydd ap Rhys.[262]

---

[257] The letter, what little is known of it, is examined in Acts, 444-5. The reasons why it is not 'Tangwystl' or any other of Llywelyn's alleged brides are discussed, but the possibility - or rather likelihood of this being Emma - is not.

[258] Giraldus Cambrensis, *Opera*, eds. J.S. Brewer, J.F. Dimock and G.F. Warner [8 vols., 1861-91] I, 13.

[259] 'Ystoria Charles, from the Red Book, Jesus College, Oxford', trans. Rhys, J., *Sechs Bearbeitungen...*, Koschwitz, E. [Heilbronn, 1879], 18, 38.

[260] Rejhon, AC., *Can Rolant: The Medieval Welsh Version of the Song of Roland* [University of California Publications, 1984]. The original Old French version would seem to date from the 1170s, *Idem*, 66-7.

[261] *Chronicon Anglicanum* of Ralph Coggeshall, ed. Stevenson, J [London, 1875], 107; *Chronica Magistri Rogeri de Hovedene*, ed. W. Stubbs [4 vols., 1868-71] IV, 142, 145.

[262] Rejhon, AC., *Can Rolant: The Medieval Welsh Version of the Song of Roland* [University of California Publications, 1984], 3.

This copy was later copied again by Ieuan the scholar in 1336[*263]. Quite obviously the copy of the work that was said to be done for Reginald is at best a third hand copy. That said, no evidence other than some rather wild and unsustainable speculation ties the first purported work of Reginald to Llanbadarn Fawr and nothing says that it was done in Welsh. It is certainly possible that the 1336 transcription was carried out at Llanbadarn Fawr, or Strata Florida, or indeed elsewhere. There is simply no evidence to suggest the place of its origin other than where men who called themselves teachers or scholars may have lived - whether that was in a household or a religious establishment or even elsewhere. Similarly, the idea that Gruffydd ap Maredudd must have ordered the book translated from Latin into Welsh before 1282, because he had been militarily defeated in 1283, cannot be taken seriously. Gruffydd was known to be fighting for Edward I in 1297 and was living until shortly before 24 March 1319[*264]. By this time he would have been at least 59 years old and had apparently spent the last 25 years of his life in freedom. It is by no means impossible that in his later years he desired to have the Latin book undertaken by King Reginald translated into Welsh.

As has been noted, some of the manuscripts containing the Can Rolant have a colophon stating that Reginald was responsible for the initial translation of the work from Romance - ie French - into Latin. Although it has been argued that the translation was done at Llanbadarn Fawr, as this was a major centre of learning in *pura Wallia*, not a single jot of evidence has been brought forward to substantiate such a claim. Indeed, it has been noted that Reginald had no known links with this establishment[*265]. The argument is simply that as Maredudd ab Owain (d.1265) was confirmed in holding the lands around Llanbadarn Fawr by Llywelyn ap Gruffydd (d.1282), who was grandnephew of Rhodri ab Owain (d.1194), it is likely there was a link between Reginald (d.1229) and Llanbadarn Fawr. These tenuous speculations have been taken further in more modern accounts where the translation is seen to be a method of King Reginald currying favour at Rome[*266]. The dating speculations that the history was translated after a visit by Reginald to London in 1219 seem unimpressive and ignore Reginald's previous trips to visit King John in 1206 and apparently also in 1212.

In summary, there can be little doubt that Can Rolant was in 1336 thought to have been translated into Latin from Old French (Romance) for King Reginald. Logically this must have happened before Reginald's death in 1229 and most likely after 1187 when he became king. Then, possibly as late as the death of Prince Gruffydd after 1319, but no earlier than 1265, Madog ap Selyf translated the Latin Pseudo-Turpin into Welsh and apparently amalgamated it with the earlier work said to have been commissioned by King Reginald. Finally, in 1336, the scholar Ieuan made a copy which survives as Peniarth 9.

Considering this, it seems most unlikely that King Reginald would have had Can Rolant translated into Latin before 1187, when he succeeded his father. That the work may date to soon after this early period is possible if it was Rhodri ab Owain (d.1194) who appeared as my brother Rhodri in the king's entourage as early as 1188. Subsequently, with his daughter married to Rhodri in 1192 and then Llywelyn ab Iorwerth around 1195, Reginald would have had a strong connection with North Wales[*267]. This would have continued beyond the divorce of his daughter from Llywelyn in 1203, due to the survival of a son, Gruffydd ap Llywelyn (d.1244), who would have been Reginald's grandson. It is therefore possible that

[*263] *Selections from the Hengwrt Mss Preserved in the Peniarth Library*, Williams, R., [2 vols, 1876-92] II, 118.
[*264] *CPR 1317-21*, 323.
[*265] Rejhon, AC., *Can Rolant: The Medieval Welsh Version of the Song of Roland* [University of California Publications, 1984], 73-4.
[*266] Hurlock, K., *Wales and the Crusades, 1095-1291* [UWP, 2011], 50-1.
[*267] Llywelyn's marriage to Reginald's daughter is examined in the next chapter.

the Can Rolant was translated into Latin at Reginald's behest with the education of his grandson in mind - certainly the poet Einion Wan noted that Gruffydd had the qualities of Charlemagne - was this alluding to the history translated by King Reginald, Gruffydd's grandfather? As Gruffydd would seem to have been born before 1200 it is possible that the translation occurred at some point from then until 1229, with the likelihood of it taking place more in the thirteenth century than the twelfth. This dating corresponds with the date arrived at via study of the linguistics[*268].

Judging from this, there is no evidence at all to place the Latin translation as being done at Llanbadarn Fawr. Further, there is no evidence that this work was undertaken by a clerical rather than a lay scribe as the term scholar (*athro*) might suggest. If the work dates to the early thirteenth century it therefore seems much more likely that it was undertaken in the Isles or North Wales, rather than Ceredigion. If the work is earlier it is possible that there may have been a connection to Ceredigion with Rhodri's first father-in-law, the Lord Rhys ap Gruffydd (d.1197), being prince of the district. Rhys was also second great grandfather to the Gruffydd ap Maredudd who later desired the work translated into Welsh.

From all of this, all that can really be said is that an unnamed scholar who could have come from anywhere in Europe, translated the work for King Reginald. It is possible that this was done after 1187 and that such a scholar could have been at Aberconwy abbey. It is also just as likely that the scholar did not come from there, but it is even more unlikely that he came from Llanbadarn Fawr. As has been noted, the subprior of Aberconwy bore the name of Roland. This is a most unusual name and it is possible that he was called this in the same way that Geoffrey Monmouth was known as Geoffrey Arthur - due to his interest in works about that king. It should also be noted that the abbey was under the control of the husbands of Princess Rhunallt ferch Reginald (1192-1203+), princes Rhodri (d.1194) and Llywelyn (d.1240), at the turn of the thirteenth century, as well as being closely associated with the princes of Gwynedd. Further, from the time of his birth about 1200, until the time of his brother Dafydd's birth about Easter 1212, Gruffydd ap Llywelyn (d.1244), King Reginald's grandson, was theoretical heir to the principality of Gwynedd and it may have been hoped by his family that he would become another Charlemagne. Finally, by the time of his death in 1244, Gruffydd was compared to Charlemagne, the subject of the book commissioned by King Reginald. This surely points more to a North Welsh and therefore possibly an Aberconwy origin for the Can Rolant rather than to a Ceredigion one.

This leads on to another work that has no known home. It has been argued that the original *Vera Historia de Morte Arthuri* was composed during the time when Giraldus was seeking the bishopric of St David's, 1199-1203, and in North Wales[*269]. It is argued that because of the fifteenth century link with Hailes abbey, the *Vera* could have been originally written at Aberconwy. This is also a possibility, but the evidence is nowhere near as strong as that offered for the origin of King Reginald's Can Rolant. Even so, together this evidence suggests that there was a strong literary tradition forming at Aberconwy and it should come as no surprise that there was once an Aberconwy version of the Brut.

Of Roland of Aberconwy there is little left to be said. According to Giraldus, after Easter (6 April) 1203, he left Giraldus at Rome and returned to England armed with a papal

---

[*268] Rejhon, AC., *Can Rolant: The Medieval Welsh Version of the Song of Roland* [University of California Publications, 1984], 75ff.
[*269] *Glastonbury abbey and the Arthurian Tradition*, ed. Carley JP, [Cambridge, 2001], *Vera Historia de Morte Arthuri*: A New Edition by Lapidge, M, 127-9, argues the case. The link between the abbey and Llywelyn ab Iorwerth would be better amended with what is shown here of that relationship and Llywelyn's lack of power in the district before March 1200.

commission[*270]. This was actually dated at the same time as Giraldus' election was quashed, 26 May 1203 (the seventh calends of June) at Faenza (*Ferentino*). In Roland's case the pope ordered the priors of Wenlock and Enlli to examine the case between the bishop of Bangor and R. sometime subprior of *Aberconwe* and send written depositions back to the pope with the two parties for judgement, but if either would not do so then to settle the case according to the papal mandate[*271]. It would appear that the case was settled by papal mandate, for Robert remained bishop of Bangor until his death in 1212[*272] and Roland is apparently not mentioned in history again.

Llywelyn's First Marriage and Aberconwy, 1192 to 1205

The status of Llywelyn ab Iorwerth's marriages played a great and devastating part in the thirteenth century history of Wales. It certainly led to much warfare, destruction and killing and much fighting on the granges of Aberconwy abbey. To consider how this came about it is necessary to look at what marriage actually meant at the time[*273]. Today marriage is thought of as a pairing of adults. In the twelfth century marriage could and did take place between young children. Pope Alexander III (1159-1181), in a letter to the archbishop of York, ordered that there should be no espousal or marriage before the age of seven. In a later ruling, he changed this age to twelve. Even so, younger marriages still took place with papal dispensations and in both the cases of Rhodri and Llywelyn without, although Llywelyn tried to rectify his irregular union after the event and Rhodri spent a year engaged and apparently even had banns read. Earlier King Henry II had obtained papal approval for the marriage of his son Henry to Princess Margaret of France. They married on 2 November 1160, the young Henry having been born on 28 February 1155 and Margaret about 1 January 1158. Therefore he was five and she not yet three.

Similarly as the age of marriage was being raised, the way marriage was performed was also being altered. At the Council of Westminster in 1076 it was ruled that:

> No one should give his daughter or other relative to anyone without priestly blessing, otherwise it will be judged not a legitimate marriage but a fornicator's marriage.

This was reiterated at the Council of Westminster in 1200 when it was stated that marriage should only take place:

> publicly in front of the church and in the presence of a priest. No marriage should be contracted without a public announcement in church on three occasions.

This was the first direction for banns to be read in England. Giraldus was well aware of this and stated that the readings of the banns should occur on the three Sundays preceding the wedding. As will be seen, Rhodri ab Owain had his banns read three times as early as the Spring of 1192.

[*270] Giraldus Cambrensis, *Opera*, eds. J.S. Brewer, J.F. Dimock and G.F. Warner [8 vols., 1861-91] III, 287-8.
[*271] *Calendar of Entries in the Papal Registers relating to GB and Ireland - Papal Letters, 1198-1304*, ed. W. H. Bliss [1893], 14 precising *Patrologiae cursus completus,... Latine*, Migne, JP., [1844-1864] CCXV, 81-2, LXXIX.
[*272] Pen, 86.
[*273] The following observations are taken from the chapter, 'Rituals of Betrothal and Marriage in the 12th and early 13th Centuries', Bartlett, R, *England Under the Norman and Angevin Kings: 1075-1225 [Oxford, 2000]*.

The wedding service subsequently carried out was somewhat similar to that still performed today. The marriage should have begun at the church door with the priest asking if there was any reason why the couple could not be legitimately married. The heart of the ceremony was still the priest's following questions to the bride and groom.

Do you take this woman...to keep in sickness and in health?

If both members of the couple replied *Volo* (I do) then the priest and the man giving the woman away would hand her to the groom. The latter would put a ring on her hand saying:

With this ring I honour you...with my body I wed you.

All this took place outside the church, before the main door. During this ceremony the husband was expected to give his wife her dower 'at the church door'. The bride's father or guardian would then present to the groom a marriage portion - property or cash to increase the size of the husband's estate. This might be done by handing over a symbolic object such as a knife or a sod of turf. It was only now, after the actual wedding had taken place, that everyone entered the church to hear mass. During the mass, the couple would lie prostrate before the altar and the altar cloth would be held over them. The husband would then kiss the bride, but first he had to give the priest the kiss of peace during the communion.

Unfortunately, there were occasional problems with marriage when things went wrong. The Church stated that for a marriage to be legal both parties had to consent, 'Marriage is contracted by consent alone.' However, this led to the well founded worry that marriages could be conducted in secret and the truth of the matter would therefore be difficult to know. Consequently, it was increasingly held that the marriage ceremony needed to be witnessed, so it became common practice for all marriages to be made in front of the church in a public ceremony before witnesses and with the blessing of a priest. Despite this, lawsuits and appeals to the clergy and even the pope show that the fact of marriage could and often was successfully appealed. Sometimes the marriage partners were willing in the absolution of their marriage, sometimes not. Indeed, whether a marriage was legal or had even occurred was also argued out in clerical courts. This bears great relevance to what happened in Wales during the first half of the thirteenth century.

Much confusion exists about Llywelyn ab Iorwerth's first marriage, with most historians having denied that any such match ever took place. It will be shown here that this view totally ignores the original evidence as accepted by Prince Llywelyn, King John and Pope Innocent III, to name but the most important. That said, the evidence is really quite straight forward.

It was during the last months of Gruffydd ap Cynan's principality of North Wales that the young Llywelyn ab Iorwerth appears to have begun to think of regularising his own marriage status. Quite obviously he was worried that he had been illegally married. This can be deduced from three surviving pieces of papal correspondence. Considering what Llywelyn called himself in the first of these, it is possible that there was either an agreement that he would succeed Gruffydd to paramountcy in North Wales or the more likely scenario, that he had forced Dafydd ab Owain to recognise him as his heir to the title of king/prince of North Wales in 1198. In favour of the former there seems to have been an easy transfer of lands from Gruffydd to Llywelyn on the former's death and there seems to have been no attempt by any other prince, even Gruffydd's brother, Maredudd, to dispute this process for at least twelve months.

It is unfortunate that the original evidence in these three papal letters has been poorly studied and consequently misconstrued by earlier historians. This has disguised both their importance and their meaning. To put this right it is best to first print the offending 'translations' and then the full letters in their precised form and finally the full text in an English translation, with the original Latin appearing in Appendix 9, p.342.

> 7 Kal Dec 1199, Lateran. Mandate to the bishop of Man, the archdeacon of Bangor and the prior of the isle of *Glannan*, to take cognisance of and decide the case of R prince of North Wales, who wishes to marry a daughter of the prince of the Isles previously betrothed to his uncle.[*274]

From this precis it has generally been assumed that Prince R must have been Llywelyn, possibly on the widely held, but erroneous belief, that he had been prince of North Wales since 1194. As noted above, this does not conform with the original evidence and if any prince was lord of North Wales in 1199 it was Gruffydd ap Cynan or even Dafydd ab Owain and not their nephew Llywelyn. Yet, before looking at the document this precis came from, it is worth commenting on the lords of North Wales to elucidate which prince appears to be being discussed in papal circles.

Although it is rarely stated, Rhodri is the only known prince of North Wales who is historically recognised to have had a Manx royal bride in the late twelfth century. In November 1199 his near relatives included Gruffydd ap Hywel[*275] the son of Hywel ab Owain (d.1170), Gruffydd ap Cynan (d.1200), Maredudd ap Cynan (d.1212), Llywelyn ab Iorwerth (d.1240), Madog ap Gruffydd (d.1236), Gwenwynwyn (d.1216), Goronwy ab Einion (d.1206+), Cadwallon ab Owain (d.bef.1231), Maredudd ab Owain (d.bef.1231), Meurig Powys (d.1200), Owain ap Dafydd (d.1212), Thomas ap Rhodri (d.bef.1243), Einion ap Rhodri (d.1209+) and Gruffydd ap Rhodri (d.1240+). Obviously there is no Prince R. amongst these and possibly the R. has been written in mistake for the initial letter of Rhodri ab Owain, the prince who had previously been married to the lady in question. Alternatively, the capital letter could have been miswritten or entered wrongly. What can be said is that the only men liable to call themselves princes of North Wales at the time were Gruffydd ap Cynan and his brother Maredudd, Madog ap Gruffydd, Gwenwynwyn and, of course, since the discomfiture of Dafydd ab Owain in 1197, Llywelyn ab Iorwerth. Of these there is evidence that Gruffydd ap Cynan did describe himself as prince of North Wales before 1199. The possibility that Llywelyn ab Iorwerth did likewise has not to my knowledge been previously demonstrated, although it has been asserted without the foundation of quoting any original documents that prove such a case. The possibility of Llywelyn using this title is not proved in the twelfth century as is shown in the above chapter, Prince Llywelyn ab Iorwerth from 1199 to 1202.

The marital status of the sons of Cynan at this time is uncertain, but Gruffydd's known children were born before 1175, so it is possible that he was seeking a new wife in 1199. Of Maredudd ap Cynan's children, Llywelyn Fawr (the real one, not Llywelyn ab Iorwerth, see Appendix 11, p.348) was born before 1200 and his brother Llywelyn Fychan before 1212 -

---

[*274] The brief precis in *Calendar of Entries in the Papal Registers relating to GB and Ireland - Papal Letters, 1198-1304*, ed. W. H. Bliss [1893], 8. The precis in *Calendar of Letters of Pope Innocent III*, 29, No.168, is equally vague.
[*275] Nothing further is recorded of him after his father's death in 1170 so he could well have been dead by now.

which would at first sight suggest that it is possible that Rhodri's widow might have been their mother[276]. Madog ap Gruffydd was married to Ysota Lacy before 1199 and she outlived him. Gwenwynwyn married Margaret Corbet around 1204. She is thought to have been his first wife. Finally, Llywelyn ab Iorwerth was having children via his 'wife' from apparently 1197 until after 1200. This does not mean that Llywelyn did not enquire about taking a Manx wife in 1199, but surely the evidence as stated above would more likely mean that one of the sons of Cynan was the prince of North Wales referred to. This is especially true when considering the title and the marital statuses of the nephews of Rhodri. It would have been beneficial for them to consider taking a bride to strengthen their political position in North Wales. Of course, none of this is provable, but it does beg the question as to why this Prince R was taken to be Llywelyn ab Iorwerth by later historians if they had not seen the original document this precis was taken from.

Concerning this 'the bards' of the sixteenth century and their later copyists state that Llywelyn ab Iorwerth was 'married' to Tangwystl ferch Llywarch Goch of Rhos[277]. As such it would initially seem possible that Gruffydd ap Cynan was the prince seeking the hand of his aunt by marriage and that no more was heard of the affair due to his death within three months of the pope asking for an inquiry to be made. It should further be remembered that a letter took about a month to go from Rome to North Wales if the weather and all else were favourable. Therefore, on this basis, it is a surprise that most historians have definitively asserted that Llywelyn was the Prince R referred to in the papal document precis.

After this discussion of the logic of the readings of the document it is necessary to print a translation of the entire original document, as copied into a contemporary papal register, as this has not previously been widely disseminated[278]. It also shows yet again how important it is to go back to the original authority and not take the judgements of previous historians as sound, especially when the logic behind these assumptions can be seen to have been suspect [279].

> To the bishop of Man[280], the archdeacon of Bangor[281] and the prior of Ynys Llannog [Ynys Seiriol or Priestholm].
> Betrothals may not be entered into before seven [years].
> At the Lateran, 24 November 1199.
> Our beloved noble man, Prince R. of North Wales, has asked our permission that it is lawful for him to take to himself for a wife the daughter of our beloved son, the prince of the Isles, notwithstanding that it has come to light that his paternal uncle was betrothed to her, when she was below marriageable years, nevertheless at the time neither side were brought together [for consummation of the marriage]. Since the

---

[276] This appears impossible as Llywelyn ab Iorwerth had 'married' the lady in or soon after 1195 as will be shown below.

[277] There is no early reference concerning this relationship. Lloyd, J.E., *History of Wales* [2 vols., 1911] II, 686, thought Tangwystl's heritage was found in Dwnn, Lewys, *Heraldic Visitations of Wales and part of the Marches between 1586 and 1613*, ed. S.R. Meyrick [2 vols., Llandovery, 1846] II, 107, yet there is no such statement about her, merely a reference to the judgment of David Powell (d.1598) on the matter of Llywelyn's children. Nor does the name Tangwystl appear in Powell when he mentions Llywelyn's marital affairs, *The History of Cambria now called Wales... by David Powel*, trans. Lhoyd, H [1811], 187, 213. In short Tangwystl ferch Llywarch Goch of Rhos seems only to have been created in the seventeenth century. A supposedly 14th century grave slab to Tangwystl ferch Ieuaf ap Maredudd is to be found at Bryneglwys church in Powys.

[278] Appendix 9. Doc 1.

[279] My thanks to Rich Price for his comments on the Latin of these three difficult papal letters.

[280] Michael was the bishop of Man from the early 1190s until his death in 1203, *Cronica Regum Mannie & Insularum*, trans Broderick, G [Manx National Heritage, 2004], fo.41r.

[281] One Gervase was archdeacon of Bangor at some point between April 1195 and December 1196, *Cartulary of Haughmond Abbey*, ed. Una Rees [Aberystwyth, 1983], No.794. It is possible that he remained in office until after February 1205.

truth to us is not apparent at what age the girl was pledged or betrothed has come to light and to who she may have been [pledged] before, [whether] pure [when] betrothed to the nephew or the paternal uncle, with the following diversities of the facts and also the diversities of the laws in this matter we have not been able to give an answer, because under canonical laws in doubtful causes it is not possible to advance an unconditional judgment. However, wishing, as much as we are able with God, that the just petitions of the before mentioned prince may be clearly heard without hindrance where you please, we direct that you come together in an inquiry of them which we have before set out in a sure fashion for your examination, that justice may be done on every point. Wherefore, through your understanding of the apostolic scriptures we entrust, to what extent you will call to your presence those summoned to be seen, with anxious care you will examine whether the girl might not have reached her seventh [year] when it appears she was espoused to the nephew, or betrothed to the paternal uncle. For in either of these before mentioned cases, because just as espoused as betrothed may not be held with justice, if they have not reached their seventh [year], notwithstanding whether that was made with the paternal uncle first or afterwards, unless there is something else which may impede [it], the same girl may lawfully be able to enter into marriage with the nephew. Nevertheless, if truly espoused or betrothed at the time she appears to have been seven years of age or older, when from which time betrothals begin to be acceptable, if the betrothal of the paternal uncle had taken place before, it is not possible for her to enter into marriage with the nephew; because, following traditions and canonical observations, no one is able to contract in marriage a blood relative or to take her as wife, and these two cases are not to be judged unequal. If however, the espousal with the nephew preceded [that with the uncle], what followed afterwards was not binding, since the following act cannot annul the first, because such a firm choice was willingly made for betrothal by the principal parties, should the marriage between them have been consummated. If truly the nephew was espoused to her before the seventh [year] and his paternal uncle in the seventh or after the seventh had been betrothed to the same, the nephew on account of the aforesaid rule will not to able to take her to wife, but, if on the contrary, it is the other way around he may be lawfully joined to her. On account of the same aforementioned recommendations we have forwarded, when you have reached agreement of the fact, you will not be able to doubt the law. Therefore, distant to appeal, following these different premises, you are enjoined to take care of the assigned task.

With respect to which whether all, etc, you, brother bishop, with another court.[*282]

The first thing to notice from examining this document is that although the original copyist has decided that it concerned Prince R, it must have originally been Prince L for Prince Llywelyn ab Iorwerth as two subsequent letters ,which will be examined later, are certainly directed towards the marriage of that prince.

If it is accepted that the letter was concerned with the marriage of Llywelyn ab Iorwerth then it appears that the pope does not ask the local court to decide the case of a prince of Wales wishing to marry his aunt, but to decide if there was an impediment to the marriage which had already taken place, as both uncle and nephew had been betrothed to the

---

[*282] *Patrologiae cursus completus,... Latine*, Migne, JP., [1844-1864], CCXIV, 791-2, No.CCXXXIII, printed in Appendix 9, Doc 1.

bride before she was seven years of age, the minimum usual age for betrothal. Obviously this had not mattered to Llywelyn or her previous spouse, Rhodri ab Owain. It was only now, some four years after the event and at least one child later[*283] that Llywelyn sought to regularise his marriage situation in the eyes of the Church. The consequence was the formation of the ecclesiastical court under local ecclesiastics who could be little but favourable to Llywelyn's wishes. The grammatical cases of the verbs of the letter are standard for this era and could imply that the marriage had not taken place, but equally they could be taken to mean that it had. Events show that the latter case is correct.

From this it can be adjudged that the court was set up to decide whether the current prince and princess of North Wales were married illegally and if they were, the logical conclusion was that the marriage was to be annulled. Further, as it had been stated that Rhodri's bride was underage when they married, as well as when Llywelyn was betrothed to her, this would have a bearing on the case. It had further been stated to the pope that the marriage between Rhodri and the girl was never consummated and therefore her remarriage to the nephew, Llywelyn, was legal. Despite this, the pope was worried that the real age of the bride appeared uncertain and he therefore asked the bishop to check into this as well as the bride's status when she married both the uncle (Rhodri) and the nephew (Llywelyn). It can therefore be seen that the statement of the precis of the papal register that Llywelyn wished 'to marry a daughter of the prince of the Isles previously betrothed to his uncle' is not a clear precis of the document and is consequently misleading. This misapprehension has bedevilled studies of thirteenth century Wales ever since. It should be noted here that the name of Llywelyn's first bride had apparently been lost by the time of Lewis Dwnn and it was only John Wynne of Gwydir who invented Tangwystl ferch Llywarch Goch as Llywelyn's first spouse[*284]. This matter shall be discussed further after the status and problems with Llywelyn's first marriage are examined.

Over three years after the commission first deliberated upon Llywelyn's marriage, another papal court of inquiry was set up as the outcome of the first had obviously proved unsatisfactory to settle the matter. Once again it is worthwhile printing the mangled precis of the papal register and then looking at what was really said. According to this tainted source, on 19 April 1203, a mandate was sent to:

> the abbot of Aberconwy (*Abenton*), the prior of Enlli (*Henli*) and Master M., a canon of Beddgelert (*Berlinton*), within the diocese of Bangor, to cause to be observed the sentence about the marriage between the daughter of the prince of the Isles and L Prince of North Wales.[*285]

Another more modern 'translation' goes slightly further than this with:

> the abbot of Aberconwy (*Abercon*), the prior of Enlli (*Henli*) and Mr M. canon of Beddgelert (*Berlincon*), of dioc. Bangor. Confirms the judgement of the delegates in the case committed to them in no.168 above, declaring that for the sake of restoring

---

[*283] *Annales Cambriae. A Translation of Harleian 3859; PRO E.164/1; Cottonian Domitian, A 1; Exeter Cathedral Library MS. 3514 and MS Exchequer DB Neath, PRO E.164/1*, ed. Remfry, P.M., [Malvern, 2007], [E, Neath], 101.

[*284] John Wynne is first to name Tangwystl as Llywelyn's mistress, elaborating on *The History of Cambria now called Wales... by David Powel*, trans. Lhoyd, H [1811], 298, who merely, without quoting any original evidence, describes Llywelyn's elder son, Gruffydd, as illegitimate.

[*285] *Calendar of Entries in the Papal Registers relating to GB and Ireland - Papal Letters, 1198-1304*, ed. W. H. Bliss [1893], 13.

peace L(lywelyn) prince of North Wales might marry the daughter of the prince of the Isles. They had been betrothed when she was 8 years old, but later she was betrothed against her will to his uncle, now dead. Mandate to cause the sentence to be observed, unless there be reasonable objection.[*286]

Again this is hardly what was stated to have been recorded in the original letter. The full text from the register of papal correspondence actually reads:

> To the abbot of Aberconwy, the prior of Enlli and Master M, a canon of Beddgelert, in Bangor Diocese.
> He confirms the sentence concerning the betrothals between the daughter of the prince of the Isles and the prince of North Wales.
> At the Lateran, 19 April 1203.
> Formerly the beloved son, the noble man, Prince L of North Wales, humbly asked us, that it be permitted by our grant [that] the same daughter of the noble man ... prince of the Isles, of which he himself wrote of his espousal, to take as wife etc. In almost the same manner, just as in the register of our second episcopal year [the 1199 entry above] during the month of December, [that] he would to be able to be always united with [her]. Accordingly, with the parties in the presence of the appointed aforesaid judges, just as they intimated to us through their letters, by the same through the witnesses it was clearly established, with respect to the girl, she having completed eight years, by Prince Llywelyn of North Wales, as much by his consent as that of her parents, he had espoused [her], but, by necessity delayed from proceeding, by his paternal uncle without his [Llywelyn's] consent after a while he [Rhodri] betrothed [her], who, though never carnally known to him, he [Rhodri] went the way of all flesh. Hence, the judges themselves, having received the advice of these prudent men, [that] the same girl by the aforesaid Prince Llywelyn of North Wales, in the form of a judicial sentence, pardoned by apostolic authority, their promise of marriage, lest the discord formerly risen between them, however at present caused to rest, might be raised again, just as they intermated to us through their letters. We therefore the same sentence, unless any reasonable cause may stand in the way, considering it authoritative and secure, we entrust to you by the authority at hand, since you in person can bring about, by this distant appeal, by ecclesiastical decree to be observed inviolably. That if not all, two etc.[*287]

Here finally we get towards the truth of the matter. The previous enquiry started in 1199 had found that Llywelyn's marriage was suspect, but the prince had persevered in it and the ecclesiastics acquiesced in this as the marriage had taken place for the political reason to stop strife between the two parties. Despite it being stated that Llywelyn's betrothed had not been carnally acquainted with his uncle, Rhodri, while they were married, the pope did not appear to believe this and was prepared for the marriage to be quashed, although he was content for it to continue for the sake of peace. It seems obvious from this that Llywelyn had persisted in the marriage since his first request to the pope in 1199. Now, nearly four years later in April 1203, the matter was before the pope again. A conclusion from this would appear to be either

---

[*286] *The Letters of Pope Innocent III (1198-1216) concerning England and Wales: A Calendar...* ed. Cheney, CR & MG [Manchester, 1967], 77, no.469.
[*287] *Patrologiae cursus completus,... Latine*, Migne, JP., [1844-1864] CCXV, 49-50, No. XLVII, printed in Appendix 9, doc 2.

that the problems with the marriage had not been suppressed by Llywelyn's actions in 1199, when he wrote to the pope, or that Llywelyn was now looking for a way out of his marriage. The birth of children in 1197 and before 1200 as well as these two appeals to the pope would suggest that Llywelyn did not put aside his bride before 1203.

It is therefore a possibility that Llywelyn stuck by his wife in this period, while coming under increasing ecclesiastical pressure to put her aside. Such pressure had been brought against previous princes of Wales to end non canonical marriages, viz. Owain Gwynedd with his cousin Christina ferch Goronwy, Rhodri ab Owain with his cousin Agnes ferch Rhys and Cadwallon ap Madog with his cousin Eva ferch Madog. Considering this, it is fantastic that Giraldus makes no mention of this affair in all his works, when obviously he should have been favouring the canons of the church and supporting his pope in bringing religious orthodoxy to Wales.

Another reason that Llywelyn was finally brought upon to relent concerning his first marriage appears to have been more political than mere ecclesiastical pressure. In mid April 1205 Llywelyn married Princess Joan, the illegitimate daughter of King John[288]. Despite this, there is some evidence that the match was contemplated as early as 27 May 1203, when King John was looking at bringing Ellesmere, the dower of his aunt, Emma Plantagenet, under his direct control[289]. The implication is that the king was thinking of using this as dower for his own daughter being given in marriage to Llywelyn. Therefore, it can be seen that all the pieces fit nicely together. Llywelyn married his aunt by marriage soon after the death of Rhodri. This was probably done to honour his alleged betrothal which would have to have been made before 15 June 1192 when Rhodri married the girl and apparently granted her lands in dower which had been granted, no doubt by Gruffydd ap Cynan, to Aberconwy abbey - hence the land claims made by King Reginald against Aberconwy abbey in September 1192. If correct this would mean that the two known children of Llywelyn, the unnamed one who died in 1197 and Gruffydd ap Llywelyn[290], were both the grandchildren of King Reginald of Man. This can virtually be confirmed by checking against the almost universally baseless assertions found in Wikipedia under the erroneous and anachronistic title of Llywelyn the Great rather than Llywelyn ab Iorwerth:

> Little is known of Llywelyn's mistress, Tangwystl Goch, except that she was the daughter of Llywarch "Goch" of Rhos. Gruffydd ap Llywelyn (c. 1196–1244) was Llywelyn's eldest son and known to be the son of Tangwystl.[291]

It is a great pity that no contemporary 'knew' that Gruffydd was the son of Tangwystl, rather than he was a child of Llywelyn's then legitimate wife. The pope's letters therefore make far more sense when considering Gruffydd ap Llywelyn's obvious grievance against his father and younger half-brother, Dafydd ap Llywelyn (d.1246); especially when it is realised what trouble Llywelyn went to in having Princess Joan declared legitimate; especially when he

---

[288] 'Annales Prioratus de Wigornia', *Annales Monastici*, ed. H.R. Luard [5 vols., 1864-9] IV, 394. Although the lady is known as Joan and that name will be used here, Johanna is more likely her correct name as appears from the records. She was probably named this as a female version of John.

[289] *Rotuli de Liberate ac de Misis et Praestitis regnante Johanne*, ed. T.D. Hardy [1844], 36. The reason for this has often been argued was the death of Dafydd ab Owain, but he may already have been dead for three years, see p.101.

[290] It has been alleged that there was a third son, Tegwared, known as Bais Wen, but there is no contemporary evidence for this, see below p. 109-10. Indeed his lack of mention in the treaty of 1211 all but proves his non-existence.

[291] https://en.wikipedia.org/wiki/Llywelyn_the_Great#Children Accessed 14 November 2015. The true nature of the name Llywelyn Fawr is given in Appendix 11, p.348.

didn't go to such trouble for his own surviving child from his ill-starred first marriage, but he did make the effort, as detailed below, to have Gruffydd castigated by the pope as 'the son of a slave girl'. Once again the world of history has been ill-served by those who wish to make events up and fill in the historical voids with their own ignorance, rather than fact.

Finally, it can be seen that despite the matter of Llywelyn's marriage being unsound, the affair was still rumbling on two years later. Consequently, the pope wrote again to his brethren of England concerning the matter - and it is immediately apparent that he wrote to the bishops of the see of Canterbury and not to the heads of lesser establishments, like abbots, priors and canons in Wales. Unfortunately, yet again, this mandate has been cruelly precised. Thus it was said to have been recorded:

> 17 February 1205 [13 Kal Mar]. Mandate to the bishops of Ely, Norwich and St Asaph to bring to an end the cause relating to the marriage of the daughter of the prince of the Isles and Prince L. of North Wales.[*292]

The more modern version at least leans a bit more towards the complexity of the subject:

> 17 Feb 1205. To bp of Ely, bp of Norwich and bp of St Asaph. Recounts the earlier history of the marriage case concerning Prince L of North Wales and the daughter of the prince of the Isles. The last judges were not satisfied that the marriage of Llywelyn was valid and sent to the pope further evidence, including evidence that L, when betrothed to the girl, had married a sister of the earl of Chester. As a result the pope decides that there has been no valid marriage between L and the daughter of the prince of the Isles. He orders the addressees to summon the parties and give judgement accordingly.[*293]

Once again, when the copy of the original document is examined, rather than the best known, but misleading 39 words of the first precis, the story told is very different and totally changes the perception of Welsh history in this period. The pope's real letter of some nine hundred words runs:

> To the bishops of Ely[*294], Norwich[*295] and St Asaph[*296].
> In order that they may conclude overturning the case of the marriage between the daughter of the prince of the Isles and the prince of North Wales.
> At St Peters, 16 February 1205.
> When formerly the beloved son, the noble man, Prince [Llywelyn] of North Wales, humbly asked of us, that from us to himself he might be allowed permission, the daughter of the noble man Prince [Reginald] of the Isles, whom he himself [Llywelyn] had claimed to espouse, to take in wife, notwithstanding that [Rhodri] his paternal uncle had been betrothed to the same woman before she was of marriageable age, since neither of them married the same [woman], we commissioned Bishop [Michael]

[*292] *Calendar of Entries in the Papal Registers relating to GB and Ireland - Papal Letters, 1198-1304*, ed. W. H. Bliss [1893], 19.
[*293] *The Letters of Pope Innocent III (1198-1216) concerning England and Wales: A Calendar...* ed. Cheney, CR & MG [Manchester, 1967], 100, No.600.
[*294] Eustace, 1197 to 4 February 1215.
[*295] John Grey, 3/24 September 1200 to 18 October 1214.
[*296] Reiner, 10 August 1186 to 1223/4.

of Man, of good memory[*297], and our beloved sons [Gervase?] the archdeacon and Prior [?] of Ynys Llannog, to conclude the actual case in the specified form [This was on 24 November 1199, Book II, No.233 above]. And so with the parties assembled in the presence of the aforesaid judges, just as they themselves intimated to us via their letters, through the witnesses it was clearly established, that the aforesaid girl, having reached eight years, by Prince L. [Llywelyn] of North Wales, so much through her assent as through her parents, she was pledged, but, due to necessity he put off marrying her in person, the paternal uncle [Rhodri] of the same Llywelyn, without the consent of the same [Llywelyn] presently in person married her, who, she by no means became known carnally [to him], went the way of all flesh. Therefore the previously named judges, having taken counsel of experienced men, granted the aforesaid prince of North Wales by apostolic authority, that he might betroth the same girl, lest the discord that once arose between himself and the parents of the girl, and was then calmed, should again arise. We therefore, being of the same opinion, unless there might be other reason certainly to oppose it, desiring strongly that it might be maintained; [so] to our beloved sons, the abbot of Aberconwy[*298], the prior of Enlli and Master M, a canon of Beddgelert, of Bangor diocese, we gave orders, by distant appeal, that they might strongly observe in person through ecclesiastical sentence. Truly the aforesaid abbot and his co-judges, on account of the terms expressed in our letters, concerning that marriage, just as we had observed contained in their letters, zealously and carefully, received from the witnesses, they undertook to seek the truth. Therefore by the production of four witnesses, and by rendering their depositions into writings, the things which they believed were sufficient to settle the case, with the assent of both parties, they undertook to transmit to us, that the truth of the business might be manifest to us, and that they might consider the conscience of the aforesaid prince; who said that the previous judges, and particularly the archdeacon and prior[*299] were ignorant of the law, and that our letters were obtained through mistaken propositions, nor did he himself believe that [the marriage] might be able to be saved with the same girl, who had been delivered over as wife to his paternal uncle [Rhodri], she often being in the one bed with him. We therefore, by carefully examining the depositions of the witnesses, find it proven by them, that the same L. [Llywelyn] had himself sworn to take the girl herself in marriage, but she herself did not proclaim it, nor was it proved by witnesses that it had been blessed, or even that she might have been on the one land with the same, in as much as their lands are divided by the sea between them. Likewise, enclosed in the records of the judges we have observed, that sufficient witnesses have been approved in court by themselves [the judges], [that] the girl was of eight years when the same L [Llywelyn] swore to take her. However, the father of the girl [King Reginald], delayed taking his daughter into North Wales at the stated time, not to mention that the same L. [Llywelyn], the sister of the noble man Earl [Ranulf] of Chester[*300], without objection anywhere, about the end of that year he

---

[*297] Michael, 1194/5 to 1203.

[*298] Abraham, was abbot about this time, Acts, 346

[*299] This was the archdeacon of Bangor and the prior of Ynys Llannog in 1199.

[*300] Earl Ranulf Blunderville was born in Oswestry in 1170 and died at Wallingford on 26 October 1232, *Annales Cestrienses, a chronicle of the abbey of St. Werburgh, Chester*, ed. and trans. Christie, R.C., Record Society for Lancashire and Cheshire XIV [1887], 24, 58; 'Annales de Theokesberia', *Annales Monastici*, ed. H.R. Luard [5 vols., 1864-9] I, 87. His sisters were Matilda (b.1171-1232), Mabel (bef.1179-bef.1232), Agnes (bef.1180-1247) and Hawise (bef.1181-1242). Matilda married Earl David of Huntington on 26 August 1190.

(continued...)

took as his wife[*301], and R. [Rhodri] his paternal uncle [Llywelyn's] was betrothed to the girl spoken of, and after a year in the presence of the Church entered into marriage with her, and from the beginning of May up to the feast of St Vitus the martyr [15 June][*302], as often as it pleased the same, in the same bed he lay down with the same, and he returned to Wales and a considerable amount of time went past. The other [Rhodri], in the second year from the time of the betrothal, truly the first from the time of their marriages, he returned to Man, peacefully cohabiting with his wife, and he took her with him through land and sea, but, at length at the court of her parents he left the same behind, he returned to Wales [1194], and there he went the way of all flesh. Therefore the judges mentioned above deduced from the words of the witnesses that the aforesaid R. [Rhodri] had by that time been betrothed to the same girl for three years and three months, not to mention during two years and two months and fifteen days since the time of their marriages; however, there has been a difference between the witnesses, with some, from the fact that the girl at that time was slim/thin/meagre, in respect of which they judged that she had not been known carnally, although she was of marriageable age and swelling maturely/early; yet, some said it was unknown to them if it had come to light that she had been carnally known, truly some might believe that she might not have been known, truly some asserted that they had heard from R. [Rhodri] himself that he had not known her carnally; although adding that they themselves did not know whether afterwards she could have been with him. In truth, the aforesaid bishop of Man, just as in his writings, and his following co-judges who examining the enclosed, with his co-judges absent, as much from the girl herself as from her parents, from her nurse and the household of the same he has been told on oath that the aforesaid R. [Rhodri] had not known the girl herself carnally. Therefore, once the paternal uncle [Rhodri] had gone the way of all flesh, when the aforesaid L. [Llywelyn] asked from the king of Man a younger daughter to join in marriage, nor was he able to obtain that from the same, in as much as he was already coupled with her another way, the frequently said girl, with the assent of the preceding judges, after a while he [Llywelyn] joined her physically to himself. Therefore it was established from the aforesaid that between the often mentioned L. [Llywelyn] and the aforesaid girl, at the time she might have been eight years, whose consent nevertheless was not found clearly expressed, before the paternal uncle, the same Llywelyn had entered into marriage with her, merely through words that in the future they would celebrate espousal; therefore, because the same Llywelyn neither took or pledged to the same, nor at the time had themselves blessed, in fact, on the contrary, they had not even been in the same land at the same time in so much as any lands, just as is expressed above, the sea divided between them: from whence it cannot be presumed that he was able to attempt anything, because they would not have been able to consummate. It was also determined from the preceding that the girl herself was in her ninth year when the often said R. [Rhodri] married her [by pledge], and in her tenth when she was

---

[*300] (...continued)

Mabel married Earl William Aubigny before 1200, Agnes married Earl William Ferrers in 1192 and Hawise married Robert Quincy before 1205. Therefore, Llywelyn had to have been betrothed to either Mabel or Hawise before they married their respective husbands, or just as likely, he was betrothed to another girl who did not survive childhood. Certainly there is no question of Llywelyn having applied to annul any other marriage as this would certainly have been mentioned in the court proceedings.

[*301] The year end was 25 March 1192, therefore it appears that Llywelyn broke the marriage negotiations off in favour of an alliance with his neighbour the earl of Chester, allowing Rhodri to marry the girl without Llywelyn's apparent knowledge on 15 June 1192.

[*302] The implication of this is that banns were read in church in the month prior to Rhodri's marriage in the Isle of Man on 15 June 1192.

conducted [married], and for a further two years was frequently in the one bed with him. From whence it is plainly deducted that the first letters were obtained by supplying a false proposition, seeing that it was maintained by the former that neither of them had taken the same. And since they might have been simultaneously in one bed together, it is to be presumed according to the law that they had been one flesh, when furthermore in her twelfth year, in which the girl freely and lawfully in this gave her consent, she was willingly with the same, it is evident that she legally consented in this marriage and was not able to enter into legal marriage with the nephew afterwards. Hence the same L. [Llywelyn] should not have been legally able to take her [as wife], and, if he has physically joined [in marriage] with her after the death of his paternal uncle, he requires to be rightly separated from her. And therefore we command through your brotherhood through these apostolic letters, to what extent, you call those who should be summoned for this, cause a verdict itself in the following form, that the appeal is set aside, concluded, done, etc.[*303]

It is quite clear from this that Llywelyn's marriage, which appears to have begun soon after Rhodri's death, ended in the period of 1203 to 1205. It also appears clear from this that Llywelyn was trying to maintain the marriage in 1199, but that his attitude had changed dramatically by 1203. The story would seem to go like this. After the initial inquest of 1199 it was decided that Llywelyn's marriage was unsound, but should not be annulled due to its benefits to all parties. Yet by 1203, Llywelyn's position seems to have changed and certainly by 1205 he denounced the archdeacon of Bangor and the prior of Ynys Llannog as having been ignorant of the law when they examined the cause in 1199. The implication of this is that he now wished to abandon his current wife and acquire the king's daughter as his spouse. The result of this was the second inquisition of 1203 and the papal confirmation of 1205 that Llywelyn's marriage was unsound and was to be quashed. The second enquiry was led by the abbot of Aberconwy and although it found that Llywelyn should not have married his current wife, it allowed matters to stand as it had brought peace to a dispute. The abbot obviously knew this as part of his lands were the bone of contention between the king of the Isles and Llywelyn. Quite obviously the abbot was protecting his own lands as well as the general well being of the land. The result was the third hearing led by English ecclesiastics which has been preserved in greater detail than the two previous ones. This shows clearly that most witnesses were of the opinion that Rhodri and his wife had not known each other carnally, but their evidence was not accepted as they were forced to make the lawyers' plea that although they knew that this had not happened, they could not swear that it had not happened out of their sight. The main proponent of this view appears to have been Llywelyn ab Iorwerth himself. It is therefore apparent that the prince had changed his viewpoint between 1199 and 1203. The most logical reason for this, after his marriage had been accepted by the pope in 1199, is that he now wished to have his marriage annulled so that he could make a better match with a Plantagenet spouse. Comparisons with his eighth great grandson, Henry VIII, are apparent.

A final point must be raised about the death of Rhodri as the dates given by the pope do not agree with the death date of the prince given in both the St David's and the Strata Florida versions of the Annales Cambriae. They both record this as the first event of 1195, yet the pope's statement that Rhodri had been betrothed for three years and three months and

---

[*303] *Patrologiae cursus completus,... Latine*, Migne, JP., [1844-1864] CCXV, 534-7, No.CCXX, printed in Appendix 9, Doc 3.

married for two years, two months and fifteen days, means that he must have died about 30 August 1194. This makes much more sense than Rhodri hanging about in limbo for twelve months after his defeat at Coedana. Llywelyn chased him back from there to Holyhead where he died, no doubt of either dysentery or his wounds. This also means that Rhodri betrothed the girl about 1 June 1191 when he was in the Isle of Man. This again suggests that Rhodri was expelled from Gwynedd in late 1190 or early 1191. Finally, the fragments of original evidence provide a plausible scenario for the events of 1190 to 1194, until and unless further original evidence might come to hand and change this reading. The alternative that Rhodri became engaged to the Manx princess about 1 June 1192 and then married her a year later does not really work, as this would mean that King Reginald complained to the Cistercian chapter in 1192 before his daughter would have been given any dower and that Rhodri would have married her immediately before his Manx invasion of Mon. In short, the 15 June 1192 marriage is the date that works best with the available evidence that survives.

The pope's final letter on the matter shows that by 1205 Prince Llywelyn had clearly repented of his former attitude and put his wife aside. What became of her is unknown, but she was only 21 in 1203. The pope's summation of the case and the appointment of the three bishops from Canterbury province in 1205 was obviously done to ensure that Llywelyn was free to marry again and this he did in mid April 1205. The pope's summary clearly shows the desire for the regularisation of Llywelyn's matrimonial affairs and this it appears was intended to ensure that Gruffydd ap Llywelyn would never inherit Gwynedd if the proposed Plantagenet marriage proved fruitful. It should also be noted that canonically illegal marriages seem commonplace at this time as is easily confirmed by a quick study of the Chronicles of the Kings of Man and the Isles.

Looking at the personages involved in settling the cause of Llywelyn's marriage it is apparent that most were of Gwynedd, viz. the bishop of Man (who may have held or claimed some influence in Mon), the archdeacon of Bangor, the prior of Ynys Llannog, the abbot of Aberconwy, the prior of Enlli and a canon of Beddgelert. All these were people directly connected with and within the patrimony of Prince Llywelyn. However in 1205, two of those appointed were from the east of England and could not have been pressurised by Llywelyn. Such might mean that the pope was worried by Llywelyn's attitude, or, more likely, he wished King John to be certain that Llywelyn was free to marry. Certainly the responses of the ecclesiastical judges from Llywelyn's principality suggest that they were not overawed by him. Further still, the princely complaints of the ignorance of two of them suggests that Llywelyn made strenuous efforts to overturn the previous finding in favour of the validity of his first marriage. It is also interesting to see that the abbot of Aberconwy was placed in charge of overseeing the dissolution of Llywelyn's marriage in 1203. This again shows the importance of the abbey after only seventeen years in existence.

It can be seen from this evidence that Llywelyn has never been known to have had any mistress or any illegitimate children, other than the surviving Gruffydd who was apparently only made illegitimate in 1203 by the dissolution of his parent's marriage. The final question about Llywelyn's matrimonial habits that must be asked is was Tangwystl Goch the real name of Llywelyn's first wife, the daughter of King Reginald. This Tangwystl, the alleged daughter of Llywarch Goch, appears to be a seventeenth century invention made simply to tidy up the family tree. That said, there may have been a real person of this name who was associated with Prince Llywelyn. Around 1336, ie over 130 years after the time being written about, the survey of Denbighshire recorded that the land of *Dyncadvel* in Llannefydd (*Carvedvennith*) was at some unknown time mortgaged to Prince Llywelyn ab Iorwerth for £13.

Certainly which prince gave the said mortgage to some friend of his named Tangwystl Goch' and he sold that to some Cynan ap Laurence whose heirs hold that...

Qui quidem Princeps dedit dictum pignus cuidam amice sue nomine Tanguestel Goch' que illam vendidit cuidam Canon ap Lauwar cuius progenies tenet illam...[304]

The word used to describe Tangwystl is *amice*. This comes from the Latin, *amic/us* and its case is vocative, singular and masculine. If *Tanguestel* was a woman then surely the word would have been *amica*. In short, it cannot be certain if this Tangwystl was male or female from the text, although the former is explicitly stated by the Latin, though this could possibly be a scribal error. Finally, this supplies no evidence as to whether he/she was a lover of Llywelyn and mother of two of his children.

If there is no evidence that Tangwystl was female or the mother of Llywelyn's first children, there is another far more credible wife for Llywelyn in the form of Rhunallt, the daughter of the king of Man[305]. By c.1500 the bard Guttyn Owen mistakenly thought that Rhunallt was the bride of Gruffydd ap Llywelyn, and not his mother. Historically it is clear that Gruffydd only had one wife and that this was Senana ferch Caradog (bef.1200-52+). Further they appear to have married before 1214 judging from the birth dates of their children[306]. This allows no time for Gruffydd to have married and had children by another wife. As Senana outlived her husband there is little chance that Gruffydd had another wife from the Isle of Man. The matter is confirmed by a poet contemporary to Owain Goch ap Gruffydd, the brother of Llywelyn ap Gruffydd (d.1282), who calls Owain of the lineage of the kings of Man[307]. Quite clearly this refers to Owain's grandmother and establishes the four brothers' lineage through Rhunallt and the kings of Man. It would therefore appear that this was not a very oblique reference to their distant ancestry through the half Irish Gruffydd ap Cynan (d.1137) as has been suggested in modern histories.

With Llywelyn ab Iorwerth's first wife clearly identified as Princess Rhunallt it is worth taking a further look at what occurred with the marriage of Llywelyn and Joan Plantagenet. On 26 May 1222, the new pope, Honorius III (1216-27), the successor to Innocent III (1198-1216) who had quashed Llywelyn's first marriage, wrote to 'his beloved noble man, Lord Llywelyn of North Wales'. This was in reply to a now lost letter of the prince asking that as Llywelyn, with the consent of King Henry III, Archbishop Stephen of Canterbury and Legate Pandulf, had abolished the detestable custom that illegitimate children should inherit just as if they were legitimate, that the pope would confirm this. Further, the prince asked that the pope would confirm Llywelyn's statute that his son Dafydd 'by his legitimate wife Joan, daughter of the late king of England' should succeed him by hereditary right in all his possessions'[308]. Various versions of this text have been printed. It is therefore once again necessary to consider them here and then see what was actually stated.

26 May [7 Kal June] 1222, Confirmation for Llywelyn Lord of North Wales, on his petition showing that there is a detestable custom in his country that the son of the handmaid should be heir with the son of the free, putting legitimate and illegitimate

---

[304] *Survey of the Honour of Denbigh, 1334*, eds. Vinogradoff, P., & Morgan, F. [London, 1914], 128.

[305] Thornton, DE., 'A neglected genealogy of Llywelyn ap Gruffydd', *Cambridge Medieval Celtic Studies*, XXIII [1992], 2-23, deals with the Cronica de Wallia. NLW Peniarth MS.129, 131.

[306] As Owain Goch and Llywelyn ap Gruffydd appear to have been born before 1215 it would appear that Gruffydd and Senana's marriage had taken place before that date, Remfry, PM. *The Killing of Prince Llywelyn of Wales, 10 December 1282* [Ceidio, 2014], 7, footnote 9.

[307] *Gwaith Bleddyn Fardd a Beirdd Eraill Ail Hanner y Drydedd Ganrif ar Ddeg*, ed. Andrews, RM. *et all* [Cardiff, 1996], 48. 21.

[308] Acts, 414-5, No.253.

sons on the same footing, of an ordinance made by him, with the consent of King Henry and by the authority of Stephen Cardinal Archbishop of Canterbury and Pandulf Bishop Elect of Norwich then acting as legate, to the effect that his son, Dafydd born of Joan, daughter of the late king of England, should succeed him.[*309]

The text this translation appears to have come from actually seems to have run:

Nobili viro Lowelino domino Norwallie. Confirmat statutum quod ipse in terra suae ditioni subiecta cum consensu Henrici regis Anglorum fecerat, consentientibus quoque Stephano Cantuariensi archiepiscopo S R E Cardinali et Pandulpho Norwiciensi electo Apostolicae Sedis Legato, contra abusum in eius terra introductum, ut illegitimi succederent in hereditates sicut et legitimi, ordinando ut David filius suus quem ex Iohanna filia cl. mem. [et] regis Angliae uxore sua legitima suscepit, haereditario iure in omnibus bonis suis ei succedat.[*310]

This literally translates as:

To the nobleman Lord Llywelyn of North Wales. Confirming a statute that [Llywelyn] himself in the land lying under his authority made with the consent of King Henry of the English, likewise acting together with Archbishop Stephen of Canterbury... and Pandulf the elect of Norwich and legate of the Apostolic See, against the abuse which has been introduced into his land, that the illegitimate may succeed in hereditary [title] just as the legitimate: orders that Dafydd his son who was born from Joanna the daughter of Clementia [*cl. mem.*] [and] of the king of England, his [Llywelyn's] lawfully accepted wife, that he might succeed him in hereditary right in all his goods.

The differences are readily apparent and at first sight the handmaidens of Llywelyn ab Iorwerth appear ready to be dispatched back into the realms of scripture from which they were summoned forth in the last century. However, recent scholarship has found and translated the original letter of the pope, filling in many blanks from standard formulae found in other papal letters, which have largely been left out in the first two extracts above[*311].

Petition stating that since a detestable custom has developed in his land, whereby the son of the handmaiden was equally heir with the son of the free woman and illegitimate sons obtained an inheritance as if they were legitimate, Llywelyn has abolished this custom, that was contrary to divine and human law, with the consent of King Henry of England, as well as the authority of Archbishop Stephen of Canterbury and Pandulf, bishop elect of Norwich and legate, and has ordained that henceforth the canonical sanctions should be inviolably followed in the aforesaid cases, issuing a statute whereby Dafydd, his son by his legitimate wife Joan, daughter of the late king of England, should succeed him by hereditary right in all his possessions. Llywelyn seeks confirmation of the statute by apostolic authority.

[*309] *Calendar of Entries in the Papal Registers relating to GB and Ireland - Papal Letters, 1198-1304*, ed. W. H. Bliss [1893], 87.
[*310] *Regesta Honorii Papae III*, ed. Pressutti, P., [Rome, 2 vols, 1884-95] II, 73, No. 3996.
[*311] Acts, 414-6, quoting Vatican City, Archivio Segreto Vaticano, Reg. Vat. 11, fo.244r-v, No.407.

The above precis had been made from the following Latin text:

Nobili viro Lowelino domino Norwallie. Cum a nobis petitur... effectum. Sane tua petitio nobis exhibita continebat quod cum quedam detestabilis consuetudo vel potius corruptela inolevisset in terra tue ditioni subiecta, ut videlicet filius ancille esset heres cum filio libere et illegitimi filii hereditatem sicut legitimi obtinerent, tu karissimi in Cristo filii nostri Henr regis Anglor illustris domini tui accedente consensu ac etiam interveniente auctoritate venerablilis fratris nostri Stephani Cantuarien archiepiscopi sancte Roman ecclesie cardinalis ac dilecti filii Pandulfi Norwicen electi tunc in partibus illis legationis officium exercentis consuetudinem seu corruptelam huiusmodi iuri divino et humano contrariam abolere ac extirpare curasti, statuendo ut in predictis casibus id decetero in prefata terra inviolabiliter conservetur quod cautum est per canonicas et legitimas sanctiones, secundum statutum huiusmodi ordinando ut David filius tuus quem ex Iohanna filia clare memorie[312] *regis Anglie uxore tua legitima suscepisti hereditario iure te succedat in omnibus bonis tuis; quare nobis humiliter supplicasti ut predictum statum apostolico roborare munimine dignaremur. Nos igitur iustis precibus tuis benignum impertientes assensum, statutum ipsum sicut provide factum est auctoritate apostolica confirmanus communimus. Nulli ergo conffirmationis infringere. Si quis autem... Dat' Alatri vii kal iunii anno sexto.*

A more literal translation of this would run:

To the nobleman Lord Llywelyn of North Wales. Bringing about from us the attached petition. Certainly your petition to us showed that since some detestable custom or rather corruption has developed in the land subject to your authority - as evidently the son of the slave girl could be the heir together with the son of the free woman and illegitimate sons could obtain the inheritance just as the legitimate - you [Llywelyn] and your Lord Henry, the illustrious king of the English, beloved sons of Christ, have agreed in harmony and also furthermore with the intervening authority of our beloved sons, our venerable brother Archbishop Stephen of Canterbury, cardinal saint of the Roman church and also Pandulf the elect of Norwich then in those parts as official legate in the customary manner, or if the corruption of this sort contrary to divine and human justice is to be abolished and rooted out in curing, it is required to be established that in the preceding case it henceforth in the before mentioned land inviolably will be followed that the provisions of the law is by canonical and lawful ordinances, according to the statute of this sort as composed [by you] that Dafydd your son, who from Joan the daughter of Clementia and the king of England, your legal wife, should succeed in receiving your inheritance by right in all your possessions; wherefore from us you asked as a supplicant that the preceding apostolic statute we might think worthy to strengthen by this fortification. We therefore to your just prayers bestow assent, the statute itself just as provident is made by the authority of the apostolic See strongly fortified and confirmed. Therefore no one is to infringe on this confirmation. However if any do.... Dated at Alatri the seventh calends of June in our sixth year.

---

[312] This would appear to be a mistranscription of Clemenita.

This important document therefore indicates that even at this late date Llywelyn was very interested in bolstering the lineage of his children by his second marriage by further downgrading the legitimacy of his children by his first wife. It also gives us the true name of Princess Joan's mother, Clementia. This adds another dimension to the story of Prince Llywelyn's marriages, for this Clementia is easily traceable in the records and she impacted appreciably on the politics of the age (Fig.13).

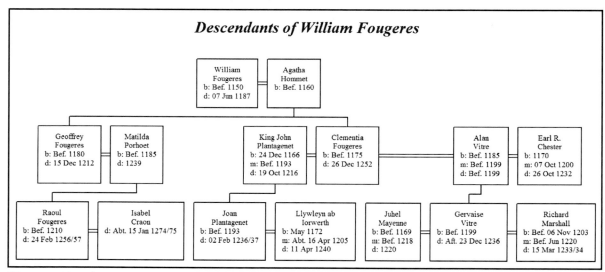

Figure 13, The extended family of Clementia Fougeres.

Clementia was born before 1180, possibly in Fougères, Brittany, to William Fougeres[313] (d.7 June 1187) and his wife, Agatha Hommet. Agatha was a granddaughter to the great Richard Humez Hommet (d.1181), the seneschal of Normandy for Henry II. Her ancestry is asserted in a copy of a charter, probably of 1232, when the widowed Clementia gave away her Lincolnshire lands of Freiston (*Fotstun*) and Bennington (*Benyngton*) on the death of her husband, Earl Ranulf of Chester[314]. In this she describes herself as *Clemenciae filiae Willielmi de Fugeres*. Before 1193 she would seem to have presented Count John with an illegitimate daughter who was named after the king himself, Johanna. Today this Johanna is better known as Princess Joan or in modern times, Siwan of Wales. Before 1199 Clementia had married Alan Vitre of Dinan, for 1199 is the last possible year in which she could have given birth to Gervaise Vitre of Dinan. Before 1218 Gervaise married Juhel Mayenne and presented him with three daughters before his death in battle in 1220. Gervaise lived on until after 23 December 1236[315]. Another reason Clementia's marriage must have taken place before 1199 is that on 7 October 1200 she, obviously as a widow, married the thirty year old Earl Ranulf Blunderville of Chester[316]. A copy of the charter by which her brother, Geoffrey Fougeres, gave her away tells much of her history[317]. In this charter Geoffrey granted lands to Earl Ranulf together with his sister, Clementia. This included all the lands that she was

[313] The Fougeres family appears in English records as at least *Fulgeriis, Fugeriis, Fulcheriis, Filgeriis, Fillgeriis, Feugeres, Feugers* and *Faugerollis*.

[314] *Monasticon Anglicanum*, ed. W. Dugdale, Revised edition by J. Caley, H. Ellis, and B. Bandinel [6 vols., 1817-30] VI ii, 1102.

[315] Du Paz, A., *Histoire Genealogique de Plusieurs Maisons Illustres de Bretagne...* [Paris, 1619], 127.

[316] On 29 May 1204, King John confirmed that Geoffrey Fougeres had granted his sister Clementia the manor of Bennington (*Belinton'*) with all appurtenances on the day of her marriage to Earl Ranulf of Chester, *Rotuli Chartarum in Turri Londonensi asservati [1204-22]*, ed. T.D. Hardy [1837], 104b.

[317] Ormerod, G., *The History of Cheshire* [3 vols, 1819] I, 39.

given when she married Alan Dinan, which was all the land the family held in the valley of Mortain (*Moretoniae*) and the manor of Bennington (*Belingtona*) in England. This was currently held by William St John by the custom of England as he had received it as the marriage portion of his wife, Olive, who was the mother of Clementia's and Geoffrey's grandfather, Ralph Fougeres. Before the witness list came a confirmation of William Hommet, the constable of Normandy, who swore that the gifts were legal. This William was maternal grandfather to Clementia and Geoffrey. A second charter made on the day of the wedding carried the seals of both Williams and Ranulf as well as confirming the lineage of Clementia and her marriage to Alan Dinan[*318]. There can be little doubt that the Queen Clementia of Wales who died in 1252 was the same woman who was wife to Earl Ranulf and Alan Dinan and mother of Princess Joan of Wales (d.1237).

From all this information it is possible to see that when Prince Llywelyn married Johanna Plantagenet in April 1205, Earl Ranulf (Fig.13) became his step father-in-law. It is also possible that he was already his brother-in-law, if Llywelyn had married Ranulf's sister in 1192. Here we finally have the coming together of Ranulf and Llywelyn in alliance and this explains much of their acting in unison in the coming years. The Tewkesbury chronicler was certainly aware of the relationship, for on the death of Princess Joan in 1237. He wrote:

> The Lady Johanna of Wales died, the wife of Llywelyn, daughter of King John and Queen Clementia, 30 March.[*319]

Queen Clementia is a bit of an overstatement, but no doubt the scribe who wrote the entry was aware that Clementia was the legitimised consort of a king and the mother of a princess. The ecclesiastical logic that as Joan was the legitimised daughter of King John then Clementia must have been lawful wife and consequently was queen dowager of England is therefore natural, if a little strange to us today.

The knowledge that these events give to us makes much more sense of the relationship between Earl Ranulf and Prince Llywelyn. It was one of father-in-law to son-in-law. This makes far more sense of Llywelyn rushing to meet Ranulf when he returned from Crusade on 16 August 1220. It is just such a great pity that this scribe never finished the sentence he was writing about the affair[*320]. This relationship explains why Earl Ranulf abandoned Cheshire's western provinces in Wales so easily to Llywelyn. He did not abandon them, he passed them on to his step-daughter and his son-in-law. There was no 'conquest' of Tegeingl by Llywelyn, it became a marriage portion and this is why the cantref was treated differently in Llywelyn's 1211 treaty with King John. This treaty and Tegeingl will be examined later. Consequently, the harmony seen between the two is more easily explainable. Especially when it is remembered that Ranulf was childless and therefore that Llywelyn, via his wife, Johanna could be considered as an heir to his wife's dower. Such a family bond tends to make a nonsense of the suggestion that Ranulf 'had a fellow-feeling for a great territorial lord whose

---

[*318] Ormerod, G., *The History of Cheshire* [3 vols, 1819] I, 39-40.

[*319] *Obiit domina Johanna domina Walliae, uxor Lewelini, filia Regis Johannis et reginae Clemenciae, iii kal Aprilis*, 'Annales de Theokesberia', *Annales Monastici*, ed. H.R. Luard [5 vols., 1864-9] I, 101.

[*320] *Rediit dominus Rannulphus comes Cestrie de Damata venitque Cestriam in crastino Assumpcionis receptus cum maxima veneratione tam cleri quam plebis. Lewelinus etiam princeps Wallie venit ad eum eodem die, cui dominus Rannulphus comes in.... Annales Cestrienses, a chronicle of the abbey of St. Werburgh, Chester*, ed. and trans. Christie, R.C., Record Society for Lancashire and Cheshire XIV [1887], 50-1.

franchises were threatened by the activity of the central government'[321]. It also makes far more sense of the contemporary statement that Ranulf was both family and friend to Llywelyn[322]. Family was the reason for their closeness, not politics.

Clementia's daughter, Johanna Plantagenet, would appear to have been at least forty years old at the time of her death in 1237, ie born before 1197. This age is suggested as the children she bore Llywelyn were born from 1208 at the latest onwards. According to the pope it was against religion and custom for husbands and wives to indulge in carnal relations before the girl had reached the age of eleven[323]. This suggests, but does not prove, that Johanna was born before 1197 to be at least eleven by that date[324]. As her mother was married to Alan Dinan before 1198 at the very latest and gave birth to his daughter, Gervaise (d.1236) before 1199, it would suggest that Johanna was born before 1198 at the very earliest to allow Clementia time to give birth to her second daughter, Gervaise, by 1199. Johanna's marriage to Prince Llywelyn in 1205 would suggest she was a minimum of eleven years old, again according to the pope's letter quoted above concerning her predecessor as Llywelyn's wife, although the evidence related above shows she was probably at least twelve. During their married life Johanna presented Llywelyn with at least seven children, Dafydd around 1213, Gwladys Ddu before 1208, Margaret before 1209, Angharad, Gwenllian and Helen/Eleanor all before 1210 and finally, after a suspiciously long gap, Susannah before 1228. These tentative dates are based upon marriage dates or contemporary mentions. It can therefore be seen that Johanna died quite young, being somewhat over forty years old, especially when considering the age her mother reached. Clementia Fougeres died on 26 December 1252[325]. She was aged at least 72. Little is recorded of her activities after her marriage to Earl Ranulf in 1200.

That the problem of succession was strong in Prince Llywelyn's mind is obvious from the great lengths he went to strengthen his second marriage. Indeed, on 29 April 1226, he, working in tandem with his nephew, King Henry III (1207-72), secured a papal dispensation which legitimised his wife. The precis of this runs:

> Dispensation to Joan wife of Prince Llywelyn of North Wales, declaring her legitimate, but without prejudice to the king or realm of England. Mandate to the bishops of St David's, Bangor, and St Asaph, on the showing of Prince Llywelyn, that he, by command of King Henry, caused an oath of fealty to be taken by the great men of Wales to his eldest son David, to give counsel and help that the oaths so taken be inviolably observed.[326]

It would appear from this that Llywelyn did everything practical, after he succeeded in having his first marriage annulled by the pope, to make as sure as possible that his marriage to his second wife was as secure as he could make it for the benefit of his youngest son, Dafydd ap Llywelyn (d.1246). It has been argued that an oath of fealty was given to Dafydd in 1226 on

---

[321] Lloyd, J.E., *History of Wales* [2 vols., 1911] II, 657.

[322] *Comes vero Cestriae, Leulini familiaris et amicus...*, 'Annales Prioratus de Dunstaplia', *Annales Monastici*, ed. H.R. Luard [5 vols., 1864-9] III, 82.

[323] *Patrologiae cursus completus,... Latine*, Migne, JP., [1844-1864] CCXV, 534-7, No.CCXX.

[324] It is apparently possible for girls to give birth from the age of five, but this must have been highly unusual. https://en.wikipedia.org/wiki/List_of_youngest_birth_mothers retrieved 12 February 2018.

[325] 'Annales de Burton', *Annales Monastici*, ed H.R. Luard [5 vols., 1864-9], I, 305

[326] *Calendar of Entries in the Papal Registers relating to GB and Ireland - Papal Letters, 1198-1304*, ed. W. H. Bliss [1893], 109.

his reaching fourteen years of age[*327]. If this is the case, Dafydd was born in March 1212, ie. about a month before the pope's reply to Llywelyn's letter, when presumably the ceremony of fealty took place. A week later, on 6 May 1226, a papal bull was issued confirming Prince Llywelyn of North Wales in all the liberties that King John had allowed him[*328]. It was at this time that Dafydd's half brother, Gruffydd, was granted a large share of Powys. It is therefore possible that Dafydd's coming of age was recognised with Gruffydd being granted Powys as his patrimony. It should be remembered that Llywelyn's mother was Margery ferch Madog, the daughter of the last king of a united Powys, Madog ap Maredudd (d.1160). It is therefore quite possible that Llywelyn was intending to substitute Gruffydd for the heirs of Gwenwynwyn as prince of Powys. If this was his intention it failed within two years and Gruffydd was condemned to six years imprisonment by his father[*329]. It is interesting to note that Gruffydd was apparently imprisoned in Degannwy castle immediately before the Ceri campaign of 1228[*330]. As Ceri was an area that had been under Gruffydd's control it is possible that Gruffydd's removal from southern Powys by his father was another factor in having the king invade the commote, and that just maybe the king was acting on behalf of his vassal, Gruffydd ap Llywelyn, just as he would later claim to do in 1241. It is to be presumed that the six years of Gruffydd's imprisonment, which seems to have begun early in the year and certainly before 26 September 1228 when Abbot William of Chester died, was used by Dafydd to tighten his grip on Wales as the only legitimate heir to his father.

Another factor that has been generally overlooked in the affairs of North Wales is the involvement of the kings of Man. King Reginald obviously wanted a good life for his daughter and seemed happy with her marrying two princes who were vying for supremacy in North Wales. He certainly was intricately involved with Rhunallt's marriage to Rhodri as he invaded Mon - unsuccessfully as it turned out - on the strength of it. His dispute with Aberconwy abbey was quite likely due to Rhunallt's marriage portion having been granted to Aberconwy abbey by Gruffydd ap Cynan after he had overwhelmed Rhodri in Mon. The dower was probably made in June 1192 when Rhodri took Rhunallt as his wife. What Reginald thought of Llywelyn's marriage to his daughter after the prince had helped hound Rhodri to his death is unknown, although he obviously consented in it as she had been left under his care in Man when Rhodri had returned to Wales. Further, the bishop of Man being appointed to oversee the cause of the marriage in 1199 would suggest that he was still favourable to it at that date. The pope's later comments would also support that view. Finally in 1205, a series of royal documents concerning the king of Man throw more light upon the affair.

On 8 February 1205, when Prince Llywelyn had set aside Rhunallt, but had yet to marry Joan Plantagenet, King John, while at Woodstock, took Reginald under his personal protection.

King John undertakes the protection of King Reginald of Man.

[*327] Stephenson, D. & Jones, CO., 'The date and context of the birth of Dafydd II ap Llywelyn', *Flintshire Historical Society Journal* XXXIX [2012], 28.
[*328] *Littere Wallie, preserved in Liber A in the Public Record Office*, ed. J.G. Edwards [Cardiff, 1940], 175-6. In this case the bull would definitely appear to call King John of clear memory, *a clare memorie j[ohanne] rege*.
[*329] RBH, 232; Pen, 103: *Annales Cambriae. A Translation of Harleian 3859; PRO E.164/1; Cottonian Domitian, A 1; Exeter Cathedral Library MS. 3514 and MS Exchequer DB Neath, PRO E.164/1*, ed. Remfry, P.M., [Malvern, 2007], 128, adds that he was given part of Llyn on his release.
[*330] *Annales Cestrienses, a chronicle of the abbey of St. Werburgh, Chester*, ed. and trans. Christie, R.C., Record Society for Lancashire and Cheshire XIV [1887], 55.

Know that we have accepted our beloved kinsman, King Reginald of Man, into our safe-keeping, protection and legal maintenance and all his lands and his men. And we prohibit anyone, to inflict injury upon, or annoyance on the same, because if any should make forfeit against him, this fact will be reflected upon by us.[*331]

That this was happening exactly when Llywelyn was finalising his wedding plans with John's daughter is too apparent a coincidence to overlook. It would appear that the king was ensuring that Reginald would not be vexed or suffer undue loss caused by the annulment. On the same day, one year later at Salisbury, the king issued a safe conduct for his 'beloved and faithful relation, King Reginald of the Isles' in coming to see him over Easter[*332]. Even the phraseology of this demands comment. In what way was King John related to King Reginald IV of Man? Strictly speaking, he was his half second cousin once removed, via his great grandmother being an illegitimate daughter of King Henry I, King John's great grandfather. If this was not the family so obliquely being alluded to in John's letters, then it seems more likely the immediate link of King John and King Reginald with Prince Llywelyn via his first wife is the answer, though neither suggestion can be directly proved.

It is not possible to state what the two kings discussed, but John's attitude is interesting in that he accepted Reginald as a king, but only ever referred to Llywelyn as prince. It is entirely possible that Reginald's continuing dealings with King John may have been due to his interest in otherwise unknown lands in Mon, held as the dower of Rhunallt. Certainly it is possible to speculate that Reginald took Llywelyn's side in the Welsh war of 1210-11 and 1212-17. Two records support this assumption. On 16 March 1212, King Reginald of Man became a liege man of King John, after John seems to have acquired military control of Man during his Irish campaign of 1211. With Llywelyn having been brought soundly to heel in August 1211 this seems a natural move to confirm John's power in the Irish Sea. The notification of the agreement also shows John's sly sense of humour, considering his struggle with the pope at this time.

Greetings to all faithful Christians and King Reginald of the Isles, I present a charter for inspection.
Know that he has come to be the liege man of the lord King John of England against all mortals as long as I live, and the same thereupon tenders faithfulness and an oath of allegiance. And in this thing I therefore make this charter thereupon. Witnessed Bishop Peter of Winchester, Earl W of Salisbury, Earl Geoffrey Fitz Peter of Essex, Earl Saer of Winchester, William Briwere and Warin Fitz Gerold at Lambeth.[*333]

If this was the king's method of binding Llywelyn's ex-father-in-law to him, the process failed as Reginald subsequently joined in the Welsh revolt. This can be seen by a letter of the regent to the king of 16 January 1218. In this Earl William Marshall states:

[*331] *Foedera, Conventiones, Litterae etc*, ed. T. Rymer and R. Sanderson, 4th edn, by A. Clarke, F. Holbrooke, and J. Caley [4 vols. in 7 parts, 1816-69] I, 44.
[*332] *Foedera, Conventiones, Litterae etc*, ed. T. Rymer and R. Sanderson, 4th edn, by A. Clarke, F. Holbrooke, and J. Caley [4 vols. in 7 parts, 1816-69] I, 44.
[*333] *Foedera, Conventiones, Litterae etc*, ed. T. Rymer and R. Sanderson, 4th edn, by A. Clarke, F. Holbrooke, and J. Caley [4 vols. in 7 parts, 1816-69] I, 51. John gave the extravagant amount of ten marks (£6 13s 4d) in conducting Reginald back to his own country, *Monumenta de Insula Manniae*, tr & ed. Oliver, JR. [2 vols, Douglas, 1860-61] II, 30.

The king of the Isles has letters of conduct to come to the king to pay his homage to the same & for the excesses made by his men against the lord king, as much in England as in Ireland, by the men of his land, & in staying and in returning. And the conduct will endure up to 15 days after Easter in the second year of the reign of King Henry, witnessed by the earl at Winchester. And the justiciar of Ireland is ordered not to interfere, or permit molestation to occur, or any unjust injury or inconvenience to the said king, or his men, or the lands of the said king of the Isles.[*334]

Quite evidently the king of the Isles had been at war with the king of England before this point. The obvious time for his rebellion was in the period leading up to Magna Carta. Unfortunately, of Reginald's actions and the status of his daughter at this time there is no further mention. Although this is the last time that Reginald seems to have been recorded in possible dealings with Wales, his family involvement with Llywelyn appears one more time, much later in 1241. This will be considered in a later Chapter, Aberconwy Abbey During the Wars of Prince Dafydd, 1240 to 1246.

In conclusion, it can be seen that the artificially created 'evidence' that Llywelyn did not have a first wife coloured the opinions of the editors of the nineteenth century papal registers, thus reinforcing a recent invention at the cost of real history. Once more 'the infallible bards' who recorded history accurately down through the generations until they could be written down in the sixteenth century can be seen to have the historical strength of nothing more than wishful thinking. The damage done to medieval history by 'bards' and 'heralds' from the Renaissance onwards concocting family trees and 'history' may possibly never be undone. As if such invention were not bad enough, a quick search of the Internet shows that modern 'bards' have given the fictional (and male) Tangwystl a birth date of c.1168 in Denbighshire and a death date of 30 March 1226 in Caernarfonshire. Such dates are totally fantastic - even more so when you consider that there were no shires in North Wales other than Cheshire and Shropshire before 1284! Mind you, this does contradict that historically woeful source, Wikipedia, which gleefully speculates that Tangwystl had obviously died in childbirth as she is heard of no more[*335]. Certainly that is a useful way to dispose of the awkward fact of the lady's non existence in contemporary records.

[*334] *Foedera, Conventiones, Litterae etc*, ed. T. Rymer and R. Sanderson, 4th edn, by A. Clarke, F. Holbrooke, and J. Caley [4 vols. in 7 parts, 1816-69] I, 75.
[*335] From the dubiously entitled entry, Gruffydd ap Llywelyn Fawr, accessed 25 November 2015: https://en.wikipedia.org/wiki/Gruffydd_ap_Llywelyn_Fawr

Owain ap Dafydd, 1204 to 1212

The rise to power of Llywelyn ab Iorwerth in Gwynedd left many of his contemporaries displaced from rule in North Wales. After his release by Prince Llywelyn in 1198, Dafydd ab Owain lived on in the borders between England and Wales until his death. On 10 April 1200 at Worcester, King John informed all his justices and sheriffs that he had assumed the custody and protection of Emma, the wife of David ab Owain, as well as all their lands, things and possessions. Consequently, no one was to molest or injure these and if that should happen amends were to be made. Especially mentioned were the manors of Ellesmere and Hales which had been given to the couple by King Henry II[*336]. It is noteworthy that John puts Emma first in this notification and does not include Dafydd the ex king of North Wales. Similarly, at the end of 1201, it was Emma and not Dafydd who received the farm of the manor of Hales[*337]. However, as this was the exact same formula that had been used for years concerning the rent of Halesowen, 'and the wife of Dafydd ab Owain £17 6s 8d in Halles'[*338], perhaps too much should not be read into this; the clerks of the Exchequer were notoriously conservative about changing their yearly entries. Other than the Aberconwy Register, which places Dafydd's death at Aber in Gwynedd at the hands of Prince Llywelyn apparently on 1 January 1190, the other Bruts date his death to 1203:

> Dafydd ab Owain died in England, after being banished from Wales by Llywelyn ap Iorwerth (*Ac yna y bu varw Dauid ap Ywein yn Lloeger, wedy y dehol o Lywelyn ap Jorwerth o Gymry*).[*339]

> In that year Llywelyn ap Iorwerth expelled Dafydd ab Owain from Gwynedd; and he died in England.[*340]

The final comment on the matter by Thomas Jones about this sentence was that the supposedly original source of all three renditions of the Brut 'is wrong here: Dafydd had been exiled in 1197'[*341]. The conclusion would therefore seem to be that the compiler of the Brut had blundered and added this statement under the wrong year. As none of the Annales Cambriae mention Dafydd's fate it is possible that this is a very late addition to the Bruts and that therefore the death of Dafydd in 1203 might be misplaced by up to three years - as the Aberconwy Register would have it. Certainly the statement he died in England might need revision - Ellesmere at this time was in Powys and therefore was more likely to be seen as Wales than England in the thirteenth century. In short, other than fourteenth or fifteenth century works, there is no evidence as to the date of Dafydd's death. Further, the protection King John granted to Emma on 10 April 1200 could well imply that he was already dead. If this is the case, the Aberconwy Register compiler may have mixed up the accession of King Richard with that of King John. In which case the murder of Dafydd at Aber would have taken place on 1 January 1199/1200, within a year of King John, not King Richard, being

---

[*336] *Rotuli Chartarum in Turri Londonensi asservati [1204-22]*, ed. T.D. Hardy [1837], 44.

[*337] The wife of Dafydd ab Owain received £17 6s 8d in Hales, *PR 1 John*, 73; *Rotulus Cancellarii vel Antigraphum Magni Rotuli Pipae de tertio anno regni regis Johannis* [1833], 121.

[*338] *PR 1 Richard I*, 92.

[*339] RBH, 185-7.

[*340] Pen, 82.

[*341] ByS, 330. The dating of Dafydd's death is also suspect in *O Oes Gwrtheyrn* where any date between 1201 and 1203 could be indicated - see Appendix 3, p.298.

crowned. Certainly there seems nothing to gainsay Dafydd's death in January 1200 and much to recommend it.

Regardless of the time of Dafydd's death, it was about a decade later when his son, Owain ap Dafydd, gave Hales its final placename, Halesowen. This occurred when a monastery was founded there in his memory by his cousin, King John. Thus the man King Dafydd named after his more successful grandfather gave his name to a moderate sized town in the Midlands of England, while his grandfather became synonymous with his country, Owain Gwynedd.

At some point obviously after Dafydd's death, the king asked the justiciar on 2 August 1203 to find other provision for Owain ap Dafydd other than Ellesmere castle and its purtenances as the king wished them to be in his own hand[*342]. This may suggest that the idea for a marriage between Llywelyn and Joanna, John's daughter, was already afoot. Certainly on 8 April 1204, the king issued another set of safe conducts for 'Prince Llywelyn of North Wales and Madog ap Gruffydd and all the others who had letters of safe conduct from 9 April until the end of Easter'[*343]. Later still on 29 July 1204, a safe conduct was issued via William Marshall and Earl William of Salisbury, for Prince Llywelyn of North Wales and Madog ap Gruffydd and their men in coming to the king at Worcester between 15 August and 8 September[*344]. With Llywelyn's marriage difficulties over it was finally possible for him to marry Joan Plantagenet and receive with her as dower the manor of Ellesmere. As a consequence on 14 October 1204, the sheriff of Warwickshire was ordered to assign to Owain ap Dafydd land in Elmdon manor in exchange for his land in Ellesmere which had been kept in the king's hand[*345]. These transactions allowed the king to grant Llywelyn ab Iorwerth Ellesmere together with the hand of his daughter in April 1205. In this manner Llywelyn finally became the heir of King Dafydd ab Owain in all the lands he had held and claimed in North Wales. With these acts Owain ap Dafydd disappeared from the stage of Welsh politics for many years to come.

By 31 October 1212, King John had decided he had made a mistake in promoting Llywelyn to paramountcy in North Wales. Whether he had heard of Llywelyn's claim that he would make:

> neither truce nor peace, nor even parley, with the English, but that, by God's grace, I and all the princes of Wales unanimously leagued together have manfully resisted our and your enemies, and by God's grace we have recovered by force of arms from the yoke of their tyranny a large part of the land and the strongly defended castles which they, by fraud and deceit, had occupied, and having recovered them, we hold them strongly in the might of the Lord.[*346]

Llywelyn concluded by stating that he and all the other princes of Wales eagerly desired and asked that King Philip of France would make no peace or truce with the English except in conjunction with his Welsh allies, since Philip can be sure that the Welsh princes will not 'for any terms or price' make any pact with the English unless they knew in advance that Philip would approve.

[*342] *Rotuli de Liberate ac de Misis et Praestitis regnante Johanne*, ed. T.D. Hardy [1844], 56.
[*343] *Rotuli Litterarum Patentium in Turri Londinensi asservati [1201-16]* ed. T.D. Hardy [1835], 40.
[*344] *Rotuli Litterarum Patentium in Turri Londinensi asservati [1201-16]* ed. T.D. Hardy [1835], 44.
[*345] *Rotuli Litterarum Clausarum in Turri Londinensi asservati [1204-27]*, ed, T.D. Hardy [2 vols., 1833-44] I, 12a.
[*346] Treharne, R.F. 'The Franco-Welsh Treaty of Alliance in 1212', *Bulletin of the Board of Celtic Studies*, XVIII, 60-75

If King John had heard of these terms, or even if he was vaguely aware of what his enemies were plotting, this would have encouraged him greatly in attempting to curb Llywelyn's power by giving his cousins, Owain ap Dafydd and Gruffydd ap Rhodri, the cantref of Rhos except for Degannwy castle within the commote of Creuddyn in which it stood[*347]. Simultaneously, John granted Rhufoniog and Dyffryn Clwyd to the cousins for a rent of twelve warhorses, a pack of hounds, ten greyhounds as well as all the hawks, tame falcons and sparrowhawks they could find and deliver at Shrewsbury every midsummer's day. The charter also tells us something of the heirs of both men. Owain was already married and had a son, who he had to give as a hostage to the king. Gruffydd was apparently unmarried and so had to supply hostages from the children of his uncles, Goronwy, Seisyll, Bleddyn and Meurig. This is peculiar as Gruffydd has no known uncles with such names, although he did apparently have two elder brothers, Thomas (bef.1170-1243+) and Einion (bef.1190-1209+). Presumably they are not mentioned in the charter as they were still loyal to Llywelyn. It would seem likely Thomas and Einion were the sons of an otherwise unknown first wife of Rhodri who must have died before 1188 by which time Giraldus states that Rhodri had recently married Agnes the daughter of Rhys ap Gruffydd of Deheubarth (d.1197). Gruffydd ap Rhodri himself would possibly be a son of Agnes as Rhodri and Rhunallt of Man apparently had no children - otherwise they would have been mentioned in the pope's three letters concerning their marriage and Llywelyn ab Iorwerth.

Finally, in the king's charter, the cousins were given the right to take possession of Arfon, Arllechwedd and Llyn for similar payments. Interestingly, this grant obviously did not include Meirionydd. Perhaps the king was reserving this district for Maredudd ap Cynan (d.1212) and his heirs, Llywelyn Fawr and Llywelyn Vychan[*348]. The grant was obviously made in reply to Llywelyn retaking the Perfeddwlad from royal forces during the summer, although once again three castles had continued to hold out, the rest falling with the king sending no one to their aid[*349]. These three castles were likely Degannwy, Rhuddlan and Denbigh or Basingwerk[*350]. Early the next year Degannwy and Rhuddlan castles fell to Llywelyn. As Owain ap Dafydd is never heard of again, it is likely that he perished with his fledgeling principality[*351].

Over a year after Owain's disappearance from the records, King John, on 27 October 1214, instructed Bishop Peter of Winchester 'to build there [in the manor of Hales] a house of religion of whatever Order he so chooses'[*352]. Thus it came about that Halesowen abbey was probably founded in memory of John's cousin, Owain ap Dafydd, who had apparently died

---

[*347] *Rotuli Chartarum in Turri Londonensi asservati [1204-22]*, ed. T.D. Hardy [1837], 188b.

[*348] Llywelyn ap Maredudd, presumably the elder brother known as Llywelyn Fawr, accompanied Llywelyn ab Iorwerth in his great campaign into Deheubarth in December 1215, Pen, 93. Possibly he was also holding Meirionydd of Llywelyn at this time.

[*349] *Annales Cambriae. A Translation of Harleian 3859; PRO E.164/1; Cottonian Domitian, A 1; Exeter Cathedral Library MS. 3514 and MS Exchequer DB Neath, PRO E.164/1*, ed. Remfry, P.M., [Malvern, 2007], 114.

[*350] RBH, 194-5. Mathrafal castle had been destroyed and then abandoned by the king himself to rebel forces on 2 August 1212, 'Itinerary of King John', ed T.Duffus Hardy, printed in, Anderson, J.C., *Shropshire: Its Early History and Antiquities* [London, 1864]. Therefore it is unlikely that Mathrafal was one of the three castles. The next year the three castles were certainly recorded as Degannwy, Rhuddlan and Basingwerk, *Annales Cambriae. A Translation of Harleian 3859; PRO E.164/1; Cottonian Domitian, A 1; Exeter Cathedral Library MS. 3514 and MS Exchequer DB Neath, PRO E.164/1*, ed. Remfry, P.M., [Malvern, 2007], 115. The castles of Oswestry, Chirk, Kinnersley and Carreghofa were still garrisoned for the Crown in Powys during August, *Rotuli Litterarum Clausarum in Turri Londinensi asservati [1204-27]*, ed, T.D. Hardy [2 vols., 1833-44] I, 132.

[*351] Gruffydd ap Rhodri was still fighting for his king on 14 August 1214, *Rotuli Litterarum Clausarum in Turri Londinensi asservati [1204-27]*, ed, T.D. Hardy [2 vols., 1833-44] I, 210. He later went over to Prince Llywelyn's cause and served him all his days by at least witnessing several of his charters. The lack of further mention of Owain indicates that he died in 1212 or the next year.

[*352] *Rotuli Litterarum Clausarum in Turri Londinensi asservati [1204-27]*, ed, T.D. Hardy [2 vols., 1833-44] I, 174b; *Monasticon Anglicanum*, ed. W. Dugdale, Revised edition by J. Caley, H. Ellis, and B. Bandinel [6 vols., 1817-30] VII, 927. The grant was confirmed by the king on 8 August 1215, *Rotuli Chartarum in Turri Londonensi asservati [1204-22]*, ed. T.D. Hardy [1837], 217.

defending his principality and King John's kingdom during 1212/3. The war he died in had come to an end by 3 June 1213 when the king arranged a truce with the Welsh, if they so wished it[353]. They obviously did and the truce was repeatedly prolonged from then on until the Magna Carta war. Of Owain and his unnamed son and wife nothing further is currently known.

Aberconwy Abbey During the Reign of King John, 1202 to 1216

As has been examined in an earlier chapter, it is claimed in the Aberconwy Register that King John granted protection to their abbey on 1 April 1202, so that 'they may have a firm peace etc. just as the charter of my father, King Henry, testifies'[354]. One implication from the granting of this charter is that the war then being waged by Llywelyn ab Iorwerth and Hywel ap Gruffydd ap Cynan against Maredudd ap Cynan was disrupting the lands of Aberconwy abbey. This would certainly seem likely as some of their lands may already have lain within Eifionydd, which fell to the aggressors in 1201. The fighting did not stop in 1201 and it is possible that the abbey feared that Maredudd would return, although all chance of this faded with Maredudd's defeat and exile from Meirionydd at the start of 1202. It is therefore possible that the abbey's lands in the west were severely disrupted at this time, viz Nant Call, Cwm, Nanhwynain and Ffriwlwyd. It is unfortunate that there is no record of who granted these lands and when, as all, some or none of them may have been Aberconwy properties in 1202 (See Appendix 8, p.336, for the dates these lands are attested as having belonged to the abbey). Certainly by September 1202, Aberconwy had been accused of being lax with holding masses, although they were accused of this with the abbots of Caerleon and Valle Crucis[355]. As these latter two were well away from war zones it is to be presumed that the cause of the malaise was other than warfare. At the same time it was noted that Roland, who was once the subprior of Aberconwy, was now considered a fugitive of the order, but that he was allowed to write to the archbishop of Canterbury[356]. Six months later, on 29 May 1203, the priors of Wenlock and Enlli in the dioceses of Hereford and Bangor were ordered to examine witnesses and send the written depositions to the pope, commanding the parties in the cause between the bishop of Bangor and Roland formerly subprior of Aberconwy, to appear before the pope. However, if either were unable to do so, then they were to proceed in the case according to the papal mandate[357]. It is to be presumed that no odium fell upon Aberconwy due to the actions of one of its former brethren.

It was apparently around this time that a prince of North Wales, in keeping with current religious feeling, attempted to put down older styles of religion and help the new. To this end he intended to dissolve Beddgelert monastery and turn that establishment over to Aberconwy abbey which was then to annex their lands. Unfortunately, the only source for this affair is Giraldus Cambrensis and, as has been noted, he was not above twisting reality to suit his own prejudices. As ever, it is worth quoting the cleric in full.

> There was in Gwynedd, which the vulgar call North Wales, a house of religious clerks under the mountains of Eyri ,which the foreigners called Snowdon, this is a mountain

---

[353] *Rotuli Litterarum Patentium in Turri Londinensi asservati [1201-16]* ed. T.D. Hardy [1835], 100, 103, 120b.

[354] Above p.10. The copy is printed below p.255 and in the *Register and Chronicle of Aberconway from the Harleian MS. 3725*, ed Ellis, H., *Camden Miscellany* [1847], 10.

[355] Statuta I, 281/35.

[356] Statuta I, 281/34.

[357] *Calendar of Entries in the Papal Registers relating to GB and Ireland - Papal Letters, 1198-1304*, ed. W. H. Bliss [1893], 14.

of snow; not far off from that place said to have been the court of Merlin Ambrosius, situated about almost on the shore of the Irish sea[*358]. However there were there clerics devoted to the service of God, the congregation in characteristic being lively and saintly, and not having their own apostolic custom, none indeed were specifically assigned to the order of monk or canon, but just as bachelors not God worshippers, that is honouring God; called equally to abstinence and given to fasting, and especially to charitable works and conspicuous for their hospitality, how excellently they followed the early authorities from before monastic religion became ordered...

However, it was at the same time and in our days that a rich house of the Cistercian order, beside the River Conwy was founded [Aberconwy, 1186], by pastures and fields, herds of cattle and granges stuffed full of abundant wheat, and remembering a house in southern Wales, adulterously said in the vernacular South Wales, and situated in the province of Dyfed, certainly one the mother of the other, as it is said, through [the boundaries of] almost the whole of Wales, the daughter or granddaughters appeared[*359]. But because it appeared from their fat unfairness and insatiableness, greed is always required to be detested, although from the said poor house through the lands [rightly amongst Wales] at remote intervals, yet very much neighbouring the same, because: "The excessive power of Mantua made poor the vicinity of Cremona"; the [abbey] pursued the whole [house] itself by pressuring the work of every sort and employing worry, and the strength of the prince of the province himself [they gained] by bribes and great gifts for bias, to induce him into agreement, to the point where the said poor house might be wholly demolished, or those clerks transformed into being their ordinary monks, and that the house and church should be destroyed and converted into a grange of theirs, they would not delay violently ruining it; [so] the said clerks sent a letter to the Roman court and they obtained letters of protection from the lord pope by great labours and costs..., finally with difficulty from the said persecutions and tyrannical oppressions they were able to defend themselves.[*360]

Whatever the truth of the matter - for no papal letters have yet been found about the affair despite the cleric's claims that they were sent - Giraldus was sure that Aberconwy was a rich and powerful Cistercian house and that it was desirous of new lands at the expense of the old order. Such is hardly impossible. Other shady deeds were occurring at Aberconwy in 1205, when a lay brother (*conversum*) was accused of selling produce irregularly[*361]. This is the first mention of Aberconwy being a wool producer. It should also be noted that Giraldus considers that Aberconwy 'beside the River Conwy was founded'. He mentions no early site move from Rhedynog Felen.

By 1209 Aberconwy abbey had developed greatly from its founding. In that year an accord was made between the Cistercian abbeys of Dore and Strata Florida in which the abbot

---

[*358] Before the nineteenth century the sea used to flow to within a few miles of Beddgelert, Remfry, PM., *Harlech Castle and it True Origins* [Ceidio, 2013], 6-9. The llys of Merlin Ambrosius is probably Castell Dinas Emrys.

[*359] The Cistercian abbey by the Afon Conwy is obviously Aberconwy and its grandmother in Dyfed is Whitland. This story was probably written in the 1210s after Giraldus' retirement from Wales to Lincoln. His reluctance to name the prince involved in the attempt to downgrade Beddgelert may suggest that Llywelyn ab Iorwerth was the man meant. Certainly the story appears to see Aberconwy well established. If this is the case the story must date to after March 1200 when Llywelyn acquired Gwynedd. If before that date then either Gruffydd ap Cynan or, if before April 1191, Rhodri ab Owain must be the prince referred to.

[*360] Giraldus Cambrensis, *Opera*, eds. J.S. Brewer, J.F. Dimock and G.F. Warner [8 vols., 1861-91] IV, 167-8.

[*361] Statuta I, 310/14.

and convent of Strata Florida withdrew their claims in Cantref Selyf and accepted that Dore held the land there and recognised their charters to that effect. The agreement was brought about by arbitrators, viz the abbots of Neath, Tintern, Margam, Whitland (*Alba Domus*) and Aberconwy (*Aberconu*) as well by 'other lieges, especially Llywelyn'[*362]. This was presumably Llywelyn ab Iorwerth, who had effectively taken over the patronage from the sons of Gruffydd ap Rhys the previous year[*363]. Presumably he had intervened in Brycheiniog as their protector in the district as some of the heirs of their grandfather, William Braose (d.1211)[*364]. Alternately, this may show the abbot of Aberconwy working hand in hand with his patron. Certainly later authorities thought that Llywelyn ab Iorwerth was the greatest patron of Aberconwy abbey.

With Llywelyn pushing his power far into central Wales during the autumn of 1208 he seems to have believed that he could ignore the royal power of his father-in-law with immunity. In the summer of 1209 Llywelyn campaigned with King John in Scotland, but in 1210 disaster faced the prince and his lands were repeatedly invaded. Firstly, Justiciar Geoffrey Fitz Peter, Earl Ranulf of Chester and Bishop Peter of Winchester marched a great army into Wales and rebuilt Degannwy and Holywell castles[*365].

> the earl of Chester with much arms and many men prepared to march against North Wales and mark out a castle at Degannwy.[*366]

According to an apparently contemporary Aberconwy source (printed in Appendix 3, p.298), during 1210:

> The following year King John proceeded to Ireland and Earl Ralph of Chester came to the castle of Degannwy to meet (or possibly 'in the place of') King John and with his army took the castle of Degannwy and restored the same with the wood of Creuddyn granary.[*367]

This, and the fall of Llandovery castle, all seem to have happened before 8 September 1210. The next year, after two royal campaigns, Prince Llywelyn was brought to the peace table by 15 August 1211, after King John had attacked Bangor, fifteen miles beyond Aberconwy[*368]. Again *O Oes Gwrtheyrn*, apparently written at Aberconwy, has:

> The following year King John, with a huge army who were collected from France, England and Scotland, came to Aber and from thence he sent his Brabantines to burn Bangor. And there was captured St Robert the bishop and escorted in the manner of a prisoner to Aber, but the king relaxed the imprisonment of the bishop. And there Llywelyn was restored to the king's goodwill and his son Gruffydd with 24 chieftains the same gave as hostages and the king returned to England.

[*362] *A Descriptive Catalogue of Ancient Deeds* [London, 1890] I, 282, referencing: TNA. E.326/727.
[*363] The sons of Gruffydd were first cousins once removed to Llywelyn through their joint descent from Madog ap Maredudd of Powys (d.1160)
[*364] The story of the sons of Gruffydd and Braose is told in Remfry, PM, *Medieval Battles: Wales, 1055 to 1216: Volume 2, part 1* [2017], 253.
[*365] 'Annales Prioratus de Dunstaplia', *Annales Monastici*, ed. H.R. Luard [5 vols., 1864-9] III, 32; Pen, 84.
[*366] *Annales Cambriae. A Translation of Harleian 3859; PRO E.164/1; Cottonian Domitian, A 1; Exeter Cathedral Library MS. 3514 and MS Exchequer DB Neath, PRO E.164/1*, ed. Remfry, P.M., [Malvern, 2007] (D, Hopton Commission?), 112.
[*367] My thanks to Rich Price for his comments on the Latin.
[*368] Lloyd, J.E., *History of Wales* [2 vols., 1911], II, 636.

No other source mentions that King John stayed at Aber, presumably at Llywelyn's llys there, but they all agree that the prince bought peace by handing over some thirty hostages[369]. Despite the threat to the hostages, this did not stop Llywelyn's disloyalty to his father-in-law and he revolted again in 1212 - an act that callously betrayed Gruffydd ap Llywelyn to King John's mercy - and it should be remembered that Gruffydd was no immediate blood relative to John. Although a truce was made between prince and his king in May 1213, it was not until Magna Carta on 15 June 1215 that Llywelyn received back his muniments and his apparently ill-regarded son. The relevant terms in the charter - clauses 56 to 58 - are:

> If we have disseised or removed Welshmen from their lands or liberties or other things, without a legal judgement of their peers in England or in Wales, they shall be immediately restored to them; and if a dispute should arise over this, then let it be decided in the Marches by the judgement of their peers; for English tenements following English law, for Welsh tenements following Welsh law, for Marcher tenements following Marcher law. The same shall be done by Welshmen for us and ours.
>
> Also of all those things which any Welshman has been disseised of or had removed without the lawful judgement of his peers through King Henry our father or King Richard our brother, and which we have in our hand, or which are held by others to whom we are bound to warrant them, we shall have respite up to the usual term for crusaders; excepting those things of which a plea has been raised or an inquest made by our writ before we took the Cross; however as soon as we return, or if we desist from our pilgrimage, immediately we will give full justice following the laws of the Welsh and the aforesaid parts.

And finally what may have been the most important chapter:

> We will return the son of Llywelyn immediately and all the hostages of Wales as well as the charters that were delivered to us as a security for the peace.

The son of Llywelyn was obviously Gruffydd who was not mentioned in the hostages handed over the previous year, and who was therefore still held by the king from 1211. The return of Gruffydd was probably allowed as he had become less valuable as a hostage following the birth of Prince Dafydd, probably in the March of 1212 at Coleshill castle. The mention of the return of Llywelyn's charters is also significant and this poses the question as to what these were. Were they all Llywelyn's charters, including any he might have made to Basingwerk, Cymer and Aberconwy abbeys and did they include Llywelyn's charter to King John in August 1211? Unfortunately we shall probably never know.

Magna Carta itself was quashed by the pope within a short while of it being sealed. Therefore it seems likely that legally the treaty of 1211 between John and Llywelyn was still in existence, apart from the fact that Llywelyn had already invalidated it by retaking the lost territories of the Perfeddwlad including its castles. He had also had a son by his lawful wife, which for the time being invalidated the clause of all Gwynedd reverting to the English

---

[369] *Margan*, 31; *Winchester*, 81; 'Annales Prioratus de Wigornia', *Annales Monastici*, ed. H.R. Luard [5 vols., 1864-9] IV, 399; *Matthaei Parisiensis, monachi Sancti Albani, Chronica Majora*, ed. H.R. Luard [7 vols., 1872-83] II, 531. For Llywelyn's llys at Aber Garth Celyn see Remfry, PM, *A Brief Report on Pen y Bryn and Aber, Gwynedd* [Ceidio, 2012].

Crown on the death of Llywelyn, unless he had a male heir by Princess Joan. The full treaty of 12 August 1211 ran:

Greetings to all in the faith of Christ, I, Prince Llywelyn of North Wales, present a charter for inspection.

Know that for having the favour and benevolence of [my] lord [King] John [of England] I give up and forever quitclaim the castle of Degannwy with Rhos and all its appurtenances and Rhufoniog with Denbigh and Ystrad and all its appurtenances and Dyffryn Clwyd with Ruthin and all its appurtenances. While concerning Edeirnion with its appurtenances I accept nothing for myself except to humbly beseech for Owain Brogyntyn my [uncle] because he has never held that land from me or any ancestor of mine but from the lord king. Also I concede that Hywel ap Gruffydd may have seisin of his land thus in so far as afterwards he will stand by his right in my court. And if he is unwilling to come into my court or in the same to stand by his right, the lord king himself will distrain him to do so. Also I concede that the lord king may do his will concerning Rhuddlan and Mold with Englefield and all their appurtenances saving my right and [... or ...] to ask for established title through justice in the same claim; in so far as I shall give up establishing a title into the hand of the lord king until it pleases the same. However the men of the land which I gave up to the lord king, if they wish to come to the lord king and to hold their lands from him, they may give to the same good security that they will serve the same faithfully and they will deliver to the same his services well and they will not search for anything recently because they should not receive [anything] from elsewhere than from the lord king. In addition I shall allow my lord king to have the allegiances of all my men of whom he wishes, and release to the same my son Gruffydd to keep always and I shall do his will henceforth so that if from the daughter of the lord king, my wife, I do not have an heir, I concede to the lord my king himself, as if he were my heir, all my lands as much as those which I retain as those others and I give up, besides those lands it pleased the same to give to my same son and mine. In addition I give to the same lord my king for his expenses 10,000 cows and forty destriers and sixty hunters, so that the men of the lands which I have given up to the lord king, as much those who have gone to the lord king as from his lands by the same they may hold, any that which remain with me, to help me they will do reasonably to pay back the aforesaid money. Furthermore I shall release to the same hostages from my land who and how many and of which you may wish to have for my faithful service, and for the aforesaid agreement needing to be held and these in good faith and without evil trick needing to be held I have sworn while touching relics and thence this charter of mine I have had made for the same lord, my king. Truly the lord bishop of Norwich, Earl William of Salisbury, Earl William Marshall, Earl William Warenne and Peter Fitz Herbert undertake that the lord king will remit all malevolence and anger from me through the aforesaid agreement which he had towards me up to Friday next after the feast of Laurence the Martyr 13 John. And for the greater safety of this matter the Lord Bishop John of Norwich, Earl William Salisbury, Earl William Marshall, Earl William

Warenne and Peter Fitz Herbert to my petition apply their seals with my seal on this charter.[*370]

This agreement brings up many matters not previously studied. Firstly, Llywelyn only handed back Rhos, Rhufoniog and Dyffryn Clwyd to the king and not the entire Perfeddwlad. Much later in the charter the remaining cantref of Tegeingl or Englefield was mentioned and here Llywelyn treated the land totally differently. He does not give and quitclaim the land, but merely stated that the king may do with the land, which included Rhuddlan and Mold, as he thought fit and that Llywelyn would waive his rights there for as long as the king wanted. The implication from this is that Llywelyn's power in Tegeingl was based upon a different basis to that of the other three cantrefs. The answer to this conundrum would seem to lie in the history of Englefield as a Mercian province and then a fief of the earldom of Chester. It therefore seems quite possible that Llywelyn had done a deal of some description with Earl Ranulf of Chester whereby Llywelyn held the cantref from the earldom of Chester, rather than as the heir of Dafydd ab Owain. This is pure supposition as no such treaty is known to survive. Yet it would make good sense of Llywelyn and Ranulf's apparent relationship if the prince did nominally hold Tegeingl of the earl. Again, this would have bound them closer together as 'family'. It also makes it possible that Princess Joan stayed at Coleshill castle to give birth over Easter 1212 while Prince Llywelyn went on to Cambridge[*371]. Whether the castle was then held by King John, Earl Ranulf or still by Llywelyn is really academic. Certainly no source mentions anyone Welsh at Cambridge but Llywelyn, and the only source that mentions the birth of Dafydd and possibly other of Llywelyn's children at Coleshill, only proves that Joan was there. Indeed there is no reason to believe, or not to believe, that Llywelyn was present at the birth of any of his children[*372].

The next interesting point concerns Hywel ap Gruffydd. Undoubtedly this is the son and heir of Gruffydd ap Cynan (d.1200). Although he has been noted elsewhere as always following Llywelyn's lead, here is direct evidence that the two were at odds concerning Hywel's inheritance in 1211. As chronicled above, Gruffydd held Arfon, Arllechwedd, Mon and possibly Llyn on his death in 1200 when Llywelyn took them over. His brother, Maredudd ap Cynan at that time held Meirionydd, Ardudwy, Eifionydd and, from 1200 at least, Llyn. There is now no evidence as to what land Hywel wished to hold in 1211, but whatever it was his early death in 1216, as described below, put the matter to rest and he was surely living under Llywelyn's lordship at that time.

The final point of interest is the terms of Llywelyn's submission. He allowed John the allegiance of any of his men that the king wanted and also he turned his son Gruffydd over to the king permanently - obviously as a pledge for his good behaviour in doing the king's will in all things from that time onwards. The mention of Gruffydd suggests without much doubt that the alleged son of Llywelyn, Tegwared of Mon, is a creation of the bards, as surely he would have been just as great a threat to King John as Gruffydd was if he were to inherit any

---

[*370] The original text is printed with a precis in Acts, 386-8, quoting Smith, J.B., 'Magna Carta and the Charters of the Welsh Princes', *English Historical Review* IC [1984], 361-2. The treaty is clearly of 12 August - the Friday after 11 August - and not 11 August - the feast of St Lawrence - as is usually stated.

[*371] *Memorials of St Edmund's Abbey*, ed. Arnold, T., [3 vols, 1890-92] II, 21, notes that the Welsh revolted under Llywelyn, who had recently celebrated Easter with the king at Cambridge.

[*372] The issue of when and where Dafydd was born is examined in Stephenson, D. & Jones, CO., 'The date and context of the birth of Dafydd II ap Llywelyn', *Flintshire Historical Society Journal* XXXIX [2012], 21-32. Although the birth of Dafydd at Coleshill is proved, the actual date is still uncertain, although the case made for 1212 is strong.

lands in Wales. Also Tegwared's lack of mention in contemporary records in relation to his alleged father and brother again condemn the bards' statements of his genealogy.

As Aberconwy abbey was so patently bound up with Prince Llywelyn's lands it is no surprise to find that King John fined them heavily. Thus in the pipe roll for Michaelmas 1211 comes the statement at the end of the Worcestershire account under the heading 'Concerning Fines by the Welsh', that the abbot of Aberconwy (*Aberkunwen*) owed the county 600 marks (£400) for having the king's goodwill as well as for having the king's letters patent allowing them to beg back this money throughout the king's lands. Regardless of this, before Michaelmas, the abbot paid 400 marks (£266 13s 4d) in two installments of 200 marks (£133 6s 8d)[373]. Obviously either the monastery was rich by this date or had a good source of credit.

Other Welsh abbeys were also fined at this time. Basingwerk was fined £100 for having 'the king's goodwill and their lands returned which were taken into the king's hands due on occasion for the malevolence the king felt for them'. They immediately paid 100 marks (£66 13s 4d) and later, after a complex set of transactions, the other fifty marks (£33 6s 8d)[374]. In the south, Strata Florida (*Stratflur*), a notorious stronghold of the king's enemies, was fined a colossal 1,200 marks (£800) to pay for being restored to its boundaries as envisaged by its charter. Of this they managed to pay 500 marks (£333 6s 8d) in two installments and remained owing 700 marks (£466 13s 4d) for many years to come[375]. The previous year the abbot of Margam (*Morgan*) had been charged £200 'for having his charters'[376]. From this it can be seen that several of the Welsh houses were hard hit at this time by the Crown and that Aberconwy had greatly annoyed its king by supporting its prince against him.

After spending Easter (25 March) 1212 with King John, Prince Llywelyn soon afterwards allied with many other Welsh princes and retook the Perfeddwlad apart from two or three castles, although these fell the next year[377]. Therefore by 1214, the prince had expelled all the royalist garrisons from North Wales as well as defeated the attempt by King John to install his relatives, Owain ap Dafydd and Gruffydd ap Rhodri, in North Wales. This fighting seems to have led to an unusual event, a dispute between the abbot of Aberconwy and the abbot of Poulton in Cheshire. Poulton had been set up as a Cistercian house in the mid 1140s in what was then central Cheshire, yet by Tudor times this area was made the actual border with Wales. About 1214 the earl of Chester is alleged to have moved the abbey eastwards to a new site at Dieulacres in Staffordshire due to Welsh pressure against the former site. According to the monks themselves:

---

[373] *PR 13 John*, 253.
[374] *PR 13 John*, 93.
[375] *reddendas ad terminos in carta, PR 13 John*, 235; *PR 2 Henry III*, 91. On 1 July 1221 the fine was placed in respite for the time being, Fine Rolls, No.220. The fine was still owing in 1230, *PR 14 Hen III*, 217. It was only in 1248 that the matter was settled with the abbot agreeing to pay off the debt in yearly installments, *CPR 1247-51*, 48, 338-9. The last of the debt was paid in 1253 by which time they had been pardoned 440 marks (£293 13s 4d) of it, *CCR 1251-53*, 398.
[376] *PR 12 John*, 110.
[377] The three castles were recorded as Degannwy, Rhuddlan and Basingwerk, *Annales Cambriae. A Translation of Harleian 3859; PRO E.164/1; Cottonian Domitian, A 1; Exeter Cathedral Library MS. 3514 and MS Exchequer DB Neath, PRO E.164/1*, ed. Remfry, P.M., [Malvern, 2007], 115, although the Bruts only mention the first two.

The monastery of Poulton was transferred to Dieulacres on 1 May 1214 by Earl Ranulf of Chester, on account of the great encroachment by the Welsh, by whom much damage was endured by them.[*378]

During 1212 and 1213 much fighting had gone on in the Perfeddwlad as control of this area was retaken by Llywelyn before he was offered and accepted a truce with King John as had been arranged by the pope and his legate by 3 June 1213[*379]. The fighting before this must have disrupted the Aberconwy granges in that district, presuming of course that they had already been granted to the abbey. It was also possible that the disturbances resulted in one or more of these granges being wrested from the control of Poulton and given to Aberconwy. Possibly this reversed recent actions when the earl of Chester may have enriched Poulton at the expense of Aberconwy. It is unlikely that the truth of the matter will ever be known, but by September 1214 the affair was laid before the general chapter in France as a dispute between the abbots of Aberconwy and Poulton[*380]. Unfortunately no details of the case were preserved other than the fact that the abbots of Strata Marcella and Basingwerk were ordered to investigate and bring the dispute to a conclusion. This they must have done as no more is heard of it. That the dispute was described as the abbot of Aberconwy bringing a complaint against the abbot of Poulton may well suggest that they were reclaiming lands taken from them by Earl Ranulf in 1210 or 1211.

It is possible that the examination of the dispute did not go all Aberconwy's way, for the next year the abbot of Aberconwy complained against the abbot of Basingwerk concerning five books and other things[*381]. Possibly this consisted of loot taken from the pro Llywelyn house of Aberconwy and given to the more royalist house of Basingwerk, or even documentary evidence for Aberconwy's holdings. Whatever the case, the Cheshire abbots of Combermere and Stanlaw were ordered to look into it and do justice. For some reason the abbot of Dieulacres was made responsible for delivering the summons - a choice that might have boded ill for Aberconwy considering their previous problems. The next year the general chapter gave their assent for the abbot of Aberconwy not making the trip to France due to illness, though the proviso was added that he should come next year[*382]. If the abbot at this time was still the Abraham mentioned around the turn of the century it is possible that he had been abbot since the foundation of the house in 1186 - in which case he would have been abbot for thirty years in 1216. Alternatively, if this man is the same as Archdeacon Abraham ap Gruffydd, then he could not have been abbot of Aberconwy before 1195. Perhaps as Abraham is such a rare name the latter case is more likely.

It was also this year, 1216, that saw another royal burial in Aberconwy abbey when Hywel ap Gruffydd ap Cynan was laid to rest:

an excellent young man, and beloved by all.[*383]

[*378] ...maxime propter intrusionem Wallensium, per quos multa damna perpessi sunt. Monasticon Anglicanum, ed. W. Dugdale, Revised edition by J. Caley, H. Ellis, and B. Bandinel [6 vols., 1817-30] V, 627a.
[*379] Rotuli Litterarum Patentium in Turri Londinensi asservati [1201-16] ed. T.D. Hardy [1835] I, 100, 103. This ended the fighting in Wales until Llywelyn again revolted in May 1215 and seized Shrewsbury, Lloyd, J.E., History of Wales [2 vols., 1911] II, 643.
[*380] Statuta I, 425/39.
[*381] Statuta I, 446/56.
[*382] Statuta I, 454/21.
[*383] Pen, 93. The same notice appears in the Chronica Wallia [D], although the Strata Florida annals [B] just mention his death before that of Gwenwynwyn, which seems to have happened soon after 27 June 1216. The St David's annals [C] did not even record this Venedotian's death, Annales Cambriae. A Translation of Harleian 3859; PRO E.164/1; Cottonian Domitian, A 1; Exeter Cathedral Library MS. 3514

(continued...)

Just one fourteenth century source states that this occurred after 28 October 1216, the day that the young Henry son of John had been ordained king[*384]. It is unfortunate that such dates in these chronicles cannot be taken as exact if they are uncorroborated as the chronicles can so often be seen to be unchronological in their composition. With the end of the reign of King John Aberconwy abbey moved into more peaceful times.

Aberconwy During the Latter Part of the Reign of Llywelyn ab Iorwerth, 1217 to 1240
In September 1217, it was recorded at the Cistercian general chapter that the abbot of Strata Florida was to be threatened with deposition at the request of the cardinal legate in England, while various priors had been removed from office and cast out to other houses[*385]. Presumably this was for their support of Louis as king of England. It is noticeable that the abbots of North Wales, viz. Cymer, Aberconwy, Basingwerk and Strata Marcella were not included amongst these rebels. This is even more surprising when it is realised that Llywelyn ab Iorwerth did not make his peace with Henry III's government until the next year. Perhaps therefore, the abbot of Strata Florida had been particularly outspoken in his comments and actions. Certainly the level of his fine demanded by King John in 1211 might suggest this.

Seven years later on 10 April 1225, Pope Honorious III (1216-27) made a rather unusual grant. This was to allow Abraham, a monk of Aberconwy, the right to be admitted to ecclesiastical dignities although he was illegitimate[*386]. As a consequence of this boon he was consecrated the new bishop of St Asaph by Stephen Langton at Westminster on 29 June the same year[*387]. Abraham is quite an unusual name at this time. Consequently, it is possible that this man is one and the same as the Abraham who was the abbot of Aberconwy mentioned before 1202. If he is the same man then it could be that he was the founding father of Aberconwy and that he had been in charge of the abbey for some 39 years. An alternative scenario is that he may have been the same as the Archdeacon Abraham ap Gruffydd mentioned in 1195. Whatever the case, Bishop Abraham died in January 1233[*388]. Earlier, on 15 October 1221, a Father Abraham of Aberconwy (*Aberthon'*) was with Prince Llywelyn at Caernarfon when he witnessed a charter to Ynys Llannog[*389]. The likelihood of two men at Aberconwy being named Abraham at this period seems remote. Hence it would seem possible that Abraham was firstly the archdeacon of Bangor and then became the second abbot of Aberconwy. He subsequently remained there as abbot until transferred and promoted to St Asaph in 1225. If he was the same man as the archdeacon he would have been at least 65 years old by the time of his death. If there were at least two men called Abraham then the abbot and later bishop would have probably been slightly older than Archdeacon Abraham ap Gruffydd. Although this is pure speculation considering the amount of Gruffydds about at the time, it is to be wondered if this Abraham might not be an illegitimate son of Gruffydd ap

[*383] (...continued)
and MS Exchequer DB Neath, PRO E.164/1, ed. Remfry, P.M., [Malvern, 2007], 120.
[*384] ByS, 217.
[*385] Statuta I, 484/83. *Abbas de Strata Florida qui praeter conscientiam abbatum, nomine ipsorum, cardinali scripsit, deponitur in instanti. Priores vero qui ad illum diem fuerunt, ab officiis suis amoveantur et ad domos alias emittantur. Pater vero abbas, qui iniunctum est a Legato ut secundum formam Ordinis puniret eum, et non punivit, similiter deponitur in instanti.*
[*386] *Calendar of Entries in the Papal Registers relating to GB and Ireland - Papal Letters, 1198-1304*, ed. W. H. Bliss [1893], 102.
[*387] 'Annales Prioratus de Wigornia', *Annales Monastici*, ed. H.R. Luard [5 vols., 1864-9] IV, 417; 'Annales Monasterii de Waverleia', *Annales Monastici*, ed. H.R. Luard [5 vols., 1864-9] II, 301, supplies the date, although Abraham's consecration is not mentioned.
[*388] Pen, 102; RBH, 231, the year ending for the chronicler's 1232 being 25 March 1233; on 4 February 1232 the dean and chapter of St Asaph's were given letters of licence to elect by the archdeacon and Philip the church chancellor who had come to the king with letters patent, *CPR 1232-47*, 10.
[*389] Acts, 411, No.250.

Cynan (d.1200). If he were an abbot of Aberconwy it would make much sense of Gruffydd's grants to this house and his becoming a monk there before his death.

The name of Abraham's successor at Aberconwy is unknown and the abbey's history for the next few years is obscure, although Llywelyn ap Maelgwn Ieunac, the short-lived grandson of Prince Llywelyn, was buried there in 1230[390]. The entry states that he 'died in Gwynedd'. This comment suggests that he was not normally in North Wales. His father, Maelgwn Ieuanc (*Fychan*) ap Maelgwn (bef.1210-57), was a grandson of the Lord Rhys (d.1197). He had at some point before 1225 married Angharad, the daughter of Llywelyn and Joan. The implication from the text is that the young man, probably no more than five years old, had come up to see his grandfather when death overtook him. That he was buried at Aberconwy again shows the place the abbey had in the affections of the princes of North Wales.

In the meantime politics continued apace with war again coming between Llywelyn and his allies and the king in May 1231. This ended in a truce soon after 27 October 1231, when the king ordered the Marchers to approach Llywelyn to end the hostilities[391]. It has been stated that Henry III planned an amphibious attack for 1232 upon Mon during this campaign, but that it came to nothing[392]. This does not appear to be correct. On 30 September 1231, the king at Hereford wrote to the justiciar of Ireland that:

> You have heard enough before of how the hostile and unfaithful Prince Llywelyn of Aberffraw and Snowdon bears himself towards us and ours, he burns and pillages our lands and he kills our men and other damage he does to us and ours.... we have written to all and each of our magnates of the land of Ireland that against the coming summer they should prepare themselves to come to Wales, to put into practice the strong hand in England to avenge us of such great excesses made upon us, which it is not possible for us to conceal. And we therefore order you strongly... that the magnates will be able themselves... to come to our service and induce them to attack the said Llywelyn diligently, you are not permitted by us and our honour diligently that any merchandise or other types of victuals, through which the Welsh may carry back support, to bring to Wales from our land of Ireland and it is to be proclaimed throughout Ireland and strongly made prohibited from our part, not for anyone, as he his person and his chattels loves, any merchandise or other types of victuals to the aforesaid parts to export or have exported... that our enemies thence should feel greatly oppressed...[393]

Quite clearly there was no thought of attacking Mon per se. This was just a vague assertion that the Irish magnates should come to England to attack Llywelyn. Presumably they were to be used by a royal army in whatever campaign should come about. More immediately pertinent was the blocking of Irish trade to the rebels. In any case the 27 October truce, not even a month after this letter was sent, probably slackened any preparations that might have been made. It is therefore doubtful if this war had any effect on Aberconwy abbey and its lands in Mon or elsewhere.

---

[390] Pen, 101.
[391] *CCR 1227-31*, 585-6. The Welsh envoys, Master Instructus and Philip, were issued with a safe-conduct to come to the king who was at Westminster on 24 November 1232, *CPR 1225-32*, 452. They no doubt brought the article of the year long truce from Wales which was witnessed by Prince Llywelyn, Owain ap Gruffydd, Rhys Gryg, Ednyfed Fychan and Gruffydd ap Rhodri, *Idem*, 453.
[392] Lloyd, J.E., *History of Wales* [2 vols., 1911] II, 676.
[393] *CCR 1227-31*, 600.

The next year passed in an uneasy truce and then, on 9 December 1232, at Shrewsbury the king issued an act of protection for the abbey of Aberconwy (*Abberconewey*) and the Cistercian monks there and all their goods and possessions. All of these were to be treated as the king's own and further the monks were to be quit of toll, passage, paage[394] and pontage as well as all customs pertaining to the king throughout his dominions. Finally, they were to have such quittance for everything which they or their servants could prove to be their own exactly as other monks of the Cistercian order had. This was to be pursuant to the charter given by King Henry II and confirmed by King John[395]. Considering that Aberconwy was a long way from the front line at this time, it is to presumed that the charter was the result of the abbot approaching the king, perhaps fearing for his outlying eastern granges in the Perfeddwlad. It should also have allowed his men to pass through the war zones to English markets. No warfare seems to have reached the abbey either now, or for the rest of Llywelyn's reign.

The events of 1233 may have had long reaching repercussions for Aberconwy. Despite the fact that Gruffydd ap Rhodri had loyally supported Llywelyn (as far as it is known), on 3 June 1233 the king granted him protection to go to Jerusalem on pilgrimage with anyone he took with him[396]. Presumably he proceeded with the consent of his prince. Whatever the case, Gruffydd survived the trip - if he went - and outlived Prince Llywelyn. His timing though appears somewhat unusual as delicate discussions were taking place from 8 June [Tuesday before the feast of St Barnabas] between Llywelyn's seneschal, Ednyfed Fychan, and possibly even the young Prince Dafydd at Gloucester. For this the king had cancelled a tournament at Northampton on 8 June [The Wednesday after Trinity Sunday] and called his barons and knights together to him at Worcester[397]. The meeting was obviously unsuccessful in securing peace and on 13 June the king began to strengthen the Shropshire frontier, looking particularly to the loyalty of Thomas Corbet and the defence of Strattondale, Bridgnorth, Montgomery and Sned[398].

With this act to secure the northern Marches, peace continued for the rest of the summer until the Clifford revolt of that August. This was already brewing as early as 15 June 1233 when the king ordered the seizing of Walter Clifford's lands in Oxfordshire, Lincolnshire, Shropshire, Kent and Herefordshire[399]. Before 4 July 1233 the king had ordered Clifford to repay 1,100 marks (£733 6 8d) he had borrowed from royal Jews, and if he defaulted the king would move against his pledges as had been named in his chirograph[400]. As a result, by 13 August, the lands of Clifford and Richard Siward were again sequestrated, despite the above order of 4 July[401]. This action brought the Earl Marshall and others into full rebellion, although on 17 August they offered terms to the king[402]. In the first days of September the king campaigned against the rebels in the Herefordshire Marches and took Clifford's castles of Glasbury, Bronllys and Clifford itself. Clifford himself would appear to have headed northwards during this period as he came to the king's peace on 17 September at

---

[394] The next charter of 1247 had panage and not paage. One transcript, probably this one, is in error.
[395] *Calendar of Charter Rolls 1226-1516* [6 vols., 1903-27] I, 1226-57, 171.
[396] *CPR 1232-47*, 17.
[397] *CPR 1232-47*, 17.
[398] *CCR 1231-34*, 311; *CPR 1232-47*, 18; *Calendar of Liberate Rolls, 1226-1272* [6 vols., 1916-64] *1226-40*, 218-9.
[399] Fine Rolls, No.225.
[400] *CCR 1231-34*, 314.
[401] Fine Rolls, Nos.277-88, 294.
[402] *CCR 1231-34*, 321.

Montgomery[*403]. During the period of his revolt Clifford acquired the hand of Llywelyn's daughter, Margaret, the widow of John Braose (d. July 1232). She had been granted royal permission not to marry for as long as she liked on 7 June 1233 at Gloucester, as long as she would only marry with royal permission[*404]. No such permission is noted in the royal records and as Walter was in considerable disfavour during the summer when the marriage must have occurred, it seems logical to assign its occurrence to late August or early September 1233. As Margaret and Walter's daughter, Matilda (d.1284), seems to have been born in 1234, it is most likely that the marriage took place between 8 June and 16 September 1233, and this was another reason for war coming between prince and king in October. On 22 September the king was still writing to Llywelyn in friendly terms and asking him his pleasure concerning the truce and his bailiffs confining themselves to their bailiwicks[*405]. As late as 14 October 1233 the king granted 'his nephew, Dafydd ap Llywelyn' the manor of Purley in Essex, while the next day he ordered the freeing of Llywelyn's envoys who had apparently been captured by Thomas Corbet before the 1231 truce[*406].

When Llywelyn finally attacked the royalists he appears to have succeeded in his military aims and brought devastation to the Herefordshire and Shropshire Marches, with his host finally coming to a rest at Shrewsbury in the January of 1234. Once more all the fighting seems to have taken place well away from Aberconwy abbey and no fighting is recorded anywhere near the abbot's lands. Although there is no evidence of fighting in the north, where in any case Llywelyn's lands were somewhat protected by the presence of the lands of his son-in-law, Earl John of Chester (1207-37). Yet it appears that famine was approaching in North Wales by 4 May 1234, as that day the king gave permission for Bishop Cadwgan of Bangor to buy grain in Ireland to alleviate the suffering of the poor in Gwynedd[*407]. Although this was an obvious humanitarian gesture, it obviously was a hopeless military action if King Henry III wished to bring Prince Llywelyn to heel.

Within three years of 1234 Gruffydd ap Llywelyn seems to have expanded his powerbase from Llyn to include Arwystli, Ceri, Cyfeiliog, Mawddwy, Mochnant and Caereinion. It is implausible that this was done without the consent, indeed the blessing, of his father. It was from this powerbase that the eldest son opposed the father's attempt to end the political impasse with their king. On 2 February 1237 Princess Joan of Wales died[*408]. Presumably thinking of his own mortality and wishing to end his life in comfort Prince Llywelyn approached King Henry. Matthew Paris wrote the following in his anti-royalist chronicle.

How Llywelyn prompted the king about making a peace treaty.
Likewise at the same time [as the fighting taking place in Spain], Prince Llywelyn of Wales through solemn nuncios wrote to the king, that, as his lifetime was coming to an end, all uproarious quarrel and all the tumult of wars should now be settled by reason at that time, following a secure peace he would be glad of the tranquillity, he would place himself and all his own under the power and guardianship of the king of the English to settle [the dispute], and of him [the king] he would hold his lands in

---

[*403] The Clifford revolt is detailed in Remfry, PM., *Clifford Castle, 1066 to 1299*, 14-6.
[*404] *CPR 1232-47*, 18.
[*405] *CCR 1231-34*, 323-4.
[*406] *CCR 1231-34*, 280, 327.
[*407] *CCR 1231-34*, 417.
[*408] *Annales Cestrienses, a chronicle of the abbey of St. Werburgh, Chester*, ed. and trans. Christie, R.C., Record Society for Lancashire and Cheshire XIV [1887], 61.

faith and friendship, entering into an indissolvable treaty. And if the king might go on an expedition, to campaign by foot and horse, and with his treasury, attended by his forces, that with his faithful men, he himself [Llywelyn] faithfully would move forward in support. Until this therefore could be confirmed they sent intermediaries, the bishops of Hereford and Chester, who spoke out diligently to bring the business about. However, this cause was regarded to be entrusted within the mandate, that the same Llywelyn was not in himself in a fit state of mind, weakened by the sickness of a partial paralysis, weighted down by the attack of Gruffydd his son, that he might put off the fight against him. While many of the magnates of Wales would accept the treaty entered into, who would likewise confirm that with Llywelyn; however several of the others gainsaid the compact immovably. But the Welsh faithful are devoid of faith, nor do they show consideration when they are able; and they follow lucky patrons of their own custom, humbled truly, or they flee or they abase [themselves]; following that poetic at no such time do they trust:

I fear Danaans, even when bringing gifts[*409].

Also Seneca the philosopher:

"You are never safe when making a treaty with the enemy."[*410]

There is no evidence of warfare in Wales during 1237, so presumably the attack of Gruffydd was no more than words in the prince's council, but they were words that held back the prince as he could not gain the full assent of his men. Madog ap Gruffydd of Powys had died the previous year and had been succeeded in his lands by his son Gruffydd ap Madog (bef.1199-1269). This Gruffydd seems to have usually taken the part of Gruffydd ap Llywelyn, who was now his neighbour in Powys. The advancement of Gruffydd ap Llywelyn in southern Powys was to the loss of Gruffydd ap Gwenwynwyn (d.1286), the second son and potential heir to the lands of Gwenwynwyn (d.1216) in Powys. Presumably there were other Welsh lords and maybe Marchers too who supported Gruffydd's position and this opposition checked the peace party led by the disabled Prince Llywelyn and his son, Dafydd.

It was probably still thinking of his soul that Prince Llywelyn made a grant of Penmon priory with a village called Trecastle (*Trefekastell*, probably now between Llangoed and Llanfaes) to Ynys Llannog on 10 April 1237 at Rhosyr (*Rosver*). The grant was witnessed by Ednyfed Fychan (*Evin Parvus*), Maredudd ab Iorwerth, Heylin ap Kewrid, Madog ap Purwyn, Maredudd ap David, David Machan, Hywel ap Heylin and Philip ab Ivor[*411]. This was some two months after the prince's second wife, Princess Joan was buried at Llanfaes[*412]. It is somewhat surprising that Joan was buried here, rather than in Aberconwy where her husband was to lie. It is also odd that Aberconwy was later to be found holding lands in Llanfaes. Possibly there was more going on with this than now survives in documentation. This land at Llanfaes does not appear in the 1291 Taxatio of Aberconwy abbey, but in the fifteenth century Register it appears as 'a holding next to Beaumaris' worth 5s. It also appears in Llywelyn's forged charter allegedly of 1199, but actually of 1318-32. This in itself, without all the evidence which will be considered later, all but proves the Llywelyn charters date to after 1291. Similarly, the abbey seems to have acquired properties at Bangor and Chester worth 6s 8d in total and one unvalued property in Conway which all appear in the Register, but

---

[*409] Danaans were the besiegers of Troy, usually claimed to have been 'Greeks'.

[*410] *Matthaei Parisiensis, monachi Sancti Albani, Chronica Majora*, ed. H.R. Luard [7 vols., 1872-83] III, 385.

[*411] *Calendar of Charter Rolls 1226-1516* [6 vols., 1903-27] II, 459-60.

[*412] See the next chapter on Venedotian burials.

nowhere else. Quite possibly the Llanfaes holding of Aberconwy was therefore obtained quite late in the abbey's life, though before 1332 when the abbey had Llywelyn's forged 1199 charter confirmed.

It would seem likely that it was at this time when Llywelyn was at Rhosyr that he sent his peace envoys to King Henry as it was on 29 May that King Henry III issued a safe conduct for Prince Dafydd in coming to him at any time up to 8 September 1237[*413]. Possibly the council of Llywelyn met and argued at Rhosyr, for Dafydd had obviously reached his king by 3 June when the king issued an order for the archbishop of Canterbury to escort Dafydd to him at Westminster. Dafydd must already have been nearby for the next day it was agreed to prolong the truce 'with our open enemies' who consisted of 'our faithful Prince Llywelyn of Aberffraw and lord of Snowdon and his open adherents and his men as much Welshmen as others' for another year until 25 July 1238[*414]. Immediately after this another blow hit Llywelyn when his son-in-law, Earl John of Chester, died on 7 June 1237[*415].

The king wrote again to Llywelyn, on 16 June 1237, confirming that the truce was to last until 25 July 1238, when he confirmed that both he and Llywelyn had sworn to it and that Llywelyn's negotiator in the matter was Brother Theodoric, the prior of the hospital of St John of Jerusalem in England. Further, the king was thankful that Llywelyn thought fit to send Dafydd to continue negotiations at Worcester in a fortnight. Yet the king found that he was not able to gather the full members of his council in time and so suggested postponing the meeting until 1 August 1237 when he would send to meet Dafydd 'the venerable fathers Ralph of Hereford and Alexander of Coventry, bishops, and our beloved and faithful Earl John Lacy of Lincoln, or Earl William of Aumale in his place, Walter Clifford, Ralph Mortimer (both of these were Llywelyn's sons-in-law) and John Lestrange' who would be at Shrewsbury on 25 July 1237 to conduct Dafydd's party to Worcester. The terms were to be sent to Llywelyn via his nuncio, Brother Geoffrey[*416]. This seems to be the basis of Matthew Paris' tale, backed in royal documents. No meeting is known to have taken place at Worcester that summer and the king made no attempt to go there. Quite obviously the attempt failed and presumably this was due to the refusal of the men of Powys under Gruffydd ap Madog and Gruffydd ap Llywelyn to adhere to such a peace deal as Llywelyn and Dafydd proposed.

As a consequence, no doubt after 25 July 1237 and apparently in early 1238, Dafydd ap Llywelyn struck, taking from his brother Gruffydd the lands of Arwystli, Ceri, Cyfeiliog, Mochnant, Caereinion and Mawddwy, leaving him just Llyn[*417]. With his half-brother shorn of his principality of Powys it might have been possible to make a settlement with the king. However, at this time the Crown was racked by what to some appeared to be the resumption of the civil war of King John's day. This was concerning the marriage of the king's sister to Simon Montfort[*418]. Dafydd's move had obviously happened before 7 March 1238, for on that day the king wrote the following letter to Morgan of Caerleon (bef.1195-1248), Rhys ap Gruffydd (bef.1210-56), Hywel ap Maredudd (bef.1211-79), Rhys Mechyll (bef.1205-44), Maredudd ap Rhys (bef.1210-71), Cynan ap Hywel (bef.1195-1238+), Maelgwn ap Maelgwn (bef.1210-57), Gruffydd ab Owain (bef.1205-60), Richard ap Hywel, Rhys ap Trahaearn

---

[*413] *CPR 1232-47*, 184.

[*414] *Foedera, Conventiones, Litterae etc*, ed. T. Rymer and R. Sanderson, 4th edn, by A. Clarke, F. Holbrooke, and J. Caley [4 vols. in 7 parts, 1816-69] I, 130.

[*415] *CPR 1232-47*, 184-5.

[*416] *CCR 1234-7*, 536-7.

[*417] *RBH*, 235.

[*418] *Matthaei Parisiensis, monachi Sancti Albani, Chronica Majora*, ed. H.R. Luard [7 vols., 1872-83] III, 475-6.

(bef.1186-1238+), Llywelyn ap Gruffydd (the future prince of Wales, d.1282), Maredudd ap Maelgwn (bef.1194-1249+), Owain ap Hywel (bef.1200-53) and his brother (Owain, Einion and Maredudd were his brothers of Ceri), Owain ap Maredudd (bef.1205-82?) and all the tenants of the honour of Brecon and Buellt and all the tenants of Richard Clare and all the tenants of the English earls and barons in Wales. In this the king complained that he had heard that Llywelyn threatens to let Dafydd take the homage of some of the magnates of Wales. He ordered the above not to let this happen as:

> the aforesaid magnates hold their lands from us and they owe homage to us and because the aforesaid Dafydd should pay homage to us and has not yet done homage to us.

They were therefore ordered that under no circumstances were they to pay homage to Dafydd. Immediately afterwards Gruffydd ap Gwenwynwyn was also ordered not to pay homage to Dafydd or anyone else for the lands and tenements that he aspired to as such homage should only be paid to the king and the king was prepared to grant him his lands and take his homage as this is what was owed for his fidelity. The same message was sent to Gruffydd ap Madog (Powys Fadog), Owain Fychan and Llywelyn his brother (Edeirnion) and Maredudd ap Robert (Cedewain)[*419]. It would seem possible from this that after stripping Gruffydd ap Llywelyn of his Powysian lands Dafydd and his father offered them to Gruffydd ap Gwenwynwyn as a peace settlement. Obviously the matter progressed no further as the king had apparently not been consulted and certainly had not consented in the potential arrangement.

As a consequence of all this manoeuvring, on 8 March 1238, the king wrote privately to William Stuteville [Richards Castle], John Fitz Alan [Clun and Oswestry], William Warenne of Whitchurch (*Albo Monasterio*), William Fitz Warin, Roger Chandos [Snodhill], Ralph Tosny [Painscastle], Roger Picard [Tretower], Thomas Corbet [Caus, father-in-law to Gruffydd ap Gwenwynwyn], Ralph Mortimer [Wigmore and son-in-law of Prince Llywelyn], Walter Clifford [Clifford & Bronllys and son-in-law of Prince Llywelyn], Walter Baskerville [Eardisley], John Monmouth [Monmouth] and Fulk Fitz Warin [Whittington] concerning the end of the truce with Prince Llywelyn on 25 July and the fact that it had been reported that Dafydd ap Llywelyn had taken the homage of the magnates of North Wales and Powys and how 'we are neither certain that this was done voluntarily, nor are we certain of the intention of the prince himself'. Consequently, he asked them to meet him at Oxford on Tuesday 13 April 1238 to discuss matters[*420].

The king then proceeded to send a second open or patent letter to various Marchers, some of whom were the same as those written to privately. These were John Fitz Alan, Walter Clifford, Herbert Fitz Peter [Bleanllynfi], Thomas Corbet, Walter Baskerville, John Lestrange [Knockin], Earl Humphrey Bohun of Hereford, Henry Audley [Weston under Redcastle], John Monmouth, Ralph Mortimer, Roger Picard and William Stuteville. These were informed that although the king had sent nuncios to Llywelyn concerning the truce they could find no peace with Llywelyn or measures to make amends. Further the king commanded them to prepare to defend the Marches of Wales in case Llywelyn should attack

---

[*419] *CCR 1237-42*, 123-4.
[*420] *Foedera, Conventiones, Litterae etc*, ed. T. Rymer and R. Sanderson, 4th edn, by A. Clarke, F. Holbrooke, and J. Caley [4 vols. in 7 parts, 1816-69] I, 132. According to *CCR 1237-42*, 124, these letters were dated 7 March.

so that effective resistence could be shown him[*421]. Obviously the king did not intend to be taken by surprise as he had been in the autumn of 1233.

Also on 8 March 1238, the king wrote to Prince Llywelyn informing him that he was sending his steward, Amaury St Amand, together with Henry Audley and John Lestrange to make amends at Montgomery ford for the attacks committed upon the Crown and against the truce[*422]. Simultaneously with this, he sent two letters to Gwynedd, one to Llywelyn and one to his son, Dafydd. The first was sent to Llywelyn concerning the homage taken without the king's permission by his son. This stated that the king understood that Llywelyn was intending to have the magnates and others of North Wales and Powys give their homage to Dafydd. This he stated was not to be attempted until Dafydd had come to the king and paid him homage as the magnates in question owed allegiance to himself in chief and have done homage for their tenements to the Crown. The king continued to complain that the archdeacon of St Asaph, who had been sent by Llywelyn to treat with the king, did not have sufficient instructions to do so, although it was signified that the prince desired a firm peace with Henry. The king concluded:

> Yet because we know nothing certain of your wish and intention in this region, and [that you] threaten to end the truce held between us, we have ordered our Marcher magnates that they are to come to us at Oxford on Tuesday 13 April about this, and that they may bring others to us and from you at that time. If you desire a firm peace between us, as you signify to us, you should send to us on that day and at that place, if you please, anyone of yours, with full power to treat for peace and establish it between us and you. Since we wish to know this from you because thus far we have understood nothing, not even from the tenor of your letters nor from others, that although you say that you aim at a strengthened peace between us.., in this we have clearly heard insincerely or even, we reflect, nothing. However, at the urging of the aforesaid archdeacon we send to you our letters patent of safe and secure conduct for any you wish to send from you, at the aforesaid day and location.[*423]

At the same time a similar letter was sent to Dafydd. This was simply a reiteration that Dafydd was not to take the homages of the magnates of North Wales and Powys before he had come to meet the king and pay homage. In blunter language he was told not to presume to take the homages of magnates, especially those that were held of the Crown in chief[*424].

The final letter in the series came the next day, 9 March 1238, when the king wrote to the prince touching what the archdeacon of St Asaph had said to him concerning:

> the attacks and trespasses done in the prince's lands by some of the king's land contrary to the truce and requesting that amends be made for the same; but as it has not been made clear to the king by any of his lieges what attacks have been made on either side, consequently he is sending Amaury St Amand, Henry Audley and John

---

[*421] *CPR 1232-47*, 235.

[*422] *CPR 1232-47*, 235.

[*423] *Foedera, Conventiones, Litterae etc*, ed. T. Rymer and R. Sanderson, 4th edn, by A. Clarke, F. Holbrooke, and J. Caley [4 vols. in 7 parts, 1816-69] I, 132.

[*424] *Foedera, Conventiones, Litterae etc*, ed. T. Rymer and R. Sanderson, 4th edn, by A. Clarke, F. Holbrooke, and J. Caley [4 vols. in 7 parts, 1816-69] I, 132-3.

Lestrange to Montgomery that they may hear the same and do thereon what should be done according to the form of the truce.[*425]

The ambiguous nature of the king's language has led some to believe that royalist Marchers had been responsible for attacks on Welsh Marchers. This letter says nothing of the sort. Judging by what has been noted above, the attacks would appear to have been done by Welsh lords to Welsh lords and refers to the fighting between Dafydd and Gruffydd and their respective adherents. Hence the repeated comments in these letters about North Wales and Powys. The lands in question where fighting may have taken place would therefore appear to be within the Powysian lands of Arwystli, Ceri, Cyfeiliog, Mochnant, Caereinion and Mawddwy - those lands which Dafydd had seized from Gruffydd and which action started the current furore of letters. If this is the case, then King Henry III was intervening on the behalf of Gruffydd ap Llywelyn against the king's own nephew, the future Prince Dafydd. Nothing further seems to have happened about this disruption and the royal records mention no more of the affair. Once more the Welsh truce was prolonged without comment concerning Dafydd's homage on 8 July[*426]. Some further correspondence had obviously passed between king and prince for on 9 August 1238 the king wrote to the prince telling him that he would not be able to meet Llywelyn's representatives on 9 September as had been agreed, however the king would be at Shrewsbury on 22 September 1238 to discuss the diverse and arduous business concerning the position of royal power between them[*427]. The king obviously kept his appointment as he was at Bridgnorth on 20 September and was certainly in Shrewsbury from the 24th to the 25th[*428]. Despite this, there is no record of any meeting between the king and his Welsh vassals.

Regardless of this, it seems likely that the meeting had gone ahead, for within the month, on 19 October 1238 (the day after St Luke the Evangelist), all the princes of Wales swore adherence to Dafydd the son of Prince Llywelyn at Strata Florida[*429]. Unfortunately the patent rolls from 15 October 1238 to 28 October 1240 are now lost, so it cannot be known if the king complained of this abuse of his majesty or whether this was done with his consent. As no hostile moves seem to have occurred the latter could be presumed.

Two years later, on 11 April 1240, the 68 year old prince was laid to rest in the abbey which he had helped make a family mausoleum[*430].

The great renowned second Achilles, that is the Lord Llywelyn ab Iorwerth ab Owain Gwynedd, then prince of Wales, died. He received the habit of a monk at the house of Aberconwy with great devotion. His deeds I am unworthy to relate. He was master of his enemies by his shield and spear; he kept the peace for the religious; he gave to the poor (of Christ) nourishment and clothes; he enlarged his boundaries through war; he

---

[*425] CPR 1232-47, 212.

[*426] Foedera, Conventiones, Litterae etc, ed. T. Rymer and R. Sanderson, 4th edn, by A. Clarke, F. Holbrooke, and J. Caley [4 vols. in 7 parts, 1816-69] I, 133.

[*427] CCR 1237-42, 143.

[*428] CCR 1237-42, 146-7.

[*429] Annales Cambriae. A Translation of Harleian 3859; PRO E.164/1; Cottonian Domitian, A 1; Exeter Cathedral Library MS. 3514 and MS Exchequer DB Neath, PRO E.164/1, ed. Remfry, P.M., [Malvern, 2007], 130.

[*430] The date is supplied by Matthew Paris, although in some manuscripts the date of 10 April is probably erroneously given. Matthaei Parisiensis, monachi Sancti Albani, Chronica Majora, ed. H.R. Luard [7 vols., 1872-83] IV, 8, is probably the earliest of Matthew's works being originally compiled before 1250. Matthaei Parisiensis, Historia Anglorum, ed. F.H. Madden [3 vols., 1866-9] II, 430, was written slightly after this date and notes that Llywelyn had been afflicted by paralysis for some time before his death. Matthew died in 1259 which should provided a terminus post quem for the recording of the date.

strove after giving good justice to all of his own men with the love and fear of God; he was sustained by those indebted to him by bonds of fear or affection.[*431]

The Burial of Llywelyn ab Iorwerth and other Venedotians in North Wales.

The chronicles quoted above provide the evidence that Prince Llywelyn was buried in Aberconwy abbey in 1240. Yet there is little evidence as to the exact place of his burial or the fate of his remains or even his tomb, despite widespread claims in recent times. The so-called tomb of Prince Llywelyn (Fig.15) is said to have survived to the present day, being moved first to Maenan in the late 1280s and then, after the Dissolution of the abbey in 1537, to the Gwydir chapel, built in 1633 on the side of Llanrwst church. Here the partial tomb now stands near to a smaller lid with an effigy of Hywel Coetmor, an adherent of Owain Glyndwr who died some time in the early fifteenth century[*432]. Hywel's lid has lost its sarcophagus and is obviously too small to seal the so-called Llywelyn tomb. Undated sarcophagi similar to this still exist at Ellington, Cambridgeshire (Fig.14) and Fulbrook, Oxfordshire (Fig.16). No doubt there are many more still to be noted, but as undated monuments they add little to our understanding of the Llanrwst tomb. At first sight the tomb said to be that of Abbot Alexander Holderness of Peterborough (d.1226, Fig.17) might suggest that the style of this sarcophagus is early thirteenth century; however the apparent breaking and reshaping of the tomb to fit the effigy suggests that the two have been matched together at a later date.

It is a pity that the lid of the Llywelyn sarcophagus has not been found. If this sarcophagus did belong to Llywelyn, it may have had a low-relief effigy to compliment that alleged to be of his wife Joan, now residing at Beaumaris (Fig.18). Before going any further it should be noted that it is quite possible that this sarcophagus does not belong to Llywelyn himself or even to any other member of the Venedotian family who are known to have been buried in Aberconwy abbey. Indeed, without any firm provenance, it is possible that this fine tomb might have belonged to any medieval noble and came from any church in the vicinity. Its association with Prince Llywelyn currently appears to rest solely upon eighteenth or nineteenth century hearsay. It has further been suggested in the 1980s that after the demoting of Aberconwy abbey to a parish church, the tomb with the body of Prince Llywelyn was moved and relaid in a stone lined grave lying centrally in the presbytery of Maenan church[*433]. If this is true, then the freestanding sarcophagus at Llanrwst can hardly be that removed from under the ground at Maenan and it should be remembered that John Wynne of Gwydir was more than happy to fabricate evidence to link himself back to Prince Llywelyn[*434]. Further, there is no recorded historical evidence that the house of Aberconwy held any reverence for Llywelyn ab Iorwerth before his forged charters were placed before King Edward III in 1332. It should also be noted that the princely burials at Strata Florida seem to have all been in the chapter house[*435]. This, of course, does not mean that all princes were buried in chapter houses. Our only source mentioning the place of Llywelyn's burial in the presence of the high altar, this Aberconwy 'chronicle', does not define what form of tomb, if any, he had. Regardless of this, what little evidence there is makes it suspect that the monks of 1283 would have regarded Llywelyn's tomb and corpse with any greater respect than that which should

---

[*431] *Annales Cambriae. A Translation of Harleian 3859; PRO E.164/1; Cottonian Domitian, A 1; Exeter Cathedral Library MS. 3514 and MS Exchequer DB Neath, PRO E.164/1*, ed. Remfry, P.M., [Malvern, 2007], B (St David's), D (Hopton Commission?), 130.

[*432] Hywel was the son of Gruffydd Fychan and this Gruffydd and his sons, amongst whom were also Rhys Gethin, had to post a bond of £100 on 23 November 1390 that they would not harm Abbot John of Maenan, amongst others, *CCR 1389-82*, 295.

[*433] Butler, LAS. and Evans, DH., 'the Cistercian abbey at... Maenan, Excavations in 1968', *Archaeologia Cambrensis* [1980], 11.

[*434] http://www.ancientwalesstudies.org/id115.html

[*435] Williams, SW., *The Cistercian Abbey of Strata Florida...* [1889], 125, 205.

have been recorded to the founder of the house, Rhodri ap Owain (d.1194), or any of his princely successors who were buried at Aberconwy.

The only contemporary source which mentions the style of Llywelyn's burial comes from the copied words of a poet. Sometime, apparently soon after Llywelyn's death, Einion Wan wrote some lines which have been translated as:

True lord of the land – how strange that today
He rules not o'er Gwynedd;
Lord of nought but the piled up stones of his tomb,
Of the seven-foot grave in which he lies.[*436]

Certainly the sarcophagus displayed at Llanrwst is not a pile of stones, but is the phrase 'piled up stones' simply poetic licence? Certainly it would appear unlikely that the abbot would have allowed a pile of stones to be dumped in his nice church over a crude grave cut through his tiled floor. The question must be asked that if the Llanrwst sarcophagus is a part of the tomb of Llywelyn, rescued by the Wynnes from their new home of Maenan abbey, then why did they not also rescue the tomb lid and possible effigy? The conclusion of this points towards the tomb not being that of Prince Llywelyn.

The Llanrwst sarcophagus is 1'4" high, 3'1" wide at the head, but only 2'4½" wide at the base and 7'11" long (Fig.14). As such this might well have contained Llywelyn's corpse if it were taken from a 7' long grave initially cut at Aberconwy as Einion Wan sang. The sarcophagus is cut out of a light grey, medium grained sandstone which is heavily stratified along the length of the box. The tomb had six quatrefoils on each side with three more at the head and two at the base. The remains of pin holes in the central upper part of each roundel shows that they once contained plaques of some description. These may possibly have been heraldic or representations of the occupant's family as 'weepers'. Further, semi-quatrefoil carvings filled in the gaps around the main roundels, while just one corner of the box was indented. This sarcophagus was undoubtedly a part of a richly decorated tomb. It also contains a mysterious groove running deeply from lid indent to indent within the centre of the crudely carved interior.

As the sarcophagus now at Llanrwst clearly once had a lid - as can be seen from the indent cut around its top - it is quite possible that this once supported an effigy that matched that found on the lid of the sarcophagus alleged to be of Princess Joan and now displayed in the porch of Beaumaris church (Fig.18). Her death is recorded in the Bruts under 1237.

Dame Joan, daughter of King John, wife of Llywelyn ab Iorwerth, died in the month of February at the court of Aber; and she was buried in a new graveyard on the shore-bank which Bishop Hywel of St Asaph had consecrated. And in her honour Llywelyn ab Iorwerth built there a monastery for the bare-footed friars, which is called Llanfaes in Anglesey.[*437]

The Lady of Wales, wife of Llywelyn ab Iorwerth and daughter to the king of England, her name was Joan, died in Llywelyn's court at Aber in the month of February and her body was buried in a consecrated enclosure which was on the shore-bank. And there

[*436] Translated in Lloyd, J.E., *History of Wales* [2 vols., 1911] II, 693 from *The Myvyrian Archaiology of Wales*, eds. O. Jones, E. Williams & W. Owen [2nd edn., Denbigh, 1870] I, 335.
[*437] RBH, 235.

after that Bishop Hywel consecrated a monastery for the Barefooted Friars to the honour of the Blessed Mary. And the prince built it all at his cost for the soul of his lady.[*438]

Neither of these versions of the apparent original chronicle mention that Joan was buried within a church, just in the graveyard on the shore-bank. This, of course, does not rule out her exhumation and placing within a tomb when the friary was built soon afterwards, or even the friary being built around her burial plot and a tomb added around the grave at the same time. The three years from her death to that of her husband would probably have allowed sufficient time for the small church of the friary to be built[*439]. Yet, it is surprising that Llywelyn did not make a 'foundation charter' for this monastery, especially considering the amount of charters he is said to have made to North Welsh religious houses, viz. Aberconwy (forgeries), Basingwerk, Beddgelert (probably a charter by Llywelyn Fawr ap Maredudd and not Llywelyn ab Iorwerth), Cymer (probable forgery), Dolgynwal, Haughmond, Strata Marcella and Ynys Llannog. Two other tombstones have been recovered from the Llanfaes site, one said to be 'twelfth century' and the other probably a 'fourteenth century' priest[*440].

The Llanfaes sarcophagus, now in Beaumaris, was cut from a fine grey cross-bedded sandstone and is six feet long, over two feet high and has sides some three inches thick. The stone is darker than that of the Llanrwst sarcophagus. The edges of the effigy on the lid have been much damaged, the moulding on the dexter side is totally missing as too is the bulk of the top edge. Further, as the lid has recently been cemented into place, thereby filling in the missing portions, it is not possible to be certain that the lid and the sarcophagus are actually a match. In addition, it is obvious that the stone of the sarcophagus and the lid are of different varieties, the sarcophagus being cut from a single set of trough cross-beds which look slightly curved in the long section, while the lid is composed of fine grained, flat laminated and current rippled grey sandstone. Quite obviously the stone required for lid and sarcophagus needed different properties for their different purposes and this may account for the differences, one for strength and the other for intricate carving. The sarcophagus is quite plain and crudely finished as it was evidently intended to be sunk into the ground, similar to that suggested for the burial at Maenan presbytery and also the original burial of King John at Worcester. This is dissimilar to the tomb displayed at Llanrwst which was carved to stand proud of the ground.

The coffin said to be that of Princess Joan had long been used as a watering trough outside Llanfaes, when 'found' in 1808 by Viscount Thomas Bulkeley (1752-1822). It was then 'face downwards in a ditch near Llanfaes, the stone coffin which it had covered being used as a water trough'[*441]. Eight years later the 'evidence' that this was the effigy of Princess Joan was questioned on the sound surmise that this rumour only dated to the early 1800s[*442]. The story proposed by these relatively well known 'sources' can now both be proven to be wrong and historically near worthless from this 1699 record[*443].

[*438] Pen, 104.

[*439] There is no apparent confirmation for the extraordinary claim that Llywelyn ab Iorwerth founded the priory in 1245, http://www.coflein.gov.uk/en/site/300910/details/llanfaes-friary-franciscangreyfriars retrieved 23 August 2017.

[*440] *Archaeologia Cambrensis* [1855], 78pl; http://www.coflein.gov.uk/en/archive/6277008/details/504 retrieved 23 August 2017. It should be noted that the 'twelfth century' tombstone lies in a cemetery apparently only founded in 1237.

[*441] *Archaeologia Cambrensis* [1847], 316.

[*442] *Archaeologia Cambrensis* [1855], 79.

[*443] The history of the legend of the Joan's coffin can be found in Gray, M., 'Four weddings, three funerals and a historical detective puzzle: a cautionary tale', *Transactions of the Anglesey Antiquarian Society and Field Club* [2014], 4-5. Here it is also shown that Joan's effigy

(continued...)

The friary chapel now turned into a tithe barn, in which have been digged up several stone coffins of the same form with that of Llywelyn ab Iorwerth's taken up at the Abbey of Nant Conway, now remaining in the chapel of Llanrwst. These coffins are now converted into swine troughs in several houses of Anglesey.[*444]

This clearly shows that many coffins were dug up from the friary and that Joan's was at this time thought to be one similar to that now in Llanrwst, ie. presumably decorated with quatrefoils or similar. This also shows that 'Llywelyn's sarcophagus' was already in Llanrwst church by the 1670s. As it was then rumoured to be Llywelyn's only 130 years after the monastery's dissolution, it seems feasible that this might represent a true remembrance. As these accounts all mention Joan's coffin, it is uncertain as to when the effigy was brought together with the rest of her alleged tomb.

The Beaumaris effigy shows the upper portion of a woman with her hands on her chest, but they are lying flat, in an apparently unique and uncomfortably open position, rather than being held together in prayer (Fig.19). Perhaps this was necessary as the effigy was cut in low relief. The even lower relief effigy of an otherwise unknown Lady Eva in Bangor cathedral, probably dates to the last half of the fourteenth century and adopts a somewhat similar pose, although the effigy is shown in full and is surrounded by a canopy and stiff leaf foliage (Fig.20). An effigy at Danby Wiske, Yorkshire[*445], although in higher relief, has her hands in a similar position, but palm downwards (Fig.21). The style of the effigy would point towards the end of the thirteenth century, or even a few decades into the fourteenth. The lady in question is also wearing two heraldic shields which look like multiple bars. These do not fit the heraldic badges of any known family of Danby Wiske - viz. The counts of Richmond, the Nevilles, the Longvilliers, the Furnivalls or the Scropes. The Maunbys had in interest in the vill, but their heraldic devices appear unknown; however their manorial interests make it unlikely that this lady belonged to their family[*446]. This leaves the possibility that the traditional identification of this effigy as Matilda, the widow of Brian Fitz Alan (d.1306) could well be correct. The idea that she was the sister of King John Balliol is apparently unsourced and the fact that she only wears what 'could' be Fitz Alan of Bedale arms and not those of Balliol would tend to mitigate against her being a member of the Balliol family. If the identification is correct it again emphasises the problems of assuming that an effigy must be related to the church where it is currently found.

Another somewhat similar effigy to the Beaumaris one can be found at East Worldham, Hampshire, where the upper part of a woman's torso has been carved deeply into a block of light grey sandstone (Fig.22). The figure displays similar headwear to Princess

[*443] (...continued)
was not found face down in a ditch by the coffin, but was already in the church when the coffin was taken from its temporary home at Baron Hill.

[*444] 'Historia Bellomarisei of circa 1669 by William Williams' in Fenton, R., Tours in Wales [1804-1813], ed. Fisher, J. [Cambrian Archaeological Association, 1917], 305.

[*445] Traditionally the effigy is said to represent Matilda, the second wife of Brian Fitz Alan (d.1306), who died sometime after 1340. The assumption appears based on the heraldry of a barry of five shown on her cloak. However, there are many such coats of arms and there seems no Fitz Alan link to the manor. From an early date Danby Wiske formed part of the demesne land of the honour of Richmond. In the early thirteenth century this was held by Earl Ranulf of Chester (d.1232), the step father in law of Llywelyn ab Iorwerth. The lordship then passed between the Crown, the Scropes and the mostly absentee dukes of Brittany until 1342 when it was resumed by the Crown and eventually granted to John of Gaunt. Possibly the lady is a wife or mother of Geoffrey le Scrope who died holding the vill a little before 11 December 1340, Calendar of Inquisitions Post Mortem, 1216-1427 [22 vols., 1898-2003] 1336-47, 206. Alternatively, the effigy might be a Neville or a Mauneby, Hugh Neville holding the manor of Thomas Mauneby, Calendar of Inquisitions Post Mortem 1336-47, No.403. In short, she is anonymous.

[*446] Calendar of Inquisitions Post Mortem 1336-47, No.403.

Joan, except for a definite lack of a coronet. She also has a fine wheel brooch under her throat, but her hands are palm down one above the other on her chest. This figure is traditionally said to be Philippa Roet, the wife of Geoffrey Chaucer (d.1400), but this identification is at least 150 years too late[447].

The Beaumaris figure is surrounded by the branches of a floriated stem which springs from the base of the lid border and is grasped by the head of a wyvern (Fig.23). The tail of the animal is formed into a love knot just before the end loops into the lower foliage of the stem. The effigy face is enclosed by a barbet. This may be worn over an apparent coif which closes tightly about the forehead. A few strands of hair appear visible at the temples (Fig.24). On the top of her head is what has been claimed to be a coronet[448] which holds in place a wimple which falls to her shoulders where it rests in three apparently pleated rolls on either shoulder. Under the fall of the wimple and over the possible coif at the base of the neck is the V shaped top of a tight fitting long sleeved gown. This is clasped at her throat by a circular wheel brooch possibly with a dove or other design within the circle. Her head rests on a plain rectangular cushion in typical early stone effigy fashion (1150-1250). As the end of the thirteenth century was reached a second cushion and sometimes tassels were added to the effigy headrest.

The headwear of the Beaumaris effigy is surprisingly similar to that worn by Isabella Plantagenet (c.1214-41), with coronet over a wimple that apparently doesn't cover the throat, but does lie in pleats on her shoulders (Fig.25[449]). Her hair is also just showing at her temples. The style of drawing of the face is also nearly identical to the Beaumaris effigy. Isabella was the younger half sister of Princess Joan of Wales. Isabella's other uterine sisters, Eleanor (c.1215-75), the wife of Simon Montfort (d.1265), and Joan (1210-38) the queen of Scotland, are shown in the same roll in exactly the same headwear (Fig.26). It is further apparent that these ladies have quite different headgear to other royal ladies represented on the roll. They also have coronets dissimilar to the crowns of the kings in the manuscript. The implication could well be that they are all daughters of King John and that this was thought to be the style of royal ladies when the roll was drawn up in the early fourteenth century.

This combined circumstantial evidence also leaves the possibility that the effigy is of Eleanor's daughter, another Eleanor (1252-82), who was wife to Prince Llywelyn ap Gruffydd from 1278. If this is so, the effigy could well have been commissioned by that Llywelyn between Eleanor's death on 19 June 1282 and his own killing on 10 December 1282. According to a contemporary chronicle made outside of Wales - no Welsh chronicle mentions her death - she died at the very end of the day of 19 June 1282 when her daughter Gwenllian was born and she was buried at Llanfaes in the house of the brothers minor[450]. Eleanor had no female siblings and so it is not possible to compare any representations of them to the Beaumaris effigy, but another genealogical chronicle of the English kings dating to between 1275 and 1300 (BL Royal MS 14 B V), does represent her (Fig.27). This looks nothing like the effigy and has a totally different headwear. Unfortunately all the other females in this roll have exactly the same headwear, so this of itself proves nothing, other than this poor sketch may have been done just within her lifetime. It can further be stated that Eleanor of

[447] http://astoft.co.uk/eastworldham.htm?fref=gc retrieved 23 August 2017.

[448] There are many effigies who are apparently not of royal blood, but sport coronets, viz. the female effigy at Norwell, Nottinghamshire.

[449] British Library, Royal MS 14 B VI, a genealogical roll of the kings of England possibly drawn up between 1300 and 1308 accessible online via http://www.bl.uk/catalogues/illuminatedmanuscripts/record.asp?MSID=18941&CollID=16&NStart=140206

[450] *Florentii Wigornensis Monachi Chronicon ex Chronicis*, ed. B. Thorpe [2 vols., English Historical Society, 1848-9] II, 226; *The Chronicle of Bury St Edmunds, 1212-1301*, ed. Gransden, A. [Nelson, 1964], 75.

Aquitaine's effigy of 1204 at Fontevrault (Fig.28) bears more than a passing resemblance to the Beaumaris headwear, as too does that of Isabella of Angouleme (d.1246), Princess Joan's stepmother (Fig.29). The effigy of Countess Aveline Fortibus of Lancaster (d.1274, Fig.30) is less of a match in headwear than the legitimate daughters of King John seem to have worn.

The argument has run for 200 years that the Beaumaris effigy must be Joan as it has a coronet (though this never seems to have been clearly seen), is obviously an early effigy and Joan was buried at Llanfaes. Yet, if the above is correct, the possibility remains that this lady is actually Princess Rhunallt ferch Reginald, the first wife of Llywelyn ab Iorwerth and daughter of the king of Man[*451]. On 3 July 1414, King Henry V reconstituted Llanfaes friary which had been abandoned due to the troubles in Wales before 28 January 1401[*452]. In Henry V's letter he notes that the daughter of King John had been buried there as well as some son of the king of Dacia, the body of Lord Clifford and others killed in the Welsh wars[*453]. When Camden saw this document many years later he thought it read *filia regis Johannis, filius Regis Daniae...*[*454]. Logically the original reading should have been *Regis Maniae* or the king of Man and not *Daciae* or *Daniae* at all. Similarly, it is possible that *filius* is a faulty expansion of *fil'* and should really have been rendered *filia* - daughter. If these deductions are correct, Llanfaes could also have been the burial place of Llywelyn's first wife. That said, at least one son of the king of Man, Godred Olafsson, did die off the coast of Gwynedd in 1237[*455]. Thus he could quite conceivably have been buried at Llanfaes. The fact that King Henry V mentioned these people would suggest that their names were remembered due to their having inscriptions or notable tombs at the friary. It may also indicate that prayers may have been maintained for them until 1401.

Further south in Wales there are some more unidentified effigies that have similarities with that of the Beaumaris effigy. The first two are in Abergavenny. One lies largely covered by a Cantilupe shield, which almost certainly makes her the effigy of the Jean Cantilupe who died in 1271 (Fig.31). Alternatively, this just might be her mother, Eva Braose, who married William Cantilupe in 1248 and died in 1255. If it is her, then she is displaying her husband's heraldry on the shield and not her own. The likelihood is therefore that this is not Eva Braose (d.1255), who was the sister of Princess Isabella Braose (d.1272+), the wife of Prince Dafydd ap Llywelyn (d.1246), but her daughter, Jean or Joanna Cantilupe (d.1271). Once more the effigy has a rather triangular face with a barbet with probable coif underneath. Again the head lies on a plain rectangular pillow. The effigy rested on a much mutilated sarcophagus. This has recently been rebuilt, showing a rectangular box with three defaced shields in each side. There are no roundels. The second Abergavenny effigy is highly defaced and obviously dates to several generations after the Cantilupe woman. However, the reconstructed tomb she lies upon has three quatrefoils on either side containing defaced heraldic shields (Fig.32). It is worth speculating here that this figure might well represent Agnes Mortimer (d.1368[*456]), the third great granddaughter of Joan Plantagenet (d.1237). The style is feasible when compared to her sister Catherine (d.1369) at Warwick and the obviously earlier effigy of another sister, Blanche (d.1347), entombed at Much Marcle in Herefordshire. The effigy of Earl Lawrence

[*451] See the above chapter, Llywelyn's Marriage and Aberconwy, 1195 to 1203.
[*452] CPR 1399-1401, 418; CPR 1413-16, 234.
[*453] *et similiter quod in eadem domo corpus tam filiae regis Johannis progenitoris nostri, quam filii regis Daciae, necnon corpora domini de Clyffort, et aliorum dominorum militum et armigerorum qui in guerris Walliae...*, Foedera, Conventiones, Litterae etc, ed. T. Rymer and R. Sanderson, 4th edn, by A. Clarke, F. Holbrooke, and J. Caley [4 vols. in 7 parts, 1816-69], IV, 1401-33, 83.
[*454] *Joannis Lelandi Antiquarii de Rebus Britannicis Collectanea*, Hearne, T., [London, 1770, 6 vols] I, 54.
[*455] *Chronicle of the kings of Mann and the Isles*, ed Broderick, G. [Douglas, 2004], f.45r-v.
[*456] *Calendar of Inquisitions Post Mortem 1365-70*, No.226.

Hastings of Pembroke, Agnes Mortimer's husband, lies nearby. He died twenty years before her, on 30 August 1348, which might explain the two having separate tombs. His sarcophagus has no roundels, but multiple canopies with weepers within them as might be fitting for a mid fourteenth century tomb.

Just over the current Welsh border at English Bicknor in Gloucestershire, is another effigy that is worth comparison with that at Beaumaris. This shows a poorly sculptured lady allegedly of the fourteenth century (Fig.33). Again she wears somewhat similar headwear to the Beaumaris effigy and her head rests on a rectangular pillow. Quite possibly then, this is thirteenth century and not later.

There is a similar coffin lid to Beaumaris in Brampton, Derbyshire, that can be dated. This belongs to Matilda le Caus who died a little before 21 May 1224[*457]. The lid, which was discovered in the graveyard in the eighteenth century, has a quatrefoil at the top through which the bust of Matilda is displayed (Fig.34). She clasps her heart to her chest and wears a veil over some kind of cap or braided hairdo. Her head rests on a rectangular pillow of typical thirteenth century style. Above the quatrefoil lobes are some indistinct decoration, while on the main part of the coffin lid is an inscription that reads: Here lies Matilda le Caus. Say a lord's prayer for her soul[*458]. In style it is not dissimilar to the Beaumaris coffin lid, although much less ornate, as might be expected for a lesser personage.

Finally with these comparisons, it is worth noting the effigy of Rose Verdun (d.10 Feb.1247) found in Belton church, Leicestershire (Fig.35). Here is an apparently defaced effigy with canopy, apparently removed to Belton church when Rose's foundation of Grace Dieu priory was dissolved in 1538. The effigy currently lies on a modern table tomb and consists of a slab supporting the effigy of a lady set under a trefoil canopy replete with ball foliage. Towards the top of the canopy, set in the angles, are a rose and the Verdun arms, one on either side. The effigy slab is unusually thick and the canopy top has five upright figures at the head and three each on the two upper sides, all kneeling in prayer or reading, apart from the topmost figure who appears to be female and is rising to heaven from her shroud aided by two surrounding figures with angel wings, uncovering her shroud[*459]. At the base of the effigy Rose's feet lie on a dragon, while on the base of the foot plate are a further three effigies, probably Rose standing with her hands raised and two women on either side kneeling in prayer. Around the side two further girls peep around the chamfered corners of the slab. The effigy is in a long flowing surcoat with loose folds, belted high at the waist. Her hands lie flat on her chest and her left forearm cradles a closed book. On her head, which rests in early style on a single rectangular cushion, she wears just a veil which flows down onto her shoulders. The apparent barbette seems caused by the refacing of the effigy which may have occurred in 1912 when the monument was 'restored'[*460]. If the scenes around the top and bottom of the slab are interpreted correctly Rose is displayed centrally at top and bottom in life and at the Resurrection. Altogether the extravagance and workmanship of the monument is vastly superior to those already examined, there appears no evidence to suggest that the effigy must be of later provenance, especially when Rose asked for lights to adorn her tomb just before her death.

It should be remembered from this brief survey that the dating of any archaeological feature by comparison with other equally undatable features is a pastime fraught with

---

[*457] *CPR 1216-25*, 439.
[*458] *Hic:Iacet:Matild:le:Caus: Orate:Pro:Anima Ei' Pat'Nos.*
[*459] My thanks go to many members of the Facebook group British Medieval History, who helped with the interpretation of this.
[*460] It is possible that some effigies had separate faces which were then glued to the main body.

historical danger, consequently it cannot be taken for granted that the Beaumaris effigy does represent Princess Joan, even if the circumstantial evidence does seem to point that way.

To help with the identification it is necessary to look at some broad statistics to place these effigies in context. Currently it is estimated that approximately 0.84% of the world population dies each year. Of the knightly class of England there were approximately 7,000 available for service around 1200, so when wives and clerics are added to this equation it gives a rough figure of some 20,000 people who may have wished to be commemorated by effigies at any one time in the thirteenth century. If this class of people capable of affording effigies or incised slabs were dying at approximately 1% per annum and each were commemorated, this would mean that some 200 new effigies were being made each year. Between the rough dates of 1200 and 1350 that would suggest a production of some 30,000 pieces of funerary art. As it can be shown that effigies were being produced in the twelfth century this figure is most certainly an underestimate for potential production of effigies before 1350. Currently there are only some 1,500 examples existing or known to have existed from the period 1100 to 1350. This is less than 5% of what might be expected if every suitably rich person was commemorated in such a fashion. Quite obviously they were not.

Regardless of the original evidence, it has recently even been suggested that the Beaumaris effigy might represent ladies as diverse as Princess Joan, Senana ferch Caradog (bef.1200-52+) the widow of Gruffydd ap Llywelyn (d.1244), or Eleanor Montfort (1252-82), the wife of Prince Llywelyn ap Gruffydd (d.1282)[461]. No doubt there will always be more suggestions than solid answers. All of the documentary evidence as well as the similar styles of the effigies and similar works of art (though few of their dates can be taken as secure), would tend to suggest that the lady represented in the effigy is indeed Joan Plantagenet (d.1237) and dates to the second quarter of the thirteenth century - probably in the period 1237 to 1241. Unfortunately suggestion is the best that the available evidence allows.

Some further evidence can be gleaned from the geological examination of both the Beaumaris and the Llanrwst sarcophagi which was carried out in 2008[462]. This showed quite conclusively that the three parts of the two tombs came from different sandstone beds, although microscopic analysis showed that both had suffered similar geological histories in terms of alteration during their laying down and diagenesis. This suggested that both original sandstone blocks had been obtained from the same or closely related quarries. Comparison with quarries in lands adjacent to Aberconwy at Bodysgallen, Degannwy, Llandudno, Conwy, Bangor and the adjacent parts of Mon all proved negative; notwithstanding it was felt that 'the nearest likely candidate quarries are those in the fluvial Carboniferous sandstone at Talacre, near Mostyn Dock'. If this is correct it may well suggest that both sarcophagi came from the lands of Basingwerk abbey, unless of course the stone was simply purchased and then brought to Llanfaes and Aberconwy in 1237 and 1240 and cut on site. If the suggestion for the origin of the sarcophagi rock is correct the fact that Tegeingl fell out of the political control of Prince Dafydd ap Llywelyn in the summer of 1241 might well offer a terminus post quem for both tombs, although there is no reason that he could purchase the stones in the period 1241-44 when he was at peace with the English king. This geological evidence therefore leads to the likelihood that both the Llanrwst and Beaumaris tombs were cut in Wales. The conclusion of this evidence would therefore appear to be that the Llanrwst sarcophagus could well be that of

[461] Gray, M., 'Four weddings, three funerals and a historical detective puzzle: a cautionary tale', *Transactions of the Anglesey Antiquarian Society and Field Club* [2014].
[462] Campbell-Bannerman, N. and Crossley, R., *North Wales Geology Association* [Jan 2008], vol.49, 4-5.

Prince Llywelyn and that the Beaumaris effigy, but not the underlying sarcophagus, could be a part of the tomb of Princess Joan. Neither case can be more than a suggestion.

With all this considered, the Llanrwst sarcophagus could conceivably belong to any of the princes buried at Aberconwy between 1200 and 1248 and possibly any number of abbots or nobles who might have been buried there up to roughly 1300. During this time six men of Venedotian princely stock are known to have been buried within the abbey. They were Gruffydd ap Cynan in 1200, Hywel ap Gruffydd in 1216, Llywelyn ap Maelgwn in 1230, Llywelyn ab Iorwerth in 1240, Dafydd ap Llywelyn in 1246 and finally Gruffydd ap Llywelyn in 1248. There is one more factor that might sway opinion towards the Llanrwst sarcophagus being that of Prince Llywelyn, and that is that his wife's aunt, Eleanor Plantagenet (1162-1214), was buried in a sarcophagus with similar decoration at Burgos in Spain in 1214 (Fig.36). Although this tomb has no effigy, but in its place a pyramidal roof, it does have 'roundels', but these are trefoil canopies, rather than quatrefoils. Regardless of this, the design seems specifically Spanish as King Alphonso X (1226-84) was buried in a similar sarcophagus (Fig.37). Back in Britain similar tombs seem to have been made for other members of King John's family. King John's tomb in Worcester cathedral has quatrefoil roundels, but these are far more sumptuous, as is the whole tomb (Fig.38). Unfortunately they are a late addition, only being made in 1529 when the tomb was modified to make it match that of Prince Arthur. Thus, although the quatrefoils contain heraldic plaques, like those postulated for the Llanrwst tomb, they cannot have had a similar provenance. When the Tudor tomb was opened in 1797 the original stone coffin containing the king's corpse was discovered within. Clearly the effigy and the sarcophagus are of the same shape - similar to that of the Llanrwst sarcophagus except that this tomb was body shaped internally (Fig.39). The effigy would appear to have originally lain directly on top of the sarcophagus which shows evidence of having been initially set in the ground, with the effigy lying directly on the church floor (Fig.40). This would appear to have been in the same style as the grave found in the excavations at Maenan abbey in 1968 and suggested as the second resting place of Prince Llywelyn. The elm boards found around the Worcester sarcophagus in 1797 probably marked an attempt to reseal the coffin after its removal to its current position and the construction of the 1529 box tomb to enclose the body and sarcophagus. The conclusion of the 1797 investigators was that the stone coffin of Higley stone had been laid in the Lady's chapel in the ground and the effigy then laid over it on the ground surface[463]. It was then later translated to its present position. Whether this was initially done in 1216, 1232 or only in 1529 remains a moot point, but the later is more likely. An interesting comment by the 1797 investigators was that the body of the king accurately reflected the image of the effigy above in both clothing and position. It therefore seems likely that the effigy of the king was placed there by the executors of his will in the immediate aftermath of the king's death, rather than later in 1232 as is currently asserted[464].

If the tomb of King John does not help with identifying the sarcophagus at Llanrwst a nearby tomb does. This is the final resting place of Matilda Longespey, nee Clifford (d.1284), the granddaughter of Prince Llywelyn and Joan Plantagenet who would appear to have been buried in Worcester priory in 1284. This tomb, as well as a masterful effigy on the lid, has six quatrefoils along its one exposed side. The other three sides are built into a wall, though it is uncertain whether this was done originally or is part of the later Tudor remodelling (Fig.41).

---

[463] The idea that John asked to be buried between the two Saxon saints, Oswald and Wulfstan, is a modern invention as a quick glance at his will shows.
[464] http://worcestercathedral.co.uk/King_John.php accessed 19 August 2017.

Certainly this sarcophagus appears the nearest match to that at Llanrwst and the identification of the effigy is proved by the multitude of Clifford arms that decorate her cloak (Fig.42).

Other tombs with quatrefoil decoration exist, or once existed, at Moccas, Herefordshire (5 quatrefoils of possibly the mid fourteenth century) and Bishop Henry Marshall (d.1210) in Exeter cathedral (three large and two small quatrefoils on either side with leaf moulding surroundings). Joan Vere (d.1293) in Chichester cathedral has similar quatrefoils, but they are more elaborate. Interestingly, they are similar to those on the tomb of Earl Richard Fitz Alan (d.1376) and his second wife Eleanor Lancaster (d.1372) which lies nearby. In both these cases the roundels are flanked by trefoil canopies. Consequently these would appear to be later variants of the Llanrwst sarcophagus design. Similarly, the tomb of King Edward III (d.1377) has quatrefoils along the base, but they are far more complex than those of Llanrwst.

Figure 14, Two tombs at Ellington, Cambridgeshire, which have similar decoration to the sarcophagus at Llanrwst.

Figure 15, The sarcophagus attributed to Prince Llywelyn in the Gwydir chapel of Llanrwst church. Note the quatrefoil roundels with central pinholes to hold the plaques in place and the central groove within the tomb. There is also an insert on the base corner (bottom left) where the tomb may have butted against an object. Similarly, the upper right corner has been chamferred away damaging a roundel. This implies that this portion of the tomb at least was moved and placed with this side between or against two objects.

Figure 16, The Fulbrook, Oxfordshire, tomb.

Figure 17, The effigy alleged to be that of Abbot Alexander Holderness of Peterborough (d.1226) set on top of a modified sarcophagus with roundels containing quatrefoils.

Figure 18, The plain and undecorated stone coffin alleged to be that of Princess Joan (d.1237). This is now sealed by a decorated sepulchral slab with a female representation upon it. Joan was buried on the seashore before Llanfaes priory was apparently built near or over the site.

Figure 19, The effigy on the tomb lid thought to represent Princess Joan (d.1237), currently within Beaumaris church porch.

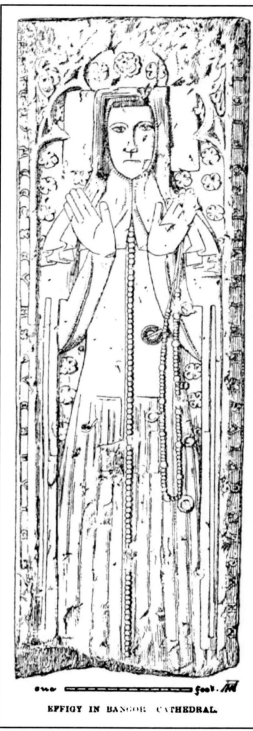

EFFIGY IN BANGOR CATHEDRAL.

Figure 20, The Lady Eva with open palms. The style of headdress and the buttons down the centre of her cloak would suggest a late 14th century date.

Figure 21, The effigy in Danby Wiske with the downturned hands. Note the more refined clothing as well as the two heraldic shields on her shoulders and the twin cushions. Such is far more 1275 to 1325 than 1200 to 1250 in style.

Figure 22, The effigy at East Worldham showing a similar wheel brooch and headwear to that worn by Princess Joan.
Photo courtesy of Allan Soedring.

Stone Coffin-lid of the Princess Joanna
Wife of Llewellyn, Prince of Wales.

Figure 23, A Victorian representation of the coffin lid assigned to Princess Joan soon after its discovery.

Figure 24, A close up of the face and headgear of the Beaumaris effigy.

Figure 25, Isabella Plantagenet, (1214-41), Empress of Germany and younger half-sister of Princess Joan of Wales.

Figure 26, Eleanor Plantagenet (1215-75), the youngest daughter of King John.

Figure 27, Princess Eleanor Montfort of Wales (d.1282).

Figure 28, The refurbished effigy of Eleanor of Aquitaine (d.1204). Note the single rectangular pillow of a type found in many early effigies.

Figure 29, The tomb effigy of Isabella of Angouleme (d.1246), the widow of King John, in Fontevrault abbey.

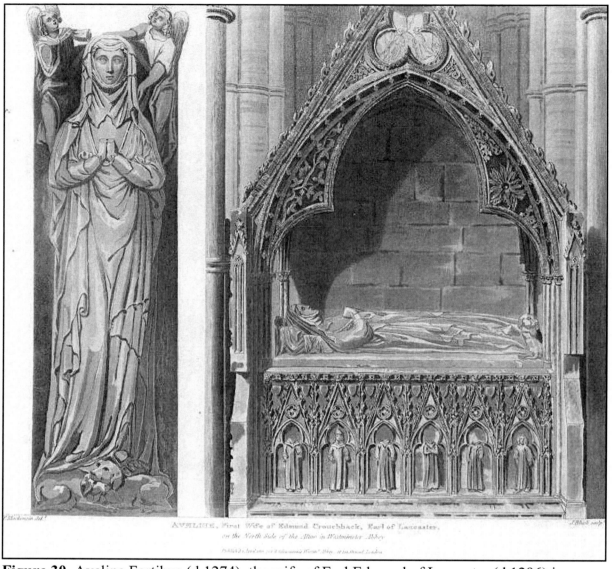

Figure 30, Aveline Fortibus (d.1274), the wife of Earl Edmund of Lancaster (d.1296) in Westminster cathedral. Note how the decoration on her tomb is trefoil, rather than quatrefoil as appears on the Llanrwst tomb.

Figure 31, The face of the effigy which seems to represent Jean Cantilupe (d.1271) at Abergavenny.

Figure 32, The second female effigy at Abergavenny set upon a modern reconstruction of a table tomb. The quatrefoils of this bear some resemblance to those on the sarcophagus at Llanrwst.

Figure 33, The rather amateurish English Bicknor effigy.

Figure 34, The effigy of Matilda le Cauz (d.1224) at Old Brampton, Derbyshire.

Figure 35, The Lady Rose Verdun (d.1246) in Belton, Leicestershire. Notice the Verdun arms on the trefoil canopy and the apparently new face glued to the defaced head.

Figure 36, The sarcophagus of Eleanor Plantagenet (rear with the three leopard heraldic device of England) and King Alphonso VIII of Castile at Burgos cathedral, Spain.

Figure 37, The tomb of King Alphonso X of Castile (d.1284).

Figure 38, King John's tomb showing the three quatrefoil roundels set in a sumptuous tomb with elaborate buttresses of a canopy style. The sarcophagus, but not the effigy, dates from 1529.

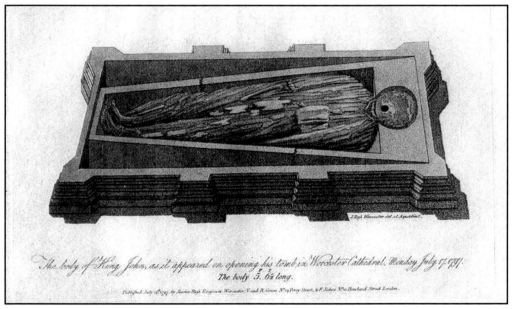

Figure 39, The body of King John as it was found in 1797, placed within in the original coffin with the head inverted, possibly in the 1529 translation.

Figure 40, A representation of the effigy of King John
showing its coffin shape which apparently matches that
of the sarcophagus below.

Figure 41, The tomb of Matilda Longespey nee Clifford (d.1284) in Worcester cathedral showing the quatrefoil roundels similar to those found on the Llanrwst sarcophagus.

Figure 42, A Victorian sketch of the heraldry on the effigy of Matilda Clifford at Worcester.

145

Aberconwy Abbey During the Wars of Prince Dafydd, 1240 to 1246

If it is uncertain if any trace of Prince Llywelyn's tomb still remains, more can be said of his last years and his successors' fight for power. The precise course of events concerning Prince Dafydd's assumption of power as well as his imprisonment of his half-brother have previously created some confusion. Once more, following the contemporary sources alleviates this confusion. The Bruts state under 1239 that:

> Dafydd ap Llywelyn seized Gruffydd, his brother, breaking faith with him and imprisoned him and his son at Criccieth (*Kruceith, Grugyeith, Krucyeith*)[*465].

> Dafydd ap Llywelyn seized Gruffydd, his brother, breaking his oath with him and he imprisoned him and his son in the castle of Criccieth.[*466]

By the implication of the juxtaposition of entires, this event occurred after the birth of the future King Edward I on 18 June 1239 and before the death of Llywelyn on 11 April 1240. However, as the Bruts were only redacted in the fourteenth century, this cannot be taken as an untainted primary source. The same is true of the Annales Cambriae, which were likewise redacted around the beginning of the fourteenth century. The probable Strata Florida and Hopton Commission versions, both have Gruffydd captured by Dafydd due to the fortunes of war, with the Strata version sandwiching this between two events, the death of Gruffydd ap Maredudd and the birth of Prince Edward[*467]. Obviously this disagrees dramatically with the Bruts which have Gruffydd captured after the birth of Edward. Further, no Gruffydd ap Maredudd is known to have died in 1239, but this year Maredudd Goeg died at Whitland[*468]. His nephew, a Gruffydd ap Maredudd, died in 1242. Whatever the case, the Strata chronicle is corrupt here. The St David's version is also corrupt and states under the year 1239:

> And Gruffydd his son was captured by his brother Dafydd and imprisoned.

The original should probably have read:

> Gruffydd, and also his son, were captured and imprisoned by his brother Dafydd.

Regardless of these renderings, it seems reasonably clear from this that the writer of the lost Welsh Chronicle believed that Dafydd had captured Gruffydd. Whether this happened at Criccieth or Criccieth castle is open to doubt. Furthermore, it is uncertain whether the prince 'and his son' were imprisoned in Criccieth as well as being captured there. Criccieth was in Eifionydd and therefore next to Gruffydd's land of Llyn.

English sources have a quite different take on Welsh affairs. Matthew Paris recorded two versions of Dafydd's takeover of power. In the first, which might have been written up near contemporaneously, he said:

[*465] RBH, 237.
[*466] Pen, 105.
[*467] *Annales Cambriae. A Translation of Harleian 3859; PRO E.164/1; Cottonian Domitian, A 1; Exeter Cathedral Library MS. 3514 and MS Exchequer DB Neath, PRO E.164/1,* ed. Remfry, P.M., [Malvern, 2007], 130.
[*468] Pen, 105.

The same year, on 11 April, which was the feast of St Guthlac, Prince Llywelyn of North Wales, after having been subdued by Gruffydd, who had already endured his heel when he made war, went the way of all flesh. After his death, Dafydd, who his father, with the consent of his eldest brother, Gruffydd, had decided should have Wales for his inheritance, now his brother, the said Gruffydd, he called treacherously to some council, in which, in order that he might allege that he might provide for the form [of peace] between them with a general agreement between each brother, agreeing peace and brotherly alliance; to which, under the conduct of Bishop Richard of Bangor and some other great men, he arrived with the intention of making peace; Dafydd, simultaneously forgetful of their fraternity and of honesty, ordered him to be seized and, even though the leaders were unwilling and cried out in protest, he ordered him to be consigned to the safe keeping of jail.[*469]

The implication of Matthew's statements is that there had been much upset before Llywelyn's death and that it had finally been agreed that Gruffydd should hold some lands in brotherly alliance with Dafydd and that Dafydd should inherit Llywelyn's title and overlordship. It was only after Llywelyn's death that Dafydd reneged on this agreement and arrested his brother when he was under safe-conduct.

Matthew's second recording of events was made after 1250 when he had to quickly concoct a new history book that was pro-royalist. This was because that year King Henry III asked to see his famous book of contemporary history. Matthew, in a blind panic as his Great Chronicle was openly and scurrilously hostile to the king and his family, produced a new, far more royalist version. This states:

The Death of Prince Llywelyn of North Wales.
Besides during the same year on the third [fourth in one ms] ides of April [11 (or 10) April], Prince Llywelyn of North Wales, troubled by a lasting palsy, went the way of all flesh. Of who's two sons, Gruffydd and Dafydd, after forsaking him to the great loss of his descendants, by whom they were born to him the sons of different mothers and were disagreeable to each other.
How Gruffydd was captured.
Indeed one day Dafydd, born legitimate from the king of England's sister, his brother Gruffydd, the firstborn but illegitimate, called him to a meeting in treachery. He [Gruffydd] came there under the conduct of Bishop Richard of Bangor imagining nothing sinister, he [Dafydd] captured him and sent the former imprisoned to his uncle the king. Who in person shackled him down in the Tower of London.[*470]

Quite obviously Matthew had written this account in hindsight and has changed its ethos. Firstly, the account was written anachronistically as it mentions the imprisonment of Gruffydd by Henry III, which only occurred on 29 August 1241 when Dafydd agreed to send Gruffydd to King Henry to be held until the dispute between the brothers was suitably resolved[*471]. Secondly, Matthew's account adds details not present in the earlier account, namely that Llywelyn had been paralysed and that the brothers had different mothers. Additionally, Matthew asserts that Gruffydd was illegitimate and that Dafydd's mother was sister to King

---

[*469] *Matthaei Parisiensis, monachi Sancti Albani, Chronica Majora*, ed. H.R. Luard [7 vols., 1872-83] IV, 8.
[*470] *Matthaei Parisiensis, Historia Anglorum*, ed. F.H. Madden [3 vols., 1866-9] II, 430.
[*471] *CPR 1232-47*, 264.

Henry. It can also be seen that Matthew thought the king would be impressed that this was now done for his benefit and that he personally was responsible for shackling Gruffydd in the Tower. Thus is history skewed for personal advancement. That said, there is nothing in the account that is demonstrably false, but the earlier section about the two brothers having come to terms before Dafydd's act of treachery is ignored as no doubt this would have made the king's conduct look dishonest - as indeed some contemporaries thought it was. It is also apparent that Matthew considered Gruffydd illegitimate, but he does not state the reason, namely that Llywelyn had repudiated his marriage to Princess Rhunallt.

Confirmation of what had happened in the dispute finally comes from a contemporary chronicle kept in East Anglia. This states in an entry under 1241:

> This year Wales was acquired by the king against Dafydd ap Llywelyn, who had imprisoned his brother Gruffydd by means of a trick a second time, who was handed over to the king, and the king, approving of the deception, imprisoned him in England. On the other hand, the land of Wales united with Dafydd, for he was of the same [royal] blood, that is the son of his [the king's] sister.[*472]

The chronicler is quite certain that Gruffydd was taken in by the same trick twice and, as Matthew had earlier reported, the king condoned this treachery. The final unravelling of this story shows that Gruffydd was initially captured, probably at Criccieth in Eifionydd and then imprisoned by Dafydd ap Llywelyn, and that this was after Gruffydd had waged war against Dafydd and his probably incapacitated father. It is interesting that Gruffydd was taken at Criccieth castle. Other castles in the Llyn peninsular that may have existed at this time were Garn Fadryn, Nefyn and Llannor castles actually in Llyn, while Dolbenmaen castle was just beyond Criccieth in Eifionydd. It is likely that Criccieth would have been the major fortress in the district since its building in the 1180s[*473]. During his lifetime Gruffydd was praised as 'Lord of the wide *Crugkaeth*'[*474], although no source names him lord of Eifionydd. Regardless of this conundrum, it seems that Gruffydd was released before his father's death and remained in harmony with his brother until treacherously captured 'a second time' in mid 1240.

Taken as a whole, these chronicle sources paint a valid picture. Gruffydd fought Prince Llywelyn for his rights as a son. After a period of uncertainty Gruffydd, Llywelyn and Dafydd came together and agreed that Dafydd would inherit the title prince of North Wales, but that Gruffydd would hold his lands, mostly in Powys, but with Llyn, under his younger brother in fraternal unity. This fighting probably took place in March 1238, when all the diplomatic activity was occurring between the king and Llywelyn. Quite possibly the agreement between the brothers only took place after Dafydd had treacherously captured Gruffydd at Criccieth. Then, after Llywelyn's death, Dafydd called Gruffydd to him for a meeting and Gruffydd complied, but asked for the bishop of Bangor and other nobles to come with him to guarantee his safe-conduct. On his arrival at court he was arrested 'a second time' by Dafydd despite the protestations of many of those present. With the standard grasp of history so rigidly employed by Wikipedia editors, it is little surprise that they take the opposite view to the original sources

---

[*472] *Chronicon Petroburgense*, ed. T. Stapleton [Camden Society, 1849], 14.

[*473] The question of whether Criccieth or Harlech was the castle built by the sons of Cynan is discussed in Remfry, PM., *Harlech Castle and its True Origins* [Ceidio, 2013], 19-20. Further research points towards Criccieth being the fortress.

[*474] Stephens, T., *The Literature of the Kymry; being a critical essay on the History of the Language and Literature of Wales* [Llandovery, 1849], 371.

and fabricate reasons and intentions for historical characters to paint Dafydd in a good light, just as Matthew Paris wished to do in the thirteenth century to please King Henry III.

> On his father's death in 1240, under Welsh law, he [Gruffydd] would have been entitled to consideration as his father's successor. Llywelyn however had excluded him from the succession and had declared Dafydd, his son by his wife Joan, to be heir to the kingdom. Llywelyn went to great lengths to strengthen Dafydd's position, probably aware that there would be considerable Welsh support for Gruffydd against the half-English Dafydd.[*475]

From the evidence it is soon clear to see that Llywelyn did all in his power to make concord and harmony between his children and that it was Dafydd who upset this with his arrest of Gruffydd after his father's death. Further, it is certainly amusing that the Wikipedia editors believe the product of a French woman (Clementia Forgeres) and a French speaking man (King John) born in Oxford to 'French' parents (Henry of Anjou and Eleanor of Aquitaine) is an Englishwoman. It has also been noted how Prince Llywelyn had changed all Welsh custom that allowed inheritance by illegitimate children and so this was no longer valid Welsh law.

Figure 43, Prince Llywelyn dying, attended by his two sons, Gruffydd and Dafydd from the Cronica Majora of Matthew Paris, probably drawn before 1250.

The resultant war does not really concern Aberconwy, but the drawing by Matthew Paris of Gruffydd and Dafydd together with their dying father does (Fig.43). Matthew was quite aware that Llywelyn died in Aberconwy abbey and therefore must have drawn his sketch knowing full well where the action was set. It may also be significant that he had Gruffydd pictured next to the dying Llywelyn with Dafydd behind him. The act of treachery by Dafydd against Gruffydd did not bode well for future relations between the prince and his magnates and before June 1241, Bishop Richard of Bangor attempted to persuade the prince to release Gruffydd. On his failure, he excommunicated Dafydd and left Wales going to King Henry and asking him to intervene on behalf of Gruffydd. Consequently, Henry asked Dafydd to release his brother or else he would come to Wales and deal with Dafydd as a rebel. Dafydd refused and at this point Gruffydd ap Madog of Powys Fadog (bef.1199-1269) promised the king his everlasting support:

> if he would invade Wales, and make deadly war against the false David and his many wrongs.[*476]

[*475] https://en.wikipedia.org/wiki/Gruffydd_ap_Llywelyn_Fawr accessed 25 November 2015.
[*476] *Matthaei Parisiensis, monachi Sancti Albani, Chronica Majora*, ed. H.R. Luard [7 vols., 1872-83] IV, 149-51.

The king took advantage of this and came with an armed host to Shrewsbury by 2 August 1241. There he made agreements with Senana, the wife of Gruffydd ap Llywelyn, who had come to gain Henry's aid in freeing her husband as early as that Easter[477]. The Shrewsbury agreement runs:

Enrolment of an agreement made at Shrewsbury on Monday 12 August (before Assumption) between the king and Senana, wife of Gruffydd the son of Llywelyn late the prince of North Wales, whom David his brother keeps in prison with Owain his son, in the name of Gruffydd, her husband, to give the king 600 marks (£400) in order that the king may deliver the said Gruffydd and Owain his son from prison on condition that he shall abide by the judgement of the king's court, whether lawfully he ought to be detained in prison; and in order that the king by judgement of his court shall cause him to have [justice] according to Welsh law, concerning the portion which ought to fall to him of the inheritance of his father Llywelyn, of which the said David now deprives him; and if the said Gruffydd and his heirs by judgement of the king's court recover the said portion, the said Senana undertakes that the said Gruffydd and his heirs shall pay yearly to the king 300 marks (£200), one third in money, one third in oxen and cows, and one third in horses by the estimation of lawful men... moreover the said Senana undertakes for the said Gruffydd and his heirs that they shall keep a firm peace with the said David touching the portion of the inheritance that shall remain to him; and if any Welshman shall rebel against the king or his heirs, the said Gruffydd and his heirs, at their own cost, shall compel him to make satisfaction to the king; and for the keeping of the these the said Senana shall give to the king her sons, Dafydd and Rhodri, as hostages... and has undertaken that Gruffydd on his liberation shall swear in a like manner; and has submitted herself in the name of Gruffydd to the spiritual censure of the bishops of Hereford and Coventry in the event of any breach of this agreement; and has undertaken that the said Gruffydd on his liberation shall ratify this agreement by an instrument in like form; and one part of this agreement she has sealed with the king's seal; moreover she has found the following pledges: Ralph Mortimer, Walter Clifford, Steward Roger Mohaut of Chester, Maelgwn ap Maelgwn, Maredudd ap Rhobert, Gruffydd ap Madog of Bromfield and Hywel and Maredudd his brothers and Gruffydd ap Gwenwynwyn, who have all given their charters thereof to the king.[478]

As can be seen from the treaty of Gwerneigron on 29 August 1241, King Henry clearly twisted the terms of his agreement with Senana for he took Gruffydd into his own prison and then tried to negotiate between the two princes. This certainly was not what Senana was asking and although Henry remained within the letter of the law, he was surely morally wrong.

In the meantime, the army continued on its way to Chester and then turned towards Gwynedd along the coast road, reaching Rhuddlan towards the middle of August. It was there on 29 August that Dafydd effectively surrendered at Gwerneigron and handed Gruffydd over to his cousin, King Henry III. Thus both king and prince betrayed the captive. Bishop Richard's opinion on this is not recorded. The opinion of the rest of the Welsh became apparent three years later when rebellion undid all Henry's achievements of 1241.

---

[477] *Curia Regis Rolls* XVI, No.1595. Easter was on 31 March 1241.
[478] Acts, 452-4; *Calendar of Charter Rolls 1226-1516* [6 vols., 1903-27] I, 262-3; *Littere Wallie, preserved in Liber A in the Public Record Office*, ed. J.G. Edwards [Cardiff, 1940], 19, 78.

Whilst this was occurring, Aberconwy continued to function as a normal Cistercian abbey and there is no evidence that it or its granges were disrupted during the desultory campaign of 1241. In the September of 1243 Aberconwy was again used to solve disputes between sister abbeys in Wales, when the case between the abbots of Margam and Caerleon were referred by the chapter general to the abbots of Aberconwy, Dore and Flaxley[*479]. This seems to have proved a failure, for the next September the same quarrel was referred to the abbots of Aberconwy, Dore and Tintern[*480].

In the meantime, war came again to Wales and once more Aberconwy was involved in the quarrel. The story can best be told by the near contemporary history recorded by Matthew Paris[*481]. He wrote that in the spring of 1244:

Prince David of North Wales sought to divest himself of the English yoke around his neck.

Around that time, Prince David of North Wales, the nephew of the lord king of England, fearing the most violent attack of the king of England would deservedly be caused against him, sent solemn envoys to the lord pope, through which he could show the same, that he himself and all his land, against the king of the English, he contemplated resigning his right to the church of Rome, nevertheless David himself and his heirs should hold it, thenceforth for an annual render of 500 marks (£333 6s 8d). And letters about this, met with the chance of justice not without the greatest outpouring of money, he obtained his deserts (whore pay) under this form:[*482]

There then follows a letter of 26 July 1244, whereby Pope Innocent, hearing that Dafydd had been forced into the treaty with Henry III 'by violence and fear', when he had been given by his parents as a ward of the Holy See, appointed the abbots of Aberconwy and Cymer to determine if Henry III had cast aside arbitration in favour of war and if so absolve Dafydd of his oath taken to the king under duress. Quite obviously this referred to the war of 1241 and the treaties of Gwerneigron and London. After the letter the pope, according to Matthew, continued:

Therefore by this secured authority, we order you that on the day before St Agnes the virgin [20 January 1245] at Caerwys in the church of *Gustefend* that you will appear in our court, to answer the above original content said by the prince, if you may see it to be expedient. When this came to the hearing of the king and his magnates, and quickly afterwards to the notice of other princes who wished to recount the news, they, with exceeding scorn, persuaded the king himself not to pay attention to the orders, and they animated hostile combat, hastening in order to attack Dafydd himself without delay. When the lord pope was acquainted with this, he conveniently ignored all this; the gift however, which he had received from the said Dafydd, he did not return.[*483]

[*479] Statuta II, 269.

[*480] Statuta II, 287.

[*481] The historical outline for the reasons for the war can be found in Richter, M., 'David ap Llywelyn, the first Prince of Wales', *The Welsh Assize Roll 1277-84*, ed. J. Conway Davies [Cardiff, 1940] V [1970-1], 208-18. Regardless, his reasoning has to be modified with reference to the real relationship between the two half brothers and Prince Llywelyn as discussed in the chapters above.

[*482] *Matthaei Parisiensis, monachi Sancti Albani, Chronica Majora*, ed. H.R. Luard [7 vols., 1872-83] IV 399-400.

[*483] *Matthaei Parisiensis, monachi Sancti Albani, Chronica Majora*, ed. H.R. Luard [7 vols., 1872-83] IV 399-400. It is interesting that in doing this Dafydd was merely copying what his step-father-in-law, King John, had done in May 1213, *Foedera, Conventiones, Litterae etc*, ed. T. Rymer and R. Sanderson, 4th edn, by A. Clarke, F. Holbrooke, and J. Caley [4 vols. in 7 parts, 1816-69] I, 79; *Monumenta de Insula*

(continued...)

The king, after receiving the pope's missive, took the opportunity to reply. Unfortunately this reply has been lost, but he had a response from the pontiff on 8 April 1245.

> Order to the bishops of Ely and Carlisle to revoke what has been done and pronounce invalid whatever may be done by the abbots of Aberconwy (*Haberconnuum*) and Cymer (*Keneri*) in pursuance of papal letters commanding them to absolve Prince David of North Wales from an oath which he took to obey the commands of the king of England. *Exposuit nobis...* Lyons, vi Id. Apr.,2 Innocent IV.[484]

This overturned the commission set up by the abbots of Aberconwy and Cymer and placed the bishops of Carlisle and Ely in their place and states that it had been found out that Dafydd 'who governs for himself the principality of North Wales' was like his ancestors 'vassals of the kings of England, the predecessors of this king, as is on record from this time and beyond memory'. Paris contemptuously states at this:

> And which Christians do not know that the prince of Wales is a vassal of the king of England?[485]

The pope, according to Matthew, went on to state that a false suggestion had been put to him that Dafydd's parents had given North Wales to the church of Rome. Quite obviously the pope was not happy that he had been misled - in this Dafydd appears to have been following the route followed by his father in his own convoluted matrimonial affairs. The pope further relaxed the sentences of interdict and excommunication set in place by the abbots of Aberconwy and Cymer. Despite this, the pope did not wish to move against Dafydd for his lie as he 'truly believes the oath' that he had taken on the matter[486]. In the meantime, ecclesiastical measures had been moved against Dafydd culminating in the king asking Bishop Walter of Worcester to have him and his adherents excommunicated for breach of faith on 29 November 1244[487]. No action seems to have been taken against the abbot of Aberconwy for his part in the affair, but events were pushing his abbey towards the forefront of military affairs.

The new war dragged on through the early months of 1245 with Dafydd taking Mold castle, only ten miles from Chester and eight miles beyond Ruthin, the caput of Dyffryn Clwyd, on 28 March[488]. Despite the fighting, on 16 June 1245, Earl Richard of Cornwall founded Hailes abbey[489]. This event would many years later allow the compilation of the Aberconwy Register. At the same time the king was finally preparing to move against Dafydd after a long and patient wait of nearly a year. Between 9 and 24 June it was recorded that

---

[483] (...continued)
Manniae, tr & ed. Oliver, JR. [2 vols, Douglas, 1860-61] II, 43-4, 53-7.
[484] Summary from TNA SC.7/20/19.
[485] *Matthaei Parisiensis, monachi Sancti Albani, Chronica Majora*, ed. H.R. Luard [7 vols., 1872-83] IV, 323-4.
[486] *Foedera, Conventiones, Litterae etc*, ed. T. Rymer and R. Sanderson, 4th edn, by A. Clarke, F. Holbrooke, and J. Caley [4 vols. in 7 parts, 1816-69] I, 149; *Councils and Ecclesiastical Documents relating to GB and Ireland*, ed. A.W. Haddan and W. Stubbs [2 vols., Oxford, 1869-78] I, 471-2.
[487] *Foedera, Conventiones, Litterae etc*, ed. T. Rymer and R. Sanderson, 4th edn, by A. Clarke, F. Holbrooke, and J. Caley [4 vols. in 7 parts, 1816-69] I, 151; *Councils and Ecclesiastical Documents relating to GB and Ireland*, ed. A.W. Haddan and W. Stubbs [2 vols., Oxford, 1869-78] I, 472. Dafydd's adherents included Ednyfed Fychan (d.1246), Maredudd ap Richard (d.1257), Gruffydd ab Owain [Brogyntyn] and Tewdwr ap Madog.
[488] *Annales Cestrienses, a chronicle of the abbey of St. Werburgh, Chester*, ed. and trans. Christie, R.C., Record Society for Lancashire and Cheshire XIV [1887], 62.
[489] 'Annales Monasterii de Waverleia', *Annales Monastici*, ed. H.R. Luard [5 vols., 1864-9] II, 337.

Justice John Lestrange of Chester at the king's command had sent directly to Dafydd ap Llywelyn once prince of North Wales and other Welshmen to account for their homicides, burnings, deprivations and other transgressions as well as damages perpetuated in the king's realm against the king's peace. This had been sent via the agency of several religious men carrying the royal letters to Gresford (*Crucem Griffini*) or similar places several times during 1244. The transgressors, listed as Dafydd ap Llywelyn, Maredudd ap Madog, Madog ap Madog, Gruffydd ab Owain, Owain ap Bleddyn, Elias ab Yarvo, Llywelyn ap Maredudd and Llywelyn his brother, Madog ap Gwenwynwyn, Llywelyn *Wahan* and his brothers, Gruffydd ab Owain, Owain ap Hywel and Iorwerth Goch (*Yaruch Gad*) ap Madog via Reginald Scot, Adam Brondlast, Ralph Ree, Thomas Hese, Roger Andeslawe, Roger ?, Robert Gerecoc and Robert Wykton... did not come. Therefore John Lestrange was ordered to go and summon them to the king's court for Easter 1245 at Westminster to reply to these charges. Once more they did not come, nor did they appear at Trinity, so finally they were summoned to appear at Chester on 16 August (the day after the Assumption of St Mary) to reply to the aforesaid transgressions[*490].

In the meantime, the king began to move militarily against his rebels. On 11 June Henry began to make his dispositions for the coming campaign[*491]. On 1 July the king finally set the date of 1 August for his campaign to begin and ordered the justiciar of Chester to begin stockpiling materials for a castle building programme as well as victuals for the coming army[*492]. The costs of such campaigns are readily apparent when the king ordered that 5,000 marks (£3,333 6s 8d) were to be prepared to take with the king for expenses in the forthcoming Welsh expedition. Simultaneously imprests of some £300 were made to the king's nearest supporters and later a further 2,000 marks (£1,333 6s 8d) were borrowed from Earl Richard of Cornwall[*493]. The result, a fortnight after its supposed start date, was the royal invasion of Wales and the assault on Aberconwy abbey. The progress of this campaign is easily followed by a contemporary chronicle.

> That year Prince David ap Llywelyn of Wales, undertook much evil in the lands of the king of England; and deceiving the court of the pope, he undertook to dominate Snowdonia against the English king. Therefore the king gathered an army from England and Ireland and around 15 August [the feast of the little Assumption] he entered Wales, and strengthened the castle of Degannwy (*Gannock*); and in that place with his army he existed in great want, enduring to the full a lack of food and drink; many were lost there though few of the Welsh were killed; from there in great wariness they returned about 11 November [the feast of St Martin].[*494]

The castle of Degannwy lay on the opposite side of the Conwy to the modern town of Conway, in the centre of which stands the old abbey church of Aberconwy. As such the abbey was moved straight into the front line of the conflict. The story of what happened is eloquently told by Matthew Paris, a man who was acquainted with many of the protagonists who fought there.

[*490] *Curia Regis Roll 1243-45*, 357-8, No.1727.
[*491] *CPR 1232-47*, 463-4; *Calendar of Liberate Rolls, 1226-1272* [6 vols., 1916-64] *1240-45*, 311.
[*492] *Matthaei Parisiensis, Historia Anglorum*, ed. F.H. Madden [3 vols., 1866-9] II, 504-5; *CCR 1242-47*, 321, 322.
[*493] *Calendar of Liberate Rolls, 1226-1272* [6 vols., 1916-64] *1240-45*, 317, 319; *CPR 1232-47*, 459.
[*494] 'Annales Prioratus de Dunstaplia', *Annales Monastici*, ed. H.R. Luard [5 vols., 1864-9] III, 168.

Concerning the casualties caused by the war at Degannwy that happened while the king stayed in that very place.

While from the week of 1ˢᵗ October while the lord king [was] on the borders of lower Wales by a river which flowed between there and Snowdon, already nearly two months he stayed there constructing a castle, impregnably sited and walled, some noble of the king's army, concerned to inform his friends about this, thus he wrote this.

Greetings. The lord king with his army made pause at Degannwy, to strengthen some castle which was already strongly established there; and we about the former live in our tents in vigils, fastings and prayers for cold and want.

In vigils due to fear of the Welsh suddenly and by night attacking us.

In fastings on accounts of the failure of provisions, because a farthing loaf costs 5d.

In prayers in order to return home alive and uninjured.

In regard to cold and exposure because our houses are linen and we lack winter clothes. Nevertheless there is some small branch of the tidal sea just like a port under the said castle where we stay; to which place ships often come during our stay bringing victuals from Ireland and Chester; and this estuary is between us and Snowdon in which place the Welsh now dwell; and it is in width as far as a crossbow can shoot when the sea is full. However on Monday 18 September [the next before the feast of St Michael] after noon it happened that some ship from the parts of Ireland came, carrying victuals to sell to us, to the entrance of the port. Which with improvident steering, the sea receded leaving it on dry land, of course on the furthest bank towards the Welsh under our aforesaid castle. Consequently the Welsh rushed to take possession of it while [it was] on dry land. And we from the near bank seeing this sent over the river by means of small boats 300 Welsh Marchers of ours from Cheshire and Shropshire, and with them crossbowmen and armoured knights to defend the said ship. When the Welsh saw this from the shelter of their usual woods and well-known mountains they conferred with each other. And our knights attended by our men, pursued them for a distance of two leagues[*495], although they were on foot because it was not possible to bring horses over the river with them, many of the Welsh were wounded and killed. Then our men turned back, as though they had completely conquered the enemy, just as the greedy and the needy, lootings, robberies and burnings they carried out over the river, amongst other profanities, an abbey of the Cistercian order, Aberconwy, all the goods and besides chalices and books, they disrespectfully plundered, burning the outbuildings of the same. Meanwhile the Welsh howling and clamouring assembled a great force of their men and attacked our men who were loaded under the worst plunder and besides enveloped with their sins, many of our men were put to flight, wounded and killed as they fled unsuccessfully back to the ship. However some of our men preferred to be covered by waves and choosing to perish under water than be killed by their enemies, voluntarily committed suicide under the waves of the sea. Even our knights were taken alive and imprisoned. But because they heard that we had killed some of their nobles and particularly Naveth ab Odo, the most elegant and strenuous of juveniles, and so they hanged ours, decapitated them and horribly tore them to pieces; and finally threw

---

[*495] A Medieval league was usually about three miles, although sometimes it was only one mile!

the wretched corpses limb by limb into the river, [cursing] their wicked greed, as the church, especially one of such devouts, they had shown so little consideration to.[496]

From this it can be seen that there was no great damage done to Aberconwy church. The building itself was pillaged, but not damaged. It was the outbuildings that were burned. This may suggest that the main building was already stone but the ancillary buildings were still of timber. Whatever the case, it was over five years before the king bothered to make any sort of reparation for the damage carried out by his Welsh soldiers of the Perfeddwlad and Powys. On 13 May 1251 he ordered the sheriff of Shropshire to let the abbot of Aberconwy (*Abercunuay*) have 50 marks (£33 6s 8d) for the damages sustained by the burning of his buildings and granges in time of war[497]. Quite possibly more damage was done to the granges, which would have been pillaged to support the royal army, than had been done to the monastery buildings. The idea that the church of St Mary was rebuilt due to the damage done in the 1245 war is therefore false.

After the king withdrew from Degannwy, he granted on 16 November 1245, to Owain ap Gruffydd, the eldest son of the recently deceased Gruffydd ap Llywelyn, two cantrefs of the Perfeddwlad. The only reference remaining to the grant runs:

> Promise by Owain ap Gruffydd that he and his heirs will be faithful to the king and his heirs for ever on pain of losing the two cantrefs of land which the king has committed to him as well as all his other land in Wales belonging to him by inheritance. Witnessed by Ralph Fitz Nicholas, Geoffrey Despenser, Hugh Vivona, Robert Muscegros, Herbert Fitz Matthew, Peter Genevre, John Lexinton, Nicholas Boleville, Walter Luton, Anketil Malore and others. Protestation by him that he has plighted his faith to the king of his own free will and not through fear or torture or prison or any other thing, and he has taken his oath that not for fear or hatred or even treaty will he stand against the king, and if he should withdraw at any time from the king's service he submits himself and his heirs to the jurisdiction and power of the archbishop of Canterbury and the bishops of Worcester and Hereford to excommunicate him without appeal or remedy of a higher court, which he hereby renounces.[498]

Presumably the cantrefs granted were Rhufoniog based on Denbigh and Dyffryn Clwyd based on Ruthin. If effective this would have left Tegeingl and Rhos, with the new castles of Degannwy and Diserth, to the king himself as heir to the county of Cheshire. The grant of the two southern cantrefs of the Perfeddwlad would have made Owain the lord of the Aberconwy granges of Pentrefoelas, Ceirniog, Llanfair Rhyd Castell, Llyn Cymmer and Llechwedd Cryn Llwyn [Hireathog]. Probably Owain was unable to occupy these lands although Dafydd was held behind the Conwy to the north. To back Owain's claim to the two southern cantrefs the king granted him the rather measly sum of 20 marks (£13 6s 8d) and wrote to the king's faithful men of Wales and the Marches.

---

[496] *Matthaei Parisiensis, monachi Sancti Albani, Chronica Majora*, ed. H.R. Luard [7 vols., 1872-83] IV, 482-3.
[497] *Calendar of Liberate Rolls, 1226-1272* [6 vols., 1916-64] *1245-51*, 352.
[498] *CPR 1232-47*, 462.

The king is well pleased that they shall come to Owain ap Gruffydd, whom he has released from prison, and give him aid in his fealty and service to the king and the king will defend him and them.[*499]

Despite these signs of royal favour it is impossible to now know to what extent Owain made any impression upon the southern Perfeddwlad against his half-uncle, Prince Dafydd and his major supporter in 1245/46, the future Prince Llywelyn ap Gruffydd (d.1282), Owain's next youngest brother. At this time Llywelyn ap Gruffydd can be seen as firmly in Prince Dafydd's camp and was lord of various lands in the early 1240s in the Middle Marches of Wales where he acted on behalf of his uncle[*500]. Indeed, Llywelyn appears as nothing less than lord of Dyffryn Clwyd for his uncle as early as 27 September 1243[*501]. There is absolutely no evidence that Owain managed to make any headway against his younger brother in what appears to be a repetition of the events of 1212. This would mean that Llywelyn and not his brother Owain Goch had control of the eastern granges of Aberconwy abbey from at least 1243 until 1245/6.

In the meanwhile the desultory war continued on its sorry course until 25 February 1246 when Prince Dafydd ap Llywelyn died at Aber, to be succeeded by his two nephews, the eldest sons of his elder half brother, Gruffydd ap Llywelyn[*502].

> The hand which last year held the breach
> At Aberconwy until put to rest.
> Grandson of the king of England, from a host of kings,
> Son of the king of Wales, of steadfast lineage,
> He was a man who sprang, great joy of the people,
> From the true royal lineage of kings...[*503]

On his death the rebellious Welsh, against those who remained loyal to King Henry III, chose Llywelyn ap Gruffydd as their prince. On hearing this his royalist brother, Owain Goch, fled his royal protection and 'unexpectedly leaped in flight like a hare to his Welsh den'[*504]. Not surprisingly the local Chester chronicle took much interest in these events and adds important details.

> Prince Dafydd ap Llywelyn of Wales died on 25 February and was buried at Aberconwy by the side of his father. In the same week Owain the son of Gruffydd the brother of Dafydd, who had been long in prison in London and had afterwards for a long time stayed in the king's peace in the parts of Cheshire, secretly fled into Wales

---

[*499] *CPR 1232-47*, 446.

[*500] *CCR 1242-47*, 347-8; Acts, 479; BL. Harliean Ms.1240, fo. 57, No.1; fo. 58, No.12; Remfry, PM. *The Killing of Prince Llywelyn of Wales, 10 December 1282* [Ceidio, 2014], 7.

[*501] Acts, 491.

[*502] 'Annales Prioratus de Wigornia', *Annales Monastici*, ed. H.R. Luard [5 vols., 1864-9] IV, 437; *Matthaei Parisiensis, monachi Sancti Albani, Chronica Majora*, ed. H.R. Luard [7 vols., 1872-83] IV, 517-8; RBH, 239; *Annales Cestrienses, a chronicle of the abbey of St. Werburgh, Chester*, ed. and trans. Christie, R.C., Record Society for Lancashire and Cheshire XIV [1887], 64.

[*503] The elegy of Dafydd Benfras to Prince Dafydd, translated by Ann Parry Owen, Smith, J.B., *Llywelyn ap Gruffydd: Prince of Wales* [UWP, 2001], 54.

[*504] *Matthaei Parisiensis, monachi Sancti Albani, Chronica Majora*, ed. H.R. Luard [7 vols., 1872-83] IV, 517-8. Although Owain had been granted the houses of Shotwick on 1 November 1245, *CPR 1232-47*, 465, there is no evidence as to his whereabouts four months later, contrary to the impression given in Lloyd, J.E., *History of Wales* [2 vols., 1911] II, 707.

and having had parley with his brother, Llywelyn, divided between themselves the lands that had been Dafydd's, their uncle.[505]

It is from this chronicle that we learn that Dafydd and his father lay side by side in Aberconwy abbey church. If this is correct it means that the monks only moved Prince Llywelyn ab Iorwerth with them when they moved to Maenan - assuming his was the grave in the centre of the presbytery. Alternatively, it might be more likely that the monks took with them Prince Dafydd, the royal nephew of King Henry III and cousin of King Edward I. It is simply impossible to say and really must be considered pointless to even speculate without the slightest evidence. It is quite possible indeed, as the abbey considered Edward I as its founder at Maenan, that they took no Venedotian remains with them to the new site. Consequently it is quite possible that the grave in the presbytery was that of an abbot or even some other notable.

With the division of Gwynedd agreed between them, by the advice of prudent men[506], Owain and Llywelyn tried to end the war. Thus on 5 March 1247, the king confirmed that a truce had been negotiated by Justice John Grey of Chester with Owain and Llywelyn and that it should come into force on Easter day (31 March 1247) and last for five weeks, 'so that all Welshmen who are of the king's party are admitted in the meantime to the lands which they held on the day when they came to the king's fealty and service'. Safe conduct was also granted to the princes or their men in coming to the king at Oxford after Easter[507]. Presumably the abbot of Aberconwy was allowed to reclaim his damaged granges in the Perfeddwlad by this agreement if he had lost control of them. Certainly around this time the princely brothers would appear to have jointly sent an emissary to the king to ask for peace[508]. Despite this, the king was not at all happy with the Welsh princes' position, or at least took up a strong negotiating position. On 20 April 1246, just after Dafydd ap Llywelyn died, Bishop Richard of Bangor professed his faith to King Henry and added the following statements to his declaration.

> We wish it clearly to be known that we well know that Dafydd, the son of Llywelyn once prince of North Wales, spontaneously willed to you, and was not coerced when he decided that the aforesaid King Henry of England his illustrious heir to all the dominion that Dafydd himself held in Wales, and this if the said Dafydd died without heirs of his body. Besides we understand and testify that the same Dafydd in the same manner bound himself to the aforesaid lord king by his charter that if at any time he went against the king's peace between them entered into between them at Rhuddlan and afterwards renewed at London, that all his land should fall to the lord king himself and his heirs, and that the same Dafydd and the heirs of his body by right that which they held in Wales or elsewhere in the kingdom of England in perpetuity.[509]

---

[505] *Annales Cestrienses, a chronicle of the abbey of St. Werburgh, Chester*, ed. and trans. Christie, R.C., Record Society for Lancashire and Cheshire XIV [1887], 67.

[506] *Annales Cambriae. A Translation of Harleian 3859; PRO E.164/1; Cottonian Domitian, A 1; Exeter Cathedral Library MS. 3514 and MS Exchequer DB Neath, PRO E.164/1*, ed. Remfry, P.M., [Malvern, 2007], 133.

[507] *CPR 1232-47*, 498.

[508] *Matthaei Parisiensis, monachi Sancti Albani, Chronica Majora*, ed. H.R. Luard [7 vols., 1872-83] iv, 551.

[509] *Littere Wallie, preserved in Liber A in the Public Record Office*, ed. J.G. Edwards [Cardiff, 1940], 21-2.

Despite this, the two princes of Gwynedd met their king deep in England and on 30 April 1247 agreed the treaty of Woodstock[*510]. The next day the two protested to the king that his land did not include all the River Conwy, but merely ran to the middle of it[*511]. Such a point would have been important to the abbots and monks of Aberconwy, lying as they now did, on the border between the kingdom of England and the subject land of North Wales. It should also be noted that the treaty as preserved in its 1290s copy states quite clearly that all the river belonged to the king.

Although not mentioned in any treaty, it seems likely that Owain Goch took the western parts of Gwynedd as his share of North Wales, viz. Aberffraw, Menai, Arfon, Llyn and Eifionydd, while his brother Llywelyn held the east and south, Cemaes, Dindaethwy, Archllechwedd and Ardudwy[*512]. Certainly later land grants seem to support such a disposition. Presumably Llywelyn also held Penllyn, although this may have been split between the brothers. With this peace agreement some form of normality returned to Aberconwy abbey and its granges, with a great portion of the monks' lands now lying in areas administered directly by the king's delegates of the Perfeddwlad, viz. the granges of Creuddyn, Pentrefoelas, Ceirniog, Llanfair Rhyd Castell [Hiraethog], Llyn Cymmer and Llechwedd Cryn Llwyn. Of the rest, Conwy Gyffin with the site of the abbey lay in the lands of Llywelyn, as did Arddau and Darlas and perhaps a small portion of southern Nanhwynain. Owain held Gelliniog and Bodgedwydd on Mon; Ffriwlwyd in Eifionydd and Cwm, Rhedynog Felen, Nant Call and Nanhwynain in Arfon. If these divisions caused any problems, none are recorded.

Aberconwy Abbey Between the Wars, 1247 to 1276

With Wales once more at peace, Waleran Teuton was ordered by the king on 11 July 1247 to allow the abbot of Aberconwy 20 marks (£13 6s 8d) of the king's gift. This was almost a year after the abbot of Basingwerk had been given the same amount[*513]. Ten days later the king must have had further dealing with the abbot, for on 21 July 1247 he issued the following statement from Marlborough.

> The king has taken into his hand and protection the abbey of Aberconwy (*Aberkonny*) and the monks of the Cistercian order there, their lands and possessions and these are to be protected as the king's own; and they are to be quit of toll, passage, panage[*514], pontage and every custom belonging to the king throughout his land; and have acquittance of all things which they or members of their community (*famuli*) and servants can show to be theirs, as other monks of that order have. And no one shall presume to put any vexation or injury or grievance upon them upon forfeiture to the king as the charters of Henry II and King John testify. Witnessed by Earl Richard of Cornwall, the king's brother, John Mansell the provost of Beverley, Ralph Fitz Nicholas, William Vescy, Paulinus Peyvre, Robert Muscegros, William Beaumont and others.[*515]

[*510] *Littere Wallie, preserved in Liber A in the Public Record Office*, ed. J.G. Edwards [Cardiff, 1940], 7.
[*511] *CPR 1232-47*, 501.
[*512] Smith, J.B., *Llywelyn ap Gruffydd: Prince of Wales* [UWP, 2001], 66-7.
[*513] *Calendar of Liberate Rolls, 1226-1272* [6 vols., 1916-64], *1245-51*, 66, 59.
[*514] The previous charter of 1232 had paage and not panage. One transcript, probably the 1232 one, is in error.
[*515] *CPR, 1232-47*, 504.

Possibly about the same time and certainly before 1254, Llywelyn ap Gruffydd granted to Aberconwy abbey the chapels of St Patrick of Cemaes (*Kenmeys*) and St Peplicius of Caernarfon (*Llanbeblig*) at their first voidance[*516]. This may have happened around the time the abbots of Strata Florida and Aberconwy went into England to recover the body of Gruffydd ap Llywelyn (d.1244) after seeking the permission of King Henry. Once more the corpse of a Welsh prince of Gwynedd was laid to rest in Aberconwy abbey, probably next to his father and half-brother[*517]. This seems to have been done 'about the month of May' in 1248 according to the elegy by Dafydd Benfras[*518]. Relations between Aberconwy and the Crown seemed stable at this time and on 13 May 1251, the sheriff of Shropshire was ordered

> to cause the abbot of Aberconwy (*Abercunuay*) to have 50 marks (£33 6s 8d) for damages sustained by the burning of his buildings and granges in war time.[*519]

Quite clearly this was in recompense for the assault on the abbey by the king's Welsh in 1244 as well as compensation for all the crops looted from the abbey's numerous Welsh granges. It is also notable that no other North Welsh abbey received any compensation, apart from that already noted to Basingwerk in 1246. Further, the abbot of Aberconwy did have a dispute with the neighbouring house of Cymer (*Comminz*) within eighteen months of this grant. This suit was ordered to be settled by the abbots of Margam, Buildwas and Combermere in September 1252[*520]. As both these abbeys had lands that had now been partitioned between Owain and Llywelyn it is possible that the dispute indicates that there was already a degree of antagonism between the two brothers concerning land access. The next year, 1253, the tithe of Norwich was carried out and this found that the church of Dwygyfylchi (*Duygenelby*) had been given to the Cistercians and was now worth 1½m 16d (£1 1s 4d)[*521]. Probably this church had been granted to Aberconwy at its foundation, it being only 3 miles away from the abbey site. Dwygyfylchi was still the abbey's property when it was dissolved in 1537. Unfortunately the church has been throughly rebuilt in 1760 and 1889[*522].

The history of Aberconwy is pretty much blank during this time of peace following the treaty of Woodstock. As ever the peace did not last and late in 1256 another war was begun against Henry III after Llywelyn had defeated his two brothers in battle and seized all of North Wales. He then proceeded to expel his cousin, Llywelyn ap Maredudd, who 'preferred fidelity to unfaithfulness', from Meirionydd the next year[*523]. By these acts Llywelyn brought all of the Aberconwy lands to the west of the Conwy under his jurisdiction. Despite this, the lands to the east lay mainly under the control of the Crown, backed as it was by the royal castles of Degannwy and Diserth. This had become part of the extensive domains of the future King

---

[*516] Unfortunately the original has not survived, but the grant was confirmed by Edward III on 24 March 1332, *Calendar of Charter Rolls 1226-1516* [6 vols., 1903-27], *1327-41*, 269; *Registrum vulgariter nuncupatum, 'The Record of Caernarvon'*, ed. Ellis, H. [London, 1838], 148. On 20 November 1388, the advowson of Llanbeblig church, together with the chapel of Caernarfon which was annexed to it, was granted by the king to the Benedictine nuns of St Mary, Chester, due to their extreme poverty, *CPR 1385-89*, 530-1. Its non appearance in the Aberconwy listing again points to the Register being later than 1388.
[*517] RBH, 243; Pen, 108.
[*518] Lloyd-Jones, J., *The Court Poets of the Welsh Princes* [The Sir John Rhys memorial lecture, London, 1948], 18-9.
[*519] *Calendar of Liberate Rolls, 1226-1272* [6 vols., 1916-64], *1245-51*, 352.
[*520] Statuta II, 381.
[*521] The list is reproduced in *Archaeologia Cambrensis* [1894], 30.
[*522] The idea that this church had been swapped for Llanbeblig does not hold water as this church was granted to the abbey by Llywelyn ap Gruffydd around 1254. The suggestion of the 1254 swap is found in Hays, RW, *The History of the Abbey of Aberconway, 1186-1537* [UWP, 1963], 117.
[*523] Smith, J.B., *Llywelyn ap Gruffydd: Prince of Wales* [UWP, 2001], 91.

Edward I (1272-1307) in 1254[*524]. Consequently, Llywelyn endeavoured to control the surrounding countryside from November 1256 onwards with increasing success. This must have caused damage to the Aberconwy granges during these years

With Llywelyn's early victories the abbot of Aberconwy appears to have joined the prince's entourage. Consequently on 26 April 1258, an agreement was made between Prince Llywelyn and Maredudd ap Rhys of Deheubarth. This was witnessed at Esgair Ddu Llanbedr (*Ekaedu Vannebedeyr*) by the abbot (unfortunately unnamed) together with the bishops of Bangor and St Asaphs, the abbot of Enlli and the priors of Beddegelert and Ynys Llannog (*Onyslannauc*)[*525]. A month later on 31 May 1258, Llywelyn appointed Master Madog ap Philip and Abbot Einion of Aberconwy as his representatives at the reforming Oxford parliament[*526]. They were apparently on their way by 2 June when King Henry ordered Peter Montfort to escort Llywelyn's men to Oxford for the parliament[*527]. This he obviously did and on 17 June they proceeded to negotiate a thirteen month truce that was to last until 1 August 1259. This was far less than Llywelyn wanted as he had offered the king 4,500 marks (£3,000) for a lasting peace, but Henry would not hear of it[*528]. Instead the proctors agreed on Llywelyn's behalf that each party was to have seisin of the lands, men, castles and other things as they currently stood. The king was allowed to provision Degannwy (*Gannok*) and Diserth (*Dissard*) castles as well as munition them via two boats of 12 oars each or less, or by land if there was a tempest or other impediments to the sea route[*529]. Despite this agreement, the two clerics did not return home, but stayed on in parliament. Consequently it was only on 24 June 1258, that Abbot Einion of *Aberconewey* and Master Madog ap Philip or other proctors or envoys of Llywelyn ap Gruffydd, who had come to the king to the number of ten horsemen, received a safe conduct to return home until the week after 29 June (octaves of St Peter's Chains)[*530]. For some reason the party did not make use of this and on 28 June they received another safe conduct which was to last a fortnight and allowed them to come to the king at Oxford with their households until they returned to their own parts[*531]. On the same day the two clerics, recorded as the proctors and special envoys of Llywelyn ap Gruffydd, promised to send 100 marks (£66 13s 4d) to the king via Justiciar Roger Mohaut of Chester in order to secure the agreed truce[*532]. While at Oxford Abbot Einion had obviously taken the opportunity to press the king on his concerns for his abbey as on 29 June the king issued a warrant allowing Einion to buy fishing nets in Chester and authorised the justiciar of Chester to let this happen[*533].

The new truce got off to a rocky start and by 8 July 1258 it was stated that Llywelyn had violated it, which apparently led to Llywelyn sending the king a peace offering[*534]. Finally on 27 July, the king replied that the truce would be better kept in future in reply to a further

[*524] The anti-Edwardian commentary of Matthew Paris is the main source for the early days of this conflict, but it should be remembered that Matthew was no unbiassed observer. *Matthaei Parisiensis, monachi Sancti Albani, Chronica Majora*, ed. H.R. Luard [7 vols., 1872-83], VI, 594, 596-8.

[*525] *Littere Wallie, preserved in Liber A in the Public Record Office*, ed. J.G. Edwards [Cardiff, 1940], 168-9, No.294; Acts, 501-2.

[*526] *Littere Wallie, preserved in Liber A in the Public Record Office*, ed. J.G. Edwards [Cardiff, 1940], 29.

[*527] *CPR 1247-58*, 632.

[*528] *Matthaei Parisiensis, monachi Sancti Albani, Chronica Majora*, ed. H.R. Luard [7 vols., 1872-83] V, 727.

[*529] *CPR 1247-58*, 636.

[*530] *CPR 1247-58*, 664.

[*531] *CPR 1247-58*, 639.

[*532] *Littere Wallie, preserved in Liber A in the Public Record Office*, ed. J.G. Edwards [Cardiff, 1940], 13.

[*533] *CCR 1256-59*, 316.

[*534] *Foedera, Conventiones, Litterae etc*, ed. T. Rymer and R. Sanderson, 4th edn, by A. Clarke, F. Holbrooke, and J. Caley [4 vols. in 7 parts, 1816-69] II, 40; *Matthaei Parisiensis, monachi Sancti Albani, Chronica Majora*, ed. H.R. Luard [7 vols., 1872-83], V, 704.

complaint sent by Llywelyn via a monk from Aberconwy[535]. The truce was renewed on 29 June 1259, but it would appear that no clerics played any part in this[536]. A year later on 18 August 1260, the king confirmed the truce negotiated by Abbot Einion of Aberconwy and Bishop Richard of Bangor at Montgomery ford[537]. This was confirmed and laid out in detail by the king on 12 March 1261 in a document that mentioned the names of Llywelyn's negotiators[538]. A year later, between 4 May and 24 June 1262, the abbot journeyed again to England and in the king's court ratified on behalf of Llywelyn an extension of the truce for another two years until August 1264[539]. Despite this, the truce collapsed at the end of 1262, while the stirrings of civil war grew in England and the Marches. During these manoeuvrings the princes of Gwynedd and Powys buried their differences and on 12 December 1263 Gruffydd ap Gwenwynwyn paid homage to the Lord Llywelyn ap Gruffydd, prince of Wales. Gruffydd also swore fealty on the Holy Gospels in the presence of Bishop Richard of Bangor and the unnamed abbots of Aberconwy, Strata Marcella, fourteen named notables and others unnamed. Almost as a matter of course the record of the agreement ended with a clause calling for the excommunication of either party who should break the agreement. This excommunication was to be performed by the bishops of Bangor and St Asaph, together with the abbots of Aberconwy and Strata Marcella[540]. It should also be noted that Bangor was the diocese in which most of Llywelyn's possessions lay, while St Asaph held sway within Gruffydd's domains. Similarly, Aberconwy was the spiritual home of the princes of Gwynedd, while Strata Marcella performed the same purpose for the princes of Powys. It is quite clear from these few references that during the period 1256 to 1263 Abbot Einion was a close confederate of Prince Llywelyn. Yet after all this activity, Aberconwy then fades from the records for nearly a decade.

Nearly ten years later on 12 April 1272 at Caernarfon, Rhodri ap Gruffydd quitclaimed his princely rights in Wales to Prince Llywelyn. In this document Rhodri promised not to disturb the prince as he had sworn to the bishops of Bangor and St Asaph, the abbots of Aberconwy, Basingwerk and Enlli and the archdeacons of Bangor and St Asaph. Presumably these men were all present, although none witnessed the charter[541]. In the mid 1270s Llywelyn seems once again closely entwined with Aberconwy, although the apparent hiatus before this date could well be simply due to no documents of this period having been preserved. On Sunday 3 September 1273, Prince Llywelyn was at Llanfair Rhyd Castell (*Rydgastell*) when he replied to a letter of King Edward's government which had happened to reach him there[542]. This place lay within the western portion of the Aberconwy granges around Pentrefoelas. Llywelyn replied that he was only attended from his council by his brother Dafydd, although the bishop of Bangor had since turned up by chance. Consequently, he was not suitably attended to reply to such important issues that the government had raised. Llywelyn was back at Llanfair Rhyd Castell (*Lanuer Kygcastel*) on 20 December 1274 when

[535] *CCR 1256-59*, 320.
[536] *Littere Wallie, preserved in Liber A in the Public Record Office*, ed. J.G. Edwards [Cardiff, 1940], 28.
[537] *CCR 1259-61*, 198.
[538] *Foedera, Conventiones, Litterae etc*, ed. T. Rymer and R. Sanderson, 4th edn, by A. Clarke, F. Holbrooke, and J. Caley [4 vols. in 7 parts, 1816-69] II, 63.
[539] *Littere Wallie, preserved in Liber A in the Public Record Office*, ed. J.G. Edwards [Cardiff, 1940], 17-18.
[540] *Littere Wallie, preserved in Liber A in the Public Record Office*, ed. J.G. Edwards [Cardiff, 1940], 77-80, 111-13, where both parts of the cirograph are preserved.
[541] *Littere Wallie, preserved in Liber A in the Public Record Office*, ed. J.G. Edwards [Cardiff, 1940], 85-6; Acts, 657-8.
[542] Acts, 555-6.

he sent another letter to King Edward I from that place[*543]. Relations with the abbot, whether this was still Einion or his replacement, Abbot Maredudd who was installed by mid 1278, were still obviously strong. On 7 March 1274 the abbots of Whitland, Strata Florida, Cwmhir, Strata Marcella, Aberconwy, Cymer and Valle Crucis wrote from Strata Florida assuring the pope that Prince Llywelyn was a prominent and vigorous champion of their order and had not been wronging monks and monasteries as the bishop of St Asaph had falsely suggested[*544]. It is interesting to note that the abbot of Basingwerk, who was often at loggerheads with Llywelyn over taxation, was not amongst those writing.

As relations with King Edward (1272-1307) continued to deteriorate Llywelyn took the step on 6 October 1275, of sending a letter to the archbishop of Canterbury and his suffragans at London via the hands of the abbots of Aberconwy and Strata Florida[*545]. This is the abbot's final known act before full scale war broke out between Edward and Llywelyn in the autumn of 1276. Again it shows that the abbot of Aberconwy was a pivotal supporter of the prince during this time.

Aberconwy Abbey in the Front Line, 1277 to 1283

The escalation into full scale war in the winter of 1276 began badly for Prince Llywelyn with Marcher armies hemming him in and pushing his forces back towards the north and west. It appears that on 15 July 1276 Llywelyn was again at the Aberconwy grange of Llanfair Rhyd Castell (*Rytgastell*) when he complained of Roger Mortimer breaking the truce at Montgomery[*546]. During the summer of 1277, King Edward advanced on Rhuddlan, pushing Llywelyn away from Chester and its environs back towards the River Conwy.

Figure 44, Llywelyn's tower and hall, built into the enceinte of Edward's later town wall.

This must have had a very destabilising effect on Aberconwy's more easterly granges in the Perfeddwlad. The king obviously recognised this and, while at Rhuddlan on 8 October 1277, granted simple protection for the abbot and convent of *Abreconeway*[*547]. It is possible that the abbot used this protection to help his prince negotiate with the king, although he is not mentioned in any of the letters concerning the ending of the war which passed between king and prince. Despite this, on 9 November 1277, the formal peace treaty with Edward was

---

[*543] Acts, 558-60; *Littere Wallie, preserved in Liber A in the Public Record Office*, ed. J.G. Edwards [Cardiff, 1940], 174-5.
[*544] *Councils and Ecclesiastical Documents relating to GB and Ireland*, ed. A.W. Haddan and W. Stubbs [2 vols., Oxford, 1869-78] I, 498-9.
[*545] Acts, 271-74.
[*546] Acts, 577-9; CACW, 126-7.
[*547] *CPR 1272-81*, 234.

signed by Llywelyn at Aberconwy (*Aberconewey*) itself, while Llywelyn's negotiators are mentioned as Tewdwr ab Ednyfed and Goronwy ap Heilyn[*548]. Three other letters to Edward were written this day at Aberconwy. It has previously been assumed that Llywelyn was staying in the abbey while these negotiations were taking place[*549]. However, there is no evidence to back up this assumption and, considering the lack of involvement of the abbot of Aberconwy as well as his protection granted by Edward, it is more likely that Llywelyn was staying at his castle, the remains of which are now built into the town walls on the west side of the town (Fig.44).

That the new peace was not made by Llywelyn from Aberconwy abbey is again suggested in the king's conduct. On 15 November 1277, the king issued a safe conduct for Orlando Podio, the king's merchant as well as his men, who were bringing to Chester twenty sacks of wool that had been bought from the abbot of Aberconwy[*550]. It is a pity that no mention is made of where this wool was kept, whether it was at Aberconwy or one of its granges. Regardless, twenty sacks was a not inconsiderable amount of wool considering the scale of other contemporary enterprises. To give an idea of the size of the load, each sack should have consisted of 300 fleeces, therefore theoretically each sack would have weighed 364 pounds (26 stone). To put the 20 sacks in proportion to the general wool output of England, in 1292 some 950 sacks were taxed at York between Easter and Michaelmas[*551]. From this it can be seen that the abbot sold some 6,000 fleeces to Orlando.

Between 1310 and probably 1320, Francesco Pegolotti, an employee of the Bardi banking house, made a list of where to buy wool in England. Many of the Cistercian houses in Wales and the Marches as well as further afield are listed in this document and they give an idea of what wool production was like in the early fourteenth century. Presumably this was not that much different from the late thirteenth century. Dieulacres produced 20 sacks per year, Margam 25, Neath 10, Llantarnam 8, Tintern 15, Abbey Dore 16, Strata Florida (*Istanforte*) 12, Whitland 15, Kingswood (*Chinchesulda*) 25, Waverley 14, Ford 10, Miravale 30, Basingwerk 10, Vale Royal (*Vareale*) none, Aberconwy (*Barcanoe*) in Wales 20 sacks *none di mome* and Cwmhir? in Wales (*Conte in Gualesi*) 6 sacks per year, *marchi 9 il sacco*[*552]. From this it can be seen that Aberconwy had an above average production of wool. It also becomes apparent that twenty sacks were the normal yearly output of Aberconwy per year, if these figures are correct and not merely what was available for sale, rather than total production[*553]. The reason for questioning this claim is the number of sheep recorded on the various lands of the Welsh abbeys under the 1291 taxation. This recorded that Aberconwy had 560 sheep. Other Welsh houses had far more stock, viz: Margam 5,285, Neath 4,897, Tintern 3,264, Basingwerk 2,000 in Penllyn (and presumably others elsewhere), Strata Florida 1,327, Whitland, 1,100 and Dore 980 in Gwent[*554]. This would suggest either that Pegolotti's figures were wrong and the abbot's 20 sacks in 1277 were a culmination of several years output, or, more likely, that not all of Aberconwy's sheep were counted in 1291. The latter seems most likely as it is glaring that Nanhwynain grange, Aberconwy's largest, was not mentioned in the Taxatio. There also appears to be no mention of Gyffin or Creddyn, the granges nearest to

---

[*548] Acts, 589-94.

[*549] Smith, J.B., *Llywelyn ap Gruffydd: Prince of Wales* [UWP, 2001], 437.

[*550] CPR 1272-81, 235. It has been calculated that there was usually 340 lbs of wool to each sack, Williams, D.H., *The Welsh Cistercians* [Norwich, 1983, 2 vols] II, 310.

[*551] TNA, SC.6/1088/13.

[*552] Francesco Balducci Pegolotti, *La Pratica della Mercatura*, edited by A. Evans, *Medieval Academy Books*, No. 24 (1936), 161-63.

[*553] Hays, RW, *The History of the Abbey of Aberconway, 1186-1537* [UWP, 1963], 112.

[*554] Williams, D.H., *The Welsh Cistercians* [Norwich, 1983, 2 vols], II, 305.

Aberconwy. The lands of Aberconwy at this time are dealt with in subsequent chapters and in the Appendices.

If Abbot Maredudd was not noticeable during the war of 1276-77 he played a more active part in subsequent affairs. On 21 July 1278 he was at his grange of Arddau near Trefriw in Nanconwy with Dean David of Arllechwedd when they undertook an enquiry into the 1274 plot against Prince Llywelyn by Gruffydd ap Gwenwynwyn and his son, Owain[555]. In this they put their seals to what they swore was an authenticated record of what had occurred before the prince at his council at Dolforwyn castle four years earlier. This was for use in the forthcoming court case before the Hopton commission at Oswestry the next day and the two clerics swore that the process they recorded 'had in no way been erased, effaced or in part revised'. Two months later on 11 September 1278, the abbot of Aberconwy came to Rhuddlan and presented the document by which Rhodri had surrendered his claims to North Wales to his elder brother Llywelyn in 1272[556]. This shows that after 1272 Aberconwy abbey had been the repository for this document on Prince Llywelyn's behalf. With this interesting snippet the abbey's history once more fades into obscurity for two years.

The close link between Aberconwy and the house of Gwynedd is again emphasized in September 1280. In this month the Cistercian chapter general at Citeaux informed Dafydd ap Gruffydd and his wife the Lady J[557] that they would have full participation in the prayers and spiritual benefits of the order and that this 'petition for these privileges had been forwarded by our co-abbot of Aberconwy' so they were promised the spiritual benefits or their prayers in full measure both in life and in death[558]. Presumably Dafydd was now involving himself with the abbey as a prelude to his eventual inheriting the curtailed principality of Wales to which he would bring his own southern two cantrefs of the Perfeddwlad on the childless death of his brother, Prince Llywelyn. It is to be wondered if these prayers were actually said for Dafydd after his execution in 1283, just three years after these privileges had been granted. Certainly the record of his grisly execution in the Aberconwy Register is one of the most detailed recorded and again points to a record of his execution being kept in a chronicle at Aberconwy.

The same year, on 1 November 1280, Dafydd's elder brother, Rhodri ap Gruffydd, was at Aberconwy abbey when he acknowledged the receipt of 100 marks (£66 13s 4d) from the abbot and convent in part payment of the monies owed to him by his brother, Prince Llywelyn[559]. Within a year of this, the abbot and community of Aberconwy offended Prince Llywelyn and as a consequence, on 5 September 1281, Abbot M[aredudd] gave £40 to 'his prince' to obtain Llywelyn's goodwill and have the predicament forgotten and the undefined rancour the prince held against him relaxed. This document was drawn up at Hafod y Llan (*Hauot y Llan*) in the grange of Nanhwynain barely a mile east of Castell Dinas Emrys[560]. Presumably Llywelyn and Maredudd were there together at the time, although we are left none the wiser as to what had caused this difficulty between them. The reconciliation between the two set the scene for further war and change at Aberconwy.

---

[555] *Littere Wallie, preserved in Liber A in the Public Record Office*, ed. J.G. Edwards [Cardiff, 1940], 108-10.

[556] *CCR 1272-79*, 506.

[557] Dafydd's wife was Elizabeth Ferrers, a younger daughter of Earl William of Derby (d.1254), so J is presumably a misreading for E.

[558] *Littere Wallie, preserved in Liber A in the Public Record Office*, ed. J.G. Edwards [Cardiff, 1940], 153.

[559] *Littere Wallie, preserved in Liber A in the Public Record Office*, ed. J.G. Edwards [Cardiff, 1940], 42; Acts, 659.

[560] *Littere Wallie, preserved in Liber A in the Public Record Office*, ed. J.G. Edwards [Cardiff, 1940], 25. Hafod was apparently synonymous with vaccary by around 1300, Waters, W.H., 'Account of the sheriff of Caernarfon' *Bulletin of the Board of Celtic Studies* XIV [1932], 149-50. However hafod may also have meant a series of dwellings or cottages which tenants had the right to erect on the wastes appurtenant to their holdings, Davies, E., 'Hafod, Hafoty and Lluest', *Ceredigion* IX: 1 [1980], 1-41. Later evidence shows that there were some 6 hafods in Nanhwynain grange.

The Downgrading of Aberconwy Abbey and the Foundation of Conway, 1283 to 1289

In 1282 Prince Llywelyn again went to war against his king. Edward moved slowly against Gwynedd and once again overwhelmed the Perfeddwlad which Llywelyn and Dafydd had briefly controlled between themselves except, crucially, for the royal castles. Then, on 16 October 1282, the king created the lordship of Denbigh by amalgamating the cantrefs of Rhos and Rhufoniog, but without the Rhos commote of Creuddyn which he retained in his own hands[561]. These changes must have affected the granges of Aberconwy, but this was not to be the biggest upset to the abbey. After the death of Llywelyn on 10 December 1282[562], but before the capture of Dafydd on 21 June 1283, the king decided to move Aberconwy abbey to make way for a new town and castle of Conway as part of his new defensive policy for North Wales. The story is told briefly in three English chronicles.

> The abbey of Aberconwy was transferred to another place and in its place a strong castle was built to check the attacks of the Welsh.[563]

> This year Aberconwy (*Abertoun*) was transferred to another site by the king and in the place that the abbey was, a strong castle was built to check the assaults of the Welsh.[564]

> And the king gave £40 to the abbot of Aberconwy in full satisfaction for taking the site of his abbey of Conway in which same place he built the castle and town of Conway from new.[565]

Once again, it should be noted that if this had occurred in the twelfth century this might have been all that was known of the transaction and the later errors in interpretation of the accounts accepted as fact - viz. the castle was not built upon the actual physical site of the abbey and £40 was not the total sum given to the abbey for compensation for the move. Again, this shows the dangers of accepting the opinions of monkish chroniclers writing many miles and often many years away from the events that they describe.

Luckily, by the late thirteenth century much more documentary evidence was kept about fiscal events and from this it is possible to follow the history of the transference of Aberconwy abbey to Maenan much more closely. It should also be noted here that these chroniclers, possibly writing up events at the year end or even years later, were all of the opinion that the transfer of Aberconwy abbey to Maenan happened before the building of Conway castle. Royal documents show that this was not the case and far more than the inconsiderable £40 was paid to the abbot for the move.

After Edward's armies crossed the River Conwy into Snowdonia during the early months of 1283 the king soon followed from Rhuddlan and between 13 March and 9 May based himself at Aberconwy[566]. It is generally written that Edward spent these two months closeted in the abbey while his great new castle and town was begun. Yet, as this was a

---

[561] *Calendar of Various Chancery Rolls: Supplementary Close Rolls, Welsh Rolls, Scutage Rolls, 1277-1326* [1912], 241.

[562] Remfry, PM. *The Killing of Prince Llywelyn of Wales, 10 December 1282* [Ceidio, 2014], contains the evidence and true date for his death.

[563] *Triveti Annales*, ed. T. Hog, [English Historical Society, London, 1845], 308.

[564] *Chronica, ascribed to William Rishanger, a monk of St. Albans*, ed. H.T. Riley [1865], 105.

[565] *Chronica Johannis de Oxenedes*, [1859], 336.

[566] Gough, H., *Itinerary of King Edward the First* [2 vols, 1900] I, 141-3 & *Calendar of Various Chancery Rolls: Supplementary Close Rolls, Welsh Rolls, Scutage Rolls, 1277-1326* [1912], 266, for his being at Conway by 13 March.

functioning abbey, surely it would be more logical that the Aberconwy in Snowdon his correspondence was actually dated at would have been from Llywelyn's hall in his castle upon the rise within bowshot of the abbey? Certainly none of the dating clauses found so far name either the abbey or the castle as his abode, so it appears once again that Edward's habitat during this time has been decided purely by guesswork.

What is known is that early in Edward's stay the treasury was moved to Aberconwy and at some point appears to have been within the abbey. However, this is by no means the full story and much more can be said from a reading of the copious original sources. As early as 5 March 1283, 1,000 marks (£666 13s 4d) were taken on three hackneys from Chester to Rhuddlan. Presumably this money was then carried on to Aberconwy, for on 10 March, 400 marks (£266 13s 4d) were sent from the wardrobe in what was described as Conway abbey (*Abbatia de Conewey*) to the river towards Mon by cart at a cost of 2d[*567]. This shows that the monies were being kept in the abbey at this time and already the distinction between the English Conway and the Welsh Aberconwy was in use. This distinction can be seen as early as 29 May 1268 when three royal justices were recorded as John Fitz Geoffrey, John Conweye and Henry Anwelton[*568]. The use of *Conweye* is quite obviously the same as the English Conway used for many centuries afterwards.

It is quite possible that in the early days of the push over the River Conwy, the abbey was the only building in suitable repair to safely house the royal money barrels. No mentions of action at Aberconwy have survived and it is to be presumed that the site was simply abandoned to Edward sometime early in 1283. Edward seems to have based himself at Rhuddlan from 7 November 1282 until 12 March 1283. By 14 March he was installed at Aberconwy, four days after a treasury had first been recorded at Aberconwy abbey. All this meant was the abbey and castle at Aberconwy were secure enough for a monarch to stay there by 12 March and were safe enough to have a large amount of ready cash on hand by 10 March. King Edward then remained at Aberconwy until 9 May 1283, before moving on the ten miles into Llanrwst on 10 May and then moving eight miles from there on the 14th or 15th to Dolwyddelan by 16 May. After some further roving at the beginning of June he was back in Aberconwy from 4 June to 16 or 17 June 1283. It was around this time he was presented with the Cross of Naid, for on 25 June 1283 it was recorded that when the king:

> was lately at *Aberconewey*, Einion ab Ifor, Llywelyn, Dafydd, Meilyr and Goronwy his sons, Goronwy ap Dafydd, Einion, Dafydd, Dayhoc and Teguaret his sons, Welshmen, rendered to him by the hands of Justice Reginald Grey of Chester, that part of the most holy wood of the Cross which is called by the Welsh *Croysseneyht*, which Llywelyn ap Gruffydd, late prince of Wales, owned....[*569]

It seems from this modern historians have of course decided that the Cross was actually kept in Aberconwy abbey[*570]. The above merely shows that it entered the historical record there, when it was taken from places unknown to the king who just happened to be residing in Aberconwy, and, as has been shown, not necessarily within the abbey.

[*567] These and the following entries are from TNA, E.101/351/9, an imperfect account of miscellaneous issues of the wardrobe, containing 13 Membranes running from 20 November 1282 to 19 November 1284. Selected sections of the account are printed in Appendix 4.
[*568] *The Great Chartulary of Glastonbury*, ed. Watkin, A., [3 vols, Glastonbury,1952-56], 357.
[*569] *Calendar of Various Chancery Rolls: Supplementary Close Rolls, Welsh Rolls, Scutage Rolls, 1277-1326* [1912], 273-4.
[*570] https://en.wikipedia.org/wiki/Cross_of_Neith accessed 19 Jan 2018.

King Edward returned again to Aberconwy on 3 July 1283, he moved off the eight miles to Aber Garth Celyn on the ninth. He then proceeded to tour North Wales before leaving Wales via Chester on 28 August[*571]. Despite being predominantly at Rhuddlan during January 1283 the king also seems to have been at Llanrwst, eighteen miles away, between 14 and 20 January before returning to Rhuddlan and then appearing on 24 January at Dolwyddelan, 26 miles away, and then Bettws y Coed, a little over five miles away, on the 26th, before returning the 22 miles to Rhuddlan on the 24th. It therefore appears quite possible that Aberconwy was abandoned to the king somewhere in the second half of January when he was obviously campaigning along the upper reaches of the Conwy.

Despite Edward's movements in January, it was March before any use was made of Aberconwy. Possibly this was because it had taken all of February to make the district secure and the castle habitable. Similar events happened at Harlech and no doubt other Welsh fortresses that came into Edward's hands during 1283[*572]. Certainly the king found Aberconwy suitable for holding his ready money in March 1283. On 19 March, a further 1,200 marks (£800) arrived via the River Conwy and was shipped up to the wardrobe at a cost of 1s 2d. Soon afterwards £80 was sent via water to Mon and another six hackneys arrived bearing £1,200 from Chester at a cost of 6s 3d. A further undefined load of pennies arrived from London by water and was delivered from the waterside to the wardrobe at a cost of 9d. The same day construction costs were accounted for the commencement of the fortification of the new borough of Conway by building brattishing around the site.

More money arrived on 12 April and was transported over the River Conwy between Degannwy and Aberconwy abbey and then up to the wardrobe at a cost of 8d. There is no certainty in this that the wardrobe was still kept in the abbey, but at this early date this would seem possible. It was only a month later that a new wardrobe had been made ready. Apparently this occurred when the king and queen had chambers for themselves made ready, most likely in Aberconwy castle. Quite clearly, Prince Llywelyn's old castle (Fig.44), once suitably rebuilt, would have been a far more secure location for both the royal family and their monies. Indeed, there is evidence in the roll that this is exactly what happened at this time.

On Tuesday 23 March 1283, 4s was accounted for four masons renewing the chimneys in the king's chamber at Conway for three days[*573]. The argument that the chimneys on Edward's temporary apartments at Aberconwy already needed repair hardly needs further comment. There is evidence for only one masonry building standing at this time that could possibly have been regarded as belonging to the king and that was Llywelyn's old castle at Aberconwy. Similar work was also later carried out at Harlech castle and other old castles of the prince[*574]. Further work undertaken the next month would suggest that much was being rebuilt in what would appear to be the damaged Welsh castle of Aberconwy. On 25 April David Wautham was given 10s for the wages of his ten men who had worked for six days at 2d per day in digging earth for plastering the house of Brother Walter and his associates at Aberconwy. He was also paid 1½d for one man carrying turf for covering this house for an entire day, as well as 6d for buying twigs (wattle) for the making of the house walls. To finish the house 12,000 nails were bought which were also used on the wardrobe and the chamber of the king and queen at a cost of 26s. Finally on 5 May 1283, David bought 5,000 lath nails for

[*571] Edward's movements are taken from Gough, H., *Itinerary of King Edward the First* [2 vols, 1900], I, 137-146.
[*572] The argument is rehearsed with full original documentation in, Remfry, PM., *Harlech Castle and its True Origins* [Ceidio, 2013].
[*573] *Et pro stipend' iiij Cement' reparantium caminum in camera Regis apud Conewey per iij dies iiij s'.*
[*574] Remfry, PM., *Harlech Castle and its True Origins* [Ceidio, 2013], with some of the evidence printed at http://www.castles99.ukprint.com/Essays/Harlech%20foundation.html

the construction of the wardrobe in Conway castle (*castro de Conewey*) at a cost of 4s 2d. As the English Conway castle was not and could not have been standing at this time, we are left with making a decision as to whether the castle referred to was a temporary new castle at Conway, as has been stated in modern times, or the old fortress of Llywelyn at Aberconwy[*575]. Once again the surviving documentary evidence points to only one conclusion.

On 12 May the wardrobe had been set up in its own building and this obviously was in a rebuilt building and not in a part of the abbey. The following entries make this reasonably clear.

Monday 10 May
Also the same for wages of 2 men digging turfs for the covering of the wardrobe, mill and granary of Conway for 2 days, 16d.

Wednesday 2 June
And David Wautham for 4,000 spike nails bought for the works of the wardrobe at Conway 9s 4d, precisely 2s 4d per 1,000.
And Richard Shrewsbury for 10 perches of great cloth and for 10,194 of lesser cloth by himself bought from various people for the building of the wardrobe and granary of the king at Conway by the hand of Henry Oxford master carpenter £11 8s 3d.

Sunday 13 June
David Wautham for the wages of carpenters, plasterers, carriers and men digging turfs for the works of the queen's wardrobe in Aberconwy castle and for buying nails for the same work just as is well known from the particulars in the book of particulars £14 2d.
And Roger the treasury chamberlain for wages of carpenters conducted to Aberconwy for making the wardrobe of the king there and for carrying timbers of wood there for the said wardrobe and for making some houses next to the said wardrobe where the clerks of the wardrobe slept before the said wardrobe was perfected and for plastering the said wardrobe and said houses made nearby just as in the particulars put in the book in the wardrobe £6 8s 4½d.
And David Wautham for wages of carpenters, plasterers, carriers and men for digging turfs and for some people carrying things around the king's wardrobe in the castle of Aberconwy just as put down in the particulars in the book of particulars 78s 7d.

Tuesday 15 June
David Wautham for the wages of carpenters, plasterers, carriers and men for digging turfs and for some people to carry things about the king's wardrobe in the castle of Aberconwy just as appears through the particulars in the book of particulars 76s 6d.
And for boating £2,600 over the water from Conway and for carrying the same from the water to the wardrobe 14d.

Wednesday 23 June
Hamo of the queen's chamber for making 500 turfs to cover the wardrobe of the queen at Conway and for the turfing of her garden there 15d.

[*575] The opposing views are given in Edwards, JG., *Edward I's Castle Building in Wales* [1944], 39 and Taylor, A., *The Welsh Castles of Edward I* [London, 1986], 46.

Thursday 1 July
And for the wages of 2 carts just as for 2 horses carrying turfs to the said garden and for the queen's wardrobe of Conway for 6 days 15s.

Sunday 4 July
And David Wautham for 1,900 turfs bought for covering the wardrobe of the king at Aberconwy for 3d per hundred, 4s 9d.
Also the same for 2,000 great spikes bought for the said wardrobe preceding at 1,000 for 2s 2d, 4s 4d.
Also the same for the wages of one man working about the said wardrobe by writ per day 3d and for the wages of 7 men helping for digging turfs and for placing them on top of the said wardrobe for 6 days 8s 6d.
Also the same for boating the said turfs from the ford next to Trefor to Aberconwy 8s 6d.

Sunday 29 August
And Nicholas Clifford for carrying timbers to make two latrines for the king and queen's wardrobe at Conway and for carpenters and roofers for the same 4s 3d.
Total £16 5s 1d.

Figure 45, The remains of Llywelyn's hall and tower stand on a boss of rock. The later enceinte of Edward I, built on a lower level, connects to it to left and right.

These entries show that the wardrobe of both the king and the queen were within Aberconwy castle. It is also quite clear that this Aberconwy castle was not in fact the new Conway castle, that had yet to be built, and the idea that Edward had his most important wardrobe built of wood on the site of the new Conway castle and then quickly demolished it to make way for the castle, just does not seem logical or credible[*576]. The only sensible remaining conclusion is that Edward made use of the castle he found standing there as the documentary evidence implies. This Welsh castle was latter incorporated into the town walls and largely demolished in 1317 by which time it was throughly obsolete. This demolition left just the outer wall of Llywelyn's hall and the adjoining tower as an obvious older relic within the newer town enceinte (Fig.45). The king also set up a temporary wardrobe at Llanrwst in early May 1283.

> ...for the wages of four men in making some ditch around the wardrobe (*gard'*) of the king at Llanrwst for half a day 4d.[*577]

This again suggests that the king needed a safe space for his ready money when he was on the move and that a ditch dug around a pre-existing building was sufficient for his purpose. This again suggests that a secular site, rather than a religious one, was preferable to Edward for his wardrobe, rather than an ecclesiastical building that was already standing like Llanrwst church.

In the meantime Edward certainly celebrated Easter at the abbey, though of course this does not imply that he was also living there.

> And in some monastery of the Cistercian order, in whose language is called Aberconwy (*Abercunewith*) and which is situated in the aforementioned province, he celebrated Easter (18 April 1283).[*578]

> The king of England, animated by favourable success, revealed to him according to the vow taken, triumphantly invaded Snowdonia, and was there at Easter in some monastery of the Cistercian order, which was called Aberconwy (*Abercunewyth*), disposing of all the principality of Wales as it pleased him.[*579]

Yet, when it is considered that one of these sources plagiarised the other, this is only one source stating that Edward was actually in the abbey, and that just for the Easter celebrations and not for residency. In the meantime, the end of Llywelyn's castle of Aberconwy as well as Aberconwy abbey was being planned. On 30 March 1283 King Edward, himself at Aberconwy, ordered the bringing of:

> divers instruments and other necessaries such as Richard the engineer will tell him on the king's behalf to make ditches at Aberconwy; and also to cause to come to Aberconwy masons and stonecutters...[*580]

This has been stated to have occasioned the commencement of Conway castle[*581]. Yet, as can be seen, the order does not say this. The ditches and masons could well be intended solely for the town walls, although, considering the site at Aberconwy, the logic of commencing the castle at the same time as the town is strong. A week later on 6 April the king further ordered John Kirkby, Hugh Kendale and Walter Odiham to:

[*576] This is the scenario in Taylor, A., *The Welsh Castles of Edward I* [London, 1986], 39. 'These buildings were apparently made of timber and were not meant to be permanent, but we may reasonably surmise that they would be located on the site destined for the castle.'
[*577] See entry for 10 May in Appendix 4, 317.
[*578] 'Annales of Osney', *Annales Monastici*, ed. H.R. Luard [5 vols., 1864-9], IV, 292.
[*579] 'Chronicon Thomae Wykes', *Annales Monastici*, ed. H.R. Luard [5 vols., 1864-9] IV, 291-2.
[*580] CACW, 265.
[*581] Edwards, JG., *Edward I's Castle Building in Wales* [1944], 39.

grant gratis to the abbot and convent of Aberconwy the king's patent of protection, quit of the hanaper [tax], with the addition that they may carry their corn and other victuals from Ireland to the king's army or elsewhere as they see fit'.[582]

He further granted a safe conduct to men of the abbot of Aberconwy from 17 April 1283 until Michaelmas providing that they paid the required customs and did not take any goods which they bought to the king's enemies or indeed make any contact with them whatsoever[583].

This leaves the question as to whether there is any difference between the names Aberconwy and Conwy/Conway. Did they differentiate different places - ie. was the Llywelyn's castle of Aberconwy and Aberconwy abbey separate from Conway castle and the town walls? An answer to such a question can be found by studying the royal accountants' differing use of the placename during 1283[584].

Date	Placename	Usage
10 March	*Aberconewey*	placename
10 March	*Conewey*	placename
10 March	*Abbatia de Conewey*	Conway abbey
28 March	*castro de Conewey*	construction of the houses and windows in Conway castle (from the date this must be Llywelyn's castle)
7 April	*Aule Regis apud Conewey*	1200 small nails for boards purchased for construction of the king's hall at Conway
7 April	*cameras Regis et Regine apud Conewey*	4,500 nails for laths bought for the king and queen's rooms at Conway
12 April	*Abbatiam de Aberconewey*	carrying money to Aberconwy abbey
20 April	*castro de Conewey*	turf to cover the house of Brother Walter, goldworker of the queen, in Conway castle
20 April	*Aberconewey*	earth for plastering the house of Brother Walter and his associates at Aberconwy
20 April	*molendinum aquaticum apud Aberconewey*	Aberconwy water mill
30 April	*domus fratris Walteri apud Conewey*	turfs to cover the house of Brother Walter at Conway

---

[582] CACW, 42.
[583] *Calendar of Various Chancery Rolls: Supplementary Close Rolls, Welsh Rolls, Scutage Rolls, 1277-1326* [1912], 269.
[584] The accounts are to be found in TNA, E.101/351/9.

30 April	*duas fabricas Regis apud Conewey*	two royal forges at Conway
5 May	*gard' in castro de Conewey*	5,000 lath nails bought for the construction of the wardrobe in Conway castle
12 May	*constructionem novarum domuum Regis Conewey*	6,000 spike nails bought for the construction of the new house of the king at Conway
12 May	*gard' molendin' et granar' de Conewey*	turfs for covering the wardrobe, mill and granary of Conway
16 May	*ville de Conewey*	400 nails bought for the brattishing around the enclosure of Conway town
16 May	*novam cameram Regis et Regine apud Conewey*	nails bought for making the new chamber of the king and queen at Conway and for other houses next to that chamber
25 May	*Aberconewey*	placename
2 June	*Aberconewey*	placename
2 June	*gard' apud Conewey*	4,000 spike nails for the works of Conway wardrobe
2 June	*Abbatiam de Conewey*	Conway abbey
8 June	*quoddam furnum apud Aberconewey*	6 masons made some oven at Aberconwy
11 June	*gard' et granar' Regis apud Conewey*	10 perches of great cloth and 10,194 of lesser cloth for the building of the wardrobe and granary of the king at Conway
13 June	*gard' Regine in castro de Aberconewey*	wages of carpenters, plasterers, carriers and men digging turfs for the works of the queen's wardrobe in Aberconwy castle and for buying nails
13 June	*Aberconewey ad faciend' gard' Regis*	carpenters conducted to Aberconwy to make the king's wardrobe and for timbers for the wardrobe and for making some houses next to the wardrobe... and for plastering the wardrobe and houses
13 June	*gard' Regis in castro de Aberconewey*	carpenters, plasterers, carriers and men for digging turfs and for some people carrying things around the king's wardrobe in the castle of Aberconwy
15 June	*gard' Regis in castro de Aberconewey*	carpenters, plasterers, carriers and men for digging turfs and for some people to carry things about the king's wardrobe in the castle of Aberconwy

19 June	*granar' Regis in Abbatia de Conewey et molendin' Regis*	carpenters, carriers of timbers and turfs, diggers of turfs, buying of canvas/hemp... concerned with the construction of the royal granary in Conway abbey and the mill of the king there
23 June	*gard' Regine apud Conewey*	wardrobe of the queen at Conway
23 June	*fabricam de Conewey*	workshop of Conway
24 June	*herbar' Regine de Conewey*	queen's garden of Conway
24 June	*granar' marescalcie de novo inceptum apud Conewey*	granary of the Marshall newly built at Conway
1 July	*herbar' Regine apud Conewey*	garden of the queen at Conway
1 July	*herbar' et ad gard' Regine de Conewey*	queen's garden and wardrobe of Conway
4 July	*quasdam domos apud Conewey*	some houses at Conway
4 July	*factur' j stabuli pro equis Regis apud Conewey*	making one stable for the king's horses at Conway
4 July	*gard' Regis apud Aberconewey*	1,900 turfs bought for covering the king's wardrobe at Aberconwy
26 July	*novum castrum de Aberconewey*	10,700 strips of metal and 25 iron picks bought for the new castle of Aberconwy
29 Aug	*gard' Regis et Regine apud Conewey*	timbers to make two latrines for the king and queen's wardrobe at Conway

These accounts make it quite plain that the names Aberconwy and Conway were synonymous to the Edwardian scribes tasked with works at Conwy. Further, they show that the castle of Aberconwy was a standing and fully functioning fortress, although in need of repair and rebuilding in its woodwork and furnishing in March 1283 while King Edward and his queen were staying there. It is also quite clear that the 'new castle of Aberconwy', which is now known as Conway or Conwy castle, was only commenced on 27 July 1283. It is difficult to know exactly what was spent at Conway, but it seems reasonable to assume that some £5,000 was spent in 1283, £3,000 in 1284 and £2,000 each in 1285 and 1286. These figures rather put in perspective Edward's purported grant of just £40 to help with the relocation of Aberconwy abbey on 11 September 1283. In total Edward gave the abbey £560, plus the new lands in Mon worth some £32 3s 8½d a year, which were in exchange for Conwy Gyffin and Creddyn grange worth £46 7s 8½d [585].

With this act for the move of the abbey sealed on 11 September 1283, the king ordered Master James St George to take seisin from Earl Henry Lacy's bailiff, in the king's name, the vill of Maenan and to hold it for three or four days so that there could be no question of title at a future date and then pass the land on to the abbot and convent of Aberconwy[586]. This was followed on 13 September 1283, by William Louth, the keeper of king's wardrobe, ordering William Perton, a king's clerk, to deliver £40 to the abbot of Aberconwy in accordance with a valuation which the king had earlier made of the abbey and adjacent lands, and which represented compensation for the first year after the proposed transfer[587]. The annual income of the abbey at this time was over £63[588]. Consequently, it is to be supposed that the £40 was meant as compensation for the loss of the land which later became Conwy borough. That same September it was recorded in the Cistercian chapter general at Citeaux that the transfer was agreed subject to the approval of inspectors and the requirement that neither the revenues nor the liabilities of the monks were to be diminished in any way and that the pope would agree to the move[589].

Despite Edward's efforts the move did not proceed smoothly. On 14 June 1284, Archbishop Peckham wrote from Rhuddlan to King Edward at Nantlle (*Baladeuthlyn*) asking him to reconsider his decision to move Aberconwy abbey to Maenan. He stated that although he was willing to dedicate the site he could not proceed without the full consent of the bishop of St Asaph and his chapter as well as the parson of Maenan, but they, with plenty of other people, had a great dread of the coming of the monks. He warned that the clergy of St Asaph already had four Cistercian white abbeys within the diocese and if Maenan was planted there that would give them five to Bangor's single one[590]. Therefore he asked the king to wait upon the matter until they could come together to discuss it in full. The archbishop also pointed out that Bishop Einion of St Asaph had taken the advice of his chapter on this matter and that they would not agree to the move in any manner[591]. Peckham duly met with the king and Bishop Robert Burnell of Bath and Wells and discussed the matter fully. As a consequence of their debate the archbishop wrote to Bishop Einion advising him to conciliate the king by consenting immediately to the foundation of a monastery at Maenan. If he did not the archbishop stated that he was prepared to consecrate the new site despite any opposition, but if Einion sent his letters patent accepting the new abbey he could also send a statement of damages expected to accrue to himself, his chapter and the local priest [probably of Eglwysbach] due to the new foundation[592]. This was obviously done and finally on 24 June 1284, Edward made his formal announcement of the move and made pains to reassure the bishop, chapter and priest that they would not suffer as a result of this. He further stated that he had already gained the assent of the chapter general of the Cistercians, the Aberconwy

[585] *Calendar of Various Chancery Rolls: Supplementary Close Rolls, Welsh Rolls, Scutage Rolls, 1277-1326* [1912], 292; *Calendar of Charter Rolls 1226-1516* [6 vols., 1903-27] II, 279.

[586] *Calendar of Various Chancery Rolls: Supplementary Close Rolls, Welsh Rolls, Scutage Rolls, 1277-1326* [1912], 275.

[587] CACW, 163.

[588] *Taxatio Ecclesiastica Angliae et Walliae auctoritate Pope Nicholai IV, circa 1291* [1802], 289, 292.

[589] *Littere Wallie, preserved in Liber A in the Public Record Office*, ed. J.G. Edwards [Cardiff, 1940], 202-3.

[590] The singular abbey in Bangor's jurisdiction would have been Cymer. Those in St Asaph would have been Basingwerk, Valle Crucis, Strata Marcella and Aberconwy. Possibly Bishop Einion was still claiming Cwmhir, which had always been in the diocese of St David, despite the apparent attempt to claim it in the late 1170s.

[591] *Registrum epistolarum Fratris Johannis Peckham*, ed. C.T. Martin [3 vols., 1882-5] II, 726-7, 769-70.

[592] *Registrum epistolarum Fratris Johannis Peckham*, ed. C.T. Martin [3 vols., 1882-5] II, 729-31.

monks themselves and that Archbishop Peckham would be arbitrator of any future disputes[*593]. Throughout this affair it would seem that the king kept Abbot David of Aberconwy with the abbot of Vale Royal and another monk close to the royal court when David was allowed £7 7s 6d for 118 day's attendance on the king[*594]. Despite the abbot's close attendance on the king at this time he, like the abbots of Neath, Cwmhir and Margam, was never called upon to attend parliament. Compared to this, the abbot of Strata Florida was called seven times, the abbot of Basingwerk six, Tintern five and Whitland twice[*595].

Despite this, there was still much to do before the move took place. On 25 June 1284, Archbishop Peckham replied to an obvious enquiry of King Edward concerning whether the piece of ground hitherto used by the monks as a cemetery had ever received episcopal consecration. Peckham replied that as the ground had been hallowed simply by the burial of Christians there, even if it may not have been specifically consecrated by a bishop, it was prudent to consult higher authorities, presumably the pope, about the matter[*596]. It is likely that the burial ground remained in use for the new parish church which used the old abbey building and is now known as St Mary's. This act was recorded by the king with two documents both issued while he was at Nantlle (*Baladeuthlyn*). The first on 24 June 1284 ran:

> Notification that the king, for the common utility of his realm and for the peace and security of his realm and of his whole land of Wales hereafter, after having communicated the counsel of his magnates whom it concerned, has caused to be built his castle of Aberconwy (*Aberconewey*) on the soil of the abbot and convent there and has caused the abbey to be transferred, with the consent of the men of religion and of the abbot of Citeaux and of all the convent of the abbots in their chapter general of that place, to the place called Maenan (*Meynan*) in the diocese of St Asaph, and that, lest any prejudice shall arise hereby to the bishop of St Asaph or others whom it concerns, the king promises and binds himself and his heirs that he will save harmless the bishop and church and chapter of St Asaph and also the parish church within the limits whereof Maenan is situated, according to the arbitration of Archbishop John of Canterbury and as the archbishop shall cause to be ordained in this matter.[*597]

The second on 28 June ran:

> Notification that the king has granted to the abbot and convent of Maenan (*Meynan*) that they may have as a parish church the old church of Aberconwy (*Aberconewey*), which they previously held as a conventual church, with the tithes, offerings and other things pertaining by parish right to that church, provided that they cause it to be served suitably by vicars and other ministers of the church and that the cure of souls in it shall not be neglected in any way in the future.[*598]

[*593] *Calendar of Various Chancery Rolls: Supplementary Close Rolls, Welsh Rolls, Scutage Rolls, 1277-1326* [1912], 285. A copy of the agreement about Rhuddlan church and Eglwysbach was obviously kept by Bishop Einion and was later recorded in the Red Book of St Asaph, 'Index to "Llyfr Coch Asaph", *Archaeologia Cambrensis* [1868], 159.
[*594] Taylor, A.J., 'Royal Alms and Oblations' in *Tribute to an Antiquary: Essays Presented to Marc Fitch...* [1976], 121.
[*595] Williams, D.H., *The Welsh Cistercians* [Bodmin, 2001], 40-1.
[*596] *Registrum epistolarum Fratris Johannis Peckham*, ed. C.T. Martin [3 vols., 1882-5] II, 735, *Littere Wallie, preserved in Liber A in the Public Record Office*, ed. J.G. Edwards [Cardiff, 1940], 123-6; *Foedera, Conventiones, Litterae etc*, ed. T. Rymer and R. Sanderson, 4th edn, by A. Clarke, F. Holbrooke, and J. Caley [4 vols. in 7 parts, 1816-69] I, 232-3.
[*597] *Calendar of Various Chancery Rolls: Supplementary Close Rolls, Welsh Rolls, Scutage Rolls, 1277-1326* [1912], 285-6.
[*598] *Calendar of Various Chancery Rolls: Supplementary Close Rolls, Welsh Rolls, Scutage Rolls, 1277-1326* [1912], 286.

Finally, the king announced on 16 July 1284 that he had confirmed the rights of the abbot and convent of Aberconwy and stated his wishes for the monastery to be transferred to Maenan. Interestingly, this charter has come down to us in two different forms, one via the charter rolls and one via the Aberconwy Register. The differences are illuminating. Firstly from the charter roll:

> The king to his archbishops etc, greetings. Know that we for the health of our soul and the souls of our ancestors and heirs have given and conceded and by this our charter confirmed to our beloved in Christ abbey and convent of Aberconwy whose site we wish to be transferred to Maenan, with the assent of the same abbot and convent and of his co-abbots of the Cistercian order who we have caused to visit that place; that all the church of Aberconwy which the convent have had and have held from others and so much as they may hold in regard to us is for their own parochial uses, with all just patronage and ownership to himself and his successors and in pure and perpetual alms with all right of possessions and other things to the aforesaid parochial church observing whatever title they may be judged, so much as within the walls as without, with all tithes, all lands and seas from each side of the region of Conwy to the aforementioned church of Aberconwy as observed from antiquity. Yet nevertheless that the same church should be served by two English chaplains both suitable and honest of which one may be continuously substitute to the other, and through themselves the abbot and convent in each calling of the substitute himself may be presented in the place of the diocesan, and also through a third distinguished Welsh chaplain on account of the difference of language.
> Whereby we wish etc. Dated by our hand at Caernarfon, 16th day of July [12 Ed I - 1284]
> And a memorandum of this charter is in the Welsh Roll of this year.*599

The second charter tells the same story, but in a much altered form.

> Edward by grace of god king of England and France, lord of Ireland and duke of Aquitaine etc*600. Know that we for the health of our soul and the souls of our predecessors and our heirs of the kingdom of England, we concede for ourselves and our heirs, beloved to us in Christ, to the abbot and convent of Maenan the old church of

---

*599 *Rex archiepiscopis etc salutem. Sciatis nos pro salute animae nostrae et animarum antecessorum et haeredum nostrorum dedisse concessisse et hac carta nostra confirmasse dilectis nobis in Christo abbati et conventui de Aberconewey quorum situm transferri volumus usque Maynan, de assensu eorundem abbatis et conventus et co-abbatum suorum ordinis Cisterciensis per quos locum illum fecimus visitari, quod totam ecclesiam de Aberconewey quam prius conventualem habuerunt et tenuerunt de caetero habeant et teneant quantum in nobis est in proprios usus parochialem, cum omni jure patronatus et proprietatis sibi et successoribus suis, et in puram et perpetuam elemosinam cum omnibus juribus possessionibus et rebus aliis ad praedictam ecclesiam parochialem spectantibus quocunque nomine censeantur, tam infra muros quam extra, cum omnibus decimationibus omnium terrarum et maris ex utraque parte de Conewey ad praefatam ecclesiam de Aberconewey spectantium ab antiquo. Ita tamen quod eidem ecclesiae deservire faciant per duos capellano Anglicos et idoneos et honestos, quorum unus sit perpetuus vicarius ineadem, et per ipsos abbatem et conventum in singulis vocationibus ipsius vicariae loci dioecesano praesentetur, et per unum tertiam capellanum Walensem honestum, propter idiomatis diversitatem. Quare volumus, etc. Dat per manu nostram apud Karnarvan, xvi die Julii. Et memorandum quod haec carta irrotulatur in rotulo Walliae de hoc anno.* This text is printed from Dugdale, *Monasticon Anglicanum*, ed. W. Dugdale, Revised edition by J. Caley, H. Ellis, and B. Bandinel [6 vols., 1817-30] V, 674. *Calendar of Charter Rolls 1226-1516* [6 vols., 1903-27] *1257-1300*, 276, contains a very brief abstract, while *Calendar of Various Chancery Rolls: Supplementary Close Rolls, Welsh Rolls, Scutage Rolls, 1277-1326* [1912], 286-7 has a translation.
*600 This title was never used by King Edward I (1272-1307) and obviously this composition dates to after 1340 when the title King of England and France and lord of Ireland was used (1340-97). This title, with various variations, remained in use until 1521. The title generally used from 1259 to 1340 was, *Rex Angliae, Dominus Hiberniae et Dux Aquitaniae* - King of England, lord of Ireland and duke of Aquitaine.

Aberconwy which convent they first had and held of others, which they may have and hold to themselves and their successors those things pertaining to the parish for their very own uses for ever, with tithes and offerings and other things for that church which pertained by right to the parish, therefore however that themselves the same church through a priest or other church ministers a suitable reputable Welsh chaplain on account of the difference of language. Hence we wish and firmly order, for us and our heirs, that the aforesaid abbey and convent and their successors have and hold for ever the aforesaid church of Aberconwy which the convent first had and held from others, they may have and hold so much from us for their very own parochial uses with all just patronage to himself and his successors in perpetual alms, with all rights and possessions and other things pertaining to the aforesaid parochial church observing wherever by title it may be judged, whether within the walls or without, with all tithes, all lands and seas from either side of the Conwy to the before mentioned church of Aberconwy as observed from antiquity.

So nevertheless that etc, this witnessed by the venerable father Bishop Robert of Bath and Wells, Earl Henry Lacy of Lincoln (1251-1311), Earl Richard Burgh of Ulster (bef.1271-1326) etc and dated at Caernarfon the 16th day of July in the year of our reign.[*601]

Quite obviously the later charter in the Register has more details, mainly the two witnesses who are missed in Dugdale's account, but this version has also been condensed from the more wordy royal proclamation. Presumably both these records are correct in what they have to tell us and presumably the royal version is nearer to the original, although the witnesses have been omitted. Despite this, the title given to King Edward in the Register clearly applies to King Edward III in the period after 1340. No such title is given in the royal records as recorded by Dugdale. This tends to confirm that the Monasticon account is superior to the Aberconwy one, which has apparently been altered to better fit in with the compiler of the Register's desires - whatever they might have been.

Despite there being no certain date at which the monks of Aberconwy left what was to become the new royal borough of Conway, it would seem likely that this happened either in or soon after this charter of 16 July 1284. Certainly they would seem to have been gone by 8 September 1284, when King Edward at Flint issued his new borough of Conway with a founding charter.

The king to his archbishops etc greetings. Know that we will and grant for ourselves and our heirs, that our town of Aberconwy becomes a free borough and our men of the same town free burgesses; and that the constable of our castle of Aberconwy for the

---

[*601] *Edwardus Dei gracia Rex Angliae et Franciae, Dominus Hiberniae et Dux Aquitaniae, &c.*
Sciatis nos pro salute animae nostrae et animabus antecessorum nostrorum et heredum nostrorum regni Angliae, concessisse pro nobis et heredibus nostris dilectis nobis in Christo Abbati et Conventui de Maynan veterem Ecclesiam de Abberconwey quam prius habuerunt et tenuerunt conventualem de ceetero habeant et teneant parochialem sibi et successoribus in proprios usus imperpetuum, cum decimis et oblacionibus et aliis ad Ecclesiam illam de jure parochiali pertinentibus, ita tamen quod ipsi eidem Ecclesiae per vicarium et alios Ecclesiee ministros ydoneos capellanum honestum Wallensem propter ydeomatum diversitatem. Quare volumus et firmiter precipimus, pro nobis et heredibus nostris, quod praedicti Abbas et Conventus et successores sui imperpetuum habeant et teneant praedictam Ecclesiam de Abberconwey quam prius conventualem habuerunt et tenuerunt de caetero habeant et teneant quantum in nobis est in proprios usus parochialem cum omni jure patronatus sibi et successoribus suis in perpetuam elemosinam, cum omnibus juribus et possessionibus et rebus aliis ad praedictam Ecclesiam parochialem spectan[tibus] quocumque nomine censeatur, tam infra muros quam extra, cum omnibus decimationibus omnium terrarum et maris ex utraque de Conwey ad prefatam Ecclesiam de Aberconwey spectantibus ab antiquo. Ita tamen quod, &c. Hiis testibus, venerabili patre Roberto Bathon et Wellen Episcopo, Henrico de Laci Comite Lincoln, Ricardo Burg Comite Ulton, &c. Dat. apud Carn'. xvj die Julij Anno regni nostri.

time being be mayor of the same borough, sworn as well as to us as to the same burgesses, who first having taken the oath to preserve our rights shall swear to the said burgesses upon the holy evangelists of God, that he will preserve the same liberties to the said burgesses by us granted, and faithfully perform that, which to the office of mayor may belong in the same borough. Also we grant that the said burgesses yearly choose from amongst themselves on the feast of St Michael, two fit and sufficient bailiffs, and to such their constable as well as their mayor present, who, in the presence of the said major and burgesses, shall swear, that the office of bailiff they will faithfully do and execute. Also, we will and grant that the said burgesses have their persons free in the borough aforesaid of all trespasses there, except in cases of life and limb, in all which cases all men as well as burgesses as others, shall be imprisoned in our castle there. Nevertheless if any of our said burgesses shall be sued, accused, or indicted upon any trespass in any of those cases we will that on that account they be imprisoned, until they shall find good and sufficient bail to abide the right thereof before our chief justice, or other our justices assigned in this behalf.

Moreover we grant to the same burgesses, that all land, to the same borough now assigned, be altogether dis-warrened and deforested and that no Jews shall dwell in the same borough at any time. We grant also for us and our heirs to the said burgesses the underwritten liberties, viz: that no one of our sheriffs on any occasion intrudes himself upon them in any plea or quarrel or cause or any other matter to the said town belonging, saving always to us and our heirs pleas of our Crown as is before mentioned, and that they have a merchant's guild with a hanse and other customs and liberties to that guild belonging. Also that no one who is not of the guild shall trade in the same town, unless from the permission of the aforesaid burgesses. We also grant to them, if any native of any one shall stay in the aforesaid town and hold land in the same, and shall be in the aforesaid guild and hanse and lot and scot with our same men for a year and a day without challenge, then he cannot be recovered by his lord, but in the same town he shall remain free. Moreover we grant to our same burgesses that they have sok and sak, tol and theam and infangenethef and that they be quit through all our land of toll, lastage, passage, murage, pontage and stallage. And of levies of Danegeld and gaywite, and all other customs and exactions through all our dominions as well in England as in all other our lands. And that they or their goods be not arrested for any debt, of which they are not the sureties or principal debtors, unless it happens that the said debtors be of their commonalty and having in their power whereof they can satisfy their debts in whole or in part and our said burgesses being deficient in justice to the creditors of the same debtors, and of this reasonable proof shall be made. And that our same burgesses for the trespass, or forfeiture of their servants, do not lose their goods and chattels found in the hands of them, or in any place deposited by their said servants, so far forth as they can sufficiently prove them to be theirs. And also that if the same burgesses or any of them die within our kingdom or dominion testate or intestate, we or our heirs will not cause the goods of such persons to be confiscated; but their heirs shall wholly enjoy the same so far as they may consist of the said chattels of the said deceased persons, provided that nevertheless sufficient knowledge, or proof can be had of the same heirs. And that our burgesses aforesaid be not convicted by any persons residing out of the said borough, upon any appeal, right, injury, trespass, crimes, damages, demands, imposed, or to be imposed upon them from Caernarfon (*Karnarvan*) unto the water of the Clwyd (*Cloyt*), but only by our aforesaid burgesses;

unless concerning anything touching the commonalty of the aforesaid borough, and then in that case they be dealt with according to the liberties approved and theretofore reasonably used in our city of Hereford... Also we will and grant for us and our heirs that the aforesaid burgesses have all other liberties and free customs above expressed well and peaceably, without let, or impediment of us, our heirs, justices, sheriffs and others our bailiffs and ministers whatsoever for ever as is above expressed. Witnessed by the venerable father, Bishop Robert of Bath and Wells our chancellor, Earl Richard Burgh of Ulster, Thomas Clare, Richard Bruce, Reginald Grey, Nicholas Segrave, Peter Champnent, John Mohault and others. Given under our hand at Flint (*Flynt*), 8th day of September 1284.[*602]

It is noticeable that the rights of the abbey are nowhere mentioned in this charter and this goes to add to the impression that the monks had already moved out by this date. This impression is confirmed on 10 October 1284, when King Edward granted the advowson of Rhuddlan church to Bishop Einion of St Asaph in compensation for a grant of advowson of Eglwysbach church by the bishop to Aberconwy abbey.

> Notification that whereas Bishop Einion of St Asaph, has, at the king's instance, granted to the abbot and convent of Aberconwy (*Aberconewey*), which monastery is now situated at Maenan (*Meynan*), the advowson of the church of Eglwysbach (*Eglwysyvach*), which belonged to the bishop, as is contained in his deed to the abbot and convent, the king has granted to the bishop as compensation the advowson of the church of Rhuddlan (*Rothelan*), with provision that in case the bishop or his successors shall in any case obtain again (*retractare*) the advowson of the former church the king shall have power to revoke his grant of the advowson of the church of Rhuddlan.[*603]

As a consequence of this grant the next day, at Aberconwy (*Aberconeweye*) itself, Bishop Einion and his chapter formerly acquitted the king of indemnifying them for the transfer of the abbey to Maenan in his diocese[*604]. Even though the monks had apparently moved from Aberconwy the new monastery at Maenan was obviously still not ready for their arrival. On 26 December 1285 the Crown enrolled:

> A deed of Brother David, abbot of Aberconwy (*Aberconeweye*),... witnessing that whereas the king has caused the abbey to be transferred to the place called Maenan (*Maynan*) and has promised to build the abbey there and make good the damages sustained by them by reason of the war in Wales, the abbot and convent, considering that the site has been usefully transferred and that the work on the new site has been well commenced by the king, have, in consideration of 580 marks (£386 13s 4d) that he voluntarily gave to them beforehand and of other goods and benefits that he has in many ways conferred upon them and their house, remitted to him and quitclaimed him from the construction of the said church and the further building of their houses in the

[*602] *Calendar of Charter Rolls 1226-1516* [6 vols., 1903-27] *1257-1300*, 276-7; Translation in Williams, R., *The History and Antiquities of the Town of Aberconwy...* [Denbigh, 1835], 24-30.
[*603] *Calendar of Various Chancery Rolls: Supplementary Close Rolls, Welsh Rolls, Scutage Rolls, 1277-1326* [1912], 290; *Councils and Ecclesiastical Documents relating to GB and Ireland*, ed. A.W. Haddan and W. Stubbs [2 vols., Oxford, 1869-78] I, 579-80; *Register and Chronicle of Aberconway from the Harleian MS. 3725*, ed Ellis, H., *Camden Miscellany* [1847], 14.
[*604] *Littere Wallie, preserved in Liber A in the Public Record Office*, ed. J.G. Edwards [Cardiff, 1940], 46.

aforesaid place, and also the damages aforesaid. Dated 15 October 1284 at Caernarfon.[*605]

This is the first mention of such a large sum being given to aid the transfer and the building of the new abbey. In total this means that the king supplied over £400 in funding the move. Such would have been sufficient to build some two or three great towers like those in the inner enceinte at Harlech. Unfortunately, as the bulk of Maenan abbey is now gone, it is impossible to say on what scale the Edwardian buildings were.

The transfer was still rumbling on throughout the rest of the year with various land transfers taking place to ensure that the monastery was built without lay interference. On 18 October 1284, it was recorded that the king had granted the vill of Rhosmawr in Mon (*Rossmaur*), to the value of £10 yearly, to Gruffydd ab Iorwerth for his lifetime, in exchange for his vill of Maenan (*Meynan*) which the king in turn had granted to the abbot and convent of Aberconwy (*Aberconewey*), which monastery was now situated at Maenan[*606]. Other landholders also had to be recompensed by the Crown. On 22 October 1284, Maredudd Grach and his brother Gwrgeneu Ruth were granted the vills of Glyn and Gronant in Caernarfonshire in recompense for their land and rent in Maenan to the value of £5 17s 8d yearly, 'the land in Maenan being granted in frank almoin to the abbot and convent of Aberconwey, whose monastery he had now founded at Maynan'[*607]. On 21/22 October it was recorded that:

> the king has granted to Tewdwr ap Karuet 10s yearly of land in Coeteos, in recompense for a messuage and a parcel of land in *Penlassok*, which Tewdwr surrendered to the king, and which the king granted in frank almoin to the abbot and convent of Aberconwy, whose monastery he had now founded at Maenan.[*608]

A further notice concerning the transfer of lands in north and east Mon to Maenan abbey, still under the name of Aberconwy, was made the same day, 22 October 1284.

> Notification that the king has granted and confirmed by this charter to the abbot and convent of *Aberconewey* whose monastery he has newly founded at Maenan, in completion and satisfaction of the lands that they surrendered to him, the manor of [Llanfairyn] Ghornwy (*Kauruwilys/Kanruwylis*, SH.326909[*609]), with the hamlets of Ucheldref (*Hucheldref/Hucheldref*, SH.344875) and Gwenynog (*Gwenenauc/Qwenenauc*, an estate within Llanfflewyn, SH.350891[*610]) in the commote of Talybolion (*Thalebolyon*), which are extended at £18 14s 5½d yearly, and the town

---

[*605] *CCR 1279-88*, 407-8.
[*606] *Calendar of Various Chancery Rolls: Supplementary Close Rolls, Welsh Rolls, Scutage Rolls, 1277-1326* [1912], 290. For Rhosmawr see Lewis, E.A., 'The Decay of Tribalism in North Wales, *Transactions of the Honourable Society of Cymmrodorion*, 1902-3, 41.
[*607] *Calendar of Various Chancery Rolls: Supplementary Close Rolls, Welsh Rolls, Scutage Rolls, 1277-1326* [1912], 290. See *Registrum vulgariter nuncupatum, 'The Record of Caernarvon'*, ed. Ellis, H. [London, 1838], 9, for the lands granted.
[*608] *Calendar of Various Chancery Rolls: Supplementary Close Rolls, Welsh Rolls, Scutage Rolls, 1277-1326* [1912], 291. *Registrum vulgariter nuncupatum, 'The Record of Caernarvon'*, ed. Ellis, H. [London, 1838], 2. According to the king's charter of 24 October where these people and their compensation is mention, one Roger Bozun owned land worth 15s yearly and he too was compensated, *Monasticon Anglicanum*, ed. W. Dugdale, Revised edition by J. Caley, H. Ellis, and B. Bandinel [6 vols., 1817-30] V, 674. Roger's name has been omitted in *Register and Chronicle of Aberconway from the Harleian MS. 3725*, ed Ellis, H., *Camden Miscellany* [1847], 19 and his 15s placed against Tewdwr ap Carwet.
[*609] The hamlets of Mynachdy, Gader Mynachdy and Cae'r Mynach (Mynach being Welsh for monk) mark their interest in the district.
[*610] The name has not survived but in 1618 it was 'little more than 242 acres', Jones, E.G., 'Hugh Owen of Gwenynog', *Trans Anglesey Antiq. Soc* [1938], 42.

of Treveibion Maelog[*611] (*Trefuebien Maelauc/Crefnebien Maelant*) in the same commote which is extended at 50s 9d yearly and a moiety of the town of Penmynydd (*Penmynyd*, SH.508744) in the commote of Dindaethwy (*Dynndaethwy*), which is extended at 118s 6d yearly, and the hamlet of *Cumrewet/Cumrewez*, with a moiety of Raulyn's meadow in the commote of Creuddyn (*Cruthyn*), which is extended at 100s yearly. Witnessed by Bishop Robert of Bath and Wells, Earl Richard Burgh of Ulster, John Vescy, Otto Grandison, Robert Tybetot, Richard Bruce, Robert Fitz John.[*612]

Thankfully, quite a lot can be said of these newly granted lands. Since Ghornwy was granted to Maenan in 1284 the manor came to be known as Llanfairynghornwy which is the church of St Mary in Ghornwy. Obviously this indicates that either the church was newly built by the monks after 1284 and dedicated to their patron saint, or that they rededicated the old church. There is also a probably contemporary petition from the community of freemen and villains of the commote of Talybolion to the king. This complained that a third part of the commote had been granted to the abbot of Maenan with a consequence that the remaining two thirds were unjustly burdened with all the works owed to the houses and mills together with hostage and other services[*613]. As no reply was made it is to be presumed that the services owed by the abbot's lands remained with the remnants of the commote.

Some of Aberconwy's lands were mentioned during the extent of Anglesey carried out in 1294. This found that Llanfairynghornwy (*Cornuchles*) consisted of four carucates of cultivated land (about 400 acres) rendering 26s 8d out of a total of 106s 8d. There was a broken mill there that rendered nothing and pasture worth 20s, the whole held for £4 10s 8d, while the villains of the town paid 6s. In total the estate was worth £8 10s[*614]. Gwenynog is not named, but is obviously the estate described as:

> *Tursemon* which is a hamlet which pertains to *Gerneweles* whose hamlet of *Westdrewy* renders... 116s 9d.

Finally comes Treveibion Maelog (*T'bonmaylok*) which rendered 25s, which gave the abbot a total valuation of £21 8s 5d. Soon after this comes the statement that the manors of Ghornwy (*Cornuthles*) with the hamlets of *Tursemon*, *Westdrewy* and Treveibion Maelog (*T'lonmaylock*) were held by the abbot of Conway (*Conewey*) by the king's charter. The discrepancies of the names are obvious, but the reason for this is unknown.

Regardless of the names of the lands by 1294, it is apparent that in 1284 the king had granted the abbey a series of probably contiguous lands running from near Llanbabo (SH.378868) diagonally north-west across Mon to the North Sea at Carmel Head (Trwyn y Gader). Nearer to Conway itself the abbey's lands in Creuddyn had been extended and it is possible to state with some certainty that they lay under what is now Llandudno Junction and consisted of the land on the opposite bank of the Conwy to the abbey and immediately under

---

[*611] Treveibion Maelog was in the parish of Llanbeulan (SH.373755). The name may partially live on in Llanfaelog (SH.336731). On the northern side of the altar in Llanbeulan church is a stone commemorating Hugh Davis of Treveibion Meyrick, Gent., 1690. As this land lay immediately north of the grange of Bodgedwydd claimed to have been given to Aberconwy by Prince Llywelyn (d.1240), it makes perfect sense to make it over to the monks. Although Bodgedwydd grange is given its boundaries in the forged charter of 1199 they are uncertain to the north, apparently running just south of Llanbeulan.

[*612] *Calendar of Various Chancery Rolls: Supplementary Close Rolls, Welsh Rolls, Scutage Rolls, 1277-1326* [1912], 292.

[*613] CAPW, 112.

[*614] These three lands are recorded in the 'Extent of Anglesey 1294', Seebohm, *The Tribal System in Wales* [London, 1904], Appendix A, 20-1.

Degannwy castle to the south and south-east. This can be gleaned from a document of 1352 which states that the abbey held a quarter of Bodysgallen vill as well as a quarter of a weir near Degannwy[*615]. As most of the drainage flows south of Degannwy castle from Bodysgallen it seems a reasonable assumption that the abbey's lands in Creuddyn lay there within site of the old abbey across the river.

While the king was commencing building his new fortress at Conway Bishop Einion of Bangor called together the representatives of the defunct kingdom of Gwynedd to discuss the running of the district immediately before and after the conquest of King Edward I. The meeting took place on 3 August 1283 at a roughly central point in Gwynedd, the Aberconwy grange of Nant Call in Arfon.

> The prince used to take townships for his own use, or to grant them to others in return for services, but the burden of that township remained upon the community or upon other such townships, and it is a great wrong to place the burden of one township upon another. The prince took great and small lands without the consent of the heirs and placed his cattle-pastures and plough lands there, and took profit from land which was sold, something which no other prince did except him alone... the prince frequently waged war against you, lord king, without consulting his people and without seeking and obtaining their agreement, and when, in the course of time, peace was made between you and him he made his men pay three pence a year for every great beast, yet he was not willing to pay anything from his treasure deposited at Dolwyddelan and elsewhere... in the time of Llywelyn the measure of wine, corn and beer was increased... the prince made the noblemen of Meirionydd bear the cost of horses to carry burden and perform his duties, and demanded pasture for other horses, something which had never occurred before his time. In Arfon, where before the time of the prince there were only one courthouse, one bailiff and two servants, now they are doubled. There the prince made villeins out of noblemen... Never in the past have these or similar wrongs been attempted or contemplated by any prince or king except by the said Prince Llywelyn. For this reason the people pray God that remedy may be brought against such matters.[*616]

It is interesting that the Aberconwy grange was pushed into use on this occasion for such a meeting. Possibly the new castle building works going on in the major centres precluded them from being meeting points for such a gathering. This would also suggest that Nant Call and therefore possibly the other nearby granges of Rhedynog Felen, Ffriwlwyd and Cwm had not been damaged in the fighting. The opposite is most likely true of the granges east of the Conwy and on Mon. Nanhwynain might also have suffered damage due to its proximity to the king's advance to Dolwyddelan and possibly beyond early in the year. This would suggest that the £100 paid in compensation by Edward I for damage done to Aberconwy was to cover damage to the lands on or east of the Conwy. As other houses had less rounded amounts paid (see below) it is to be presumed that this was a generous figure, rather than being paid from an audited account of damages done.

On 23 October 1284, the king granted Bishop Einion of St Asaph acquittance of the 200 marks (£133 6s 8d) of the 500 marks (£333 6s 8d) which he owed for the king's goodwill

---

[*615] Ministers' Accounts for Nant Conway manor, TNA, SC.6/1171/7, m.1.
[*616] Beverley-Smith, L., The Gravamina of the Community of Gwynedd against Llywelyn ap Gruffydd', *Bulletin of the Board of Celtic Studies* XXXI [1984], 173-6.

as he had paid this sum to the abbot of Aberconwy to be used towards the building of the new abbey at Maenan[617]. Presumably this sum was to be added to the £400 plus that the king had already given. On the same day the king issued his full and long grant to the abbey concerning the exchange that had taken place[618]. What follows is one of the longest charters issued to any monastery with a full description of the new abbey lands at Maenan. Further, the king listed the liberties granted to the translated abbey. These included ordinary rights of seigneurial jurisdiction and less common rights having to do with the apprehension and punishment of felons - the rights to capture and hang thieves both within and without the abbey's lands, take those accused of housebreaking with violence, failure to raise hue and cry, the right to punish those who aided felons and those guilty of civil disturbances[619]. Many of these are obviously of English origin and many appear in the Domesday Book concerning the rights of Chester inhabitants. It would appear that the monks therefore were aware of the rights of Chester and took advantage of that fact to add these to their new royal charter. King Edward was obviously also willing to grant these to his new foundation. These should be compared with those later claimed in 1332 to have been granted to the abbey by Prince Llywelyn in 1199.

All these grants were added to the immunities from direct and indirect taxes and from personal service such as suit of court that the monks had held since the early grant of Henry II some hundred years earlier. Further rights now granted included provisions that the abbey's woods should not be taken for the king's works and that its grain should not be taken for the provisioning of castles. The monks were even granted immunity from forest law, a law that kings usually sought to uphold, especially when they were renowned hunters like King Edward. Then there were the more normal grants that the monks and their brethren should have freedom from toll as was stated in their earlier royal charters as well as their being allowed to enjoy all reasonable gifts of lands, churches, men and money that they already possessed and might be given in the future and that if any man under the monastery's jurisdiction should have been put to death, or have fled, or have committed a crime for which loss of his possessions was the penalty, such possessions were to become the property of the monks. Similarly if one of the abbey's men should be fined, the abbey was to receive the money collected. As usual the right of justice involving loss of life or limb was reserved to the king. This was similar to the reservation granted in Edwardian borough charters. Interestingly, all men were prohibited on penalty of £20 from exacting forfeiture from the abbey since it was under royal protection and it was granted that the abbey should not be impleaded in matters relating to any of its holdings except in the presence of the king himself. In these grants Edward would appear to be following the alleged 1199 charter of Llywelyn ab Iorwerth as the words *in puram et perpetuam elemosinam* appear in both that charter and Edward's. As this concept is undoubtedly English and not Welsh it would suggest that Llywelyn's charter was indeed forged and based upon Edward's charter and not the other way around as is usually claimed[620]. It therefore seems increasingly likely that the similar Prince Llywelyn charter claimed by the abbot of Cymer which stated that he had the right of fishing in all waters and shores of the sea; the right of wreck for all goods of the monastery wrecked

---

[617] *Calendar of Various Chancery Rolls: Supplementary Close Rolls, Welsh Rolls, Scutage Rolls, 1277-1326* [1912], 291.

[618] The entry in *Calendar of Charter Rolls 1226-1516* [6 vols., 1903-27] *1257-1300*, 279 is next to useless, but the full text appears in *Monasticon Anglicanum*, ed. W. Dugdale, Revised edition by J. Caley, H. Ellis, and B. Bandinel [6 vols., 1817-30] V, 674-5, and is found in Appendix 1, p.277-9.

[619] Davies, J.C., 'Felony in Edwardian Wales', *Trans. of the Honourable Society of Cymmrodorian*, [1916-17], 190.

[620] Similarly Llywelyn's alleged chaplain in the 1199 charters, Ydon, seems to be taken from the phrase in Edward I's charter of 16 July 1284, copied into the Register as *ydoneos capellanum honestum*. The original would seem to have run, *duos capellano Anglicos et idoneos et honestos*.

wherever found; the right to fell trees and pursue and kill game and to graze animals in their woods and lands; the right to dig and carry away metals and minerals which might be reduced to another form and sea coal and other minerals which could not be so reduced and the right to accept a lease of lands would also appear to be a forgery[621]. In short, the claims of both Aberconwy and Cymer to great rights granted by Prince Llywelyn ab Iorwerth should be held in great suspicion and that of Aberconwy should be regarded as a total forgery. It should also be noted here that the abbot of Cymer did not claim similar rights of jurisdiction to Aberconwy[622]. Similarly, the abbot of Strata Florida never claimed any exemptions from the normal operation of secular courts, while in 1254, Valle Crucis claimed no right of judgement on homicide and theft, while it was only in 1302 that Tintern was granted the right of gallows and judgement of life and limbs[623]. More can be said of this as a charter was issued between 1219 and 1231 to Tintern abbey when William Marshall Junior (d.1231) expressly reserved the right of *utfangenethef* to himself and not to Tintern abbey[624]. It would appear that the monks of Aberconwy decided to claim this right to themselves as well and so go one up on Tintern and most other religious houses. It is to be wondered if they did not use the Tintern abbey charter as their exemplar and add to this various rights then customary in Chester. Certainly a second Tintern abbey charter, this time by Earl Gilbert Marshall of Pembroke (1234-41), granted the abbey that they should hold their lands:

> with soc and sac and tol and them and infangenethef and that they and their men and serjeants shall be quit of shires and hundreds and suit of shires and hundreds and from summonses and all else; and from amercements of the county save from those who hold by secular service and from toll, pontage, pannage, passage, tallage, blodwyte, flithwyte, hengwite and flemeneswite; and that the abbey shall be without the forest... so that the monks may do in their woods and waters what they will and be without the danger of foresters and all other serjeants touching puture (*pastu*) and any such exaction; and that they shall have all the forfeitures of their men arising from justice saving to the grantor and his heirs justice of life and limb and in all the grantor's forests free pasture for their beasts and their needs for burning and building; provided that if any one claim any of the things granted to the abbey the grantor and his heirs shall answer thereto and satisfy the claim by exchange or in any other manner....[625]

This charter certainly suggests that such rights could be granted by English earls in the first half of the thirteenth century to their favoured abbeys. Presumably this was also the same of Welsh princes, yet there is no evidence they ever did apart from the forged Aberconwy and Cymer charters, and a possible one of Llywelyn ap Gruffydd (d.1282) which was rejected in 1348, almost certainly correctly, as a forgery. Consequently, it can be seen that there is no evidence that any Welsh prince granted such rights to a religious house within his own domains. The main examples of princely charters not including such extensive 'English' rights include those of Maredudd ap Rhobert to Llanllugan between 1216 and 1236, Rhys ap

---

[621] *Archaeologia Cambrensis* [1873], 170.
[622] The last historian to examine the Cymer charter of 1209 concluded, 'But it may fairly be claimed that, despite the fact that no 'chancery' of Llywelyn's could have issued such a document as it stands in its entirety, and despite the fact that it harbours many unusual and obsolescent forms, the authenticity of the 1209 charter cannot be gainsaid'. Williams-Jones, K., 'Llywelyn's Charter to Cymer Abbey in 1209', *Journal of the Merioneth Historical Society* III [1957], 54
[623] Williams, D.H., *The Welsh Cistercians* [Norwich, 1983, 2 vols] II, 248.
[624] *Monasticon Anglicanum*, ed. W. Dugdale, Revised edition by J. Caley, H. Ellis, and B. Bandinel [6 vols., 1817-30] V, 267-9.
[625] *Calendar of Charter Rolls 1226-1516* [6 vols., 1903-27] III, 98.

Gruffydd to Chertsey abbey between 1165 and 1197, the same to Strata Florida in 1184, Maelgwn ap Rhys to Strata Florida on 22 January 1198, Rhys Ieuanc to Strata Florida in 1202, Maelgwn Fychan to Strata Florida between 1198 and 1227, Maredudd ab Owain to Talley abbey between 1235 and 1265, Cynan ap Maredudd to Strata Florida between 1280 and 1282 (a possible forgery), Llywelyn ab Iorwerth to Ynys Llannog on 15 October 1221, Llywelyn ap Gruffydd to Basingwerk on 8 April 1247, Llywelyn ap Gruffydd to Beddgelert priory on 25 July 1271 (declared a forgery in 1348[626]), Hywel ab Iorwerth to Goldcliff priory between 1184 and 1217, Madog ap Gruffydd Maelor to Combermere on 5 January 1197 and the same founding Valle Crucis abbey on 28 January 1201 as well as making a grant and confirmation to Strata Marcella in 1207, Owain ap Gruffydd founding Strata Marcella in 1170 and the (possibly forged) confirmation of Gwenwynwyn on 9 May 1185[627]. In short, the fact that these two houses (or three if you include Beddgelert and the forgery of 1348) have clauses granting their occupants very 'English' rights and all are set in charters which are highly aberrant makes it appear that all three charters of Llywelyn ab Iorwerth are forgeries, made when the abbots of these houses were being pressured by Quo Warranto enquiries.

Regardless of these forgeries, the original documentation gives the impression that the move of the abbey from Aberconwy to Maenan was completed around this date. In the aftermath further abbey business was completed. On 26 October 1284 a debt of 11 marks (£7 6s 8d) owed by the abbot of Aberconwy to Bishop Robert Burnell was pardoned[628]. The next day Abbot David of Aberconwy issued a letter which Adam the subprior and Madog a monk of Aberconwy were to take to Chester to the royal commission hearing war claims cases. Consequently, on 3 November the commission delivered £100 to the two representatives to cover the claims of the abbey for war damage[629]. This puts the abbey in the higher bracket for damage done during the war of 1282-83. For comparison, the compensation issued to other houses were a surprisingly large amount of £160 for Valle Crucis, a similar £100 for Basingwerk, £80 for Cymer, £78 for Strata Florida and £43 for Strata Marcella. The non-Cistercian houses of Beddgelert received £50, Priestholm £46, Enlli 10 marks (£6 13s 4d), Llanllyr nunnery 40 marks (£26 13s 4d), the Rhuddlan friars £17 10s, the Llanfaes friars £8 and the Dominican friars of Bangor the surprisingly large amount of £100. These recompenses were augmented by other amounts to various churches as well as to the two North Welsh bishops. Further compensation of a non-warlike manner was given on 5 November 1284, when King Edward granted Bishop Einion of Bangor three vills valued at 50s yearly in recompense for the loss of the tithes of Ghornwy and Penmynydd which had recently been granted to Aberconwy abbey[630].

> Notification that the king has granted to Bishop Einion of St Asaph and to *Effeyriat Teulu* (the domestic or court chaplain) of Wales, in recompense for the tithes of the king's demesnes at Ghornwy (*Kauruwylus*) and Penmynydd (*Peynmeynyd*), which are extended at 50s yearly, which they granted at the king's instance to the abbot and convent of *Aberconewey*, whose monastery the king has now caused to be founded anew at *Meynan* and to whom he has granted his demesnes aforesaid, the townships of

---

[626] *Registrum vulgariter nuncupatum, 'The Record of Caernarvon'*, ed. Ellis, H. [London, 1838], 166-7.
[627] Acts, 162-3; 168; 171-5, 180-82,194, 197-201, 203-4, 216-22, 411-2, 492-94, 550, 667-8, 696-8, 698-700; 704-6, 744-5, 746-8.
[628] *CCR 1279-88*, 306.
[629] *Littere Wallie, preserved in Liber A in the Public Record Office*, ed. J.G. Edwards [Cardiff, 1940], 95-6.
[630] *Councils and Ecclesiastical Documents relating to GB and Ireland*, ed. A.W. Haddan and W. Stubbs [2 vols., Oxford, 1869-78] I, 550 [misdated 1283]; Episcopal Acts II, 437, n.97; *CPR 1377-81*, 291.

Trefieuan (*Trefyevan*[631]), *Abydon* and Bodychen (SH.389780), which are also extended at 50s yearly, provided that the bishop and his successors shall satisfy the said *Effeiryat Teulu* of Wales and his successors for the portion due to him of the tithes aforesaid.[632]

It is also apparent that the king showed favour to his new house of Maenan by cancelling payments assessed on Aberconwy during the time of Prince Llywelyn ap Gruffydd (d.1282). Consequently on 10 June 1285, King Edward ordered that the monks should not pay a yearly puture which he had caused to be extended at 8s 3d, for their grange of Ffriwlwyd (*Friwilwith*) as had previously been done for certain serjeants of Llywelyn ap Gruffydd which the 'late prince of Wales and his ministers had extorted from them in their lifetime'. Instead the king ordered the exchequer of Caernarfon to acquit the monks of payment[633]. Similarly, the abbot of Basingwerk and the prior of the Hospital of St John of Jerusalem also had their novel payments to the serjeants of the deceased Prince Llywelyn cancelled. The order for Aberconwy alone was repeated on 26 August 1295 when the king emphasized that the remission was permanent and included arrears from the time of the conquest in 1283[634].

With the abbey moved to Maenan the king finally applied for papal sanction for this translation and this was obtained on 24 April 1286[635]. The bull of the unconsecrated Pope Honorius IV confirmed the king's very own foundation and endowment of a Cistercian monastery in the diocese of St Asaph with the bishop's assent and the union to it with the consent of the bishops of St Asaph and Bangor, of the monastery of Aberconwy, it being transferred from Bangor diocese to that of St Asaph. As such the pope confirmed this for the abbot and convent, 'whose possessions the king had largely increased as well as all the privileges and indults of the said monastery'. The king himself confirmed this document on 4 October 1288, but someone may have sensed an error in the bull for on 21 August 1289 Pope Nicholas IV confirmed the transfer of the abbey as appeared in the bull of his predecessor. He finished his bull with the statement that the pope's bulls which were issued before their consecration bear no name on the lead seal, so that this should not have given rise to the popular error that such bulls were defective[636]. Presumably this bull was in answer to a question from Edward I concerning the apparently defective seal. There is no evidence to suggest that there were any problems with the moving of the abbey after 1284 or that anyone was dissatisfied with the outcome.

---

[631] A study of the parish church records in the tref of Llanidan, SH.495669, shows: "The ancient parish of Llanidan comprised the ten townships of Bodowyr, Bryn Gwyn, Brynsiencyn, Cefnyfyrwen, Gwydryn, Llysllew, Porthamel, Trefarthen, Trefieuan and Tre'r Dryw".
[632] *Calendar of Various Chancery Rolls: Supplementary Close Rolls, Welsh Rolls, Scutage Rolls, 1277-1326* [1912], 292.
[633] *Calendar of Various Chancery Rolls: Supplementary Close Rolls, Welsh Rolls, Scutage Rolls, 1277-1326* [1912], 301, 304
[634] *CPR 1292-1301*, 143.
[635] *Calendar of Entries in the Papal Registers relating to GB and Ireland - Papal Letters, 1198-1304*, ed. W. H. Bliss [1893], 480; the full document is transcribed in *Littere Wallie, preserved in Liber A in the Public Record Office*, ed. J.G. Edwards [Cardiff, 1940], 182-3.
[636] *Calendar of Entries in the Papal Registers relating to GB and Ireland - Papal Letters, 1198-1304*, ed. W. H. Bliss [1893], 500; *Councils and Ecclesiastical Documents relating to GB and Ireland*, ed. A.W. Haddan and W. Stubbs [2 vols., Oxford, 1869-78] I, 588-9; *Monasticon Anglicanum*, ed. W. Dugdale, Revised edition by J. Caley, H. Ellis, and B. Bandinel [6 vols., 1817-30] VI, III, 1627; *Foedera, Conventiones, Litterae etc*, ed. T. Rymer and R. Sanderson, 4th edn, by A. Clarke, F. Holbrooke, and J. Caley [4 vols. in 7 parts, 1816-69] I ii, 49.

The Ecclesiastical Taxation of Maenan Abbey, 1291 to 1295

Some five years after the abbey's move to Maenan, Pope Nicholas IV ordered an assessment for the taxation of the church in England. Consequently the returns of 1291/92 throw much light on the state and value of the lands of Aberconwy and other churches at the end of the thirteenth century. It also gives the first solid account of what lands Maenan abbey was holding at the end of the thirteenth century. As such the full account is rendered below and printed with the Latin in Appendix 7, p.329.

The goods of the abbot of Conwy in St Asaph diocese.

The abbot holds the vill of Maenan (*Maurnant*); he renders for the mills and perquisites, as well as for two carucates, income £6 1s 7d, tithe 12s 2d.

Also Hiraethog (*Hir'hadok*) and the vaccaria of *Trekedewe* 3 carucates with other profits, income £1 5s, tithe 2s 6d.

Also the grange of Ceirniog (*Karennock*), Pentrefoelas (*veylas*), Llanfair Rhyd Castell (*Demoetjerstn/demoe q'stu*), Llyn Cymmer (*Kenekenea/kenenkennea*), Lechwedd Cryn Llwyn (*Lewes' et Kylwen*), five carucates with other profits, income £2 5s, tithe 4s 6d.

Also *Herlygaret & Lanwueiri & henkesche*, 2 carucates with pasture, income £1 4s 8d, tithe 2s 5¾d.

The income of animals.

The abbot has 106 cows, income £6 6s, tithe 12s 7¼d.

He also has 560 sheep, income £8 5s, tithe 16s 6d[*637].

He also has 15 horses, income 15s, tithe 1s 6d.

The sum of the goods of the abbot of Conway (*Conewey*) £26 2s 4d, tithe £2 12 3d.

The temporal goods of the abbot of Conway (*Conewey*), diocese of St Asaph, existing in the diocese of Bangor.

The abbot has the grange of Ffriwlwyd (*Frithlwyd/Fryleyt*), two carucates of land with profits, £1, tithe 2s.

Also he has the grange of Cwm (*Cor'/Corano*) 1 carucate of land with profits 10s, tithe 1s.

Also he has the grange of Nant Call (*Nankal/Namall*) 1 carucate of land with profits 10s, tithe 1s.

Also he has the grange of Rhedynog Felen (*Reddenaut'*) and *Havailyn/Hanoclyv'*, with a fulling mill and other profits, 21s 8d, tithe 2s 2d.

Also he has the manor of Ghornwy (*Cornoles*) three carucates of land with profits, a mill and other profits £15 10s.

Also he has the grange of Gelliniog (*Killiniog/Keneloe*) seven carucates of land with profits £12, [£1 4s] tithe.

Also he has the grange of Bodgedwydd (*Bodgedwyadhes/Dodgedewez*) three carucates of land with other profits £1 10s, tithe 3s.

Also the abbot has a moiety of the vill of Penmynydd (*Penmir/Pennenuz*) a carucate of land with profits and a mill, £4 10s, tithe 9s.

[*637] For comparison at this time the following houses had the following amount of sheep: Margam 5,285, Neath 4,897, Tintern 3,264, Basingwerk 2,000 in Penllyn, Strata Florida 1,327, Whitland, 1,100 and Dore 980 in Gwent, Williams, D.H., *The Welsh Cistercians* [Norwich, 1983, 2 vols], II, 305. The 560 sheep of Aberconwy therefore suggests that these were not a major staple of this house, but as three granges are missing from the taxatio, viz. Nanhwynain, Creuddyn and just possibly Gyffin Conwy, these figures cannot be taken as definitive.

Also he has the grange of Arddau (*Herduw*) a carucate of land with Dulyn (*Nauthlyn/Nanthlyne*) with profits 15s, tithe 1s 6d.
In total £37 6s 8d, total tithe £3 14s 8d.

When the totals of the two dioceses are added together this gives Maenan abbey an annual income of £63 9s. This is exactly half way down the list of the ten recorded Cistercian abbeys in Wales in the Taxation. These values were Neath £236 1s 5d; Margam, £225 7s 4½d; Basingwerk £104 1s; Strata Florida £98 6s 9d; Maenan £63 9s; Whitland £43 15s; Cwmhir £35 12s; Cymer £25 8s 3d; Strata Marcella £19 1s 2d and Valle Crucis £14 14s 8d. Therefore it can be seen that Aberconwy was for the purposes of this taxation worth nearly four times less than the value of the richest house, Neath, but was over four times the value of the poorest house, Valle Crucis. It is also apparent that the survey appears incomplete for it misses Nanhwynain grange altogether and makes no mention of the abbey's lands in Creuddyn. Obviously Gyffin Conwy is not mentioned either as this had been swopped for the royal lands in northern Mon.

According to these 1291 figures Aberconwy had 31 carucates of land. This was lower than the southern abbeys, Margam and Neath, but much higher than their neighbours. Similarly, the North Welsh priories of Enlli, Beddgelert and Ynys Llannog had much less. Depending on the quality of the land a carucate was reckoned in the reign of King Richard I to be either sixty or one hundred acres[638]. By the reign of Edward I a carucate was reckoned as between 96 and 108 acres. It would therefore seem likely that in 1291 each carucate was roughly one hundred acres put under the plough. The table below therefore gives a relatively rough estimate of the amount of acres each house had in cultivation. The southern abbeys like Neath and Margam also had much more land described in acres rather than carucates. This suggests that many more donors of lesser status had granted lands to the abbey in amounts of much less than a hundred acres.

Religious House	Carucates Recorded	Acres Under Cultivation
Abbeys		
Margam	53½	5,350
Whitland	44	4,400
Neath	40	4,000
Strata Florida	32	3,200
Aberconwy	31	3,100
Strata Marcella	18	1,800
Basingwerk	13½	1,350
Cymer	9½	950

---

[638] The subject is examined in Zupko, RE, *A Dictionary of Weights and Measures for the British Isles: the Middle Ages to the Twentieth Century* [1985], 74.

Cwmhir	4	400
Valle Crucis	3	300
Priories		
Enlli	6	600
Beddgelert	3	300
Ynys Llannog	3	300

Whatever the Taxatio and the above figures show, they do not reveal the total landholdings of these houses, merely the land they had under cultivation. Abbey Cwmhir for one had massive landholdings and the idea that this amounted to only 400 acres is absurd. Further, it must be remembered that Nanhwynain, Aberconwy's largest grange, is not mentioned. Possibly, as this is very much hill country on the slopes of Snowdon, there were no ploughlands here and this explains its absence and it simply provided the land for the abbot's animals. The same could well be true of the other houses with a low carucate reading.

In the aftermath of the taxation assessment[639], probably in 1294 for his Gascon war, King Edward in parliament was granted a moiety of the value of the clergy. The moiety would seem to have been a half as sometime after the Welsh war of 1294-95 began, the abbot of Aberconwy, writing as the king's 'especial chaplain' begged the king for a pardon from raising the £30 demanded of him because the goods taxed to this date on 29 September (1294 almost certainly meant) had been ruined and destroyed by both the English and the Welsh during the war and that his house could not pay the money if it was not to be ruined for ever[640]. That £30 had been demanded agrees that the income of the house was about £60 per annum which would agree with the Taxatio figure. The abbot had been appointed collector for the tax in St Asaph diocese on 30 September 1294 and had agreed to make payments in three thirds on 1 November 1294, 17 April 1295 and the final payment on 8 July 1295[641]. The request of the abbot could well date to immediately after 21 October 1294 when the king ordered him and a host of other clergy to supply the first third of the monies owed on time on 1 November[642]. During this period the abbey granges would no doubt have been pillaged once more with the ongoing war in North Wales between Michaelmas 1294 and 20 July 1295. During the hostilities King Edward was at Conway castle from Christmas 1294 until 9 April 1295. He then campaigned in Mon for a month before leaving Bangor for South Wales on 6 May 1295[643]. He was back in North Wales on 29 June 1295 when he stayed at Trefriw, opposite Maenan abbey and just south of their grange of Arddau. He then moved on to Conway until 6 July[644].

With the fall of the major princes of Gwynedd the abbot of Aberconwy was obviously considered a good go-between by the people of the land. Consequently, they petitioned the

---

[639] It seems possible that many of the Welsh abbots were ordered to remain in the kingdom, certainly on 10 August 1293 Edward I ordered that the abbot of Citeaux should be informed that the abbot of Aberconwy was remaining in England this year as the king required him and that he would therefore not be going to the general chapter and asking that the abbot should not be troubled on this, *Calendar of Chancery Warrants 1244-1326* [1927], 37.

[640] CAPW, 311.

[641] *CPR 1292-1301*, 89.

[642] *CCR 1288-96*, 397.

[643] Gough, H., *Itinerary of King Edward the First* [2 vols, 1900] II, 124-8.

[644] Gough, H., *Itinerary of King Edward the First* [2 vols, 1900] II, 130-1.

abbot as well as some local lords to greet the king in person and intercede on their behalf. In reply the king sent the following on 3 December 1296.

> Letter to the good men and community of Snowdon and Anglesey, informing them that the abbot of Aberconwy, Thomas Danvers, Tewdwr ap Goronwy and Hywel ap Cynwrig, sent by them to the king's presence, have related to the king rumour which disturbed and grieved them, to wit, that the king held them in suspicion; and begging them not to believe such rumours for the future, as no sinister rumours of their state and behaviour has reached the king in these days and he has no suspicion towards them, but rather, by reason of their late good service, holds them for his faithful and devoted subjects.[*645]

With the end of the war the history of Aberconwy fades back into more run of the mill routine. Although once again, this time on 6 May 1298, the abbot of Citeaux was informed that the king had ordered the abbot of Aberconwy to stay in Wales 'on the king's business and the quiet of the land' and not travel to Citeaux and further that he was 'not in a fit bodily state to travel' in any case[*646].

On 28 April 1301 Abbot David of Maenan (*Meignon*) paid his fealty to the new prince of Wales, later to be King Edward II[*647]. It was some two years later that his successor, Abbot Tewdwr, with the agreement of Prince Edward and Sir Cadwgan, the bishop of Bangor, made a charter concerning Conway church.

> This composition made and indented between the Venerable Sir Tewdwr, abbot of the monastery and convent of Conwy and Sir Rowland Badchey, chaplain and first vicar of the parochial church of the Blessed Virgin in the town of Conway... that the said vicar and his successors in time to come, shall have a half or second part of the tithes of the said parish church of Conway...[*648]

This was followed by a list of the sources of income to be divided and a provision that certain lands on the north-east side of the church should belong to the vicar:

> on condition that the said vicar shall bear and support half the burden, ordinary and extraordinary, belonging to the said church etc.

Within a hundred years of Edward I's 1284 grant, only one vicar served the church of Aberconwy, the services of the other two chaplains' having been allowed to lapse. This state of affairs was regularised by King Richard II on 10 October 1386 when it was found that the church was worth more than ten marks (£6 13s 4d) due to the pestilences and other misfortunes[*649].

[*645] *CPR 1292–1301*, 223.
[*646] *Calendar of Chancery Warrants 1244-1326* [1927], 92.
[*647] *CPR 1343-45*, 231.
[*648] The original deed is in the Bangor Diocesan Register, but the above is taken from the extracts printed in, *The Registers of Conway* ed. Hadley, L [1900], x.
[*649] *CPR 1385-89*, 237.

Aberconwy Abbey at Maenan during the Fourteenth Century

Sometime during 1308 the pope had instructed the abbot of Aberconwy to collect the tithe for the Holy Land[*650]. It was probably some time after this, during the summer of 1313, that the abbot of Aberconwy decided to act against purported financial pressure brought on his house by royal agents in North Wales. Consequently, he decided to write to King Edward II (1307-27) complaining that the royal sheriffs and bailiffs had been amercing Aberconwy against the terms of the charter of Edward I and:

> do not forbear frequently to amerce the abbot and the convent in shires and in hundreds and often molest them by that means and harass them unduly and unjustly and against the tenor of the aforementioned charter'[*651].

The auditors of petitions, to whom the complaint had been addressed, replied that they were not empowered to make any reply to a request that anyone should be quit of any amercements made before the king's representatives. They therefore asked the abbot to present the charter he claimed made him quit of all amercements before chancery. The follow up to this exchange seems to have led the king writing on 13 October 1313 to Roger Mortimer, his justiciar of Wales, stating that the abbot of Aberconwy had complained to him of unlawful amercements being raised against his abbey by the sheriffs of Caernarfon and Anglesey in contradiction of the charter granted by Edward I. As a consequence, the king was informing Mortimer that he was not to impede the abbot and monks coming to the November parliament at Westminster to state their case. In the meantime, Mortimer was to send to parliament, if he could in the limited time available, a list of the misdeeds of the abbey and their amercements. This reply shows that Edward, or his government, appears to have taken the plea personally, as the letter was said to have been witnessed by the king in person. The writ was obviously answered by Mortimer and this was copied down with the original writ on four membranes of parchment under the title: Writs and returns of the Justice of Wales as to the amercements claimed by the abbey of Aberconwy under its charter[*652].

The Mortimer list is then copied out. Firstly he found that on Monday 8 March 1311 (the first Monday after St David's day - which was Monday 1 March) at the Clynnog (*Kelleneth/Kellennock*) tourn, that the abbot of Aberconwy was fined £5 for unjustly obstructing the course of the River Gwyrfai (*Gwyleth*) bank in Uwch Gwyrfai (*Ughcorney*) commote between their land of Rhedynog Felen (*Redeynok Velyn*) and the land of the king's free tenants at Dinlle (*Dynthleu*). The jury also found that in 1305 the abbey had raised a new mill within the grange which had resulted in a fall of revenue at the royal mill for which the monks were fined £5. At the same time the abbot had appropriated four bovates (half a carucate) of land that had belonged to Einion ap Gwyn for which the abbey was amerced £20. Presumably Einion had joined the abbey and brought his lands with him. This was against the ordinance proclaimed at Kennington (*Kenyton*) near London by King Edward II in 1305 when he had been prince of Wales[*653]. At the same time the jurors complained that the abbey had accepted Einion Ddu, a royal villain, with his progeny and his land of Tynywedd? (*Tusnevyth*

[*650] 'Index to "Llyfr Coch Asaph", *Archaeologia Cambrensis* [1868], 160.
[*651] CAPW, 40. The wording of this is similar to the monks' complaint to Edward II and therefore almost certainly dates to 1311 and not 1307 as was suggested in the *Calendar*.
[*652] TNA, C.47/10/32/9. This is transcribed in Appendix 5, p.324.
[*653] This happened in 1305, *Registrum vulgariter nuncupatum, 'The Record of Caernarvon'*, ed. Ellis, H. [London, 1838], 212-25. This petition also confirmed that the abbey's lands in Rhos and Rhufoniog were held directly of the prince of Wales and not of the earl of Lincoln as lord of Denbigh.

above the hamlet of Nant Call into their ranks. For this they were fined £5. During the same tourn and on the same day a local jury at Aber again amerced the monks for a total of £10. This time for receiving another royal villain, Adam Best of Aber and his brother Cynddelw, into their fellowship of monks to the damage and contempt of the king.

In Mon the sheriff replied to Mortimer that during his tourn of Aberffraw the abbot was amerced £2 for receiving a royal villain as a lay brother without licence.

> And also it was found there that the same abbot had since ploughed his carucate above the king's highway between Aberffraw and Tal-y-llyn' (*Talethlen*), longwise and lengthwise two acres of land for which he was amerced... 13s 4d.
> And also it was found there that the same abbot had received David ab Ieuan ap David a villain of the lord king of the maerdraef of Aberffraw with his chattels above his land in Penmynydd (*Penmenyth*) without the licence of the lord king for which he was amerced... 6s 8d.[654]

Tal-y-llyn is three miles north-north-east of Aberffraw at SH.367734 immediately north of Bodgedwydd (SH.362716) and obviously a part of the abbey's grange of Bodgedwydd as the forged charter of 1315-32 shows (Appendix 2). This would suggest that the abbot was bringing these lands within the granges of Bodgedwydd and Penmynydd into production at the end of the reign of Edward I (1272-1307).

Nothing is recorded further of these complaints and it appears obvious that the abbot failed to get respite from the sheriffs' control. This can be deduced as they must have approached the king again, as on 27 April 1314 Edward II wrote further to Roger Mortimer on the same matter as is recorded in the roll, repeating the complaints that the abbot had earlier brought before the king and which the king repeated to Mortimer in his letter[655]. King Edward again emphasised that he did not want the abbey further vexed until the matter was dealt with by the Michaelmas parliament of that year (29 September 1315).

The result was another missive from Mortimer which reiterated what had been done. In this he claimed that he had:

> ordered the sheriffs of Caernarfon and Anglesey that they might certify by me of all the misdeeds of the abbot and monks of Aberconwy by themselves in his bail touching on just as in the form of the disputed writ...

He then repeated the complaints listed above concerning the monks actions in Rhedynog Felen, the appropriation of Einion ap Gwyn's lands as well as those of Einion Ddu, Adam Best and his brother Cynddelw, David ab Ieuan ap David and another man in Mon and in ploughing land between Aberffraw and Tal-y-llyn (SH.367734)[656]. It seems obvious from this that no further amercements were admitted by Mortimer since the king's first writ of 1313. Despite all this work by king, abbot and justiciar there is also no evidence that these amercements were ever paid and it is likely that they never were. This, of course, would be in line with Edward I's charter to Maenan where the abbot and convent were freed of all amercements. However, the total lack of a mention of the 1199 charters of Llywelyn shows that these did not then exist. The idea that the monks would not have used them as they would have believed that Edward's

---

[654] Appendix 5, No.19.
[655] Appendix 5, No.20.
[656] Appendix 5, No.21.

charter, that was much less expansive than that of Llywelyn's and that Edward's, 'would hold greater weight with the king'[657], must be seen as wishful modern thinking that no abbey would seriously contemplate in the fourteenth century. Certainly there is no evidence of any of the Edwards showing animosity towards charters granted by the Welsh princes. In conclusion, it can be seen that the abbot lost his case for Edward I's charter did not allow these activities to take place, but it did give the monks exemption from amercement. Therefore, it is to be presumed that they had to make good their offenses, but they were not amerced for their crimes. Certainly there is no record of the overturning of the fines, but neither is there any evidence that they were ever paid.

That the monks had been defeated in their actions (even if they had not paid fines for them) is confirmed the next year, a little before 2 March 1315, when the abbot wrote in French to the king and his council asking to be granted the right to build a water mill to grind corn on their own land of Gwydir on the side of the Carrog Gwydir. This they had not done with the mill on the Gwyrfai, which had led them to fall foul of the royal administration of Gwynedd as documented above. Consequently, they were now asking for permission, permission they would not have needed if they had the 1199 charters of Prince Llywelyn. Again this shows that these documents are forgeries made after 1315. Similarly, they pointed out to the king on 4 January 1315 that they should not receive Dafydd Goch at the abbey as they were exempt from secular exactions as stated in the charter of Edward I[658]. Once again the charters of Llywelyn ab Iorwerth were not even mentioned.

The original petition of 1315 is hard to read, but it states that when Edward moved the abbey to Maenan they had three mills - presumably in Maenan - and presumably above 'the bridge' which was likely at Llanrwst. The text runs:

> To the king and his council the abbot and monks of Aberconwy in Wales wish to be granted the power to make on their demesne land which is called Gwydir next to the side of their Carrog Gwydir a water mill for the demesne grain itself which the abbot and monks milled because they have the right just as the abbey had from the foundation by King Edward the father of our lord king when he translated the said abbey [with?] three mills for their grain, milled and golden, in the ... bridge of which he promised, our great lord the king.[659]

On 2 March 1315 the king wrote to his new justiciar of North Wales, John Grey, asking him to investigate whether granting the abbot's petition would damage or prejudice the king or any other interested parties and return the findings in haste so that the petition could be answered in parliament[660]. Unfortunately Grey's reply has suffered over the ages, but enough remains of it to state that Grey seems to have been asked:

> if it might be to the damage or prejudice of the aforesaid lord king or others if the same lord king conceded to the abbot and monks of Aberconwy that they could raise a water mill in their own land to mill their own grain and others.

---

[657] Hays, RW, *The History of the Abbey of Aberconway, 1186-1537* [UWP, 1963], 91.

[658] *CCR 1313-18*, 319. The story is rehearsed in Hays, RW, *The History of the Abbey of Aberconway, 1186-1537* [UWP, 1963], 92.

[659] TNA, C.143/109/20. The document is transcribed in Appendix 6, Doc 1.

[660] Appendix 6, Doc 2. Grey is also supposed to have chased the abbot of Aberconwy amongst others for their failure to pay arrears of taxation for which he was collector during 1316, Hays, RW, *The History of the Abbey of Aberconway, 1186-1537* [UWP, 1963], 84-5. However, this and the other tax collecting roles of the abbot are not really relevant to the history of Maenan abbey and so haven't been pursued here.

Consequently, he replied that he had held an inquiry at the proposed mill site by the Carrog Gwydir - Carrog being Welsh for the rushing white water - on 16 April 1315 and that he could:

> certify that the water of Carrog Gwydir discharges into some pool called *Thlynka Loyt* which pool indeed is the lord king's who owns its course up to the water of the Conwy and it is the end and boundary between the land of the lord king on the one part and the land of the said abbot and monks on the other and it is the centre of the same water of the lord king and the other centre of the aforesaid abbot and monks through which if the same lord king to the same abbot and monks might concede the same centre of the water it is not otherwise to the damage nor prejudice of the same king nor in this because as far as that middle of the water it is his. Nor is it to the damage of others if the same lord king concedes to the aforesaid abbot and monks the contents in their petition.[*661]

It is to be presumed that the petition was therefore allowed, although no evidence for the mill being built has been found. On another level this petition shows that the monks plainly did not have either forged charter allegedly by Llywelyn ab Iorwerth available at this time as these allowed them to raise mills wherever they chose on their own lands. Considering Llywelyn's career by 1199, as well as this evidence, it is quite obvious that the prince's charters alleged to date to 1199 were therefore forged between this date in 1315 and the confirmation of 'Llywelyn's charters' in 1332.

It was therefore in the seventeen years after 1315 that an abbot of Aberconwy took the momentous decision to illegally expand his abbey's rights with a fake charter to augment the extensive rights granted to them by Edward I in 1284. Presumably this was done nearer to the charter being used in 1332 than in 1315. On 24 March 1332, the abbot paid £3 to have his charters confirmed, namely King Edward I's charter of 23 October 1284; Llywelyn ab Iorwerth's two charters of 7 January 1199; and the grant by Llywelyn ap Gruffydd of two of his chapels. This is the first time that the charters of Llywelyn ab Iorwerth appear in the historical record. As the abbot did not make use of these in the 1313 petition to parliament it seems quite clear that the abbot of Aberconwy had these two 'new' charters fabricated for this confirmation as he had failed to win his case in 1313. It therefore seems logical that the two charters of Llywelyn were forged about 130 years after their alleged writing. This certainly explains all the obvious problems with accepting either charter as genuine. It is to be assumed, that due to this royal confirmation of the abbey's charters, the abbot and the monks were no longer vexed by royal officials. It is interesting to note what happened to the prior of Beddgelert who tried to have a forged charter confirmed in 1348[*662]. That year the justices of the Black Prince held a *Quo Warranto* at Caernarfon, which was attended by the abbots of Aberconwy and Cymer as well as the prior of Beddgelert. The proceedings went well for the two abbots, but not for the prior, whose forged charter was detected. It is notable that the two abbots' forgeries were accepted, apparently as they had been confirmed by previous kings. The prior fell by the wayside as his charter was recorded as having been destroyed by fire by no less an authority as King Edward I. It is therefore to be presumed that all three charters otherwise seemed authentic to the justices. Obviously there was a master forger at work in Gwynedd at the time.

[*661] Appendix 6, Doc 3.
[*662] *Registrum vulgariter nuncupatum, 'The Record of Caernarvon'*, ed. Ellis, H. [London, 1838], 166-7.

Consequently, the abbot of Cymer appears to have got away with his forged charter from Llywelyn ab Iorwerth at the same time as the abbot of Maenan made his successful bid to pass off his two forgeries ascribed to the same Llywelyn. The Cymer charter is undoubtedly the best produced of the three and despite its 'many unusual and obsolescent forms'[663] both abbots got away with the scam which still fools historians to this day. Despite the success of the fraud, the tone of the record suggests that the justices believed the charters were not above board and they noted that it was probable that the abbey had made improper uses of its liberties and this was remitted for further consideration, although nothing seems to have come of this[664]. Indeed, it is possible that there was some collusion at the hearing, for although the abbot claimed that the charter of Edward I had confirmed the grant of privileges of Llywelyn ab Iorwerth, no one in court pointed out that this was clearly not true from a simple reading of Edward's charter.

The years before the Quo Warranto proceedings were very taxing for Maenan as can be seen in the few records that survive. In 1336-37 the abbot placed Henry Eccleshall in his place to collect the clerical tenth taxation. The next year he was allowed to pay his tax off in installments[665]. Presumably this was done, possibly by the abbot borrowing the money, for on 4 February 1344, it was recorded that Abbot Clement of Aberconwy and Parson Henry Eccleshall of Caernarfon church owed £200 to the merchants of Florence which was to be levied on their lands and chattels and ecclesiastical goods in Shropshire[666]. This of course is most odd as Aberconwy had no lands in Shropshire. To add to the burden of the abbey, on 12 March 1345, it was recorded that Dean Bleddyn ab Einion of St Asaph, Abbot Cynfrig of Aberconwy and 24 named others had been attainted on a charge of conspiracy. Two others were attainted of diverse felonies and one man, Gruffydd ap Cynfrig ap Bleddyn, was convicted of conspiracy and assault on the castle and town of Rhuddlan, while one further man was convicted of trespass. It was also recorded that a further 31 named Welshmen, including two deans, were attained of conspiracy and were still at large, while another 14 were attainted of felony and still at large. This was probably to do with instability in the lordship of Denbigh after the death of its lord, William Montacute in January 1344 and the murder of Henry Shaldeford on 14 February[667]. The final outcome of this is unknown, but the abbot seems to have suffered no great damage by this. Indeed he was again nominated to raise a tax for the Crown and in 1347 Abbot Cynfrig was ordered to pay £93 to the Black Prince as quickly as feasible[668]. This was presumably after the 18 May visit of John Burnham Junior, the clerk of the prince of Wales. He had:

> been to the monastery of the abbot of Aberconway on the same business [arrears of the clerical tenth taxation] and the abbot was and is still in South Wales, and according to what the prior and convent of the said monastery told Brunham, the abbot had done nothing about levying the tenth of which he was deputed to be collector by the bishop of St Asaph; for he refused the commission... on the ground that he has long been a collector, to the great damage of his monastery wherefore he sued to be discharged, but

---

[663] Williams-Jones, K, 'Llywelyn's charter to Cymer Abbey in 1209', *Journal of the Merioneth Historical and Record Society*, III [1957-1960], 45-78.

[664] *Registrum vulgariter nuncupatum, 'The Record of Caernarvon'*, ed. Ellis, H. [London, 1838], 144-50.

[665] Fryde, N., *List of Welsh Entries in the Memoranda Rolls* [1974], 101, No.893, 103, No.910.

[666] *CCR 1333-37*, 338.

[667] CACW, 227-30ff.

[668] *The Register of Edward the Black Prince...*, ed. Dawes, MCB., [4 vols, 1930-33] I, 121.

he has now accepted a new commission and Brunham will sue as far as he can for the said money as he has been charged...[669]

Presumably the sum was paid, for nothing further seems to have been recorded of it. Cynfrig remained abbot until at least 1356[670].

A change to the abbey's landholdings occurred on 1 October 1350 when the abbot swopped the grange of Ffriwlwyd, 25 miles distant from Maenan, but directly across the main peaks of Snowdonia, with Edward III in exchange for the advowson of the church of Eglwysrhos[671]. This lay due north of the abbey's grange in Creuddyn known as *Cumrewet/Cumrewez* and to the south of the site of Degannwy castle, being set between the river estuary opposite Conway and Bodysgallen. The grange of Ffriwlwyd came to the king with a mill, a disused weir and another weir joining to the sea. It gave the king £4 10s in rents for the manor and vill[672]. The fact that the Aberconwy Register includes Eglwysrhos, but not Ffriwlwyd indicates that this could not have been written before October 1350 at the earliest.

The possessions of Maenan continued to be augmented as on 16 February 1355, the Black Prince ordered the abbot of Aberconwy to appropriate Aber church[673]. Yet next year, on 3 December 1356, the Black Prince ordered John Delves, lieutenant to the justice of North Wales, to dispossess the abbot of Aberconwy of lands he had acquired within the franchise of the town of Conway 'which thing is contrary to common law'. Consequently he was to:

> seize these lands into the prince's hand without delay and deliver them to the abbot to hold until Michaelmas (1357) next on his giving security to answer then for the issues thereof.

In the meantime the value of the lands were to be assessed and they were to be rented out for the prince's profit[674].

After the death of the Black Prince and his father Edward III, Abbot John[675] obviously found it wise to have the government of King Richard II (1377-99) confirm the privileges of his house. Consequently on 12 July 1379, an inspeximus and confirmation was issued in favour of the abbot and convent of *Aberconeweye* of a charter dated Westminster 24 March 1332[676], inspecting and confirming a charter dated Caernarfon 23 October 1284 and two of Llywelyn ab Iorwerth, formerly prince of North Wales, dated Aberconwy 7 January 1199[677]. Nearly fifty years later on 28 October 1426, the inspection and confirmation was carried out again, this time of letters patent made by Henry V when he was prince of Wales, to the abbot and convent of *Aberconewey*, which were dated at Westminster on 20 February 1401. This in turn inspected and confirmed letters patent dated 12 July 1379, inspecting and confirming a charter dated 24 March 1332 which inspected and confirmed with additions, the four standard

---

[669] CACW, 237-8.
[670] Hays, RW, *The History of the Abbey of Aberconway, 1186-1537* [UWP, 1963], 95, quoting a now lost source.
[671] This is now Llanrhos in Creuddyn, SH.794804.
[672] The various comments are found in the ministers accounts of 25 January 1350 to 24 January 1352 in TNA, Sc.6/1171/7, ms. 8, 11, 11b: Gresham, C.A., 'The Aberconwy Charter', *Archaeologia Cambrensis* XCIV [1939], 159.
[673] *The Register of Edward the Black Prince...*, ed. Dawes, MCB., [4 vols, 1930-33] III, 490.
[674] *The Register of Edward the Black Prince...*, ed. Dawes, MCB., [4 vols, 1930-33] III, 496.
[675] He was certainly abbot before the year was out, Hays, RW, *The History of the Abbey of Aberconway, 1186-1537* [UWP, 1963], 128, quoting TNA, MS. Clerical Subsidies 1/4.
[676] *Calendar of Charter Rolls 1226-1516* [6 vols., 1903-27] *1327-41*, 267-9, No.36, as noted above.
[677] *Registrum vulgariter nuncupatum, 'The Record of Caernarvon'*, ed. Ellis, H. [London, 1838], 145-8. This 1332 confirmation had also been confirmed by the Black Prince on his return from France on 16 October 1347.

charters put forward by the monks for previous inspections[678]. Quite obviously, once the establishment had been fooled in 1332 it was merely a bureaucratic process to have the right's of the abbey confirmed and no serious checking was done to the Llywelyn charters. Consequently, King Edward's true, but less generous charter was quietly allowed to be ignored. In this manner did Llywelyn ab Iorwerth finally usurp the true founders of the house, Rhodri ab Owain and King Edward I.

On 3 June 1371, the abbot of Aberconwy was one of those chosen of St Asaph diocese to collect a royal tax for Edward III[679]. At this time there would seem to have been only six monks left in the abbey[680]. In the next reign, during 1390, a dispute blew up between the abbot of Maenan and the bishop of Bangor[681]. Initially the bishop appointed the abbot to collect and levy the tenth ordered to be raised in the diocese of Bangor. On hearing this the abbot had gone to Westminster and effectively lied that he held no lands of importance in the county and was in any case from an abbey from the diocese of St Asaph as had been proved many times in chancery. As a result the king had ordered the bishop to find another collector on 24 May 1390. Consequently, the bishop replied on 22 June that the abbot was lying and that:

> the said abbot has obtained the parish churches of Conwy, Dwygyfylchi (*Deygevythi*) and St Patrick of Cemaes (*Llanpadric*) within Bangor diocese, for his own use, and for these has given canonical obedience to the bishop as he is bound and the said abbot and his monks are known to have the whole substance of their sustenance in the diocese of Bangor, through the granges of Gelliniog (*Peleniok*), Penmynydd (*Penmynyt*), Ghornwy Llys (*Cornwy Lles*) and diverse other granges and other lands and many rents there. On account of these churches, granges, woods, lands and his other temporalities he is considered more suitable to collect these tenths for the king than other ecclesiastics, whether regular or secular. Nor ought he to be excluded from the collection of these tenths, although his abbey was translated a stone's throw outside the diocese of Bangor by King Edward, when he conquered Wales, from the town of Conwy to a place called Maenan, in the county of Caernarfon, for the said abbot and his predecessors have been customarily called abbots of Conwy and not otherwise, and that he should be so named was ordained both by... and also the possessions and estates with the churches of the aforesaid abbey within....

This quite clearly puts the case that Maenan was still in Gwynedd and that the abbot's lands in Mon at least were still largely as they were fifty years before, though it is interesting that the bishop didn't also mention the abbot's Arfon granges of Rhedynog Felen, Arddau, Nanhwynain, Cwm and Nant Call.

---

[678] *CPR 1422-29*, 408.
[679] CACW, 187-8. The abbot undertook a similar operation for the bishop of St Asaph in 1478-9, *Archaeologia Cambrensis* [1882], 156-8.
[680] Hays, RW, *The History of the Abbey of Aberconway, 1186-1537* [UWP, 1963], 120, quoting TNA, MS. Clerical Subsidies 1/4.
[681] CAPW, 254-6.

Maenan Abbey in the Fifteenth Century

The abbot of Aberconwy seems to have supported both sides in the Welsh wars of the early fifteenth century. On 9 October 1400 the abbot of *Conewe* in North Wales and his fellow monks and their men and possessions obtained royal protection from Henry IV at Caernarfon 'during their good behaviour'[682]. Such good behaviour was obviously still ongoing on 26 February 1404, when the lieutenant of Conway castle wrote to the constable of Chester that the Abbot of Maenan had recently sent word to him that six fully laden French ships had just been spotted off the Llyn peninsula[683]. Soon after this Abbot Hywel ap Gwilym was held in custody as 'a rebel', although he received a royal pardon in 1409[684]. From this it appears likely that in 1404 he began to think that Owain Glyndwr's alliance with the French might prove successful in expelling Henry IV's influence from Wales. Excavation of Maenan abbey last century discovered a charcoal layer that was interpreted as the burning of the abbey, though whether this occurred during the war and by which side is unknown[685]. Certainly Maenan abbey would appear to have been pillaged during the wars of Owain Glyndwr (1400-13) as, some forty years later on 17 October 1448, a pardon was granted:

> to the abbot and convent of the house of St Mary, Conway (*Conwey*), North Wales... for the sum of £10 on their petition showing that the house was burned in the time of the war of Wales and that all the books, vestments, chalices and other of their ornaments had been spoiled and carried away and that they have since repaired a great part of their houses on account whereof and of their charges in the collection of tenths they are indebted to the king and the abbot is blind and aged eighty years and is indebted to the king for the said sum of £10 for the said tenths[686].

This pardon obviously did not end the problems of the house for interest or fines may have been attached to the above debt. Consequently on 6 November 1449, the king again pardoned the abbot of Maenan, who had been:

> appointed on 22 June 1446 as collector of a tenth granted to the king in the deaneries of Rhos (*Roos*), Rhufoniog (*Rewyneok*), Dinmael (*Dynmaill*), Penllyn and Edeirnion (*Ediernyon*) in the diocese of St Asaph, whereby he is accountable and in arrears of £10, of all accounts of the said tenth, contempts of accounts and issues thereof; in consideration of the poverty of the abbey and the costs in building the same.[687]

The note of the destruction of the abbey's books in the first entry once more indicates that the Aberconwy Register dates to after the Glyndwr revolt.

---

[682] *CPR 1399-1401*, 555.

[683] *Original Letters Illustrative of English History...*, ed. Ellis, H., [3 vols, 1825] I, 30.

[684] Hywel had been a monk of Maenan before 1378, Williams, DH., 'Fasti Cistercienses Cambrenses', *Bulletin of the Board of Celtic Studies* XXIV part 1. The abbot was recorded as a rebel as early as 12 July 1406, 'Recognizance Rolls of Chester, now part of the Records of the Palatinate of Chester', *Annual Reports of the Deputy Keeper of the Public Records* [1874] XXXVI, Appendix II, 236. Hywel came to the royal peace on 3 November 1409, *CPR 1408-13*, 141.

[685] Butler, LAS, 'The Cistercian Abbey at Maenan: Excavations in 1968', *Archaeologia Cambrensis* CXXIX [1980], 14.

[686] *CPR 1446-52*, 227.

[687] *CPR 1446-52*, 296.

A little before this, a modern text has stated that Abbot John ap Rhys of Conway attacked and occupied Strata Florida abbey in 1442/3[*688]. This appears to be the result of a misreading of Cymer for Conway as other documents show quite clearly that the man involved was John ap Rhys, the former abbot of Cymer[*689]. About this time, Richard Kirkby was a monk at Maenan, before he became abbot of Cymer and then attempted to make himself abbot of Basingwerk in 1465 and he remained such until at least 1476 despite the general council's admonishments[*690].

In the last quarter of the fifteenth century the house of Maenan seems to have degenerated from the standards required, for in 1480 the abbots of Louth Park (Lincolnshire), Woburn (Bedfordshire) and Hailes (Gloucestershire) were ordered by the General Chapter of the Cistercian Order to undertake a visitation of the Cistercian houses in Wales with a view to reforming them, due to the fact they had 'digressed from the path of holy religion as well in habit and tonsure as in other usages'[*691]. Two years later in 1482, the General Chapter sent the abbots of Hailes and Sawley in Craven (Yorkshire) to investigate reports of new abuses at Aberconwy, namely the giving out of pensions since the death of Abbot Reginald around 1480[*692]. In the meantime, the abbey had been under the control of Prior Gruffydd Goch as an interim measure. He had granted one pension to a son of Abbot Reginald called David and had also installed David's mother in an abbey building. The investigators were to confirm what was done was legal and find other accommodation for the lady as well as confirm the pensions if they were legal and make David 'learn the observance of holy religion in a cloister of the order'[*693]. The same year a monk of Hailes, David Winchcombe, was 'elected' abbot of Maenan[*694]. He later appeared at Shrewsbury in that position, but soon afterwards was challenged. The dispute between him and David Lloyd about who should be abbot was continuing during the first year of King Richard III, viz. between 26 June 1483 and 25 June 1484[*695]. By 20 November 1489 David Lloyd was recognised as abbot of Maenan[*696]. Possibly, he had succeeded to this position after the coronation of Henry VII as he was said to be influential at court. It therefore seems, when all the evidence is considered, that it is most likely that it was during Abbot David Winchcombe's tenure that the Register of Aberconwy and its chronicle was drawn up and inserted within a book containing otherwise just Hailes abbey material. Consequently, it seems best to assign the production of that work to the years 1482 to 1485/9.

In 1490 Abbot David Lloyd of Maenan met an unfortunate end. He had been at the royal court where he had much influence and, on returning to Aberconwy, he was thrown from his horse, breaking his neck[*697]. As a consequence Prior Gruffydd again took up the reins in an interim capacity, though by 1494 he was abbot of Cymer[*698]. The next year, David

[*688] Williams, D.H., *The Welsh Cistercians* [Bodmin, 2001], 57 quoting CAPW, 235; and Hays, RW, *The History of the Abbey of Aberconway, 1186-1537* [UWP, 1963], 132-3, who dates these events to 1427-8, apparently following Williams, SW., *The Cistercian Abbey of Strata Florida...* [1889], xxxix-xli.
[*689] *CPR 1441-46*, 151-2; CAPW, 503.
[*690] Williams, D.H., *The Welsh Cistercians* [Bodmin, 2001], 58.
[*691] Williams, The Welsh Cistercians [1984] I, 81; *Letters From English Abbots to Citeaux*, ed.Talbot, CH [Camden Soc, 1967], 188, 208.
[*692] Williams, The Welsh Cistercians [1984] I, 86; *Letters From English Abbots to Citeaux*, ed.Talbot, CH [Camden Soc, 1967], 81-3.
[*693] Statuta V, 438-9.
[*694] Statuta V, 432.
[*695] A copy of a warrant sent to the farmers of Maenan abbey to pay their rents to Prior Gruffydd Gogh during the controversy between David Winchcombe and David Lloyd over who should be abbot is contained in BL. Harliean Ms.433, f.175, printed in *Archaeologia Cambrensis* [1882], 71.
[*696] Hays, RW, *The History of the Abbey of Aberconway, 1186-1537* [UWP, 1963], 136.
[*697] *Letters From English Abbots to Citeaux*, ed.Talbot, CH [Camden Soc, 1967], 127-30.
[*698] University of North Wales, Penrhyn Castle Deed, 257; TNA, LR 1/213, fo.270d.

Winchcombe had become abbot of Cymer[*699]. It seems quite likely that David was much used in the 1480s and 1490s as Abbot Huby of Fountain abbey's troubleshooter in Wales. In 1496, possibly at Huby's prompting, the general chapter appointed the abbots of Aberconwy and Valle Crucis its commissaries in Wales[*700]. Some twenty years later it was reported that Abbot David Floyd of Maenan had been translated first to Cymer and then Strata Marcella all within the period of two years[*701]. Quite obviously religious life was continuing at Maenan abbey during the reign of Henry VII (1485-1507).

It was probably some time around this that the Welsh poet Tudur Aled (bef.1470-1525) wrote his poem to the unnamed abbot of Aberconwy on behalf of Lewis ap Madog. In this quite long poem he says something of the state and environs of the abbey. It is therefore worth repeating some of these lines.

> With one who safeguards Gwynedd
> I would feast on Conwy's bank,
> Abbot over eight districts,
> Aberconwy field of vines...
> His cook works hard at turning.
>
> Conwy in a warm valley,
> White stream where I'd have fresh wine,
> Wine-rich house, shrine of honey,
> Passage and pantry below:
> In choosing his wines at once
> He was best of all nations...
> White and red the robes they wear.
> If his breast and cope were white,
> So dressed he'd pass for bishop...
> They'd have a thousand small rents,
> He wished the rent of Maenan.
> For him on Meirionydd's face
> A band like woodland blossoms,
> soldiers from Maelor to Rhos,
> Tegeingl, his close relations.[*702]

All in all this gives an attractive view of the abbey as a place to live, but not necessarily of a place of learning and religion.

In 1502 the abbot of Aberconwy was granted a site for the building of a fulling mill[*703]. This suggests that not only was the abbey still a going concern, but the abbot was making arrangements to increase their financial security, rather than doing something for the public good. In around 1533 the bishop of Bangor and Abbot Geoffrey of Maenan were 'indited for

[*699] *Letters From English Abbots to Citeaux*, ed.Talbot, CH [Camden Soc, 1967], 176.
[*700] Statuta VI, 151-2.
[*701] *Letters From English Abbots to Citeaux*, ed.Talbot, CH [Camden Soc, 1967], 251-2.
[*702] Jones, G., *Oxford Book of Welsh Verse in English* [1977], 67-9.
[*703] NLW, Cernioge MS, 48.

extortion' by the vicar of Llanfair[*704]. Soon after this Geoffrey must have died, or been removed, for the final abbot of the house under Henry VIII was Richard ap Rhys.

At the time of the dissolution of the abbeys in 1534, Aberconwy had an income of £162 15s from a gross revenue of £179 10s 10d[*705]. Even at this late date, in mid February 1534, the abbot with his brother abbots of Cwmhir and Cymer met at Valle Crucis in an attempt to reform that house[*706]. It was also this year that Hiraethog grange was mortgaged for £240[*707]. This was roughly ten times its annual value. The next year, 1535, it was noted that Aberconwy had the appropriations of the churches of Eglwysbach, Eglwysrhos, Conwy, Dwygyfylchi and Llanbadrig[*708]. Quite obviously the church of Aber, which the abbot had been granted by the Black Prince in 1355, had fallen away from their control after that time. In 1536 a further survey of Maenan found that the abbey lands were worth a total of £289 8s 5d as is tabled in Appendix 8[*709]. The same year on 3 June, Abbot Richard Price wrote to Thomas Cromwell begging him to suffer his abbey to continue for financial considerations as he had borrowed some £200 and had debts of nigh on the same[*710]. On 24 January 1537 Price tried again, also sending £40 in recompense of Cromwell's pains[*711]. Despite this, the abbey was closed just two months later[*712], leaving only Strata Florida, Whitland and Neath as Welsh abbeys surviving until 1539. Part of Maenan's suppression included the leasing of Quirt grange in Gelliniog in Mon to William Stumpe, the Crown Receiver[*713].

The site of Maenan abbey was granted in 1563 to Elizaeus Wynne by Queen Elizabeth. As early as 1 July 1539 the abbey was already being demolished according to the following record. Of the ruins the stone was taken to repair the king's hall, the shire or justice court, the Exchequer (Eagle Tower), treasury and the quay of the castle as well as the town walls of Caernarfon itself[*714].

> The coosts and chargs that were done in taking downe of the churche rouffe of the alte abbeye of Conweye and the kariage of stones and tymbre from the said abbeye to Caern'
>
> Imprimis payde to Thomas Hervey and Robert ap Willm carpenters by the space of vi days after the rate of vid the day unto euy of them, vi s.
>
> It'm payde to the same carpynters for theire labor in taking downe the said rouffe iiiid a pese, viii d...
>
> It'm paid to Richarde Maynwaring for the fraighte of his pykarde loden with stones from the abbey of Conewye to Caern'.. xi s iii d.
>
> It'm paid for the fraighte of an other pykarde laden with stones of iii tonne from the said abbey to Caern' v s iii d...
>
> It'm paide for the taking downe of xxxv sparres in the abbey and for ale to the tenaunts that caryed stones to the water syde viii d.

[*704] TNA, STAC 2/2, ff.76-8 quoted in Williams, D.H., *The Welsh Cistercians* [Bodmin, 2001], 46.

[*705] *Monasticon Anglicanum*, ed. W. Dugdale, Revised edition by J. Caley, H. Ellis, and B. Bandinel [6 vols., 1817-30], Conway, 675.

[*706] Williams, D.H., *The Welsh Cistercians* [Bodmin, 2001], 67.

[*707] Hays, RW, *The History of the Abbey of Aberconway, 1186-1537* [UWP, 1963], 176.

[*708] Williams, D.H., *The Welsh Cistercians* [Norwich, 1983, 2 vols] II, 335.

[*709] A translation of the inspeximus of 1332 and a full translation of the Ministers Accompts of 1535-37 of Maenan were made during the period 1688-1710, BL. Additional MS.15,632 and 15,633.

[*710] *Letters and Papers, Foreign and Domestic of the Reign of Henry VIII*, X, 434.

[*711] *Letters and Papers, Foreign and Domestic of the Reign of Henry VIII*, XII i, 108.

[*712] *Letters and Papers, Foreign and Domestic of the Reign of Henry VIII*, XIII i, 577.

[*713] *Letters and Papers, Foreign and Domestic of the Reign of Henry VIII*, XIII i, 584.

[*714] Owen, E., 'The Fate of the Structures of Conway Abbey and Bangor and Beaumaris Friaries', *Trans. of the Honourable Society of Cymmrodorion* XXVII [1917], 70-114.

Also several loose loads of timber were taken from the grange of Rhedynog Felen to Caernarfon for the works as well as much wood cut from around Maenan. What doesn't seem to have happened though, is a full scale demolition of the stonework of the abbey. Presumably the spars were part of the roof and the implication is that much stonework was left standing. Certainly it did not take much longer for the rest of the structure to disappear. Further in 1773-6, Thomas Pennant recorded that much of the rebuilding at Gwydir castle had been 'built out of abbey materials'. This no doubt marked the end of the standing abbey structure.

The Physical Remains of the Abbey Church
Aberconwy appears to have been a typical abbey church with a nave, chancel, aisles and transepts - see the Introduction. As ever it is next to impossible to accurately date masonry remains and so all the conclusions put forward here have to be tentative, but they appear to show a logical progression of the building from abbey to parish church (Fig.46).

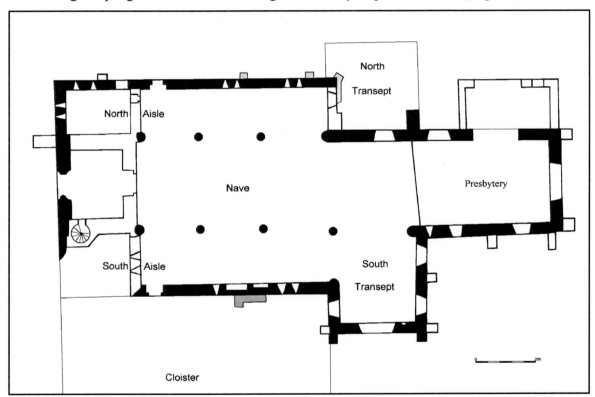

Figure 46, The now covered foundations, in lighter shading, on either side of the aisles. Those to the north would appear to be buttresses to the aisle, while that to the south appears to be a corner of a lost building of uncertain purpose.

Despite popular opinion, as expressed in most works on this subject, there is no evidence that the cloisters and conventual buildings of Aberconwy lay to the north of the abbey church, even though the 'remains of walls and a sepulchral slab' had been found in the Castle Inn grounds in 1832[*715]. Other Victorian finds have included an ancient tombstone with a

---

[*715] *Royal Commission on Ancient Monuments in England and Wales, for Caernarvonshire* [3 vols, 1960], 39b, quoting Williams, R., *The History and Antiquities of the Town of Aberconwy...* [Denbigh, 1835], 75.

crois fleuris decoration, another slab with a plain cross cut into it from the Castle Hotel yard and a stone font from a site a little east of the same hotel[716]. Some years before this 'a long vaulted room of good masonry, worked with clay, but plastered with lime; and a Saxon door' were still standing[717]. As all the other cloisters and conventual buildings at Cistercian sites in Wales lay south of the church it is to be presumed that the same was true at Aberconwy. The only exception to this rule is Tintern at the opposite end of Wales and with a very different provenance to Aberconwy. Without any certain evidence it is probably best to assume that Aberconwy followed the general Cistercian plan and that the cloisters and associated buildings lay to the south.

The West End of the Abbey Church

The apparent remains of the original twelfth century abbey now consist of an east and west end as was perceptively recognised by Harold Hughes in the last decade of the nineteenth century[718]. Between these it would appear that the first abbey church lay. It is therefore fitting to start with an examination of these walls and then work backwards into the abbey church remains.

The west end of St Mary's consists of a rubble wall some fifty feet long and some five feet thick in its central, nave portion (Fig.47). It consists of a 'local' sandstone formed from long dark red sandstone slabs, most being around 18 inches long. Sandstone outcrops are found just west of Conwy town and on the east side of the river in the Creuddyn. Here and there, much lighter red sandstone sneker stones are found in the wall. Judging from the exterior masonry style, the original wall seems to rise some 25 feet high or just above what may be the original three west lights of the abbey nave (Fig.48). These lancet lights are much smaller than those found at the east end of Cymer abbey and have a simpler, chamfered decoration. At Cymer the three much bigger and lower set lancet windows are positioned in the east wall in the presbytery and had a further two lights set above them (Fig.49). These were still intact in the eighteenth century (Fig.50). It therefore seems strange that the physically larger and more ornate Aberconwy abbey had a lesser setup. However, the west end at Cymer has been destroyed by the addition of a later external tower and its original layout is now hard to assess and may have once been similar to that at Aberconwy. Strata Florida (1201, Fig.51) had a central round-headed west doorway, somewhat similar to the one found at Llanidloes church which in turn seems to have been made from parts of Cwmhir abbey (1176, Fig.52). The west door at Aberconwy is nothing like these (Fig.53). Instead it has been credibly asserted that the doorway comes from the old abbey chapter house (Fig.54), as originally it was not intended to hold a door and has obviously been reset in its present position[719]. The moulding on the pillar tops is stiff leafed and therefore could date to any period from 1150 to 1250 (Fig.55). The doorway is quite dissimilar in style from the nave arches of the nave arcades or the transept, so it was not made of the demolished west end of the arcades or the north transept. Supporting the surmise that the doorway was reset in the late thirteenth century are the two heavily worn headstops on either side of the doorway. These have a late thirteenth or early fourteenth century look about them. Above the doorway itself,

---

[716] Elias, T., 'The history and associations of the abbeys and convents of the Vale of Conwy and district', *Journal of the British Archaeological Association*, ns IV [1898], 38. All these finds really tell us is that much digging has taken place in the vicinity of the hotel.
[717] Pennant, T., *Tours in Wales* [3 vols, London, 1810] III, 120.
[718] Hughes, H, 'The Architectural History of St Mary's Church, Conway', *Archaeologia Cambrensis* [1895], 161-79
[719] Hughes, Arch Camb [1895]Hughes, H, 'The Architectural History of St Mary's Church, Conway', *Archaeologia Cambrensis* [1895], 166-7.

inserted into the sloping plinth, is a decorative stone with 'Celtic' style foliage (Fig.53). Possibly this too was carved in the twelfth century before being reset here, probably when the new west doorway was made after the abbey had been transferred to Maenan. As a west door into the nave is common in Cistercian monasteries this thirteenth century doorway probably replaces an earlier door which may have been similar to the ones at Strata Florida and Abbey Cwmhir. Both these were constructed around the same time as Aberconwy was built. A tentative reconstruction has been made of the original look of the west end of Aberconwy (Fig.56).

It seems likely that the original Aberconwy roof was gabled immediately above the lancets. Above this is what appears to be a later heightening of the wall which consists of a less ordered rubble build with more and larger, lighter red sandstone blocks. This rises up to a roll moulded string course, whose southern quarter has been destroyed by the inserted stair well (Fig.47&48). Above this is the later work of the tower, whose rubble brickwork is quite dissimilar to the phase 2 build below. It is uncertain whether this second phase work was part of the abbey or the later parish church after 1284. As the formation of the west tower may have come soon after the moving of the abbey to Maenan, it seems likely that this raising of the wall belongs to the second phase of the abbey.

Immediately under the abbey's potentially first phase west windows is a sloping sandstone plinth that runs the entire length of the west face of the wall. Its last few feet to the north at the corner of the north aisle have obviously been replaced in modern times. The same is true of the quoining along the north-west corner of the north aisle. At the base of the wall three or four apparently original sandstone quoins remain, but above this the corner is made up simply of larger slabs of rock (Fig.47). At the other end of this original wall the southern aisle has been totally demolished, but the shadow of the wall is clearly visible in the south stair turret of the later tower (Fig.57). This shows that the west wall of the south aisle was about four feet thick, against the five feet of the nave west wall. The same appears to be true of the north aisle where the wall thins at the line of the north wall of the west tower. This was most likely done as the aisles were always intended to be low structures with a clerestorey in the nave above, as remains today. The nave was obviously taller than the aisles and as such needed thicker and therefore stronger walls to support the extra weight. In the last century the foundations of the west wall of the south aisle were uncovered for some six feet, although the junction with the old south wall was not reached[*720]. The roof line of the original south aisle is still visible as a crease on the west tower wall and lines up perfectly with the new roof of the surviving portion of the south aisle. This shows that the current aisle roofs occupy the position of their predecessors. It also shows that the now external flight of stairs up to the entrance to the stair turret was originally internal in the post 1284 design. It is unknown when this portion of the south aisle collapsed or was simply taken down.

[*720] *Archaeologia Cambrensis* [1937], 371.

Width of tower East of turret-staircase

Cement Weathering late 19th century!!

Two Lancets above are modern.

Conway Church . West End .

Harold H. Hughes 1894

feet 10 . . . . 5 . . . . . . 0 . . . . . 10 . . . . . 20 feet

Figure 47, Howard Hughes' 1894 drawing of the west end of the abbey. The original wall seems to end above the three lancets on a line with the current aisle roof. This is marked by the commencement of the white plaster on the sketch. Note how the stonework is looser above this point.

Figure 48, The west wall of the abbey church. The possible first roof line was just above the central lancet window. The looser masonry of the second phase is above this and later work still can be clearly seen the left and right of both, it being clearly defined by a prominent fissure on both sides.

Figure 49, The east end of Cymer abbey about 1900. Notice the three lancet windows with the remains of two offset lights set above them. Notice too the single sloping plinth and low aisles which are similar to those at Aberconwy.

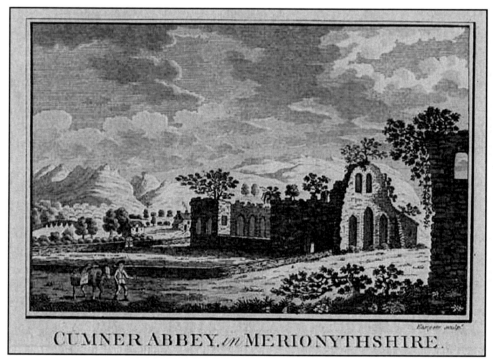

CUMNER ABBEY, *in* MERIONYTHSHIRE.

Figure 50, Cymer abbey at the end of the eighteenth century showing the surviving two offset windows above the triple lancets in the east wall. Note also the north aisle beyond the buttress with traces of a window in it which are now not to be seen.

Figure 51, The great west doorway at Strata Florida with one surviving round headed light to the right. Both should date to the pre 1201 building phase.

Figure 52, The door at Llanidloes, apparently built from the remains of the west door of Cwmhir. The pillars and jambs would appear to be twelfth century, but the arch is more likely sixteenth.

Figure 53, The inserted west door at Aberconwy with the three lancets above. Notice also the finely carved stiff leafed foliage above the door keystone and the two carved headstops at either end of the label. The foliage has a late twelfth century look, while the heavily worn heads look more late thirteenth century or even early fourteenth.

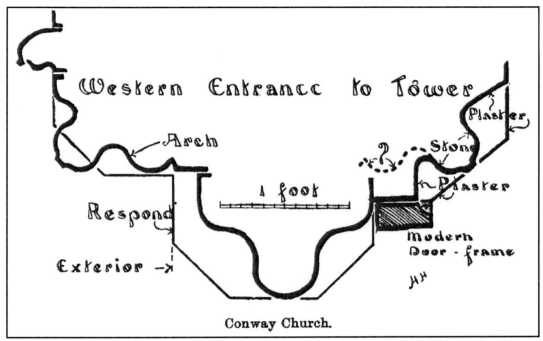

Figure 54, A cross section of the northern door jamb of the west door of Conwy church by Howard Hughes. This shows its composite construction and later fitting to hold a door frame.

Conway Church: carved Capital of W. Entrance to Tower.

Figure 55, A close up drawing of the northern side of the west entrance of Conwy church as drawn by Harold Hughes at the end of the nineteenth century before the headstop was virtually weathered away.

Figure 56, A tentative reconstruction of how the west end of Aberconwy abbey may have looked when a Cistercian monastery. The doorway is superimposed from that at Strata Florida abbey while the background church with the side aisles is taken from Grosmont, Gwent. The three lancets are from Aberconwy.

Figure 57, The old west wall of the abbey (a) can be seen fossilised within the later west tower stair turret. The roof crease line (b) above the top of this wall runs over the stair turret doorway to join up with the rebuilt wall of the south aisle. This clearly shows that the south aisle originally covered the south-western corner of the nave. Notice how the quoins (c) above the aisle roof line are made of fine dark red sandstone blocks. This again delimits the interior and exterior of the church and shows that the south aisle was still standing when the west tower was constructed post 1283.

The East End of the Church or Abbey Presbytery

At the east end of the church it was long ago concluded that the base of this wall was a part of the original abbey. This wall consists of thin eighteen inch slabs with the odd snecker stone and is generally similar to the early west wall. It appears also to be only some four feet thick, like the low western aisle walls. Unlike the west end there is an external projecting rolled string course of a grey, gritty sandstone, set some three feet above current ground level (Fig.58). This is totally lacking at the west end and would not have worked well with a west door. This could well explain its non appearance in the west face of the abbey. Conversely, the east end at Cymer has a sloping plinth solely on this side of the abbey (Fig.49). Presumably this is mirroring the string course at Aberconwy. The east end design at Valle Crucis is quite different, having three lancet windows set between integral ashlar pilaster buttresses in an ashlar facing (Fig.59). Obviously this is far more elegant and ostentatious than Aberconwy.

At the east end of the Aberconwy presbytery, a foot above the string course, is a fine, large, probably late fifteenth century window. This is an obvious replacement of an earlier, larger window whose shadow can still be clearly seen (Fig.58). This window shadow[*721] lies in the apparent phase 2 work which begins where the tracery of the fifteenth century window starts, as is clearly shown by the change in masonry style. It is possible that the two eastward projecting buttresses from the presbytery wall are also from an early phase - although their butt joint with the main masonry would suggest that they post date it at least slightly. The similarity in style can be seen at the base of the buttresses which appear to be of the same masonry as the base of the east wall. Both buttresses have fine sloping plinths and quoins of sandstone and grey gritstone. Quite possibly they have been much rebuilt.

The centre part of the wall around the east window has obviously been much rebuilt to house the new light. Possibly, most of the wall above the string course is rebuilt. The east end of the early nave at Cymer had three tall lancet windows with simple decoration (Fig.60), with the remains of two more above. This seems to be the original design and it is possible that the Cymer setup was copied from Aberconwy, where it may be that the original three windows were moved from the east wall to the west when the new west doorway was added post 1284. It is certainly possible that the east and west ends at Aberconwy have been heavily altered with only the lowest few feet remaining as truly original work.

A close inspection of the south wall of the presbytery clearly shows the old style of masonry running along the base of the wall to the height of the two south window bases and rising up to some five feet high on either side of the central buttress (Fig.61). This differentiation was missed by Hughes in his 1894 sketch of the wall (Fig.62). The phase above the early south wall is obviously different from the phase 2 work in the west end of the abbey, as this contains many large rectangular blocks of limestone, probably from Creuddyn. These are distinctly absent in the second phase of the western end. It should also be noted that Creuddyn was removed from the abbey's lands as part of the move to Maenan in 1284. Therefore this phase quite likely predates the formation of the parish church here in 1284. Alternatively, these blocks may have come from Degannwy castle, whose remains were used as a quarry for the town walls of Conwy in the mid 1280s. The buttresses of the south and east walls also contain many well cut limestone and red sandstone blocks and so may likewise date to this later phase.

[*721] It has been suggested that this is a relieving arch, *Royal Commission on Ancient Monuments in England and Wales, for Caernarvonshire* [3 vols, 1960] I, 41a, but as the arch made of crude voussoirs is smaller than the window beneath it this seems unlikely.

Inserted into the wall are two major windows, of which the easternmost one is supposed to be some fifty years older than the western one (Figs.61&62). The quatrefoil in the allegedly older eastern window is identical with the windows in the clerestorey. If this is correctly dated to the second half of the thirteenth century, it has been suggested that these windows all date to any rebuilding done after the war of 1244-46. However, the history of the abbey related above, shows that there appears to have been no damage done to the main abbey structure during this war. Therefore this work might date to any time from 1200 to 1300 and seems to fit in with the phase 2 masonry stage of the abbey. Beneath the possibly later western window is a low, blocked doorway. This appears to be the priest's door and therefore probably dates to immediately after the abandonment of the monastery and its conversion into a parish church. This would suggest a date of soon after 1284 for the insertion of this doorway into the new chancel on the site of the old abbey presbytery. It consists of a crudely inserted series of jambs which have been roll moulded rather than chamfered. Internally the doorway has a shoulder-headed arch, typical of the late thirteenth century. The whole is made from red and creamy sandstone blocks, which again seems to point towards the Creuddyn and possibly the reuse of stone from Degannwy castle. These facts together strengthen a late thirteenth century date for the rebuilding of this section of the presbytery wall and the insertion of both the doorway and the window above it. Both fit comfortably into the time when this portion of the abbey was converted into a parish church chancel.

There was obviously some problem at the junction of the new chancel and the south transept, for apparently in the late fifteenth century this section of wall either collapsed or was taken down and rebuilt. This may well have occurred when the current rood screen was installed. The fissure through the south wall of the chancel was apparently obvious at the turn of the twentieth century (Fig.62), but is not now (Fig.63). On the west side of the break two new windows were inserted one above the other, set very tightly against the transept wall. The lower window is slightly larger than the upper and both may be reused as they appear of a late thirteenth century style, both having trefoil heads.

The north wall of the presbytery has been much hidden by the later addition of the vestry, but was thought in the early twentieth century to be built of 'rubble similar to the east wall'[722]. It has been suggested that this addition occurred 'around 1300' and is dated by the twin light east window which does not appear to be an insertion (Fig.64). As such the vestry would be phase 3 of the build, completed soon after the 1284 creation of the parish church.

At some point the bulk of the north wall of the presbytery was demolished to make way for an organ partially set within the vestry (v). There was previously 'a drop arch' doorway here[723]. Further, the only exposed external side of the presbytery has been later modified by the insertion of a probably fifteenth century window (a). This is the only window to be headed by crude voussoirs. Above the voussoirs appears to be a crease that may mark a boundary line of a new masonry phase. Certainly the line aligns with the roof of the vestry to the east. Immediately west of the window is a buttress (b) which may mask the east wall of the now demolished north transept. The ghost of the parish church rood loft window can still be seen above where the buttress fades into the current nave wall. This wall was some five feet thick, which would suggest that like the nave west wall, this wall carried more weight than those of the aisles. Consequently, it is possible to suggest that a small squat tower once lorded it over

[722] *Royal Commission on Ancient Monuments in England and Wales, for Caernarvonshire* [3 vols, 1960], 41a.
[723] Hughes, H, 'The Architectural History of St Mary's Church, Conway', *Archaeologia Cambrensis* [1895], 179.

the choir of the abbey between the two transepts. The transepts will be examined individually later.

Figure 58, The east end of the abbey showing the two phase vestry to the right. Notice the shadow of the older, larger window above the current east window. The string course is visible below this window.

Figure 59, The east end of Vale Crucis abbey showing its superior ashlar finish and pilaster buttresses. Notice too the finer quality of the stonework of the three lancet windows as well as those two on the higher level. The two windows to the left are in the east wall of the south transept.

Figure 60, The eastern lancet windows at Cymer abbey showing the simple indented jambs.

Figure 61, The south wall of the presbytery showing the line of the original walling (a). The eastern of the two windows (b) with its label is said to predate the western one (c). The low blocked doorway (d) is certainly a later insertion.

Figure 62, The 1894 sketch of the presbytery wall which clearly misses the masonry differentiation shown in the preceding photograph, although the join with the much later rebuild at the junction with the south transept is clearly shown and is not so prominent now (Fig.63). The Victorian brick chimney has also been seamlessly removed in the last century.

Figure 63, The eastern end of the presbytery with the south transept to the left. The junction between the two is not so readily apparent as in the sketch above (Fig.62).

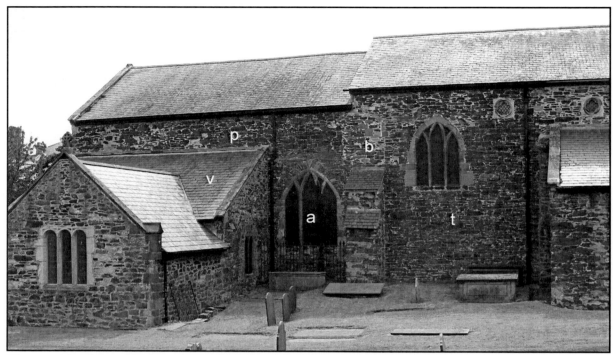

Figure 64, The north face of the presbytery (p) much covered by the later vestry (v). The inserted window (a) with voussoirs means that little can be seen of any early walling. Above the buttress in the centre can be seen the ghosting (b) of a rectangular later window that once lit the rood loft of the post 1284 parish church. Presumably this was inserted after the north transept (t) was taken down. Above the buttress (b) the change in roof height, probably marks the end of the original presbytery and the beginning of the choir which almost certainly lay under the cross between the two transepts. The twin lights are visible in the vestry (v) east wall.

The North Aisle

The original north aisle of the abbey has been almost totally rebuilt, but enough would seem to remain of it to make some broad statements. The external north-western corner of the aisle has already been examined when analysing the west wall of the abbey. The outer wall of this seems to have run some eighty feet eastwards to join up with the north transept. Not much remains of this four feet thick wall and most of it has been replaced by a poor quality wall probably of the seventeenth century. Next to a small buttress about half way between the west end of the church and the north porch, is a small lancet light with chamfered jambs of the original yellow gritty sandstone (Fig.65). This, and the short piece of wall around it, shows every sign of dating back to the first phase of the church, although the nature of the rubble build around it might suggest that it has been reset. Certainly this light would appear to have been in an original position as it is at a totally different level from all the other lights in the aisles. The lower window slightly west of it would seem to be a mutilated original light inserted into the wall possibly in the seventeenth century. The other four lights in the wall are very modern.

Figure 65, The northen face of Conwy church from the presbytery north window (left) to the west end (under the tower). A single possibly original twelfth century lancet window can be seen in the aisle to the far right.

Towards the northern third of the aisle is a seventeenth century porch which overlies an earlier door into the nave. This was probably inserted when the abbey was moved to Maenan or afterwards as it better serves a parish church than an abbey. The doorway is obviously reset and consists of chamfered jambs which are all poorly constructed and mutilated. The rear arch is elliptical. Such poor construction would suggest a rebuilding date of the aisle in the late fifteenth century or later.

The possibly seventeenth century rebuild of the north aisle ends slightly before its medieval counterpart did. Indeed, the end of the original aisle wall can still be made out partially overlain by the current east wall. Although it has been stated that this was solely a buttress, it appears that the wall here doubled as the west wall of the north transept. Foundations of this wall were traced during the Victorian era further north than they extend today and partially underlying the current nave east wall. Two further wall foundations have also been uncovered and are displayed on the attached plan (Fig.90).

The South Aisle

The south aisle presently has a totally altered appearance to its northern counterpart. Firstly, it has lost its western third and has a new west wall, parallel to the rear of the later west tower. This wall, with two inserted modern lights, makes a right angled joint with the old original wall which runs eastwards to the south transept. Towards the new west end it is broken by the south doorway which has almost certainly been inserted here after the old cloisters were demolished. The style of doorway also places it in the period 1284 or later. Previously there would have been a doorway close to the south transept and possibly another near the west end which led to the east and west sides of the cloister. Some abbeys only have the eastern door. This type includes Basingwerk (1133/57), Cwmhir (1176), Margam (1147), Strata Marcella (1170/72) and Valle Crucis (1200). Cwmhir also seems to have a south doorway west of the cloisters, leading to the exterior. Neath (1180), Strata Florida (1201) and Whitland (1140/53) seem to have had doors to east and west. Therefore either hypothesis is possible at Aberconwy.

Four modern lights are positioned irregularly along the south wall (Fig.66) and there is also a piscina in a niche at the east end (Fig.67). One of the modern four windows is a half light that has been inserted over the junction between two wall tombs cut into the thickness of the earlier wall (Fig.68). These now contain carved slabs for which they were obviously not built. The first is a foliated cross on a coffin shaped slab (fig.69). The other is a low relief effigy of a lady possibly of the fifteenth century (Fig.70). Quite plainly neither fit the current spaces and so both are later insertions held in place by Victorian concrete. Considering the age of this wall base, which probably dates back into the pre-1284 era, it would seem possible that this marks the last resting place of Prince Gruffydd ap Cynan (d.1200) and his son Hywel (d.1216), as history records the burial of both princes in the abbey. It is most unlikely that either wall tomb was designed for Llywelyn ab Iorwerth as he was, according to the abbey's own Register, buried before the high altar. Presumably his sons were buried near him. As such a high-status grave has been excavated at Maenan abbey under the cross, it is possible that the Register, written many years after Llywelyn's death, referred to his reburial at Maenan. If so it is still possible that these two tomb recesses might be the first resting places of the prince (1240) and his son, Prince Dafydd ap Llywelyn (1246). Against this scenario is the fact that there is then no grave for Llywelyn's other son, Gruffydd ap Llywelyn (d.1244), who was reburied at Aberconwy abbey with all honour in 1248. The tombs associated with the abbey are discussed in the chapter above, The Burial of Llywelyn ab Iorwerth and other Venedotians in North Wales.

Externally, the south aisle wall consists of a poorly laid build of red sandstone slabs which contrast unfavourably with the clerestorey above (Fig.66). Most likely the aisle is a seventeenth or eighteenth century rebuild lying on top of the remains of the original twelfth century wall. Surprisingly, an L shaped foundation is said to have been uncovered half way along the aisle wall. This is where the cloisters should have been, so presumably these foundations represent post abbatial use of the site. Further projecting foundations have been found against the north aisle wall, but these seem to have largely marked buttresses rather than buildings.

Figure 66, The south aisle showing the four modern windows. The churchyard is some three to four feet higher than the interior, as can be seen by the internal picture below when the bases of the windows are compared inside and out (Fig.68). Notice how the aisle wall consists of an irregular patchwork of sandstone slabs. The clerestory above, with its five round windows, consists of superior masonry with several snecker stones. In this it most closely resembles the phase 2 masonry in the west wall.

Figure 67, The much damaged piscina in a niche at the east end of the aisle south wall.

Figure 68, The two tomb recesses cut into the north face of the south wall of the aisle. Notice the height of the modern half light between the two compared to the two full size embrasures just visible to right and left. The top of both arches have been recut and replaced in modern times. The three unadorned coping stones under the half window are also totally modern.

Figure 69, The foliated cross on the coffin shaped lid cemented into place.

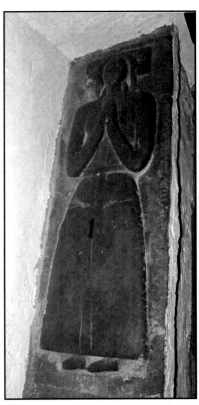

Figure 70, The low relief female effigy cemented into the niche.

The Transepts

Virtually nothing remains above ground of the presumed north transept (Fig.64). The same has been said of the original south transept (Fig.71), but is this correct? Close study of the masonry style of the current transept, which joins the south aisle wall in a seamless junction, would appear to be far more of the phase one style around and above the western door than anything else. As such it does not appear to be a later rebuild as has been alleged. It is therefore very difficult to reconcile the remains on the ground with the statement that 'this is the work of finer craftsmen, probably English, whose ambitious plan of reconstruction was cut short'[*724]. If the similarity with the earliest masonry style is correct then the transept is more likely to date to the late twelfth or early thirteenth century rather than the fourteenth. The old chestnut that Welsh princes could not hire masons hardly holds true with our current knowledge of medieval affairs. In deference to the old interpretation of the transept this seems to have been based largely on the presence of the string course surmounted by a single course of grey ashlar. This continues from the south east corner of the presbytery right around the south transept to some three feet along the south aisle where it is suddenly broken off at the remains of a destroyed window (Fig.72), never to reappear elsewhere in the current church. Despite the fact that a plinth is visible on all the church buttresses it is not the same as the plinth around the south side of the main building as described above. It would therefore appear that the buttresses are later than the wall, as can be seen in the manner that they butt onto it, rather than being an integral part of it. It is therefore quite feasible that the main plinth post dates the construction of the wall or that this was copied from the east end of the presbytery in the newer builds. It is also apparent that the transept buttresses and the two on the southern wall of the presbytery are all of a similar style and build (Fig.71). The two on the east end of the church are similar, but not as tall (Fig.74). The singular buttress against the north-west corner of the west tower is much larger and taller than any other (Fig.48). Quite possibly it is more modern too (Fig.47). The surviving buttress on the north wall of the presbytery has already been examined and is totally dissimilar to those on the south and east sides of the church (Fig.64). This, it has been suggested, is because this is not a true buttress, but was built upon the modified remains of the old north transept east wall. The junction of the south transept with the south aisle has been noted and commented on above (Fig.71).

Considering the masonry styles of the transept it is surprising that the two eastern windows are stated to be original. In style they are quite different and it seems likely that both are later additions (Fig.73). The northern of the two is slightly taller and is possibly somewhat the elder in having quatrefoil tracery over three ogee headed lights. The southern window appears slightly later in design, but is also of three lights with complex tracery above (Fig.74). The twin light window in the east wall has been heavily restored, but also has a pointed head (Fig.71). All are probably fourteenth century and post date the abbey. The south window of 5 lights is also modern and the wall immediately around it shows clear signs of it having been inserted.

Within the church, entrance to the transept is gained via two arches of similar style and design, but dissimilar size. The pointed north arch into the choir rises nearly 25 feet high and consists of three orders. Unlike the nave arches it is not set on pillars, but rises from decorative floor bases (Fig.75). There is a singular headstop of a long haired man above the north-western respond (Fig.80). A date of 1250 to 1350 would be acceptable for this and the similar label headstops on the transept arches. The relative smallness of the three transept

---

[*724] *Royal Commission on Ancient Monuments in England and Wales, for Caernarvonshire* [3 vols, 1960] I, 41a.

heads to those of the nave arcade clearly indicate that the transept arches are of a slightly later date than those of the nave. As such they could date to the time of some rebuilding in the time of the parish church after 1284.

A second arch, similar, but slightly lower at twenty feet, allows access between the transept and the south aisle (Fig.81). This has carved headstops to the east to both north and south, which are similar to the single example on the main arch to the north. There is no label to the west. The more elaborate decoration of the arches would suggest that they are of a later date than the nave arcades and could date from anytime between 1250 and 1350. Probably they date to after the translation of the abbey in 1284.

The roof of the transept has been clearly raised, with the east and west walls being heightened some two feet each (Fig.74). In the south wall is an apparently original piscina which has a similar style arch to the transept arches, while nine feet up the east wall, is a small doorway leading to a mural passage to the rood loft. The organ loft was still in use here at the turn of the nineteenth century[725].

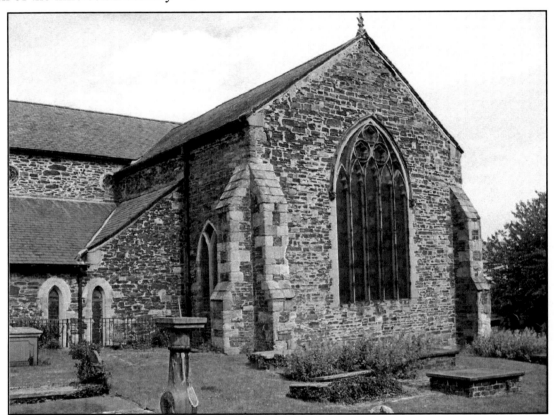

Figure 71, The south transept showing the odd junction with the south aisle. Notice the change in masonry style over the south transept south window, where it becomes a much more regular rubble build. The seamless junction with the south aisle is also seen before the wall height drops dramatically to a building style change at the first modern lancet window. The original transept roof height seems to have been at aisle roof level, the side walls having been raised some two feet on each side in a poorly laid masonry.

---

[725] Williams, R., *The History and Antiquities of the Town of Aberconwy...* [Denbigh, 1835], 103.

Figure 72, The junction of the south transept (right) and south aisle (left). The projecting string course with single line of ashlar masonry above can be seen proceeding from bottom right to top centre. Here it ends abruptly with one side of a blocked window in the aisle above.

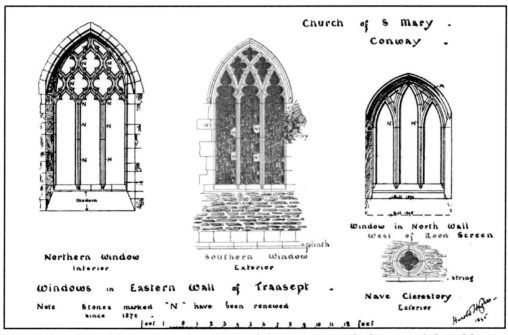

Figure 73, Harold Hughes' drawings of the transept windows and the older clerestory light.

Figure 75, The presbytery and south transept from the south showing the uniform buttresses along this front of the church. The slight raising of the transept east wall for a higher or less sloped roof can clearly be seen at the line of the tops of the buttresses.

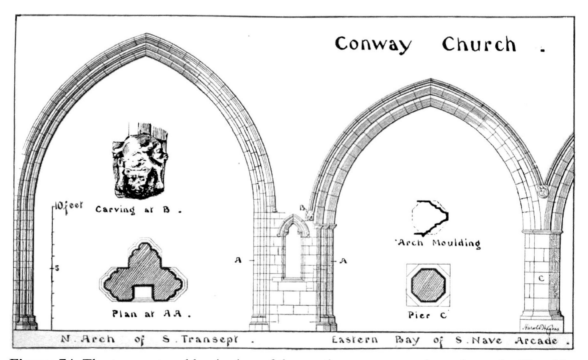

Figure 74, The transept and beginning of the southern nave arcade as drawn by Harold Hughes in 1895.

227

The Nave and Arcades

It should immediately be noted that the layout of the nave and aisles at Cymer abbey (1199) is virtually identical to the remains found at Aberconwy (1186). Both aisle arcades are of three bays and both have 'early English' style pointed arches of two orders set on piers and responds[726]. However, it should also be noted that the westernmost bays at Aberconwy would appear to have been taken down and replaced by the west tower, which means that Aberconwy would have had four bays a side and not three as at present (Fig.76). Similarly the Aberconwy bays are taller and more ornate than those at Cymer, although they both have octagonal ashlar piers (Fig.77). In this case there can hardly be any doubt that they date to similar building periods, in the case of Aberconwy the late 1180s and in the case of Cymer the period immediately after 1199. As Cymer was a poorer house than Aberconwy it is not surprising that the arcades here were smaller and less ornate and also that the east end was apparently never finished. Instead a new east blocking wall was added at the eastern end of the cloisters where the transepts should have begun. It is noticeable that both these north-western Welsh houses are smaller than their many southern counterparts. A simple comparison can be made with the surviving arcade at Llanidloes church. These were taken from Cwmhir abbey at the dissolution. Cwmhir's probably earlier work of the late 1170s is grander, taller and generally vastly superior to that of its northern daughter and niece houses (Fig.78). The idea that the masonry of Cwmhir abbey was the work of Llywelyn ab Iorwerth (d.1240) can be dismissed, for there is no logical reason to dismiss the work as beginning in the 1170s[727].

On the top of the easternmost pier of the nave array is a single animal with a large human-like grotesque face acting as a headstop (Fig.79). This is set on a respond on the west side of the transept wall. A niche possibly for a piscina is then set in the transept wall end. This has a damaged trefoil head which is arched by a pointed 'Early English' style label (Fig.80). Again the earlier work of the aisle is possibly contemporaneous with the abbey church, while the transept work could date to after 1284. The ashlar masonry blends seamlessly between the pier and the transept wall with the niche and the transept arch beyond. Obviously the transept masons knew their job well enough to make a seamless junction between the two phases. It seems likely that the niche and the bulk of the pillar are of a similar date to the transept. The arch between the transept and the south aisle would appear to be of a similar date (Fig.81).

There are three relatively large character heads on the two remaining octagonal piers and associated respond on the label of the nave side of the southern arcade. Moving westwards along the southern arcade, the first is of a rather round faced knight who appears to be wearing a coif and an arming cap, possibly with a turban of some description (Fig.82). If this is a turban it might again link to an early phase of the abbey and perhaps the fall of Jerusalem in 1187. The next figure to the west is that of a clean shaven young man, apparently wearing an arming cap similar to that on the previous figure, but without the coif or turban effect (Fig.83). The final respond shows a quite surprisingly wry face pulled markedly to one side (Fig.84). This appears to have been reset in a clumsy manner and is not an integrated part of the structure as the previous two heads. Despite this, it does appear to be part of the same set, as the eyes of them all are quite distinctive. As the final bay of the arcade has been taken down, or bricked up when the west tower was built, it is to be presumed that this head, whose shape indicates that it was designed to fit against the wall on the last respond of the arcade, has

---

[726] *Royal Commission on Ancient Monuments in England and Wales, for Caernarvonshire* [3 vols, 1960] I, 42a, thought that the piers slightly predated the arches by up to fifty years. The two are just as convincingly of the same date.
[727] Remfry, PM., *Abbey Cwmhir* [forthcoming].

been moved one bay to the east. The pudding-bowl haircut and wry look may suggest that this is a portrayal of a monk, perhaps someone intimately known to the stone-cutter who made it, or even a founder member of the abbey. It is also apparent that the three heads and the animal make a set, with the two central heads set several feet higher than the end two. This again shows that the arcade form was well thought out and was maintained as such even with the converting of the abbey into a parish church.

The northern arcade is similar to the southern one in layout and design, although there are no arches to the northern transept which has disappeared (Fig.85). The east wall of the aisle has been replaced with a thinner, probably seventeenth century one on the site of the north transept arch. Similarly, the arch from the choir into the north transept has been replaced by a later wall, together with a probably inserted window of the fourteenth century (Fig.64). Once again, four carved figures grace the two cusps and two responds, although in this case all of them are heads and no animals are portrayed. The westernmost head is largely obscured by a bookcase, but appears to show a knight's head encased in a coif and again wearing an arming cap (Fig.86). The head is set in the final stone of the outer order of the arch and as such is obviously one cut for the end of the arcade. Yet this head does not curve into the arch like its opposite number (Fig.84). Perhaps this indicates that this head has not been reset like the monk opposite.

The next two heads on the arcade label are set higher up in the cusps of the arches, just like their two companions opposite. The first is that of a fully bearded man, again wearing a cap. His is the only face covered by a beard and the face is somewhat Christlike (Fig.87). The next head is mustachioed and appears to sport a peculiar hat or headband. The face is also very long and fits nicely into the narrow space at the join between the two arches (Fig.88). Is this supposed to be a representation of a Jew? The final head is perhaps the most disturbing and grotesque having much the appearance of a death mask (Fig.89). In total these five heads and an animal seem very similar in style and design. They would therefore appear to be a conceptual whole and there seems no logical reason to assume that they were not here from the conception of the abbey. It is therefore possible that these very distinct faces were those of personages connected with the abbey or its times. It should be remembered that 1187 saw the fall of Jerusalem and the knight in a possible turban might be a reflection of this, as too could the Jewish or Christlike representations. There are also a few masons' marks on the piers (Fig.90).

Above the arcades are a series of round quatrefoil lights in the clerestorey. To the south are a series of five, which end close to the transept. These are all stated to have been raised when the wall was heightened for the new roof in the 1870s. Therefore, although they are reset, they may contain old stones. On the north side there are six windows, where at least one has been added in the wall which replaced the lost north transept. This and its neighbour are in a different style to all the rest, having a square exterior rather than circular (Fig.91). These would seem to have been added in 1872[*728]. The crease of a steep nave roof line still exists on the tower east face. This shows the level of the nave roof from probably before as well as after 1284, remembering that the tower could not have been built before this date when the abbey moved to Maenen, but the roof line might have been from earlier. This crease was visible around 1860 when the entire church had a single roof (Fig.92), rather than the several it has now.

[*728] *Royal Commission on Ancient Monuments in England and Wales, for Caernarvonshire* [3 vols, 1960] I, 41a, where it is also stated that all but the westernmost two lights are replacements. Judging by the remains this might be an error for all but the easternmost two being originals as is noted here in the main text above.

The only other feature that may have survived from the abbey church is the reset doorway in the south porch (Fig.93). It has been suggested that the porch is of fourteenth century date[*729]. Certainly it must post date the abbey, as originally the cloisters would have stood here. The arch is poorly reconstructed and the stones it consists of are badly mauled, therefore the date of its reconstruction must be purely hypothetical without further evidence.

It should finally be noted, that the stairs in the west tower vice are made up in the lower steps of reused sepulchral slabs as too is one of the corbels on the second floor of the tower. This sacrilegious use of the old gravestones raises certain issues. If the monks took the tomb and body of Llywelyn ab Iorwerth with them to Maenan, then what happened to the bodies of Llywelyn's sons? Were they left behind as they were not 'the founders' of the abbey? Indeed, was Llywelyn even considered the founder in 1284? Surely then his memory was too close to be used in such a manner. The same may be asked of the more real founder, Gruffydd ap Cynan (d.1200), who died here as a monk. Was his body abandoned? Were their graves defiled and their tombs reused as building materials in the new parish church? The doorway into the vice is certainly correct for the period immediately after 1284, being a shoulder headed doorway which was so common in North Wales in this period. This therefore suggests that the twelfth and thirteenth century burials were not much regarded by the builders of the new parish church of Edward I.

This brief resume of the remains of Aberconwy abbey shows the extent of masonry probably remaining from the period 1186 to 1284. It was during this period that several of the documents contained in the Aberconwy Register were composed. Therefore, with the church remains and their history examined, it is finally possible to look at the so-called Aberconwy Register with its chronicle.

[*729] *Royal Commission on Ancient Monuments in England and Wales, for Caernarvonshire* [3 vols, 1960] I, 43a.

Figure 76, The southern arcade of Aberconwy. Notice the fine octagonal ashlar pillars and twin tier 'early English' arches. In conception these are almost identical to those found at Cymer (1199). Notice too the two central carved heads between the arches and the lower two headstops to east and west at pillar top level.

Figure 77, The northern arcade at Cymer abbey with the remains of the north aisle beyond. This looks like a simpler and smaller version of Aberconwy.

Figure 78, The abbey Cwmhir arcade reconstructed at Llanidloes church. Note the arches of five orders are much less pointed than the later arches of Aberconwy and Cymer. The standard of decoration at the northern abbeys are similarly much lower and the arcades are much less impressive than Cwmhir appears to have been overall. There is also a lack of labels and their decorative heads as found at Aberconwy.

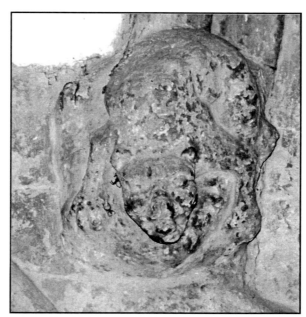

Figure 79, The cat-like creature with grotesque face on the easternmost pillar of the southern aisle arcade.

Figure 80, The southern transept to aisle pillar complete with head on the transept side and animal towards the aisle. Between them is the trefoil head of a niche under an 'Early English' style label. As can be seen the ashlar is seamless between the two, although the style is slightly different. The animal on the aisle side is also lower and more integral with the structure than the head on the transept side.

Figure 81, The archway into the southern aisle from the south transept showing the similarity in style of this to the main transept arch as well as the small headstops.

Figure 82, The carved knight's head in a coif. He
appears to be wearing an arming cap with some kind of
turban or wreath-like decoration on it. He also appears to
have a moustache. Perhaps his turban is an allusion to the
fall of Jerusalem in 1188.

Figure 83, The second carved head to the west in the southern
nave arcade set on the pillar between the arches. This head is
unarmoured, but appears to be wearing another arming cap.
He is also clean shaven. The style of the eyes suggests that he
is of a similar provenance to the knight in Fig.82.

Figure 84, The possible face of a monk staring wryly from the western end of the southern arcade. Note how the head seems poorly positioned as if placed here as an afterthought, or more likely reset here when the west tower was inserted into the parish church destroying the westernmost arch of the arcade. Again the style of the eyes is similar to the previous two heads, even if the head does show signs of being reset in its uncomfortable position.

Figure 85, The north arcade from the east. Once again a symmetry is maintained with the southern array with the two central heads being set high up in the cusps of the arches, while the two end stops are lower down at pillar top level.

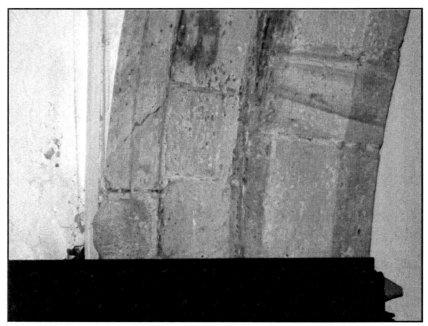

Figure 86, The westernmost armed head of the north arcade.
Note how the head is set properly in the outer order of the arch,
rather than the unsatisfactory positioning of the monk's head
opposite (Fig.84).

Figure 87, The western, bearded head in the northern arcade. This is the only
fully bearded head of the set and appears to be wearing a cap with a rolled
banded edge. Again the eyes mark it out as part of a set.

Figure 88, The next easternmost head in the northern arcade has a large dropping moustache and possible a small goatee beard. He wears a cap similar to the next head to the east and his triangular face was obviously made to fit easily into the gap between the two arches. The pyramidal nose and rounded eyes of the faces strongly suggests that one man was responsible for the creation of all these heads.

Figure 89, The final easternmost head in the north arcade is a grotesque, almost like a death mask. The figure apparently has thick lips, although the upper one might possibly be a moustache. He has wide set eyes and a small forehead and unlike the rest of his fellows wears no apparent head gear. Perhaps this is the face of a monk or patron who died during the building? Its dissimilarity from the other faces, but its similarity in style, show that it was part of the set. Presumably two heads are missing from the demolished westernmost bay.

Figure 90, Harold Hughes' 1894 sketches of the masons' marks on the arcade piers.

Figure 91, The nave and north aisle showing the six quatrefoil windows of the clerestory. Note that the two windows to the east (left) have square exteriors which shows them up to be replacements, notwithstanding that one of them is now within the probable site of the line of the old north transept.

Figure 92, Francis Bedford's photograph of St Mary's church about 1860. Note the single roof blocking all trace of the clerestory and the single large window on the north aisle which has since been replaced by the four modern ones. It is also apparent that the north aisle has been reduced in height since this photograph was taken, as the roof line is now beneath the roof of the north porch. Note the rectangular leaded window above the site of the north transept east wall. The possible remains of the transept projects from the nave wall as a buttress.

Figure 93, The rebuilt south door of the parish church. This certainly post dates 1284 as does its surrounding porch. The poor craftsmanship and the reuse of good quality material suggests a fifteenth century date.

The Register and Chronicle of Aberconwy Abbey

The Register of Aberconwy and the chronicle it contains have over the years been dismissed as either a botched abridgment of an original chronicle or a useless later medieval compilation[*730]. Unfortunately, close study of the document confirms the latter pronouncement for its creation, but it does show that the manuscript is far from useless. Before the contents of any document can be seriously studied it is first necessary to arrive at a reasonable compilation date for the only version that has come down to us and to compare it with similar documents.

The only surviving copy of the Register which seems to have been a singular exemplar, is to be found in Harleian MS. 3725 between folios 40v and 65v. This work both starts and finishes in the middle of a page. It commences immediately after the chronicle of Hailes abbey ends and the implication is that this was intentional. Indeed, the chronicles share many features of a single composition. After the Aberconwy section ends, the lower part of folio 65v is 'covered with fifteenth or sixteenth century memoranda of no importance'[*731]. The whole Aberconwy Register was obviously written by one hand and the compiler patently left spaces at the beginning of each paragraph for rubricated initial letters. These were never added. It is also obvious, other than the missing rubrication, that the work was never completed. After the list of the abbatial property values on folio 45 the remainder of the page is left blank, as is the whole of the following folio, 45b. Quite obviously it was the intention to add further details here and this was never done. The rest of the manuscript is in another hand, which might suggest that the Aberconwy material comes from elsewhere than Hailes and was merely bound into the one book at Hailes abbey.

The provenance of the whole Hailes/Aberconwy manuscript is obscure. It appears to have belonged to the antiquary Nicholas Batteley and was sold by his son to Earl Robert Harley of Oxford (d.1724) in 1723. Before that its provenance is unknown, although there seems little doubt that it began its life in Hailes abbey in Gloucestershire. The manuscript commences with the chronicle of Hailes abbey and concludes with more Hailes material. The entire manuscript is in two separate hands, although apparently both are of the fourteenth or fifteenth century. As the Aberconwy Register contains matter relating to an agreement of 1 October 1350, this must have been the earliest possible date of the writing of the manuscript. However, this does not help with dating the original chronicle which was obviously abridged and copied into the manuscript by one scribe after 1350. The dating of handwriting, like the dating of masonry, is a notoriously dangerous black art and often the possible dates of writing are narrowed down far too closely. Hence the idea that this manuscript is post 1350 should also be stated with the fact that it was written probably before 1535 by which time the monastic era had ended in the kingdom of England. Further, the inclusion of some of the lands of Strata Florida in the 'Aberconwy' Register tends to suggest a date in the early 1480s[*732]. The idea that the manuscript dates to the 1440s when the alleged Abbot John ap Rhys of Aberconwy apparently attempted to annex Aberconwy's mother house is not based on solid evidence. It has been suggested that before 1443 John ap Rhys, the abbot of Cymer, was also abbot of Aberconwy and therefore his interest in both this place and Strata Florida suggested a date for drawing up the document[*733]. Certainly this would explain the otherwise apparently nonsensical appearance of the Strata Florida data in an Aberconwy document. This thesis

---

[*730] Hays, RW, *The History of the Abbey of Aberconway, 1186-1537* [UWP, 1963], 144-5; Hardy, T.D., *A Descriptive Catalogue of Materials for Great Britain* [London, 3 vols, 1862-71] III, 352-3.

[*731] Owen, *Catalogue of Manuscripts in the British Museum relating to Wales*, 404-6.

[*732] The information alleged to refer to Cwmhir is more likely Aberconwy related as will be shown later in the proper place.

[*733] Hays, RW, *The History of the Abbey of Aberconway, 1186-1537* [UWP, 1963], 132-3.

tends to fall down on the confusion that John ap Rhys was never associated with Aberconwy as is discussed in the chapter, Maenan Abbey in the Fifteenth Century. Consequently, this idea falls flat and can be counted as disproved. That the abbey was said to have had all its books burned during the Glyndwr revolt would also suggest that the Register dates to after this time.

The evidence in the figures given in the assessments of land would suggest a late fourteenth or fifteenth century date for the original compilation of the values in the Register. As the manuscript in which the Register is found is a composite volume, with the Aberconwy sections contained on folios with different numbers of quires to the rest of the work, the conclusion remains that the current copy of the Register was certainly written after 1350 and probably after 1410 and likewise before 1535 and quite possibly at or for Hailes abbey. As the Hailes material before and after the Aberconwy material is said to be in a different hand, it can be assumed with some confidence that the Aberconwy work was inserted into the current manuscript and therefore is not necessarily related to Hailes abbey[*734]. Yet, as it is pertinently noted, the lack of a common origin for the texts does not preclude that there is not a link between them. It is certainly peculiar that the Aberconwy text 'follows immediately upon a chronicle of the abbey of Hayles in Gloucestershire'. As has been noted the only known link between the two houses is that a monk of Hailes went on to become abbot of Aberconwy in 1482 after Hailes was involved in reforming the Welsh Cistercian houses in 1480. As such it seems reasonable to date this part of the manuscript to the early 1480s. That said, none of the recognizable sources used for the chronicle, except for Tewkesbury (which appears to have been written in the late 1260s), would seem to have been available as early as the end of the Aberconwy chronicle in 1283. Therefore, the compilation of the chronicle could not have taken place until the last source had been written. In this case it would appear to be the Hailes chronicle itself which apparently was not written before 1314.

When looking at the content of the whole Aberconwy Register, including the part referred to as its chronicle, it is obviously a composite creation. Possibly this was created using an original chronicle, which itself was built from several sources, to form a chronology from 1170 until the translation of the abbey in 1283. This also helps to explain various charters related to the lands, rights and extent of Aberconwy abbey, even though these obviously date to a later period than the thirteenth century. That 'original' Aberconwy charters are used in the chronicle's creation would therefore suggest that some copies were kept in the abbey into the fifteenth century and therefore survived the burnings of 1245 and 1404/10. The format of the chronicle might also suggest, but by no means prove, that there was also once an Aberconwy chronicle that formed the basis of the historical section of the annals. So too would the survival of an apparent basis of a similar chronicle which is now known as *O Oes Gwrtheyrn* (see Appendix 3). However, this proto-chronicle cannot have been the basis of the surviving Aberconwy chronicle due to the different materials both contain. What the compiler of the Aberconwy Register did seem to have access to, was an Aberconwy archive where various original manuscripts, or copies thereof, existed. The only logical places for these to have been retained is Aberconwy abbey itself, or a royal archive. The charters of Gruffydd ap Cynan (d.1200), King John (d.1216) and those of Edward I (d.1307) obviously existed and those of Edward are certainly not forgeries as they exist in various other copies, although there are certain differences which suggest that the compiler was not fastidious in the treatment of his sources. The compiler obviously also had access to the 1348 Quo Warranto proceedings,

---

[*734] Stephenson, D., *Kathleen Hughes Memorial Lectures, The Aberconwy Chronicle* [2002], 2, quoting Huws, D., *Medieval Welsh Manuscripts* [Cardiff, 2000], 277, note 29.

but not to the 'original' spurious charters of Llywelyn ab Iorwerth (d.1240), as otherwise he would surely have copied them from the original rather than the Quo Warranto report. In conclusion, it can be said that the chronicle within the Aberconwy Register was written by a competent compiler who had much older sources at his disposal and that this was later bound up within a Hailes abbey manuscript. More will be said of this after examining the chronicle itself.

The Constituent parts of the Aberconwy Register

This century, in an attempt to make the Register and chronicle more understandable, the text was divided up into what were seen as thirteen logical parts[*735]. For clarity these are listed below and are followed in the main text, even though it is evident that the work was the composition of one compiler and should be seen as an integral whole.

Part I is an introduction consisting of the fall of Britain running from Cadfan to the death of Cadwaladr dated in 389. It is obviously based on the unreliable history of Geoffrey Monmouth (d.1154).

Part II is a continuation of Part I which deals with the ninth century division of Wales amongst the sons of Rhodri Mawr (d.878).

Part III is a set of just two anachronistic annals for the years 1170 and 1186. They possibly are based upon a lost North Welsh Brut, although why they show such an interest in Strata Marcella is peculiar, unless this detail was contained in one of the chronicle's sources. This might suggest a Strata Marcella and therefore a Powysian origin for a lost Brut.

Part IV is the 1190s charter of Gruffydd ab Cynan.

Part V is a complete list of Aberconwy possessions with values made after 1350/1410 and before 1536.

Part VI is a similar list of Strata Florida possessions made after 1376. The inclusion of this list in error - otherwise it would surely have been noted as belonging to Strata and not Maenan - would suggest that the compiler was unaware of the lands of both abbeys. Such ignorance again points to the compiler not being a monk of Aberconwy or Strata Florida.

Part VII is a summary of events from 1190 to an undated 1211 in a similar format to Part III.

Part VIII is a copy of the 1202 Aberconwy charter of King John.

Part IX consists of a further anachronistic summary of events in 1205 (sa.1206), 1231 (sa.1230), 1240 (undated) and 1241. That the compiler thought that Gruffydd ap Llywelyn's death came 'a few days' after his journey to London instead of nearly three years later, again shows how far removed in time he was from the events he was recording.

[*735] Stephenson, D., *Kathleen Hughes Memorial Lectures, The Aberconwy Chronicle* [2002].

Part X is a proper set of anachronistic annals running from 1277 to 1279 and then 1282 and 1283. This seems to be based on the Hailes abbey chronicle, but again the placing of the events of 1281 [year end 25 March 1282] under 1279 shows that this is the distant past being recorded.

Part XI consists of three grants made by Edward I in relation to the transfer of Aberconwy abbey to Maenan and date from 1284.

Part XII is a list of lands around Maenan which obviously belonged to the abbey. It has previously been suggested that this referred to various lands of Abbey Cwmhir as two placenames, Cefncelynnog near Betws y Crwyn and Pennant in Bugeildy, were in the Maelienydd/Clun region. However, neither place is recorded as ever having been properties of Cwmhir or any other abbey. Many of these placenames can be seen around Maenan.

Finally, Part XIII is a partial version of the Quo Warranto proceedings concerning Aberconwy in 1348.

Although this makes an interesting starting point, these suggestions cannot be allowed to stand and a detailed study of the evidence shows that the text breaks down into two certain parts. Copies (some not so good) of original documents and a somewhat annalistic text that tries to tie these disparate documents together. Thus the texts begin with a foundation story for Wales which runs rapidly from Cadfan to Llywelyn ap Gruffydd (d.1282). This is followed by the foundation of Aberconwy abbey and what is presumed to be the only early charter that could be found concerning the twelfth century history of the church. This format continues throughout its length with the list of the abbey's and Strata Florida's lands dropped incongruously in the middle. In short, the entire text is built around an attempt to make sense of the few original documents that the compiler had to hand. As such it is worth analysing the document in some detail.

    The early portion of the work (Parts I & II) consists of an essay explaining the formation of Wales from late and unreliable sources, mainly Geoffrey of Monmouth (d.1154) and Giraldus Cambrensis (d.1223, see Appendix 3, p.300). This seems largely based upon Giraldus Cambrensis, who makes a similar error concerning the sons of Rhodri Mawr, by making Merfyn the heir to Gwynedd instead of Anarawd[736]. Perhaps this was a common fifteenth century misconception for the Aberconwy text ignores the supremacy of Deheubarth as put forward by Giraldus[737]. This may not be surprising as Cambrensis came from South Wales and was a great grandson of King Rhys ap Tewdwr of Deheubarth (d.1093). This could explain his claim and possibly the reason why other compilers would not accept his conclusion and would go with what had happened in reality - ie. Deheubarth being eclipsed by Gwynedd. The manner of the detail in this section appears unique to Aberconwy, but some of the text, and especially the story of the nobles drowning one another and the prophesy of the angel, also appear in a brief history of Britain written in 1429 (Appendix 3, p.302). If the dating of the Aberconwy chronicle is correct, then this might well have been the source of the early 'chronicle' section. This would concur with a 1480s writing date as has already been advanced. The Aberconwy foundation of Wales story, concludes with a section that explains,

---

[736] *Early Welsh Genealogical Tracts*, ed. P.C. Bartrum [Cardiff, 1966], 95, quoting Achau Brenhinoedd a Thywysogion Cymru.
[737] Giraldus Cambrensis, *Opera*, eds. J.S. Brewer, J.F. Dimock and G.F. Warner [8 vols., 1861-91] VI, 166-8.

wrongly as it turns out, that there were only three principalities of Wales (and no kingdoms, which an early source would undoubtedly have described them as) and that this state of affairs ended with Llywelyn ab Iorwerth (d.1240) and Llywelyn ap Gruffydd (d.1282). There follows a skimpy and abbreviated 'chronicle' running directly from the foundation of the Cistercian house of Strata Marcella in 1170 (the year 1170 ended on 25 March 1171, so the foundation date of 1171 could be correct) to the foundation of Aberconwy abbey in 1186 and noting no years or details of events inbetween. This is followed by Gruffydd ap Cynan's 'foundation' charter with explanatory sentences before and after. These sentences contain obvious chronological and genealogical errors. Then comes a list of the abbey's possessions with values which can be compared to values given in other ages (Appendix 8, p.338). The range of these values would again suggest that this list dates to the fifteenth century. Surprisingly, there then follows a similar list for Strata Florida abbey, which was the mother house of Aberconwy, but otherwise unconnected with that abbey. After this, the skimpy 'chronicle' resumes from 1190 to 1211. This section is ended with King John's charter of 1202. Then comes the final part of the chronicle which runs from 1205 [sa.1206] to the death of Gruffydd ap Llywelyn in 1244.

Although there is no noticeable break in style or manner, the chronicle then takes up in more detail from the year 1277 and runs to 1283 with the death of Prince Dafydd. Tellingly, the start of the last war of 1282 to 1283 is commenced in the chronicle during 1279. A similar error occurs in the Bermondsey chronicle which was compiled in or soon after 1432[*738]. This in turn could suggest that the original Aberconwy chronicle was not compiled until the mid fifteenth century, as too does the statement 'after whose death [Llywelyn ap Gruffydd, d.1282] none thus far has been prince of their own descent'. Otherwise the date of the commencement of the war would more likely be far more accurate and the date of the death of Llywelyn would have been more accurate. Finally, the text of the war is similar to that found in the Teweksbury annals. This entire section seems to be based upon the Hailes chronicle, which itself dates only to around 1314 and may have used the Tewkesbury annals as a source[*739].

The Register then continues with a series of three documents concerning the move of the abbey from Conway to Maenen between 1283 and 1284. These survive in other forms and show significant differences (see Appendix 1, p.274ff). Again the implication of this is that the compiler had the originals available to him, but changed them slightly, for what reason though, is now difficult to ascertain.

The penultimate section consists of a list of lands which have in modern times been curiously said to refer to the Tempseter holdings of Abbey Cwmhir. These lands in the Register are assigned to various people and they seem to be set in the land of Maenan itself. Certainly, most of the placenames are still easily identifiable, unlike the few seen in Tempseter which were never recorded as having belonged to Abbey Cwmhir. The clinching argument is the inclusion of Hugh Conway in the list. He was an important landholder in North Wales and around Alcester, but is known to have held nothing in the lands of Abbey Cwmhir. The identifiable Register placenames in the Perfeddwlad follow.

Register Placename	Modern Placename	Grid reference

[*738] 'Annales Monasterii de Bermondeseia', *Annales Monastici*, ed. H.R. Luard [5 vols., 1864-9] III, 466. There is no evidence that the compiler of Aberconwy took any material from the Bermondsey chronicle, so his misdating of the events of March 1281/2 cannot come from here.
[*739] Remfry, PM. *The Killing of Prince Llywelyn of Wales, 10 December 1282* [Ceidio, 2014], 168.

Kevynkelynnocke	Cefncelynnog	
Bryn y vrane	Bryn y Fran, or possibly Bryn gwian	SH.811702 SH.679822
Bulth y gerwyn	Bwlchwern Hir	SH.820743
ll'etir Clochyth i bren y gofe	Cloliau	SH.848709
llemdire	Llindir	SH.825715
Pennant	Pennant	SH.816673

After this section the Aberconwy Register concludes with an incomplete version of the *Quo Warranto* proceedings of 1348 relating to Maenan abbey.

This mix of documents is at once surprising for both its omissions and its inclusions. Two of the recorded grants of King Edward I were to people outside of Aberconwy, namely Bishop Einion of St Asaph and Tewdwr ap Carwet, although both of these men were concerned with the abbey's move to Maenen. Further, why did the compiler choose his three charters to the abbey and exclude the presumed original foundation charter of 1186 or Henry II's confirmation charter before his death in July 1189? The obvious answer would tend to be because he only had what he used and the rest had been lost or destroyed by the time of his compilation. The same must be said of the extensive charters allegedly made by Llywelyn ab Iorwerth in 1199, especially when it is considered that in 1332 they thought these the most valuable charters of the house. These questions are of course insoluble, but they might suggest that this document was drawn up far from any possible archive kept at Maenen, perhaps by a monk in distant exile from his North Welsh home or a Hailes monk trying to make sense of what had happened at Aberconwy before 1482. Alternatively, the compiler may have been working at Aberconwy and those missing documents were not available to him. It is to be noted that the abbey never again produced the forged Llwyelyn charters after King Edward III confirmed them in 1332. Instead they had Edward's 1332 confirmation confirmed and not the original documents. Perhaps they were disposed of soon after Edward's 1332 confirmation of them, rather than run the risk of having their fraud exposed.

It is apparent from this that the Register and Chronicle as they stand are part of a coherent whole and although it may make some sense to break them down into various parts these are not constituent parts and what was assembled for the compilation was done with thought and some degree of planning. Consequently it seems that this document was put in this peculiar format for a reason at a date long after the originals had been written. This leaves the question as to whether the compiler used an older Brut that had been kept at Aberconwy to form his 'chronicle'. This is possible, but the chronicle does not hold the same information, nor the same style of the *O Oes Gwrtheyrn* which it can be said with some confidence originated in Aberconwy abbey. It therefore seems likely that the current Aberconwy chronicle was put together from sources other than any chronicle with which *O Oes Gwrtheyrn* was linked. To prove this point it is therefore necessary to proceed with a translation of the Register and Chronicle and then other documents and a version of the *O Oes Gwrtheyrn* proto-chronicle itself.

Conventions of the Translation

The translation will be as literal as possible with modern additions, to make the meaning clearer, placed within square brackets. The expanded Latin text will appear at the year end in italics or for the charters in footnotes. Where dates appear in square brackets they have been added from independent sources to help make more chronological sense of the current text or point out errors of chronology. Modern dates follow medieval ones in brackets. Punctuation has been altered as little as possible, although full stops and capital letters follow modern convention. It has also been deemed necessary to attempt a standardisation of titles throughout. Although a literal translation has been chosen for accuracy, it has been necessary to reverse certain orders. Therefore kings and popes will commence with their titles, rather than have them simply follow their names as happened in the Latin. Therefore King Henry of England has been used rather than Henry, king of England (*Henricus Rex Anglie*) as it appears in the Latin. Similarly, single names attached to a title have often been reversed in translation, thus Pope Serge has been used rather than the Serge pope (*Sergium Papam*) of the original Latin.

Throughout the *de* of surnames have been ignored as unnecessary, so Peter Stokes has been translated for *Petro de Stokys* rather then the more literal, Peter of Stokes - Stokes being the vill from which the family hailed. When the Latin of the compiler contains an error of transcription or similar this will be followed by [*sic*] to indicate that these are original errors. Finally, all parts that appear similar to *Epitome Historiae Britanniae* are emboldened in the Epitome Latin text in Appendix 3, p.302. This shows the similarities of these sources - verb endings, expansions etc. notwithstanding.

The Register and Chronicle of the Abbey of Aberconwy
[Part I]

After Charles[*740] reigned in Britain Cadfan. After Cadfan Cadwallon. Truly in the time of Cadwallon there was a great dearth, so much plague, and so great a famine intensified that the magnates mutually embraced themselves and drowned themselves in the waters. At which it was said through the voice of an angel that his son [Cadwaladr] himself was to be driven out of the kingdom, and that he would die at Rome, and that he would be numbered in the catalogue of the saints[*741]. At which even the king searched for the cause of such great evil in his kingdom. To which the angel answered saying, "Because of the negligence of the prelates, the robbery of the nobles, the usury of the Jews [could also be read as the covetousness of the judges], the detestable luxury, the ravings of perjurers, the inordinate worship of clothings."

Post Karolum regnavit in Britania Caduanus. Post Caduanum Cadwallanus. Tempore vero Cadwallani fuit tanta caristia, tantae pestilentiae, et tanta fames invalescebat quod magnates mutuo se amplexantes submerserunt se in aquis. Cui dictum est in voce per angelum quod filius ejus expelleret seipsum de regno, et quod moriturus esset Romae, et quod deberet numerari in de catalogo Sanctorum. Qui quidem rex quaesivit causam tanti mali in regno suo. Cui respondens Angelus dixit, Negligentia prelatorum; Rapina potentum; Cupiditas Judicum; detestanda Luxuria; Rabies perjuriorum; inordinatus Cultus Vestimentorum.

[*740] According to Geoffrey of Monmouth this was Kareticus, Hays, RW, *The History of the Abbey of Aberconway, 1186-1537* [UWP, 1963], 150.

[*741] The angel and the story of the magnates drowning themselves only appears in this and the *Epitome Historiae Britanniae*, see Appendix 3, p.302ff.

After Cadwallon reigned Cadwaladr his son. This Cadwaladr, known as the Blessed, reigned a short time, but besides because of the mortality which almost laid waste his people, then on account of diverse sufferings which he was enduring continually from the Saxon barbarians, he relinquished his kingdom. He made for Lesser Britain [Brittany]. And there after an interval of time he assembled a great army in order that he might return and expel the foreign heathens from his kingdom. To which warning was given by an angel in order that he should give up his claim of ownership. Indeed God was unwilling for the Britons to reign for a long time in the island of Britain until the time came of which Merlin had prophesied to Arthur. Besides he warned the former [Cadwallon] that he was to go to Pope Serge in Rome, and there, when penitence was completed, he was to be classified amongst the saints. Furthermore he said that the people of Britain through the merit of their faith would obtain the island in the future. Then Cadwaladr, casting aside worldly things on account of God came to Rome and there was confirmed by Pope Serge, he was restored to the best of health[*742], and on the 12th calends of May in the year of our lord 389[*743] by contagion was released from his flesh. Indeed the Welsh bards firmly hold the belief that when the bones of Cadwaladr might be roused from the ground the former power of the Britons which they once had would be restored through the promise of the angel.

Post Cadwallanum regnavit Kadwalladrus filius ejus. Iste Kadwalladrus, cognomine Benedictus, regnavit modico tempore, sed tum propter mortalitatem quo populum suum fere devastabat, tum propter diversas persecutiones quas patiebatur assidue per Saxones barbaricos, reliquid regnum suum. Minorem Britanniam petiit. Ibique post intervallum temporis congregavit magnum exercitum ut rediret et expelleret externas nationes a regno suo. Cui nunciatum est per Angelum ut a proprio suo desisteret. Nolebat enim Deus Britones in Insula Britanniae diutius regnare antequam tempus venisset quod Merlinus Arthuro prophetaverat. Precepit illi etiam ut Romam ad Sergium Papam iret, et ibi, peracta penitentia, inter beatos annumeretur. Dicebat etiam populum Britannicum per meritum fidei sui insulam in futurum adepturum. Tunc Cadwalladrus, abjectis mundialibus, propter Deum venit Romam, et ibi a Sergio Papa confirmatus, in optimo langore correctus est, & xxij. kal. Maij Anno domini CCC.lxxxix. a contagione carnis solutus est. Bardi enim Kambrenses istam opinionem firmiter tenent, quod cum ossa Cadwalladri in terra suscitarentur Britones pristinae potestati quam habuerunt per promissionem Angeli restaurantur.

[Part II]

After Cadwallon the remains of the Britons lost their name and kingdom. Now they are not called Britons but Welsh. They suffered so much disturbance through the barbarian Saxons that they were not able to further resist them, and thus weakened they gathered in Cambria, presently Wales; and there for a long time they were ruled by princes of their own stock, that is to say they were ruled by one prince alone up to the time of Rhodri Mawr, that is Roderick the Great/Senior. This Roderick the Great/Senior ruled all Wales in his time. After whose death his three sons, namely Merfyn, Anarawd and Cadell, divided between themselves all Wales in

---

[*742] The opposite is surely meant here and should be compared with the *Epitome Historiae Britanniae* in Appendix 3, p.302ff.

[*743] The date should have been twelfth calends of May, ie. 20 April 689, Hays, RW, *The History of the Abbey of Aberconway, 1186-1537* [UWP, 1963], 150. The *O Oes Gwrtheyrn* more 'accurately' dates this event to [6]48, Humphrey Llwyd, *Britannicæ descriptionis commentariolum: necnon de Mona insula et Britannica arce, sive armamentario Romano disceptatio epistolaris. Accedunt æræ Cambrobritannicæ*, ed. by M. Williams [London, 1731], 146. Cadwaladr ap Cadwallon actually died on 12 November 664 of the plague in Wales and was buried at Llangadwaladr, Lloyd, J.E., *History of Wales* [2 vols., 1911] I, 230; Bartrum, P.C., *Welsh Classical Dictionary* [NLW, 1993], 80-1.

three parts, Merfyn the principality of Gwynedd, that is North Wales, Anarawd the principality of Powys and Cadell the principality of Deheubarth, that is South Wales; and each one of those mentioned with their descendants ruled their part as prince for many years. And after many years had unfolded, two of those parts, namely Powys and South Wales, lost the title of their prince and principality. Truly the prince of North Wales reassumed the integral name of prince of all Wales, which was always enjoyed among his descendants up to Prince Llywelyn ap Gruffydd ap Llywelyn ab Iorwerth Drwyndwn, after whose death none thus far has been prince of their own descent just as clearly the following will testify.

Post Kadwalladrum reliquiae Britonum perdiderunt nomen suum et regnum. Jam non vocantur Britones sed Wallenses. Tantam inquietationem patiebantur per barbaricos Saxones quod non potuerunt eis amplius resistere, et sic debilitati petierunt Cambriam, modo Walliam; et ibi per multa tempora regebantur per Principes generis sui, regebantur enim omnes per unum Principem solum usque ad tempus Rothri vawr, i Rodrici magni. Iste Rodricus magnus regebat totam Walliam tempore suo. Post cujus mortem iij filii ejus, videlicet Merwynus Anaraud et Cadell diviserunt inter se totam Walliam in iij partes, Merthwin principatum Gwyneth, i. Northwalliam, Anaraud principatum Powysiae, Cadett principatum deheuparth, i. Sowthwalliam; unusquisque istorum cum posteris suis regebat partem suam ut Princeps post multos annos. Et postquam multi anni essent evoluti, istae duae partes, videlicet Powysia et Sowthwallia, perdiderunt nomen Principis sui et Principatus. Princeps vero Northwalliae reassumpsit nomen integrum tocius Principatus Walliae, quo gaudebat usque cum posteris suis usque ad Lewelinum Principem Wap gruff' Wap Ll Wap Jerwarth Droyndon, post cujus mortem nullum hucusque habuerunt Principem de genere suo sicut manifeste sequentibus declarabitur.

[Part III]

In the year of our lord 1170 Prince Owain ap Gruffydd of Powys, the lord of Cyfeiliog, founded the monastery of Strata Marcella of the Cistercian order, in which he himself now on the northern side next to the high altar lies buried, and this is his epitaph[*744].

Anno Domini Millesimo Centesimo lxx Owynus ap Gruff princeps Powysiae dominus de Keueliauc fundavit Monasterium de Strattamarcella, Cisterciensis Ordinis, in quo ipse jam prope summo altare quod parte boriali jacet sepultus, et hoc est ephitafium ejus.

> Alas here lies the cultivator of the church, the great Owain
> Attacker/Trampler of his enemies, who himself was begot from Gruffydd

> *Ecclesise cultor jacet hic heu major Owynus*
> *Hostibus insultor, genuit quem ipse Griffinus.*

The same year Archbishop Thomas Becket of Canterbury on the fourth calends of January in his cathedral seat, struck by a sword, departed to the Lord, in the [17th] year of the reign of King Henry the second since the conquest of England[*745], just as these verses declare.

[*744] Owain died in 1197, RBH, 181; Pen 79-80.
[*745] *Xvii* has likely been omitted from the text by the compiler.

In the year one thousand one hundred and seventy
Thomas the primate of the English came to grief by the sword[*746].

Eodem anno Thomas Beket Archiepiscopus Cantuariensis iiij. kal Januarii in basilica sedis suae gladio percussus migravit ad dominum. Anno regni regis Henrici secundi post Conquestum Angliae, sicut istea versus declarant:

> *Anno milleno Centeno septuageno*
> *Anglorum primas corruit ense Thomas.*

In the year of the Lord one thousand one hundred 86 on the ninth calends of August [24 July] the monastery of Aberconwy of the Cistercian order in the bishopric of Bangor was founded during the reign over England of the Lord Henry Fitz Empress Matilda in the 60th year of his reign.[*747]

Anno Domini Millesimo Centesimo lxxxvj. nono kalendas Augusti fundatum est Monasterium de Aberconwey Cisterciensis Ordinis in episcopatu Bang. regnante super Angliam domino Henrico filio Matildis imperatricis Anno regni ejus lx.

[Part IV]

Let it be known to all of the sons of the Holy Mother Church so much as in the present as in the future that I, [Llywelyn ap[*748]] Cynan, prince of North Wales, considering divine piety, for the health of my soul and of my ancestors, I give and concede in pure and perpetual alms to God, St Mary and the monks of Aberconwy, under the Cistercian order being servants of God, Gelliniog with all its appurtenances, Rhuddgaer with all its lands, *Stawenan* with its lands and all its purtenances, and the mill of Talybont. And I will to the same monks, so much in the present as in the future, all the prenamed lands with everything on the same appurtenances in perpetual alms that they may hold rightly and quietly, and freely in peace, fully, honestly and honourably, in the wood and on the plain in meadows and pastures, in waters and in mills, with all customary freedoms and free of all earthly service and secular exaction. Moreover in order that this my gift and concession remains valid perpetually this present charter is strengthened and reinforced by the impression of my seal. This is witnessed by Gwyn ab Ednowain, Teg ap Robert, Cadwgan ab Iorwerth, Hywel ab Idrys and many others. Dated at Menai Bridge (*Porthaethwy*) in the year from the incarnation of the lord, one thousand, 100, in the month of June[*749].

[*746] *MCLXXI. Anno xviiii Henrici II regis, Sanctus Thomas **archiepiscopus Cantuariae in basilica sedis suae** ob defensionem justitiae **gladio percussus**, feliciter **migravit ad Dominum iv kal. Januarii.***
"Annus millenus centus septuagenus
Primus** erat, primas cum **ruit ense Thomas". 'Annales Monasterii de Waverleia', *Annales Monastici*, ed. H.R. Luard [5 vols., 1864-9] II, 239.
[*747] The 32nd year of Henry II was actually 1186, the year in which Henry reached 53 years of age, he having been born in 1133. From this it can be seen that neither of these years were the source of the compiler's error.
[*748] There is an erasure at this point. In the margin Humphrey Wanley (21 March 1672 – 6 July 1726) has added *Lewelinus ap*. The original Register text would probably have been the same, but a later corrector probably removed this. The original would undoubtedly have been *Griffinus ap*, but for some reason the fifteenth century compiler of the Aberconwy Register wished this grant to have been made by a fictitious Llywelyn ap Cynan whom he inserts into the family genealogy as the father of Owain Gwynedd. The true genealogy is Owain ap Gruffydd ap Cynan and is attested by numerous sources.
[*749] This was possibly in June 1192, before King Reginald of Man complained that the monks of Aberconwy had appropriated his lands, 36. It was also on 15 June 1192 that Rhodri married Princess Rhunallt of Man, so this grant may have been in answer to Rhodri promising her land on Mon as dower. Alternatively, the date given may be correct, in which case Rhodri was chased from North Wales by June 1190.

Notum sit omnibus Sanctae Matris Ecclesise filiis tam presentibus quam futuris quod Ego [Lewelinus ap] Kynan filius, Northwalliae princeps, intuitu divinae pietatis, pro salute animae meae et antecessorum meorum, dedi et concessi in puram et perpetuam elemosinam Deo beatae Mariae et Monachis de Aberconwey, sub Ordine Cistercien Deo famulantibus, Kelliuioc cum omnibus pertinentiis suis, Rudgaer cum omnibus finibus suis, Stawenan cum finibus et omnibus pertinentiis suis, et molendinum de Talepont. Et volo ut idem monachi, tam presentes quam futuri, omnes prenominatas terras cum omnibus ad eas pertinentibus in perpetuam elemosinam possideant bene et quiete, et libere, in pace, plenarie, integre et honorifice, in bosco et plano, in pratis et pasturis, in aquis et molendinis, cum omnibus libertatibus solitis et liberis ab omni terreno servitio et exactione seculari. Ut autem haec mea donatio et concessio imperpetuum firma permaneat eam presentis cartae munimine et sigilli mei impressione roboravi. Hiis testibus, Owyn ap Eduywan, Teg ap Robert, Cadwen Jeweryth ffilio, Howelo Ydrys filio, et multis aliis. Datum apud Porthaethay Anno ab incamatione domini Millesimo. C. Mense Junii.

After that Llywelyn ap Cynan the principality of North Wales was ruled by Owain Gwynedd ap Gruffydd his son. Then Dafydd ab Owain ap Gruffydd[*750].

Post istum Lewelinum wap Kynan regebat Principatum Northwalliae Owynus Gwyneth ap Gruff' filius ejus. Deinde David ap Owen ap Gruff'.

[Part V]

In the island of Anglesey Ghornwy	£13 2s
Also Bodgedwydd	£3 6s 8d[*751]
Gelliniog	£10 16s 8d
Penmynydd	£4 13s 4d
Also the water mill in the manor of Ghornwy	10s
Also one tenement next to Beaumaris	5s
Also the big field[*752]	£2
Also Nanhwynain	£21 18s 4d
Also Cwm	£5
Also Nant Call	£2
Also Rhedynog Felen	£1 6s 8d
Also Arddau mountain	£13
Also Maenan	£9
Also Creuddyn	£1 13s 4d
Also a tenement in Bangor	6s 8d
Also Chester[*753]	6s 8d
Also a tenement in Conwy	
Also the windmill	

[*750] Here the compiler has the correct genealogy of Owain Gwynedd mixed up with the fictitious Llywelyn ap Cynan and in one sentence makes Llywelyn and Gruffydd the same person. It seems unbelievable that he did not realise that Owain Gwynedd and Owain ap Gruffydd were one and the same.

[*751] This figure is incorrectly given as £12 6s 8d in the printed version of the Register.

[*752] It has been suggested that this was the abbey's holding in Llanfaes, however there was a 'great field' in Gelliniog, *Records of Court of Augmentation Relating to Wales and Monmouthshire* ed. Lewis, EA & Davies, JC. [UWP, 1954], 7.

[*753] The mention of land at Chester would suggest a date after 20 November 1388, when Llanbeblig church was granted by Aberconwy to the Benedictine nuns of St Mary, Chester, *CPR 1385-89*, 530. Possibly the monks were granted lands in Chester in compensation.

Also the other water mill next to the monastery

Also the church of Eglwysbach	12 marks (£8)
Also the church of St Patrick [Cemaes]	5 marks (£3 6s 8d)
Also the church of Rhos	10 marks (£6 13s 4d)
Also the church of Conway	£3
Also the chapel of Dwgyfylchi	£2*754

[Total £113 4s]

[Part VI]

In Commote Mefenydd	£20
Also in Penardd commote	£20 20d exc'
Also in Cwmystwyth	£8
Also in Blaenaeron	£6
Also in Hafodwen	£6
Also in Anhuniog	£6
Also in Nant-bau	£8
Also in Cwmwdteuddwr	£6
Also in Aberdihonw with Cae'r Mynach?	£6 13s 4d
Also in Y Dwyarachen	£1 13s 4d
Also in Morfa Bychan	£4 13s
Also in Aber-miwl	£10 4d
Also in the church of Llangurig	£20
Also in the church of Pencarreg*755	£10

[£133 1s 8d]

---

*754 *In Insula de Anglesia Cowrnoylis*   *xiii li. ii s.*
Item Bobgedwid   *xii li. vi s. viii d.*
Kellyuiok   *x li. xvi. viii d.*
Penmynyd   *iiii li xiii s iiiid*
Item Molendinum aquaticum in manerio de Cowrnylis x s
Item unum tenement iuxta Bellum Moriscum   *v s*
Item y kae mawr   *ii li*
Item Nanthoynayn   *xxi li xviii s iiiid*
Item Come   *v li*
Item Nankall'   *ii li*
Item Redinoc Velyn   *i li vi s viii d*
Item Arthe mynethe   *xiii li*
Item Maynan   *ix li*
Item Creuthyn   *i li xiii s iiiid*
Item tenement in Bangor   *vi s viiid*
Item in Cestr'   *vi s viiid*
Item tenement in Conway
Item molendinum ventriticum: Item al' molendinum aquaticum juxta monasterium
Item ecclesia de Vagh   *xii m*
Item ecclesia Sancti Patricii   *v m*
Item ecclesia de Rose   *x m*
Item ecclesia de Conway   *iii li*
Item capella de y gyvichy   *ii li*

*755 Pencarrog church, Carmarthenshire, was apparently granted to Strata Florida by King Richard II in memory of his father, the Black Prince. Therefore this list must date to after 1376.

Pennardd	28 troc'
Mefenydd	92 troc'
Blaenaeron	88 troc'
Hafodwen	232 troc'
Anhuniog	48 troc'
Morfa Mawr	192 troc'
Morfa Bychan	12 troc'
Y Dwyarachen	five nobles (coins)
Cwmteuddwr	£6[*756]

[Part VII]

In the year of our Lord one thousand one hundred 90, Richard called the heart of a lion was king reigning over England, on 1 January, which is the day of the Circumcision of the Lord, Llywelyn ab Iorwerth Drwyndwn strangled and killed his prince, Dafydd ab Owain, at Aber[*757], and thus he raised himself over the principality of all North Wales, also he brought together the diverse properties of the abbot and monks of the abbey of Aberconwy with its liberties as written below. John, the son of Henry II the illustrious king of England, which John was certainly crowned king of England in the year of our lord one thousand, one hundred and ninety nine at Westminster, he led a well equipped army into Wales against Llywelyn ab Iorwerth Drwyndwn, all the way to Snowdon, where Llywelyn in person made peace with the said king of England and homage was done to him and hostages given and many lands with ten thousand cows, the king founded many castles there and returned into England[*758].

Anno domini millesimo centesimo lxxxx, Regnante Ricardo vocato cor de lyon rege super Angliam, primo die Januarii, hoc est die Circumsisionis domini, Lewelinus ap Jerwarth Droyndun David ap Owen principem suum suffocavit et occidit apud Aber, et sic Principatum tocius Northwalliae super se assumpsit, qui et diversas possessiones contulit Abbati et

---

[*756] *In Comot Mevenith*   *xx li*
Item in comot Pennarth   *xx li xxd exc;*
Item in Cu'wstwith   *viii li*
Item in Blaen ayron   *vi li*
Item in Havodwen   *vi li*
Item in Ruhrniok   *vi li*
Item in Nantvay   *viii li*
Item in Comottewthur   *vi li*
Item in Aberdehonwy cum Ken   *vi li xiiis iiiid*
Item Dywarthen   *xxxiii s iiiid*
Item Morua Vichan   *iiii li xiii s*
Item Aber Mywl'   *x li iiiid*
Item ecclesia de Llangirak   *xx li*
Item ecclesia de Pencarrek   *x li*

Pennarth   *28 troc'*
Mevenith   *92 troc'*
Blaen Ayron   *88 troc'*
Havodwen   *232 troc'*
Hanhvniok   *48 troc'*
Morva Mawr   *192 troc'*
Morva Vychan   *12 troc'*
Y dewarchen   *quinque nobl'*
Commot Devddor   *vi li*

[*757] The expulsion of Dafydd ab Owain from Gwynedd and his alleged death in England is examined above p.101.

[*758] The last sentence may have come from 'Annales de Theokesberia', *Annales Monastici*, ed. H.R. Luard [5 vols., 1864-9] I, 60, *Debellata [desellata] Norwallia per Johannem regem Angliae, princeps ejus ewelinus **cum rege pacificatur, datis obsidibus et terris multis cum decima uaccarum** et aliis monilibus multis.*

Monachis Monasterii de Aberconwey cum libertatibus subscriptis. Johannes filius Henrici secundi illustris regis Angliae, qui quidem Johannes Anno domini Millesimo Centesimo Nonagesimo ix. apud Westm' coronatus erat in regem Angliae, duxit copiosum exercitum in Walliam contra Lewellinum ap Jerwarth Droyndun usque ad Snowdon, ubi ipse Lewellinus cum dicto rege Angliae pacificatur, factoque ei homagio et datis obsidibus, et terris multis, cum decem milibus vaccis, rex illuc Castella plura fundavit, et in Angliam reversus est.

[Part VIII]

John by the grace of God king of England, lord of Ireland, duke of Normandy and count of Anjou, greets his justices, sheriffs and all his bailiffs in England and Wales and all his lands and sea ports, greetings[*759]. Know that we have received into [our] hand and protection our abbey of Aberconwy and the monks of the Cistercian order there serving god, and all their things and their possessions. And for that reason we order that that abbey and the monks serving the same and all their things and possessions and all which they consider the same, you will preserve and maintain as if it were our own, nor will you allow any of the same to be molested or injured or troubled by others. And they are to have a secure peace, and they may be quit of tholoni, passio, paage and pontage and all custom which pertains to us through all our land, and such thenceforth that they may have quittance from all which themselves or their households or servants are able to assure to be their own possessions, like other monks of the Cistercian order have. And we forbid lest anyone to the same above the truth of this may presume to inflict injury or annoyance, above our just deed, just as the charter of King Henry our father reasonably testifies. Witnessed by Peter Pratellis, Ingram Pratellis (bef.1175-1226/9), Peter Stokes (d.bef Aug 1206). Dated by the hand of the archdeacon of Wells[*760] at Montfort-sur-Risle, the first day of April in the third [year] of our reign. [1 April 1202]

Johannes Dei gratia Rex Angliae Dominus Hiberniae Dux Normanniae et Comes Andegaviee, Justiciariis, Vicecomitibus, et omnibus Ballivis suis Angliae et Walliae, et totius terrae suae, et Portuum Maris, salutem. Sciatis quod suscepimus in manum et protectionem nostram Abbatiam de Aberconwey, et Monachos Ordinis Cisterciensis ibidem Deo servientes, et omnes res et possessiones suas. Et ideo precipimus quod Abbatiam illam et monachos in eadem servientes, et omnes res et possessiones suas, et omnia quae ad eos spectant, custodiatis et manuteneatis sicut nostra propria, ne quis eis de aliquo molestiam vel injuriam aut gravamen faciat. Et firmam pacem habeant, et quieti sint de tholonio, et passio, et paagio, et pontagio, et omni consuetudine quae ad nos pertinent per totam terram nostram, et talem inde quietantiam habeant de omnibus quae ipsi vel famuli et servientes sui poterunt assecurare, sua esse propria, qualem alii monachi habent de Ordine Cisterciensi. Et prohibemus ne quis eis super hoc veracionem vel injuriam aut gravamen inferre presumat, super foros facturam nostram, sicut Carta Henrici Regis patris nostri rationabiliter testatur.
Teste Petro de Pratellis. Engelranum de pratellis, Petro de Stokys. Datum per manum Archidiaconi Wellen'. apud Mountford, primo die Aprilis Anno regni nostri tercii.

[*759] This was certainly a valid form of charter and is similar to the one issued by the king on 31 May 1203. See Appendix 13 for more of John's contemporary charters.
[*760] Presumably this was Simon Fitz Robert Whatley who became archdeacon of Wells by 15 June 1198 and was elected bishop of Chichester immediately before 9 April 1204.

[Part IX]

In the year of the lord one thousand 206, Llywelyn ab Iorwerth Drwyndwn, prince of North wales, took to wife the Lady Isabella[*761], daughter of John, the illustrious king of England. This Llywelyn was buried in the monastery of Aberconwy, of the Cistercian order, in the presence of the high altar, of which he enlarged the liberties and gave great possessions.

In the year of the Lord one thousand 230, Llywelyn prince of North Wales greatly harassed all Wales outside his marches, thus the churches he spared with respect[*762]. Against whom King Henry of England advanced with a great army and strengthened Maud's Castle, yet he left many in that place who might guard it, as many knights as sergeants, he burned all the neighbouring regions he was able to[*763]. In the year of the lord one thousand 240 and one, King Henry of England, the third from the Conquest, attacked parts of the Marches with his army against Dafydd ap Llywelyn, but Dafydd took himself into the interior regions. And the king of England, with a great army pursued him towards Snowdon. When Dafydd saw this, he submitted himself and all his possessions to the king of England and handed over as security his brother Gruffydd ap Llywelyn whom the king imprisoned in London, but Gruffydd himself [after] a few days in the Tower of London broke his neck[*764].

Anno domini Millesimo .CC.vi. Lewellinus ap Jerwarth Droyndun princeps Northwalliae Dominam Isabellam filiam Johannis Regis Anglie illustris duxit in uxorem. Iste Lewellinus sepultus est in Monasterio de Aberconwey Cisterciensis Ordinis coram summo altare; cui largas libertates et amplas possessiones dedit. Anno domini Millesimo .CC.xxx. Lewellinus Princeps Northwallie multum infestavit totam Walliam extra fines suos, ita quod ecclesiis parceret. Contra quem Henricus rex Angliae cum grande exercitu ivit et firmavit Castrum Maud. relictis tamen illic qui custodirent illud multis, tam militibus quam servientibus, omnes finitimas partes quas potuit accendit. Anno domini Millesimo .CC.xl. primo. Henricus tertius a Conquestu Rex Angliae adivit partes Marchiee cum exercitu suo contra David ap Ll. sed David misit se in interiora loca. Et rex Angliae cum exercitu magno persecutus est eum versus Snowdon. Quod videns David, subjecit se regi Angliae et omnia sua, et reddit ei in obsidem Griffinum ap Ll fratrem suum quem Rex incarceravit London, sed ipse Griffinus paucos dies in turre Londoniarum collum suum rupit.

[*761] The compiler must have mis expanded his I to Isabella instead of Joan. 'Annales Prioratus de Wigornia', *Annales Monastici*, ed. H.R. Luard [5 vols., 1864-9] IV, 394, also misdates this event, stating that it occurred after Ascension in 1206 - *Lewelinus desponsavit filiam regis Anglie post Ascensionem.* This comment obviously wasn't copied directly by Aberconwy, but may be the source of the misdating of the event.

[*762] 'Annales de Theokesberia', *Annales Monastici*, ed. H.R. Luard [5 vols., 1864-9] I, 79, dates this event to the right year, 1231. **Lewelinus princeps Norwalliae multum infestavit totam Walliam extra fines suos, ita quod neque ecclesiis parceret, contra quem** *dominus* **Henricus rex** *obviam* **ivit cum** *magno* **exercitu**, *circa festum beatae mariae Magdalenae*, **et firmavit castellum Maud.**

[*763] 'Annales de Theokesberia', *Annales Monastici*, ed. H.R. Luard [5 vols., 1864-9] I, 80; *Lewleinus princeps Norwalliae circa festum Sancti Michaelis, rege recedente et aliis magnatibus angliae a munitione castelli Maud,* **relictis illic tamen qui custodirent illud multis tam militibus quam servientibus, omnes finitimas partes quas potuit** *incedit atque praedavit, ita ut prior Leministre propter vexationem ejus vitandam, pacem compulsus est facere cum eo, ad magnam pecuniae quantitatem.* 'Annales Prioratus de Wigornia', *Annales Monastici*, ed. H.R. Luard [5 vols., 1864-9] IV, 422, clearly put the slaughters done down to the actions of Llywelyn. Obviously this was not used as a source by Aberconwy for this era.

[*764] 'Annales de Theokesberia', *Annales Monastici*, ed. H.R. Luard [5 vols., 1864-9] I, 120: *Dominus Henricus rex Angliae veniens apud Salopesburiam, cum orta esset discordia inter ipsum et Walenses, David filius Leweleni venit circa festum Sancti Bartholomaei ad eundem locum, et satisfecit domino regi, tradens ei fratrem suum Grifinum, qui ad Londoniam ductus incarceratur.*
'Annales de Theokesberia', *Annales Monastici*, ed. H.R. Luard [5 vols., 1864-9] I, 133: *Griffinus filius Lewelini cadens de turri Lundoniae interiit.*

[Part X]

In the year of the Lord one thousand 277 war arose between the Lord King Edward of England, ['the first' probably missed out] after the conquest of England, called Longshanks, and the Welsh. Indeed in which war the king occupied the island of Anglesey. And Llywelyn ap Gruffydd ap Llywelyn ab Iorwerth Drwyndwn the prince of North Wales, at length humbly returned himself to the king's peace, and came afterwards to the London parliament of the said king, and did homage to the king, as well as holding the greatest banquet there[*765].

Anno domini Millesimo .CC.lxxvii. orta est gwerra inter dominum Edwardum Regem Angliee post conquestum Angliae dictura Longescankes et Wallenses. In qua quidem gwerra rex insulam de Anglesey cepit. Et Lewellinus ap Gruffith ap Ll ap Jerwarth Droindun Princeps Northwalliae tandem ad pacem regis se humiliter reddit, et ad Parliamentum dicti Regis London postea venit et Homagium fecit Regi, atque convivium ibidem permaximum tenuit.

In the year of the Lord one thousand 278, Llywelyn ap Gruffydd, prince of North Wales, in the presence of the Lord Edward called Longshanks, king of England, as well as the lady queen and also Edmund earl of Cornwall and many others who were magnates of the king of England, took to wife at Worcester Eleanor the daughter of Simon Montfort, earl of Leicester and kinswoman of the said king[*766]. Likewise in the same year, during the summer, that is at the feast called St Peter in Chains, the statutes of Gloucester were composed in the castle of the same town.

Anno domini Millesimo .CC.lxxviij. Lewellinus ap Gruffud Princeps Northwalliae, presente domino Edwardo vocato Longescankes Rege Angliae, atque domina regina, necnon Edmundo comite Cornubise et aliis quam pluribus regni Angliae magnatibus, Alienoram filiam Simonis Montis fortis comitis Leycestriae et dicti Regis consangwineam apud Wygorniam duxit in uxorem. Eodem quoque anno, tempore aestivo, videlicet in festo Sancti Petri quod dicitur ad vincula, facta sunt statuta Gloverniae in Castro ejusdem villae.

In the year of the Lord one thousand 279, an unexpected war began in Wales. For Dafydd ap Gruffydd the brother of Llywelyn prince of Wales on the eleventh calends of April [22 March], which was Palm Sunday, captured Roger Clifford and killed many others, and besieged the castles of Flint and Rhuddlan[*767]. Previously to this, Dafydd was one of the most intimate friends of the Lord King Edward.

Anno domini Millesimo .CC.lxxix. Orta est gwerra inopinata in Wallia. Nam David ap Gruffud frater Lewelini principis Walliae, undecimo kall' Aprilis qui tunc erat dies Palmarum,

---

[*765] All this appears in much greater detail in 'Annales Prioratus de Wigornia', *Annales Monastici*, ed. H.R. Luard [5 vols., 1864-9] IV, 472-3.

[*766] 'Annales Prioratus de Wigornia', *Annales Monastici*, ed. H.R. Luard [5 vols., 1864-9] IV, 476, **Princeps Walliae Leolinus duxit in uxorem A. filiam Symonis Montis Fortis**, *quondam* **comitis Leycestriae**, *et sororis bonae memoriae regis henrici tertii*. Similarly, 'Annales Monasterii de Waverleia', *Annales Monastici*, ed. H.R. Luard [5 vols., 1864-9] II, 389: **Princeps Walliae Leulinus duxit in uxorem Alienoram, filiam Simonis de Monteforti**, *quodam* **comitis Leycestriae**.

[*767] 'Annales Prioratus de Wigornia', *Annales Monastici*, ed. H.R. Luard [5 vols., 1864-9] IV, 481: *undecimo kal. Aprilis David frater Lewelini venit cum multis subito apud Haworthin, et cepit Rogerum de Clifford vivum, et milites ejus occidit, et omnes Anglicos quos capere potuit*. 'Annales Prioratus de Wigornia', *Annales Monastici*, ed. H.R. Luard [5 vols., 1864-9] IV 485: 1283 ...Prince Llywelyn of Wales and Dafydd his brother with a great army surrounded the castles of Rhuddlan and Flint and other castles of the king which they entered they destroyed... *MCCLXXXIII. Qui est annus regni Edwardi decimi, intempesta noctis hora dominicae in Ramis Palmarum, princeps Walliae Leulinus et David frater ejus cum magno exercitu castra de Rothelaunde et de Flint circumdederunt, alique castra regis ad quae ingressum habere poterant destruentes....*

Rogerum Clifford cepit, et caeteros quamplures interfecit, et Castrum de Flynt et Ruthland obsedit. Iste David domino Regi Edwardo ante hoc factum specialissimus fuit.

In the year of our Lord one thousand 282, Lord Edward Longshanks, king of England, led an army into Wales and vigorously drove off the besiegers of Flint castle, and remained there with his men for some time.

Anno domini Millesimo .CC.lxxxij. Dominus Edwardus Longescankes Rex Angliae duxit exercitum in Walliam et obsessores castrorum de Flynt virihter ammovit, et ipse ibidem cum suis aliquamdiu permansit.

In the year of the Lord one thousand 282, Llywelyn ap Gruffydd ap Llywelyn ab Iorwerth Drwyndwn, prince of North Wales, on the third ides of September[*768] [11 September], at night, was captured and killed by the conceived deceit of Edmund Mortimer and moreover he was beheaded at Builth[*769]. Whose head was sent to London and affixed over the Tower. Consequently the Welsh were frightened and disturbed beyond measure at the aforesaid prince's death, they delivered to the Lord Edward, king of England, all the castles of North Wales together with a precious portion of the cross of the Lord, truly of Wales, called the Cross of Naid with many other noted relics[*770]. They also handed over the crown of the famous Arthur, once king of Britain, and so the glory of Wales and of the Welsh rulers and magnates was taken to England[*771].

Anno domini Millesimo .CC.lxxxij. Lewellinus ap Gruffud ap Ll ap Jerwarth Droyndun Princeps Northwal tercio idus Septembris, nocte, per Eadmundum de Mortuo mari, imaginata fraude, captus et interfectus, atque decollatus est apud Beelte. Cujus caput Londonias fuit missum, et super turrem affixum. Igitur Wallenses territi sunt et turbati ultra modum de morte praedicti Principis, reddiderunt domino Edwardo Regi Angliae omnia Castra Northwalliae, una cum portiuncula pretiosse Crucis Dominicae, Cambriae vero, dicta Cros de Neth', cum multis aliis famosis rehquiis. Reddiderunt etiam Coronam famosissimi Arthuri quondam regis Britanniae; et sic gloria Walliae et etiam Wallencium regibus et magnatibus Angliae translata est.

[*768] This is surely an error for 3rd ides of December [11 December], the oft reported, but erroneous day of Llywelyn's killing, Remfry, PM. *The Killing of Prince Llywelyn of Wales, 10 December 1282* [Ceidio, 2014]. Quite obviously the Aberconwy compiler is here plagiarizing Hailes, even down to the getting the month wrong.

[*769] 'Annales Prioratus de Wigornia', *Annales Monastici*, ed. H.R. Luard [5 vols., 1864-9] IV, 484-5: **Tertio idus** *Decembris* **Edmundus de Mortuomari** *nondum miles, cum fratribus suis militibus Rogero, Willelmo, et Galfrido et aliis amicis quorum nomina novit Deus, et Robertus de Mortuomari, nepos ejus, scilicet dominus castelli Ricardi, leulinum principem Walliae...* leaf ends here without the verb and begins on the next page Nono Kal. Junii about a totally different matter.

[*770] 'Annales Prioratus de Wigornia', *Annales Monastici*, ed. H.R. Luard [5 vols., 1864-9] IV, 486: after the death of Llywelyn, *Wallenses vero pro morte sui principis* **territi et turbati**, **regi Angliae omnia castra de** *Snoudone reddiderunt*. Worcs 489 after the execution of Dafydd has: *Portio Dominicae crucis magna, quae lingua Wallensium dicebatur Croizneth, domino Edwardo regi Angliae cum multis famosis reliquiis tradebatur.*

[*771] 'Annales Prioratus de Wigornia', *Annales Monastici*, ed. H.R. Luard [5 vols., 1864-9] IV, 589, again after execution of Dafydd, **Corona** *quondam* **famosi regis Britonum** *Arturi regi Angliae cum aliis jocalibus reddebatur.* **Sic ad Anglicos gloria Wallensium**, *invite Anglorum legibus subditorum, per Dei providentiam* **est translata**. Similarly in Rishanger the first comments on the Cross of Naid, p.104, are quite clearly different from the Aberconwy version, but the second entry, p.107, is much nearer. Chronica Rishanger, 107, **Corona etiam quondam famosi regis Britonum, Arthuri**, *Regi Angliae, cum aliis jocalibus*, **reddebatur. Et sic ad Anglos gloria Wallensium**, *incivem Anglorum legibus subditorum, per Dei providentiam*, **est translata**. Quite possibly the latter entry and Aberconwy shared a common exemplar.

In the next year, that is the year of our Lord one thousand 283, Dafydd ap Gruffydd, the brother of the same Prince Llywelyn, was captured about the nativity of St John the Baptist and was taken to Rhuddlan where he was held by a prison guard until the feast of the Blessed Michael the archangel. And thus from Rhuddlan he was taken to Amwythig, that is Shrewsbury. There, by the judgment of the barons of England, he was first dragged by horses to the gibbet; next he was hanged; thirdly he was beheaded while half alive because he had held the king's peace in contempt; fourthly he was disembowelled and his entrails burned because he had been an enemy of the Catholic faith and of the church besides being a destroyer of justice; fifthly his body was divided into four parts and hung up through the four parts of the kingdom of England because he had disturbed the peace of the kingdom; sixthly his head was sent to London and was fixed above the Tower beside the head of his brother Llywelyn, so that other traitors would be deterred by his example, and in witness that the king is just and an extirpator of traitors[*772]. This sentence was made on the fifth nones of October [3 October] and on the same day was fully carried out. And so the said Edward Longshanks, king of England, wishing to strengthen Wales greatly as was his habit, moved the abbey of Aberconwy of the Cistercian order, fashioned near to the entrance to Snowdon, and built a castle and town there, truly the monks were given another site called Maenan and great payments for new buildings: and besides he conceded all the possessions that they had previously held and also those that they might henceforward acquire, and granted unparalleled liberties to them and their successors. Likewise the same year, the above named king built Caernarfon castle.

In anno sequenti, videlicet Anno domini Millesimo .CC.lxxxiij. David ap Gruff' frater ejusdem Lewellini Principis, circa Nativitatem Sancti Johannis Baptistse capitur, et apud Ruthland ducitur, ubi carcerali custodia detinebatur usque ad festum Beati Michaelis Archangeli. Et sic de Ruthlande usque Amoythie id est Salopiam perducitur, ibique judicio Baronum Angliae primo usque ad patibulum equis trahitur, secundo suspenditur, tertio semivivus decollatur, quia pacis Regis erat contemptor, quarto evisceratur et viscera ejus concremantur quia Catholicae fidei et Ecclesise inimicus ac Justorum interfector, quinto corpus ejus in quatuor partes dividitur et per quatuor partes regni Angliae suspenditur quia pacis regni erat perturbator, sexto caput ejus London mittitur atque super turrem juxta caput Lewellini fratris sui defigitur, ut ejus exemplo caeteri proditores terreantur et in signum quod Rex justus est et proditorum extirpator. Hoc judicium quinto nonas Octobris factum fuit, et eodem die plene executum. Volens itaque Edwardus dictus longescankes rex Angliae Walliam plus solito firmare, Abbathiam de Abberconwey Cisterciensis Ordinis juxta introitum Snowdon factam ammovit, et castrum et villam ibi construxit, Monachis vero situm alterum videlicet Maynan et expensas largas ad nova edificia dedit: ac omnes possessiones quas prius habuerunt et imposterum adquirere possent concessit, et libertates inauditas eis et successoribus eorum concessit. Eodem quoque Anno Rex prenominatus construxit Castrum de Karnarvon.

[*772] 'Annales Prioratus de Wigornia', *Annales Monastici*, ed. H.R. Luard [5 vols., 1864-9] IV, 488-9, has the execution of Dafydd after his capture in much less detail as too does *Chronica, ascribed to William Rishanger, a monk of St. Albans*, ed. H.T. Riley [1865], 104.

[Part XI]

Edward by grace of God king of England and France, lord of Ireland and duke of Aquitaine etc*773. Know that we for the health of our soul and the souls of our predecessors and our heirs of the kingdom of England, concede for ourselves and our heirs, beloved to us in Christ, to the abbot and convent of Maenan the old church of Aberconwy which convent they first had and held of others, which they may have and hold to themselves and their successors those things pertaining to the parish for their very own uses for ever, with tithes and offerings and other things for that church which pertained by right to the parish, on condition however that they themselves through a priest or other church ministers [keep in] the same church a suitable reputable Welsh chaplain on account of the difference of language. Hence we wish and firmly order, for us and our heirs, that the aforesaid abbey and convent and their successors have and hold forever the aforesaid church of Aberconwy which the convent first had and held from others, [that] they may have and hold so much from us for their very own parochial uses with all just patronage to themselves and their successors in perpetual alms, with all rights and possessions and other things pertaining to the aforesaid parochial church observing wherever by title as it may be judged, whether within the walls or without, with all tithes, all lands and seas from either side of the Conwy to the before mentioned church of Aberconwy as observed from antiquity. So nevertheless that etc, this witnessed by the venerable father Bishop Robert of Bath and Wells, Earl Henry Lacy of Lincoln (1251-1311), Earl Richard Burgh of Ulster (bef.1271-1326) etc and dated at Caernarfon the 16th day of July in the [12th*774] year of our reign.

Edwardus Dei gracia Rex Angliae et Franciae, Dominus Hiberniae et Dux Aquitaniae, &c. Sciatis nos pro salute animae nostrae et animabus antecessorum nostrorum et heredum nostrorum regni Angliae, concessisse pro nobis et heredibus nostris dilectis nobis in Christo Abbati et Conventui de Maynan veterem Ecclesiam de Abberconwey quam prius habuerunt et tenuerunt conventualem de ceetero habeant et teneant parochialem sibi et successoribus in proprios usus imperpetuum, cum decimis et oblacionibus et aliis ad Ecclesiam illam de jure parochiali pertinentibus, ita tamen quod ipsi eidem Ecclesiae per vicarium et alios Ecclesiee ministros ydoneos capellanum honestum Wallensem propter ydeomatum diversitatem. Quare volumus et firmiter precipimus, pro nobis et heredibus nostris, quod praedicti Abbas et Conventus et successores sui imperpetuum habeant et teneant praedictam Ecclesiam de Abberconwey quam prius conventualem habuerunt et tenuerunt de caetero habeant et teneant quantum in nobis est in proprios usus parochialem cum omni jure patronatus sibi et successoribus suis in perpetuam elemosinam, cum omnibus juribus et possessionibus et rebus allis ad praedictam Ecclesiam parochialem spectan[tibus] quocumque nomine censeatur, tam infra muros quam extra, cum omnibus decimationibus omnium terrarum et maris ex utraque de Conwey ad prefatam Ecclesiam de Aberconwey spectantibus ab antiquo.
Ita tamen quod, &c. Hiis testibus, venerabili patre Roberto Bathon et Wellen Episcopo, Henrico de Laci Comite Lincoln, Ricardo Burg Comite Ulton, &c. Dat. apud Carn'. xvj die Julij Anno regni nostri.

---

*773 This title was never used by Edward I, so obviously this composition dates to after 1340 when the title King of England and France and lord of Ireland was used (1340-97). This title, with various variations, remained in use until 1521. The title generally used from 1259 to 1340 was, *Rex Angliae, Dominus Hiberniae et Dux Aquitaniae* - King of England, lord of Ireland and duke of Aquitaine.
*774 This has obviously been omitted by the compiler.

Edward by grace of God king of England, lord of Ireland, duke of Aquitaine, to all men that these present letters might reach, greetings[*775]. Know that with the venerable father Einion, bishop of St Asaph, for himself and his successors at our insistence has given and concedes with our approval in Christ, to the abbey and convent of Aberconwy and their successors, because indeed the monastery now is sited at Maenan, the advowson of the church of Eglwysbach which pertains to the aforementioned bishop, just as in the writing of the said abbey and convent henceforth made fully secured. Wishing to compensate the said bishop for that donation, we give and concede to the same the advowson of the church of Rhuddlan, to be held by himself and his successors in perpetuity, without complaint from us or our heirs or successors to us what so ever. Therefore, still because if we or our heirs or successors whatsoever lay hands upon the advowson of the aforesaid church of Rhuddlan from the bishop himself or his successors or by chance retract anything, it is permitted for the aforesaid bishop and his successors to be entirely regained of the advowson of the aforesaid church of Eglwysbach from the aforesaid abbot and convent. In this business the testimony of these our letters which we have made openly. Witnessed by me at Aberconwy the tenth day of October in the twelfth year of our reign [1284].

Edwardus Dei gratia Rex Angliae, Dominus Hybemiae, Dux Aquitaniae, Omnibus ad quos praesentes literae pervenerint Salutem. Sciatis quod cum venerabilis pater Anianus, Assaven' episcopus, pro se et successoribus suis ad instantiam nostram dederit et concesserit dilectis nobis in Christo Abbati et Conventui Monasterii de Aberconwey et eorum successoribus, quod quidem Monasterium nunc est situm Maynan, Advocationem Ecclesise de Eglwyswath quae ad praefatum Episcopum pertinuit, prout in scriptis dictis Abbati et Conventui inde confecto plenius continetur. Nos dicto episcopo donationem illam compensare volentes, dedimus et concessimus eidem advocationem Ecclesiee de Ruthlande, habendam sibi et successoribus suis imperpetuum, absque reclamatione nostri vel heredum aut successorum nostrorum quorumcumque. Ita tamen quod si nos vel heredes aut successores nostros quoscumque contingat advocationem preedictae Ecclesiae de Ruthlande ab ipso episcopo vel successoribus suis casu aliquo retractare, licet praefat' Episcopo et successoribus suis Advocationem praedictse Ecclesiae de Eglwys Wath a praefat' Abb et Conventu totaliter revocare. In cujus rei testimonium has litteras nostras fieri fecimus patentes. Teste meipso apud Aberconwey decimo die Octobris Anno regni nostri duodecimo.

[*775] Once more the king's titles are given incorrectly - see the above charter.

Edward by grace of God king of England etc. Know that in recompense for one messuage and one small parcel of land in Penlassok which Tewdwr ap Garwette surrendered into our hands peacefully for himself and his heirs for ever, and which our beloved in Christ abbot and convent of Aberconwy, which monastery at Maenan we founded, in free and pure alms we bestowed, we give and concede to the aforementioned Tewdwr ten shillings of land with purtenances in Creuddyn, to have and to hold to himself and his heirs, of us and our heirs in perpetuity, paying from that place the services owed and accustomed. About which business this testimony. (usually translated as 'In testimony whereof').

Edwardus Dei gracia Rex Angliae &c. Sciatis quod in recompensationem unius mesuagii et unius particulae terrae in Penlassok quae Tuderius ap Garwette in manus nostras reddidit quiete de se et heredibus suis imperpetuum, et quae dilectis nobis in Christo Abbati et Conventui de Abberconwey, quarum Monasterium apud Maynan fundamus, in liberam et puram elemosinam contulimus, dedimus et concessimus prefato Tudero decem solidat terrae cum pertinen' in Crethyn, habend et tenend sibi et heredibus suis de nobis et heredibus nostris imperpetuum, faciend inde servitia debita et consueta. In cujus rei testimonium.

[Part XII]

Among first in the fields of Dafydd? ap Tudor Taylor	5 virgates
Also in Cefncelynnog	4 virgates
Also in Bryn y Fran (SH.811702)	3 virgates
Also in the field of Gruffydd ap Robin	1½ virgates
Also in the same place where the house of Lord David[*776] formerly was	2½ virgates
Also in Bwlchwern Hir (SH.820743)	4 virgates
Also in *ll'etir Clochyth i bren y gofe*	2 virgates
Also in Dyffryn (SH.807695) between the lands of Gruffydd ap Robin and the lands of Dafydd ap Tona and this is Abbuttan' above *gweirgledd y thwaley*	2 virgates.
Also for the same lands between the land of Hugh Conway[*777] and the land of Gruffydd Gethyn	2 virgates
Also the other small parcel situated towards/against the same meadow between Llywelyn ab Ieuan ab Egn' and *Erwr groes*	2 virgates
Also in the place where there was once a tithe-barn for grain in Llindir (SH.825715)	1 virgate
Also between Gruffydd ap Robin and Dafydd Gethyn in the wood	2 virgates
Also at Pennant (SH.816673) from the tenement of John ab Ieuan ap Hywel	7 virgates
Also between the lands of Gruffydd ap Robin and Dafydd ap Tudwr Taylor in Cefncelynnog	1½ virgates
	[39½ virgates]

In primis in campis dd' ap Tud Taylor	*v ug'*
Item in Kevynkelynnocke	*iiii ug*

[*776] Was this the David Winchcombeb the abbot installed in 1482, in which case this may have been Maenan manor house.
[*777] Hugh Conway was lord of Rhuddlan on 14 May 1488, *CPR 1485-94*, 226. The Conway's ancestors, the Crevecours held land at Penmaen Rhos SH.880783 and Llysfaen (SH.887772) in the thirteenth century, *Registrum epistolarum Fratris Johannis Peckham*, ed. C.T. Martin [3 vols., 1882-5] II, 459. These places were only 7 miles from Eglwysbach in Maenan.

Item in Bryn y vrane   *iii ug*

It in campo Gruff ap Robyn   *1 vg & di.*

Item in illo loco ubi domus dompni Dauid olim erat   *2 ug & di.*

Item in Bulth y gerwyn   *iiii ug.*

Item in ll'etir Clochyth i bren y gofe   *ii vg*

Item in diffren inter terras Gruff' ap Robyn et terras Dauid ap Tona,
*   et hoc est abbuttan' super gweirgledd y thwaley*   *ii vg*

Item per easdem terras inter terram Hvgonis Conwey
*   et terram Gruffini Gethyn*   *2 vg*

Item alia parcella jacens versus eundem pratum inter
*   Lewelinum ap Jeun' ap Egn' et Erwr' groes*   *ii vg.*

Item in loco ubi erat olim horrium pro granis in llemdire   *i vg*

Item inter Gruff' ap Robyn et David Gethyn in silva   *ii virg*

Item apud Pennant ad tenementum Johannis ap Jeun' ap Howel   *vii vig*

Item inter terras Gruff' ap Robyn et David ap Tuder taylor
*   in Keuynkelynnocke*   *i vg et dim.*

[Part XIII]

The abbey and convent were founded, in the reply to the request of the lord prince of Wales from what warrant they claimed to have sok and sak, toll and them, *infangentheff et utfangentheff, homsokenne, Gryuthbruch, Blodwyte, ffyttewyte, fferewyth, hongewyth, Leirwyth, fflemenfrith*, and to be quit of murder, brigandage, *fforstall', horedel', horest*, within time and without, in all regions and in all lawsuits which they are actually able to bring, and of all misdeeds. And that they themselves and all their men may be free from all *theloneo*, passage, paage, pontage, scutage and gildage and all aids by kings, sheriffs and all their ministers, and of hideage, carucateage, danegeld and horngled and of armies, scutages, tallages, x3, assizes and assarts, of wasting the woods, carrying timber, carrying arms, carrying treasure, x2, scotall of the king, of perquisites, of the hundred, of the Wapentake, placita and querel, ward duty, ward penny, and of works on castles, parks, bridges and enclosures, and of all carriage, summages, arrerages, passages, wallage, building the houses of the princes, and of every sort of work, except for those which are of their woods for the works aforesaid or for anything else that they might hold, either any of their grain or their men which may be taken towards munition for the castles, and also that all of their tenements, all the same in wood as in plain, may be deforested and outside all rule of the forests. And also the same abbot and monks, their men or their servants are to be free and quit of all customs in every market and on all market days, and in all passage of sea ports and of the sea and through all lands in which the Lord Edward king of England holds power, 23rd day of the month of October in his reign 12th, to them he was able to give [this] liberty, and also in all territories of the lord prince. And each [and] every market of his and his men may be similarly in the aforesaid places quit from all customs and any ships of the same abbot and monks may have free transit through all the aforesaid realm without any exaction or custom. And that the same abbot and monks may be free and quit of all pasturage and bridge work by men, horses, dogs and birds and they are not to be compelled to require to feed the lord prince himself or his ministers or other any such laymen, unless by their spontaneous desire; and concerning any elections, depositions, or resignations of the abbot, in the time of vacancy or other time, the lord prince nor his ministers nor other laymen will admit none, but all [will be done] in the said abbey through religious ordination according to rule and discussion.

Abbas et Conventus fundati fuerunt ad respondendum domino principi Walliae de placito quo war' clamant habere sok et sak, tol et them, infangentheff et utfangentheff, homsokenne, Gryuthbruch, Blodwyte, ffyttewyte, fferewyth, hongewyth, Leirwyth, fflemenfrith, et quietos esse de Murdredo, latrocinio, fforstall', horedel', horest, infra tempus et extra, in omnibus locis et omnibus causis quae sunt vel esse possunt, et de omnibus misericordiis. Et quod ipsi et omnes homines sui liberi sint ab omni theloneo, passagio, paagio, pontagio, scotto, et Gildo, et omnibus auxiliis Regum, Vicecomitum, et omnium ministralium eorum, et de hidagio, carucagio, denegild, et hornegild, et exercitibus, scutagiis, tallagiis, lestagiis, stallagiis, schiris, assisis, et assartis, de wasto nemorum, meremio cariando, armis portandis, thesauris portandis, Chaceis, establiis, scotall' regum, de perpresturis, hundred, Wapentake, placita et querel', warda, wardepeny, et de operibus Castellorum, parcarum, pontium, et de clausuris, et de omnibus carragiis, summagiis, arreragiis, passagiis, muragiis, domorum Principum edificatione, et de omnimoda operatione, absque hoc quod bosci eorum ad opera praedicta vel ad aliqua alia capiantur, seu quod blada sua vel hominum suorum ad Castella munienda capiantur, et etiam quod omnia tenementa eorum, tam in bosco quam in plano, sint deforestata et extra omnem potestatem forestarum. Et quod idem Abbas et monachi, homines et servi sui, sint liberi et quieti de omni theloneo in omni foro et in omnibus nundinis, et in omni transitu portuum marium et maris per omnem potestatem et per omnes terras in quibus Dominus Edwardus Rex Angliae xxiij die mensis Octobris Anno Regni sui xij. eis libertatem dare potuit, et in omnibus terris domini Principis. Et quod omnia Mercata sua et hominum suorum sint similiter in predictis locis ab omni theloneo quieti, et quod naves eorundem Abbatis et Monachorum liberum transitum per omnem potestatem praedictam habeant absque omni exactione et consuetudine. Et quod iidem Abbas et Monachi sint liberi et quieti ab omnibus pascubus et ponturis hominum, equorum, canum, et avium, et non compellantur ad pascendum ipsum dominum Principem aut ministros suos, aut alios quoscumque seculares, nisi eorum spontanea voluntate; et quod circa electiones, depositiones, seu resignationes Abbatum, tempore vacationis aut alio tempore, dominus Princeps nec ministri sui, nec alii seculares in nullo intromittant, sed omnia in dicta Abbathia per religiosos ordinentur regulariter et tractentur.

And that the same abbot and monks may have all the chattels of all their men for whatever misdeed or felony of the forest, and similarly all the amercements of all their men, they may have in [any] case which they may have been fined against the lord prince or his ministers for whatsoever cause or offense. And they may keep anything from sea wrecks in all their lands and on all the seashores adjoining their lands, and all vessels and their other goods through the intemperateness of the sea or other perilous misfortune, broken or submerged, and discovered in their lands. And any themselves and their men and their servants and also all their goods are to be free and without cost wherever bought when they may be transported over the Menai, the Conwy, the Abermaw and the Dyfi, and all passage through all the principality and power of the lord prince, unhindered by whatever law or custom. And if any of his animals or any other such goods should be stolen, ravaged, or removed or ruined by the weather, then quickly the same abbot and monks will be called that they may prove [them] to be theirs, and if any animals should be found stamped with the mark of the abbot and monks themselves, they may be returned to the monks themselves, and any themselves for whatever cause, said, done, whether by forfeit in the court of the lord prince, or in whatever lay court, they will by no means be judged, punished or amerced. And because it is permitted that they are able to travel over the waters between the lands of the lord prince or his men in so far as from one part of his lands to another, they are freed from mills and building them and the same with canalising his water to alter or deflect all the way to the land of the abbot himself and of the monks. And that they themselves may be able to freely accept to their habit, and to their fraternity and service, freemen of the prince, swordman and men under oath of the lord prince, as well as having all first tonsures, and whomsoever by recorded agreement, without trouble or damage by whomsoever. And that no minister of the lord prince for whatever cause may enter the lands of the abbot and monks themselves for any duty or requiring the same to be done, and because no goods of them or ser[vices]...

Et quod iidem Abbas et Monachi habeant omnia catalla omnium hominum suorum pro quocumque delicto seu felonia forisfacta, et similiter omnia amerciamenta omnium hominum suorum habeant in casu quo erga dominum Principem vel ministros suos fuerint amerciari, pro quacumque causa seu delicto. Et quod habeant wreccum maris in omnibus terris suis et in omnibus littoribus eisdem terris adjacentibus, et omnia vasa et alia bona sua per intemperiem maris vel aliud infortunium periclitata, fracta, aut submersa, et in terris suis inventa fuerint. Et quod ipsi et homines sui et servientes sui, ac omnia bona sua libere et sine quocumque pretio paratum habeant transitum per Meney, Conwey Ab'man, et Devi, et in omnibus passagiis per totum Principatum et potestatem domini Principis, non obstante quacumque lege seu consuetudine. Et quod si animalia sua aut alia quaecumque bona furata, rapta, vel ablata, vel ad tempus perdita fuerint, tm' cito Idem abbas et Monachi illa probauerint esse sua, et si animalia quorumibus inuenta fuerint signo ipsorum Abbatis et Monachorum signata, ipsis monachis liberentur, et quod ipsi pro quacumque causa, dicto, facto, seu forisfacto in curia domini Principis, aut in quacumque curia laicali, nullatenus judicentur, punientur, seu amercientur. Et quod licite possint super aquas currentes inter terras domini Principis seu hominum suorum quod una parte et terras ipsorum ex altera, molendina levare et edificare et easdem aquas de canalibus suis usque ad terram ipsorum Abbatis et monachorum vertere et declinare. Et quod ipsi libere possint recipere ad habitum suum, et ad famulatum suum et servitia, liberos principis spadarios et hominea de advocatione domini Principis, atque omnes primam tonsurara habentes, cujuscumque condicionis extiterint, sine molestia et calumpnia cujuscumque. Et quod nullus minister domini Principis pro quacumque causa ingrediatur terras ipsorum Abbatis et Monachorum ad aliqua officia in eisdem facienda, et quod nullus bona ipsorum aut ser. . .

[new leaf]
To the convent, of which monastery the same King Edward, the great-grandfather of the lord prince [the Black Prince of Wales, 1343-76], at Maenan in honour of the omnipotent God and St Mary and All Saints, and for the salvation of his soul and the souls of all his ancestors and his heirs, he founded, and the aforesaid vill of Maenan with appurtenances, together with all their liberties, as they were had and were held by the aforementioned abbot and his successors, and his church, he gave in perpetuity. Also anything to the liberty aforesaid, that is that aforesaid abbot and monks may be free and quit of all acquisitions etc. and for all other following liberties contained in the aforesaid declaration, it is said that one Llywelyn ab Iorwerth, once prince of North Wales, by two of his charters conceded to the abbot of Aberconwy who then was and the predecessors of the abbot himself, now was to have the same liberties to himself and his successors and his church aforesaid in perpetuity. And it is said that afterwards the Lord Edward, presently king of England (1327-77), inspected the aforesaid charter of the aforesaid king, the great grandfather of the aforesaid lord prince, and

indeed the charters of the aforesaid Llywelyn, those which were of the then abbot and convent and their successors, through his own charter ratified, accepted and confirmed [them]; indeed which charter of the lord king, the same lord prince inspected today and through his letters patent accepted and ratified it and the aforesaid current abbot and his successors and his church aforesaid, for himself and his heirs, and the same lord prince bringing this forward in his letters patent testified that in these words.

Conventui, quorum monasterium idem Rex Edwardus proavus domini Principis apud Maynan in honore omnipotentis Dei et beatae Mariae et omnium Sanctorum, et pro salute animae suae et animarum omnium antecessorum et heredum suorum fundavit, et praedictam villam de Maynan cum pertinentiis, una cum omnibus libertatibus suis, habendam et tenendam praefato Abbati et successoribus suis, et Ecclesiae suae, imperpetuum dedit. Item quo ad libertatem supradictam, videlicet quod praedicti Abbas et Monachi liberi sint et quieti ab omnibus potituris, etc. et ad omnes alias libertates subsequentes in praedicto clameo contentas, dicit quod quidam Lewelinus Gervasii filius quondam Princeps Northwalliae per duas cartas suas concessit Abbati de Aberconwey qui tunc fuit et predecessoribus ipsius Abbatis nunc easdem libertates habendum sibi et successoribus et ecclesiee suae praedictae imperpetuum. Et dicit quod postea dominus Edwardus Rex Angliae nunc inspexit praedictam cartam praedicti regis proavi praedicti domini Principis, necnon cartas praedicti Lewelini, eas Abbati et Conventui qui tunc fuerunt, et successoribus suis, per cartam suam ratificavit, acceptavit, et confirmavit; quam quidem cartam domini Regis nunc idem Dominus Princeps inspexit, et per litteras suas patentes acceptavit et ratificavit, et praedicto Abbati nunc et successoribus suis, et Ecclesise suae praedictae, pro se et heredibus suis, Et profert hic easdem domini principis litteras patentes quae premissa testantur in haec verba.

Edward [III] by the grace of God etc, to the archbishops etc greetings.
We have examined the charter of the Lord Edward [1239-1307], once king of England, our grandfather in these words, Edward by the grace of god king of England, lord of Ireland and duke of Aquitaine, to the archbishops, bishops, abbots, priors, dukes[*778], earls, barons, justiciars, sheriffs, mayors, ministers and other bailiffs and faithful men of his to which these present letters may have come, greetings. Know that in compensation for the site of the former abbey of Aberconwy and for the lands adjacent, and the grange of Creuddyn with appurtenances near the same abbey thereupon considering, which the abbot and convent in the same place restored into our hand, we give and concede and by this our charter confirmed the aforesaid abbot and convent of the Cistercian order, which monastery afterwards from new at Maenan in honour of the omnipotent God and St Mary and All Saints, for the health of our soul and the souls of all our ancestors and heirs or of any other successors of ours, we founded, the aforesaid vill of Maenan with appurtenances that together with some other lands of Earl Henry Lacy of Lincoln and his heirs, and that himself the same earl afterwards quit for himself and his heirs restoring it into our hand. And also 107 shillings and eight pennies of land which Maredudd Grath and Goronwy his brother, and fifteen shillings of land which Roger Borun and ten shillings of land which Twdwr ap Carwet held in the same vill of Maenan, and which in our hand they similarly peacefully restored, to be had and held by the aforesaid abbot and

---

[*778] The first English dukedom, Cornwall, was created by Edward III in 1337 for his son. This word is therefore either anachronistic or was a scribal error.

convent and their successors in the same monastery serving god and St Mary, with all their appurtenances in free, pure and perpetual alms.

Edwardus Dei gratia etc. Archiepiscopis, &c. salutem.
Inspeximus cartam domini Edwardi quondam Regis Angliae avi nostri in haec verba, Edwardus Dei gratia Rex Angliae, Dominus Hiberniae, et Dux Aquitaniae, archiepiscopis, Episcopis, Abbatibus, Prioribus, Ducibus, Comitibus, Baronibus, Justiciariis, Vicecomitibus, Praepositis, Ministris, et omnibus Ballivis et ffidelibus suis ad quos praesentes litterae pervenerint, salutem. Sciatis quod in recompensationem situs quondam Abbathiee de Aberconwey, et terrarum adjacentium, et Grangise de Crethyn cum pertinentiis ad eandem Abbatiam tunc spectantium, quas Abbas et Conventus loci ejusdem in manus nostras reddiderunt, dedimus et concessimus et hac carta nostra confirmavimus praedictis Abbati et Conventui Ordinis Cisterciensis, quorum Monasterium postmodum de novo apud Maynan in honore omnipotentis Dei et beatae Mariae et omnium sanctorum, pro salute animae nostrae et animarum omnium antecessorum et haeredum seu aliorum successorum nostrorum, fundavimus, praedictam villam de Maynan cum pertinentiis quam una cum quibusdam aliis terris Henrico de Lacy comiti Lyncoln et heredibus suis, et quam ipse idem comes postmodum quietam de se et heredibus suis in manus nostras reddidit. Et etiam centum et decem et septem solidatas et octo denariatas terrae quas M'educus grath et gornonen frater ejus, et quindecim solidatas terrae quas Rogerus Borun et decem solidatas terrae quas Tuderius ap Carweit tenuerunt in eadem villa de Maynan, et quas in manus nostras quiete similiter reddiderunt, habendum et tenendum praefatis Abbati et Conventui et eorum successoribus in eodem Monasterio Deo et beatae Mariae servituris, cum omnibus suis pertinentiis in liberam puram et perpetuam elemosinam.

Besides we concede to the same abbot and convent all reasonable gifts of lands, churches, men and alms to the same by anyone at any time already conveyed and henceforward should they need to be conferred or acquired. Whereby we wish and strongly order on behalf of ourselves and our heirs that the aforesaid abbot and monks and their successors have and hold the vill, lands and delivered as before said with all of the customary liberties and freedoms for the same observed, that is in woods, meadows, pastures, grazing, mills, pools, game enclosures, fisheries, roads, waters, paths and marsh crossings and [within] the boundary as written below, that is ascending the Conwy towards the mountains of Abercambwll where it descends the river which is called Cumogan into the River Conwy, and climbs by that river Cingonan up to the well/spring of Tangwre, and from that spring/well by the great road straight up to Rytyllwydieirth, and thence by the little river up to the stream of Gwydenging, and thus it ascends by that stream up to the little brook which descends to Dewlwyn, and thence up to Grasiwy'chwydant, and thus direct to the pool in the middle of Gwenn gennarwan, and then up to the pool in the middle of Gwennd Bythyne, and so up to Dynon yr Heol, then the moor Kaelerth, then up to Clawd next to the workmens/smiths' houses, then up to the head Grw y Ranallen, thence up to the River Gretlyn, then up to Wennbowys and thus to near Ewen'bowys up to the pool Budyr, and thence up to Nantuwrath, and then descend all the way to the moor which is called Gwennce, and then up to y bwlch'cho, then up to the lake which is between Gwernelanc and Garthgynnanuelt, and then up to the waterway which is called Balenllechane, and thus by that water up to the long ford/causeway, then up to the moor which is called Gwerun Vaenan, and thus via some river up to Pwll y don, all the way to the Conwy, and following the course of the River Conwy up to Abercambwll.

Concessimus etiam eisdem Abbati et Conventui omnes rationabiles donationes terrarum, Ecclesiarum, hominum et Elemosinarum eis a quibuscumque jam collatas et imposterum conferendas vel adquirendas. Quare volumus et firmiter praecipimus pro nobis et heredibus nostris quod praedicti Abbas et Monachi et eorum successores habeant et teneant villam, terras, et redditus praedictos cum omnibus libertatibus et liberis consuetudinibus ad eos spectantibus, ut in boscis, pratis, pascuis, pasturis, molendinis, stagnis; vivariis, piscariis, viis, aquis, semitis, et mariscis permetas et bundas subscriptas, videlicet ascendendo de Conwey[779] *versus montes Abercambwll' ubi descendit fluvius qui appellatur Cumogan in flumine de Conwey, et ascendendo per illum fluvium de Cingonan usque ad fontem de Tangwre, et de fonte illa per viam magnam directe usque ad Rytyllwydieirth, et exinde per rivulum parvum usque ad fluvium de Gwydenging, et sic ascendendo per illum fluvium usque ad rivulum parvum qui descendit de Dewlwyn, et inde usque Grasiwy'chwydant/Graflwyn-chwydauc, et sic directe usque Pwll' in medio Gwenn gennarwan/Gweun-Benarwan, et deinde usque Pwll' in medio y Gwennd bythyne/ygweinud Bycheyne, et sic usque dynon yr heol/Aynon yr Heol, deinde moram Kaelerth'/Ykaekeirch, deinde usque Clawd' juxta domos fabrorum, deinde usque ad caput Grw y ranallen/Erw Yranallen, exinde usque ad flumen Gretlyn/Erethlin, deinde usque ad Wennbowys/Gweun-Bowys et sic iuxtatus ewen' bowys/Gweun-Bowys usque pull' bndir/Pwll-Budyr, et exinde usque Nantuwrath/Nantiwrach, et deinde descendendo usque ad moram quae dicitur Gwennce/Gwennyco, et deinde usque y bwlch'cho/Ybwlch-coch, deinde usque ad maram quae est inter Gwernnelanc/Gwernnelauc et Garthgynnanuelt/Garthgynannel, et deinde usque ad aquam quae appellatur Balenllechane/Balenllechauc, et sic per illam aquam usque longum vadum, deinde usque ad moram quae appellatur Gwerun vaenan/Gwernnvaenan, et sic per quendam rivulum usque Pull y don/Pwllydon, usque Conwey, et filum aquae Conwey usque ad Avercambwll'.*

And because they may have all reasonable gifts of lands, churches, men and alms to them by anyone whomsoever now to them conferred and conveyed in posterity or to be acquired, well and in peace, free and quit, honestly, fully and honourably, with sok and sak, tol and theam, infangenetheff et outfangenethef, hamsoken, *gridbruigh, bolwyke, ffythwyth, fferewyth,* hengwite, *leirwyth,* flemefrith, murdredo, *latrocinio,* forsteal, *hordell' et horest* before this time and after, and in all places and with all causes in which they are or may be in. We concede also that the aforesaid abbot and monks are to be quit in perpetuity of all misdeeds and that they themselves and all their men and tenants are to be free of all scutage and geld and all aids for the king, sheriff and all their ministers, and of hideage, carucatage, Danegeld, hornegeld and army duty, scutage, tallage, lastage, stallage, shire moot (county court) and assizes, and assarts of waste in the woods, of timber carriage, of arms carrying, of treasury transport, of chasing, stabling, compulsory royal feasts, of encroachment of the hundred, wapentakage, pleas and suits, ward, ward penny, hall? penny, hundred penny, borough[780] penny, trithing[781] penny, of castles works, of parks, of bridges, and of enclosures, and all carriage, reckonings, sailings, passages, wallings and at the house of the royal feast, and all works. And we prohibit not of their wood for the aforesaid works or for any other thing is to be taken, and similarly neither their grain or their men are to be taken for munitioning castles. We also concede that all of their tenements, so much as in wood or in the plain, may be

---

[779] Corrections to the following placename spellings have been made Hays, RW, *The History of the Abbey of Aberconway, 1186-1537* [UWP, 1963], 186.
[780] Usually such boroughs referred to Sussex or Kent.
[781] a Yorkshire riding.

defforested and outside of all forest law. We also order that the aforesaid abbot and monks, and their men and tenants, are to be free and quit of all customs in all markets and on all market days, and in all crossings over bridges, roads and seas and through all our power and through all our lands in which their freedoms are given by us, and all their merchants and their men may be similarly in the aforesaid places, quit from all customs. And that the ships of the same abbot and monks have free transit through all our power, without any exaction or custom. We also concede and confirm to the same abbot and monks that if any men of theirs through crime ought to lose his members or his life, or if he had fled, he may refuse to stand trial, or if he should do another misdemeanour for which his chattels ought to be forfeit, those chattels may be [made over] to the aforesaid abbot and monks; similarly if any man of theirs made fine against us or our bailiffs for whatever cause or fault, or forfeited, the fine may be rendered to the said abbot and monks, saving to the king the power of justice of death and members. All these things aforesaid and any other things peacefully, freedoms and free customs of which in this script are dealt with, and the liberties to force back to the house any member of the religious order we concede to the aforesaid abbot and monks for the love of God and the glory of the Virgin Mary, and for the health of our soul and all our ancestors and our heirs, in free and pure alms in perpetuity. And we prohibit moreover our forfeit that no one to the same abbot and monks or their men against this our charter may forfeit under the penalty of £20, because themselves and all things and all their possessions and their men we have received into our custody and protection. And we prohibit assuredly the abbot and monks in person to be placed in a plea over any of his tenements, unless in our court or that of our heirs. This is witnessed. Dated by our hand at Caernafon the 23rd day of the month of October in the year of our reign twelve [1284].

Et quod habeant omnes racionabiles donationes terrarum, Ecclesiarum, Hominum, et Elemosinarum eis a quibuscumque jam eis collatas et in posterum conferendas vel adquirendas, bene et in pace, libere et quiete, integre, plenarie, et honorifice, cum sok et sak, tol et them, infangtheff et outfangethef, hamesok, gridbruigh, Bolwyke, ffythwyth, fferewyth, hengwith, leirwyth, fflemfrid, murdredo, latrocinio, fforstall', hordell', et horest infra tempus et extra, et in omnibus locis et cum omnibus causis quae sunt et esse possunt. Concedimus etiam quod praedicti Abbas et Monachi quieti sint imperpetuum de omnibus misericordiis, et quod ipsi et omnes homines et tenentes sui liberi sint et ab omni Scotto et Gildo et omnibus auxiliis Regis, Vicecomitum, et omnium Ministerialium eorum, et de hidagio, carucagio, danegeld, hornegeld et exercitibus, scutagiis, talagiis, lestagiis, stallagiis, siris, et assisis, et assartis de wasto nemorum, de meremio cariando, de armis portandis, de thesauro portando, de chaciis, establiis, scotall' regis, de purprestura hundred, wapentachiis, placitis, et quereit, ward, et wardpeni, auerpeny, hundredespeny, borthalpeny, Trithingpeny, de operibus castellorum, parcorum, pontium, et de clausuris, et omni cariagio, summagio, navagio, passagio, muragio, et dominium regalium edificatione, et omnimoda operatione. Et prohibemus ne bosci eorum ad praedicta opera vel ad aliqua alia capiantur, et similiter ne blada illorum vel hominum suorum ad castella munienda capiantur. Concedimus etiam quod omnia tenementa ipsorum, tam in bosco quam in plano, sint deafforestata et extra omnem potestatem forestariorum. Precipimus etiam quod praedicti Abbas et Monachi, et homines et tenentes sui, liberi sint et quieti ab omni theoloneo in omni foro et in omnibus nundinis, et in omni transitu pontium, viarum, et maris, et per omnem potestatem nostram et per omnes terras nostras in quibus eis libertatem dare possumus, et omnia mercata sua et hominum suorum sint similiter in praedictis locis ab omni theoloneo quieta. Et quod naves eorundem Abbatis et

Monachorum liberum transitum per omnem potestatem nostram habeant, absque omni
exactione et consuetudine. Concedimus etiam et confirmamus eisdem Abbati et Monachis
quod si aliquis hominum suorum pro delicto suo vitam vel membra debeat amittere, vel
fugerat, in judicio stare noluerit, vel aliud delictum fecerit pro quo catalla sua debeat perdere,
ipsa catalla sint praedictorum Abbatis et Monachorum; similiter si aliquis hominum suorum
sit amerciatus erga nos vel Ballivos nostros pro quacumque causa vel delicto, vel forisfacto,
amerciamenta dictis Abbati et Monachis reddantur, servata regise potestati justitia mortis et
membrorum. Haec omnia praedicta et omnes alias quietantias, libertates, et liberas
consuetudines quae in hoc scripto comprehenduntur, et liberiores quae domui aliquo religioso
referri possunt, concedimus praedictis Abbati et Monachis pro dei amore et gloriosae Virginis
Mariae, et pro salute animae nostrae, et omnium antecessorum et haeredum nostrorum, in
liberam et puram Elemosinam imperpetuum. Et prohibemus super forisfacturam nostram
quod nullus eisdem Abbati et Monachis vel hominibus suis contra hanc Cartam nostram
forisfaciat sub poena viginti librarum, quia ipsos et omnes res et omnes possessiones suas et
hominum suorum in custodiam et protectionem nostram recepimus.
Et prohibemus ne ipsi Abbas et Monachi ponantur in placitum super aliquo tenemento suo,
nisi coram nobis vel haeredibus nostris. Hiis testibus. Datum per manum nostram apud
Caren' .xxiij. die mensis Octobris Anno regni nostri .xij.

Furthermore we have inspected a charter of Llywelyn ab Iorwerth once prince of North Wales
in these words. Let it be known to all the sons of the sainted mother of the church as much in
the present as the future that I, Llywelyn ab Iorwerth, prince of all North Wales, considering
divine responsibility, for the health of my soul and the souls of all the ancestors and heirs and
successors of me, I give and concede as well as confirm by my present charter for me and my
heirs and my successors in pure and perpetual alms for ever, to God and St Mary and the
monks of Aberconwy under the canonical habit of the servants of God, the place itself in
which the same monastery is founded through these terms etc. I concede in addition to the
same monks any liberty they may have in perpetuity and quit from all service of providing
pasture or food to men, horses, dogs and birds, and that they are not compelled to feed me or
my ministers or any other layman at anytime under prevailing custom. And that concerning
elections, depositions, or resignations of abbots in time of vacancy, or any other time, I in no
way will intervene, or my ministers or other seculars may not at all intervene, but all in the said
monastery may bring it about through the religious devotees according to rule and discussion.
I furthermore concede to the same as in order that they are able and glad to have [the right of]
shipwreck in all their lands and valid shores in the same manner that I enjoy in my lands, viz
any goods or things which at any time through submersion or breakage, or through other
misfortune are carried by the sea to their lands or the shores of their lands just as it happens,
these goods [are to be] totally and wholly for the abbot and monks themselves. Similarly if
ships or skiffs or goods of the same monks under my lordship, through the storm of the sea, or
shipwreck, or through another misfortune being broken or submerged, the vessels and goods
themselves will belong to the monks themselves. In addition I concede to the same monks that
themselves and all their servants, with all their goods, are to be quit of all customs, passagio,
pavagio and pontage in all my lands, and that they themselves and all their servants in their
lands are to be free to buy and sell animals, food and drink as well as any other goods at any
time. Also similarly even themselves and their servants, and besides all their goods, are to be
free and without charge wherever prepared to have transit over the Menai or the Conwy or the

[blank*782] or the Dyfi and all passage, through all my power/realm, and not hindered by law or custom in any manner. In addition I concede to the same monks that no men may extort from them the vicinity [of their lands?] or part of their pastures, woods, or mills; but the monks themselves against all customs and seizures, their marches and boundaries drawn up in this charter, and between the same boundaries the plough lands, the buildings, the mills, cultivations and any other thing they may acquire at any time.

Inspeximus etiam Cartam Lewellini filii Gervasii quondam principis Northwalliae in haec verba. Notum sit omnibus Sanctae Matris Ecclesiae filiis tam praesentibus quam futuris quod Ego Lewellinus Gervasii filius, totius Northwalliae princeps, intuitu divinae pietatis, pro salute animae meae et animarum omnium antecessorum et haeredum ac successorum meorum, dedi et concessi atque praesenti carta mea confimavi pro me et heredibus meis et successoribus meis in puram et perpetuam elemosinam imperpetuum, Deo et Sanctae Mariae et Monachis de Aberconwey sub regulari habitu Deo servituris, locum ipsum in quo idem Monasterium fundatum est per hos sz terminos, &c. Concessi insuper eisdem Monachis quod liberi sint imperpetuum et quieti ab omnibus pascubus et poturis hominum, equorum, canum, et avium, et quod non compellantur ad pascendum me aut ministros meos aut alios quoscumque seculares sub optentu consuetudinis. Et quod circa electiones, depositiones, seu resignaciones Abbatum tempore vacationis, aut alio tempore, ego nullatenus intromittam, seu ministri mei aut alii seculares minime intromittant, sed omnia in dicto Monasterio facienda per religiosos ordinentur regulariter et tractentur. Concessi etiam eisdem ut uti possunt et gaudere naufragio in omnibus terris suis et litoribus meliori modo quo in terris meis ego utor vz quaecumque bona seu res per submersionem aut fractionem, seu per aliud infortunium, ad terras suas seu littora terrarum suarum conuict' de mari evenerint, ipsa bona totaliter et integre ipsorum Abbatis et Monachorum. Similiter si navae aut scaphae, aut bona ipsorum Monachorum infra dominium meum per procellam maris, aut Naufragium, aut per aliud infortunium fracta aut submersa fuerint, ipsa vasa et bona sint ipsorum Monachorum. Concessi etiam eisdem Monachis quod ipsi et omnes servi sui, cum omnibus bonis suis, quieti sint ab omni theoloneo, passagio, pavagio, et pontagio in omnibus terris meis, et quod ipsi et omnes servi sui in terris suis libere possint emere et vendere animalia, cibum, et potum, atque alia quaecumque bona. Et similiter et ipsi et servi sui, ac omnia bona sua, libere et sine quocumque pretio paratum transitum habeant per Meney et Conwey et [blank] et Devy et omnibus passagiis, per omnem potestatem meam, non obstante quacumque lege aut consuetudine. Concessi etiam eisdem Monachis quod nullus hominum extorqueat ab eis vicinitatem aut partem de pasturis, silvis, aut molendinis suis; sed ipsi Monachi contra omnes custodiant et possideant fines et terminos suos in hac carta contentos, et intra eosdem terminos araturas, edificia, molendina, culturas et alios quoscumque faciant.

---

*782 Other charters show this to be Abermaw. That these are renderings appear botched in other charters suggests that either the original in a pre Llywelyn ab Iorwerth charter was unclear or that the Edwardian forger was uncertain of his geography.

Appendix 1
The Surviving Charters of Aberconwy Abbey

[Gruffydd ap Cynan to Aberconwy, June 1190-99: Register]

Let it be known by all of the sons of holy mother church so much as in the present as in the future that I, [Gruffydd[*783]] ap Cynan, prince of North Wales, considering divine piety, for the health of my soul and of my ancestors, I give and concede in pure and perpetual alms to God, St Mary and the monks of Aberconwy, being servants of God under the Cistercian order, Gelliniog with all its appurtenances, Rhuddgaer with all its lands, *Stawenan* with its lands and all its purtenances, and the mill of Talybont. And I will to the same monks, so much in the present as in the future, all the prenamed lands with everything on the same appurtenances in perpetual alms that they may hold rightly and quietly, and freely in peace, fully, honestly and honourably, in the wood and on the plain in meadows and pastures, in waters and in mills, with all customary freedoms and free of all earthly service and secular exaction. Moreover in order that this my gift and concession that it remains valid perpetually this present charter is strengthened and reinforced by the impression of my seal. This is witnessed by Gwyn ab Ednywain, Teg ap Robert, Cadwgan ab Iorwerth, Hywel ab Idrys and many others. Dated at Menai Bridge (*Porthaethwy*) in the year from the incarnation of the Lord, one thousand 100. In the month of June.

[King John to Aberconwy, 1 April 1202: Register]

John by the grace of God king of England, lord of Ireland, duke of Normandy and count of Anjou, greets his justices, sheriffs and all his bailiffs in England and Wales and all his lands and sea ports, greetings[*784]. Know that we have received into [our] hand and protection our abbey of Aberconwy and the monks of the Cistercian order there serving God, and all their things and their possessions. And for that reason we order that that abbey and the monks serving the same and all their things and possessions and all which they consider the same, you will preserve and maintain as if it were our own, nor will you allow any of the same to be molested or injured or troubled by others. And they are to have a secure peace, and they may be quit of tholoni, passio, paage and pontage and all custom which pertains to us through all our land, and such thenceforth that they may have quittance from all which themselves or their households or servants are able to assure to be their own possessions, like other monks of the Cistercian order have. And we forbid lest anyone to the same above the truth of this may presume to inflict injury or annoyance, above our just deed, just as the charter of King Henry our father reasonably testifies. Witnessed by Peter Pratellis, Ingram Pratellis (bef.1175-1226/9), Peter Stokes (d.bef Aug 1206).

Dated by the hand of the archdeacon of Wells[*785] at Montfort-sur-Risle, the first day of April in the third [year] of our reign. [1 April 1202]

[*783] There is an erasure at this point. In the margin Humphrey Wanley has added *Lewelinus ap.* The original text would probably have run *Griffinus ap.*

[*784] This was certainly a valid form of charter and is similar to the one issued by the king on 31 May 1203. See Appendix 13 for more of John's contemporary charters.

[*785] Presumably this was Simon Fitz Robert Whatley who became archdeacon of Wells by 15 June 1198 and was elected bishop of Chichester immediately before 9 April 1204.

[King Henry III to Aberconwy, 9 Dec 1232: Charter Roll]

Protection for the abbey of *Abberconewey* and the Cistercian monks there and all their goods and possessions, all which are to be treated as the king's own; moreover the said monks are to be quit of toll, passage, paage, and pontage and all customs pertaining to the king throughout his domains, and they are to have such quittance for everything which they or their servants can prove to be their own as other monks of the Cistercian order have, pursuant to a charter of King Henry II and a confirmation of King John.[*786]

[King Henry III to Aberconwy, 21 July 1247: Patent Roll]

The king has taken into his hand and protection the abbey of Aberconwy (*Aberkonny*) and the monks of the Cistercian order there, their lands and possessions and these are to be protected as the king's own; and they are to be quit of toll, passage, panage[*787], pontage and every custom belonging to the king throughout his land; and have acquittance of all things which they or members of their community (*famuli*) and servants can show to be theirs, as other monks of that order have. And no one shall presume to put any vexation or injury or grievance upon them upon forfeiture to the king as the charters of Henry II and King John testify. Witnessed by Earl Richard of Cornwall, the king's brother, John Mansell the provost of Beverley, Ralph Fitz Nicholas, William Vescy, Paulinus Peyvre, Robert Muscegros, William Beaumont and others.[*788]

[Llywelyn ap Gruffydd to Aberconwy, 1247-54: Record of Carnarvon]

With further confirmation of the grant of Llywelyn ap Gruffydd of the first voidance of his two chapels, to wit the chapel of St Patrick of Cemaes (*Kenmeys*) and the chapel of St Peplicius of Caernarfon (*Carnarvon*, now Llanbeblig) to be held by the monks as freely as any rector held them in the time of Llywelyn his ancestor.[*789]

[Edward I to Aberconwy, 24 Jun 1284: Welsh Rolls]

Notification that the king, for the common utility of his realm and for the peace and security of his realm and of his whole land of Wales hereafter, after having communicated the counsel of his magnates whom it concerned, has caused to be built his castle of Aberconwy (*Aberconewey*) on the soil of the abbot and convent there and has caused the abbey to be transferred, with the consent of the men of religion and of the abbot of Citeaux and of all the convent of the abbots in their chapter general of that place, to the place called Maenan (*Meynan*) in the diocese of St Asaph, and that, lest any prejudice shall arise hereby to the bishop of St Asaph or others whom it concerns, the king promises and binds himself and his heirs that he will save harmless the bishop and church and chapter of St Asaph and also the parish church within the limits whereof Maenan is situated, according to the arbitration of Archbishop John of Canterbury and as the archbishop shall cause to be ordained in this matter.[*790]

[*786] *Calendar of Charter Rolls 1226-1516* [6 vols., 1903-27], *1226-57*, 171.
[*787] The previous charter of 1232 had paage and not panage. One transcript, probably the 1232 one, is in error.
[*788] *CPR, 1232-47*, 504.
[*789] Unfortunately the original has not survived, but the grant was confirmed by Edward III on 24 March 1332, *Calendar of Charter Rolls 1226-1516* [6 vols., 1903-27] *1327-41*, 269; *Registrum vulgariter nuncupatum, 'The Record of Caernarvon'*, ed. Ellis, H. [London, 1838], 148. On 20 November 1388 Llanbeblig church was granted by Aberconwy to the Benedictine nuns of St Mary, Chester, *CPR 1385-89*, 530. This is possibly when they acquired land in Chester which they are holding in the Register.
[*790] *Calendar of Various Chancery Rolls: Supplementary Close Rolls, Welsh Rolls, Scutage Rolls, 1277-1326* [1912], 285-6.

[King Edward I to Aberconwy, 28 June 1284: Welsh Rolls]

Notification that the king has granted to the abbot and convent of Maenan (*Meynan*) that they may have as a parish church the old church of Aberconwy (*Aberconewey*), which they previously held as a conventual church, with the tithes, offerings and other things pertaining by parish right to that church, provided that they cause it to be served suitably by vicars and other ministers of the church and that the cure of souls in it shall not be neglected in any way in the future.[*791]

[King Edward I to Aberconwy, 16 Jul 1284: Welsh Rolls, Charter Rolls]

The king has granted to the abbot and convent of Aberconwy (*Aberconewey*), whose site he wills shall be transferred to Maenan (*Maynan*) by the assent of the abbot and convent and of their fellow abbots of the Cistercian order, by whom the king has caused that place to be visited, that they shall have and hold all the church of Aberconwy, which they previously had and held as a conventual church, henceforth as a parish church appropriated to them with all rights of patronage and ownership in frank almoin, with all rights, possessions and things pertaining to the said parish church both within the walls and without, with all tithes of all lands and of the sea on both sides of the Conwy (*Conewey*) pertaining of old time to the said church of Aberconwy, on condition that they cause the said church to be served by two fit and honest English chaplains, one of whom shall be perpetual vicar in the same and shall be presented by the abbot and convent to the diocesan upon each voidance and by a third honest Welsh chaplain by reason of the difference of language. Witnessed by Bishop Robert of Bath and Wells, Earl Henry Lacy of Lincoln, Earl Richard Burgh of Ulster, Otto Grandison, Reginald Grey, John Mohaut, Peter Chaumpvent by the king's hand at Caernarfon.[*792]

[King Edward I to Aberconwy, 16 Jul 1284: Monasticon]

Know that we for the health of our soul and the souls of our ancestors and heirs have given and conceded and by this our charter confirmed to our beloved in Christ abbey and convent of Aberconwy whose site we wish to be transferred to Maenan, with the assent of the same abbot and convent and of his co-abbots of the Cistercian order who we have caused to visit that place; that all the church of Aberconwy which the convent have had and have held from others and so much as they may hold in regard to us is for their own parochial uses, with all just patronage and ownership to himself and his successors and in pure and perpetual alms with all right of possessions and other things to the aforesaid parochial church observing whatever title they may be judged, so much as within the walls as without, with all tithes, all lands and seas from each side of the region of Conwy to the aforementioned church of Aberconwy as observed from antiquity. Yet nevertheless that the same church should be served by two English chaplains both suitable and honest of which one may be continuously substitute to the other, and through themselves the abbot and convent in each calling of the substitute himself may be presented in the place of the diocesan, and also through a third distinguished Welsh chaplain on account of the difference of language.

Whereby we wish etc. Dated by our hand at Caernarfon, 16th day of July [12 Ed I - 1284].[*793]

[*791] *Calendar of Various Chancery Rolls: Supplementary Close Rolls, Welsh Rolls, Scutage Rolls, 1277-1326* [1912], 286.

[*792] *Calendar of Various Chancery Rolls: Supplementary Close Rolls, Welsh Rolls, Scutage Rolls, 1277-1326* [1912], 286-7; *Register and Chronicle of Aberconway from the Harleian MS. 3725*, ed Ellis, H., *Camden Miscellany* [1847], 13-14, *Calendar of Charter Rolls 1226-1516* [6 vols., 1903-27] *1257-1300*, 276 [very brief abstract].

[*793] *Rex archiepiscopis etc salutem. Sciatis nos pro salute animae nostrae et animarum antecessorum et haeredum nostrorum dedisse concessisse et hac carta nostra confirmasse dilectis nobis in Christo abbati et conventui de Aberconewey quorum situm transferri volumus*

(continued...)

[King Edward I to Aberconwy, 16 Jul 1284: Register]

Edward by grace of God king of England and France, lord of Ireland and duke of Aquitaine etc[*794]. Know that we for the health of our soul and the souls of our predecessors and our heirs of the kingdom of England, we concede for ourselves and our heirs, beloved to us in Christ, to the abbot and convent of Maenan the old church of Aberconwy which convent they first had and held of others, which they may have and hold to themselves and their successors those things pertaining to the parish for their very own uses for ever, with tithes and offerings and other things for that church which pertained by right to the parish, therefore however that themselves the same church through a priest or other church ministers a suitable reputable Welsh chaplain on account of the difference of language. Hence we wish and firmly order, for us and our heirs, that the aforesaid abbey and convent and their successors have and hold for ever the aforesaid church of Aberconwy which the convent first had and held from others, they may have and hold so much from us for their very own parochial uses with all just patronage to themselves and their successors in perpetual alms, with all rights and possessions and other things pertaining to the aforesaid parochial church observing wherever by title it may be judged, whether within the walls or without, with all tithes, all lands and seas from either side of the Conwy to the before mentioned church of Aberconwy as observed from antiquity.

So nevertheless that etc, this is witnessed by the venerable father Bishop Robert of Bath and Wells, Earl Henry Lacy of Lincoln (1251-1311), Earl Richard Burgh of Ulster (bef.1271-1326) etc and dated at Caernarfon the 16th day of July in the [14th] year of our reign.

[King Edward I to Aberconwy, 10 October 1284: Welsh Rolls]

Notification that whereas Bishop Einion of St Asaph, has, at the king's instance, granted to the abbot and convent of Aberconwy (*Aberconewey*), which monastery is now situated at Maenan (*Meynan*), the advowson of the church of Eglwysbach (*Eglwysyvach*), which belonged to the bishop, as is contained in his deed to the abbot and convent, the king has granted to the bishop as compensation the advowson of the church of Rhuddlan (*Rothelan*), with provision that in case the bishop or his successors shall in any case obtain again (*retractare*) the advowson of the former church the king shall have power to revoke his grant of the advowson of the church of Rhuddlan.[*795]

[*793] (...continued)

usque Maynan, de assensu eorundem abbatis et conventus et co-abbatum suorum ordinis Cisterciensis per quos locum illum fecimus visitari, quod totam ecclesiam de Aberconewey quam prius conventualem habuerunt et tenuerunt de caetero habeant et teneant quantum in nobis est in proprios usus parochialem, cum omni jure patronatus et proprietatis sibi et successoribus suis, et in puram et perpetuam elemosinam cum omnibus juribus possessionibus et rebus aliis ad praedictam ecclesiam parochialem spectantibus quocunque nomine censeantur, tam infra muros quam extra, cum omnibus decimationibus omnium terrarum et maris ex utraque parte de Conewey ad praefatam ecclesiam de Aberconewey spectantium ab antiquo. Ita tamen quod eidem ecclesiae deservire faciant per duos capellano Anglicos et idoneos et honestos, quorum unus sit perpetuus vicarius ineadem, et per ipsos abbatem et conventum in singulis vocationibus ipsius vicariae loci dioecesano praesentetur, et per unum tertiam capellanum Walensem honestum, propter idiomatis diversitatem. Quare volumus, etc. Dat per manu nostram apud Karnarvan, xvi die Julii. Et memorandum quod haec carta irrotulatur in rotulo Walliae de hoc anno. Dugdale, *Monasticon Anglicanum*, ed. W. Dugdale, Revised edition by J. Caley, H. Ellis, and B. Bandinel [6 vols., 1817-30] V, 674.

[*794] This title was never used and obviously this composition dates to after 1340 when the title 'king of England and France and lord of Ireland' was used (1340-97). This title with various variations remained in use until 1521. The title generally used from 1259 to 1340 was, *Rex Angliae, Dominus Hiberniae et Dux Aquitaniae* - King of England, lord of Ireland and duke of Aquitaine.

[*795] *Calendar of Various Chancery Rolls: Supplementary Close Rolls, Welsh Rolls, Scutage Rolls, 1277-1326* [1912], 290; *Councils and Ecclesiastical Documents relating to GB and Ireland*, ed. A.W. Haddan and W. Stubbs [2 vols., Oxford, 1869-78] I, 579-80.

[King Edward I to Aberconwy, 10 October 1284: Register]
Edward by grace of God king of England, lord of Ireland, duke of Aquitaine, to all men that these present letters might reach, greetings[*796]. Know that with the venerable father Einion, bishop of St Asaph, for himself and his successors at our insistence has given and concedes with our approval in Christ, to the abbey and convent of Aberconwy and their successors, because indeed the monastery now is sited at Maenan, the advowson of the church of Eglwysbach which pertains to the aforementioned bishop, just as in the writing of the said abbey and convent henceforth made fully secured. Wishing to compensate the said bishop for that donation, we give and concede to the same the advowson of the church of Rhuddlan, to be held by himself and his successors in perpetuity, without complaint from us or our heirs or successors to us whatsoever. Therefore, still because if we or our heirs or successors whatsoever lay hands upon the advowson of the aforesaid church of Rhuddlan from the bishop himself or his successors or by chance retract anything, it is permitted for the aforesaid bishop and his successors to be entirely regained of the advowson of the aforesaid church of Eglwysbach from the aforesaid abbot and convent. In this business the testimony of these our letters which we have made openly. Witnessed by me at Aberconwy the tenth day of October in the twelfth year of our reign [1284].

[King Edward I to Aberconwy, 18 Oct 1284: Welsh Rolls]
To all to whom it concerns etc. Notification that the king has granted to Gruffydd ab Iorwerth - in recompence for £10 yearly in land in Maenan (*Meynan*) surrendered by him to the king, who has granted it to the abbot and convent of Aberconwy (*Aberconewey*), which monastery was now situated at Maenan - the vill of Rhosmawr (*Rossmaur*) for life.[*797]

[King Edward I to Aberconwy, 22 Oct 1284: Welsh Rolls]
To all to whom it concerns etc. Notification that the king has granted to Maredudd Grach (*Mereduc Cragh*) and his brother Gwrgeneu Rhuddlan (*Gurgennew Ruth'*) - in recompense for 117s yearly of land and rent in Maenan (*Maynan*) that they have surrendered to him, which he granted in frank almoin to the abbot and convent of *Aberconwey*, whose monastery he had now founded at Maenan - his vills of Glyn and Gronant.[*798]

[King Edward I to Aberconwy, 21/22 Oct 1284: Welsh Rolls]
To all to whom it concerns etc. Notification that the king has granted to Tewdwr ap Karuet 10s yearly of land in *Coeteos*, in recompense for a messuage and a parcel of land in *Penlassok*, which Tewdwr surrendered to the king, and which the king granted in frank almoin to the abbot and convent of Aberconwy, whose monastery he has now founded at *Maynan*.[*799]

[*796] Once more the king's titles are given incorrectly - see the above charter in the Register.
[*797] *Calendar of Various Chancery Rolls: Supplementary Close Rolls, Welsh Rolls, Scutage Rolls, 1277-1326* [1912], 290. For Rhosmawr see Lewis, E.A., 'The Decay of Tribalism in North Wales, *Trans. of the Honourable Society of Cymmrodorion* [1902-3], 41.
[*798] *Calendar of Various Chancery Rolls: Supplementary Close Rolls, Welsh Rolls, Scutage Rolls, 1277-1326* [1912], 290. See *Registrum vulgariter nuncupatum, 'The Record of Caernarvon'*, ed. Ellis, H. [London, 1838], 9, for the lands granted.
[*799] *Calendar of Various Chancery Rolls: Supplementary Close Rolls, Welsh Rolls, Scutage Rolls, 1277-1326* [1912], 291; *Registrum vulgariter nuncupatum, 'The Record of Caernarvon'*, ed. Ellis, H. [London, 1838], 2. According to the king's charter of 24 October where these people and their compensation is mention, one Roger Bozun owned land worth 15s yearly and he too was compensated, *Monasticon Anglicanum*, ed. W. Dugdale, Revised edition by J. Caley, H. Ellis, and B. Bandinel [6 vols., 1817-30] V, 674. Roger's name has been omitted in *Register and Chronicle of Aberconway from the Harleian MS. 3725*, ed Ellis, H., *Camden Miscellany* [1847], 19 and his 15s placed against Tewdwr ap Carwet.

[King Edward I to Aberconwy, 22/3 Oct 1284: Welsh Rolls, Charter Rolls]

To the archbishops etc. Notification that the king has granted and confirmed by this charter to the abbot and convent of *Aberconewey* whose monastery he has newly founded at Maenan, in completion and satisfaction of the lands that they surrendered to him, the manor of [Llanfairyn] Ghornwy (*Kauruwilys/Kanruwylis*, SH.326909[*800]), with the hamlets of Ucheldref (*Hucheldref/Hucheldref*, SH.344875) and Gwenynog (*Gwenenauc/Qwenenauc*, an estate within Llanfflewyn, SH.350891[*801]) in the commote of Talybolion (*Thalebolyon*), which are extended at £18 14s 5½d yearly, and the town of Treveibion Maelog (*Trefuebien Maelauc/Crefnebien Maelant*) in the same commote which is extended at 50s 9d yearly and a moiety of the town of Penmynydd (*Penmynyd*, SH.508744) in the commote of Dindaethwy (*Dynndaethwy*), which is extended at 118s 6d yearly, and the hamlet of *Cumrewet/Cumrewez*, with a moiety of Raulin's meadow in the commote of Creuddyn (*Cruthyn*), which is extended at 100s yearly, to be held by the said abbot and convent in frank almoin. Witnessed by Bishop Robert of Bath and Wells, Earl Richard Burgh of Ulster, John Vescy, Otto Grandison, Robert Tybetot, Richard Bruce, Robert Fitz John.[*802]

[King Edward I to Aberconwy, 23 Oct 1284: Monasticon taken from Charter Rolls]

The king greets his archbishops etc. Know that in recompense for the site once belonging to the abbey of Aberconwy and the adjacent lands and the grange of Creuddyn with appurtenances for the same abbey then observing, which abbey and convent of the same place into our hands they restored, we give and concede and confirm with this charter to the aforesaid abbot and convent of the Cistercian order, of which monastery afterwards newly at Maenan in honour of omnipotent God and St Mary and All Saints, for the health of our soul and the souls of all our predecessors and heirs or other of our successors we have founded, at the aforesaid vill of Maenan with appurtenances, as one with some other lands of Earl Henry Lacy of Lincoln and his heirs and which same earl afterwards/presently quit for himself and his heirs, he has restored to our hands. And furthermore 117s 8d of land which Maredudd Grath and Gorgon his brother, and 50s of land which Tewdwr ab Karwet held in the same vill of Maenan and which into our hands they similarly peacefully restored. It is to be had and held by the aforesaid abbot and convent and their successors in the same monastery serving God and St Mary, with all their appurtenances, in free, pure and perpetual alms in perpetuity. We concede to the same abbot and convent and confirm all reasonable gifts of lands, churches, men and alms to them by anyone already conferred and about to be conferred henceforward or acquired. By which means I will etc, that the aforesaid abbot and monks and their successors may have and hold the vill lands and restored the preceding with all liberties and free customs to them observing that in woods, meadows etc through the boundaries and bounds written below; clearly ascending from the Conwy towards the mountains of Abercamwl; where a river which is called Cynnogan descends into the River Conwy; and thus ascends through that river to Cynnogan up to the spring/fountain of Tangwre; and from that font via the great road direct to Rytyllwydieirche; and thence via the small rivulet up to the River Gwydenging; and thus ascending via that river up to the small rivulet which descends to Dewlwyn and thence up to Graflwynchwydaue; and this directly up to the pool in the middle of Gwenn Benarwann; and

[*800] The hamlets of Mynachdy, Gader Mynachdy and Cae'r Mynach (Mynach being Welsh for monk) mark their interest in the district.

[*801] The name has not survived but in 1618 it was 'little more than 242 acres', Jones, E.G., 'Hugh Owen of Gwenynog', *Transactions of the Anglesey Antiq. Society* [1938], 42.

[*802] *Calendar of Various Chancery Rolls: Supplementary Close Rolls, Welsh Rolls, Scutage Rolls, 1277-1326* [1912], 292; *Calendar of Charter Rolls 1226-1516* [6 vols., 1903-27] II, 279.

then up to the pool in the middle of Ywemud Bycheyn and thus up to Axnonyr, Heol, then up to the sea of yhaekeirth; then up to an enclosure next to the smiths'/workmens' houses; then up to Pen Erw Yranallen; then up to the River Erethlin; then up to Gwen Bowys; and then hard by Gwenn Bowys up to Pool Budyr and thence up to Nantiwrach; and then descend to the moor which is called Gwennyco; and then up to Y Bwlch Coch, then up to the moor which is between Gwenaelog and Garthgynannel; and thence up to the water which is called Ballenllathog, and thus through that water up to the long valley, then up to the moor called Gwernnvaenan and thus via some rivulet up to Pwll Ydon, and through the water of Pwllydon up to Conwy; and thus via the thread of water Conwy up to Abercambwll. And because they may have all reasonable gifts of lands, churches, men and alms to them by anyone already conferred and about to be conferred henceforward or acquired may be held freely, well and in peace, quietly, wholly, fully and honourably with sok and sak, tol & theam, infangenethef, & utfangenethef, hamsoken, *gridbrich, bolwyk, fichwych, Ferwych, kengwyek, leirwych,* flemeneswite, murder, *latrocinio, forstal, hordel, & horest* beyond time, and in all places and with all things which they have and are able to have.[*803]

We also concede to them in so far as the aforesaid abbot and monks are to be at peace in perpetuity from all misdeeds, and that themselves and all their men are to be free and from all scutage and geld and all aids of the king by sheriffs and all other of his ministers and of hidage, carucatage, danegeld, hornegelde, & of the army, scutage, tallage, lastage, stallage, *siris, & sesisie* & assarts, of waste of woods, of carrying timber, of carrying arms, of carrying treasure, of cooking, *establiis, scetallis Regalibus,* of pouture, hundreds, wapentakes, pleas & *querdis* ward & ward penny, everpenny, hundred penny, hearth penny, trithing penny, and of castles works, of parks, of bridges and enclosures and of all carriage, *summagio*, shipping, passage, murage and building royal houses and all works. And we prohibit neither the woods of them to the aforesaid works or to some other seizure and similarly neither their grain nor their men shall be taken to garrison castles.

[*803] *Rex Archiepiscopis etc salutem. Sciatis quod in recompensationem situs quondam abbacie de Aberconewey & terrarum adjacentium, & grangiae de Creuthyn cum pertinentiis ad eandem abbaciam tunc spectantium, quas abbas & conventus loci ejusdem in manus nostras reddiderunt, dedimus & concessimus & hac carta nostra confirmavimus praedictis abbati & conventui ordinis Cisterciensis, quorum monasterium postmodum de novo apud Maynan in honore omnipotentis Dei, & beatae Mariae & omnium Sanctorum, pro salute animae nostrae & animarum omnium antecessorum & haeredum seu aliorum nostrorum successorum fundavimus, praedictam villam de Maynan cum pertinentiis, quam una cum quibusdam aliis terris Henrico de Lacy comiti Lincolniae & haeredibus suis & quam idem comes postmodum quietam de se & haeredibus suis in manus nostras reddidit. Et etiam centum decem & septem solidatas, & octo denaratas terrae quas Mereducus Grath, & Gorgonen frater ejus, & quindecim solidatas terrae quas Tuderius ab Karwet tenuerunt in eadem villa de Maynam & quas in manus nostras quiete similiter reddiderunt. Habendas & tenendas praefatis abbati & conventui & eorum successoribus in eodem monasterio Deo & beatae Mariae servituris, cum omnibus suis pertinentiis, in liberam puram & perpetuam elemosinam imperpetuum. Concessimus eisdem abbati & conventui & confirmavimus omnes rationabiles donationes terrarum ecclesiarum hominum & elemosinarum eis a quibuscunque jam collatas & imposterum conferendas vel adquirendas. Quare volumus &c. quod praedicti abbas & monachi & eorum successores habeant & teneant villam terras & redditus praedictos cum omnibus libertatibus & liberis consuetudinibus ad eos spectantibus ut in boscis, pratis &c per metas & bundas subscriptas; videlicet ascendendo de Conewey versus montes de Abercamwl; ubi descendit fluvius qui appellatur Cynnogan in flumine de Conewey; & sic ascendendo per illum fluvium de Cynnogan usque ad fontem de Tangwre; & de fonte illo per viam magnam directe usque ad Rytyllwydieirche; & exinde per rivulum parvum usque ad fluvium de Gwydenging; & sic ascendendo per illum fluvium usque ad rivulum parvum qui descendit de Dewlwyn & deinde usque Graflwyn-chwydaue; et sic directe usque Pwll in medio Gwenn-Benarwann; & deinde usque Pwll in medio Ywemud Bycheyn & sic usque Axnonyr, Heol, deinde usque maram yhaekeirth; deinde usque Clawd juxta domos fabrorum; deinde usque ad capud Erw Yranallen; exinde usque flumen Erethlin; deinde usque Gwen-Bowys; & sic juxta latus Gwenn-Bowys usque Pwll-Budyr & exinde usque Nantiwrach; & deinde descendendo usque ad moram quae dicitur Gwennyco; & deinde usque Y bwlch-coch, deinde usque ad moram quae est inter Gwernaelanc, & Garthgynannel; & inde usque ad aquam quae appellatur Ballenllethauc, & sic per illam aquam usque longum vadum, deinde usque ad moram quae appellatur Gwernnvaenan & sic per quendam rivulum usque Pwll-ydon, & per aquam Pwllydon, usque Conewey; & sic per filum aque Conewey usque Aberycambwll. Et quod habeant omnes rationabiles donationes terrarum ecclesiarum hominum & elemosinarum eis a quibuscumque jam collatas & imposterum conferendas vel adquirendas bene & in pace libere, quiete, integre, plenarie, & honorifice, cum sok & sak, tol & theam, infangenethef, & utfangenethef, hamesock, gridbrich, bolwyk, fichwych, Ferwych, kengwyek, leirwych, flemmefirid, murdro, latrocinio, forstal, hordel, & horest infra tempus & extra tempus, & in omnibus locis & cum omnibus causis quae sunt & esse possunt.* [The text of this charter has been divided into two for convenience.]

And also we concede that all of their tenements as much in the wood as in the plain are to be deforested and outside all powers of the foresters. Furthermore we order that the said abbot and monks and men are free and quit of all tolls in all markets and in all places and in all crossing of bridges, roads and seas through everywhere in our power, and through all our lands in which we are able to give freedom and in all their trade and similarly of their men in the aforesaid places they are to be quit of all tolls; and because the ships of the same abbot and monks are to have free passage through all our power without any tax or custom.

Also we concede and confirm to the same abbot and monks, that if any of their men may owe through life or member should lose or flee and be unwilling to stand judgement or cause other fault for which their chattels should be lost, those chattels may be [held] by the aforesaid abbot and monks. Similarly if any of their men may be fined against us or our bailiffs for whatever reason or for fault or forfeit the penalty it will be rendered to the aforesaid said abbot and monks, saving the righteousness of the king's power of life and limb. All this aforesaid and all other peaceful liberties and free customs which in this writing are not included and freemen of this particular religious house they are able to bring together, we concede to the aforesaid abbot and monks for the love of God and the glory of the Virgin Mary and for the health of our soul and those of all our ancestors and our heirs, in free pure and perpetual alms forever. And we forbid upon our forfeiture that no one the same abbot and monks or their men against this our charter will forfeit under penalty of £20, because themselves and all their things and possessions and their men we have received into our custody and protection. And we do not hinder the same abbot and all which may be put in place of some of his tenement unless to our court himself or that of our heirs. This is witnessed by the venerable father Robert of Bath and Wells, our chancellor etc dated by our hand at Caernarfon 23rd day of October [12 Ed I - 1284].*804

---

*804 An irrelevant precis appears in *Calendar of Charter Rolls 1226-1516* [6 vols., 1903-27] *1300-26* III, 267. The text comes from *Monasticon Anglicanum*, ed. W. Dugdale, Revised edition by J. Caley, H. Ellis, and B. Bandinel [6 vols., 1817-30] V, 674-5. [Continued]

Concessimus etiam quod praedicti abbas & monachi quieti sint imperpetuum de omnibus misericordiis, & quod ipsi & omnes homines sui liberi sint & ab omni scoto & geldo & omnibus auxiliis regum vice-comitum & omnium ministerialium eorum & de hidagio, carucagio, danegeld, hornegelde, & exercitibus, scutagiis, tallagiis, lestagiis, stallagiis, siris, & sesisie & assartis, de vaste nemorum, de maeremio cariando, de armis portandis, de thesauro portando, de chociis, establiis, scetallis Regalibus, de purprestura, hundredis, wapentachiis, placitis & querdis warda & wardepeny, everpeny, hundrederpeny, herthalpeny, trythingpeny, & de operibus castellorum, parcoram, pontium, & de clauauris & omni carragio summagio navagie passagio muragio & domunum regalium edificatione & omnimoda operatione. Et prohibemus ne bosci eorum ad praedicta opera vel ad aliqua alia capiantur, & similiter ne blada illorum vel hominum suorum ad castella munienda capiantur.

Concedimus eciam quod omnia tenementa eorum tam in bosco quam in plano sint deaforestata & extra omnem potestatem forestariorum. Praecipimus eciam quod praedicti abbas & monachi & homines sui liberi sint & quieti ab omni theolonio in omni foro & in omnibus mundinis & in omni transitu pontium viarum & maris per omnem potestatem nostram, & per omnes terras nostras in quibus eis libertatem dare possumus & omnia mercata sua & hominum suorum sint similiter in praedictis locis ab omni theolonio quieta; & quod naves eorundem abbatis & monachorum liberum transitum per omnem potestatem nostram habeant absque omni exactione & consuetudine.

Concedimus eciam & confirmavimus eisdem abbati & monachis, quod si aliquis hominum suorum pro delicto suo vitam vel membra debeat amittere vel fugerit & judicio stare noluerit vel aliud delictum fecerit pro quo catalla sua debeat perdere, ipsa catalla sint praedictorum abbatis & monachorum. Similiter si aliquis hominum suorum sit amerciatus erga nos vel ballivos nostros pro quacumque causa vel delicto seu forisfacto amerciamenta praedicta dictis abbati & monachis reddantur, servata regiae potestati justitia mortis & membrorum. Haec omnia praedicta & omnes alias quietancias libertates & liberas consuetudines quae in hoc scripto non comprehenduntur & liberiores alicui domui religiosae conferri possunt, concedimus praedictis abbati & monachis pro Dei amore & gloriosae virginis Mariae & pro salute animae nostrae & omnium antecessorum & haeredum nostrorum, in liberam puram & perpetuam elemosinam imperpetuum. Et prohibemus super forisfacturam nostram quod nullus eisdem abbati & monachis vel hominibus suis contra hanc cartam nostram forisfaciat sub poena viginti librarum, quia ipsos & omnes res & possessiones suas & hominum suorum in custodiam & protectionem nostram recepimus. Et prohibemus ne iidem abbas & omnachi ponantur in placitum de aliquo tenemento suo nisi coram nobismet ipsis vel haeredibus nostris. Hiis testibus venerabili patre Roberto Bathonensi & Wellensi ipiscopo cancellario nostro, &c Dat. Per manum nostram, Apud Kaernarfan xxiii die Octobris. [The year has been omitted.]

[King Edward I to Aberconwy, 5 Nov 1284: Welsh Rolls]

Notification that the king has granted to Bishop Einion of St Asaph and to *Effeyriat Teulu* (the domestic or court chaplain) of Wales, in recompense for the tithes of the king's demesnes at Ghornwy (*Kauruwylus*) and Penmynydd (*Peynmeynyd*), which are extended at 50s yearly, which they granted at the king's instance to the abbot and convent of *Aberconewey*, whose monastery the king has now caused to be founded anew at *Meynan* and to whom he has granted his demesnes aforesaid, the townships of Trefieuan (*Trefyevan*[805]), *Abydon* and Bodychen (SH.389780), which are also extended at 50s yearly, provided that the bishop and his successors shall satisfy the said *Effeiryat Teulu* of Wales and his successors for the portion due to him of the tithes aforesaid.[806]

[Abbot of Aberconwy to the king, 26 Dec 1285: Close Rolls]

A deed of Brother David, abbot of Aberconwy (*Aberconeweye*),... witnessing that whereas the king has caused the abbey to be transferred to the place called Maenan (*Maynan*) and has promised to build the abbey there and make good the damages sustained by them by reason of the war in Wales, the abbot and convent, considering that the site has been usefully transferred and that the work on the new site has been well commenced by the king, have, in consideration of 580 marks (£386 13s 4d) that he voluntarily gave to them beforehand and of other goods and benefits that he has in many ways conferred upon them and their house, remitted to him and quitclaimed him from the construction of the said church and the further building of their houses in the aforesaid place, and also the damages aforesaid. Dated 15 October 1285 at Caernarfon.[807]

---

[805] Apparently once in the tref of Llanidan, SH.495669.
[806] *Calendar of Various Chancery Rolls: Supplementary Close Rolls, Welsh Rolls, Scutage Rolls, 1277-1326* [1912], 292; *Councils and Ecclesiastical Documents relating to GB and Ireland*, ed. A.W. Haddan and W. Stubbs [2 vols., Oxford, 1869-78] I, 550 [misdated 1283]; *Episcopal Acts and cognate documents relating to Welsh Dioceses, 1066 - 1272*, ed. J.C. Davies, [2 vols., Historical Society of the Church in Wales, 1946] II, 437, n.97; *CPR 1377-81*, 291.
[807] *CCR 1279-88*, 407-8.

Appendix 2
The Forgeries of 1315-32 Attributed to Prince Llywelyn in 1199

[Transcribed from the 1332 Confirmation[*808]]

Let it be known to all the consecrated mother churches by the daughters so present, as in the future, that I, Llywelyn ab Iorwerth, prince of all Wales, considering divine piety, for the health of my soul and the souls of all my ancestors and heirs or successors, I give and concede, together with my present charter confirm for me and my heirs or successors in pure and perpetual alms forever to God and St Mary and the monastery of Aberconwy, serving God under a canonical habit, the place itself in which the said monastery is founded, by these certain limits.[*809]

[Conwy Gyffin]

Rising away from the River Conwy up to the mouth of the Gyffin, then all the River Gyffin up to some enclosure next to Gwerydros (in Henryd manor[*810]), hence diverting to the right through some enclosure marked by stones up to the rivulet *Perhey*, hence ascending through that rivulet up to some enclosure next to Coed Mawr (SH756724), hence through that enclosure up to some rock/cliff close by this by means of a high rocky hill up to the bone/s of the Christian, hence it descends to the sea and then by the River Conwy, up to Abergyffin.[*811]

[Creuddyn]

Furthermore I give and concede as well as confirm to the same monks these lands at Creuddyn, through these evident bounds. Ascending the Conwy up to that spring which appears in the furthest part of the arable land of the monks at *Hemiron*; Hence via the higher part of the same cultivated land up to the great stones standing in *Erw-voruran*, thence up to the common road, hence following the way up to the enclosure above *Erwedus* (Erw Goch? SH.819733), hence up to the head *Carrec-Wyber*, hence via the higher part of *Ryoryn*, and the arable lands of the monks up to the furthest part of *Gwernegof*, hence through the hollow below *Gwernegof* to the land of *Crocuryn*; Hence via the stones arranged in a boundary up to the rivulet next to Llanrhos (SH.794804), hence through the rivulet up to the hollow which is in the extreme part of the meadow of the monks below *Crocuryn*, hence through the hollows up to the pleasing rivulets which are between Bodysgallen (SH.798794) and *Brongoch* and descend in the said hollow. Hence up to some spring/fountain, hence via the nearest overhanging cliff all the way to the stone which is called the square/quadrant, hence to the rock in which is a pit, hence up to Creigiau Rhiwledyn? (SH 813824, *Carrecerue*), hence up to the second rock/cliff beyond Carrecwalth, hence via the higher part of the cultivated land of the monks up to the enclosure between *Trefwarth* and *Callaurwerth*, and thus leading through that enclosure up to the marsh/swamp below, hence via the furthest part of the arable land of the monks up to the wood

---

[*808] The full copy of the first charter is in *Monasticon Anglicanum*, ed. W. Dugdale, Revised edition by J. Caley, H. Ellis, and B. Bandinel [6 vols., 1817-30] V, 672-4. *Calendar of Charter Rolls 1226-1516* [6 vols., 1903-27] *1327-41*, 267, simply has a wrongly dated notice of the first charter and a full, wrongly dated translation of the second. The charter also appears in the Aberconwy Register as it was inspected, without the extensive land boundaries, in the Quo Warranto proceedings of 1348.

[*809] *Notim sit omnibus sanctae matris ecclesiae filiis, tam presentibus, quam futuris, quod ego Lewelinus Gervasii filius, totius Norwalliae princeps, intuitu divine pietatis, pro salute animae meae & animarum omnium antecessorum & haeredum ac successorum meorum dedi & concessi, atque presenti Carta mea confirmavi pro me & haeredibus ac successoribus meis, in puram & perpetuam eleemosinam imperpetuum Deo & Sanctae Mariae & monachis de Aberconwey, sub regulari habitu Deo servituris, locum ipsum in quo idem monasterium fundatum est, per hos scilicet terminos.*

[*810] Richards, M., *Welsh Administrative and Territorial Units, Medieval and Modern* [Cardiff, 1969], 82.

[*811] *Ascendendo de flumine Conwy usque ad Abergeffyn, deinde totum fluvium Geffeyn usque ad quoddam claud juxta Gweridros, hinc divertendo ad dextram per illud claud lapidibus signatum usque ad rivulum Perhey, hinc ascendendo per illum rivulum usque ad quoddam claud juxta Coetmaur, hinc per illud claud usque ad quandam rupem prope hinc per altitudinem collium petrosarum usque ad os Christiani, hinc descendendo usque ad mare & deinde per flumen Conwy, usque ad Abergeffyn.*

of Eardur ap Kendelu, hence via the enclosure to the head of that enclosure. Thence via the banks of the marsh between the arable land and the swamp up to *Argaevelin*, hence following the water up to Conwy.[*812]

[Conwy]

Furthermore I concede to the same monastery all the water of the Conwy and passage of the same water as well as the fishing from Abergyffin up to Aberconwy.[*813]

[Ffriwlwyd]

In addition I concede and confirm to the same monks Ffriwlwyd (SH.439375) through these evident bounds. Ascending from the sea via the middle of some ditch made for a boundary up to the River *Karroc*, hence through the middle of the Carrog? up to the rivulet *Chwilogen*, hence through the middle of the *Chwilogen* up to *Blaen-chwilogen*, hence ascending through the marsh up to *Pwllberwr*, hence through the marshy hollow to *Gwernebleideu*, hence through the middle of *Gwernebleidu* up to Ynys Wen? (SH.444431, *Wennbanc*), then via the middle of *Wennbanc* descending by some rivulet (SH.465448) flowing through some small valley up to the River Dwyfach (SH.479425, *Dwynech*), and thus descending all the water of the Dwyfach and the mill house as well as the all the fishing and wholly up to the River Dwyfor (SH.465380, *Dwynaur*), then by the middle of the waters of the Dwyfor, with half the fishing, up to the sea, and from this place by the shore up to the aforesaid ditch.[*814]

[Cwm]

Furthermore I concede and confirm to the same monks *Kwin* withing these evident bounds. Ascending to *Hensarngwiu* next to Penyffridd (SH506569, *Pentyrth*) through some hollow up to the River Carrog (SH.4657, *Keiloc*). Hence through the middle of the Carrog up to some stream flowing to *Sichnanc*, hence through the same stream up to the sown enclosure, hence descending via the stream flowing from the sown enclosure up to *Blaen stream Efelanc*, hence via the middle of the Llifon (SH.490558, *Efelanc*) stream up to Rhiwfallen (SH.463563, *Rytefelanc*). Hence ascending through some hollow up to *Rytnerkvoessen*, hence through the furthest hollow beyond *Bryn-brych* and *Enys-las* up to the River Carrog and from hence descending through some hollow to *Hensarngwin*.[*815]

[*812] *Dedi etiam & concessi atque confirmavi eisdem Monachis has terras apud Creudyn, per hos videlicet terminos. Ascendendo de Conwy usque ad quendam fonticulum existentem in extrema parte terrae arabilis monachorum apud Hemiron; Hinc per superiorem partem terrae ab eisdem cultae usque ad lapides grandes existentes in Erw-voruran, inde usque ad communem viam, hinc per ductum viae usque ad claud supra Erwedus, hinc usque ad caput Carrec-Wyber, hinc per superiorem partem Ryuoryn, & terrae arabilis Monachorum usque ad extremam partem Gwernegof, hinc per alveum desubtus Gwernegof usque ad terram Crocuryn; hinc per lapides in termino constitutos usque ad rivulum juxta Eglwys-Ros, hinc per ductum rivuli usque ad alveum qui est in extrema parte prati monachorum subtus Crocuryn, hinc per ductum alvei usque ad decensum rivuli qui est inter Bodesgallen & Brongoch & descendit in dictum alveum. Hinc usque ad fontem quendam, hinc per rupem proximam desuper pendentem usque ad lapidem quem vocant quadratum, hinc usque ad rupem in qua est fovea, hinc usque ad Carrecereu, hinc usque ad secundam rupem ultra Carrecwalth, hinc per superiorem partem terrae cultae monachorum usque ad claud inter Trefwarth & Callaurwerth, & sic per ductum illius claud usque ad paludem subtus, hinc per extremam partem terrae arabilis monachorum usque ad nemus Eardur filii Kendelu, hinc per claud usque ad caput illius claud. Inde per ripam paludis inter terram arabilem & paludem usque ad Argaevelin, hinc per ductum aquae usque ad Conwy.*

[*813] *Concessi etiam eisdem monachis totam aquam Conwy & ejusdem aquae transitum atque piscariam de Abergeffyn usque Aberconwy.* These rights are not mentioned in the 1247 treaty of Woodstock, as they would have been if they existed. This again condemns this alleged 1199 charter as a forgery.

[*814] *Concessi insuper & confirmavi eisdem monachis Frywlwyd per hos scilicet terminos. Ascendendo de mari per medium cujusdam fossae in terminum factae usque ad fluvium Karroc, hinc per medium Karroc usque ad rivulum Chwilogen, hinc per medium Chwilogen usque Blaen-chwilogen, hinc ascendendo per paludem usque pwllberwr, hinc per alveum paludis usque Gwernebleideu, hinc per medium Gwernebleidu usque Wennbanc, hinc per medium Wennbanc descendendo per quendam rivulum fluentem per quendam valliculum usque ad fluvium Dwynech, & sic descendendo totam aquam Dwynech & molendinum atque piscariam totaliter & integre usque ad fluvium Dwynaur, deinde per medium aquae Dwynaur, cum medietate piscarie, usque ad mare, & abhinc per litus usque ad fossam supradictam.*

[*815] *Concessi etiam & confirmavi eisdem monachis Kwin per hos videlicet terminos. Ascendendo de hensarngwiu juxta Pentyrth per quendam alveum usque ad fluvium Keiloc. Hinc per medium keiloc usque ad quendam rivum fluentem de Sichnanc, hinc per illum rivum usque ad claud-seri, hinc descendendo per aquam fluentem de claud-seri usque Blaen rivi Efelanc, hinc per medium rivi Efelanc usque Rytefelanc. Hinc ascendendo per quendam alveum usque Rytnertkvoessen, hinc per extremum alveum ultra Bryn-brych & Enys-las usque*

(continued...)

[Rhedynog Felen]

I also give and confirm to the same Rhedynog Felen (*Redenocuelen*), through these evident bounds; from by that place where the River Carrog flows next to some spring which appears near Llanwnda (SH.474578) up to some hollow which is between *Gefenys Fychan* and *Enys Keubren* towards *Gerthic*, from here it is diverted to the right via some hollow on the other side of *Enys Keubren* up to *Werndofyn*, hence through the middle of *Werndofyn* descending to the River Gwyrfai (SH.500598, *Gwyleyt*), hence via the middle of the Gwyrfai up to Aber Carrog (SH.447583, Aberkarroc) next to Morfa Dinlle (SH.436583, *Morua-Duillen*), and thus ascending through the middle waters of the Carrog towards Llanwnda up to the said place next to the aforesaid spring.[*816]

[Nant Call]

Furthermore I concede and confirm to the same Nant Call (*Nankall*) through these evident boundaries. Ascending from Aber Colwyn (SH.462479?) via the river Call (*Kall*) up to *Brieth-du* hence up to the height of Llwyd Mawr (*Llwytmaur*, SH.505462), hence to the peak of *Llwytmaur* mountain all the way to *Blaengwennyd Gwyneon*. Hence up to *Blaen-Meyc*, hence descending via the middle of *Meyc* up to the Dwyfach (*Dwynech*); and from hence through the River Dwyfach up to Aber Call.[*817]

[Gelliniog]

In addition I concede to the same and confirm *Kellhineoc*, by these evident bounds. Ascending from the Menai via the River Braint (SH.436638) up to Aber Pwllgwyngyll (SH.513715), hence through the middle of the water of Pwllewyrran up to Siglan? (SH.531725, *Sarnigerd*), hence via some enclosure of marker stones up to some pool next to *Treferiken*, hence via the middle of this pool up to *Clauderadwy*, hence via this enclosure up to bank of the pool up to *Clauderadwy*, hence through that enclosure up to the bank, hence directly up to the Menai strait, and thus through the middle of the water of Menai up to Aber-Braint.[*818]

[Talybont]

Furthermore I concede and confirm to the same the mill of Talebont with appurtenances; actually the water and ditch from Sarn y Felin up to Carreg Elgar, as well as the common way each side from Gelliniog up to the mill aforesaid without impediment by whomsoever.[*819]

[Bodgedwydd]

Furthermore I give and confirm to the same Bodgedwydd (SH.363715), by these evident bounds. Ascending from some small island arising in Llyn Coron (SH.378700) through the middle of Claudyago up to Carned Iorwerth (SH.418751). Hence turning away towards Aberffraw (SH.355689) through some enclosure marked by stones up to Lain Wen

---

[*815] (...continued)

ad fluvium karroc, & abhinc descendendo per quendam alveum usque Hensarngwin.

[*816] *Dedi etiam & confirmavi eisdem Redenocuelen, per hos videlicet terminos; ab illo loco quo fluvius Karroc fluit juxta quendam fontem existentem prope Llanwnda usque ad quendam alveum qui est inter Gefenys-vechan & Enys-keubren versus Gerthic, hinc divertendo ad dexteram per quendam alveum ultra Enys-Keubren usque Werndofyn, hinc per medium Werndofyn descendendo usque ad fiuvium Gwyleyt, hinc per medium Gwyleit usque Aberkarroc juxta Morua-Duillen, & sic ascendendo per medium aquae Karroc versus Llanwnda usque ad dictum locum juxta praedictum fontem.*

[*817] *Concessi etiam & confirmavi eisdem Nankall per hos scilicet terminos. Ascendendo de Aberkall per fluvium Kall usque Brieth-du, hinc usque ad altitudinem Llwytmaur, hinc ad cacumen montis Llwytmaur usque Blaengwennyd Gwyneon. Hinc usque Blaen-Meyc hinc descendendo per medium Meyc usque Dwynech; & ab hinc per aquam Dwynech usque Aberkall.*

[*818] *Concessi insuper eisdem & confirmavi Kellhineoc, per hos scilicet terminos. Ascendendo de Meney per fluvium Breint usque Aber-Pwllewyrran, hinc per medium aquae Pwllewyrran usque Sarnigerd, hinc per quoddam claud lapidibus signatum usque ad quoddam stagnum juxta Treferiken, hinc per medium illius stagni usque Clauderadwy, hinc per illud claud usque ad litus stagni usque Clauderadwy, hinc per illud claud usque ad litus, hic directe usque ad alveum Meney, & sic per medium aquae Meney usque Aber-Breint.*

[*819] *Concessi etiam & confirmavi eisdem molendinum de Talebont cum pertinentiis; aquam quoque & fossam de Sarn y Velyn usque Carreg-Elgar, atque viam communem omni tempore de Kellhineoc usque ad molendinum praedictum sine impedimento cujuscunque.*

(SH.357744). Hence via an enclosure by some marked stones up to Merddyn-y-bit?
(SH.349701). Hence directly towards Henllys (SH.354709) up to Penhenllys (SH.356178,
Korsenllys). Hence divert to the right through the middle of the hollow up to *Rytdu*. Hence
through the middle of that hollow up to Afon Gwna (*Abergoner Garanen*), as it descends into
Korscallellyn. Hence ascend through *Gonergaranen* next to some enclosure marked by stones
up to *Wennlas*. Hence via the middle of *Wenlas* up to *Wennfaur*. Hence ascend via a hollow
up to the well of the monks/horses. Hence via some enclosure marked by stones up to the
side/flank of Bodwrdin (SH.392719). Hence by means of following the stones up to *Cerric
poethion*. Hence by some enclosure digress towards Trefdraeth (SH.409702) up to the
side/flank of Trefdraeth. Hence by the middle of the hollow arising on the bounds of
Trefdraeth through the middle of Cors Ddyga (*Korsygirvran* Maltreath Marsh) up to *Pwlleu-
Haloc*, and from hence through the hollow up to the aforesaid island.[*820]

[Llanfaes]

Furthermore I give and confirm to the same the water meadow of Llanfaes by its boundaries
with all its appurtenances.[*821]

[Pentrefoelas]

In addition I concede and confirm to the same monks Pentre Voelas (SH.872515) and Hen
Voelas (SH.870522, Llanfair Rhydd Castell), through these evident boundaries. Ascending
from Abergwrysgog (SH.833523) by the River Gwrysgog up to some wide/broad ford/stream
in *Blaengwrysgog*. Hence through the hollow up *Maenesartyr*. Hence up to *Cerric
Llwynogod*. Hence up to Cairn Merddyn (SH.858546). Hence up to the springs under Moel
Seisiog (SH.862563). Hence up to the summit of Moel Seisiog (SH.861573). Hence descend
via the hollow up to *Hentytbeli*. Hence via the Nant Caledfryn (SH.886572) up to *Blaen
Katletwyn* (SH.893589) under *Kers Geranan*. Hence follow the direct line up to *Esgynvaen
Gwgann*. Hence up to Llyn Alwen (SH.898565). Hence via the middle of Llyn Alwen and the
middle of the River Alwen up to *Rhtgwynn*. Hence by Nant Heilyn (SH.928555) up to a great
valley/ditch separating to the left and through that valley/ditch ascending up to the head of that
deep hollow under *Broadengynlboyn*. Hence leave behind *Brondengym-Llwyn* to the right
hand side within the boundaries of the monks via the valley up to Blaen Llaethog
(SH.915530). Hence through the middle of Llaethog up to the River Nug (SH.892509).
Hence through the middle of the Nug up to the River Conwy (SH.856512) and through the
middle of the water of the Conwy up to Abergwrysgog.[*822]

[*820] *Dedi etiam & confirmavi eisdem Bodgedwyd, per hos videlicet terminos. Ascendendo de quadam parva insula existente in Llyn-coron
per medium claudyago usque Carned-Yerwerth.*
Hinc divertendo versus Aberfraw per quoddam claud lapidibus signatum usque Wenn-wenn.
*Hinc per claud quoddam lapidibus signatum usque Merdynen-kefnerth. Hinc directe versus Henllys usque Korsenllys. Hinc divertendo
ad dexteram per medium alvei usque Rytdu. Hinc per medium illius alvei usque Abergoner garanen, prout descendit in Korscallellyn.
Hinc ascendendo per Gonergaranen juxta quoddam claud lapidibus signatum usque Wenn-las. Hinc per medium Wen-las usque Wenn-
vaur. Hinc ascendendo per alveum usque Fynnon-y-meyirch. Hinc per quoddam claud lapidibus signatum usque ad latus Bodwrdyn.
Hinc per ductum lapidum usque Cerric-poethion. Hinc per quoddam claud divertens versus Trefdraeth usque ad latus Trefdraeth. Hinc
per medium alvei existentis in confinio Trefdraeth per medium Korsygirvran usque Pylleu-Haloc, & ab hinc per alveum usque ad
praedictam insulam.*
[*821] *Dedi etiam & confirmavi eisdem plateam de Lemnaes per terminos suos cum omnibus pertinentiis suis.*
[*822] *Concessi insuper & confirmavi eisdem monachis Voelas-Keirnauc & Llanveir-Ryt-castell, per hos videlicet terminos. Ascndendo de
Abergwrysganc per fluvium Gwrysgune usque ad quoddam latum vadum in Blaengwrysgene. Hinc per alveum usque Maenesartyr.
Hinc usque Cerric-Llwynogod. Hinc usque Carnedrun. Hinc usque ad fontum subtus Moel-seissauc. Hinc usque ad summitatem Moel-
seissauc. Hinc descendendo per alveum usque Hentytbeli. Hinc per fluvium Kaletwyn usque Blaen Katletwyn subtus Kers-geranan.
Hinc directe ducta linea usque Esgynvaen-gwgann. Hinc usque Llyn-alwen. Hinc per medium Llyn-alwen & medium fluvi Alwen usque
Rytgwynn. Hinc per Nant-heilynsets usque ad quandam valliculam divertentem ad sinistram, & per illam valliculam ascendendo usque
ad capud cujusdam alvei profundi subtus Broadengynlboyn. Hinc relinquendo Brondengym-llwyn ad dexteram intra terminos
monachorum per vallem usque blaen-Llaethanc. Hinc per medium Llaethauc usque ad fluvium Nue. Hinc per medium Nue usque ad*

(continued...)

[Llyn Cymmer]

In addition I concede and confirm to the same Llyn Cymmer (SH.972525), by these evident bounds; ascending through Llyn Kymmer via the River Alwen up to *Aber Drywes*. Hence through the middle of the water of the *Drywes* up to *Bonerelicbras*. Hence up to *Nant Ringhylleyt*. Hence to the River Brenig and through the middle of the Brenig up to Llyn Cymmer.[*823]

[Llechwedd Cryn Llwyn]

Furthermore I concede and confirm to the same Llechwedd Cryn Llwyn through these known boundaries, by the pool near Caer Ddunod (SH.985510, *Taldinas-Dindunant*) facing Alwen up to near the place where the rivulets descend into Alwen from *Bwlchdinewyt*. Thence facing the very same rivulet up to Tan y Bwlch? (*Bwlchelinewryt*, SH.941525). Thence by descending the rivulet out of the other part of the mountain towards Cerrigydrudion (SH.954488) up to *Enyserheid*. Hence by the higher part of the same *Enys* via the swamp/marsh up to the far rivulet flowing to a former spring. Thence via the length of the same valley up to the head of the large swamp towards the east. Hence via the length of that swamp up to the rivulet rushing from the farthest spring towards the east out of the Alwen neighbourhood and from the same spring up to the lower enclosure below the road. Thence through the length of that enclosure to *Heliclwynen* near Nant y Felin? *Blaen Nant* which descends towards Alwen. Thence up to Llechwedd-y-Gaer (SH.975481) towards the north into some protruding hill. Hence up to above Blaen by the valley which descends towards Caer Ddunod. Hence via the same valley all the way along to above the said Pool next to Tal (Tal y Cefn? SH.994520) the actual Dinas.[*824]

[Nanhwynain]

In addition I concede and confirm to the same monks these lands at Nanhwynain, that is *Gwascat Onnos Bryngwynem, Hafat, Tandrec, Llyndu, Chromygoret, Scubordynemrsis, Hendrefwynein, Wernosdet, Pennant, Morgenen, Pennant Crwnn* with *Llem* from the other part of *Llem, Chwmerth* from the other part of *Erth, Chwmdelif* from the other part of *Delif, Kemen Trinemt* and *Gwrty, Kei* from the other part of *Degymm*, through the boundaries one may see clearly written below. Ascending from *Abereolwyn* just as it descends in *ferlas* through the middle of Colwyn up to Blaencolwyn just as it descends to Bwlch Chwmllem. Hence through the rim of the cliffs up to the head of *Wedduavaur*. Hence up to the head/source of *Grybgoek*. Hence up to the head of *Wregyssant*. Hence via the highest rock up to the seat/residence/settlement/chair of Peris. Hence up to the head Moel-berned. Hence directly up to that place in which the River Member begins as a torrent precipitating downwards. Hence through the middle of the water Member up to *Eranongoch*. Hence ascending by that water up to *Llegat-Erych*. Hence up to the height of *Cerric Eryylch*. Hence

---

[*822] (...continued)
fluvium Conwy & per medium aque Conwy usque ad Aber-gwriscane.

[*823] *Concessi etiam & confirmavi eisdem Llynkemer, per hos scilicet terminos; ascendendo per Llynkemer per fluvium Alwen usque Aber Drywes. Hinc per medium aque Drywes usque Bonerelicbras. Hinc usque Nant Ringhylleyt. Hinc ad fluvium Breint & per medium Breint usque Llynkemer.*

[*824] *Concessi etiam & confirmavi eisdem Llethwed-krynllwyn per hos scilicet terminos, a Pwlle propinquiori Taldinas-Dindunant contra Alwen usque ad locum ubi rivulus descendit in Alwen de Bwlchdinewyt. Inde contra eundem rivulam usque Bwlchelinewryt. Inde per discensum rivuli ex alia parte montis versus Kerrieedrudson usque ad Enyserheid. Hinc a superiori parte ejusdem Enys per paludem usque ad rivulum ulteriorem fluentem de quondam fonte. Inde per longitudinem cujusdam valliculae usque ad caput magnae paludis versus orientem. Hinc per longitudinem illius paludis usque ad rivulum decurrentem de fonte ulteriori versus orientem e regione Alwen, & ab eodem fonte usque ad claud inferius subtus viam. Inde per longitudinem illius claud ad heliclwynen apud blaen-nant quod descendit versus Alwen. Inde usque ad Kerricllwydeen versus aquilonem in supercilio cujusdam collis.*
Hinc usque super blaen vallis qui descendit versus dinas dundunant. Hinc per ejusdam vallis longitudinem usque ad supradictum Pwlle juxta Tal ipsius dinas.

up to *Lleth Edear*. Hence up to *Bankarw*. Hence via the top of the cliffs of Bancaru up to *Blaen Teyrw*. Hence via the River Teyru up to the rock which descends in the Teyru near above *Ryt Teyru*. Hence through the small rocky hills by the side of *Gerrynt* up to *Llethwedgwelvau*. Hence follow an indirect line up to the hillock which appears to resemble a castle by the right side of *Llethwedgwellvau*. Hence via the height up to the head of *Carrecereryr*. Hence by the summit of the cliffs up to *Gorssed Ressygynt* exactly as it hangs over the valley. Hence turn towards Llyndinas along some arm of the rocky place appearing from above the valley up to the head of the urine enclosure. Hence through the middle of that enclosure up to the River Ferlas, and then via the middle of the Ferlas up to Abercolwyn as it descends into *Llynekemer*.[*825]

[Arddau and Dulyn]

Furthermore I give and confirm to the same monks *Arden* and Dulyn, by these evident boundaries; ascend from Aberpwlldulyn through the middle of the water to the pool Melynllyn? (SH.702657, *Cawlwyd*). Hence through the middle of that pool up to the marsh that is above the pool and through that swamp directly up to *Vygynforthant*. Hence via the top of the cliffs to Pen Llithrig y Wrach (SH.716624). Hence from the top of that mountain towards the east up to Blaen y nant? (SH.738603, *Bwlcherylvarthant*). Hence descend through that valley and via that rivulet descend through that valley which is called Friw-ddu (ie Trefriw, *Frwt-ddu*) which is directly below *Carrec-gwennolyod* and descends into the River *Eygyen* and via the River *Engyen* up to the pool *Eygyen* and through that pool and via the river which descends from the pool up to the River Conwy and through the middle of the Conwy up to Aberpwlledarlas.[*826]

In addition I concede to the same monks that they may be free in perpetuity and quit from all pasturage and potage of men, horses, dogs and birds and not compelled to feed me or my ministers or any other such laity under maintaining any custom. And that concerning elections, dispositions or resignations of the abbot in the time of vacancy or other time I will in no way intervene, or my ministers or other laity may make the slightest admission; but all in the said monastery will be done through the religious devotees regularly composed and led. I furthermore concede to the same in order that to use and to be glad to be able to have shipwreck in all their lands and shores in a good manner which in my lands I enjoy, and that is with those goods or things through submersion or breakage or through other misfortune to their lands or to the shores of their lands contiguous to the shores they will have,

---

[*825] *Concessi insuper & confirmavi eisdem monachis has terras apud Nanhoenem, scilicet gwascat onnos Bryngwynem, Hafat, Tandrec, Llyndu, Chromygoret, Scubordynemrsis, Hendrefwynein, Wernosdet, Pennant, Morgenen, Pennant crwnn cum llem ex utraque parte Llem, Chwmerth ex utraque parte Erth, Chwmdelif ex utraque parte delif, kemen trinemt, & gwrty, kei ex utraque parte Degymm, per videlicet terminos subscriptos. Ascendendo de Abereolwyn prout descendit in ferlas per medium Colwyn usque blaencolwyn prout descendit de bwlch chwmllem. Hinc per crepidinem rupium usque ad caput Wedduavaur. Hinc usque ad capud Gryhgoek. Hinc usque ad capud Wregyssant. Hinc per altitudinem rupium usque ad sedem peris. Hinc usque ad capud Moel-berned. Hinc directe usque ad illum locum in quo fluvius Member incipit sicut torrens precipitanter descendere. Hinc per medium aque Member usque Eranongoch. Hinc ascendendo per illam aquam usque Llegat-Erych. Hinc usque ad altitudinem Cerric-eryylch. Hinc usque Lleth-edear. Hinc usque bankarw. Hinc per cacumen rupium Bancaru usque blaen-teyrw. Hinc per parvos colles petrosos a latere Gerrynt usque Llethwedgwelvau. Hinc ducta linea indirecte usque ad monticulum qui in similitudinem castelli apparet a dextera parte Llethwedgwellvau. Hinc per altitudinem usque ad capud carrecereryr. Hinc per summitatem rupium usque ad Gorssed Ressygynt prout pendet desuper vallem. Hinc divertendo versus Llyndinas per longitudinem cujusdam brachii petrosi desuper vallem apparentis usque ad capud claud mein. Hinc per medium illius claud usque ad fluvium ferlas, & deinde per medium ferlas usque ad Abercolwyn prout descendit in Llynekemer.*
[*826] *Dedi etiam & confirmavi eisdem monachis Arden & Darlas, per hos scilicet terminos; ascendendo de Aberpwlledarlas per medium aque usque ad stagnum Cawlwyd. Hinc per medium illius stagni usque ad paludem quae est supra capud stagni & per illam directe paludem usque ad Vygynforthant. Hinc per altitudinem rupium usque ad capud Llithretewrath. Hinc per altitudinem illius montis versus occidentem usque Bwlcherylvarthant. Hinc descendendo per illam vallem, & per illum rivulum descendentem per illam vallem qui dicitur frwt-du qui est directe subtus Carrec-gwennolyod & descendit in fluvium Eygyen, & per fluvium Eygyen usque ad stagnum Eygyen & per illud stagnum & per fluvium descendentem de stagno usque ad flumen Conwy & per medium Conwy usque ad Aberpwlledarlas.*

the goods themselves totally and fully may be of the monks themselves, similarly if the ships or skiffs or goods of the monks themselves within my dominion through sea storms or shipwreck or through other misfortune may have been broken or submerged, the vessels and goods themselves will belong to the monks themselves.[*827]

I furthermore concede to the same monks that themselves and all their servants with all their goods are to be quit of all tolls, ferry toll, toll paid by travellers and pontage in all my lands. And that themselves and all their servants and also all their goods may be freely without any payoff whatsoever may be obtained for passage via the Menai, Conwy, Abermaw and Dyfi, and in all toll paid by travellers through all in my domain not opposed by law or custom whatsoever. I further concede to the same that if their animals or other goods whatsoever are stolen, dragged off or snatched away or may be ruined by the weather, nevertheless quickly the same monks those examined goods of theirs [are] to be themselves [returned] without delay to be acquitted pacifically. Similarly I prohibit any person either secular or religious from my rule except the said monks to make use of that iron sign which they themselves are in the habit of marking their animals with and beasts of burden and if the animals any of them at any time are to be found marked themselves with the sign they are to be returned to the monks. In addition I conceded to the same monks in perpetuity that for wherever by cause said or done or by forfeit in my court or in a lay court wherever in no wise may they be judged, amerced or punished, but in their chapter house following their order they are to be corrected.[*828]

Besides I concede to the same monks that no men may extort from their neighbourhood or part of grazing in the woods or their mills, but the monks themselves against all may protect and be master of their lands and boundaries drawn out in this charter, and within the same boundaries ploughings, buildings, agricultures and other any such labours they may make for their pleasure without objections of any kind. Furthermore I concede to the same monks that no men themselves may be able to make charge or action on account of the recovery of some persons for his men attending whatsoever may be agreed, after themselves have received they may declare in the said monastery; but if any such persons to the religious from the secular flee above are charged by some, they may remain a year on probation and not behind the declaration made they may exhibit his deed/suit. I likewise concede to the same monks that if any professed of the said monastery without the licence and the consent of his abbot the money or other goods from the creditors they made receive the unexpected borrowing or by the faithful order of seculars himself may confuse, the aforesaid monastery for such borrowed and

---

[*827] *Concessi insuper eisdem monachis quod liberi sint imperpetuum & quieti ab omnibus pastibus & poturis hominum equorum, canum, & avium, & non compellantur ad pascendum me aut ministros meos aut alios quoscunque seculares sub obtentu consuetudinis, & quod circa electiones depositiones seu resignationes abbatum tempore vacationis aut alio tempore ego nullatenus intromittam, seu ministri mei aut alii seculares minime intromittant; set omnia in dicto monasterio facienda per religiosos ordinentur regulariter & tractentur. Concessi etiam eisdem ut uti & gaudere possint naufragio in omnibus terris suis & litoribus meliori modo quo in terris meis ego utor, videlicet quecumque bona seu res per submersionem aut fractionem seu per aliud infortunium ad terras suas seu ad litora terris suis conjuncta de mari evenerint, ipsa bona totaliter & integre sint ipsorum monachorum similiter si naves aut scaphae aut bona ipsorum monachorum infra dominium meum per procellam maris aut naufragium aut per aliud infortunium fracta aut submersa fuerint, ipsa vasa & bona sint ipsorum monachorum.*

[*828] *Concessi etiam eisdem monachis quod ipsi & omnes servientes sui cum omnibus bonis suis quieti sint ab omni theoloneo, passagio, paagio, & pontagio in omnibus terris meis. Et quod ipsi & omnes servientes sui ac omnia bona sua libere sine quocunque precio paratum transitum habeant per Meney, Conwy, Abermaw & Dyui, & in omnibus passagiis per omnem potestatem meam non obstante quacumque lege aut consuetudine. Concessi etiam eisdem quod si animalia sua aut alia quaecumque bona furata rapta seu ablata vel ad tempus perdita fuerint, tam cito iidem monachi illa bona probaverint esse sua ipsis sine dilatione pacifice liberentur. Similiter prohibeo ne aliqua persona secularis aut religiosa de dominio meo preter dictos monachos utatur illo signeo ferreo quo ipsi signare solent animalia sua & jumenta & si animalia quarumcumque inventa fuerint signo ipso signata ipsi monachis liberentur. Concessi insuper eisdem monachis imperpetuum quod pro quacumque causa dicto aut facto seu forisfacto in curiis meis aut in quacunque curia laicali nullatenus judicentur amercientur seu puniantur, set in capitulis suis secundum ordinem suum corrigantur.*

by faith ordered he may give insufficient amends. In addition I concede to the same that they are permitted to be able to hasten over the waters between my lands or my mens' from one part and the lands of themselves from the other to be freed from and building mills and also the same to turn and deflect the waters of their canals to their lands without any impediment whatsoever. I furthermore concede to the same that they are permitted to be able to receive to their habit and their service my free swordsmen and the men of my advocates, as well as all who have the first/best tonsure of contract whatsoever they will have existed, without molestation and charge whatsoever. And because he is devout as in all things, any foolishness by seculars and worldly riches they forsake and to the king of kings they are converted willingly by obedience, first they may be near protection and tutelage, I wish for me and my heirs and successors that the same monks so present or future have and possess all the aforesaid territories by the limits and territories and also boundaries before named. In wood and fields, cultivated and uncultivated, meadows, pastures, grazing, fisheries, pools, game enclosures, waters, mills, roads, paths, moors, glebes, stones, metals, approaches and all nesting pathless regions, shores, ports, shipwrecks, treasuries and all things all the same above their grounds just as beneath their grounds as found, rightly and in peace, free and wholly peacefully, in full honour, firmly and unshakenly in free, pure and perpetual alms in perpetuity, unrestrained and freely from all pertaining secular service and exaction.[*829]

Furthermore I will that the same monks nevertheless present and future all the aforesaid liberties, quitances and other freedoms by customs through all my lands and through all of my principality in perpetuity they may use and enjoy; and I prohibit under danger of my anger that no men of the same monks or their servants against this my charter make prejudice or trouble. Seeing that themselves and all things and also their possessions under my protection I have accepted. And in order that this my gift as well as confirmation in perpetuity in solidity and unshaken it may endure, nor anyone take opportunity to contend or perturb the aforesaid monks or be able henceforth to bring forth, I presently fortify the charter and reinforce it with the impression of my seal. This is witnessed by Iorwerth Gam, Gwyn ab Ednewein, Ydon my chaplain and Madog ap Cadwgan. Dated at Aberconwy in the year of the incarnation of the lord, one thousand, [one] hundred, ninety eight on the seventh ides of January and in the tenth year of my principality.[*830]

[*829] *Concessi etiam eisdem monachis ut nullus hominum extorqueat ab eis vicinitatem aut partem de pasturis silvis aut molendinis suis, set ipsi monachi contra omnes custodiant & possideant fines & terminos suos in hac carta contentos, & intra eosdem terminos araturas, aedificia, culturas, & alios quoscumque labores pro libito suo faciant sine contradictione cujuscumque. Concessi etiam eisdem monachis quod nullus hominum possit super ipsos calumpniam seu actionem facere propter receptionem aliquarum personarum ad hobitum suum cujuscumque conditionis sint, postquam ipsi recepti in dicto monasterio profiteantur; set si qui tales personas ad religionem de seculo fugientes super aliquibus calumpniaverint, durante anno probationis, & non post professionem factam actionem suam ostendant. Concessi etiam eisdem monachis ut si qui professorum dicti monasterii sine licentia & consensu abbatis sui pecuniam aut alia bona a creditoribus incaute mutuo acceperint aut secularibus fide jussionibus se immiscuerint, monasterium praedictum pro talibus mutuis & fide jussionibus minime satisfaciat. Concessi insuper eisdem quod licite possint super aquas currentes inter terras meas seu hominum meorum ex una parte & terras ipsorum ex altera levare et aedificare molendina, & etiam easdem aquas de canalibus suis ad terras suas vertere & declinare sine impedimento cujuscumque. Concessi etiam eisdem quod licite possint recipere ad habitum suum & ad famulatum suum & servicia liberos meos spadarios & homines de advocatione mea, atque omnes primam tonsuram habentes cujuscunque conditionis extiterint, sine molestia & calumpnia cujuscunque. Et quia pium est ut omnibus, qui seculi vanitates & mundanas divitias derelinquunt & ad regis regum obesquia voluntarie convertuntur, principum assint presidium & tutela, volo pro me & haeredibus ac successoribus meis quod iidem monachi tam praesentes quam futuri habeant & possideant omnes terras praedictas per limites & fines ac terminos praenominatos. In silvia & campis, cultis & incultis, pratis, pascuis, pasturis, piscariis, stagnis, vivariis, aquis, molendinis, viis, semitis, moris, glebariis, lapidibus, metallis, avibas, omniumque avium nidis, litoribus, portubus, naufragiis, thesauris, omnibusque rebus tam super terras suas quam sub terris suis inventis, bene & in pace, libere quiete integre, plenarie honoricie, firmiter & inconcusse in liberam puram & perpetuam elemosinam imperpetuum, solutas & liberas ab omni tereno servicio & exactione seculari.*
[*830] *Volo etiam ut iidem monachi tam praesentes quam futuri omnibus praedictis libertatibus quietanciis & aliis liberis consuetudinibus per omnes terras meas & per totam principitatam meum imperpetuum gaudeant & utantur; Et prohibeo sub periculo indignationis mea ut nullas hominum eisdem monachis aut servientibus suis contra hanc cartam meam prejudicium faciat aut gravamaen. Quoniam ipsos &*

(continued...)

Transcription of the second charter from the 1332 Confirmation[*831]

Llywelyn ab Iorwerth, prince of North Wales for his soul and those of his ancestors, heirs and successors, gave in frank almoin to St Mary and the monks of *Aberconewey* the enjoyment of the following liberties throughout his principality; to wit that they should be quit of all feeding and drinking of men, horses, dogs and birds; and that they should not be compelled to feed the prince or his ministers or other seculars by way of custom and that in the election, deposition or resignation of abbots, in time of vacancy or at other times, the prince will not intermeddle nor any of his ministers nor any secular persons; but that all things in the said monastery shall be ordered and treated by religious persons; and that the monks shall enjoy wreck in all their lands and shores as fully as the prince does in his lands, so that all things that shall come from the sea to the shores bordering their lands by sinking, breaking or other misfortune, shall be the monks'; and if ships, boats or goods of the monks shall be broken or sunk within the prince's domain by storm, tempest of the sea, shipwreck or other misfortune, the said vessels and goods shall fall to the monks; and the monks and all their servants and household and all their goods shall be quit of all toll, passage, payage and pontage in all the prince's lands and may freely buy and sell therein beasts, food and drink and other goods and shall have free and ready passage by Menai, Conwy, Abermaw and Dyvi and in all passages through all the prince's power, notwithstanding any law or custom; and if any of the beasts or goods of the monks be carried off, stolen, taken away or lost for a time, they shall be delivered to the monks as soon as they can prove their ownership; no secular or religious person of the domain of the prince, save only the monks, shall use the brand with which they are wont to brand their beasts and horses and if any beasts are found marked with that brand, they shall be delivered to the monks; the monks for any cause, word, deed or offence shall not be judged, fined or punished in the prince's courts or in any lay court, but shall be corrected in their chapters according to their order; no man shall extort from them common or a share of their pastures, woods or mills but the monks shall keep against all men the metes and bounds contained in the great charter granted to them by the prince, and within those bounds shall plough, build, set up mills, till and do anything else that they will without contradiction; no man shall have any claim or action against them by reason of the reception of any person into their habit, of whatever condition he may be, when once the person so received has become professed in the said monastery; but if any shall claim such persons flying from the world to religion during their year of probation and not after profession, those persons claiming shall show their cause of action, but the monks may lawfully receive into their habit and service and household the prince's free men and men of his protection and swordmen and men of his household and all having the first tonsure of any condition without claim; if any person professed of the said monastery without the licence of the abbot take money from creditors or anything else by way of loan, or incautiously involve himself with secular bonds, the monastery shall not be compelled to satisfy the same; the monks may build mills on the waters running between the lands of the prince and his men and their own lands and may even divert the waters from their channels to their own lands if needful; none of the prince's ministers for any cause shall enter

---

[*830] (...continued)

omnes res ac possessiones suas sub protectione mea suscepi. Et ut haec mea donatio atque confirmatio imperpetuum firma & inconcussa permaneat, ne aliqua contentionis aut perturbationis occasio contra praedictos monachos possit imposterum suboriri, eam praesenti cartae munimine & sigilli mei impressionae roboravi. Testibus hiis Yorwerthgam, gwynn filio Ednewein, ydon capellano meo & Madoco filio Cadur. Dat apud Aberconwy anno ab incarnatione Domini millesimo centesimo nonagesimo octavo, septimo idus Januarii, & principatus mei anno decimo.

[*831] *Registrum vulgariter nuncupatum, 'The Record of Caernarvon'*, ed. Ellis, H. [London, 1838], 145-8. Translation taken from *Calendar of Charter Rolls 1226-1516* [6 vols., 1903-27] *1327-41*, 267-9.

the monks' lands to do any office there, and no man shall take the goods of the monks or those of their servants and households from their lands, save by the special mandate of the prince or leave of the abbot; whenever ships or their boats laden with wine, corn or other merchandise shall put in to the lands of the prince or the monks, the monks may freely buy such merchandise and the sellers thereof freely sell to them, their servants and households, without licence of any; if thieves or evil doers shall be taken in the granges, houses or lands of the monks by the prince's ministers, the monks shall not be troubled therefore, since it belongs to the prince's ministers to take such persons, and to the monks to give food and lodging to travellers and guests; the monks, their servants and households shall enjoy these and other liberties, too many to be here set out through all the prince's land and principality, and no man shall prejudice them therein; witnessed by Iorwerth Gam, Gwynn ab Ednewein, Ydon the prince's chaplain, Madog ab Eardu, dated at *Aberconeweye*, AD 1198, seventh ides of January in the 10th year of the prince.

Appendix 3
The Chronicles Associated with Aberconwy

Several chronicles can be seen to have either copied the chronicle in the Aberconwy Register, or, far more likely considering its late date, to have been one of several sources for it. Despite this, it must always be remembered that any of these chronicles may have used similar sources which have not survived and possibly have not even been considered as once having existed, our knowledge of medieval chronicles being so imperfect.

The probable sources of the Aberconwy 'chronicle', or those associated with Aberconwy abbey, are listed here and then discussed below under the following headings:

O Oes Gwrtheyrn	Tewkesbury Annals
Giraldus Cambrensis	Waverley Annals
Epitome Historiae Britanniae	William Rishanger
Hailes Abbey Chronicle	Worcester Annals

O Oes Gwrtheyrn
Strictly *O Oes Gwrtheyrn* is not related to the Aberconwy Register, but as it appears that it was compiled for or in Aberconwy abbey, quite probably before the move to Maenan, it is necessary to look at this work in some detail.

O Oes Gwrtheyrn is an odd composition, being not set out in a standard chronicle form. Fortunately, it has recently been one subject within a thesis that puts its origin in perspective in relation to other annals[*832]. The chronicle, or perhaps more accurately proto-chronicle, as it appears to attempt to form a chronology for other chronicles, is based upon three fixed dates. These are the only 'solid' dates mentioned in the text. They are the battle fought near Machawy [Glasbury] on 16 June 1056, which is wrongly dated to 1055 in the proto-chronicle; the battle of *Wadiece* fought in 1132, which is again wrongly dated to

---

[*832] Jones, O.W., *Historical Writing in Medieval Wales* [Phd, Bangor, 2013].

1133[*833]; and the battle of Bryn Derwin fought in 1255, which is correctly dated. As two of the three dates fixed in the text are wrong, it also means that the chronology of the whole is unstable and several date calculations are wide of the mark, even when compared to other versions of *O Oes Gwrtheyrn*. This is before the unreliable elements of the stories of Geoffrey Monmouth (d.1151) are brought into the equation. Quite obviously the compiler of this proto-chronicle was working from one or more chronicle sources and trying to make sense of the time spans involved. Possibly this was a precursor to his writing his own history, or it was simply done as an academic exercise. Whatever the case, *O Oes Gwrtheyrn* was well copied in the Middle Ages and several versions have come down to us. The version printed below is from a Latin translation of the Welsh versions preserved in the Red Book of Hergest (compiled 1382x1410) and Llansteffan Ms.28 (1455-66)[*834]. Consequently it can be seen that *O Oes Gwrtheyrn* in its earliest surviving form is as early as any of the surviving copies of the Bruts. This by itself would suggest a late thirteenth century date for the original compilation of the work. It certainly fits in with the correctly dated events of the late thirteenth century, but the rather varied dating of earlier sections suggests that it was compiled some distance from the twelfth century. In any case, its composition must post date the publications of Geoffrey Monmouth (d.1151) and predate the Red Book of Hergest, written 1382-1410 and Peniarth 32, written c.1404 as a copy appears in these.

There is no known reason why the *O Oes Gwrtheyrn* was such a popular work. It appears in over a dozen different manuscripts between 1382 and 1768. These divide into two separate traditions with differing formats. However, in the Victorian period its worth was denigrated and apart from a brief rehabilitation by JE Lloyd, has languished in obscurity until 2013. As it can be suggested with some degree of certitude that this work had its provenance in the scriptorium of Aberconwy abbey it is worth spending some time on its contents.

The early section of the compilation uses the expression 'from... to' for dating events. This stops in the year 1193 when 'the following year' is used until the death of Dafydd ab Owain, after which (and a gap of at least 5 years) the bland text expands somewhat to become a meagre chronicle for the years from 1208 to 1212. As the old format is retained to date the battle of Painscastle in 1198, it is possible that the original source (if there was one) ended with the twelfth century. After the meagre chronicle 'ends' in 1212 there follows two sentences which take the story up to 1216 when the compiler reverts to the 'from... to' formula until the 1265 finish of the work. The implication of this is that the entire exercise was the work of just the one compiler, but he may have used older sources for the period before 1198 and another one for the period 1208 to 1212. He then used personal recollections for the period 1216 to 1265. This is possibly the most logical account for his changes in style.

The contents of *O Oes Gwrtheyrn* point quite clearly to a thirteenth century Venedotian origin. Firstly, of the 46 people mentioned in it, 27 are specifically related to Gwynedd and a further ten are kings or lords of England who either held a real or theoretical overlordship of Wales or Gwynedd. Then there is the solitary obituary of Caradog the monk of Rhos (Dyfed), who began his religious career before 1093 as a religious fugitive from Brycheiniog[*835]. Why Caradog should be included in the chronicle is a mystery for he appears in neither the Bruts

[*833] Both battles are covered in detail from the original sources in Remfry, PM, *Medieval Battles: Wales, 1055 to 1216: Volume 2, part 1* [2017].

[*834] Humphrey Llwyd, *Britannicæ descriptionis commentariolum: necnon de Mona insula et Britannica arce, sive armamentario Romano disceptatio epistolaris. Accedunt æræ Cambrobritannicæ*, ed. by M. Williams [London, 1731], 141–64, the extracts printed below are from pages 152-64.

[*835] His career is briefly charted in Lloyd, J.E., *History of Wales* [2 vols., 1911] II, 591-3. Giraldus had had a papal commission to investigate Caradog for sainthood in 1200, Butler, HE. & Williams, CH., *The Autobiography of Giraldus Cambrensis*, [1937], 200.

nor the Annales. Possibly the compiler confused him with Caradog of Llancarfan who appears in Geoffrey Monmouth, although Caradog of Rhos was highly thought of by Giraldus Cambrensis[*836]. Giraldus, it should also be remembered, was a source for the Aberconwy Register as well as *O Oes Gwrtheyrn*. It is possible that the compiler saw the name, or knew of Caradog, and simply guessed that he was from Rhos in North Wales, rather than the Rhos of Dyfed in South Wales, and thus erroneously included him in his text.

People mentioned in *O Oes Gwrtheyrn*			
Person	**Area**	**Person**	**Area**
Vortigan	Britain	Arthur	Britain
Maelgwn	Gwynedd	Gwrgius	Britain/Wales
Perdur	Britain/Wales	Cadwaladr	Mon/Gwynedd
King Offa	Mercia	Owain ap Maredudd	Dyfed
Merfyn Frych	Gwynedd	Rhodri Mawr	Gwynedd
Anarawd ap Rhodri	Gwynedd	Merfyn ap Rhodri	Gwynedd
Cadell ap Rhodri	Gwynedd	Hywel Dda	Wales/Gwynedd
Owain ap Hywel	Deheubarth	Canute (Fitz Swan)	England
Gruffydd ap Llywelyn	Gwynedd/Wales	William the Bastard	England/Wales
Bleddyn ap Cynfyn	Gwynedd	Gruffydd ap Cynan	Gwynedd
Rhys ap Tewdwr	Deheubarth	Trahaearn ap Caradog	Gwynedd/Arwystli
King William Rufus	England/Wales	Caradog the monk	Rhos/Dyfed
Cadwallon ap Gruffydd	Gwynedd	Maredudd ap Bleddyn	Powys
Owain ap Cynan	Gwynedd	Cadwaladr ap Cynan	Gwynedd
Llywelyn ab Iorwerth	Gwynedd	Owain ap Madog	Powys
Rhodri ab Owain	Gwynedd	Gruffydd ap Cynan	Gwynedd
Dafydd ab Owain	Gwynedd	King John	England/Wales
Archbishop Stephen of Canterbury	England/Wales	Hywel ap Gruffydd	Gwynedd
Harold Pic	Denmark/Mon	Earl Ralph of Chester	England/Wales
St Robert the bishop	Gwynedd	Maredudd ap Cynan	Gwynedd

[*836] Lloyd, J.E., *History of Wales* [2 vols., 1911] II, 528.

Gruffydd ap Llywelyn	Gwynedd	Hywel ap Gruffydd	Gwynedd
Lady Joan	Gwynedd	Dafydd ap Llywelyn	Gwynedd
Owain ap Gruffydd	Gwynedd	Llywelyn ap Gruffydd	Gwynedd

If the people mentioned in *O Oes Gwrtheyrn* are Gwyneddcentric so too are the places, 7 of the 28 places mentioned being at or near Aberconwy granges (marked with an * in the below table). Ten of these places are within fifty miles of Aberconwy itself and the rest were of 'national' importance to the principality of Gwynedd.

Placename	Geographical area	Miles from Conwy
battle of Badon	Geoffrey Monmouth	
battle at Camlan	Geoffrey Monmouth	
battle at Arderydd	said to be Arthuret north of Carlisle	200
battle at Chester	Cheshire	45
battle at Meigen/Hatfield Chace	near Cuckney, Yorkshire	110
Degannwy castle*	Creuddyn	2
Conwy*	Gwynedd	0
battle of Carno	Powys	60
battle near Machawy	Brycheiniog	110
battle on Mynydd Carn	Dyfed	130
Cardigan	Ceredigion	115
Tal Moelfre*	Mon	25
wood of Ceiriog	Powys	40
Rhuddlan castle	Tegeingl	15
Carrog Hwfa (*Gwern y firogl*)	Powys	45
battle at Coedana*	Mon	25
battle next to Painscastle	Elfael	100
Gwyddrug/Mold	Tegeingl	30
Scotland		200
Llanfaes*	Mon	15
Ireland		100

Creuddyn granary*	Creuddyn	1
Aber	Gwynedd	8
Bangor	Gwynedd	15
battle on Derwyn*	Gwynedd	30
Cymerau	Deheubarth	120
Diserth castle	Tegeingl	18
Pennardd Halawg [Hawarden]	Tegeingl	35

As a final compelling point in linking *O Oes Gwrtheyrn* with Aberconwy is the entry for 1210. This specifically mentions Creuddyn grange and it seems incredible that anyone writing at the time other than the monks of Aberconwy would be concerned with this being pulled down and utilised to repair Degannwy castle, especially when it is considered how many granges would have been demolished to repair fortresses in military emergencies during the years covered by similar chronicles. Further, although there is a predominance of information on the Gwynedd royal house, it is clear that Llywelyn ab Iorwerth is singled out for more detailed treatment and it is this work which is the only near original source that mentions the time of his birth. It also shows an interest in Gruffydd ap Llywelyn (d.1244), rather than his younger half brother Dafydd (d.1246). If this work was carried out at the scriptorium of Aberconwy abbey and was so widely distributed as it seems to have been, it is peculiar that it does not show up in material in the Aberconwy Register. This again points to the fact that the Register might not have been drawn up in Aberconwy abbey itself, and this in turn possibly points to a Hailes abbey origin in the time of the dispute between the two Davids who were vying to be abbot in the early 1480s.

All the evidence therefore seems to suggest that the chronicle as it now stands was a singular post 1265 work, making use of some contemporary notes of the period around 1210 which were certainly written at Aberconwy abbey. It was later much copied and altered in various forms. The fact that this proto-chronicle was so copied in the post medieval period indicates just how poor surviving chronicle material from the Middle Ages was in Wales.

In the translation below the following conventions have been used, [] to indicate a secure or reasonably secure date by modern reckoning. The earlier dating within these brackets is based upon a variety of medieval sources and before the ninth century is subject to variation. The symbol {} has been used to supply the probable date arrived at via the compiler's computation - if he had written it from his base years (a-1055, and c-1255). There is a second version of the chronicle which uses the 1211 date of the hostageship of Gruffydd ap Llywelyn as an anchor (b-1211), but that is not used in this apparently earlier series of renditions of the chronicle. Blank lines have been added to this text to help demonstrate the apparent changes in format by either writing style or fixed date. The work has no title and is simply know by the first three Welsh words of the text - *O Oes Gwrtheyrn*.

From the time of Vortigan to the battle of Badon where Arthur and his knights fought with the Saxons and gained the victory [516], 128 years {a-407}.
A tempore Vortigerni ad proelium in Badonico, ubi Arthurus & milites sui cum Saxonibus dimicavere, & victoriam adepti sunt erant anni CXXVIII.

From the battle of Badon [516] to the battle at Camlan [537] being joined, 22 years {a-535}.

A proelio in Badonico ad proelium apud Camlan commissum erant anni XXII.

From Camlan [537] to the death of Maelgwn [551], 10 years {a-557}.

A proelio apud Camlan commisso ad obitum Maglocuni, erant anni X.

From the death of Maelgwn [551] to the battle at Arderydd [573] being joined, 25 years {a-567}.

Ab obitu Maglocuni ad proelium apud Arderydd commissum erant anni XXV.

From the battle at Arderydd being joined [573] to the time when Gwrgius and Perdur were killed [580], 7 years {a-592}.

A proelio apud Arderydd commisso ad tempus quo Gwrgius & Peredurus interfecti sunt erant anni VII.

From the killing of Gwrgius and Peredur [580] to the battle at Chester [616] being joined, 9 years {a-599}.

Ab interemtione Gwrgii & Pereduri ad proelium apud Castrum legionis commissum erant anni IX.

From the battle at Chester [616] to the battle at Meigen [633] being joined, 14 years {a-608}.

A proelio apud Castrum Legionis ad proelium apud Meigen commissum erant anni XIV.

From the battle at Meigen [633] to the time Cadwaladr the Blessed departed for Rome [682*837], 48 years {a-622}.

A proelio apud Meigen ad tempus quo Cadwaladrus Benedictus Romam profectus est erant anni XLVIII.

From Cadwaladr departing [682] to the death of King Offa [26 Jul 796], 128 years {a-670}.

A Cadwaladri Romam profectione ad Offae regis Obitum erant anni CXXVIII.

From the death of Offa [26 Jul 796] to the year when the town of Degannwy was burned by a lightening strike [822/3] during the time of Owain ap Maredudd [d.811], 20 years {a-798}.

Ab Offae obitu ad annum quo urbs Diganwy caelo tacta combusta est tempore Oweni F. Mareduddi erant anni XX.

From the time when Degannwy was chastised by fire [822/3] from heaven to the death of Merfyn Frych [844], 33 years {a-818}.

A tempore quo Diganwy igne caelesti correpta est ad obitum Mervini Maculosi erant anni XXXIII.

From the death of Merfyn [844] to the killing of Rhodri and his son [873], 27 years {a-851}.

Ab obitu Mervini ad Interemtionem Roderici filii ejus erant anni XXVII.

From the killing of Rhodri [873] to the year when Anarawd his son avenged the killing of the same [881], 3 years {a-878}.

Ab interemtione Roderici ad annum quo Anarawdus filius necem ejus ultus est erant anni III.

From the battle near Conwy [881] being joined to the killing of Merfyn ap Rhodri [904], 17 years {a-881}.

A proelio juxta Conovium commisso ad Intersectionem Mervini F. Roderici erant anni XVII.

From the killing of Merfyn [904] to the death of Cadell ap Rhodri [910], 10 years {a-898}.

Ab interfectione Mervini ad obitum Cadelli F. Roderici erant anni X.

From the death of Cadell [910] to the death of Anarawd ap Rhodri [916], 6 years {a-908}.

Ab obitu Cadelli ad obitum Anarawdi F. Roderici erant anni VI.

---

*837 *Annales Cambriae. A Translation of Harleian 3859; PRO E.164/1; Cottonian Domitian, A 1; Exeter Cathedral Library MS. 3514 and MS Exchequer DB Neath, PRO E.164/1*, ed. Remfry, P.M., [Malvern, 2007], 48-9. This is a fake annal, as Cadwaladr had actually died in 664.

From the death of Anarawd [916] to the departure of Hywel Dda ap Cadell to Rome [929], 18 years {a-914}.

Ab obitu Anarawdi ad Hoeli Boni Cadelli F. Romam profectionem erant anni XVIII.

From the proceeding of Hywel to Rome [929] to his death [949], 19 years {a-932}.

Ab Heoli Romam prosectione ad obitum ejus erant anni IXX.

From the death of Hywel [949] to the battle of Carno [949] being joined, 7 years {a-(954)/951}.

Ab obitu Hoeli ad proelium in Monte Carno commissum erant anni VII.

From Carno [949] to the battle of the sons of Idwel there was 1 year (or 4 years) {a-961-958}.

A proelio praedicto ad proelium filiorum Idwali erat annus I (al.anni IV).

From the battle of the sons of Idwel [954] to the death of Owain ap Hywel Dda [988], 24 years {a-962}.

A proelio filiorum Idwali ad obitum Oweini F. Hoeli Boni erant anni XXIV.

From the death of Owain [988] to the year when Canute (Fitz Swan) began to reign [1016], 27 years {a-986}.

Ab obitu Oweni ad annum quo Canutus Swani F. regnare coepit erant anni XXVII.

From the year when King Canute began to reign [1016] to Machawy [1056], where Gruffydd ap Llywelyn escaped victorious and the Saxon bishop was killed, 42 years {a-1013}.

Ab anno quo Canutus rex regnare coepit ad proelium juxta Machawy commissum, ubi Griffinus F. Leolini victor evasit, & Episcopus Saxonum interfectus est erant anni XLII.

From the battle near Machawy being joined [16 June 1056] to the killing of Gruffydd [4 Aug 1064], 9 years. [act. 8 years]

A proelio juxta Machawy commisso ad interemtionem Griffini erant anni ix.

From the birth of Christ to that year referred to, 1055 years. [this battle is not in the Bruts or Annales Cambriae so it is a mystery why it was included as a (wrong) fixed date]

Ab incarnatione Christi ad annum istum erant anni MLV.

From the killing of Gruffydd [1064] to the coming of William the Bastard into this island, 5 years [1066]. Also he reigned 21 years. [1066-87]

Ab interemtione Griffini ad adventum Gulielmi Nothi in hanc insulam erant anni V.

Is autem regnavit annis xxi.

From the coming of William the Bastard [1066] to the killing of Bleddyn ap Cynfyn [1075], 7 years. [act.9]

Ab adventu Guilelmi Nothi ad interemtionem Blethini F. Convini erant anni VII.

From the killing of Bleddyn [1075] to the battle on Mynydd Carn being joined [1081], 6 years. Gruffydd ap Cynan and Rhys ap Tewdwr conquered in that place Trahaearn ap Caradog.

Ab interemtione Blethini ad proelium in Monte Carn commissum erant anni vi.

Griffinus F. Conani & Rhesus F Theodori ibi vicerunt Trahaiarnum f Caradoci.

From the battle of Mynydd Carn [1081] to the killing of Rhys ap Tewdwr [1093], 13 years [act.12].

A proelio in Monte Carn ad interemtionem Rhesi F. Theodori erant anni XIII.

[1100] From the killing of Rhys to the killing of King William Rufus, 7 years. The former truly reigned 13 years [1087-1100].

Ab interemtione Rhesi ad interemtionem Guilelmi Regis Rufi erant anni VII.

Ille vero regnavit annis xiii.

From the killing of King Rufus [1100] to the death of Caradog the monk [13 Apr 1124], 25 years. [act.24]

Ab interemtione Regis Rufi ad obitum Caradoci Monachi erant anni XXV.

From the death of Caradog to the killing of Cadwallon ap Gruffydd and the death of Maredudd ap Bleddyn [1132], 8 years [act.7].

Ab obitu Caradoci ad interfectionem Cadwallawni F. Griffini & obitum Mareduddi F Blethini erant anni X.

From the incarnation of Christ to this year, 1133 years. [1132]

Ab incarnatione Christi ad annum istum erant anni MCXXXIII.

From the beginning of the world to the death of Maredudd ap Bleddyn and the killing of Cadwallon, 6,332 years.

Ab orbe condito ad obitum Maredudii F. Blethini & interemtionem Cadwallawni erant anni VIMCCCXXXII.

From the killing of Cadwallon [1132] to the year when Owain and Cadwaladr devastated Cardigan [1136] (*Aber-Teifi*, 1139), 6 years. [act.4]

Ab interemtione Cadwallawni ad annum quo Owenus & Cadwaladrus terram Cereticam populbantur erant anni VI.

From the year when the sons of Cynan devastated Cardigan [1136] to the slaughter of the French at the place of Tal Moelfre [1157] it was said, 20 years. [act 19]

Ab anno quo Conani filii teram Cereticam populabantur, ad interfectionem Normannorum apud locum Tal Moelfre dictum erant anni xx (1159).

From the fight at Tal Moelfre [1165] to the year when the eyes of the hostages were plucked out at the wood of Ceiriog [1165], 8 years. [act.0]

A proelio apud Tal Moelfre ad annum quo obsidum oculi erut sunt apud Coed Ceirjawg erant anni viii.

From the fight at Coed Ceiriog being joined [1165] to the time when Owain and Cadwaladr tore down Rhuddlan castle [1167], 2 years.

A proelio apud Coed Ceirjawg commisso ad tempus quo Owenus & Cadwaladrus Rudlanium castrum diripiebant erant anni II.

From the year when Rhuddlan castle was torn down [1167] to the death of Owain [22 Nov 1170], 5 years. [act.3]

Ab anno quo Rudlanium diripiebatur ad obitum Oweni erant anni V.

From the death of Owain [22 Nov 1170] to the death of Cadwaladr [29 Feb 1171/2] there was a year and the time between the feast of St Clement (23 Nov) to the beginning of Lent.

Ab obitu Oweni ad obitumCadwaladri erat annus & spatium a Festo S Clementis ad initium Quadragesimae.

From the death of Owain [22 Nov 1170] to the birth of Llywelyn ab Iorwerth [May 1172] , 2½ years.

Ab obitu Oweni ad natum Leolinum F. Jorwerthi erant anni II & dimidium anni.

From the birth of Llywelyn [May 1172] to the killing of Owain ap Madog at the fight at Carrog Hwfa (Gwern y firogl) [1187], 14 years. [act.15]

A nato Leolino ad interfectionem Oweni F. Madoci in proelio apud Gwern y firogl erant anni XIV.

From the killing of Owain ap Madog [1187] to the Summer of the Irish [1193], 7 years. [act.6]

Ab interfectione Oweni F. Madoci ad aestatem Hibernorum erant anni VII.

In the following year was the battle at Coedana [1194].

Anno insequenti fuit proelium apud Coettaneu.

Three years afterwards [act.1] Rhodri ab Owain died [1194]*838*.

Tertio post anno obiit Rodericus F. Oweni.

From the summer of the Irish [1193] to the battle next to Painscastle [1198], 5 years.

Ab aestate Hibernorum ad proelium juxta Castrum Pagani erant anni V.

The following winter Llywelyn is said to have torn down Gwyddrug [1199].

Hyeme insequenti Leolinus Gwyddrug dictum diripuit.

The second year after the battle next to Painscastle [1198] Gruffydd ap Cynan died [1200] .

Anno secundo post proelium juxta Castrum Pagani obiit Griffinus F. Conani.

The year after [act.0?] the death of Gruffydd [1200], Dafydd ab Owain died [1200?].

Anno post obitum Griffini obiit David F Oweni.

From the death of Dafydd ab Owain [1200?] to the year when an interdict was placed through all England and Wales due to the difference between King John and Archbishop Stephen of Canterbury [1208], 5 years [act.8 or 5 according to the Bruts]. However this interdict in England lasted 7 years [1215] and in Wales 5 years [1212].

Ab obitu Davidis F. Oweni ad annum quo missae interdictae sunt per totam Lloegriam & Cambriam ob dissidium inter Joannem Regem & Stephanum Archiepiscopum Cantuariensem erant anni V. Interdictum autem istud per Lloegriam VII & per Cambriam V annos duravit.

Certainly the next year [1209] following from the former first interdict cast on England and Wales [1208], Llywelyn ab Iorwerth and Hywel ap Gruffydd set out with King John of England for Scotland in order that the king of Scotland paid obedience to King John of England.

Anno insequenti proximo nempe ab illo quo primum missae interdicebantur per Lloegriam & cambriam, Leolinus f Jorwerthi & Hoelus f Griffini profecti sunt cum Joanne Lloegriae rege in Scotiam ut Scotiae regem Joanni Lloegriae regi obedientem facerent.

[1209] The same year on the vigil of the feast of Sts Simon and Jude [27 October] the commander of the palace of the king of the Danes, who's name was Harold Pic*839*, with six piratical ships put ashore at Llanfaes to plunder and burn the town; and there Harold Pic and his chieftains were killed.

Eodem anno in vigilia festi SS Simonis & Judea praefectus palatio regis Daniae, cui nomen Heraldus Pic, cum sex navibus piraticis appulit ad Llann Faes ad spoliandum & comburendum oppidum; & ibi Heraldus Pic & optimates ejus occisi sunt.

The following year King John proceeded to Ireland [1210] and Earl Ralph of Chester came to the castle of Degannwy to meet (or just possibly 'in the place of') King John and with his army took the castle of Degannwy, and restored the same with the wood of Creuddyn granary.

Anno insequenti profectus est Joannes Rex Hiberniam, & Radulphus Comes Cestriae ad oppidum Diganwy veniebat obviam Joanni Regi & cum exercitu suo oppidum Diganwy cepit, idemque materia Horrei Creuddyn refecit. Ac a'i cadarnhaodd o waith ysgubor y Creuddyn.

The following year King John with a huge army who were collected from France, England and Scotland came to Aber and from thence he sent his Brabantines to burn Bangor [1211].

And there was captured St Robert the bishop and escorted in the manner of a prisoner to Aber, but the king relaxed the imprisonment of the bishop. And there Llywelyn was restored to the

---

838 The Welsh versions state: From when Owain was killed until the summer of the Irish 7 years and the next year was the battle of Coedanau. In the third year Rhodri ab Owain died, Jones, O.W., *Historical Writing in Medieval Wales* [Phd, Bangor, 2013], 425.
839 Erlendr Pikr was joint leader of a raid on Iona and an abortive raid on Man this year and is obviously the man described in this chronicle, Jones, O.W., *Historical Writing in Medieval Wales* [Phd, Bangor, 2013], 433.

king's goodwill and his son Gruffydd with 24 chieftains the same gave as hostages and the king returned to England.

Anno insequenti Joannes Rex cum ingenti exercitu quem e Normannia, lloegria & Scotia comparaverat, ad Aber veniebat, & inde Brabantinos suos misit Bangorium comburere. Et ibi captus est Sanctus Robertus Episcopus & in carcerem deducebatur apud Aber, sed rex episcopum a vinculis laxavit. Et ibi Leolinus gratiam cum rege reconciliavit & filium suum Griffinum cum 24 optimatibus ea de caussa obsidio dedit & rex Lloegriam reversus est.

[1212] The following year the day [of Saturday before Whitsun, viz. 19 May 1212[*840]] died Maredudd ap Cynan.

Anno insequenti diem obiit Maredudius f Conani.

For five years [act.4] Gruffydd ap Llywelyn was held in prison [1211-15], then truly with the help of God, by the advice of Archbishop Stephen Langton, he was freed from custody.

Quinque annis Griffinus f Leolini carcere attentus erat; tum vero adjuvante Deo, consilio Stephani Archiepiscopi Cantuariensis custodia liberatus est.

Three years [act.1] after Gruffydd was freed from prison [1215], late in the day died King John on the feast of St Luke (18 October - John died 19th Oct 1216). Also at the same time Hywel ap Gruffydd died[*841].

Anno tertio postquam Griffinus carcere liberatus est, diem obiit Joannes Rex in Festo S. Lucae. Eodem etiam tempore obiit Hoelus F. Griffini.

From the death of King John [19 Oct 1216] to the death of the Lady Joan [2 Feb 1237] the wife of Llywelyn, twenty years. [act.21]

Ab obitu Joannis Regis ad obitum Dominae Joannae uxoris Leolini erant anni XX.

From the death of the aforesaid lady to the death of Llywelyn [11 Apr 1240] 3 years.

Ab obitu dominae praedictae ad obitum Leolini erant anni III.

From the death of Llywelyn to the death of Gruffydd his son [30 Apr 1244], 4 years.

Ab obitu Leolini ad obitum Griffini filii ejus, erant anni IV.

From the death of Gruffydd to the death of Dafydd ap Llywelyn [25 Feb 1246], 2 years.

Ab obitu Griffini ad obitum Davidis F. Leolini erant anni II.

From the death of Dafydd ap Llywelyn [1246] to the battle on Derwyn between Owain and Llywelyn [1255], 11 years [act.9].

Ab obitu Davidis F Leolini ad proelium in monte Derwyn dicto commissum inter Owenum & Leolinum erant anni XI.

From the said battle on Derwyn [1255] to the killing of the French in the place said to be called Cymerau [1257], 2 years.

A proelio in monte Derwyn dicto ad interfectionem Normannorum in loco Cymmereu dicto erant anni II.

From the battle on Derwyn [1255] to the destruction of Diserth castle [4 Aug 1263], 10 years. [act.8]

A proelio in monte Derwyn dicto ad excidium castri Diserth dicti erant anni X.

The same harvest Degannwy was captured [28 Sep 1263].

Eadem mess captum fuit Diganwy.

[*840] Taken from the Welsh versions, Jones, O.W., *Historical Writing in Medieval Wales* [Phd, Bangor, 2013], 426.
[*841] He died soon after 28 October 1216, Pen, 93.

From the capture of Degannwy [1263] to the capture of Pennardd Halawg [Hawarden, 1265*842] was 1 year. [act.2]

A capto Diganwy ad captum Pennardd y lag dictum erat annus I.

From the forming of the world to the battle on Derwyn, 6,454 years.

Ab orbe condito ad proelium in Derwyn erant anni VIM CCCCLIV.

From the birth of Christ to the battle on Derwyn, 1255 years.*843

A nato Christo ad proelium in Derwyn erant anni MCCLV.

From the advent of the Welsh into this island to the battle on Derwyn, 2,366 years.

Ab adventu Cambrorum in hanc insulam ad proelium in Derwyn commissum erant anni IIMCCCCLXVI.

From the time when Christianity came to Wales in the reign of Lucius ap Coel to the battle on Derwyn, 111 years {c-1144}.

A tempore quo Cambri Christianismum amplexi sunt regnante Lucio F. Coel ad proelium in Derwyn erant anni CXI.

From the coming of the Saxons to this island to the battle on Derwyn, 601 years {c-654AD}.

A Saxonum in hanc insulam adventu ad proelium in Derwyn erant anni DCI.

From the first coming of the Normans [1066] to the battle on Derwyn [1255], 606 years {c-649AD - should be 189 years}.

A primo Normannorum adventu ad proelium in Derwyn erant anni DCVI.

Giraldus Cambrensis

Two sections of Giraldus Cambrensis are translated below as they seem to have been used in the Aberconwy Register as the basis for the division of Wales in the ninth century*844. Whether this source was utilised directly or came through later plagiarising is unknown. The text has been made bold where various portions seem close to the terms used in the Aberconwy Register. *O Oes Gwrtheyrn* seems to have made more use of this source, but again whether directly or indirectly via another work is unknown.

> Concerning the division of all Wales into three parts
> In antiquity all Wales was divided into three almost equal parts, nevertheless greater equivalence than just quantity or proportion was made through consideration; that is to say Venedotia, which is today North Wales, that is called Northern Wales; South Wales that is Southern Wales, which is Deheubarth in Cambrian, that is designated the southern part; which part is further joined to the seven cantrefs of Demetia; and Powys is about the middle and east.
> *De divisione Walliae totalis in tres partes*
> *Divisa est antiquitus Wallia totalis in tres partes tanquam eaquales; plus equivalentiae tamen quam justae quantitatis et proportionis habita consideratione; venedotiam scilicet quae nunc Nortwallia, id est Borealis Wallia dicitur; sudwalliam id est Australem Walliam, quae kambrice Deheubarth, id est Dextralis pars dicitur; cujus*

---

*842 Prince Llywelyn had met Henry Montfort, acting on behalf of Earl Simon and his captive King Henry III, at Hawarden in January 1265, *Annales Cestrienses, a chronicle of the abbey of St. Werburgh, Chester*, ed. and trans. Christie, R.C., Record Society for Lancashire and Cheshire XIV [1887], 90. It is therefore possible that the castle was handed over to him then, but then reverted to royalist control and changed hands again after 14 September after being besieged before 8 September, 'Annales Monasterii de Waverleia', *Annales Monastici*, ed. H.R. Luard [5 vols., 1864-9] II, 372; *CPR 1258-66*, 489.
*843 At this point the various Welsh versions have different endings which add nothing to the history contained in the main work.
*844 Giraldus Cambrensis, *Opera*, eds. J.S. Brewer, J.F. Dimock and G.F. Warner [8 vols., 1861-91] VI, 166-8; Book I, chaps 2&3.

etiam portio septem cantaredis est conserta Demetia; et Powisiam, quasi mediam et orientalem.

However of this division this was the underlying cause. Roderick the Great/Senior, who the Britons called Rhodri Mawr, and governor of the whole of Wales, had three sons, Merfyn, Anarawd and Cadell. These three divided all of Wales between themselves. Merfyn was granted North Wales, Anarawd Powys, Cadell with the blessing of all the people and of his brothers, South Wales, for nevertheless although [Deheubarth] itself by size was by far the greatest, nevertheless on account of the nobles, who in Cambrian were uchelwyr, just as superior men are called, who abounded, who also were in the habit of being rebellious to their lords and refused to receive a lord, [so Deheubarth] was seen to be inferior. But Cadell, his brothers dying before him, finally obtained the monarchy of all Wales, and similarly his successors until Tewdwr, In fact his descendants until Tewdwr occupied only South Wales just as his father [had], these being namely Rhys ap Tewdwr, Gruffydd ap Rhys, and Rhys ap Gruffydd who nowadays rules.

Divisionis autem hujus haec causa suberat. **Rothericus magnus qui Britannice Rotheri Maur** *dicebatur,* **totique Walliae** *praesidebat,* **tres filios habuerat, Mervinum, Anaraut, et Cadelh.** *Hi tres* **totam inter se Walliam diviserunt.** *Mervino cessit* **Nortwallia, Anaraut Powisia, Cadelh** *vero, cum populi totius et fratrum benedictione, Sudwallia. Ipsa nimirum quanquam quantitate longe major, propter nobiles tamen qui Kambrice Hucheilwer quasi superiors viri vocantur, quibus abundabat, qui et dominis rebelles esse solebant dominumque ferre detrectabant, deterior esse videbatur. Cadelh autem praemortuis fratribus, totius Walliae demum monarchiam obtinuit; et successores sui similiter usque ad Theodorum. Descendentes enim a Theodoro tantum Sudwalliam obtinuerunt, sicut et pater eorum; hi scilicet Resus filius Theodori, Griphinus filius Resi, et Resus filius Griphini qui hodie praeest.*

Chapter III
Concerning the procreation of the princes of Wales
Therefore this is the process of the begetting of the princes of South Wales: Rhys ap Gruffydd, Gruffydd ap Rhys, Rhys ap Tewdwr; Tewdwr ap Cadell, Cadell ab Einion, Einion ab Owain, Owain ap Hywel Dda, that is Hywel the Good, Hywel ap Cadell, Cadell ap Rhodri the Great/Senior. Therefore from Cadell, the son of Rodri the Great/Senior, descended the princes of South Wales. From Merfyn the princes of North Wales [descended] in this manner: Dafydd ab Owain, Owain ap Gruffydd, Gruffydd ap Cynan, Cynan ab Iago; Iago ab Idwal, Idwal ap Meurig; Meurig ab Anarawd; Anarawd ap Merfyn, Merfyn ap Rodri the Great/Senior.

De generatione principum Walliae.
Haec itaque est generatio principum Sudwalliae: Resus filius Griphini, Griphinus filius Resi, Resus filius theodori, Theodorus filius Cadelh, Cadelh filius Eneae, Eneas filius Oenei, Oeneus filius Hoeli da, id est Hoeli boni, Hoelus filius Cadelh, Cadelh filius Roderici magni. De Cadelo igitur, filio Rotherici magni, descenderunt principes Sudwalliae. De Mervino principes Nortwalliae, in hunc modum; David filius Oenei, Oeneus filius Griphini, Griphinus filius Canani, Cananus filius Iago, Iago filius Ythewal, Ythewal filius Meuric, Meuric filius Anaudrech, Anaudrech filius Mervini, Mervinus filius Rotherici magni.

However Anarawd did not procreate. Yet from him himself the princes of Powys consider themselves descended. Besides that to me it appears worthy to record that the Welsh bards and poets or reciters, have the genealogy of the aforesaid princes in their ancient and authentic books, but nevertheless written in Welsh and likewise master them from memory from Rhodri the Great/Senior up to the Blessed Virgin; and from thence up to Sylvius, Ascanius, and Aeneas; and from Aeneas up to Adam they produce the lineal generation. But being that they are so distant and remote the descents recounted might be seen to be more meritless rather than historical, so these in our compendium we will refrain from inserting from diligence.

De Anaraut autem generatio non provenit. Unde et principes Powisiae suam habent per se generationem. Hoc etiam mihi notandum videtur quod bardi Kambrenses et cantores seu recitatores genealogiam habent praedictorum principum in libris eorum antiquis et authenticis, sed tamen Kambrice scriptam; eandemque memoriter tenent a Rotherico magno usque ad beatam Virginem et inde usque ad silvium Ascanium et Eneam; et ab Enea usque ad Adam generationem linealiter producunt. Sed quoniam tam longinqua tam remotissima generis enarratio multis trutanica potius quam historica esse videretur, eam huic nostro compendio inserere ex industria supersedimus.

Epitome Historiae Britanniae

The Epitome is undoubtedly related to the Aberconwy Register, but whether as a source, a derivative or a companion text is uncertain. This short Latin Chronicle in British Library, Cotton Titus D. xxi - An Epitome (brief summary) of the History of Britain, is dated 1429 in the text. Another version, Cotton Nero A iv, is late 15th or early 16th century, but copies a version written in 1399. Another abbreviated version of this text was written in 1404[*845]. This latter work, within the book known as *Y Llyfr Teg*, was possibly made at Llantarnam abbey in Gwent. Therefore, when compared with the timescale of the creation of the Aberconwy Register some time in the period 1388 to 1536, it is apparent that both existed at around the same time, although both obviously use older source material.

The chronicle summaries events from the arrival of Brutus in Britain in 1230BC until 1375AD in a series of disparate jumps. The first section begins in 1230BC, jumps to 156AD and then 446AD. The 1230BC date may be taken wrongly from Henry Huntington, who dates the coming of Brutus to 1130BC. This is deduced as he states he was writing in 1135 and that this was 2,265 years after the coming of Brutus. Perhaps the Epitome compiler did his maths wrong on this, for the Book of Hyde and a short Welsh chronicle in the Red Book of Hergest both have Henry's 1130BC date.

The introduction is followed by a discussion on the foundation of Llandaff church in the fifth century before telling the Hengist Horsa story which is dated (far too early) to 349AD and is followed by the crowning of King Arthur by Archbishop Dubricius of Llandaff in 506AD. After a fanciful trip through Arthurian legend, ending with his burial at Avalon otherwise now known as Glastonbury and Dubricius going to Ynys Enlli, there then follows a fanciful review of the history of post Arthur Britain. This section, from Brutus to the death of Cadwaladr, which is wrongly said to have occurred in 689, draws chiefly on Geoffrey Monmouth, supplemented by other sources such as the texts in the Book of Llandaff and

---

[*845] Aberystwyth NLW, Peniarth 32.

Bede's *Historia Ecclesiastica*. The mention of Glastonbury would suggest a post mid twelfth century date for the chronicle's inception.

There follows a section which bears many similarities to the Galfridian mythology at the beginning of the Aberconwy Register as well as subsequent sections which take the Epitome's history up to the death of Dafydd in 1283 and then beyond in a series of almost random entries up to 1375. The early section obviously uses parts of Giraldus' *Descriptio Kambriae* as well as the Gildasian recension of the *Historia Brittonum*. The later more annalistic section uses as its source information that seems linked to the Waverley and Worcester annals, and further provides an account of events from a Glamorgan perspective, one piece of information - the founding of Cardiff in 1081 - seems linked to work at Neath abbey around the turn of the fourteenth century[*846]. The part relevant to Aberconwy is printed in translation with the original Latin printed below. Where one appears to have plagiarized the other, being similar to the matter in the Aberconwy Register, the text had been made bold. The extracts below are taken from *The Lives of Cambro British Saints* [1853], 282-5. The full text runs from page 278 to page 286.

After Ceredig reigned Cadfan. After Cadfan, Cadwallon. Truly in the time of Cadwallon there were so much dearth, so much pestilence, so much the famine intensified that the magnates mutually embracing each other submerged themselves in the waters; at which point it was said to have been expressed through the voice of an angel that his son would banish himself from the kingdom and that he would die in the middle of Rome and that he was destined to be numbered in the list of the saints. Which king indeed enquired the cause of so much calamity in his kingdom; to which the angel replied saying, "The negligence of the prelates, the plundering of the nobles, the usury of the Jews [could also be read as 'the fraud of the judges'], the detestable luxury, the rage of the purjurers, the inordinate ornamentation of clothes."

*Post Kareticum regnavit Cadvanus. Post Cadvanum, Cadwalanus. Tempore vero Cadwalani fuerunt tanta karistia tante pentilentie, tanta fames invalescebant, quod magnates mutuo se amplexantes, submerserunt se in aquis. Cui dictum est in voce per angelum, quod filius ejus expelleret se ipsum de regno, et quod moriturus eta Rome, et quod deberet numerari in cathalogo sanctorum. Qui quidem rex quesivit causam tanti mali in regno suo; cui respondens angelus dicens, "Necligencia prelatorum, rapina potentium, cubiditas judicum, detestanda luxuria, rabies perjuriorum, inordinatus cultus vestimentorum."[*847]*

After him reigned Cadwaladr his son. Truly this Cadwaladr, surnamed the Blessed, reigned a short time, who, as much as on account of the mortality which nearly destroyed his people, than on account of the diverse persecutions, which he continually suffered from the barbarous Saxons, he left his kingdom and made for Lesser Britain [Brittany]. And there after an interval of time, he assembled a great army that he might return and expel the foreign peoples from his kingdom, but it was announced by an angel that he should desist from his purpose.

[*846] The Neath annals are printed in *Annales Cambriae. A Translation of Harleian 3859; PRO E.164/1; Cottonian Domitian, A 1; Exeter Cathedral Library MS. 3514 and MS Exchequer DB Neath, PRO E.164/1*, ed. Remfry, P.M., [Malvern, 2007].

[*847] Peniarth MS.32 has: King Cadwaladr inquired about the cause of so many evils in his kingdom, to which an angel responded saying, 'The negligence of officials, the plundering by powerful men, the greed/usury of Jews/judges, detestable extravagance, the madness of false oaths, inordinate finery in clothings'.

Rex Kadwaladrus quesiuit causam tanti mali in regno suo, cui respondens angles dicens, "Necgligencia prelatorum, rapina potentum, cupiditas iudicum, detestanda luxuria, rabies periuriorum, inordinatus cultus uestimentorum".

For God was unwilling that the Britons should reign for a long time in the island of Britain before the time should come of which Merlin had prophesied to Arthur. And he ordered the former [Cadwallon] to go to Rome to Pope Sergius in order that there he should perform penance that he could be numbered among the saints. He also asserted that the British people, through the merit of their faith, would gain their island in the future. Then Cadwaladr, setting aside worldly things on account of God, came to Rome and there was confirmed by Sergius and unexpectedly was seized by illness and on the 22nd day of the calends of May in the year of our Lord 689 by a contagion was liberated from his flesh, he entered the hall of the heavenly kingdom. Indeed the Welsh bards firmly hold such belief which they have written in their authentic books that when the bones of the blessed Cadwaladr shall be roused from the earth the Britons will be restored to their former power, which they had held, through the promise of the angel.

Post eum regnavit Kadwaladrus filius suus. Iste *vero* ***Kadwaladrus, cognomine Benedictus, regnavit modico tempore, qui tam propter mortalitatem que populum suum fere devastabat, quam propter diversas persecuciones, quas paciebatur assidue per*** *barbaricos Saxones,* ***reliquit regnum suum*** *et* ***Minorem Britanniam peciit. Ibique post intervallum temporis, congregavit magnum excercitum ut rediet, et expelleret externas naciones a regno suo, cui nunciatum est per angelum ut a*** *proposito* ***suo desisteret. Nolebat enim Deus Britones in insula Britanie diucius regnare, antequam tempus venisset quod Merlinus Arthuro prophetaverat. Precepit illi*** *et* ***ut Romam ad Sergium papam iret, ut ibi peracta penitencia inter beatos annumeretur. Dicebat populum*** *etiam* ***Britannicum per meritum fidei sue insulam in futuro adepturum. Tunc Kadwaladrus abjectis mundialibus propter Deum, venit Romam, et ibi a Sergio confirmatus,*** *inopino et languore correptus* ***est xxii*** *die* ***Kalendarum Maie Anno Domini DCLXXXIX a contagione carnis solutus,*** *celesti regni aulam ingressus* ***est. Bardi enim Kambrenses istam opinionem*** *quam in libris suis autenticis habent scripta,* ***firmiter tenent quod cum ossa beati Kadwaladri*** *a* ***terra suscitarentur, Britones pristine potestati, quam habuerunt, per promissionem Angeli restaurarentur.***

Truly after Cadwaladr the remains of the Britons lost their name, already they were not called Britons but Welshmen; they suffered so much disturbance from the attacks of the barbarous Saxons that they could not resist them and thus weakened they gathered in Cambria, recently Wales and there for a long time reigned through princes of their own stock. For they were ruled by only one prince up to the time of Rhodri Mawr, that is Roderick the Great/Senior.

Post *vero* ***Kadwaladrum reliqui Britonum perdiderunt nomen suum jam non vocabantur Britones, sed Wallenses; tantam inquietacionem paciebantur per barbaricos Saxones, quod non potuerunt eis resistere, et sic debilitati pecierunt Kambriam, modo Walliam, et ibi per multa tempora regnabant per principes generis sui. Regebant enim omnes per unum principem solum usque ad tempus Rodri Vawr,*** *id est* ***Roderici magni.***

And after many years had unfolded, two of those parts mentioned, that is Powys and South Wales, lost their title of prince and principality. Certainly the prince of North Wales reassumed the title of prince of all Wales which he possessed continually with his posterity up to Prince Llywelyn ap Gruffydd ap Llywelyn ab Iorwerth Dryndwyn, after whose death none to this point have been prince of his descent just as it will be revealed clearly in the following. That Rhodri the Great reigned over all Wales in his time. After his death his three sons, namely: Merfyn, Anarawd and Cadell divided between themselves all Wales in three principalities: Merfyn the principality of Gwynedd, that is North Wales; Anarawd the principality of Powys and Cadell the principality of Deheubarth, that is South Wales. And each of them with their posterity ruled over his portion as prince for many years.

Et postquam multi anni essent evoluti, istae duae partes, videlicet Powysia et Sowthwallia, perdiderunt nomen Principis sui et Principatus. Princeps vero Northwalliae reassumpsit nomen integrum tocius Principatus Walliae, quo gaudebat usque cum posteris suis usque ad Lewelinum Principem Wap gruff' Wap Ll Wap Jerwarth Droyndon, post cujus mortem nullum hucusque habuerunt Principem de genere suo sicut manifeste sequentibus declarabitur. Iste Rodricus magnus regebat totam Walliam tempore suo. Post cujus obitum tres filii sui, videlicet Merthwynus Anarawd et Cadell diviserunt inter se totam Walliam in tres principatus, Merthwyno principatum Gwyneth, id est. Northwalliam, Anarawd principatum Powysie, Cadell principatum Deheubarth, id est Suth Wallia; unusquisque istorum cum posteris suis regebat partem suam ut princeps per multos annos.

And after many years had passed two of those portions, namely Powys and South Wales, lost the name of prince and principality. Truly Cadell ruled his portion with his offspring until the time of Rhys ap Gruffydd, the son of Rhys ap Tewdwr, of whose family this is: Rhys ap Gruffydd ap Rhys ap Tewdwr ap Cadell ab Eneas ab Owain ap Hywel Dda ap Cadell ap Rhodri Mawr ap Mervfyn the king of Mon (Anglesey). From Roderick the Great the genealogy of the princes is recited up to the blessed Virgin[848], as is to be fully found in the authentic books of the Welsh bards. And from the blessed Virgin up to Aeneas Ysgwyddwyn ab Aeneas it stretches out lineally.

Et postquam plures anni essent devoluti, iste due partes, videlicet Powysia et Sothwallia, perdiderunt nomen principis et Principatus. Cadell vero regebat portionem suam cum genere suo, usque ad tempus Rees vap Gruffuth, vap Rees vap Teudwr; cujus generacio est hec. Rees vap Gruffuth vap Rees vap Teudwr vap Cadell vap Eneas, vap Owein vap Howel dda vap Cadell vap Rodri Vawr vap meruin brenin Manaw. A Roderico magno recitatur genealogia principum usque Beatam Virginem, ut in libris autenticis Bardorum Kambrencium plenarie reperitur. Et a Beata Virgine usque ad Eneas yscoythwyn ab Eneas usque ad linealiter producant.

Truly after these two portions, namely Powys and South Wales, as it is said above, themselves lost the title of prince and principality; the prince of North Wales reassumed the complete whole, the title of all Wales, and also the rulership; which afterwards he enjoyed with his posterity until Prince Llywelyn ap Gruffydd ap Llywelyn ab Iorwerth Drwyndwn. Truly in the time of that Llywelyn there arose a great discord between him and Edward king of England called Longshanks, who for a long time was fatally envious of him, on account of which he assembled an army and entered Wales with a multitude of oppressive people and cruelly laid waste the country with fire and sword; because while the Welsh experienced so much suffering they began manfully with strength joining with them in battle and from them as many armed men as foot they exterminated by death, but nothing benefited them in the end. For early in the night by a contrived deceit Llywelyn, their prince, was captured by Roger Mortimer his kinsman and by means of him killed and beheaded. After whose death up to this point they had no prince of his race.

---

[848] The genealogy of Owain ap Hywel Dda in BL. Harliean Ms.3859 states that the ancestor of Rhodri was Anna, the cousin of the Virgin Mary and mother of God, *Archaeologia Cambrensis* [1860], x.

Postquam vero iste due partes, videlicet Powysia et Suthwallia, ut dictum est supra, perdiderunt nomen principis sui et principatus, princeps Northwallie reassumpsit totum integrum nomen totius Wallie, et principatus; quo deinceps gaudebat, cum posteris suis usque ad Lewelinum principem, vap Gruffuth vap Llewelin vap Ioruerth droyndon. Tempore vero istius Lewelini orta est magna discordia inter ipsum et Edwardum, regem Anglie dictum Longeschankys, qui ei diu mortaliter invidebat, propter quod congregavit exercitum et ingressus est Walliam cum multitudine gravi gentem et patriam igne et gladio crudeliter devastabat; quod cum Wallenses tantam persecucionem senciebant, sumptis viribus viriliter congressi sunt cum eis, et ex eis tam armatorum quam peditum per mortem exterminaverunt; sed nichil eis in fine profuit. Nam de nocte ymaginata fraude Lewelinus, princeps suus, captus fuit per Rogerum de mortuomari affinem suum et per eum interfectus et decollatus. Post cujus mortem nullum hucusque habuerunt principem de genere suo.

In the year of our Lord 1282 the said Llywelyn prince of Wales was slain; on account of whose death the Welsh were terrified beyond measure and thrown into confusion; they delivered to the king of England all the castles of North Wales with a small portion of the Cross of our Lord, truly in Welsh called Croes Naid, with many other noted relics.

*Anno Domini MCCLXXXII interfectus est dictus Lewelinus princeps Wallie; de cujus morte territi sunt Wallenses ultra modum et turbati **reddiderunt regi Anglie omnia castra Norwallie una cum porciuncula crucis dominice Kambrice vero dicta Croes Neide, cum multis aliis famosis reliquiis.***[*849]

They also gave up the crown of the most famous Arthur, once king of the Britons and thus the glory of Wales and the Welsh was transferred to the kings and nobles of England.

Reddiderunt eciam coronam famocissimi Arthuri quodam regis Brittanie et sic gloria Wallie et Wallensium Regibus et magnatibus Anglie translata est.[*850]

Truly in the following year, David the brother of the said Llywelyn was captured and at Amwythig, that is Shrewsbury, was drawn, beheaded and butchered.

***In sequenti** vero **anno** captus est **David frater dicti Lewelini** et apud **Amoythic, id es Schorrysburi**, tractus decoltus et trucidatus.*[*851]

After the execution of Dafydd there follows a series of isolated and usually misdated chronicle entries which are summarised below.
1296, the revolt of Morgan ap Maredudd.
1315, the war of Llywelyn Bren.

[*849] This is similar to the text in Peniarth Ms.32: In the year 1282, Llywelyn prince of Wales was killed, because of whose death all of the Welsh were terrified beyond measure and, being thrown into confusion, they delivered up all the castles of North Wales to the king of England, along with one small portion of the cross of the Lord, which in Welsh is called Croes Naid, as well as many other famous relics. *Anno domini MCCLXXXII, interfectus est Leuelinus princeps Walie, de cuius morte territi sunt Walenses ultra modum [et] turbati, reddiderunt regi Anglie omnia castra Northwalie, una cum porciuncula crucis dominice, Cambrice uero dicta Croes neide, cum multis aliis famosis reliquiis.* For this chronicle see, Luft, D., 'The NLW Peniarth 32 Latin Chronicle', Studia Celtica XLIV [2010], 47-70.

[*850] Once again, Peniarth Ms.32: They even delivered up the very famous crown of Arthur, once king of the Britons, and thus the glory of Wales and the Welsh was translated to the kings and nobles of England. *Reddiderunt etiam coronam famocissum Arthuri quondam regis Brittannie et sic gloria Walie et Wallencium regibus [et] magnatibus Anglie translata est.*

[*851] Peniarth Ms.32: In the following year Dafydd, the brother of the said Llywelyn, was captured at *Amwythig*, that is Shrewsbury, and drawn, beheaded and maimed. *In sequenti uero anno captus est Dauid frater dicti Lewelini, et apud Amoythic, id est Schorouisburi, tractus decollatus et trunctatus.* The Aberconwy Register, although possibly based on this, is much more interested and detailed on the last days of Dafydd.

1321, the barons' war.

1327, the queen's war - where it is stated that the king and Hugh Despenser and other magnates were taken at Llantrissant (*Lantressen in Meiskyn*).

1348, the great pestilence.

1361, the second pestilence.

1370, the third pestilence.

1375, the fourth pestilence.

The text then jumps back to Noah and the great flood and finishes with the encouraging news that the end of the world would occur after 7330 years.

The final entry runs:

In the year of the Lord 1081 the town of Cardiff was built under King William of England.

Anno Domini MLXXXI edificata fuit villa de Kerdyf sub Willielmo rege anglie.

Hailes Abbey Chronicles

The Hailes abbey chronicle is important to the Aberconwy Register as one version appears immediately before it in the only surviving manuscript, BL. Harliean MS 3725. This version of Hailes runs to 1364. Other versions of the Hailes Abbey Chronicle are in the Bodliean and BL. Cotton MS Cleopatra D III, ff.59-72. These run from the time of Brutus (1230BC) until 1314AD, in which year it was probably compiled, or soon afterwards.

It therefore seems that the first medieval portion of the Hailes abbey chronicle which influenced the Aberconwy Register appears to have been compiled around 1314. One passage of this is taken virtually verbatum and the other is slightly altered, but the date of Llywelyn's death is not corrected. As one obviously copies the other it would appear that the Aberconwy version is the copyist, it being likely that the Hailes version was compiled around 1314 and the Aberconwy Register not until some 170 years afterwards. It is interesting that the Aberconwy compiler seems to have made the mistake of miscopying the *lxxxi* of Hailes as *lxxix* to get 79 instead of 81 for his dating. Whether this was a deliberate act as by the fifteenth century the war was erroneously thought to have begun in 1279, or whether this was carelessness will probably never be known[852].

Where the Hailes chronicle appears to have been plagiarized by the Aberconwy Register the text has been made bold.

> In the year 1281. An unexpected [second[853]] war began in Wales. For Dafydd ap Gruffydd the brother of Prince Llywelyn of Wales on the eleventh calends of April (22 March), which then was the Palm festival, captured Roger Clifford and killed many others, and besieged the castles of Flint and Rhuddlan. Before this, this Dafydd had been the most favoured of King Edward.
>
> *Anno mcclxxxi.* **Orta est [secunda] gwerra in Wallia inopinata. Nam Dauid ab Griffin frater Lewelini principis Wallie xi kal Aprilis que tunc erat dies palmarum Rogerum de Clifford cepit et ceteros quamplures interfecit, et castra de Flint et de Rothelan obsedit. Iste Dauid regi Edwardo ante hoc factum specialissimus fuit.**

---

[852] The fifteenth century 'Annales Monasterii de Bermondeseia', *Annales Monastici*, ed. H.R. Luard [5 vols., 1864-9] III, 466, misdates the war to 1279, but this chronicle does not appear to have been used by Aberconwy.

[853] *Secunda* has been added here in the margin, as this was the second war between Edward and Llywelyn.

In the year 1282. The king led an army into Wales and caused the besiegers of Flint and Rhuddlan castles to retire and with his men in that very place remained for a considerable amount of time... The same year Prince Llywelyn of Wales was killed on the third ides of September by the army of Lord Edmund Mortimer and decapitated in Buellt. Whose head was sent to London by the king and affixed over the Tower.[*854]
Anno mcclxxxii. Rex duxit exercitum in Walliam et obsessores castrorum de Flint et de Rothelan amouit et cum suis ibidem aliquamdiu permansit.... Eodem anno Lewelinus princeps Wallie iii idus Septembris occisus fuit per exercitum domini Edmundi de Mortuo mari et decollatus in Beolt. Cuius capud Londoniis per regem fuit missum et super turrim affixum.

The Bodliean version ended with the additional statement:

> ...it is said that had Llywelyn lived for just two days more all those of the Welsh tongue would have turned to his cause.[*855]

This seems to suggest that the Bodleian version was not used by the Aberconwy compiler, but that the other versions may have been, with the Harliean copy obviously being odds on favourite. The Hailes chronicle used Giraldus Cambrensis (d.c.1223), William Malmesbury (d.c.1143) and Sigebert of Gembloux (d.1112) amongst its sources.

Tewkesbury Annals, 1066 to 1263
The Tewkesbury annals appear to have been a source for the Aberconwy Register between 1211 and 1231 when several statements show direct parallels between the texts. These are shown in bold in the main Aberconwy Register text footnotes. It seems possible that the Aberconwy compiler also precised Tewkesbury for the events of 1241-44.

The Tewkesbury annals have much in common with the Worcester priory chronicle, which was also used as a source by Aberconwy. Tewkesbury's content is meagre up to 1200, but it becomes fuller with the new century. This suggests a mid-thirteenth century origin for the annals. Many passages are similar to those found in the Worcester chronicle which continued after the end of Tewkesbury in 1263 to 1308/9. Yet it appears that this Worcester chronicle does not copy Tewkesbury, although Worcester appears to copy the Wigmore chronicle which seems to have been written in or soon after 1295[*856]. Both Worcester and Tewkesbury seem to have used a now probably lost original. In the Tewkesbury chronicle during1219 there is an eye-witness account which would suggest that one author was not born any later than 1210 and would suggest that he could well have been living when the current manuscript comes to an end in June 1262. Again the funeral of Earl Gilbert in 1230 would suggest an eye-witness account. However, there was obviously also some copying going on from at least two other sources which can be seen by the death of Bishop Richard of Durham being recorded correctly under 1226 and also wrongly under 1228. Double entries like this

---

[*854] Hailes Chronicle, BL MS. Cotton Cleopatra D. iii, f.45v, printed in Stephenson, D., *Kathleen Hughes Memorial Lectures, The Aberconwy Chronicle* [2002], 15.
[*855] Hailes Chronicle, Bodley MS. Laud Misc., 529; Smith, J.B., *Llywelyn ap Gruffydd: Prince of Wales* [UWP, 2001], 210. This appears to be copied directly from the Wigmore chronicle, *The Wigmore Chronicle 1066 to 1377. A Translation of John Rylands Manuscript 215, ff. 1-8 and Trinity College, Dublin, MS.488, ff. 295-9*, ed. Remfry, P.M. [Ceidio, 2013].
[*856] *The Wigmore Chronicle 1066 to 1377. A Translation of John Rylands Manuscript 215, ff. 1-8 and Trinity College, Dublin, MS.488, ff. 295-9*, ed. Remfry, P.M. [Ceidio, 2013].

usually occur when one or more copyists enter data from two sources under conflicting years, probably due to them being unsure as to which year was correct. The Tewkesbury chronicle ends with an entry for 27 June 1262, which may suggest that the chronicler died soon afterwards. Then, probably in late 1262 or 1263, another scribe copied with minor variations the section from 1258 to 1262[*857]. This is followed by another hand who wrote up events from 1258 to 1263 in an entirely different manner from his two predecessors[*858]. Unfortunately his chronicle ends abruptly, with the end being lost. Possibly this is why the Aberconwy compiler used the Worcester and Hailes chronicles for his section on the Welsh Wars of 1276-83.

Waverley Annals, Incarnation to 1291

The Waverley annals seem to have been the source for Aberconwy's commentary on the killing of Becket in 1170. Other than this there is no evidence of any plagiarism. Presumably the comment was lifted from another work that had plagiarised Waverley, or vice versa, as no further sections are obviously related to Aberconwy, although most of the story of the war of 1282-83 is to be found in this chronicle[*859].

The only copy of the Waverley Annals is found in MS Cotton Vespasian A xvi and runs from the incarnation to 1291. In the earlier part of the work the Anglo Saxon Chronicle has been freely used and this also shows up in the Wigmore Chronicle[*860]. As Waverley itself was only founded in 1128 it seems reasonable to presume that any entry before this date is certainly derivative. Only the one medieval manuscript of this chronicle survives and that appears to be the original. The survival of such an apparently unpopular work is therefore somewhat surprising, especially as it is a good source for events in the thirteenth century.

Three main hands wrote this work. The first scribe wrote up to 999. Judging from the style of his handwriting he wrote some time in the late twelfth century. He is followed by a second scribe who brought the chronicle up to 1201. It is therefore presumably in the last quarter of the twelfth century that the chronicle was commenced. A third scribe takes the chronicle on to 1219 after which a variety of hands become involved with events clearly being written up contemporaneously - indeed from at least 1218 there are internal comments which most certainly suggest a contemporaneous account[*861]. This section of the work also contains numerous blanks which suggest that space was deliberately left for future insertions of data. The text after 1158 is also riddled with marginal insertions which all seem to be of the thirteenth century. It can therefore be judged that the Waverley annals are a prime historical source from the mid-twelfth century onwards and may carry copied snippets from earlier times from now otherwise lost sources. Presumably the chronicle was amended and added to until 1291, its end date.

[*857] 'Annales de Theokesberia', *Annales Monastici*, ed. H.R. Luard [5 vols., 1864-9] I, 170.
[*858] 'Annales de Theokesberia', *Annales Monastici*, ed. H.R. Luard [5 vols., 1864-9] I, 170-80.
[*859] 'Annales Monasterii de Waverleia', *Annales Monastici*, ed. H.R. Luard [5 vols., 1864-9] II, 397-401.
[*860] *The Wigmore Chronicle 1066 to 1377. A Translation of John Rylands Manuscript 215, ff. 1-8 and Trinity College, Dublin, MS.488, ff. 295-9*, ed. Remfry, P.M. [Ceidio, 2013].
[*861] 'Annales Monasterii de Waverleia', *Annales Monastici*, ed. H.R. Luard [5 vols., 1864-9] II, xlix

William Rishanger, 1250-1327+

The chronicle of William Rishanger does not seem to have been a direct source for the Aberconwy Register, but as some information may have enjoyed a common exemplar some comments on the chronicle are included here.

William was born in Rishangles, Suffolk, in 1250 and died sometime, certainly after 1312 and probably after 1327. He entered the Benedictine abbey of St. Alban's in 1271 and revived the custom of composing chronicles which had languished since the time of Matthew Paris. He is mainly remembered for his history of the Barons' Wars, *Narratio de bellis apud Lewes et Evesham* covering the period from 1258 to 1267. It is extant in only one manuscript, Cotton. MS. Claudius D. vi. ff. 97–114. Within this was his own statement, now detached, from the autobiographical memorandum, which became MS. Bibl. Reg. 14 C. 1, that he was a monk of 41 years' standing, and 62 years of age, on 3 May 1312. This means he was born in 1250 and became a Benedictine at St. Albans Abbey in 1271. The date, 3 May, is probably that of his 'profession' rather than that of his birth. In the work he describes himself as *cronigraphus* or *cronicator*, which probably means simply writer of chronicles, though it might well refer to the definite position of official abbey chronicler which Roger Wendover and Matthew Paris may have held in earlier times. The *Narratio de bellis* is primarily derived from Matthew Paris and his continuators and appears to have played no part in the formation of the Aberconwy Register.

William also wrote a short chronicle about Edward I, *Quaedam recapitulatio brevis de gestis domini Edwardi* found in MS. Bibl. Reg. 14 C. i. and Cotton MS. Claudius, D. vi[862]. However, his main work, *Willelmi Rishanger, quondam monachi S. Albani, Chronica et Annales*, does seem to have had some influence on the Aberconwy Register. The idea that Rishanger couldn't have written this chronicle is based on the assumption that as the author makes a reference to the death of Edward II in 1327[863] and William, born in 1250 by his own statement, could not possibly have lived to the grand old age of 77 in the early fourteenth century to be the author of the work. Obviously such an argument is nonsense and there are numerous undoubtedly true examples of people from those times living past the age of 77, viz. Robert Curthose (1051/55-1134), Eleanor of Aquitaine (1122-1204), Bishop William Wykeham of Winchester (1320/4-1404).

Rishanger's chronicle forms a lengthy record which is extant in several manuscripts. Of these MS. Bibl. Reg. 14 C. vii. (1259–1272), Cotton. MS. Claudius E. iii. (1259–1297), Cotton. MS. Faustina B. ix. (1259–1306) seem the three oldest. The last of these is the fullest and is the main basis of the main printed text and is used in comparison with the Aberconwy Register annals. The inception of the chronicle, which appears to have been worked upon in fits and starts, would seem to have been after 1303, but before 1308, when Abbot John Maryns (1303-08), who had apparently asked for it to be written, died. Obviously additions were still being made to the chronicle after 1327. Several other works attributed to Rishanger by Bale seem not be his. Regardless of the origin of this chronicle it seems likely that it used many sources and may have been formed by many hands as is shown by the great variations in style and diction as well as the discrepancies in chronology and of different accounts of the same event being given at different times. Quite clearly if this was used as a source by the compiler of Aberconwy it must have been used after the early fourteenth century when it was written.

---

[862] Printed in *Chronica, ascribed to William Rishanger, a monk of St. Albans*, ed. H.T. Riley [1865], 411-23.
[863] *Chronica, ascribed to William Rishanger, a monk of St. Albans*, ed. H.T. Riley [1865], 119.

Worcester Annals, Incarnation to 1308

The main Worcester priory annals run from the incarnation down to 1308/9, although there are a few entries added in later hands down to 1377. The text is preserved in a single quarto manuscript, Cotton Caligula A x, of 133 leaves. Within this the Worcester annals occupy folios 153 to 201. The entire copy as it now exists was written in one hand of the early fourteenth century and runs to 1303. This text has been added to at different times by apparently the same hand using different inks. There have also been other additions by other hands. In the earlier sections especially there are many blanks. These have been left to be filled in later according to the preface, which the compiler has lifted from the Winchester annals. Unfortunately, the later updaters of the manuscript have used these spaces to insert additions in blank spaces opposite or adjacent to the years they should have occupied. This makes the early chronology very unstable. In some cases the original numbering has been altered to the correct date for the later additions, but in others the insertions have been left under incorrect dates simply because there was no room for it in its proper place.

The entire Worcester chronicle has been largely based upon the Winchester annals with a singular surprising gap from 1202 to 1260. Other than this the work is competently transcribed. Before 1138 the main additions to the Winchester annals come from Florence Worcester. After that date Roger Wendover is occasionally used. From 1141 Tewkesbury and Waverley seem to have been used as sources, although there seems little doubt that the Tewkesbury entries share a common ancestry, rather than one copying the other. The Tewkesbury manuscript, although older than Worcester, has many blunders which are missing in the Worcester annals. Presumably then, the Worcester compiler was a more accomplished scholar than his Tewkesbury counterpart.

The parts of the text relevant to Aberconwy are printed in the footnotes under the main Register with those parts that seem lifted directly into the Aberconwy text being marked in bold. As can be seen from this Worcester was not plagiarized wholesale, but it does seem to have been the source for much of Aberconwy's history for Welsh affairs between 1277 and 1283. Alternatively both works may share a common source.

Appendix 4
Extracts concerning Aberconwy Abbey

TNA E.101/351/9 - Issues of the Wardrobe, 20 Nov 1282 to 19 Nov 1284[*864]
Taken from an imperfect account of miscellaneous issues of the wardrobe on 13 membranes.

Wednesday 10 March 1283
And William Burdet, clerk, earlier appearing at Aberconwy for 5 days for pledging payment of the foot soldiers for his expenses and wages through the same time 3s.

And William Pennesby for boating 10 tuns of wine from Chester to Aberconwy to sustain the army 50s.

And for boating 6 tuns of wine through the hand of Matthew Checker through the same manner 30s.

And John Shelton for the watching and custody of the king's wine on the sea at Chester, Rhuddlan and Conway for 30 days for his wages through the same time 5s.

And Henry Mont Pess for carrying 400 marks from the wardrobe in Conway abbey to the water towards Anglesey by cart 2d.

And the same Henry for collecting that money in that place Ralph Brouchton gives for his bodily expenses for 3 days 13½d.

And Albino the king's squire for wages 1 cart and 2 horses carry to the king's equipment from Rhuddlan to *Cogar* and Conwy and elsewhere for 4 days to the king 3s 4d.

And Hugh le Hare and Robert Secomb for boating 7 tuns of wine from Rhuddlan to Conway 35s clearly for sustaining the army.

And for the wages of 2 men looking after the said wine for 8 days 2s 8d.[*865]

Friday 19 March 1283
... Gilbert Briddeshale knight for 511 light sections of fencing (clays) through himself bought to make the brattishing at Conway 7s 10d.

And for carrying 1200 marks from the water of Conway to the wardrobe 14d.

And for carrying £80 to the water of Conwy outside the wardrobe to be taken to Anglesey, Ralph Broughton 4d.

And Royal Squire John Geyton for his wages of 6 hackneys bearing £1200 from Chester to Conwy to sustain the army 6s 3d.

And the same also Peter Chilham, king's squire fetching and conducting the said money for the expenses of his body for 4 days 3s.

[*864] TNA. E.101/351/9. My thanks to Simon Neal for transcribing the relevant parts of the document.

[*865] *Die mercur' x° die Martij. Et Willelmo Burdet clerico prius existenti apud Aberconewey per v dies ad pacand' vadia peditum pro expensis et vadiis suis per idem tempus iij s'.*

Et Willelmo de Pennesby pro Batillag' x dol' vini de Cestr' usque Aberconewey ad sustent' exercitus L s'.

Et pro Batillag' vj dol' vini per manus Mathei Cheker per eandem viam xxx s'.

Et Johanni de Shelton vigilanti et custod' vina Regis in mari apud Cestr' Rothel' et Conewey per xxx dies pro stipendiis suis per idem tempus v s'.

Et Henrico de Monte Pess' pro portag' iiij^C marcarum de Gard' in Abbatia de Conewey usque ad aquam car' versus Angles' ij d'.

Et eidem Henrico conducent' illam pecuniam ibidem Radulpo de Brouchton lib' pro expens' corporis sui ad iij dies xiij d' ob'.

Et Albyno Scut' Regis pro stipend' j carrete ad ij equos car' armatur' Regis de Rothel' usque Cogar et Conewey et alibi per iiij^or dietas Regis iij s' iiij d'.

Et Hugoni le Hare et Roberto Secomb pro Batill' vij dol' vini de Rothelan' usque Conewey xxxv s' videlicet pro sustentacione exercitus.

Et pro stipend' ij hominum custod' dicta vina per viij dies ij s' viij d'.

And for boating spades and forks beyond the water of Conway 4d.

And William Chicoun knight for carrying boards from the water of Conway up to the abbey in the same place to make brattishes in that place for the wages of 20 men for 1 day 3s 4d.

And for wages of 9 men carrying brattishing for the hedge/fence of the queen enclosed within Conway abbey for 1 day by the hand of Reginald Port 18d.

And for hiring one boat fetching and leading 8 wooden ladders beyond Conway over the water up to the said castle 18d.

And for 4 boards bought for some windows of the queen's chamber 6d.

And for hiring 2 boats to carry timber from Conway up to some bridge made in some marsh above Conway for 1 day 2s.

And Lord Hugh Turbeville for wages for 1 unshod horse bearing £112 from Conway to Shrewsbury 7s 6d.

And Ralph Scot king's squire going from Conway to Chester for fetching money to sustain the army for the expenses of his body for 4 days 18d.

And the same for 12 forearms of hemp/canvas for himself bought for the queen's chamber through the hands of Roger Dover 2s 9d.*866

Tuesday 23 March 1283

And for William Wynyn himself and 19 associates leading and passing from Aberconwy for their wages from the said Tuesday up to the Monday next following for 7 days 7s.

And Richard de la Lynde for the wages of 4 boats taking bread and wine from Denewell to Conway to sustain the army 56s.

And for the wages of 4 valets custodians of the aforesaid at sea for the same time 4s.

And the Tuesday aforesaid Henry Mont Pess' took the money from Conway to Bangor Ralph Broughton libertate 12d for his expenses.

And the same for expenses of 6 valets conducting with him the said money for 2 days 2s.

And for the wages of 4 masons renewing the chimneys in the king's chamber at Conway for 3 days 4s.

And Ralph Scot going to the barons at Welshpool on the king's business for his bodily expenses for 6 days 2s 3d.

And the same for passage over the water of Conwy 4d.

And for carrying pennies which Matthew Columbaris recently brought from London from the water of the Conwy to the wardrobe 9d.

---

*866 *Die Veneris xix die Martii.*

Gilberto de Briddeshale militi pro Lxj claiis per ipsum empt' ad faciend' Brettach' apud Conewey vij s' x d'.

Et pro portag' m^l CC marcarum de aqua de Conewey usque gard' xiiij d'.

Et pro portag' iiij^C li' ad aquam de Conewey extra gard' mittend' apud Angles' Radulpho de Broucthon iiij d'.

Et Johanni de Geyton Scut' Regis pro stipend' vj haken' defer' m^l CC li' de Cestr' usque Conewey ad sustent' exercitus vj s' iiij d'.

Et eidem et Petro de Chilham scut' Regis querent' et conduc' dictam pecuniam pro expens' corporum suorum ad iiij^{or} dies iij s'.

Et pro Batill' vangarum et Bechiarum ultra aquam de Conewey iiij d'.

Et Willelmo Chicoun militi pro portag' Bordarum de aqua de aqua de Conewey usque in Abbatiam eiusdem loci ad Brittach' inde fac' pro stipend' xx hominum pro j diem iij s' iiij d'.

Et pro stipend' ix hominum portant' briscam pro sepe Regine includend' in Abbatia de Conewey per j diem per manus Reginaldi de Porta xviij d'.

Et pro conduccione j Batelli querent' et ducentis viij scalas de Bosco ultra Conewey super aquam usque ad dictum castrum xviij d'.

Et pro iiij bord' empt' ad quamdam fenestr' camere Regine vj d'.

Et pro conductione ij Batill' car' merem' de Conewey usque ad quemdam pontem fac' in quadam mora supra Conewey per j diem ij s'.

Et domino Hugoni de Turbevill pro stipend' j equi defer' Cxij li' de Conewey usque Salop' vij s' vj d'.

Et Ranulpho Scoto Scut' Regis eunti de Conewey usque Cestr' pro pecunia querend' ad sustent' exercitus pro expens' corporis sui ad iiij dies xviij d'.

Et eidem pro xij ulnis de canab' per ipsum empt' pro camera Regine per manus Rogeri de Doveria ij s' ix d'.

And Matthew Columbaris for the wages of 9 hackneys taking money from Chester to Conwy for 2 days and for his expenses and with him conducting the said money for 2 days 28s.
And the same for a boat for the same money over the water of the Conwy and for carrying the same from the said water to the wardrobe 2s.[*867]

Sunday 28 March 1283

... Nicholas Smallwood Newcastle for 7,200 nails all bigger than small bought by himself for the construction of the houses and windows in the castle of Conway 15s 10d.
And the same for hanging hooks and hinges bought by himself for the aforesaid 4s 4d.
And for the shipping of spades, shovels and picks from Bangor to Conway 2s.
And Henry Cheval for boating, loading and unloading and hoisting with a windlass 30 tuns of wine coming from Lomas to Conway to sustain the army 47s.
And Henry Monte Pess for carrying pennies recently come from Ireland from the water of the Conwy up to the abbey 6d.
And for coal bought to make diverse iron works at Conway 2s 6d.
And Baldwin Hostiar for wages of 20 horses bearing victuals from Conway to Dolwyddelan for the garrison of the same castle 20s namely for the wages of any horses that you please 12d.
And Henry Bantesham for wages of 2 carts anyone to 3 horses carrying iron, steel, hoes and picks from Chester to Degannwy for 3 days 7s.
From that place by W Parton 2s and in this place 5s. And for boating the same over the water of Conwy 2d.[*868]

Wednesday 7 April 1283

And Henry Oxford master carpenter for 1200 small nails for boards purchased by himself for construction of the king's hall at Conway 3s 7½d.

[*867] *Die Martis xxiij die Martis. Et Willelmo Wynyn se xix socio custod' gued' seu passag' de Aberconewey pro vadiis suis a dicto die Martis usque diem Lune proxim' sequend' per vij dies vij s'.*
Et Ricardo de la Lynde pro stipend' iiij Batill' defer' pan' et vinum de Denewell usque Conewey ad sustent' exercitus Lvj s'.
Et pro stipend' iiij vallett' custod' predicta in mari per idem tempus iiij s'.
Et die Martis predicto Henrico de Monte Pess' ducent' pecuniam de Conewey usque Bangor' Radulpho de Broucthon lib' ad suas expensas xij d'.
Et eidem pro expens' vj ?valens' secum conduc' dictam pecuniam per duos dies ij s'.
Et pro stipend' iiij Cement' reparantium caminum in camera Regis apud Conewey per iij dies iiij s'.
Et Ranulpho Scoto eunti ad Barones apud la Pole in negotiis Regis pro expens' corporis sui ad sex dies ij s' iij d'.
Et eidem pro passag' ultra aquam de Conewey iiij d'.
Et pro portag' denar' quos Matheus de Columbar' nuper duxit de London de aqua de Conewey usque in gard' ix d'.
Et Matheo de Columbar' pro stipend' ix Haken' defer' pecuniam de Cestr' usque Conewey per ij dies et pro expensis suis et secum conduc' dictam pecuniam per ij dies xxviij s'.
Et eidem pro Batill' eiusdem pecunie ultra aquam de Conewey et pro portag' eiusdem a dicta aqua usque ad gard' ij s'.
[*868] *Die Dominico xxviij die Martii.*
Nicholao Smalwode Nove Castro pro vij^m CC clavis tam grossis quam minutis ab ipso emptis ad construccionem domuum et fenestrarum in castro de Conewey xv s' x d'. Et eidem pro pendulis Gunphis et vertevell' ab ipso emptis ad predictam iiij s' iiij d'.
Et pro Ba-tillag' Howarum vangarum tribulorum et Pykoys' de Bangor' usque Conewey ij s'.
Et Henrico Cheval pro Batill' cariag' et discariag' et Windag' xxx dol' vini venient' de Lommas usque Conewey ad sustentacionem exercitus xlvij s'.
Et Henrico de Monte Pess' pro portag' den' nuper venient' de Hibern' de aqua de Conewey usque ad Abbatiam vj d'.
Et pro carbon' empt' ad fabricand' diversa opera ferrea apud Conewey ij s' vj d'.
Et Baldewyno Hostiar' pro stipend' xx equorum defer' victual' de Conewey usque Dolindaleyn pro municione eiusdem castri xx s' videlicet pro stipend' cuiuslibet equi <u>xij</u> d'.
Et Henrico de Bantesham pro stipend' ij carett' quilibet ad iij equos car' ferr' calib' Howyes et Pycoys' de Cestr' usque Gannoch per iij dies <u>vij</u> s'.
Inde per W. de Parton <u>ij</u> s' et hic v s'. Et pro Batill' eorumdem ultra aquam de Conewey ij d'.

And Thomas, Edmund and Peter from Chester and Robert from Ireland boatmen coming with their boats to some grange next to the water[*869] to fetch lead from there for their wages for 2 days 7s 6d.

And the aforesaid David Wautham for 4,500 nails for laths bought by himself for the king and queen's rooms at Conway 7s 6d.

And for old iron bought for hoes and picks for the work of improvement 18d.

And for making 9 axes for the work of croping the trees of Batlefeud at the queen's writ 17d.

And for the bedding bought for the plasterers of the walls of the chambers of the king and queen 6½d.

And the same David going out of the court at Rhuddlan on the king's business for 4 days for his wages 12d.

And the same for boating iron utensils from Battlefield over the water of the Conwy 4½d.

And Nicholas Newcastle for 2,000 spike nails and 4,000 lath nails purchased in person for the work of Conway 11s.

And for the passage of Lord Anthony Bek over the water of the Conwy through the hand of the king to Waterville 4d.

And Andrew Butler for boating 20 tuns of wine from Lammas to Conway and for windlassing the same tuns at Conway 23s 4d.

And for the wages of a valet for custody of the said wine for 10 days 20d.

And for carrying £400 from Conway to the water for carriage towards Anglesey 2d.

And for the wages of 1 hackney in regard to £200 from Conway to Criccieth for 3 days through the hand of Nicholas Ramage 2s.[*870]

Monday 12 April 1283

And Henry Whetele for 1 cart with 3 horses to carry steel arrow-heads and arrows from Chester to Degannwy for 3 days inclusive 3s 8d.

And the same for passage of the same on the water of Aberconwy between Degannwy and Aberconwy abbey and for carrying the same from the water to the wardrobe 8d.

And Peter Chester and Adam Ulmo boatmen of Chester leading in their boat Lord Elias Hauville and some serjeants of his to the army of Conway up to some grange in which bronze utensils of Llywelyn were found for their wages and their boats 5s 4d.

[*869] Presumably this was Creuddyn grange.

[*870] *Die Mercur' vij die Aprilis. Et Henrico de Oxon' magistro Carpentar' pro m¹ CC clav' minutis ad bord' per ipsum empt' ad construccionem Aule Regis apud Conewey iij s' vij d' ob'.*

Et Thome Edmund Petro de Cestr' et Roberto de Hibern' Batill' eunt' cum Batill' suis ad quamdam grangeam iuxta aquam ad querend' plumbum ibidem pro stipendiis suis ad ij dies vij s' vj d'.

Et predicto David de Wautham pro iiij^m D clavis ad Lathas per ipsum emptis ad cameras Regis et Regine apud Conewey vij s' vj d'.

Et pro veteri ferro empto ad Howas et Pycos' operar' emendand' xviij d'.

Et pro fabricacione ix securium ad opus coupatorum de Batlefeud precepto Regine xvij d'.

Et pro Litera empt' ad plastracionem parietum camerarum Regis et Regine vj d' ob'.

Et eidem David exeunti extra cur' apud Rothel' in negot' Regis per iiij dies pro stipendiis suis xij d'.

Et eidem pro Batillag' utens' fabrorum de Batlefeud ultra aquam de Conewey iiij d' ob'.

Et Nicholao de Novo Castro pro m¹m¹ clavis de Spykyng et iiij^m clavis ad Lath' ab ipso empt' ad operacionem de Conewey xj s'.

Et pro passag' domini Anton' de Bek ultra aquam de Conewey per manus Regis de Waterville iiij d'.

Et Andr' de Boteler' pro Batillag' xx dol' vini de Lammas usque Conewey et pro Wyndag' eorumdem dol' apud Conewey xxiij s' iiij d'.

Et pro vad' j garcionis custod' dicta vina per x dies xx d'.

Et pro portagio iiij^C li' de Conewey usque ad aquam car' versus Angles' ij d'.

Et pro stipend' j haken' defer' CC li' de Conewey usque Crukyn per iij dies per manus Nicholai Ramage ij s'.

And Brian Faxcote himself and 18 royal squires safely conducting £1,000 silver from Conwy to Criccieth liberated to Walter Nottingham, clerk, for their provisioning at Bere for the expenses of their bodies for 4 days coming and returning 30s.[*871]

Tuesday 20 April 1283

Reginald Janitor for wages of 5 hackneys bearing £1,000 from Conway to Criccieth and returning for 3 days 15s.

And the same for boating of the horses beyond the water of Conwy 5d.

And Baldwin the host of the hall for the boat loading and unloading 13 quarters of grain from Conway to Dolwyddelan and for his expenses oris for 2 days leading to that very place the said grain 27s 9d.

And David Wautham for turf through himself bought to cover the house of Brother Walter also goldworker of the queen in Conway castle 7s 1d.

And the same for 2 stone grindstones bought by himself for the workmen of Conway 18d.[*872]

Sunday 25 April 1283

... David Wautham for the wages of 10 men digging earth for plastering the house of Brother Walter and his associates at Aberconwy for 6 days, 10s which is 2d per day.

And the same for the wages of 1 man carrying turf for covering the said house for 1 entire day 1½d.

And the same bought for twigs (wattle) for the making of the said walls of the house aforesaid 6d.

And the same for 12,000 nails bought for the house of the said brother and for the wardrobe and chamber of the king and queen 26s.

And Robert Le Warr' for cleaning the plot for the granary of the king's grain next to the water mill at Aberconwy 20½d.

And the same for 20 men hired for carrying timber for the said granary for 1 full day 3s 6d.

And the same for 20 men hired to bring timber and for digging turfs for another full day 3s 6d.

And the same for the wages of 18 men for half a day's work about the aforesaid granary 18d.[*873]

[*871] *Die Lune xij die Aprilis Et Henrico de Whetele pro j caretta ad iij equos conduct' ad car' ferr' calibem et sagittas de Cestr' usque usque Gannow per iij dies integros iij s' viij d'.*

Et eidem pro Passagio eiusdem ad aquam de Aberconewey inter Gannou et Abbatiam de Aberconewey et pro portag' eiusdem de aqua usque ad gard' viij d'.

Et Petro de Cestr' et Ade de Ulmo Batillar' Cestr' ducent' in Batill' suis dominum Elyam de ?Hauvile et quosdam servientes eius ad arma de Conewey usque ad quamdam grangeam in qua utens' erea Leu-lini fuerunt inventa pro stipendiis suis et Batillorum suorum v s' iiij d'.

Et Bryano de Faxcote se xviij^{mo} scut' Regis salvo conduc' m^l li' argenti de Conewey usque Creukyn lib' Waltero de Notingham clerico pro garnistura existent' apud Bere pro expens' corporum suorum ad iiij dies eundo et redeundo xxx s'.

[*872] *Die Martis xx die Aprilis.*

Reginaldo Janitori pro stipend' v Haken' defer' m^l li' de Conewey usque Creukyn et redeundo per iij dies xv s'.

Et eidem pro Batill' eorumdem equorum ultra aquam de Conewey v d'.

Et Baldewyno Hostiar' Aule pro Batill' cariag' cariag' et discarg' xiij quarter' bladi de Conewey usque Dolindaleyn et pro expens' oris sui per ij dies ducent' ibidem dictum blad' xxvij s' ix d'.

Et David de Wautham pro Turb' per ipsum empt' ad cooperiend' domos fratris Walteri et aurifabri Regine in castro de Conewey vij s' j d'.

Et eidem pro ij lapid' molar' per ipsum empt' ad fabros de Conewey xviij d'.

[*873] *Die Dominica xxv die Aprilis. David de Wautham pro vad' x hominum fodiend' terram ad plastracionem domus fratris Walteri et sociorum suorum apud Aberconewey per vj dies x s' cuilibet per diem ij d'.*

Et eidem pro vad' j hominis portant' Turb' ad dictam domum cooperiend' per j diem integrum j d' ob'.

Et eidem pro virgis empt' ad dictos parietes domus predicte faciende vj d'.

Et eidem pro xij^m clav' empt' ad domum dictorum fratrum et ad gard' et ad cameram Regis et Regine xxvj s'.

Et Roberto le Warr' pro mundacione placei pro granar' frumenti Regis iuxta molendinum aquaticum apud Aberconewey xx d' ob'.

(continued...)

Friday 30 April 1283

And David Wautham for turfs bought to cover the house of Brother Walter at Conway 3s... And David Wautham for 12 quarters of coal bought for two royal forges at Conway 3s. And the same for the wages of one many carrying the coal from the wood to the forges aforesaid through diverse lots 2s 6d.[*874]

Wednesday 5 May 1283

... for wages of 1 hackney bearing the tools of 6 carpenters from Conway to Bangor for 1 day 8d.

And for the expenses of the same carpenters for the same day 12d.

Thursday 6 May Robert Dorset tentmaker of the king for his wages 10 cartloads where they please for 5 horse carts for pavilions and tents of the king from London to Shrewsbury £20... Also the same for their wages carrying the aforesaid carts from Chester to Conway for 2 days £6 13s 4d.

Also the same Robert for the wages of 2 carters carting some tents and pavilions of the king who was residing at Rhuddlan after the withdrawal of the king from thence away from Rhuddlan to Conway 4s.

And David Wautham for 5,000 lath nails bought by himself for the construction of the wardrobe in Conway castle 4s 2d.

And Henry St Stephen going to Chester for fetching 21 hostages and taking them to Conway for his expenses and the carriage of them to Degannwy and for passage over the water of Conwy 14s 7d.[*875]

Monday 10 May 1283 (Monday was actually on the 12ᵗʰ)

And David Wautham for 6,000 spike nails bought by himself for the construction of the new house of the king at Conway 15s.

And the same for 5,000 lath nails bought for the same 5s 2½d.

Also the same for wages of 2 men digging turfs for the covering of the wardrobe, mill and granary of Conway for 2 days 16d.

Also the same for the wages of 4 men making some ditch around the garderobe of the king at Llanrwst for half a day 4d.

And Peter Chilham for wages of 34 hackneys bearing victuals for the king's business and his army from Conway to Llanrwst and divers equipment of the king and queen for 5 days £4 5s evidently any one hackney per day 6d.

[*873] (...continued)
Et eidem pro xx hominibus conductas ad portand' merem' ad dictum granar' per j diem integrum iij s' vj d'.
Et eidem pro xx hominibus conduct' ad portand' merem' et ad fodiend' turbas per alium diem integrum iij s' vj d'.
Et eidem pro stipend' xviij hominum per dimid' dietam operant' circa granar' predictum xviij d'
[*874] *Die Veneris xxxᵐᵒ die Aprilis... Et David de Wautham pro turb' empt' ad coopertum domus fratris Walteri apud Conewey iiij s'...*
Et David de Wautham pro xij quarter' carbon' empt' ad duas fabricas Regis apud Conewey iij s. Et eidem pro stipend' j hominis portant' carbon' de nemore usque ad fabricas predictas per diversas vices ij s' vj d'
[*875] *Die Mercur' vᵒ die Maii pro stipend' j Haken' defer' utens' vj carpentar' de Conewey usque Bangor per j diem viij d'.*
Et pro expens' eorumdem vj carpent' per eundem diem xij d'.
Die Jovis vjᵒ die Maii Roberto de Dors' papilon' Regis pro stipend' x carrettar' quelibet ad v equos car' Papilon' et tentor' Regis de Lond' usque Salop xx li'
Item eidem pro stipend' earumdem car' predicta car' de Cestr' usque Conewey per ij dies vj li' xiij s' iiij d'.
Item eidem Roberto pro stipend' ij carr' car' quedam tentor' papilon' Regis que residebant apud Rothel' post recessum Regis ab inde de Rothel' usque Co-newey iiij s'
Et David de Wautham pro vᵐ clavis Latharum per ipsum empt' ad constructionem gard' in castro de Conewey iiij s' ij d'
Et Henrico de sancto Stephano eunti apud Cestr' pro xxj hostag' querend' et ipsos ducend' usque Conewey pro expensis suis et cariag' eorum usque Gannouth et pro passag' eorum ultra aquam de Conewey xiiij s' vij d'

And Hanekyno the Forestor boatman carrying in his boat 7 tuns flour from Chester to Conway and on to Llanrwst for 8 days for his wages and his boat 16s.

And William Pannesbury boatman carrying in his boat 7 tuns flour and hay from Chester to Conway and Llanrwst for 5 days for his wages 11s 3d.[*876]

Sunday 16 May 1283

...William Chicoun for 400 nails bought by himself for the brattishing around the enclosure of the town of Conway 66s 8d.

And John Conyers for expenses that he recently had in conducting £2,651 sterling from Shrewsbury to Conway and for the wages of 13 hackneys bearing the said money and for cord, baskets and hemp bought by himself to tie up the said money 67s 6d.

And Hamon of the queen's chamber for nails so big or small bought by himself for making the new chamber of the king and queen at Conway and for other houses next to the aforesaid chamber 15s 2d.

Wednesday 25 May [the 25th was a Tuesday]

Esegero Page of Colepole for providing one ship for carrying 703½ quarters of grain from Sandwich to Aberconwy minus 6 quarters taken for his victuals also which would be subtracted for however many quarters you please 6s 8d and in such a way for unloading.

And the same for his own expenses and the expenses of the said hostages remaining at Conway for 3 days acquitted 20s 4d.[*877]

Wednesday 2 June 1283

And Asgero Paye, master of a boat from Colpole carried 696 quarters of grain from Ladmas to Aberconwy through his narrow boat 6s 8d.

And David Wautham for 4,000 spike nails bought for the works of the wardrobe at Conway 9s 4d, precisely 2s 4d per 1,000.

And Baldwin the host of the hall for the wages of 20 men for clearing the place where the tents and pavilions of the king were put next to Conway abbey for 4 days 13s 8d.

And John London for carrying iron coming from Dolwyddelan castle to the water of Conwy up to the abbey 6d.

[*876] *Die Lune xº die Maii... Et David de Wautham pro vjᵐ clavis de Spyking per ipsum empt' ad constructionem novarum domuum Regis Conewey xv s'.*

Item eidem pro vᵐ clavis ad Lath' empt' ad predicta v s' ij d' ob'.

Item eidem pro stipend' ij hominum fodient' Turbas ad gard' molendin' et granar' de Conewey cooperiend' per ij dies xvj d'.

Item eidem pro stipend' iiij hominum facient' quoddam fossatum circa gard' Regis apud Thlanhurst per dimid' diet' iiij d'.

Et Petro de Chilham pro stipend' xxxiiij Haken' defer' victual' ad opus Regis et exercitus sui de Conewey usque Thlanhurst et diversa hernes' Regis et Regine per v dies iiij li' v s' videlicet cuilibet Haken' per diem vj d'.

Et Hanekyno le Forester Batillar' car' in Batello suo vij dol' farine de Cestr' usque Conewey et usque Thlanhurst per viij dies pro stipendiis suis et Batelli sui xvj s'...

Et Willelmo de Pannesbur' Batill' car' in Batillo suo vij dol' farine et fenum de Cestr' usque Conewey et Thlanhurst per v dies pro stipendiis suis xj s' iij d'.

[*877] *Die Dominico 16 die Maii... Willelmo Chicoun pro iiijᶜ clavis per ipsum empt' ad Brittach' circa Claustruram ville de Conewey lxvj s' viij d'.*

Et Johanni le Convers pro expensis quas nuper fecit in conducendo mⁱmⁱ DC li' sterling' de Salop' usque Conewey et pro stipend' xiij Haken' defer' dictam pecuniam et pro cord' paner' et canab' per ipsum empt' ad intrussand' dictam pecuniam Lxvj s' ob'.

Et Hamoni de Camera Regine pro clavis tam grossis quam minutis per ipsum empt' ad no-vam cameram Regis et Regine apud Conewey factam et ad alias domos iuxta cameram predictam xv s' ij d'.

Die mercur' xxv die Maij Esegero Page de Colepole pro fretto j navis car' DCC iij quart' et dimid' frumenti de Sandwyco usque Aberconewey subtractis vj quart' que ceperunt pro victualibus suis et debet subtrahi pro quolibet quarterio vj s' viij d' et sic discarcaverunt.

Et Henrico de sancto Stephano... Et eidem pro expensis suis propriis et expensis dictorum hostagiorum morantium apud Conewey per iij dies acquiet' xx s' iiij d'.

And William the sergeant boatman carrying grain flour from Conway to Trefor and carrying back part of the king's armour for 5 days inclusive 7s 6d.[*878]

Tuesday 8 June 1283

And John Conyers conducting lords Arsinum Novayles, Arnold Gaveston and Amadeus de le Bret, Gascon barons from Conway to Dover at the king's writ for the expenses of his body for 29 days 10s 10½d.

And Peter Columbaris for the wages of 18 hackneys bearing £2,600 from Chester to Conway which he took with him from the treasury in London 17s 4d.

The same for boating the same money over the water of Conwy and for carrying from the water to the garderobe 2s 9d.

And Robert Penllyn mariner for taking 70 quarters of grain from Dublin to Conway in payment in full 112s 4d which ought to be received for hiring his boat 56s 2d because of that which remained to himself making amends through the hand of Adam Wetenhal at Dublin.

And the same regarding 160 quarters of grain, 54 quarters of oats from Aberconwy to Rhuddlan for hiring his ship 20s.

Also the same Robert for wages of 2 carts where they please for 4 horses carrying the pavilion of the king from Chester and Aberconwy to Llanrwst for 12 days which is carts 18d 36s.

Also for wages of the same carters ? at Conwy for 5 days which is receieved per day 9d: 7s 6d.

And Robert Thorney carrying 24 quarters of grain from Aberconwy to Rhuddlan for hiring his boat 8s.

And William of the king for 6 masons conducted to make some oven at the king's writ at Aberconwy which is given per day 2s 3d.[*879]

Friday 11 June 1283

Reginald Portitori for boating hostages to the other side of the water of Conwy towards Degannwy 2s.

And for boating the king's arms from Conway to Llanrwst 2s 6d.

[*878] *Die Mercur' ij die Junii... Et Asgero Paye magistro navis de Colpole car' DC iiijᶜˣ xvj quart' frumenti de Ladmas usque Aberconewey pro fretto navis sue vj s' viij d'...*

Et David de Wautham pro iiijᵐ clavis de Spikyng empt' ad operacionem gard' apud Conewey ix s' iiij d' prec' mˡ ij s' iiij d'...

Et Baldewyno Hostiar' aule pro stipend' xx hominum mundant' placeam ubi tentor' et papil' Regis ponebantur iuxta Abbatiam de Conewey per iiij dies xiij s'viij d'.

Et Johanni de Lond' pro portag' ferr' ve-nientis de castro de Dolindaloyn de aqua de Conewey usque in Abbatiam vj d'...

Et Willelmo le Serjaunt Batill' car' farrinam frumenti de Conewey usque ?Trevor et recariant' partem hernes' Regis per v dies integros vij s' vj d'.

[*879] *Die Martis viij Junii... Et Johanni le Convers conduc' dominos Arsinum de ?Novayles Arnald' de Gaveston et ?Amanenum de le Bret Barones Vascon' de Conewey usque Dover' precepto Regis pro expensis corporis sui per xxix dies... x s' x d' ob'.*

Et Petro de Columbar' pro stipend' xviij Haken' defer' mˡmˡ DC li' de Cestr' usque Conewey quas Thesaur' duxit secum de London' xvij s' iiij d'. Eidem pro Batill' eorumdam den' ultra aquam de Conewey et pro portag' de aqua usque in gard' ij s' ix d'...

Et Roberto de Penaleyn marinar' ducent' lxx quart' frumenti de Dublynna usque Conewey in perpacacionem Cxij s' iiij d' quos receipere deberet pro fretto navis sue Lvj s' ij d' quia de residuo fuit sibi satisfactum per manus domini Ade de Wetenhal apud Dublyn'.

Et eidem ducenti Clx quart' frumenti liiij quart' avene de Aberconewey usque Rothel' pro fretto navis sue xx s'...

Item eidem Roberto pro stipend' ij carr' quelibet ad iiij equos car' papil' Regis de Cestr' et Aberco-newey usque Thlanrust per xij dies cuilibet caretta xviij d' xxxvj s'.

Item pro stipend' earumdem carr' perhendinanc' apud Conewey per v dies quelibet percip' per diem ix d' vij s' vj d'...

Et Roberto de Thorney car' xxiiij quart' frumenti de Aberconewey usque Rothel' pro fretto Batilli sui viij s'.

Et Willelmo Pistori Regis pro vj cement' conduct' ad faciend' quoddam furnum precepto Regis apud Aberconewey quolibet percip' per diem ij s' iij d'.

And Richard Shrewsbury for 10 perches of great cloth and for 10,194 of lesser cloth by himself bought from various people for the building of the wardrobe and granary of the king at Conwy by the hand of Henry Oxford master carpenter £11 8s 3d.[880]

Sunday 13 June 1283

Alexander Geddyng for expenses of 10 hostages from Snowdon being at Conway for 2 days acquitted 11s 11d.

David Wautham for the wages of carpenters, plasterers, carriers and men digging turfs for the works of the queen's wardrobe in Aberconwy castle and for buying nails for the same work just as is well known from the particulars in the book of particulars £14 2d.

And Roger the treasury chamberlain for wages of carpenters conducted to Aberconwy for making the wardrobe of the king there and for carrying timbers of wood there for the said wardrobe and for making some houses next to the said wardrobe where the clerks of the wardrobe slept before the said wardrobe was perfected and for plastering the said wardrobe and said houses made nearby just as in the particulars put in the book in the wardrobe £6 8s 4½d.

And David Wautham for wages of carpenters, plasterers, carriers and men for digging turfs and for some people carrying things around the king's wardrobe in the castle of Aberconwy just as put down in the particulars in the book of particulars 78s 7d.

And Reginald the king's porter for the wages of 5 boatmen conducting for passage of the squire of the king's hospice going to Dafydd ap Gruffydd 2s 6d.

The same for carrying anchors and ropes from ships at Aberconwy up to the abbey 6d.

Summa Lvij li' x s' j d' ob'.[881]

Tuesday 15 June 1283

David Wautham for the wages of carpenters, plasterers, carriers and men for digging turfs and for some people to carry things about the king's wardrobe in the castle of Aberconwy just as appears through the particulars in the book of particulars 76s 6d.

And Adam Bot of Strode for hiring his boat to carry 122 quarters of grain and 130 quarters of oats from Sandwich to Aberconwy to sustain the army £8 11s 11d.

And Thomas Ippegrave, king's serjeant conducting to arms the Basques footmen from Conway to Dover going from the court for 77 days for his bodily expenses for the said time 28s 10½d.

And for boating £2,600 over the water from Conway and for carrying the same from the water to the wardrobe 14d.

---

[880] *Die Veneris xj Junii. Reginaldo Portitori pro Batill' hostag' ultra aquam de Conewey versus Gannou ij s'.*
Et pro Batill' armorum Regis de Conewey usque Thlanrust ij s' vj d'.
Et Ricardo de Salop' pro x perticat' magnarum Bord' et pro xᵐ C iiijᶜˣ xiiij minutarum bord' ab ipso et per ipsum empt' a diversis personis ad constructionem gard' et granar' Regis apud Conewey per manus Henrici de Oxon' magistri carpentar' xj li' viij s' iij d'
[881] *Die Dominico xiij die Junii.*
Alexand' de Geddyngg pro expensis x obsid' de Snoudoun' existent' apud Conewey per ij dies acquiet' xj s' xj d'.
Die Dominico xiij die Julii. David de Wautham pro stipend' carpentar' plastr' portitorum et hominum fodient' Turbas ad opus gard' Regine in castro de Aberconewey et pro clavis emptis ad opus eiusdem prout patet per particulas in libro particularum xiiij li' ij d'.
Et Rogero Camer' Thesaur' pro stipend' carpentar' conductor' apud Aberconewey ad faciend' gard' Regis ibidem et pro car' meremii de Bosco ibidem usque ad dictam gard' et pro factura cuiusdam domus iuxta dictam gard' ubi clerici de gard' iacuerunt priusquam dicta gard' erat perfecta et pro Plastracione dicte gard' et dicte domus iuxta facte prout patet per particulas inde lib' in gard' vj li' viij s' iiij d' ob'.
Et David de Wautham pro stipend' carpent' plastr' portitorum et hominum fodient' turb' et pro quibusdam cariag' factis circa gard' Regis in castro de Aberconewey prout patet per particulas in libro particularum lxxviij s vij d'.
Et Reginald' de Porta Regis pro stipend' v Batill' conduct' ad passand' scut' hospic' Regis eunt' ad querend' David fil' Griffini ij s' vj d'.
Eidem pro portag' Ancorarum et cordarum de Navibus apud Aberconewey usque ad Abbatiam vj d'...

Friday 18th June John Norwich for wages of 13 men carrying the pavilions and tents of the king from the water of the Conwy up to the abbey 13d.

And John Marreys boatman by writ per day 4d having in his boat 3 men who by writ 3d per day for carrying the pavilions and tents of the king from Aberconwy to Degannwy and returning for 1 full day 14d.[*882]

Saturday 19 June 1283

...Robert la Warr, draper, for wages of various carpenters, carriers of timbers and turfs as well as diggers of turfs and for buying of canvas/hemp and other diverse carriage and porterage made through himself for 30 days concerned about the construction of the royal granary in Conway abbey and the mill of the king there begun from new just as shown through the particulars in the book of particulars £22 15s 3d.

And Eustace Everard sailor of Calais carrying 222 quarters of grain from Sandwich to Conway in his ship for hiring his same ship £10.[*883]

Wednesday 23 June 1283

Hamo of the queen's chamber for making 500 turfs to cover the wardrobe of the queen at Conway and for the turfing of her garden there 15d.

And for boating the same from Ford and Terfor to Conway 15d.

And for the wages of 2 men putting down turfs in the garden for 2 days 5d.

And Thomas Carbonar for 15 quarters of coal bought for the same to make spades and picks and other utensils for the works of Conway 3s 1½d.

And for carrying the same coal from the wood up to the workshop of Conway 15d.[*884]

Thursday 24 June 1283

And Roger Dover for the wages of 1 hackney bringing tools of some masons and stone workers from Conway to Harlech (*Hardelowe*) for 4 days going and returning 2s 8d.

And Roger le Fykoys squire of the queen for digging 700 turfs near the ford of Trefor and for carrying the same from the said ford to the said garden of the queen of Conway 4s 1d.

And for 1 empty tun bought to enclose the said garden 5½d.

[*882] *Die Martis xv die Junii. David de Wautham pro stipend' carpent' plastrorum portitorum et hominum fodient' turb' et pro quibusdam cariag' factis circa gard' Regis in castro de Aberconewey prout patet per particulas in libro parti-cularum lxxvj s' vj d'.*

Et Ade Bot de Strode pro fretto navis sue car' Cxxij quarter' frumenti et Cxxx quart' avene de Sandwyco usque Aberconewey ad sustentacionem exercitus viij li' xj s' xj d'.

Et Thome de Ippegrave servienti Regis ad arma conduc' Basculos pedit' de Conewey usque Dover' exunti extra Cur' per lxxvij dies pro expensis corporis sui per idem tempus xxviij s' x d' ob'.

Et pro Batillag' m¹m¹ DC li' ultra aquam de Conewey et pro portag' earumdem de aqua usque in gard' xiiij d'

Die Veneris xviij die Junii [Fri 18 Jun] Johanni de Norwyco pro stipend' xiij hominum portant' papilon' et tentor' Regis de aqua de Conewey usque ad Abbatiam xiij d'.

Et Johanni de Marreys Batillar' percip' per diem iiij d' habenti in Batello suo iij homines quolibet percip' per diem iij d' car' papil' et tentor' Regis de Aberconewey usque Gannou et revertendo per j diem integrum xiij d'.

[*883] *Die Sabbati xix die Junii... Roberti la Warr' panetar' pro stipend' diversorum carpent' portitorum meremii et turbarum et fodient' turb' et pro canabo empt' et aliis diversis car' et portag' per ipsum factis per xxx dies preter' circa constructionem granar' Regis in Abbatia de Conewey et molendin' Regis ibidem de novo incepti prout patet per particulas in libro particularum xxij li' xv s' iij d'...*

Et Eustachio Everard marinar' de Caleys car' CC xxij quart' frumenti de Sandwyco usque Conewey in navi sua pro fretto eiusdem navis sue x li'...

[*884] *Die Mercur' xxiij die Junii. Hamoni de Camera Regine pro factura D turbarum ad cooperiend' gard' Regine apud Conewey et ad turband' herbarium suum ibidem xv d'.*

Et pro Batill' earumdem de Ford et Trevor usque Conewey xv d'.

Et pro stipend' ij hominum ponent' turbas in herbar' per ij dies v d'.

Et Thome Carbonar' pro xv quart' carbon' empt' ab eodem ad Bech' et Pycoys' et alia utens' pro operar' de Conewey fabricand' iij s' j d' ob'.

Et pro cariag' eiusdem carbon' de Bosco usque ad fabricam de Conewey xv d'.

And Eustace Everard shipman carrying timbers from Conway to Caernarfon to construct the town and castle located there for the 2 last days of the month of June by the hand of Hamon chamberlain 4s 10d.

And John Fitz Roger of Brouchwode shipman carrying in his ship timber from Conway to Caernarfon through Thursday 1 July 3s 4d.

And Robert Ireland for the wages of 18 men carrying timbers from the wood beneath Conway to the granary of the Marshall newly built at Conway through 1 day and for the wages of 16 men that accomplished the same through another day 5s 8d.

And William Pountfroyt for boating the pavilions and tents of the king from Degannwy over the water of Conwy.[*885]

Thursday 1 July 1283

Adam the goldworker of Hach for boating two long royal carts and their attached horses for them over the water of Conwy for to take the king's tent to Degannwy in reply to the king's arrival there 5d.

And for Roger the Fykeys for spraying water over the garden of the queen at Conwy for 1 night 3d.

And for the wages of 2 carts just as for 2 horses carrying turfs to the said garden and for the queen's wardrobe of Conwy for 6 days 15s...[*886]

Sunday 4 July 1283

David Wautham for wages 1 cart for 2 horses carting turfs for covering some houses at Conway for 4 days against the king's coming there 3s 4d.

And John Gillyngham for making one stable for the king's horses at Conway 24s 4d just as is patent in the book of particulars

And David Wautham for 1,900 turfs bought for covering the wardrobe of the king at Aberconwy for 3d per hundred, 4s 9d.

Also the same for 2,000 great spikes bought for the said wardrobe preceding 1,000 2s 2d, 4s 4d.

Also the same for the wages of one man working about the said wardrobe by writ per day 3d and for the wages of 7 men helping for digging turfs and for placing them on top of the said wardrobe for 6 days 8s 6d.

Also the same for boating the said turfs from Ford next to Trefor to Aberconwy 8s 6d.[*887]

[*885] *Die Jovis in festo sancti Johannis Baptiste... Et Rogero de Doveria pro stipend' j haken' defer' utens' quorumdam Cementar' et fractorum lapid' de Conewey usque Hardelowe per iiij dies eundo et redeundo ij s' viij d'...*
Et Rogero le Fykoys scut' Regine pro fossur' DCC tur-barum iuxta Fordam de Travor et pro cariag' earumdem de eadem ford' usque ad dictum herbar' Regine de Conewey iiij s' j d'.
Et pro j doleo vacuo empto as claustrur' dicti herbar' v ob'.
Et Eustachio Everard naute car' merem' de Conewey usque Carnarvan ad constructionem ville et castri loci eiusdem per ij ultimos dies mensis Junii per manus Hamonis de Camera iiij s' x d'...
Et Johanni filio Rogeri de Brouchwode naute car' in nave sua merem' de Conewey usque Carnarvan per diem Jovis prim' Julii iij s' iiij d'.
Et Roberto de Hibern' pro stipend' xviij hominum portant' merem' de Bosco subter Conewey usque ad granar' marescalcie de novo inceptum apud Conewey per j diem et pro stipend' xvj hominum illud idem facient' per alium diem v s' viij d'.
Et Willelmo de Pountfroyt pro Batillag' Papil' et tentor' Regis de Gannou usque ultra aquam de Conewey viij d'.
[*886] *Die Jovis primo Julij. Ade Aurifabro de Hach pro Batillag' duarum longarum carrettarum Regis et equorum pertinent' ad eas ultra aquam de Conewey ad tentor' Regis ducend' apud le Gannou contra adventum Regis ibidem v d'.*
Et Rogero le Fykeys pro aspersione aque super herbar' Regine apud Conewey per j noctem iij d'.
Et pro stipend' ij carr' quelibet ad ij equos car' turbas ad dictum herbar' et ad gard' Regine de Conewey per vj dies xv s'...
[*887] *Die Dominico iiij⁰ die Julij David de Wautham pro stipend' j carr' ad ij equos car' turb' ad quasdam domos cooperiend' apud Conewey per iiij dies contra adventum Regis ibidem iij s' iiij d'... Et Johanni de Gillyngham pro factur' j stabuli pro equis Regis apud*

(continued...)

Friday 9 July 1283.

William le Noble of Gascony for hiring his boat carrying 162 quarters of grain and 54 quarters of oats from Sandwich to Aberconwy £8 2s.

And David Wautham for wages of 20 workers working at Aber for digging the same (turfs) there and for covering 2 houses newly made with turfs where the king's pantry was and the buttery was, just as prescribed each day 2d and their leaders of 20 men 4d a day from Thursday 8 July until Saturday (10th) next following which day complete for 3 days 10s 6d.

Also the same for the wages of 2 men digging turfs for the same houses as shown by writ per day 4d for the same time 2s.

And for 1 cart conducting with 2 horses for the cart the said turfs for 1 day 10d.

And David Fitz Adam for carrying the pavilions and tents of the king from Conwy to Caernarfon in his boat for 6 days 10s.[*888]

Sunday 26 July 1283 [Monday was the 26th]

John Coupland for 10,700 strips of metal and 25 iron picks bought for the new castle of Aberconwy £10 18s by the hand of Richard Gentlecors the strips at 2s and anyhow the strips held together the 25 iron picks.

And William Hertford for carrying some pavillions of the queen from Caernarfon to Aberconwy 8d.[*889]

Sunday 29 Aug 1283

And Nicholas Clifford for carrying timbers to make two latrines for the king and queen's wardrobe at Conway and for carpenters and roofers for the same 4s 3d.

Summa xvj li' v s' j d'.[*890]

---

*[*887] (...continued)*

Conewey xxiiij s' iiij d'prout patet in libro de particulis...

Et David de Wautham pro m^l et ix^C turb' empt' ad cooperiend' gard' Regis apud Aberconewey pro qualibet C^{na} iij d' iiij s' ix d'.

Item eidem pro m^lm^l grossis Spykyngis emptis ad dictam gard' prec' m^l ij s' ij d' iiij s' iiij d'.

Item eidem pro stipend' j hominis operantis circa dictam gard' percip' per diem iij d' et pro stipend' vij hominum auxiliant' ad fodiend' turbas et ad figend' eas super dictam gard' per vj dies viij s' vj d'.

Item eidem pro Batillag' dictarum turbarum de Ford' iuxta Trevor usque ad Aberconewey iij s' vj d'.

*[*888] Die Veneris ix die Julii. Willelmo le Noble de Geruennie pro fretto navis sue car' Clxij quart' frumenti et liiij quart' aven' de Sandwyco usque Aberconewey viij li' ij s'.*

Et David de Wautham pro stipend' xx operar' operant' apud Aber ad fodiend' ibidem et ad cooperiend' duas domos de novo factas cum turbis ubi panetria Regis fuit et pincerna quolibet percip' per diem ij d' et vinte-nario iiij d' a die Jovis viij Julij usque diem Sabbati proximo sequend' utroque die comp' per iij dies x s' vj d'.

Item eidem pro stipend' ij hominum fodient' turbas ad easdem domos quolibet percip' per diem iiij d' per idem tempus ij s'.

Et pro j carretta conducta cum ij equis ad car' dictas turbas per j diem x d'...

Et David filio Ade pro cariag' papil' et tentorum Regis de Conewey usque Carnarvan in Batello suo per vj dies x s'...

*[*889] Die Dominica xxvj Julij. Johanni de Couplaund pro x^m vij^C Bend' et xxv peciis ferri empt' ad novum castrum de Aberconewey x li' xviij s' per manus Ricardi Gentilcors prec' bende ij s' et quelibet benda continet xxv pecias ferri.*

Et Willelmo de Hertfeud pro cariag' cuiusdam papil' Regine de Carnarvaran usque Aberconewey viij d'...

*[*890] Die Dominico xxix die Augusti... Et Nicholao de Clyfford pro cariag' meremii ad fac' duas Latrinas ad gard' Regis et Regine apud Conewey et pro carpentar' et coopertar' earumdem iiij s' iij d'.*

Appendix 5
TNA C.47/10/32/9: Writs and Returns of the Justice of Wales concerning the amercements claimed by Aberconwy Abbey under its charter 8 July 1313 to 7 July 1314[*891]

Edwardus dei gratia Rex Anglie Dominus Hibernie et Dux Aquit' dilecto et fideli suo Rogero de Mortuo Mari Justiciario suo Walliens' salutem. Cum nuper ad querelam dilecti nobis in Christo Abbatis de Aberconewey nobis suggerentis ipsum et monachos suos per cartam celebris memorie domini Edwardi quondam Regis Anglie patris nostri quam inspeximus quietos esse imperpetuum eosdemque Abbatem et monachos ac eorum predecessores Abbates et monachos eiusdem loci semper hactenus a tempore confectionis carte predicte quietos fuisse de omnibus misericordiis ac vicecomites nostros de Carnarvan et Angleseye et quosdam alios ballivos nostros partium illarum ipsos Abbatem et monachos quominus de huiusmodi misericordiis quieti esse possint multipliciter impedivisse et ipsos ea occasione distrinxisset inquietasse minus iuste pluries vobis mandaverimus quod si ita esset tunc vicecomites et ballivos nostros predictos ad huiusmodi districcionibus et inquietacionibus indebitis prefatis Abbati et monachis occasione premissa faciendis desistere faceretis et exaccionem prefatis Abbati et monachis ea de causa factam poneretis in respectum usque ad festum omnium sanctorum proximo futur' certificantes nos in presenti parliamento nostro apud Westmonasterium qualiter et quo modo et ex quibus causis et a quo tempore huiusmodi misericordie ab ipsis Abbate et monachis exiguntur ad opus nostrum seu alterius cuiuscumque vel causam nobis significaretis quare mandata nostra pluries vobis inde directa minime fuistis executi ac vos nobis retornaveritis quod breve nostrum vobis inde directum vobis liberatum fuit apud Westmonasterium ad parliamentum predictum et quod nos super contentis in eodem brevi ad idem parliamentum propter locorum distanciam et temporis brevitatem certificare non potuistis: Nos nolentes predictos Abbatem et monachos in hac parte indebite pregravari vobis mandamus quod vicecomites et ballivos nostros predictos ab huiusmodi districcionibus et inquietacionibus prefatis Abbati et monachis occasione predicta faciend' desistere faciatis et exaccionem eisdem Abbati et monachis ea de causa factam ponatis in respectum usque ad quindenam Pasche proximo futur'. Certificantes nos interim qualiter et quo modo et ex quibus causis et a quo tempore huiusmodi misericordie ab ipsis Abbate et monachis exiguntur ad opus nostrum seu alterius cuiuscumque ut est dictum. Hoc breve nobis remittentes Teste me ipso apud Westmonasterium xiij die Octobris Anno regni nostri septimo.

No. 19

Pretextu istius mandati mandavi vicecomitibus de Caern' et Angles' quod me certificarent de omnibus misericordiis Abbatem et monachis ... ... coram ipsis in ballivis suis tangentibus in forma in brevi contenta.

Et unde vic' de Caern' michi retornavit certificando quod in turno suo vic' tento apud Kelleneth die Lune proxim' post fest' sancti David confessoris anno regni regis Edwardi nunc quarto. Compertum fuit coram et per xij lib' et Jur' quod Abbas et Conventus de Abercon' injuste obstuparunt cursum aque Riparie que vocatur Gwyleth in Commoto de Ughcorney que

---

[*891] TNA C.47/10/32/9. My thanks to Simon Neal for transcribing the relevant parts of the document.

quidem Riparia est bundus Regal' inter terras liber' tenentium de Dynthleu et terr' dictorum Abbatie et Conventus in Redeynok Velyn pro qua transgr' amerciati fuerunt et amerciamentum taxatum per afforatores Juratos ad C s'.

Et quod compertum fuit ibidem quod dicti Abbas et Conventus injuste et absque licencia domini Regis vel eius justic' levaverunt unum novum molendinum aquaticm in Redeynock Veleyn sex annis tunc transactis ubi numquam fuerat prius molendinum levatum recipiend' ibidem tolneta diversorum hominum ibidem molantium qui prius ad molendina domini Regis sectam facere consueverant pro qua transgr' amerciati fuerunt et amerciamentum illud taxatum ut supra ad C s'.

Et quod compertum coram eo ibidem quod ijdem Abas et Conventus injuste sibi apropriarunt et tenent quatuor bovatas terre et amplius Eynon ap Gwyn sex annis transactis subtrahendo pro eisdem sect' ad comitatus et hundr' contra ordinacionem inde per dominum Regem et eius consilium tempore quo fuit princeps Wallie apud Kenyton iuxta London factam et computatis quolibet anno de sex annis predictis defaltis xvij parvorum hundr' que tenentur de tribus septumen' in tres septum' et de xiij Com' tent' die mense in mensem sic est summa ix^{xx} defalt' pro quibus Idem Abbas et Conventus amerciati fuerunt et amerciamentum illud taxatum ut supra ad xx li'.

Et etiam quod compertum fuit coram eo ibidem quod iidem Abbas et Conventus in prejudicium domini regis et contra proclamacionem et defensionem inde factas per justic' receptarunt Amanum Duy villanum domini Regis de ?Tusnevyth cum sequela sua super terr' eorumdem in hameletto de Nantcall per quod amerciati fuerunt et amerciamentum illud taxatum ut supra ad C s

Et etiam quod compertum fuit ibidem quod iidem Abbas et Conventus injuste receptaverunt Candalo fratrem dicti Ade villanum domini Regis de Maerdreff de Aber super terris suis in Maynan cum tota sequela sua contra defensionem et proclamacionem predictas per quod amerciati fuerunt et amerciamentum cum illud taxatum ut supra ad C s'
Et vic' de Angles' michi retornavit certificando quod presentatum fuit coram se in turno vic' apud Aberfrau quod Abbas de Abercon' cepit quedam ... villanum domini Regis et ipsum fratrem laicum in ordine suo fecit sine licencia unde amerciatus fuit et amerciamentum illud taxatum ut supra ad xl s'

Et etiam quod compertum fuit ibidem quod idem Abbas arare fecit cum caruc' suis super regalem viam inter Aberfrau et Talethlen in longitudine et latitudine duarum acrarum terre per quod amerciatus fuit et amerciamentum illud taxatum ut supra ad xiij s' iiij d'

Et etiam quod compertum fuit ibidem quod idem Abbas receptavit David ap Jevan ap David villanum domini Regis de Meredr' de Aberfrau cum catallis suis super terram suam in Penmenyth sine licencia domini Regis per quod amerciatus amerciatus fuit et amerciamentum illud taxatum ut supra ad vj s' viij d'

No. 20

Edwardus dei gratia Rex Anglie Dominus Hibernie et Dux Aquit' dilecto et fideli suo Rogero de Mortuo Mari Justiciario suo Walliens' salutem
Cum nuper ad querelam dilecti nobis in Christo Abbatis de Aberconewey nobis suggerentis ipsum et monachos suos per cartam celebris memorie domini Edwardi quondam Regis Anglie patris nostri quam inspeximus, quietos esse imperpetuum, eosdemque Abbatem et monachos ac eorum predecessores Abbates et monachos eiusdem loci semper hactenus a tempore

confectionis carte predicte quietos fuisse de omnibus misericordiis, ac vicecomites nostros de Carnarvan et Angleseye et quosdam alios ballivos nostros partium illarum ipsos Abbatem et monachos quominus de huiusmodi misericordiis quieti esse possint multipliciter impedevisse, et ipsos ea occasione distrinxisse, et inquietasse minus iuste pluries vobis mandaverimus quod si ita esset tunc vicecomites et ballivos nostros predictos ad huiusmodi districcionibus et inquietacionibus indebitis prefatis Abbati et monachis occasione premissa faciendis desistere faceretis, et exaccionem prefatis Abbati et monachis ea de causa factam poneretis in respectum, usque ad parliamentm nostrum quod ad quindenam Pasche proxim' preteritam apud Westmonasterium summoneri fecimus certificantes nos in dicto parliamento qualiter et quo modo et ex quibus causis et a quo tempore huiusmodi misericordie ab ipsis Abbate et monachis exiguntur ad opus nostrum, seu alterius cuiuscumque, ac vos predictum breve nostrum ad dictam quindenam retornare, vel causam aliquam pro qua predicti Abbas et monachi amerciati fuerunt nobis significare non curaveritis de quo plurimum admiramur. Nos nolentes predictos Abbatem et monachos indebite pregravari vobis mandamus quod vicecomites et ballivos nostros predictos ab huiusmodi districcionibus et inquietacionibus prefatis Abbati et monachis occasione premissa faciendis desistere faciatis, ac exaccionem eisdem Abbati et monachis ea de causa factam ponatis in respectum usque ad quindenam sancti Michaelis proxim' futur' certificantes nos tunc qualiter et quo modo et ex quibus causis et a quo tempore huiusmodi misericordie ab ipsis Abbate et monachis exiguntur ad opus nostrum seu alterius cuiuscumque ut est dictum, Hoc breve nobis remittentes. Teste me ipso apud Beverlacu xxvij die Aprilis Anno regni nostri septimo.

No. 21

Pretextu comsimul' brevis michi alias inde directi mandavi vicecomitibus de Caern' et Angles' quod me certificarent de omnibus misericordiis Abbatem et monachis de Abe… … ipsis in ballivis suis tangentibus iuxta formam in brevi contentam.
Et unde vic' de Caern' michi retornavit certificando quod in turno suo vic' tento apud Kellennock … proxima post festum sancti David confessoris anno regni Regis Edwardi nunc quarto Compertum fuit coram et per xij lib' et Jur' quod Abbas et Conventus de Abercon' injuste obstuparunt cursum aque … que vocatur Gwyleth in Commoto de Ughcorney que quidem Riparia est bundus Regal' inter terras libere tenentium de Dynthleu et terram dictorum Abbatis et Conventus in Redy… Velyn pro qua transgr' amerciati fuerunt et amerciamentum taxatum per afforatores Jur' ad C s'.
Et quod compertum fuit ibidem quod dicti Abbas et Conventus injuste et absque licencia domini Regis … vel eius Justic' levaverunt unum novum molendinum aquaticum in Reydeynock Velyn sex annis tunc transactis ubi numquam prius fuerat molendinum levatum Recipiend' inde … tolneta diversorum hominum ibidem molantium qui prius ad molendina domini Regis sectam facere consueverant pro qua transgr' amerciati fuerunt et amerciamentum illud taxatum ut supra ad C s'
Et quod Compertum coram eo ibidem quod iidem Abbas et Conventus injuste sibi apropriarunt et tenent quatuor bovatas terre et amplius Eynon ap Gwyn liberi sex annis transactis subtrahendo pro eisdem sect' ad Comitatus et hundr' contra ordinacionem inde per dominum Regem nunc et eius consilium tempore quo fuit princeps Wallie apud Kenyton iuxta London factam et computatis quolibet anno de sex annis predictis defaltis xvij parvorum hundr' que tenentur de tribus septum' in tres septum' et xiij Com' die mense in mensem sic est

summa ix^{xx} defalt' pro quibus iidem Abbas et Conventus amerciati fuerunt et amerciamentum illud taxatum ut supra ad xx li'.

Et etiam quod compertum fuit coram eo ibidem quod iidem Abbas et Conventus in prejudicium domini Regis et contra proclamacionem et defensionem inde factas per justic' receptaverunt Amanum Duy villanum domini Regis de ?Tusnenyth cum sequela sua super terr' eorumdem in hameletto de Nantcall per quod amerciati fuerunt et amerciamentum illud taxatum ut supra ad C s.

Et etiam quod in turno vic' coram eo tento apud Aber die Mercur' proxim' post festum sancti David anno predicto compertum fuit per xij Juratores ut supra quod iidem Abbas et Conventus injuste receptarunt Adam Best villanum domini Regis de Aber et eidem habitum monachalem tradiderunt ad dampnum domini Regis et contempt' et cetera per quod amerciati fuerunt et amerciamentum illud taxatum ut supra ad C s'.

Et etiam quod compertum fuit ibidem quod iidem Abbas et Conventus injuste receptaverunt Candalo fratrem dicti Ade villanum domini Regis de Maerdreff de Aber super terris suis in Maynan cum tota sequela sua contra defensionem et proclamacionem predictas per quod amerciati fuerunt et amerciamentum cum illud taxatum ut supra ad C s'.

Et vic' de Angles' mihi mandavit certificando quod presentatum fuit coram se in turno vic' apud Aberfrau quod Abbas de Abercon' cepit quendam ?Nich' ?Bogl' villanum domini Regis et ipsum fratrem laycum in ordine suo fecit sine licencia domini Regis et cetera. unde amerciatus fuit et amerciamentum illud taxatum ut supra ad xl s'.

Et etiam quod compertum fuit ibidem quod idem Abbas arare fecit cum caruc' suis super regalem viam inter Aberfrau et Talethlen in longitudine et latitudine duarum acrarum terre per quod amerciatus fuit et amerciamentum illud taxatum ut supra ad xiij s' iiij d'.

Et etiam quod compertum fuit ibidem quod idem Abbas receptavit David ap Jevan ap David villanum domini Regis de ?Maerdred' de Aberfrau cum catallis suis super terram suam in Penmenyth sine licencia domini Regis per quod amerciatus fuit et amerciamentum illud taxatum ut supra ad vj s' viij d'.

Demandas supradictas respectuari feci prout in brevi continentur. Et ad aliud breve michi inde directum simile feci retornum.

Appendix 6
TNA C.143/109/20: A Maenan Abbey Petition of 1315 to Build a Mill at Gwydir*892

Document 1

*Aur… signor le Roi & a son conseil prio… Labbe et les moignes de Aberconeweye en Gales qe
il lour voille graunter quil puissent en lour terre demeigne qe est apelle Gwedir prosde le
cawe de Carrou Gwedir leuer un molyn ewerette por le demeine ble ^{de} mesmes ceuz Abbe et
moignes mondre qar il aveient en le leu ou labbeye fust avant assise & funde avant qe le Roi
Edward piere nostre seignor le Roi ore translata la dite Abbeye trois molyns por lour blee
mondre & ore in … ponte De quei il priomit le grate nostre seignour le Roi*

Document 2

*Edwardus dei gratia Rex Anglie Dominus Hibernie et Dux Aquitanie dilecto et fideli suo
Johanni de Grey Justiciario suo Northwall' salutem.
Peticionem dilectorum nobis in Christo Abbatis et monachorum de Aberconeweye coram
nobis et consilio nostro in parliamento nostro exhibitam vobis mittimus presentibus
interclusam mandantes quod inspecta peticione illa et plenius intellecta omnibus modis et viis
quibus melius expedire videritis vos informatis super contentis in eadem si sit ad dampnum vel
preiudicium nostrum aut aliorum si concedamus eisdem Abbati et monachis ea que in
peticione continentur. Et si sit ad dampnum vel preiudicium nostrum aut aliorum tunc ad
quod dampnum et quod preiudicium nostrum et ad quod dampnum et quod preiudicium
aliorum et quorum et qualiter et quo modo. Et de eo quod inde inveneritis nos sub sigillo
vestro distincte et aperte quam citius peteritis reddatis certiores. Remittentes nobis hoc breve
cum peticione predicta. Teste me ipso apud Westmonasterium secundo die Martij Anno regni
nostri octavo* [2 March 1315].

Document 3

*… diligent… … … …cionem quam fieri feci apud Gwedir iuxta quam de Carrou Gwedir xvj
die Aprilis anno regni regis nostri viij …si sit ad dampnum vel preiudicium predicti domini
Regis vel aliorum si idem dominus Rex concedat Abbati et monachis de Aberconewey quod
possint levare unum molendinum aquaticum in terra sua propria ad molend' blada sua et
cetera vos per presentes certifico quod aqua de Carrou Gwedir exit a quodam stagno vocato
Thlynka Loyt quod quidem stagnum est domino Regi et habet cursum suum usque ad aquam de
Conewey et est meta et bunda inter terram domini Regis ex una parte et terram dictorum
Abbatis et monachorum ex altera et est medietas eiusdem aque domino Regi et altera medietas
predictis Abbati et monachis per quod si idem dominus Rex eisdem Abbati et monachis
concedat eandem medietatem aque non est aliter ad dampnum nec preiudicium eiusdem*

---

*892 TNA. C 143/109/20. My thanks to Simon Neal for transcribing the relevant parts of the document.

domini Regis nisi in hoc quod quod illa medietas aque est sua. Non est ad dampnum aliorum si idem dominus Rex concedat predictis Abbati et monachis contenta in peticione sua et cetera.

Appendix 7
The 1291 Taxatio of Maenan Abbey

The goods of the abbot of Conwy in St Asaph diocese.
The abbot holds the vill of Maenan (*Maurnant*); he renders for the mills and perquisites, as well as for two carucates, income £6 1s 7d, tithe 12s 2d.

Also Hiraethog (*Hir'hadok*) and the vaccaria of *Trekedewe* 3 carucates with other profits, income £1 5s, tithe 2s 6d.

Also the grange of Ceirniog (*Karennock*), Pentrefoelas (*veylas*), Llanfair Rhyd Castell (*Demoetjerstn/demoe q'stu*), Llyn Cymmer (*Kenekenea/kenenkennea*), Lechwedd Cryn Llwyn (*Lewes'* et *Kylwen*), five carucates with other profits, income £2 5s, tithe 4s 6d.

Also *Herlygaret & Lanwueiri & henkesche*, 2 carucates with pasture, income £1 4s 8d, tithe 2s 5¾d.

The income of animals.
The abbot has 106 cows, income £6 6s, tithe 12s 7.1/4d.

He also has 560 sheep, income £8 5s, tithe 16s 6d.

He also has 15 horses, income 15s, tithe1s 6d.

The sum of the goods of the abbot of Conway (*Conewey*) £26 2s 4d, tithe £2 12 3d.[*893]

The temporal goods of the abbot of Conway (*Conewey*), diocese of St Asaph, existing in the diocese of Bangor.
The abbot has the grange of Ffriwlwyd (*Frithlwyd/Fryleyt*), two carucates of land with profits, £1, tithe 2s.

Also he has the grange of *Cor'/Corano*) 1 carucate of land with profits 10s, tithe 1s.

Also he has the grange of Nant Call (*Nankal/Namcall*) 1 carucate of land with profits 10s, tithe 1s.

Also he has the grange of Rhedynog Felen (*Reddenaut'*) and Havailyn (*Hanoclyv'*), with a fulling mill and other profits, 21s 8d, tithe 2s 2d.

Also he has the manor of Ghornwy (*Corwylys/Cornoles*) three carucates of land with profits, a mill and other profits £15 10s.

Also he has the grange of Gelliniog (*Killiniog/Keneloe*) seven carucates of land with profits £12, tithe.

Also he has the grange of Bodgedwydd (*Bodgedwyadhes/Dodgedewez*) three carucates of land with other profits £1 10s, tithe 3s.

[*893] **Bona Abbatis de Conway.** *Abbas habet villam de Maynant, Reddit cum molendinis et perquisitis, cum carrucis, vi l is viid, xiis iid. Item Hirhadocks et Vaccariam de Trebedewe iii carucatarum cum aliis commoditatibus i l vs, iis vid. Item grangiam de Karennock, Voylas, Demoetjerstn, Kenekenea, Lewes, et Kylwen, v carucatas, cum aliis commoditatibus, i l iv s viiid, ivs vid. Item Herlygaret & Lanwueiri & henkesche duas caruc' cu' pastur' i l ivs viiid   iis v.3/4d*

Exitus al. *Abbas habet cvi vaccas, exitus vi l vjs, xiis vii ob d. Item habet ccccclx oves. Exitus viii l vs, xvis vid. Item habet xv equas, exitus xvs, is vid. Summa Bonorum abbatis de Conwey xxvi l iis ivd, ii l xii s iiid, Taxatio [1802], 289.*

Also the abbot has a moiety of the vill of Penmynydd (*Penmir/Pennenuz*) a carucate of land with profits and a mill, £4 10s, tithe 9s.

Also he has the grange of Arddau (*Herduw*) a carucate of land with Nantllyn (*Nauthlyn/Nanthlyne* possibly now Afon Porth-llwyd) with profits 15s, tithe 1s 6d. In total £37 6s 8d, total tithe £3 14s 8d.[*894]

Appendix 8 - The Lands of Aberconwy
The Lands of Maenan Abbey at the Dissolution[*895]

Minister's Account 28 Henry VIII, 1536		
Land	**Holding**	**Value**
Conway	Farm	£4 1s 4d
Maenan (*Maynan*)	Rents and indenture	£9 13s 4d
Arddau (*Arthey*)	Rents and indenture	£15 1s 8d
Ceirniog or Brenig (*Brened*)	Rents and indenture	£3 1s
Nanhwynain (*Nayboynan*)	Rents and indenture	£21 18s 4d
Cwm (*Come*)	Rent of two tenements	£5 1s 8d
Nant Call (*Nancallo*)	Rent of the vill[*896]	£2
Rhedynog Felen (*Rednokvelyn*)	Rent of the vill and hamlet	£1 7s 8d
Hiraethog (*Hirathoge*)	Rents and indenture in town	£22 8s 2d
Gelliniog (*Kellynyoke*)	Rents and indenture	£10 13s 4d
Ghornwy (*Courney*)	Rents of free and at will tenants	£13 1s 10d
Bodgedwydd (*Bodgeweth*)	Rents of Tenants	£3 7s 8d
Penmynydd (*Penmeneth*)	Rents of tenants	£3 13s 11d

[*894] **Bona temporal' Abbath' de Conewey Assavens Dyoc' existent' in Doic' Bang**. *Abbas het grangiam de Fryloyr (Fryleyt) duas caruc' cu' commodi', 20s, 2s. Item het grangiam de Cor' (Corano) 1 caruc' terr' cu' commod' 10s, 1s. Item het grang' de Namall (Namcall) un' caruc' cu' comod' 10s, 1s. Item het grang' de Reddenaut' & Hanoclyv' cu' molend' fullonar' & aliis commodis £1 0(1)s 8d, 2s 2d. Item het (Man'ui' de Cornoles') tres caruc' terr' cu' reddit' molend' & aliis commod' £15 10s. Item het grang' de Keneloe sept' caruc' cu' commodit' £12, £1 4s. Item het grang' de Bodgedewez (Dodgedewez) tres caruc' cu' aliis commodit' 30s, 3s. Item abbas het medietatem ville de Pennenuz un' car' terre cu' redd' & molend' £4 10s, 9s. Item het grang' de Herduw una caruc' terr' cu' Nantblyne (Nanthlyne) cu' commodit' 15s, 1s 6d. Summa bonor' tempal' Abb' de Coneweye £37 6s 8d. Summa dicime £3 14s 8d,* Taxatio [1802], 292. Later this total appeared under the deaconry of *Dyffrin Clyd* as the temporalia of the abbot of Conway and was valued at £37 6s 8d, but the tithe was recorded as £3 14s 0d instead of 8d, *Idem*, 294.
[*895] *Monasticon Anglicanum*, ed. W. Dugdale, Revised edition by J. Caley, H. Ellis, and B. Bandinel [6 vols., 1817-30] V, 675.
[*896] It is also possible that chapel known as *Buarth yn y Capel* within the grange was a Cistercian construction, University College of North Wales, Plas Coch Deed, 377.

Maenan, Arddau, Ceirniog/Brenig, Nanhwynain, Nant Call and Rhedynog Felen	Returns of comartha that is 4 years from the vills	£2
Maynan, Arthey, Brynney, Nanboynan, Nancoll & Radnokvelyn	Arrears in same	6s 8d
Dwgyfylchi (*Gwelthie*)	Farm of rector	£1 6s 8d
Conway	Farm of rector	£6
Eglwysrhos (*Eglos Roose*)	Farm of rector	£18 6s 8d
Eglwysbach (*Vagh*)	Farm of rector	£13 6s 8d
Llanpatrick, ie.Cemaes (*Lanpatrike*)	Farm of rector	£13 6s 8d

Value of Maenan lands in the Valor and Account of 1536

Holding	Valor 1536	1536 Account
Demesne lands		£4 1s 4d
Maenan	£10 12s 8d	£9 13s 6d
Arddau	£14 13s 8d	£15 1s 8d
Demesne	£1 3s 4d	
Ceirniog or Brenig (*Bryned/Brened*)	£3 1s	£3 1s
Nanhwynain	£21 18s 4d	£21 18s 4d
Cwm	£5	£5 1s 8d
Nant Call	£2	£2
Rhedynog Felen	£1 6s 8d	£1 7s 8d
Gelliniog	£12 7s 2d	£10 18s 4d
Bodgedwydd	£3 6s 8d	£3 7s 8d
Penmynydd	£5 3s 5d	£3 7s 8d
Ghornwy Llys	£9 14s 7d	£13 1s 10d
Ucheldref	£2 5s 2d	

Llanydusant	£1 14s 2d	
Hiraethog	£22 4s 6d	£22 8s 2d
Comortha:[897]		
Caernarvonshire	£10	
Anglesey	£6 8s	
Anregis:[898]		
Caernarvonshire	£13 4s	£13 4s
Anglesey	£6 8s	£6 8s
Denbighshire	£6 8s	
Perquisites:		
Caernarvonshire	13s 4d	
Anglesey	£1	
Denbighshire	10s	
Total	**£123 2s**	**£116 15s 1d**

Name	Valor Value	Account Value	No of holdings
Demesne lands		£4 1s 4d	
Maenan	£10 12s 8d	£9 13s 6d	23
fishery	4s		
demesne	13s 4d		
mill	£1 6s 8d		
Arddau	£14 13s 3d	£15 1s 8d	11
demesne	£1 3s 4d		
Ceirniog or Brenig (*Bryned/Brened*)	£3 1s	£3 1s	4
Nanhwynain	£21 18s 4d	£21 18s 4d	9
Cwm	£5	£5 1s 8d	2
Nant Call	£2	£2	1

[897] Comortha was a tax payable every fourth year, Hays, RW, *The History of the Abbey of Aberconway, 1186-1537* [UWP, 1963], 171-2.
[898] Anregis or Anregyon was a service or tax, Hays, RW, *The History of the Abbey of Aberconway, 1186-1537* [UWP, 1963], 171-2.

Rhedynog Felen	£1 6s 8d	£1 7s 8d	1
Gelliniog	£12 7s 2d	£10 18s 4d	10
Bodgedwydd	£3 6s 8d	£3 7s 8d	5
Penmynydd	£5 3s 5d	£3 13s 11d	5
Ghornwy Llys	£9 14s 7d	£13 1s 10d	21
Ucheldref vill	£2 5s 2d		
Llanydusant vill	£1 14s 2d		
Hiraethog	£22 4s 6d	£22 8s 2d	14
Comortha:			
Caerns	10s	(10s)	
Mon	6s 8d	(6s 8d)	
Anregis:			
Caerns	13s 4d	13s 4d	
Mon	6s 8d	6s 8d	
Denbighs	6s 8d		
Perquisites of courts:			
Caerns	13s 4d		
Mon	£1		
Denbighs	10s		
Entire Domain	£123 2s	£116 15s 1d	106

Carnarvon: Creuddyn etc. Possession of the dissolved abbey of Conway, 27-28 Henry VIII (22 April 1535-21 April 1537)[*899]

Holdings in Maenan
Tudyn Argon Lan Rice
Kay Ieuan ap Creweth
Kay I gough
Croverred
Tudyn Due
Tythyn Dycg gwythe
Ffryth ymaen hyre
Frythwen
Kaye ythel Verchan
Kay kynwryck Llooyd
Tythyn Eigyan ap William
ffryth coed bryn dan owen
Ffryth Kevan bryth vownocke
Kevyn bryth bryn gwyn

Arddau
Tudyn Arthay Bryney Voyll
Tythyn Pelthy
Tythyn I Dalthey
Breynocke Yssa
Tydyn Elyn
Breynocke Ucha
Cumcolwyd (Cwmcowlyd)

Ceirniog or Brenig
Bryned/Brened
Apprynney

Nanhwynain
Iwasdainas
boughmorhtan
Hawod Thlan
Havod Taurek
Thlyndy
Havod Porthe
Iwonoysedeg
Haywod Kyske
Comyenly
Havod nether
Havod Llwywoc
Crafflayne

[*899] TNA. SC.6/HENVIII/4972.

Glas Treane
(survived as Hafod y Llan, Llyndy, Hafod y Porth & Craflwyn)

Cwm
Tithyn Ithell

Rhedynog Felen
Tuthyn Nest Duy

Gelliniog[*900]
Rithkayre
Iquerly (Chwarelau)
Ymarle
Iperyn Eyere
Tythyn Kaye Llegche (Cae'r Llechau)
Kay Mawre
Kay Veddell
Kay Ikevan
Gwyrt Grange (Quirt[*901])
Rithkayre (Rhuddgaer)
Kay Mawre (Cae Mawr/Comoigne or the great haye, Records of Court of Augmentations, 53)
[Windmill tower (Towre Melyn Wynt) stood at Rhuddgaer, Letters and Papers of Henry VIII, xv, 565]

Bodgedwydd
Tythyn I Mollyn (Tae-moelion)
Tythyn Isaythe Ugewy

Penmynydd
Tythyn Lann
Tythyn Llowerth
Tythyn Llan
Tythyn Glan Iegrose
Tythyn Gwen Ithallen
Tythyn Llwynoglen (Llwyn-ogan)
Ymanaughty (Y Mynachdy)
Tythyn I kymrowe

Hiraethog
Tethyn Vollas (Pentrefoelas?)
Iryothed
Brennebithen (Bryniaubrithion)
Kayatha
Eriott vill

[*900] Rowlands, 'Antiquitates Parochiales, Mona Medieva', *Archaeologia Cambrensis* [1846], 312-17.
[*901] Remains of a small chapel (of the grange of Gelliniog) in the eastern end, *Archaeologia Cambrensis* [1847], 41.

Kevengarro (Cefngarw)
Mayse I Kerneved
Y Kowitte Ighllyn (Ycourt Uch Ll'n and Keyernog Vawre or Keyernogvahan or Kenynyrred presently, Ceirnioge-bach or Cwrt)
Kernyog Vawre (Ceirnioge-mawr)
Courte Uthen
Leven
Tydyn y Pandy on Foelas
Tydyn Tonna/Tomkyn
Bryne Hallyn (Cryn Heilyn)
Llanayre Issa
Iller Igarrege (Elorgarreg)

The Known Acquisition Dates of the Lands of Aberconwy Abbey

Land[902]	First Mention	Acquired by	District
Rhedynog Felen*	1186	1186	Arfon
Conwy Gyffin*	bef. 1188	1186	Arfon
Gelliniog*	bef. 1199	1193	Mon
Rhuddgaer	bef. 1199	1193	Mon
Stawenan	bef. 1199	1193	Mon
Talybont*	bef. 1199	1193	Mon
Dwygyfylchi	bef. 1253		Arfon
St Patrick of Cemaes	bef. 1254	aft. 1246	Mon
St Peplicius of Caernarfon	bef. 1254	aft. 1246	Arfon
Pentrefoelas, Rhyd Castle*	bef. 1273	1194	Rhufoniog
Arddau*	bef. 1278	bef. 1240	Arfon
Nanhwynain*	bef. 1281	bef. 1240	Arfon
Creuddyn*	bef. 1284	aft. 1263?	Arllechwedd
Eglwysbach	1284	1284	Rhos
Maenan	1284	1284	Rhos
Penlassok in Maenan	1284	1284	Rhos

[902] Those lands mentioned in the forged Llywelyn charters of 1315-32 are astrixed.

Ghornwy	1284	1284	Mon
Ucheldref	1284	1284	Mon
Gwenynog	1284	1284	Mon
Treveibion Maelog	1284	1284	Mon
Penmynydd	1284	1284	Mon
Cumrewet/Cumrewez in Creuddyn	1284	1284	Mon
Bodgedwydd*	bef.1291	bef. 1193?	Mon
Llanfaes*	bef. 1332	bef.1282	Mon
Hiraethog	bef. 1291	bef. 1240	Rhufoniog
Ceirniog	bef. 1291	bef. 1240	Rhufoniog
Llyn Cymmer*	bef. 1291	bef. 1240	Rhufoniog
Lechwedd Cryn Llwyn*	bef. 1291	bef. 1240	Rhufoniog
Ffriwlwyd*	bef. 1291	bef. 1202	Eifionydd
Cwm*	bef. 1291	bef. 1240	Arfon
Nant Call*	bef. 1291	bef. 1240	Arfon

The Changing Values of the lands of Aberconwy Abbey

Land	Value	Value	Value	Value	Value	Value	Value
	1253	1284/5	1291 carucates	1294	1350	Register	1536
Gwynedd							
Rhedynog Felen			£2 1s 8d			£1 6s 8d	£1 7s 8d
Gyffin		(£41 7s 8½d) the sum of recompense + Creddyn					
Conway						£3	£10 1s 4d
Dwygyfylchi	£1 1s 4d					£2	£1 6s 8d
Llanbeblig							
Nanhwynain						£21 18s 4d	£21 18s 4d
Ffriwlwyd			£1		£4 10s		
Cwm grange *Cor'/Corano*			10s			£5	£5 1s 8d
Nant Call			10s			£2	£2
Arddau with Dulyn			15s			£13	£15 1s 8d
Maenan		£16 7s 8d	£6 1s 7d			£9	£9 13s 4d
Total	**£1 1s 4d**	**£16 7s 8d**	**£10 18s 4d**		**£4 10s**	**£57 1s**	**£66 10s 8d**

338

Mon	1253	1284/5	1291 carucates	1294	1350	Register	1536
Gelliniog			£12			£10 16s 8d	£10 13s 4d
Rhuddgaer							
Stawenan							
Talybont							
Bodgedwydd			£1 10s			£3 6s 8d	£3 7s 8d
Cemaes						£3 6s 8d	£13 6s 8d
Ghornwy		£18 14s 5½d	£15 10s	£8 10s		£13 12s	£13 1s 10d
Ucheldref							£2 5s 2d
Gwenynog				£5 16s 9d			
Llanfflewyn in Talybolion							Llanydusant £1 14s 2d
Treveibion Maelog		£2 10s 9d		£1 5s			
Penmynydd		£5 18s 6d	£4 10s			£4 13s 4d	£3 13s 11d
Total		**£27 3s 8½d**	**£33 10s**	**£15 11s 9d**		**£35 13s 4d**	**£49 2s 10d**

Perfeddwlad	1253	1284/5	1291 carucates	1294	1350	Register	1536
Hiraethog			£1 5s				£22 8s 2d
Ceirniog (*Karennock*)							£3 1s
Pentrefoelas (*veylas*)							
Llanfair Rhyd Castell *demoe q'stu*			£2 5s				
Llyn Cymmer *kenenkennea*							
Lechwedd Cryn Llwyn Lewes *Kylwen*							
Herlygaret & Lanwueiri & henkesche			£1 4s 8d				
Bodesgallen in Creuddyn		£5				£1 13s 4d	
Eglwysrhos						£6 13s 4d	£18 6s 8d
Eglwysbach						£8	£13 6s 8d
		£5	**£4 14s 8d**			**£16 6s 8d**	**£47 2s 6d**
Total Valuation	**£1 4s 4d**	**£48 11s 4½d**	**£49 3s, over £63 with rents**	**£15 11s 9d**	**£4 10s**	**£109 1s**	**£162 16s**

The Abbots of Aberconwy and their known dates				
Abbot	**Inauguration**	**First Mention**	**Last Mention**	**Death**
Abraham[903]	1186?	<1202	1225	Jan 1233
?	1225			
Einion		17 Jun 1258	22 Aug 1260	
Maredudd		21 Jul 1278	5 Sep 1281	
David		15 Oct 1284	28 Apr 1301	
Tewdwr		1303		
Clement		2 Feb 1344		
Cynfrig		12 Mar 1345	1356	
Ieuan ap Rhys[904]?		1379	1399	
Hywel ap Gwilym		26 Feb 1404	1409	
David		1431		
?		1448	1448	aged 80
Reginald		[1478]		abt 1480
Prior Gruffydd Goch	Interim abbot	abt 1480	1482	
David Winchcombe	1482		1484	
David Lloyd		1483	1490	
Prior Gruffydd Goch	Interim abbot	1490		
[John]		1490		
David Owen	1501?	1509	1513	
Geoffrey Kyffin		1514	1526	
Hugh Price		1527		1528
Geoffrey Johns		1529	30 August 1535	
Richard Price	1535	3 Jun 1536	1537	

[903] Abraham ap Gruffydd was an archdeacon in 1195 and therefore could not have been abbot of Aberconwy before this date. It therefore seems unlikely that he is the same man who became bishop of Bangor in 1225 and died in 1233.
[904] This is probably the same as Abbot John, TNA, MS. Welsh Plea Roll 1 (Caernarfon).

Appendix 9
The Latin Texts of the Pope's Letters to Llywelyn

Document 1

Mannensi episcopo, archidiacono Bangorensi et priori de Insula Glannavo. Ne ante septennium sponsalia contrahantur.

Laterani, viii kal. Decembris

Postulavit a nobis dilectus filius vir nobilis R. princeps Norwaliae, ut de conccessione nostra sibi liceret filiam dilecti filii principis Insularum subarrhatam ab ipso accipere in uxorem, non obstante quod patruo ejus eadem infra nubiles annos exstitit desponsata, cum tamen a neutro traducta fuisset. Verum quoniam nobis constare non potuit cujus aetatis puella tempore subarrhationis vel desponsationis exstiterit et cui antea fuerit, puta nepoti vel patruo, desponsata, cum secundum diversitates factorum jura etiam sint diversa, in hujusmodi certum non potuimus dare responsum, quoniam juxta canonicas sanctiones in rebus ambiguis non est absolutum judicium proferendum. Volentes autem, quantum cum Deo possumus, justas postulationes praefati principis sine difficultate qualibet exaudire, inquisitionem eorum quae praemisimus sub certa forma examini vestro duximus committendam, quid juris sit in singulis articulis supponentes. Quocirca discretioni vestrae per apostolica scripta mandamus quatenus vocatis ad praesentiam vestram quos videritis evocandos, sollicite inquiratis utrum puella septennium non attigerit quando subarrhata exstitit a nepote, vel patruo desponsata. In utroque namque istorum casuum, quia tam subarrhatio quam desponsatio de jure non tenuit, quae non potest septennium praevenire, quod factum est a patruo primo vel postea non obstante, nisi aliud quid impediat, puella eadem legitime contrahere poterit cum nepote. Si vero tam subarrhationis quam desponsationis tempore septennis exstitit vel majoris aetatis, cum ex tunc incipiant placere sponsalia, si praecessit desponsatio patrui, non potuit contrahere cum nepote; quoniam secundum traditiones et observantias regulares nullus potest sponsam consanguinei sui accipere in uxorem, et hi due casus non ad imparia judicantur. Si autem subarrhatio facta cum nepote praecessit, quod secutum fuit postea non tenente, cum per secundum factum non potuerit primum dissolvi, quod quantum ad sponsalia sortitum fuerit firmitatem, volentibus personis principalibus, matrimonium inter eas poterit consummari. Si vero nepos eam ante septennium subarrhavit et patruus in septennio vel post septennium desponsavit eamdem, nepos eam propter rationem praemissam ducere non poterit in uxorem, sin, vice versa, eam sibi legitime poterit copulare. Pro iis quae praemisimus memoriae commendatis, cum de facto vobis constiterit, de jure non poteritis dubitare. Vos ergo, appellatione remota, secundum praemissas distinctiones injunctum vobis curetis negotium diffinire. Quod si omnes, etc, tu, frater episcope, cum corum altero.[905]

---

[905] *Patrologiae cursus completus,... Latine*, Migne, JP. [1844-1864], CCXIV, 791-2, No.CCXXXIII.

Document 2

Abbati de Abenton, priori de Henli et Magistro M. Canonico de Berlinton, Bangorensis Dioeceseos. Confirmat sententiam de sponsalibus inter filiam principis Insularum et principem Norwalliae. Laterani, xiii kal Maii.

Olim dilectus filius, nobilis vir, N. [or R.] princeps Norwalliae, a nobis humiliter postulavit, ut de concessione nostra liceret eidem illam nobilis viri .... principis Insularum, quam se subarrhasse scribebat, ducere in uxorem etc. In eumdem fere modum, sicut in Regesto secundi anni [Epistola 233 above], mense Decembri usque poterit copulare. Partibus itaque in praedictorum judicum praesentia constitutis, sicut ipsi per suas nobis litteras intimarunt, eis per testes constitit evidenter, quod puella, completis octa annis, a L. principe Norwalliae, tam suo quam suorum consensu parentum, subarrhata fuerat, sed, eo ex necessitate traducere differente, a patruo sine suo consensu postmodum desponsata, qui, ea nequaquam carnaliter cognita, viam fuerat universae carnis ingressus. Unde, ipsi judices, communicato prudentum virorum consilio, puellam eamdem a L. praedicto, Norwalliae principe, sententialiter concesserunt aucioritate apostolica desponsari, ne discordia inter illos olim exorta, nunc autem sopita iterum oriatur, sicut nobis per suas litteras intimarunt. Nos igitur eorumdem sententiam, nisi aliud rationabile quid obsistat, ratam et firmam habentes, praesentium vobis auctoritate mandamus, quatenus ipsam faciatis, appellatione remota, per censuram ecclesiasticam inviolabiliter observari. Nullis litteris veritati, etc. Quod si non omnes, ... duo, etc.[906]

Document 3

.... Eliensi, ... Norvicensi, ... et ..... de Sancto Asaph, Episcopis.

Ut causam matrimonii, inter filiam principis Insularum, et principem Norwalliae, vertentem terminent.

Apud S. Petrum, xiii kal Martii

Cum olim dilectus filius, nobilis vir ... princeps Norwalliae, a nobis humiliter postulasset, ut de nostra sibi permissione liceret filiam nobilis viri.... principis Insularum, quam se asseruit subarrasse, ducere in uxorem, non obstante, quod... patruo ejus eadem mulier infra nubiles annos fuerat desponsata, cum neuter eorum transduxisset eamdem, bonae memoriae.. Mannen. Episcopo, et dilectis filiis... archidiacono, et ... priori de Insula Glannav, sub certa forma causam ipsam commisimus terminandam. Partibus itaque in praedictorum judicum praesentia constitutis, sicut ipsi per suas nobis litteras intimarunt, per testes ejus constitit evidenter, quod praedicta puella, octo annis expletis, ab L. principe Norwalliae, tam suo quam suorum assensu parentum, fuerat subarrhata, sed, eo ex necessitate ipsam transducere differente, ejusdem L. patruus ipsam sine consensu ejus postmodum desponsavit, qui, ea nequaquam carnaliter cognita, viam fuerat universae carnis ingressus. Judices ergo praedicti, communicato prudentium virorum consilio, praedicto Norwalliae principi auctoritate apostolica concesserunt, ut puellam desponsaret eamdem, ne discordia inter ipsum et parentes puellae olim exorta, et tunc sopita, iterum oriretur. Nos igitur, eorumdem sententiam, nisi aliud rationabile quidem obstaret, volentes firmitatem debitam obtinere, dilectis filiis, abbati de Abenton... priori de henli, et magistro M. canonico de Berlinton, Bangorensis dioeceseos, dedimus (649) in mandatis, ut ipsam facerent, appellatione remota, per censuram ecclesiasticam firmiter observari. Abbas vero praedictus, et conjudices sui, propter conditionem in litteris nostris expressam, super matrimonio illo, sicut in eorum litteris

---

[906] *Patrologiae cursus completus,... Latine*, Migne, JP., [1844-1864] CCXV, 49-50, No. XLVII.

perspeximus contineri, studiose ac sollicite, receptis testibus, veritatem inquirere curaverunt. Habitis ergo quatuor productionibus testium, et redactis in scriptis depositionibus eorumdem, ea, quae ad decisionem causae credebant sufficere, de utriusque partis assensu, nobis transmittere curaverunt, ut nobis rei veritas eluceret, et consuleretur conscientiae principis supradicti; qui priores judices, et praesertim archidiaconum et priorem dicebat juris ignaros, et litteras nostras per falsam suggestionem obtentas, nec se credebat cum eadem puella posse salvari, quae patruo ejus tradita in uxorem in uno lecto saepius fuerat cum eodem. Nos igitur, depositionibus testium diligenter inspectis, probatum invenimus per easdem, quod idem L. puellam ipsam ducturum se juraverat in uxorem, sed nec ipsam transduxerat, nec probabatur per testes, quod benedictus fuerit, aut in una terra fuerit cum eadem, utpote quorum terras mare medium dividebat. In actis quoque judicum perspeximus contineri, quod sufficientibus testimoniis probatum fuerat coram ipsis, octo annorum fuisse puellam, quando idem L. eam juraverat se ducturum. Cumque pater puellae filiam suam in Norwalliam ad statutum terminum ducere distulis set, idem L. sororem nobilis viri.. Comitis Castriae, sine contradictione qualibet, circa finem illius anni duxerat in uxorem, et R. patruus ejus puellam desponsaverat memoratam, et post annum in facie Ecclesiae, cum illa contraxerat, et a principio Maii usque ad festum beati Viti martyris, quoties ei placuit, in eodem lecto jacuerat cum eadem, et in Walliam fuerat elapso tempore aliquanto reversus. Caeterum, transacto secundo anno a tempore desponsationis, primo vero a tempore nuptiarum, in Manniam rediens, pacifice cohabitavit uxori, et eam secum per terram et mare deduxit, sed, ea tandem sub parentum cura relicta, in Walliam rediit, ibique fuit viam universae carnis ingressus. Ex dictis igitur testium collegerunt judices supradicti quod praedictus R. puellam eamdem a tempore desponsationis habuerat per triennium, et tres menses, sed per biennium, duos menses, et dies quindecim a tempore nuptiarum; fuit autem diversitas inter testes, cum quidam, ex eo quod puella erat tunc temporis macilenta, quod non fuisset carnaliter cognita existimarent, licet esset aetate nubilis, et toro matura; quidam autem nescire se dicerent, si carnaliter cognita exstitisset, quidam vero crederent, quod cognita non fuisset, quidam vero ab ipso R. assererent se audisse, quod eam carnaliter non cognovit; licet adjicerent se nescire, utrum postmodum fuerit eum eadem. Verum, praedictus epsicopus Manniae, sicut in scriptis ejus, et suorum conjudieum secundo delegati perspexerant contineri, conjudicibus ejus absentibus, tam ex ipsius puellae quam parentum, nutricis et famularum ejus didicit juramentis, quod praedictus R. puellam ipsam carnaliter non cognovit. Patruo ergo viam universae carnis ingresso, cum praedictus L a rege Manniae juniorem filiam in conjugem postulasset [postutasset], nec id obtinere potuisset ab eo, utpote cum ipsa fuisset alii copulata, saepedictam puellam de assensu priorum judicum sibi postmodum copulavit. Constitit igitur ex praedictis quod inter saepedictum L et praedictam puellam, cum octo esset annorum, cujus tamen consensus non invenitur expressus, antequam cum ipsa ejusdem L. patruus contraxisset, tantummodo per verba de futuro fuerunt sponsalia celebrata, ita quod nec idem L. transduxerat aut subarrharat eamdem, nec cum ipsa fuerat benedictus, quin imo nec in eadem fuerant terra simul, utpote quorum terras, sicut superius est expressum, mare medium dividebat: unde praesumi non potest quod aliquid attentarint, quod non potuerint consummare. Constitit etiam per praedicta quod puella ipsa in nono anno saepedicto R. desponsata fuerat, et in decimo ab ipso transducta, et ultra biennium in uno lecto frequenter fuerat cum eodem. Unde colligitur manifeste quod primae litterae per falsam fuerunt suggestionem obtentae, cum contineatur in illis quod neuter eorum transduxit eamdem. Cumque tandin simul in uno lecto fuissent, de jure praesumitur quod facti fuerint una caro, cum etiam in duodecimo anno, in quo liberum et legitimum habet in hujusmodo puella *consensum, voluntarie fuerit cum eodem, patet eam in ejus matrimonium legitime consensisse, nec potuisse contrahere postmodum cum nepote. Unde idem L. ducere ipsam de jure non potuit, et, si de facto ipsam sibi post mortem patrui copulavit, ab ea est merito separandus. Ideoque fraternitati vestrae per apostolica scripta mandamus, quatenus, vocatis qui propter hoc fuerint evocandi, causam ipsam secundum praecriptam formam, appellatione postposita, terminetis, facientes, etc.*

Datum Romae, apud St Petrum, xiii kal. Martii.[907]

---

[907] *Patrologiae cursus completus,... Latine*, Migne, JP., [1844-1864] CCXV, 534-7, No.CCXX

Appendix 10
The Levelinus stone

It is generally assumed by most government bodies that the Llywelyn stone was raised in honour of Llywelyn ab Iorwerth in the period 1198 to 1230. Indeed, to quote the National Museum of Wales in Cardiff:

> This stone from near Pentrefoelas, Conwy, commemorates a gift of land from Llywelyn ab Iorwerth (1194–1240) to the Cistercian abbey at Aberconwy nearby. The inscription, cut between 1198 and 1230, can be read like a document. It plays on words, in a clever mixture of Welsh and Latin. This elaborate compliment explains Llywelyn's Latinised name.

> ED vidh LN DI enw alevon[e]
> Fortitvdi[n]e brachii mesure
> Leveline pri[n]ceps Norhv[a]llie

> The name Levelin is from 'llew' – lion
> And from the might of 'elin' – arm
> O Levelinus, Prince of North Wales

This is backed up by the following photograph and shows that at best the reading is tentative.

Figure 94, The Levelinus Stone as kept in the National Museum of Wales.

A Cadw backed and presumably checked organisation goes as far as stating:

> The stone was set up by the monks of the Cistercian Abbey of Aberconwy... It marks their gratitude to Llywelyn for the gift of farmlands around Pentrefoelas in the early 13th century. The monks had good reason to be grateful. Llywelyn had put them in control of nearly 3,000 acres, on which they could graze the livestock for which they were famous.[*908]

As has been seen in the main text, absolutely none of these claimed facts are verifiable and much can be gainsaid. Once again it is necessary to start with what is actually known of the stone, rather than looking at its fabricated history.

First of all it is obvious from the photograph that the text is of a highly poor quality, rather unlike any of the text seen in 13th C monuments elsewhere. Indeed the quality of text rather places the stone in the sub Roman era of the 5th to 10th centuries rather than the 13th. Further, the text is clearly not overly legible and the supposedly Latin-Welsh script is highly unusual. The nearest example would seem to be in Tywyn church, Meirionydd, which commemorates two women and carries the old Welsh phrase, *tricet nitanam*, 'the grief-loss remains'. Again older readings of this were different. Despite these worries, the uniqueness of the Levelinus stone does not necessarily mean that the stone itself is not ancient, but the question must be asked if the inscription does not actually date to the seventeenth century and then not many years before it was

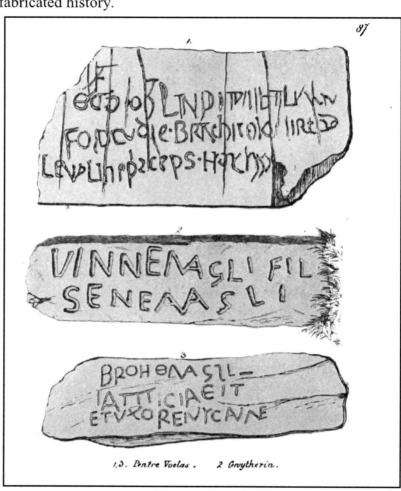

Figure 95, The inscription on the Levelinus stone can here be compared with another found nearby and one from Gwytherin. The difference in text quality is immediately apparent.

[*908] www.snowdoniaheritage.info/en/location/135/the-levelinus-stone/ accessed 18 March 2018.

apparently first mentioned in 1695 when it was near the old hall[*909]. Pentrefoelas itself had been in the hands of the Wynne family since well before 1645[*910]. Again, it is to be wondered, as with John Wynne's foundationless attributing of the birth of Llywelyn ab Iorwerth to Dolwyddelan castle, if the Wynnes did not also concoct this unusual monument. The reading of the text has always been problematical and there is no other exemplar of this alleged Latin-Welsh monument.

Appendix 11
Wikipedia versus the sources, Llywelyn Fawr

In the twelfth century Llywelyn ab Iorwerth (1172-1240), a grandson of Owain Gwynedd (bef.1105-70), was a most unimportant prince and no one could have foreseen what a great future lay in store for him in the first decade of the thirteenth century. It is therefore worth propounding that he was never referred to by contemporaries as Llywelyn Fawr - Llywelyn the Great. Indeed there appears to be no mention of him under such a name during the Middle Ages. In consequence it seems that this name is a relatively modern conceit that distorts history.

Research into the subject suggests that Llywelyn's well known epithet is based solely upon the singular evidence that a document of Edward I (1272-1307) is said to have once referred to him as *Lewelini Magni* - or Llywelyn the Great. However, it should immediately be noted that the common Latin word magnus has a wide variety of meanings and so could have meant, large, great, big, vast, huge, powerful, tall, long, broad, extensive, spacious, mighty, distinguished, skilled, bold, confident, proud, complete, pure, intense, loud, expensive, notably famous, old or simply, in its most common and most likely form in this context, senior. Quite obviously to understand the meaning of the words *Lewelini Magni* it is necessary to examine the surviving evidence concerning the commonly used name, Llywelyn Fawr.

The only place to begin and end looking for evidence is in original sources, in whatever form they have come down to us. The statement of a modern historian is not really worth anything, unless it is backed by solid original facts. A quick glance reveals that there are a myriad of letters from the kings of England and their ministers to Llywelyn and even some from various barons[*911]. None of these use the epithet Llywelyn Fawr and only one allegedly calls him *Lewelini Magni*. Leaving this one singular occurrence to examine later, it is first necessary to scrutinise other contemporary sources in the form they have come down to us. Relatively speaking a vast amount of contemporary poetry was written to Prince Llywelyn and not one of these poets, Cynddelw, Prydydd y Moch, Llywarch ab Llywelyn, Dafydd Benfras, Einion ap Gwgon, Einion ap Gwalchmai, Einion Wan, Gwgon Brydydd, Elidyr Sais or Llywelyn Vard, ever gave the prince the epitaph Fawr or indeed anything similar[*912]. Similarly, when Llywelyn was mentioned in poems to his sons or grandsons by Prydydd y Moch, Dafydd Benfras, Einion Wan, Llygad Gwr, Bleddyn Uart or Prydydd Fychan of

[*909] *Lapidarium Walliae: The Early Inscribed and Sculptured Stones of Wales*, Westwood, JO. [Oxford, 1876-79], 201.
[*910] *Archaeologia Cambrensis* [1890], 334.
[*911] A good place to start the examination of all the rolls of the era is *The Acts of the Welsh Rulers, 1120-1283*, ed. Pryce, H. [Cardiff, 2005]. The public record office has also, over the years, produced many books with valuable indexes. It should also be noted here that it would be unlikely that Llywelyn or his sons would use any epithet in any formal charter.
[*912] The many poems to Llywelyn and his descendants appear in *The Myvyrian Archaiology of Wales*, eds. O. Jones, E. Williams & W. Owen [2nd edn., Denbigh, 1870] between pages 175 and 266.

Deheubarth, he was never more than Llywelyn ab Iorwerth Drwyndwn and usually just Llywelyn. Again, in the Annales Cambriae and the Welsh Bruts, Llywelyn was either Llywelyn, Llywelyn ab Iorwerth or Prince Llywelyn. In brief the original evidence shows absolutely no indication that Llywelyn was ever known as Llywelyn the Great during his own lifetime.

What then can be said of the idea that near-contemporaries dubbed him Llywelyn Fawr due to what he had achieved while he was living? Matthew Paris (d.1259) actually calls him *magni*, but again the words indicate that he was not using it to mean great, but senior. He actually states that there were three sons of the senior Llywelyn and one of them was Dafydd who won a battle in 1258 - *David junior trium fratrum scilicet, trium filiorum magni Leolini principis Northwalliae*[*913]. Even in this Matthew gets it wrong, as Dafydd ap Gruffydd was the grandson of Llywelyn and in any case the younger Dafydd was one of four surviving brothers - Owain Goch, Llywelyn, Rhodri and Dafydd. The term *magni Leolini* obviously refers to Llywelyn the elder or the previous Llywelyn to the current Prince of Wales, Llywelyn ap Gruffydd, the brother of the Dafydd mentioned fighting in 1258. If Matthew could confuse this Dafydd with his uncle, Dafydd ap Llywelyn (d.1246), it again serves as a stark warning about the validity of original sources without corroborating evidence. Previously Matthew had referred to Llywelyn ab Iorwerth as King Llywelyn of Wales before reverting to the normal Prince Llywelyn of North Wales or even Prince Llywelyn of the Welsh[*914]. What is clear is that he never referred to him as Llywelyn the Great. Neither, apparently did any other chronicler or contemporary.

In the royal records, up to the end of the principality of Wales in 1283, there is only one singular source that may suggest that Llywelyn used the epithet Fawr and this comes in a royal confirmation of a charter that had been lost by 25 March 1286. Around that time, 46 years after the death of Llywelyn ab Iorwerth and four years after the death of Llywelyn ap Gruffydd, Bishop Einion of Bangor (1267-1307) stated that he had seen and examined a charter by *Lewelini Magni* before its recent destruction when the interior of Beddgelert priory was burned by mischance. A few weeks later King Edward I (1272-1307) confirmed this document and other recently lost charters at the request of the prior of Beddgelert and with the aid of Bishop Einion's confirmation:

> by the praiseworthy testimony of the aforesaid bishop through his inspection of the preceding charters faithfully consulted in full.

The result was two charters made in the spring of 1286 soon after the fire had swept through the interior of the priory church and destroyed its outbuildings. Einion's charter was made at Maesyllan in the week of the feast of the Annunciation which occurred on 25 March 1286 and reads:

> To all those faithful in Christ, these letters whether seen or heard, Einion by divine sanction the humble servant bishop of Bangor, [sends] everlasting salvation in the lord. Know that we have seen various charters by divers princes [made] to the prior and convent of St Mary of the valley by Snowdon.

[*913] MP CM V, 717-8.
[*914] *Matthaei Parisiensis, monachi Sancti Albani, Chronica Majora*, ed. H.R. Luard [7 vols., 1872-83] III, 64, 76, 222; 82, 261, 264; 194.

Namely a charter of Llywelyn Senior (*Lewelini Magni*) concerning all the land of Cynddelw (*Cynderick*) of Pennant (*Rennaut*).

Also a charter of Llywelyn ap Gruffydd concerning all the lands of the sons of Ithel of Pennant (*Penard*).

Also a charter of Llywelyn ap Gruffydd concerning all the land of the men of Traian (*Trehan*) at *Kenybeind* and Llecheidior (*Lecheitaur*).

Also a charter of the Lord Owain concerning all the vill called Tre'r beirdd in commote Menai.

Also a charter of the Lord Llywelyn ap Gruffydd concerning all that land at the place of Beddgelert (*Beckellers*).

Also the charter of the Lord David concerning all the land which Iorwerth ab Yerfynt held, also *Feraul* in Pennant.

And in addition to the said lands we have seen papal letters of confirmation, bulls, neither cancelled nor rescinded, nor in any part damaged. This may be known to all, that the said house of St Mary is the senior religious house in all Wales except for the island of the saints at Bardsey, and the best hospice for the common needy and those English and Welsh travelling from England and West Wales to North Wales and from Ireland and North Wales going into England. But, in immoderate damage and the common frailty of all things, the said house, by chance had the interior destroyed by fire, although it suffered destruction at the time of greatest hospitality, however through the blessed king, the catholic, the liberal, by the will of God, the Lord Edward has restored it to the full; and because it is blessed to come to the help of the afflicted and oppressed. We, through the compassion of God, and through the intercession of his same mother, and trusting in the judgement of all his saints, to all of the benefactors to the said house, whencesoever they come to help, who by goods, by God collected, pious alms or favours, they might have collected, we relax for 40 days any repented misdeeds brought against them; as long as they are truly found guilty and confessed.[*915]

Some six weeks later King Edward himself had a charter made which confirmed what had happened. However, it is noticeable that the charters and associated lands confirmed to Beddgelert were not quite the same. It would seem that the prior and his canon who met the king had remembered slightly more than the bishop. This would account for the discrepancies, but probably the full truth of the matter will never be known. Leastways on 10 May 1286 at Canterbury the king set out his charter.

> It happened that our father, Prior Madog of the house in the Vale of St Mary and Brother Hugh his co-canon of the same house, came to us humbly with devoted prayers, that with all its buildings the priory itself, and also its charters and other instruments of divers lands and tenements acquired by the same priory, with the same buildings by misfortune were recently burned, the safety of any lands and tenements aforesaid to themselves and their successors, the servants of God in the same place, we might undertake to do for charity. And because the venerable father, Bishop Einion of Bangor, sent to us his letters patent, through which he has testified to have seen himself charters of various princes made to the priory and convent in the aforesaid place;

[*915] *Monasticon Anglicanum*, ed. W. Dugdale, Revised edition by J. Caley, H. Ellis, and B. Bandinel [6 vols., 1817-30], VI i, 200, No.1.

that is the charter of Llywelyn Senior (*Lewelini magni*) of all the land of Cynddelw (*Kindeluluyt*) of Pennant (*Fennant*);

the charter of Llywelyn ap Gruffydd of all the lands of the sons of Ithel of Pennant (*Pennard*);

the charter of Llywelyn ap Gruffydd of all the land of the men of Traian (*Treban*) at *Kenybemd* and Llecheidior (*Letheyeaur*);

the charter of the Lord Owain of all the vill which is called Tre'r beirdd in Commote Menai;

the charter of Llywelyn ap Gruffydd of all their land and the place of Beddgelert;

the charter of the Lord Dafydd of all the land of Oerddwr at Pennant (*Adver apud Epennant*);

the charter of the Lord Dafydd of all the land of Legwaret, Llanfair is Gaer of Pennardd (*Vayre Gneyr de Penaut*)

And the charter of the Lord Dafydd of the land which was held by Iorwerth ab Yrefeyrat and Steyral at Llanfihangel y Pennant (*Epennant*).

We by the immense damage, which the aforesaid prior and convent sustained from the burning of the aforesaid pious companionates, and also by the praiseworthy testimony of the aforesaid bishop of his inspection of the preceding charters faithfully consulted in full, the preceding gifts on account of the safety of our soul and of the souls of our ancestors and heirs accept the preceding donations of lands to the aforesaid priory made previously, and the same for us and our heirs, as far as it is in us, the aforesaid priory and convent, exactly as the gifts have reasonably been used by them and the successors of them to this time, we concede and confirm forever. This is witnessed by the venerable Bishop Robert of Bath and Wells our chancellor, Earl Gilbert Clare of Gloucester, Earl Edmund of Cornwall our cousin, Edmund Mortimer, William Braose, Robert Fitz John, William Leybourne and others.[*916]

It is quite clear from this that Llywelyn ap Gruffydd (d.1282) was the main charter giver to Beddgelert priory, although his two brothers, particularly Dafydd (d.1283), also played a substantial part[*917]. However many of the lands 'granted' seem to be more like repeat confirmations as internecine struggles changed the political landscape of North Wales.

Regardless of this, these lost charters lead to another question which further muddies the water concerning the name *Lewelini magni*. Is this man the same as Prince Llywelyn ab Iorwerth and did he found the Augustinian house of Beddgelert as has been suggested from this charter evidence alone? The entire evidence for this comes from these two records of one charter and rests upon the doubtful identification of *Lewelini Magni* with Llywelyn ab Iorwerth. Even if Llywelyn ab Iorwerth were the founder, then the translation would not be Llywelyn the Great, but the senior Llywelyn to contrast him with the second Llywelyn who is described as *Lewelini filii Griffini*. Although this deduction is logical it is not proof. Proof is very difficult to obtain, and can only come by examining what lands the senior Llywelyn granted. Thankfully this is largely possible, not least due to the survival of later surveys, namely those of 1291 and 1535[*918]. These allow many of the lands of Beddgelert priory to be

---

[*916] *Monasticon Anglicanum*, ed. W. Dugdale, Revised edition by J. Caley, H. Ellis, and B. Bandinel [6 vols., 1817-30] VI, 200, No.2.

[*917] The lands of Beddgelert priory are examined in Bott, A & Dunn, M, *A Guide to the Priory and Parish Church of St Mary, Beddgelert, Gwynedd*. This shows there is much work still to be done on the lands held by the priory and who granted them and when.

[*918] Taxatio of Pope Nicholas IV, *Registrum vulgariter nuncupatum, 'The Record of Caernarvon'*, ed. Ellis, H. [London, 1838], 230. Valor Ecclesiasticus 26 Henry VIII printed in *Archaeologia Cambrensis* [1847], 164-5.

reasonably identified. These are listed below after this appendix. From these we can see that Llywelyn Senior granted the Pennant valley to Beddgelert. As this, like Beddgelert, was in Eifionydd and not Arfon, it would seem more likely that this land was granted by Llywelyn Fawr ap Maredudd, the cousin and enemy of Prince Llywelyn ab Iorwerth and his sons[919]. If Beddgelert priory, the major religious institution of Eifionydd was refounded by the family of Cynan ab Owain Gwynedd (d.1174), it would make much more sense of Llywelyn ab Iorwerth trying to quash the priory, if indeed Llywelyn is the prince mentioned in a contemporary text as trying to do so. According to Giraldus Cambrensis (1146-1223), Aberconwy abbey intended to annex Beddgelert priory and to this end:

> [Aberconwy Abbey] pursued the whole [priory of Beddgelert] itself by pressuring the work of every sort and employing worry, and the strength of the prince of the province himself [they gained] by bribes and great gifts for his bias, to induce him into agreement, to the point where the said poor house might be wholly demolished, or those clerks transformed into being their ordinary monks, and that the house and church should be destroyed and converted into a grange of theirs, they would not delay violently ruining it; [so] the said clerks sent a letter to the Roman court and they obtained letters of protection from the lord pope by great labours and costs..., finally with difficulty from the said persecutions and tyrannical oppressions they were able to defend themselves.[920]

This story was probably written in the 1210s after Giraldus retired from Wales to Lincoln, but as he is the only source for this affair it should be remembered that Giraldus was not above twisting reality to suit his own prejudices and he seems not to have liked Cistercians in general. Whatever the truth of the matter - for no papal letters have yet been found about the affair - Giraldus was sure that Aberconwy was a rich and powerful Cistercian house and that it was desirous of new lands at the expense of the old order.

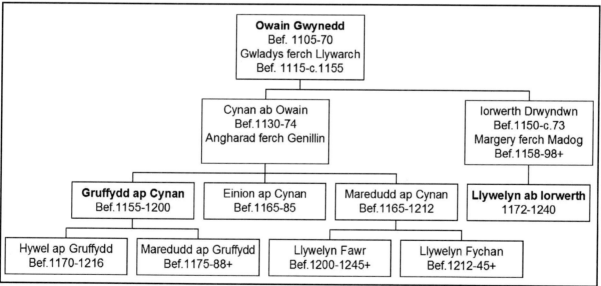

Figure 96, Some of the princes of Gwynedd descended from Owain Gwynedd and his Arwystlian bride. Those in bold ruled the bulk of Gwynedd.

---

[919] The historical Llywelyn Fawr ap Maredudd was the first cousin once removed of Llywelyn ab Iorwerth. See Figure 1.
[920] Giraldus Cambrensis, *Opera*, eds. J.S. Brewer, J.F. Dimock and G.F. Warner [8 vols., 1861-91] IV, 167-8.

If the above story is true, Giraldus must have referred to events some years after 1186 when Aberconwy was founded. His reluctance to name the prince involved in the attempt to subvert Beddgelert may suggest that Llywelyn ab Iorwerth was the prince meant - Llywelyn had been one of Giraldus' greatest supporters in his fight against the archbishop of Canterbury and King John. If this is the case, the story must date to after March 1200 when Llywelyn acquired Gwynedd. If before that date then either Gruffydd ap Cynan (d.1200) or Rhodri ab Owain (d.1195) must be the prince referred to. If it was Llywelyn ab Iorwerth moving against the priory it makes the grant of Llanfihangel y Pennant by him rather odd, unless this was granted after 1202 in recompense for his earlier hostility to the religious house. However, if Maredudd ap Cynan (d.1212), Llywelyn ab Iorwerth's enemy who he had vanquished in 1201-02, was the main grantor or even the refounder of Beddgelert the story would make sense of Llywelyn attempting to quash an enemy founded house and a possible centre of opposition to his rule in the district. It would also make sense for Maredudd ap Cynan's son, Llywelyn Fawr ap Maredudd, to make a confirmatory grant of Llanfihangel y Pennant after his reinstatement in Meirionydd and Eifionydd in 1241[*921]. Presumably the original charters of his founding ancestors had never existed or had been destroyed during the annexation of Eifionydd by Llywelyn ab Iorwerth in 1201.

The conclusion of this brief summary of the grants to Beddgelert priory is therefore that the likelihood is that the *Lewelini Magni* of the Beddgelert charters is in fact Llywelyn Fawr ap Maredudd, the lord of Eifionydd, and that Beddgelert priory had little to do with Prince Llywelyn ab Iorwerth either before or after he assumed rule of the district in 1201. Hence it is the grandchildren of Llywelyn ab Iorwerth, Owain, Llywelyn and Dafydd, after the all but destruction of the princes of Eifionydd/Meirionydd, who donated the bulk of the pre 1286 charters to Beddgelert priory.

The evidence quoted above therefore shows not a single shred of evidence that Prince Llywelyn ab Iorwerth was ever known as Llywelyn Fawr, either during his lifetime or for a century afterwards. Instead there is evidence that his first cousin once removed may have been known as Llywelyn Fawr, but never as the term is used today, viz. Llywelyn the Great. This prince appears in various genealogies as Llywelyn Fawr ap Maredudd. Quite obviously Fawr is used to differentiate him from his younger brother, Llywelyn Fychan ap Maredudd. In 1215 this Llywelyn, as Llywelyn ap Maredudd ap Cynan, accompanied Prince Llywelyn ab Iorwerth in his attack upon Deheubarth[*922]. In 1241 the king stated that he would return to 'the sons of Maredudd ap Cynan all their rights in Meirionydd'[*923]. Presumably these sons were Llywelyn Fawr and Llywelyn Vychan. Certainly, on 10 January 1245, King Henry III complained that amongst the barons of North Wales who had sworn fealty to him and were now in rebellion under Prince Dafydd ap Llywelyn were *Lewelino filio Mereduc* and *Lewelino fratri ejus*[*924]. It was probably a year later when Llywelyn had made his peace with King Henry that he wrote to him as *Lewelin senior filius Mored filii Kanani de mennoyth*[*925]. This could easily be translated as Llywelyn Fawr ap Maredudd ap Cynan of Meirionydd. It is not

[*921] *Annales Cambriae. A Translation of Harleian 3859; PRO E.164/1; Cottonian Domitian, A 1; Exeter Cathedral Library MS. 3514 and MS Exchequer DB Neath, PRO E.164/1*, ed. Remfry, P.M., [Malvern, 2007], 83-4.

[*922] *Brut y Tywysogyon or The Chronicle of the Princes. Red Book of Hergest version*, ed. and trans. T. Jones [Cardiff, 1955], 206-7.

[*923] *Idem*, 237.

[*924] *Foedera, Conventiones, Litterae etc*, ed. T. Rymer and R. Sanderson, 4th edn, by A. Clarke, F. Holbrooke, and J. Caley [4 vols. in 7 parts, 1816-69], 151; *Calendar of the Close Rolls 1272-1500* [46 vols., 1892-1955] 1242-47, 347-8.

[*925] *The Acts of the Welsh Rulers, 1120-1283*, ed. Pryce, H. [Cardiff, 2005], 342-3; *Littere Wallie, preserved in Liber A in the Public Record Office*, ed. J.G. Edwards [Cardiff, 1940], No.8.

difficult to see from this that there was apparently only one prince of Wales ever known as Llywelyn Fawr and that was the elder Llywelyn ap Maredudd of Meirionydd.

It therefore seems quite clear that the charter of *Lewelini Magni* to Beddgelert priory seen by the bishop of Bangor before 1286 was made by the prince of Meirionydd and not by Prince Llywelyn ab Iorwerth. From this it can consequently be seen that Llywelyn the Great of Wales is yet another anachronism that distorts true history. Although arguing over such minor errors may seem pedantic, such small errors lead inevitably to greater ones. Indeed, the reckless and unfounded use of Llywelyn's alleged cognomen leads naturally to even greater distortions. In one recent book, Maelgwn ap Rhys (d.1230) is exaggerated to Maelgwn the Great simply due to the fact that he was described as the older Maelgwn to differentiate him from his son, Maelgwn the younger[926]. The original text ran *Maylgim Rumor filius Magni Maylgonis*[927]. *Rumor* was most likely originally Junior before being miscopied. This is a simple example of the damage done by accepting foundationless claims as historical fact. It is also a fact that even the best historians can easily fall into this trap and therefore it is fitting to end this section with the words of Professor J.E. Lloyd and ask whether historians should set their opinions in stone for their public?

> Among the chieftains who battled against the Anglo-Norman power his place will always be high, if not indeed the highest of all, for no man ever made better or more judicious use of the native force of the Welsh people for adequate national ends; his patriotic statesmanship will always entitle him to wear the proud style of Llywelyn the Great.[928]

A Table of Lands Granted to Beddgelert Priory

Granter	Mar 1286	May 1286	1291	1535	Today
Llywelyn Magni	Kyndewewic of Rennaut	Kindeluluyt of Fennant		Llanviangell y Pennaunt	Llanfihangel y Pennant
Llywelyn ap Gruffydd	Ithael of Penard	Izthael of Pennard	Ippennant	Penant	Llanfihangel y Pennant
Llywelyn ap Gruffydd	Trehan at Kenybeind and Lecheitaur	Treban at Kenybemd and Letheyeaur	Lecheydor	Llechither	Traian? Llecheidior
Owain	Tref Ybeyrd	Ferynerd		Llanredan	Tre'r beirdd
Llywelyn ap Gruffydd	Beckellers	Betkelert	Bethkellard	Bethkylhert	Beddgelert
David		Adoer at Epennant			Oerddwr in Pennant[929]

[926] Hurlock, K. *Wales and the Crusades c.1095-1291* [Cardiff, 2011], 165
[927] Charles, BG., 'The Records of Slebech', *National Library of Wales Journal* [1947-8] V, 179-98, Appendix II, 194.
[928] Lloyd, J.E., *History of Wales* [2 vols., 1911], 693.
[929] Oerddwr was removed from Pennant and added to Beddgelert parish after the Reformation.

David		Legwaret, Vayre, Gneyr and Penaut		Llan Vaire	Llanfair is Gaer
David	Iorwert ab Yerfynt and Feraul in Pennant	Iorwerth ab Yrefeyrat and Steyral at Epennant.			Llanfihangel y Pennant
			Fenhidell Geibi		
			Haberreich		Abererch
				Dolwethlan	Dolwyddelan

Appendix 12
Two Contemporary Charters of King John to Religious Houses[*930]

John, by the grace of God, king of England, lord of Ireland, duke of Normandy and Aquitaine and count of Anjou, to his archbishops, bishops, abbots, earls, barons, justiciars, sheriffs, mayors and all his faithful bailiffs, greetings. We wish and strongly order that the brothers of Grandmont and their men are quit of tallage, pontage, theloneo, passagio, vinagio, ditching, army, misdeeds and all customs and all things and pretexts that pertain to us, and we forbid no one the brothers themselves or their men to trouble or disturb over this, and if anyone vexes them over this they are to be at our mercy for £10 sterling. Witnessed by Earl Robert of Leicester, Earl Baldwin of Aumale, Earl William of Salisbury, William Braose, Roger Tosny, Gerald Furnival. Dated by the hand of Mayor Simon of Bevereley and archdeacon of Wells at Rouen, 31 March in the year of our reign four [1203].[*931]

Johannes Dei gratia rex Angl(ie) dominus Hib(ernie) dux Norm(annie) Aquit(anie) et com(es) Andeg(auie) archiepiscopis, episcopis, abb(at)ibus, com(itibus), baron(ibus), iustic(iis), vicecom(itibus), prepositis et omnibus baill(iu)is et fidelibus suis salutem. Volumus et firmiter precipimus quod fratres Grand'montis et homines sui sint quieti de talliagio, pontagio, theloneo, passagio, vinagio, fossagio, exercitu, misericordia et omni consuetudine et de omnibus rebus et occasionibus ad nos pertinentibus, et prohibemus ne aliquis ipsos fratres vel homines suos super hoc vexet vel disturbet, et si aliquis eos super hoc vexauerit, in misericordia nostra sit de decem libr(is) sterlengorum. Test(ibus): R(oberto) com(ite) Leic', B(aldewino) com(ite) Albemarl', W(illelmo) com(ite) Sar', W(illelmo) de Brehos', Rog(ero) de Toeny, G(erardo) de Furniuall'. Dat' per manum S(imonis) prepositi Beuerl' et archid(iaconi) Well' apud Rothom', xxxi. die Marc(ii) anno regni nostri quarto.

John by the grace of God king of England, lord of Ireland, duke of Aquitaine, count of Anjou to his justices, sheriffs, ministers and other bailiffs and faithful men French and English of all England and Normandy and named sea ports greetings. Know that we concede and present

---

[*930] The texts from both charters are taken from: http://magnacarta.cmp.uea.ac.uk/read/original_charters
[*931] Oxford, All Souls College Muniments Alberbury Charter 109.

confirmation by this our script that all things of the monks of Foucarmont which the monks or convent which they are able to speak of as their own are to be quit throughout our domain of toll and passage and pontage and all customs, and no one is to unjustly disturb them against a forfeiture of £10 just as in the letters patent of King Henry our father reasonably testify. Witnessed by me myself at Pont L'Arche, 31st day of May in the 4th year of our reign.

Ioh(ann)es Dei gratia rex Angl(ie) dominus Hibernie dux Norm(annie) Aquit(anie) com(es) And(egauie) iustic(iis), vic(ecomitibus), ministris et omnibus baill(iu)is et fidelibus suis Franc(is) et Anglicis totius Angl(ie) et Norm(annie) et nominatim portuum maris salutema. Sciatis nos concessisse et presenti scripto nostro confirmasse quod omnes res monachorum de Focardi Monte quas monachi vel conuersi sui poterint affidare suas esse proprias sint quiete per omnia d(omi)nia nostra de theloneo et passagio et pontagio et omni consuetudine, et nullus eos super hoc iniuste disturbet super x. libr(as) forisfacture sicut littere patentes. H(enrici) reg(is) patris nostri quas inde h(abe)nt r(ati)onabiliter testantur. T(este) me ipso apud Pontem Archeh, xxxi. die Maii anno regni nostri quintoi.[*932]

Appendix 13
Contemporary Charters to Various Abbeys

On 22 Feb 1191, Prince Gwenwynwyn had written on his confirmation charter to Strata Marcella abbey, 'Because nothing opposes forgetfulness and false claim more effectively than writing and no circumstance should be allowed to impede the practice of holiness, he has decided that in order to perpetuate the remembrance of his gift and almoin the terms thereof ought to be recorded in writing[*933]. Quite obviously the original twelfth century donors to religious establishments were aware of the pitfalls, as too, no doubt, were the forgers who came later. Of the multitude of various charters made to Welsh religious houses the following appear relevant to the charters granted (and forged) to Aberconwy.

Neath Abbey, 6 January 1208
As part of the confirmation of the lands of the order of Savigny (*Sauvenie*), King John confirmed the letters patent and charter of King Henry my father which ran:

I also will that they hold all their tenements with their purtenances for ever in peace, free, quite, integral and full and honourably in wood, plain, meadows, pascuis, in water and mills, in roads and paths, in waters and marshes, in boroughs and without and in all places and all things with soco, saca, thol, theam and infangedepos and all other liberties and are quite themselves and their men of sisis, hundr', placitis, q'rel', murdr', hidag', scutag', geld, danegeld, and all aids and chiveward and customary dues and customs and all secular services and exactions through our alms...[*934]

Tintern Abbey, between March and July 1155

[*932] TNA C 53/5 (Charter Roll 5 John) m.26, s.xiii in.

[*933] *Quoniam obliuioni et calumpnie nichil efficatius aduersatur quam scriptura et operationis sancte propositum nulla debet occasio impedire, huius siquidem rationis intuitu ad perpetuendam memoriam donationis et elemosine meae formam eius scripto decreuimus annotandam, The Charters of the Abbey of Ystrad Marchell*, ed. Thomas, G.C.G. [Aberystwyth, 1997], 155-6, No.14.

[*934] *Rot Chart*, 174.

King Henry of the English, duke of Normandy and Aquitaine and count of Anjou to his justiciars, sheriffs and ministers of the sea ports of Southampton, Hastings, Dover, Dieppe, Ouistreham and Barfleur greetings. I order that the horses and all the things of the monks of Tintern are to be quit of toll and passage and pontage and all customs, not just that above, but similar or their things which may be wrongfully disturbed upon a forfeit of £10. Witnessed by Thomas the chancellor (Becket), Richard Humez the constable at Bridgnorth.[*935]

Margam Abbey, 1155

1155

Henry king of the English, duke of the Normans and Aquitainians, count of the Angevins to his justiciars, sheriffs and ministers, English, Welsh and Norman and the sea ports, the officials of Southampton, Hastings, Dover, Barfleet and Oisterham, greetings. I order that the horses and all things of the monks of Margam are to be quit of toll, passage and pontage and all custom. And I prohibit that any of them are unjustly disturbed upon a £10 forfeit.[*936]

1154-89

Henry by grace of God king of the English, duke of the Normans and Aquitainians and count of the Angevins, to his archbishops, bishops, abbots, earls, barons, justiciars, sheriffs and all ministers and the faithful, greetings. Know that I have received in my hand, custody and protection of the abbey of Margam and the abbot and monks of the same place and the lands, men and all their things and possessions. And accordingly I warn you that the abbey itself and all things that pertain to it and you will maintain, preserve and protect it just as if it were my own property so that no injury to them or indignity or inconvenience will be made, nor permit any to be made by others. However, if anyone usurps the same abbot or his things at any market without delay to the same thenceforth justice will be entirely done. I forbid also lest the abbot or monks of the same place may be pleaded against for any lordship tenement of his unless in my court. Witnessed...[*937]

Scanned copies of Royal Charters granted to Margam Abbey 12th cent.-1441.
Copies of original documents in the National Library of Wales, Aberystwyth, part of the Penrice and Margam mss.

[*935] *H. rex Anglorum et dux Normannorum et Aquitanorum et comes Andegaxorum justiciariis suis, vicecomitibus et ministris portuum maris de hantona, Hastingis, Doura, Depa, Oistreham et Barbefluetu salutem. Precipio quod equi et omnes res monachorum de Tinterna sint quieti de theloneo et passagio et pontagio et omni consuetudine, ne quis super hoc eos vel res suas injuste disturbet super decem libris forisfacture. Test, Thomas Chancellor, Richard Humez constable, at Brug. Calendar of Charter Rolls 1226-1516* [6 vols., 1903-27], *1300-26, 88.*

[*936] *Henricus rex Anglorum dux Normannorum et Aquitanorum, comes Andegavorum justiciariis et vicecomitibus et ministris Anglie et Wallie et Normannie et Portuum maris, et moniatim Hamtone et Hastinges et Dour' et Deope et Barbeflet' et Oistreham salutem. Precipio quod equi et omnes res monachorum de Margam sint quieti de teloneo et passagio et pontagio et omni consuetudine. Et prohibeo ne quis eos injuste disturbet super x li forisfactione. Test... Cartae et alia munimenta quae ad dominium de Glamorgan pertinent, ed G.T. Clark* [6 vols., Cardiff, 1910] *VI, 2270-1.*

[*937] *Henricus Dei gratia Rex Anglorum duc Normannorum et Aquitanorum et comes Andegavorum, archiepiscopis, episcopis, abbatibus, comitibus, baronibus, justiciariis, vicecomitibus, et omnibus ministris et fidelibus suis salutem. Sciatis me suscepisse in manu mea et custodia et protectione abbatiam de margan et abbatem et monachos ejusdem loci et terras et homines et omnes res et possessiones suas. Et ideo vobis precipio quod ipsam abbatiam et omnia que ad eam pertinent manuteneatis et custodiatis et protegatis sicut res meas proprias ita quod nullam eis injuriam vel contumeliam aut gravamen faciatis nec ab aliquo fieri permittatis. Si quis autem eidem abbatie vel rebus suis in aliquo foris-facere presumpserit plenariam sine dilatione eis inde justiciam fieri faciatis. Prohibeo et ne abbas aut monachi ejusdem loci ponantur in placitum de ullo dominico tenemento suo nisi coram me. Test.... Clarke, Cart Glam VI, 2270.*

[1157-1166]

Charter of King Henry II, notifying 'all his lieges, French and English of the whole of England, Normandy and Wales' that he has confirmed to the Church of St Mary of Margam and the monks therein, for the soul of Henry I, his grandfather, and the soul of the Count of Anjou, his father, whatever Earl Robert of Gloucester (d.1147) and others have given or are about to give to the monks, viz., of the gift of Earl Robert, the land between Kenfig (*Chenfec*) and Afan (*Aven*), the fisheries of Afan (*Aven*) and the grange of *Langewi*; of the gift of William Ponchardun, the land of *Kinewerdesham*; of the gift of Hugh Raleigh (*Raelega*, bef.1140-67), the grange of *Grenedona*; and moreover granting quittance from toll, passage, pontage and all custom for all things bought, sold or carried for their own use, 'because they and all their things are in my hands, custody and protection'. Witnesses: Master Geoffrey Ridell', Count Reginald (d.1175), William Fitz Hamon, Peter Beauchamp, Geoffrey Valognes (bef.1141-69). Dated at Leon (ie Lions-la-Forêt, in Normandy). Second great seal of Henry II, dark red wax, imperfect.[*938]

[1174-1179]

Charter of Henry II confirming to Margam Abbey the grant which Roger Albertona made to the same by gift of William Scurlage, of land at *Langewi*; that of William Scurlage Junior at *Langewi*; that of Geoffrey Sturmi and Roger his son, of land held of Earl William of Gloucester (bef.1120-83) in Margam; that of Odo Sorus, of Canterel's houses in Bristol; that of Gillebert Burdin, Agnes his wife and Geoffrey and William his sons in Sturmi Wood; that of Geoffrey, Reiner and William, sons of Gillebert Burdin, of the land called 'The mountain of Laholemede', and that of Helias Turre, clerk of Queen A(lienor), of the land which Earl William of Gloucester gave to Gregory and afterwards to him at Kenfig (*Kenefech*). Witnesses: Bishop R(ichard) of Winchester (1173-88), Bishop G(eoffrey Ridel) of Ely (1173-89), Bishop R(oger) of Worcester (1164-9 Aug 1179), Richard Lucy, Earl William Mandeville (bef.1144-89), Reginald Courtney (*Curtenai*, bef.1130-90), William Mandeville, Reginald Villa, Saher Quincy, Reginald Paueilli, Robert Stut(evilla), William Stut(evilla), Gerald Camville (*Canuilli*, bef.1145-1215); dated at Westminster. Imperfect great seal of Henry II, second type.[*939]

[1174-1179]

Charter of Henry II, notifying that he has confirmed to the monks of Clairvaux (*Clarevallis*) the gift which Earl Robert of Gloucester and the Countess Mabilia his wife and that Earl William their son (bef.1120-83) made to them of all the land between Kenfig (*Kenefeg*) and *Auen-ulterior*, to the west of the Hermitage of Theodoric; all the fisheries of Aven, the fishery in the water of Kenfig; all wreck on their lands; a burgage in Kenfig; a burgage in Cardiff, viz., Siward Palmer with his house and curtilage; and land in Margam, in exchange for that which they had from Baldwin the Harper near Newborough; and the liberty of buying and selling free victuals which Earl William granted to them; in accordance with the charters of Earl Robert of Gloucester and Earl William his son. Witnesses: Bishop R(ichard) of Winchester (1173-88), Bishop G(eoffrey) of Ely (1173-89), Bishop R(oger) of Worcester (1164-9 Aug 1179), Richard the treasurer, Richard Lucy, Earl William Mandeville (bef.1144-89), William Fitz Audeli, steward, Reginald Courtney (*Curtenai*, bef.1130-90), Saher Quincy, Thomas Basset, Ranulf

---

[*938] National Library of Wales, Penrice and Margam, 12.
[*939] National Library of Wales, Penrice and Margam, 13.

Glanville (bef.1150-90), Robert Stut(evilla), William Stut(evilla), Gerard Camville (bef.1145-1215). Dated at Westminster. Imperfect great seal of Henry II, second type.[*940]

[22 July 1207]
Charter of King John confirming to the abbot and monks of Margam the gift of Geoffrey Sturmy, of land lying between land of Herbert Fitz Godwineth and the stream of *Knithwini*; the gift of Roger Sturmy his son, viz., the rest of the land which his father held of the fee of the earl of Gloucester in Margam; the gift of Res Coh, half the land of *Kethereh* in Newcastle; the gift of Einion ap Ririd, viz., the other half of the said land; and the gift of William London, between the rivers Ogwr (*Ukgemore*) and Garw (*Garewe*). Witnesses: William Briwerre, Eustace Vescy, Robert Turneham, Geoffrey Nieuille, William Cantilupe, Geoffrey Lucy, Peter Maulay. Dated by the hand of Archdeacon Hugh Welles of Wells, at Broc. Great seal of King John, green wax, imperfect.[*941]

[*940] National Library of Wales, Penrice and Margam, 14.
[*941] National Library of Wales, Penrice and Margam 98.